THE GREAT CENTRAL RAILWAY
WHAT REALLY HAPPENED

THE GREAT CENTRAL RAILWAY
WHAT REALLY HAPPENED

John Palmer

First published in Great Britain in 2020 by
Pen and Sword Transport
An imprint of
Pen & Sword Books Ltd.
Yorkshire - Philadelphia

Copyright © John Palmer, 2020

ISBN 978 1 52677 789 8

The right of John Palmer to be identified as Author of this work has been asserted by him in accordance with the Copyright, Designs and Patents Act 1988.

A CIP catalogue record for this book is available from the British Library.

All rights reserved. No part of this book may be reproduced or transmitted in any form or by any means, electronic or mechanical including photocopying, recording or by any information storage and retrieval system, without permission from the Publisher in writing.

Typeset in Palatino 10.5/14pt by SJmagic DESIGN SERVICES, India.

Printed and bound by Printworks Global Ltd., London/Hong Kong.

Pen & Sword Books Ltd. incorporates the Imprints of Pen & Sword Books Archaeology, Atlas, Aviation, Battleground, Discovery, Family History, History, Maritime, Military, Naval, Politics, Railways, Select, Transport, True Crime, Fiction, Frontline Books, Leo Cooper, Praetorian Press, Seaforth Publishing, Wharncliffe and White Owl.

For a complete list of Pen & Sword titles please contact

PEN & SWORD BOOKS LIMITED
47 Church Street, Barnsley, South Yorkshire, S70 2AS, England
E-mail: enquiries@pen-and-sword.co.uk
Website: www.pen-and-sword.co.uk

or

PEN AND SWORD BOOKS
1950 Lawrence Rd, Havertown, PA 19083, USA
E-mail: Uspen-and-sword@casematepublishers.com
Website: www.penandswordbooks.com

CONTENTS

Acknowledgements		7
Maps, illustrations, diagrams and photographs		8
Glossary of terms		9
Preface		11
Foreword		11
CHAPTER 1	Sir Edward Watkin's time with the GCR	12
CHAPTER 2	Sir Sam Fay's time with the GCR	46
CHAPTER 3	The Great Central Railway's financial structure and performance	73
CHAPTER 4	LNER times	98
CHAPTER 5	Programme of Nationalisation and planning to 1955	150
CHAPTER 6	Developments from 1955 to 1959 and longer term consequences	179
CHAPTER 7	The former GCR lines in the 1950s	203
CHAPTER 8	Movement of coal South by rail	226
CHAPTER 9	Dr Beeching and the Transport Act 1962	253
CHAPTER 10	The political process of change for railways in the 1950s and 1960s	263
CHAPTER 11	The former GCR lines in the 1960s	267
CHAPTER 12	Accidents of timing	289
CHAPTER 13	Extant/preserved/restored examples of route, architecture and traction and rolling stock of the former GCR	291
	Conclusions	308
APPENDIX 1	Capital investment in years 1900-12	310
APPENDIX 2	Extracts from BTC Freight Charges 1957	315
APPENDIX 3	Examples of Working Timetables and their interpretation	319
APPENDIX 4	Development of competing railways in East Midlands coalfields	321

APPENDIX 5	Memorandum to British Railways Board dated 11 December 1963	323
APPENDIX 6	Meeting of representatives of British Railways Board and of three Regions held on 14 July 1964	327
APPENDIX 7	Meeting with Minister of Transport and representatives of that Ministry with representatives of BRB on 11 February 1965	331
APPENDIX 8	Meeting with Members of Parliament at BRB headquarters on 26 February 1965 and press coverage 27 February 1965	334
APPENDIX 9	Alternative passenger transport facilities following proposed closure 3/4 September 1966	337
	Bibliography	338
	Index	341

ACKNOWLEDGEMENTS

This book has been three years in the making. It started as a purely personal project to try to answer a few questions in my mind regarding the Great Central Railway, mainly in BR days.

Shortly after the outset, I sourced the Search Engine website of the National Railway Museum. During a visit to York, I discovered a treasure trove of factual information which forms the basis for much of the content of chapters 3-11 inclusive. My thanks are extended to the staff at the Museum for their individual and collective guidance.

The scope of my enquiries then widened to include establishing factual understandings of financial structures and performance over time and the extent of the reliance of the Great Central Railway upon the then private coal industry. The official history of the coal industry is well documented and proved invaluable, as did the autobiography of Lord Alfred Robens in later days. The history of the much younger electricity industry – which in turn influenced the planning and production of the nationalised coal industry – is not so well documented, but what is available was also useful in giving insights into the political aspects. At that stage, the basis for a book was clear.

Although many books have been written about the Great Central, none – as far as I am aware – covered the subject from a business history perspective and most concentrated on motive power and nostalgia.

The history of British Railways (since 1948) has been well documented and increasingly so in periodicals produced to meet a growing level of interest. A jigsaw of events and hypotheses emerged (NCB/CEGB/BTC/BRB/governments of the days), but with missing pieces, particularly with regard to policy decisions in the 1960s. Visits to the National Archives (Public Records Office) at Kew enabled several pieces of the jigsaw to be added. The purely personal project had produced a sizeable manuscript based upon facts drawn from credible sources (listed in the bibliography) and some analysis and co-ordination of events across industry and political decision making.

In an attempt to locate any government papers held by various ministries, particularly Transport, I contacted and received help from Mrs Heather Wheeler MP and Andrew Jones MP; my thanks go to both. Similarly, a request to the Editor of the ASLEF magazine produced publication of my letter seeking any old Branch papers that had been retained and not passed on to the official archive. Records from the Area and Central Transport Users Consultative Committees seem to have had only a very short life.

Throughout the research and drafting the theme of an operational railway was retained, but the questions of 'is it logical?' and 'is it readable?' remained. Two friends kindly undertook to review the most challenging chapter – financial structure and performance – and their response resulted in a necessary re-write. My thanks are extended to Nigel Tilly and to David Rayner for their advice.

For purely railway matters, I acknowledge Steve Leyland (information relating to locomotive allocations and histories), Alen Grice (for information about Annesley and local trip workings) and Albert Fennell (for information about Woodford Halse and workings South and West). Jack Pickford very helpfully was able to add insights into fuel technology developments and aspects of life at NCB headquarters.

My thanks are also extended to Karen Proudler who has patiently dealt with several trees worth of paper drafts and produced for me a professional manuscript.

MAPS, ILLUSTRATIONS, DIAGRAMS AND PHOTOGRAPHS

Although this book is primarily concerned with some 400 route miles of the Great Central Railway and its associated railways, it necessarily makes reference to other routes. That, plus a need for reference to a multitude of junctions that were used to direct traffic flows, will make it worthwhile for many readers to be able to make reference to a wide selection of maps. The maps are supplemented by some illustrations relevant to significant events along the way and also by diagrams to show the scale of operations involved. For the photographs, I have opted to include a wide range depicting developments throughout the period covered by the book; selection of that option allowed greater use of colour to support the monochrome images. Unless otherwise credited the photographs were taken by the author. Photographs on and about the track at heritage railways were taken with authorisation and regard to safety. The selection was taken from an archive that has evolved over several decades and it should not be assumed that a particular subject will still be operational at the same railway today

GLOSSARY OF TERMS

As the readership of this book may extend beyond railway enthusiasts, I have included the following glossary as a guide. At the end of the glossary are conversion tables for distance, volume and weight and a listing of distances between railway locations of particular relevance to this book.

Term	Meaning
ASLEF	Associated Society of Locomotive Engineers and Firemen
banking of trains	the use of a locomotive at the rear of a train to push the train up an incline
BEA	British Electricity Authority
block working	used in relation to trainloads of petroleum products
blooms, billets and slabs	descriptions of steel in a semi-finished state being sent between steelworks
BRB	British Railways Board
BTC	British Transport Commission
CBP	Carriage Building Programme
CEGB	Central Electricity Generating Board
CLC	Cheshire Lines Committee
CME	Chief Mechanical Engineer
CTCC	Central Transport Consultative Committee
down	direction of travel away from London
ECJS	East Coast Joint Stock (carriages)
fitted freight	trains having continuous vacuum brakes on at least a proportion of the total number of wagons
GC/GCR	Great Central Railway
GDC	Grimsby Docks Company
GENJ	Great Eastern Northern Junction Railway
GER	Great Eastern Railway
GN/GE Jt	Great Northern and Great Eastern Joint(ly) owned line
GN/LNW/Jt	Great Northern, London and North Western Joint(ly) owned line
GNR	Great Northern Railway
GTR	Grand Trunk Railway of Canada
GW/GC	Great Western/Great Central line
GWR	Great Western Railway
H&B	Hull & Barnsley Railway
IFS	International Finance Society
L&B	London and Birmingham Railway
LCDR	London Chatham and Dover Railway
LDECR	Lancashire Derbyshire and East Coast Railway
Liner trains	Concept of BRB which was a forerunner of Freightliner trains conveying demountable containers on flat wagons
London extension	the route of the MS&LR/GCR South from Annesley
L&M	Liverpool & Manchester Railway
LMS	London Midland and Scottish Railway
LNER	London and North Eastern Railway
LNWR	London and North Western Railway
LSWR	London and South Western Railway
L&YR	Lancashire & Yorkshire Railway
M&B	Manchester and Birmingham Railway
MetR/GC	Metropolitan Railway Great Central jointly operated railway
MR	Midland Railway
MSJ&A	Manchester South Junction & Altrincham railway

MS&LR	Manchester, Sheffield & Lincolnshire Railway	WTT	Working Timetable for internal railway use
NB	North British Railway	1 in 100	a gradient where the track rises or falls at a rate of one foot in one hundred feet
NCB	National Coal Board		
NER	North Eastern Railway		
NE/SW	North East/South West cross-country route	4V34	later BRB method of identifying trains. The first character represented the classification (0-9), the second the Region/location of destination and the third/fourth the train number. Shown on power signal box panels and on front of locomotives.
NLR/North Ldn	North London Railway		
OAGBM	Oldham Ashton and Guide Bridge Railway		
pick up goods	goods train calling at intermediate stations to collect/leave wagons as required		
Q	train within Working Timetable which was run only as traffic or other circumstance required		
railway mania	speculation led trading in railway shares		
RCH	Railway Clearing House		
RE	Railway Executive		
route miles	distance between locations irrespective of whether single or more tracks		
ruling gradient	the limit of gradients along a route		
S&LJR	Sheffield and Lincolnshire Junction Railway		
S&MR	Sheffield and Manchester Railway		
SER	South Eastern Railway		
SR	Southern Railway		
S&T	Signal & Telegraph/Telecommunications		
track miles	distance between locations for all tracks as laid		
TUCC	Transport Users Consultative Committee		
turn	a working for a crew or locomotive		
up	direction of travel towards London		
WM&CQR	Wrexham Mold & Connahs Quay Railway		

Conversion tables:

1 mile	=	1.60934 kilometres
1 yard	=	0.9164 metre
1 foot	=	0.3048 metre
1 inch	=	2.54 centimetres
1 gallon	=	4.54596 litres
1 ton	=	1.016 tonne

Distances in miles between major railway locations:

London (Marylebone)-Manchester (London Road) via MetR/GC route: 201

London (Euston)-Manchester (London Road) via Crewe and Wilmslow: 189

London (St Pancras)-Manchester (Central) via Sharnbrook/Leicester/Trent/Derby: 189

London (King's Cross)-Manchester (London Road) via Welwyn/Retford/Sheffield (Victoria): 201

Shortest route	GC	MR	GNR
London – Leicester	103	99	
London – Nottingham	126½	123½	129
London – Sheffield	164½	158½	156½

PREFACE

The Great Central Railway from North Nottinghamshire towards London was the last main line to be built in the UK and the first to be closed.

Conceived as part of a much wider vision of the future, for the expansion of free trade across international borders, by a man who had earned the support and loyalty of those who were willing to risk capital investment, the railway was controversial from the start.

This is not, by far, the first book to be written about the Great Central Railway, but it takes as its theme a wider perspective than those previously written. The book examines the railway from a business perspective, seeks to identify how the efforts of its chairmen were necessarily applied to raising capital and then expanding the business and gross profit at a faster rate than the capital debt accumulated.

The book then follows the relative fortunes of the railway through the years of ownership of the LNER and finally British Railways.

The final fifteen years of the existence of the London extension were filled with controversy as traffic flows reduced. The book identifies the roles and policies of the National Coal Board and the Central Electricity Generating Board, the effect of transport and environmental legislation, government and railway decisions, all of which influenced what actually happened. The recent availability of archived material has enabled more pieces of a complex jigsaw to be added.

Whilst primarily concerned with the London extension, the book includes details of other parts of the network of the Great Central Railway; some of which exist and provide service to this day.

FOREWORD

From: Mr Adrian Shooter, President, Great Central Railway Society

John Palmer has produced a scholarly work, meticulously researched, which, to a much greater extent than previous works, examines and analyses the political and economic surroundings of the Great Central Railway.

Having, myself, twice in my career worked on truncated parts of the route, I can readily visualise many of the circumstances that he describes.

I only travelled the length of the Great Central mainline once on a grey day in November 1965 behind 70013 *Oliver Cromwell*. However, over more than 50 years I have come across many examples of Sir Edward Watkin's vision. For example, I saw the foundations of the Wembley Tower when the present Wembley Stadium was built.

In 2003, when I was running Chiltern Railways, we needed to renew our track access agreement with London Underground for the section of their railway from Harrow to Amersham. In an outrageous move London Underground announced that they were going to double the access charge. It was quite obvious that they did not know their history as Chiltern Railways (as successors in title to the Great Central Railway) were able to benefit from the provisions of the Manchester, Sheffield and Lincolnshire (Railway) Act of 1891, which allowed free access over the Metropolitan Railway (predecessor of London Underground). Sir Edward had, in his time chaired both companies. Chiltern Railways and London Underground settled upon a 2% increase!

As often happens, visionaries are followed by 'small' men who do not have the imagination or means to follow through with ideas.

Nowhere is this more evident than the sorry tale of political and management bungling that followed the nationalisation of the railways by the Labour Government of 1945-51.

John has managed to produce an erudite piece of work which, unusually for a scholarly piece, is very readable. When reading the manuscript I found it difficult to put it down.

Adrian Shooter, Oxfordshire, UK
April 2020

CHAPTER 1

SIR EDWARD WATKIN'S TIME WITH THE GCR

No book about the Great Central Railway would be complete without an extensive reference to Sir Edward Watkin. The development of the Manchester, Sheffield & Lincolnshire Railway (MS&L) – which later became known as the Great Central Railway (GC) – covered over forty years of his working life. A man who at the end of his days on earth attracted such diverse obituary notes as the following must surely be worth understanding:

> 'He could not claim to be a financier or administrator.'
> The *Railway Times*, 20 April 1901
> 'As a railway financier he was unequalled.'
> *Finance*, 20 April 1901
> 'He was a great railway administrator'
> The *Sphere*, 20 April 1901
> 'Of the details of railway management, he had no mastery whatever.'
> *Engineering*, 19 April 1901
> 'His talent for reducing chaos to order ... was little short of genius.'
> *Commerce*, 17 April 1901

Watkin was far more than the man who was held as responsible for the building of the last main line railway in Britain – the GC. He held general management, director and chairman roles with several railways, he was inter alia also a Justice of the Peace, a Member of Parliament, an editor and a benefactor to causes he held dear throughout his life.

The limits of my research were to try to 'find' and understand the context of the time in which Watkin lived and worked, what 'drove' him and what, in particular, shaped his approach to the management of finance. To understand Watkin is to largely understand the Great Central.

Born in 1819 in Salford, Edward was the first of three sons of Absalom Watkin. Absalom was the owner of a textile business and, being the owner, it allowed time to devote himself to more pleasurable activities in supporting cultural and intellectual societies, facing up to social and political aspects of those turbulent years of industrialisation, poverty, unemployment and poor working conditions. He had been disturbed by the putting down by militia of the Peterloo protest of 1819 against conditions and civil indignity of the workforce of the developing industries and the imprisonment of a friend who had spoken out on behalf of the working classes. Edward and his brothers, as well as their older sister, were fortunate to be raised by parents who provided a safe, Christian environment for development, exploring the home library containing books on history, grammar, politics, travel, medicine, poetry, religion, science and philosophy. No doubt the young Edward would have had explained to him the significance of the Great Reform Act of 1832 and, as he grew, he was taken to large public gatherings to hear the visiting orators speak on politics, expansion of the British Empire and the benefits to all of free trade. That Edward became confident from an early age and was influenced by his father's beliefs and approach to working hard to modestly and unobtrusively improve the lot of working people cannot be in any doubt. Edward attended grammar school and at age 14 started work in the warehouse of his father's business.

The late 1820s and into the 1830s provided demonstrations of the power of steam locomotion and the proximity to his home of the continuing construction of the Liverpool & Manchester Railway (L&M) – opened in 1830 – allowed Edward to witness the century's then most revolutionary sign of change and became a formative part of his young life. The spread of railways in the North West of England to support the needs of the Industrial Revolution was close at hand; the Manchester & Leeds (M&L) was opened in difficult stages between 1835 and 1840, the Bolton & Preston in 1837 and the Preston & Wyre (Docks) in 1835-37.

As a boy, Edward Watkin was taken by his father to see the newly constructed railway between Liverpool and Manchester which linked the dock city of the former with the cotton mills and industry of the latter. In 1992, the Museum of Science and Industry at Manchester had built a replica of one of the L&M locomotives, *Planet*. The locomotive and two replica carriages were taken to the Great Central Railway at Loughborough for trial running and are seen here near Woodthorpe.

Edward continued to work for his father's business and whilst doing so was willingly drawn into the political and public activities, acting as a check clerk at a by-election in Manchester in 1835 and becoming committed to helping organise large scale events for the Anti Corn Law Association; an ability to conceive ideas and organise in pursuit of his convictions was developing naturally. In 1835, Absalom had helped found the Manchester Athenaeum for the encouragement of discussion on the arts, sciences and technology and in 1843, Edward appeared recorded in the Minutes as a Director, acting as Secretary to a sub-committee to organise events involving leading orators of that time: Richard Cobden and Benjamin Disraeli.

In 1845, Edward married Mary Mellor, the daughter of Jonathan Mellor, a cotton manufacturer, a man of high integrity as a Justice of the Peace and High Constable. At the end of August 1845, Edward had consulted his father about an offer he had received to become Secretary of the newly authorised Trent Valley Railway Company (TV). The prospectus for the proposed Company included men prominent in the Manchester cotton trade and members of the Athenaeum. Edward was advised to accept the offer and did so.

As with many of the new railways at that time, the passing by parliament of the Bill on 21 July 1845 had been preceded by years of arguments and opposition; the latter in this case from the London and Birmingham Railway (L&B) who could see that the proposed TV company represented a threat in providing a more direct route between Stone/Stafford and Rugby, where the Manchester and Birmingham Railway (which would use the TV route) would make a

The early locomotives of industry displayed the ingenuity of their designers. Replica locomotives have been built of two of the pioneers: *Locomotion No 1* (built 1975) and *Puffing Billy* (built 2006). Both are based at Beamish Museum.

The early transportation of coal from the mines was in caldrons, as depicted here at Beamish Museum.

connection for onward travel directly to London. The Act as passed in 1845 for the TV provided that the Company could lease itself to the L&B, the Grand Junction Railway and to the M&B Railway (which three Companies formed the London and North Western Railway (LNWR) from July 1846). The TV was not to last long as a separate entity and was purchased in Spring 1846 by the L&B Railway; and purchased at a surprisingly high price negotiated on behalf of the TV by Edward Watkin. As Secretary, he was responsible for the winding up of the Company business, balancing the books and paying off the grateful shareholders. The TV route opened on 1 December 1847, from which date the LNWR announced that its trains would use the route (rather than the longer option via Birmingham) between London and Preston; at that time the busiest commercial corridor in the country for which all station clocks and timetables were in accordance with Greenwich time (Manchester being ten minutes after Greenwich time, Liverpool twelve and Birmingham seven). The TV route now forms part of the Network Rail West Coast Main Line.

Edward and his wife (now with a son, Alfred, born in 1846) moved to London in mid-1848. His meticulous approach to the winding up of the TV – plus his negotiating skills – had been noted at the headquarters of the LNWR and in early 1849 he was taken into employment with that railway. He was to be Secretary of Committees, reporting directly to the Board of Directors. The multiple committees covered all aspects of the running of the company and, as such, represented a rare opportunity to see, hear and learn how to best manage a railway company. In his duties, he would have met the (first) chairman George Carr Glyn (later Lord Wolverton) and the General Manager (Captain) Mark Huish. Having a railway system that was more linear than the then more usual regional, the Chairman and General Manager had little option but to fight off competition by the pursuit of policies of alliances and at times aggressive acquisition. In 1851/52, proposals to amalgamate with the Midland Railway (MR) and the much smaller North Staffordshire Railway (NSR) were abortive and they were equally unsuccessful in preventing the broad gauge Great Western Railway (GWR) from reaching (via Oxford) Birmingham, Shrewsbury and Birkenhead (for Liverpool across the Mersey). As a widely travelling Secretary, Watkin found himself as a protégé of Glyn and Huish, taking up additional responsibilities and becoming a member (reporting to the Board of the LNWR) of the committees of the Coventry Nuneaton Birmingham and Leicester Railway, the Buckinghamshire, the Warwick to Stratford upon Avon, the Worcester and Hereford, the Oxford Worcester and Wolverhampton, the Shrewsbury and Crewe railways.

For Edward Watkin, work was demanding and family life was demanding (a second child, a daughter, having been born in 1850). He had to develop new skills of survival in a fiercely competitive world. Huish meantime was at the foremost in railway diplomacy and finding how best things could be done for the benefit of the LNWR. He developed traffic cartels and divided receipts between participating companies. Parallels with the later approach of Watkin have not been lost on some historians.

In 1851 Edward needed a spell of recuperation from overwork and spent time on a visit to North America.

Towards the end of 1853, Edward was contemplating leaving the LNWR; his wife and children were spending increasing time in Lancashire. He was unsettled and if he did decide to leave, several railway companies would be eager to offer him employment.

As part of understanding the context of the time through which Watkin worked, it is worth reflecting upon the general development of railways in the UK between 1844 and 1852. In 1844, eighteen new railway companies were set up and in 1846 a Commission recommended that in future, all such companies should build to a standard track gauge already adopted by most, though not the Great Western Railway (GWR) which persisted with a broad gauge until 1892. By 1852, there were 6,628 route miles (up from 2,236 in 1844) and within a decade that figure would increase by 40 per cent. The increase in route mileage between 1844 and 1852 was significantly less than that envisaged in aggregate in roundly 600 schemes put forward in 1845, the majority of which never reached the parliamentary consideration for approval stage. 1846 saw parliament inundated with Bills, 219 Acts being passed. In 1847 a further 112 Acts, but increasing financial stringency in terms of the bank rate for borrowing, crop failures at home and a need to import grain, and high cotton imports needed 'spare' capital which may otherwise have been used to purchase speculative shares in support of company prospectuses. The market settled somewhat in 1848 and in that year and the next, a total of only 53 Acts for new lines (totalling some 400 miles) were passed. The time lag from Act to physical railway meant that in 1848 alone the operational scope of the railway system was extended by nearly a third. The same time lag effect meant that by 1852, the construction phase of the railway mania of 1844-48 had virtually worked its way out. The next stage was the workings of the balance of power between the 214 companies and between them and parliament. Amalgamations such as that which formed the LNWR as already mentioned became commonplace (twenty in 1846) and the Lancashire & Yorkshire (LYR) was formed from six companies. Of relevance to this book is the formation of four companies into the Manchester, Sheffield & Lincolnshire Railway (MS&LR). Also of later relevance was the ability of a resolute company such as the South Eastern Railway (SER) to buy or lease by 1853 its way across seven adjoining railway companies' lines, thus enabling it to extend its operations quickly and relatively cheaply without the need for Acts of Parliament.

In the maelstrom of railway life, the MS&LR was a conglomerate of three companies: the Sheffield and Manchester Railway (S&MR), the (prospected) Sheffield and Lincolnshire Junction Railway (S&LJR), the Great Grimsby and Sheffield Junction Railway and the Grimsby Docks Company (GDC). This gave, from 1 January 1847, a continuous line from Manchester to the North Sea, later (August 1849) connected to the L&M to enable Liverpool to be reached. The conglomerate was referred to as 'The Sheffield Company', though its headquarters were in Manchester. The line S&MR had to traverse the Pennine ridge and included the building of the then longest railway tunnel to its summit at Woodhead – a six year effort throughout which time passengers were taken by coach and horses to 'bridge' the gap in the railway. Opened in 1849, the single bore tunnel was unable to cater for all the traffic and a second bore was driven parallel to the original, opened in 1852. As a sign of the technological times, the electric telegraph wire was installed along the route and as a measure of success of the route, a new dock was opened at Grimsby in 1852. From January 1850, the General Manager of the MS&LR was James Allport and he felt that he had to enter a commercial agreement put forward by Huish of the LNWR, a move that upset the rapidly developing GNR and its aims to have running rights

4

Above and opposite: As early enclosed railway carriage bodies were wooden and built in workshops that also built road vehicles of the stagecoach type, the resemblance between the types is unsurprising. From the 1840s the Midlands of England became the centre for railway carriage building. Depicted here are preserved examples of early types as used by the Midland Railway (4), Lancashire Derbyshire and East Coast Railway (5), North Eastern Railway (6) and South Eastern and Chatham Railway (7). Photos 4 and 5 at the Midland Railway Centre, 6 at Beamish and 7 at the Bluebell Railway. Manchester, Sheffield & Lincolnshire Railway carriage 946 has also been restored and is usually at the Great Central Railway, Ruddington.

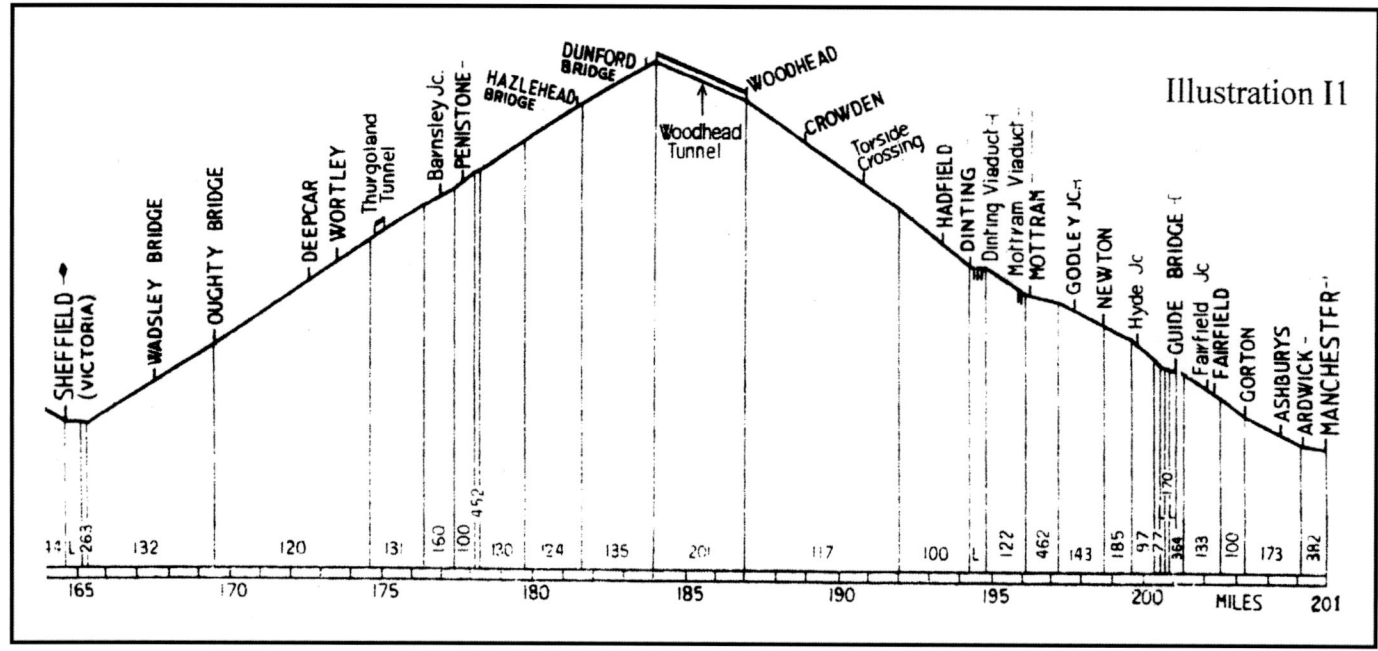

In steam days the 37 miles between Sheffield (Victoria) and Manchester (London Road) via Woodhead included challenging gradients in both directions. The illustration shows the gradient profile for the line.

towards the North West of England. Allport resigned in July 1853 to join the MR. Watkin was offered the post of General Manager of the MS&LR, which he took up from 1 January 1854 and moved to Timperley, Cheshire. An early task was to start to disentangle the Huish agreement (which was both secret and illegal) which had sought to maximise profits by minimising the competition from the GNR and the GWR. Huish then turned unsuccessfully to the GNR with a view to dividing traffic. The GNR did not trust Huish and furthermore advised Watkin of the approach that had been made. In July 1857, the GNR and MS&LR entered an agreement providing a basis for common usage of stations at Lincoln (GNR), Sheffield, Retford, Gainsborough and Grimsby (MS&LR). A route from Manchester to London to rival that of the LNWR was thus formed and led to a King's Cross to Manchester (via Retford) passenger service. The LNWR was not impressed by the moves of a former assistant manager by the name of Watkin.

Relationship difficulties between railway companies and their General Managers were commonplace and during his initial tenure, Watkin had to find ways to resolve a succession of matters. Examples were the poor state of some of the sections of infrastructure shared with the L&YR, the operational arrangements for conflicting traffic flows with the MR at Lincoln and with the GNR for goods traffic in West Yorkshire.

Watkin became drained by the parliamentary processes and constantly demanding interpersonal requirements of dealing with his peer group also seeking the best deal, but he had proven to his Board of Directors and shareholders his considerable value as a General Manager. He had also come to realise his personal strengths built upon the basic principles and moral compass from his founding years and that he would resolve matters in his own way. When his Board of Directors approached him with a view to extending his contract of employment beyond 1858, he was sufficiently confident in his position to state the condition upon which he would be willing to continue for periods up to seven years (i.e. to the end of 1865). The Board accepted on the basis that Watkin would be responsible for the proper conduct and management of the MS&LR, but not required to give his whole time to the Company. What a contract to have negotiated! By 1861, Watkin had become auditor to the Oldham Ashton-under-Lyne and Guide Bridge Railway (OAGBR), was representative of the MS&LR on three railways and a Director of four others – the West Midland, formerly Oxford Worcester and Wolverhampton; the Hereford, Hay and

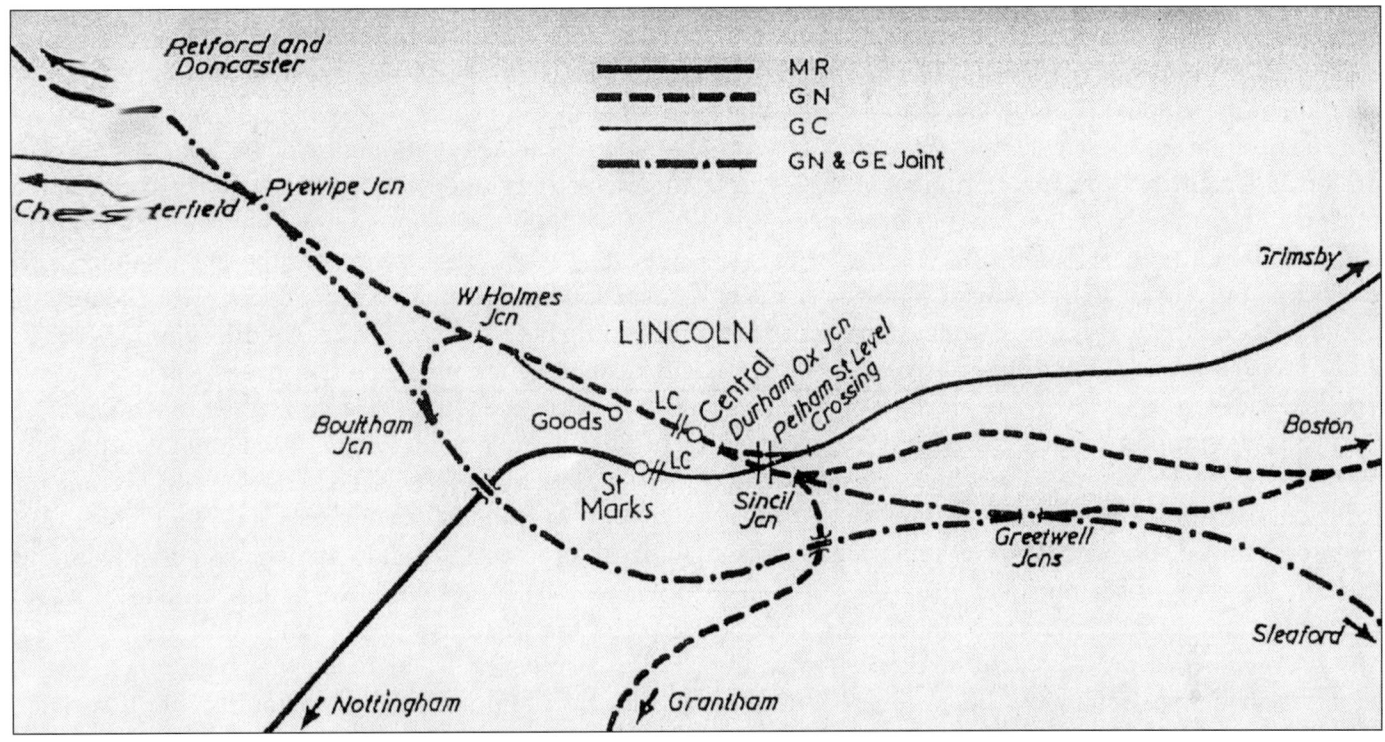

As a town Lincoln owes much to the arrival of the railways and much of its later road traffic congestion also to the railway level crossings. The map shows how four railways routed their competing traffic.

Brecon; the Boston, Sleaford and Midland Counties; and the GTR. In June 1861, the MS&LR granted Watkin a period of leave of absence to enable him to recover his strength.

The previous year or so had been demanding also upon Watkin's personal life. In 1860 a close friend – Herbert Ingram, founder of the *Illustrated London News* – drowned and his widow, Ann, requested his support. He placed the fortunes of the paper and her whole estate on a firm basis and took a role in editing the paper. During that time, he published an article he wrote entitled 'A British railway from the Atlantic to the Pacific' ... across Canada. He had visited Canada in 1851 and, following his return, had written and had published his thoughts about the future of that part of the British Colonial Empire. Sadly, 1861 also saw the death of his father.

In 1854, Watkin had been asked by his then Chairman at the LNWR – Glyn – to visit Canada and attempt to sort out the unsatisfactory state of affairs with the GTR. Glyn, with fellow banker Sir Thomas Baring, were financiers to that Railway and rightly had concerns about the investment. However, at that time the request was wrong for Watkin but clearly he had a personal interest in following developments in Canada and in 1858 had written to Samuel Cunard (born in Halifax, Nova Scotia) commending a projected new railway from Quebec to the Atlantic port of Halifax.

For various reasons the building and development of the GTR had proved difficult. The railway had been projected in 1852 and as such represented the first big business opportunity for Canadians. The advantage to them from furthering trade to bring increased prosperity were clear, but risk capital investment without early returns proved to be a barrier. Not having railway constructional skills, the Premier of Nova Scotia turned to Morton Peto (builder of several railways in England and France) to explore the possibilities for a line between Riviere du Loup and Port Huron. He joined up with three other railway contractors, including Thomas Brassey, and in 1853 a prospectus had been issued. Their choice of track gauge (5ft 6in rather than the generally applicable in England and the USA of 4ft 8½in) was based upon smoothness of ride, greater capacity of rolling stock vehicles, more powerful locomotives and prevention of military use by others with standard gauge rolling stock were sound, but commercially weak in terms of the transhipment of goods to/from other operations. The railway as constructed had engineering weaknesses in terms of track component design and integrity, drainage, alignment of curves and track laying, leading to endless trouble with operations. Glyn and Baring were correct to be concerned; they had not fully appreciated the lengthy sections of sparsely populated country over which trains moved slowly and conveyed goods of low value between centres having little industry. Over the first five years of operation (1855-59), the ratio of outlays to receipts averaged an alarming 89.8 per cent, the railway was close to bankruptcy and with the provincial government not intent on supporting it, Baring and Glyn came to its rescue in 1860. Meetings of shareholders in 1861 resulted in a recommendation that 'a man of great skill, experience and energy should proceed ... to take over the entire supervision of the Company and negotiate with the Government'. The response was that Edward Watkin was invited to undertake the considerable responsibility. As it turned out, the problem of the then longest railway in the world was not the limiting horizon for Watkin. He was far from convinced about the prospects of early success for the GTR and, although he was confident about his skills to improve the efficiency of the railway (via scheduling, management of physical and human assets, negotiations with the stake holders), he thought that early returns for investors and the strengthening of the role of the Railway would prove difficult unless ... The way to do both of those he felt would be through an extension right across Canada to link the Atlantic and Pacific Oceans. Possibly recalling his earlier visit to a Paris Exhibition, where he had studied a map of Europe and realised the potential for growth of trade and transportation by railways, the same potential surely existed in Canada. Such breadth of vision was a characteristic of Watkin which he was to retain for later projects involving a link between England and mainland Europe.

First, though, he had to turn around the fortunes of the GTR and gradually did so; by early 1864, the fleet of freight wagons and locomotives had become totally inadequate for the traffic on offer. By the end of 1865, the Company felt that its credit had been re-established. Traffic had risen by over 50 per cent in less than three years, the operating ratio improved by ten points and by 1873 the track gauge allowed ease of trans-shipment with other operators (initially via a third rail).

One of the factors over which no railway General Manager can exert influence is fluctuations in economic activity. 1866 was particularly difficult for the GTR, with the reduction in trade between Canada and the US, a stock market crisis in the UK together with suspicions of speculation in GTR shares. Although the operating ratio had by then been reduced to 55 per cent, its nearest geographical rival was at 41 per cent. 1867 proved to be no better (in terms of the ratio) and in fact deteriorated to a point where new capital was needed. The shareholders were critical, having little regard for the scale of challenges Watkin as President (since 1862 when he replaced Thomas Baring) faced in trying to increase the net earning power of the Company. Having crossed the Atlantic a dozen times and improving the Railway physically, he had exhausted himself in a futile effort to put the Company on its feet financially. He lacked good health and a willingness to serve any longer than 1869 when his term of office was due to expire.

In parallel with his duties for the GTR, Watkin was also heavily involved with the development of an Atlantic to Pacific railway, the Intercolonial Railway. The work involved him in meetings with the Duke of Newcastle, Hudson's Bay Company, the British North American Association, the International Finance Society (IFS), which later agreed the transfer to parties represented by Mr Edward Watkin of the whole interests in land of the Hudson's Bay Company. As such it was probably the greatest single transfer of a territory ever accomplished unheralded by war. The IFS then set up a subsidiary company to build a telegraph line to the Pacific. Although Watkin had no further direct involvement, it provides an example of his vision and drive. For his role in progressing the development of the Canadian Dominion, Watkin was offered a knighthood in 1867. He declined on the basis that certain enabling legislation was not yet in place but accepted when again offered a year later. A baronetcy followed in 1880, linked to his work for Grimsby.

Watkin's time (from summer 1861) and exposure to business and political pressures in the frequently hostile Canada quickly made him stronger, more assertive and hardened his resolve to maintain any position upon which he was sure he was right. Upon his return in November 1861 he was incensed to find that some of his MS&LR colleagues had agreed to an agreement with the MR which had upset the management of the GNR with whom Watkin had worked to put in place a post-Huish commercial agreement that was to last half a century. Watkin resigned over the matter, but after criss-crossing the Atlantic a few times he was invited back onto the Board in March 1863. In his development years, Watkin had been a protégé of his Chairman – John Chapman – but found himself in 1863 dissatisfied with aspects of the direction the MS&LR seemed to be taken in by the Chairman and his Deputy. Chapman – not in the best of health and with parliamentary duties as MP for Grimsby – recognised that the younger man had matured and become impatient for an opportunity to lead and exert control.

In January 1864, Watkin (still with responsibilities in Canada) was elected Chairman, a seat he was to occupy for thirty years. He was to need all of the attributes mentioned previously and as someone who found delegation of authority difficult merged many of the duties of Chairman with those of a General Manager to become what we would now refer to as a Chief Executive or Chief Executive Officer. Life as the demoted General Manager – Robert Underdown to 1885 and then William Pollitt, previously the Accountant – must have been challenging in the extreme.

As evidence of Watkin's stamina and ambition here is a summary of his business and political involvements 1864-94:

Chairman, MS&LR 1864-94
President, Grand Trunk Railway Canada, to 1869
Member of Parliament, 1864-68 and 1874-95
Chairman, South Eastern Railway (SER), 1864-94
Director, Great Eastern Railway (GER) 1868-72 and 1876-77
Chairman, Metropolitan Railway (Met R) 1872-94
Chairman, North London Railway (NLR) 1870s-93
Chairman, East London Railway (ELR) 1878-93
Chairman, Trustees of the New York, Lake Erie and West Railway USA
Director, Great Western Railway (GWR) 1863-67
Director, Black Sea and Danube Railway 1860s
Director, Belgian Congo Railway
Director, Athens - Piraeus Railway 1877
Director, Brazilian Electric Telegraph Co.
Director, Manchester Fire Assurance Co.
Director, Humber Iron Works, 1860s
Promoter, The Submarine Continental Railway Co. 1881 (renamed The Channel Tunnel Co. 1887)
Adviser on Indian railways, 1888
Knighted, 1868
Baronetcy, 1880
Freedom of the Borough of Hythe 1885, Grimsby 1891

Although from time to time Watkin faced challenges and difficulties with factions of shareholders – often because he was spreading his time too thinly across many interests – the key to understanding this lengthy list is that he earned and retained the support of his colleagues, proprietors, shareholders, constituents who invited him, nominated or elected him. He may have been very willing, or perhaps let it be known that he would be willing, to stand for election for the railway companies that particularly suited his vision (the SER, MetR, ELR, NLR) or even let prominent stakeholders chase him until he caught them!

Throughout the thirty year tenure of the MS&LR financial considerations formed a unifying thread and whilst these are developed in detail later (in chapter 3) it is worthy of note here that Watkin had earned and retained the support of wealthy backers in Lancashire who had played a leading role in the funding for railways in the 1830s/40s. Whilst the MS&LR had many holders of Ordinary shares (which performed poorly in terms of dividends), a majority of the capital was in the hands of a relatively small group of holders of Debenture shares bearing a fixed rate of interest – holders of Debenture shares did not enjoy voting rights but could hold meetings, thus creating opportunities for Watkin to seek to address them with his plans and to then encourage their development as an informed influential pressure group. This may explain references in books to proprietors as distinct from 'shareholders' and 'half yearly meetings of shareholders'. Having a group of say 20 per cent of the total number of holders of equity who owned 80 per cent of the cost of the equity would have given Watkin and his Board knowledge of the fixed interest burden year on year and the net income required to support that 'first' charge on profit. Prevailing economic conditions (in terms of inflation, minimum lending rates and alternative markets attracting investment monies) would have allowed Watkin and his Board to set the fixed rate of interest in line with confidence in business expectations and what contemporary railway companies were offering. The risks of downturns and uncontrollable variables were present then, just as today, but continuity of support was present within the Board of the MS&LR.

In the short term of his early years as Chairman, Watkin had to grapple with the demands of a fast growing economy and population, planning for the profitable expansion of the MS&LR, protecting lines and rights enjoyed as a monopoly or shared by trading running rights of others (e.g. with the GNR), joining forces with other companies to mutual advantage and/or repel the intended advances of competitor companies. In such a competitive environment and his standing within a peer group of similar dominant personalities, Watkin would much rather be a man who would lead through acquisitions or mergers and not be the chairman of a company acquired by another, or be seen to fail. At times, Watkin would have been content to work with the GNR and MR (perhaps to repel the GER, the LYR and, or, LNWR/GWR) whilst at other times quite the opposite would apply. The way it worked was via the parliamentary process whereby each railway put forward proposals or Bills, preceded or followed by correspondence between chairmen or in some cases delegated. Many were the (gentlemanly) clashes between Watkin and his contemporaries and, of course, the GNR wanted the same things, access to coalfields in the Midlands in particular, with which the MR was most unhappy; the MR wanted its own line into London to rid itself of a dependence south of Hitchin along the congested GNR and South of Rugby on the congested LNWR; the fledgling GER wanted access to Yorkshire; the LYR just wanted to be left alone until it made up its mind and the GWR wanted a route into Liverpool.

As examples, the LNWR prospected a line between Chapel-en-le-Frith and Sheffield; that spurred the MS&LR to complete its Marple, New Mills and Hayfield Junction Railway. The LNWR countered by withdrawing running rights, enjoyed by the MS&LR through parts of Manchester. Watkin responded by proposing to build a new railway which, though passed by the House of Commons, was rejected in the House of Lords in the parliamentary session 1864. The MS&LR sought powers relating to steamship service, to construct a line to Macclesfield, to lease the South Yorkshire Railway, to work jointly with the MR and/or North Staffordshire Railway, to join with the GNR in a line in Liverpool; and amongst the proposals it was opposing was a proposed GER Great Eastern Northern Junction (railway) and the GNR joined forces in that opposition as success would potentially allow access to coalfields.

Out of the complex mix came initiatives that were successful to varying degrees over differing periods of time. The MS&LR was successful in its attempt to lease the South Yorkshire Railway, essentially five separate lines: the Sheffield extension connection; the West Riding & Grimsby Railway giving access to Wakefield; the Trent, Ancholme & Grimsby Railway enabling a route crossing the River Trent and into the ironstone deposits; the Barnsley Coal Railway; and projected route improvements. A strategically valuable initial lease of 76 miles of a largely profitable railway received assent in June 1864. The MS&LR took over operations, loaned rolling stock and after ten years proposed a takeover which was agreed and enacted, providing the MS&LR not only with the railway, but also 60 miles of canals. The Tinsley-Mexborough eight mile line effectively knitted together the former South Yorkshire Railway by allowing a direct route between Sheffield and Doncaster via Mexborough, but it was very expensive and a drain on an otherwise worthy investment. The sale of the canal in 1894 brought in cash of £600,000 and fully paid ordinary shares of £540,000.

An initiative which brought the GNR and MS&LR together was for the Great Eastern Northern Junction Railway; 108 miles of easily graded trunk railway for coal from near Cambridge to Askern, where there would be routes to the West Riding and to Grimsby. The recently formed GER would provide half the capital with the aim of tapping the coalfields of South Yorkshire. Well thought out, it proposed connections with the MS&LR at Doncaster, Gainsborough and Lincoln and, commercially, sought to sway the parliamentarians with an offer to carry 'train load' coal at one farthing per mile. After 25 sittings, the Committee rejected it and that would have been the end of the matter except that the LYR – finally into action as a result of GNR influence increasing in the West Riding – decided to support the GENJ, though with an amended route North of Sleaford to Lincoln, thence to Askern for junctions with the LYR, the NER and the West Riding & Grimsby. The proposal was re-submitted in 1865 and prompted Watkin to propose a 25 mile 'blocking' line between Althorpe-on-Trent and Lincoln at a cost of £250,000. Watkin's proposal won the day, but the railway was never built. The output from the process was that agreements over running rights were entered by the MS&LR, GWR and GER with the latter being able to reach Wakefield.

A vexed question between the MS&LR and the MR relating to access to Mansfield was also resolved in 1865; the MS&LR having running rights from Shireoaks and the MR gained a similar right between Shireoaks and Retford.

Watkin judged the time right (1864/5) to expand in Lancashire and Cheshire by means of jointly owned lines with invited partners and at the expense of the LNWR upon whose patch they would be encroaching. The MS&LR could not hope to fund on its own such an expensive project involving four railways at different stages of development. They were the Cheshire Midland, already in operation and part owned with the GNR; the Stockport and Woodley Junction Railway and the Stockport, Timperley and Woodley Junction Railway which were both nearing completion; and the Garston and Liverpool Railway which opened on 1 June 1864.

A new line would be built from Old Trafford to Cressington and from Glazebrook to Timperley, thus negating any need for running powers over the LNWR between Timperley and Garston. The Cheshire Lines Transfer Act 1865 legalised the arrangement involving then the MS&LR and GNR; the MR joined as an equal partner by another Act (1866) and full independent status for the CLC was achieved in 1867, with additional mileage added for Godley to Woodford as part of sourcing lucrative contracts for transport of salt from the area around Northwich. All this represented a severe defeat for the LNWR and relationships were strained to say the least. Through the 1870s, the CLC took greater shape and in 1874, a new passenger service of 16 through trains between Manchester London Road and Liverpool Central, via Warrington Central (34 miles). CLC services to Chester were switched to Manchester Central in 1878 when the Old Trafford-Cornbrook link was completed.

The three partner railways shared costs, with the MS&LR being responsible for provision of motive power and the GNR/MR for rolling stock. The CLC was 'driven through' by one man: Watkin. Not content with the 'basic' CLC, Watkin's expansionist drive identified three further opportunities, none of which proved to be inspired successes and cost the MS&LR dear.

At the Manchester end of the CLC, there was in 1874 a perceived opportunity for local industrialists to promote an 11 mile line to access the coalfield of Platt Bridge, Bickershaw and West Leigh near Wigan. With neither the GNR or MR being keen on this, but with support of the MS&LR alone, in 1876 the first sod was cut of the Wigan Junction Railways. Progress was difficult and in 1877, the promoters sought from the MS&LR an assurance that the MS&LR would work the line when it was completed. Watkin felt obliged to protect the interests of his Company (and to prevent it falling into the hands of the LYR/LNWR) but provided financial support to the promoters. The contract proved costly for the MS&LR and it was not until autumn 1879 that the line opened to coal traffic.

A junction with the Wigan Junction Railways near Lowton St Mary was one end of the 1885 St Helens & Wigan Junction Railway later named the Liverpool, St Helens & South Lancashire Railway which, without substantial financial backing by the MS&LR, would never have been built. As it was, the line was built in part between 1885-95, traversed a coalfield and enabled access at high land purchase cost to the glass production facilities being developed by the Pilkington brothers. The line did not extend beyond St Helens and was an expensive 8 ⅜ miles of railway.

The 44 salt works in Cheshire needed coal for their production process. Adequate for that purpose was the slack coal available in the coalfields of North Wales. The Western (Chester) end of the CLC enabled access to the coal via a new railway from Chester to Hawarden. That railway became known as the Chester & Connahs Quay, having been enacted in 1884, and following construction of a bridge across the River Dee at Hawarden was opened in early 1890 by William Gladstone who lived locally and was a good friend of Watkin. Useful though it was, it was insufficient for Watkin, who wished to use it as a 'stepping stone' further South into Wales (via the Cambrian Railways) and also North from Hawarden to the coast (docks) at Bidston. The former route gap could be partially filled by an agreement with the Wrexham, Mold & Connahs Quay Railway, the owner of the controlling interest in which died in 1888. Pollitt (the GM of the MS&LR) then negotiated with the trustees of the line and achieved a purchase on what looked like very favourable terms. That left a short section between Wrexham and a connection with the Cambrian Railways at Ellesmere, for which authorisation had been received in 1885. After much wrangling with potential partners, the LNWR and GWR, the MS&LR eventually went ahead in 1892 and the line was opened in November 1895. For the projected 15 mile line to Bidston, Pollitt had in 1888 gained the agreement of the LNWR to transfer the rights to the line to the MS&LR/WM&CQR, but due to financial restraints there was a delay in proceeding. Spotting in 1892 that the MS&LR had some £476,000 to its credit, Watkin decided it was time to make a start and advised the trustees of the impoverished WM&CQR that they would be expected to pay 10 per cent interest on the share of the capital cost (more later in chapter 2). The line was opened in 1896.

Finally, whilst still just with the CLC connection, a reference has to be made to the eventually aborted Blackpool Railway into which Watkin was drawn by the promoters in 1882. The plan was to connect the Wigan Junction Railways to an extension of the West Lancashire Railway. With a possibility of invading LYR territory, Watkin was drawn in to the extent of some £300,000. By 1894, the MS&LR felt obliged to protect itself by appointing a Receiver. Within months, the Blackpool Railway was in liquidation and the best the MS&LR could hope for was the proceeds of sales of railway owned property to the LYR/LNWR.

Despite its differences and strained relationship with the LNWR, that railway company and the MS&LR worked together and effectively on the profitable Manchester South Junction & Altrincham Railway opened in 1849, though with an arbitrator present at all meetings! The MSJ&A owned its own rolling stock, but locomotives were provided by the MS&LR.

In January 1862, a group of Lancashire based supporters of the South Eastern Railway (SER) – led by Watkin's brother-in-law – who were dissatisfied with the then current management, agreed that Watkin should be their candidate if and when a vacancy upon the Board became available. In 1842, the SER had received £100,000 from various bankers on account of instalments on shares remitted through them. Glyn & Company had remitted £64,700 and much of the balance came from three Lancashire banks. It may have been a case of the group pursuing Watkin until such time as he caught them, or that group was fully aware of Watkin's intention. In 1850, Watkin had been with his father to see the 'panorama' of an overland route to India, the idea of linking cotton garment producers with their biggest customer pleasing them. Separately, in 1856/57 a plan instigated by a Frenchman, Thomé de Gamond, to link his country to England via a tunnel had been given coverage in the *Illustrated London News*. Those separate potential ventures, together with the vision for Canada he formed at the end of the 1850s/early 1860s, probably had sown the seed in the mind of Watkin to link the MS&L with the South of England portal to a tunnel under the English Channel. If that hypothesis is accepted, the pursuit of influence over the activities of the railways for which Watkin became a Director (D) and/or Chairman (C) makes a lot of sense:

- the MS&LR D 1863 (pt) C 1864-94
- the SER D 1865-66 C 1866-94
- the Great Eastern Railway (GER) C 1868 (pt) D 1868-1872 and D 1877 (pt)
- the Metropolitan Railway (MetR) C 1872-94
- the East London Railway (ELR) C 1878-93
- the North London Railway (NLR) C 1870-93

Each railway had challenges to be faced. When Watkin took office as Chairman at the SER it was in difficult financial circumstances and in 1866 a banking crisis resulted in the markets being shaken and with resultant bankruptcies. The LCDR which operated in the same geographical area as the SER was taken into Chancery and one of the Watkin non-railway companies of which he was Chairman – Humberside Ironworks – was declared bankrupt. However, attempts were made by Watkin to promote an amalgamation of the SER with the LCDR, London Brighton & South Coast Railway and London and South Western Railway, but the Bill was voted down by a parliament becoming more sensitive to monopoly positions being taken at the potential cost to the travelling public. At various times in the late 1860s and 1870s, further efforts made by Watkin with the LCDR were viewed by some as being a wasteful use of resources, by others as a personal battle of wits and egos of the respective chairmen. On several occasions, Watkin ran into trouble with factions of his Board. Firstly, following the contentious appointment of his son Alfred to the post of Locomotive Engineer (Alfred was also a Director of the MS&LR and MetR), he lost a vote and Watkin junior was dismissed. Secondly, in response to what some perceived as his dictatorial style of management, he received a vote of censure and, thirdly, following complaints that he was 'spreading himself too thinly' across his various railway chairmanships and his role as a Member of Parliament and in pursuit of a Channel tunnel. Finally, another vote was lost with discontent over his attempts to secure a connection between the MetR and the SER via the ELR at New Cross (and for the SER to gain access to the GER at the same point). Despite all of these expressions of concern, Watkin prevailed; the new line at New Cross was worked from April 1879 and his son was restored to the Board of the SER in the same month. In 1893, a further attempt at a union with the LCDR was withdrawn and by that time the two railways were working well together at all levels except between the chairmen. From 1899, they were worked as a unified system, but retained separate identities, Boards and shareholders with net receipts split 59 to 41 per cent in favour of the SER.

The Metropolitan Railway

The MetR had been conceived in the 1830s as an underground system to relieve the congested thoroughfares above. This was extended to allow the urban poor to be housed on the edge of the quickly growing conurbation and travel cheaply to their places of work. Watkin arrived to find a railway in need of management of records, of all aspects of finance and very disgruntled shareholders. Watkin's early reforms included the election of a new, smaller, Board and the appointment of an external auditor. A union with the Metropolitan District Railway had much to commend it, but for several years until 1878 all such thoughts were stifled by difficulties between Watkin and his equivalent – who just happened also to be Chairman of the LCDR – and between the MetR and the proposed Metropolitan District Railway.

All the years of Watkin's involvement saw the promotion of plans to expand to the North to Willesden, Harrow and Aylesbury. The MetR was in essence two railways; the underground section in London and (by the end of his Chairmanship) a 50½ mile extension into rural Buckinghamshire.

The ECR had been authorised in 1865 as a link to connect all railways entering London North and South of the Thames. The line was opened from New Cross to Shoreditch (5¼ miles) in 1876 and owned no rolling stock. In 1882, five companies (including the SER and Metropolitan District Railway) leased it and operated its services, joined in 1885 by the Great Eastern. The Metropolitan District was quite separate from the MetR and for financial reasons was promoted as a means of completing a circular railway for London. The Inner Circle was completed in 1884 and by 1889 its trains ran to various points, including Whitechapel in the East and to New Cross on the SER over the ECR. That part of Watkin's plan was, therefore, achieved. However, the ECR never had an adequate connection for the North and so failed as a 'through' route.

By 1880, the railway had reached Harrow-on-the-Hill, Pinner in 1885, Rickmansworth in 1887, Chesham in 1889 and Aylesbury in 1892, some 38 miles from Baker Street in London. At Aylesbury, the MetR made a connection with the GWR line from Princes Risborough. With an eye to future possibilities, Watkin became Chairman of the Aylesbury and Buckingham Railway to ensure that particular link (to the LNWR) did not fall into anyone else's plans.

The motivation for this expansion into an area then generating very low levels of traffic was either visionary, in terms of predicting the growths of population, London and its economy, or selfish, based upon his constant search in the 1880s for suitable Northern connections with the MetR. The Worcester and Broom Railway (Extension to Aylesbury) Bill of 1888 (to which the MetR subscribed £100,000) received a second reading, but a Parliamentary Committee rejected it in 1889. Had it been successful it would have offered the prospect of a lengthy route to within 60 miles of Ellesmere, the connection with the MSLR via Wrexham.

Arising from negotiations with landowners who would not sell strips of land, the MetR accumulated a considerable estate of land surplus to its railway activities. Watkin envisaged using some of this land to be used for London's finest sports leisure and exhibition centre; Wembley Park Estate between Neasden and Harrow, purchased in 1890. Upon part of the estate, Watkin wished to have built a structure housing the popular and commercially very attractive appeal of the Eiffel Tower in Paris. Into this venture the MetR invested £300,000 and Watkin, personally, was its largest single shareholder. The tower did not progress beyond its first physical stage of construction and remained until 1906 as something of a folly. However, much of the estate proved to be a success, the exhibition centre forming the venue for the British Empire Exhibition of 1924. The football pitch of the Wembley stadium was laid on the land formerly occupied by the folly.

North London Railway

Frustration with the timescale for the joining up of the MetR with the SER may have influenced Watkin accepting the role of Chairman of the North London Railway (NLR) although it is unclear as to the start date and also

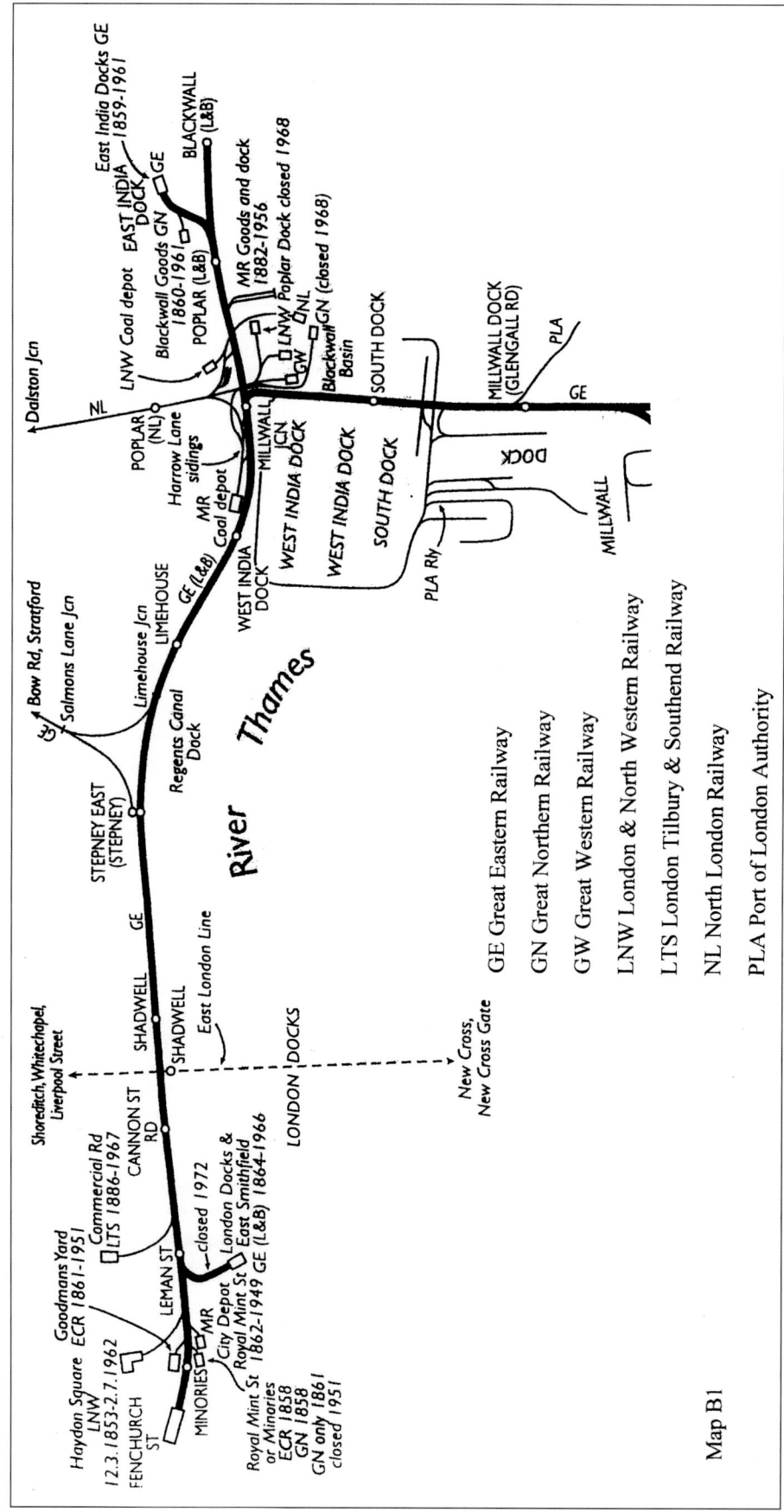

Map B1

The various docks of the River Thames in London were much sought after by competing railway companies for coal and import/export traffic. The North London Railway was of particular relevance to Edward Watkin and the Great Central Railway.

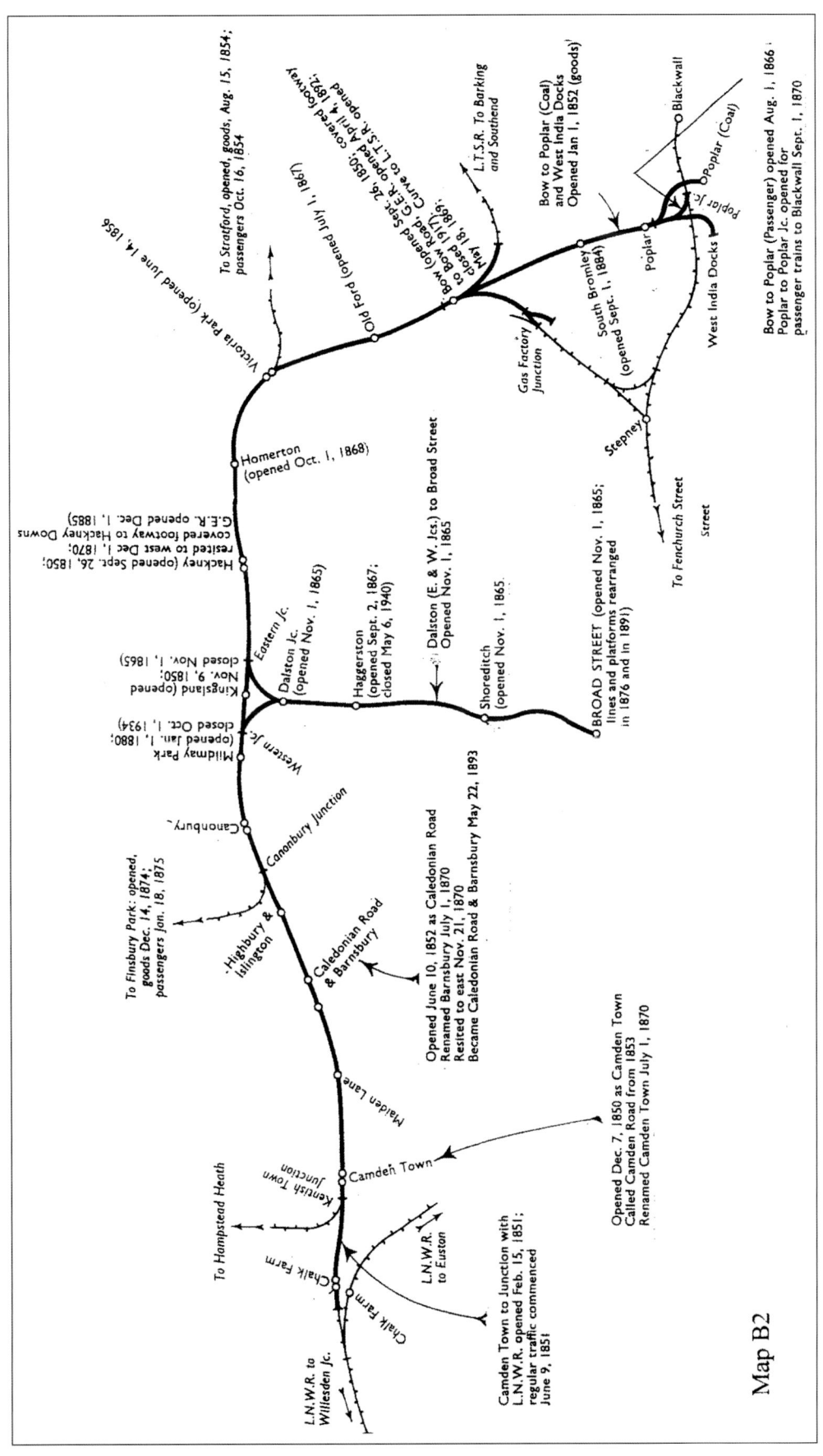

Map B2

This map shows in greater detail the route and connections onto/from the North London Railway. The Great Northern, Great Eastern, Midland and London & North Western railway companies as well as later, the Great Central, sought to use its tracks and pay for the privilege.

why the LNWR (who enjoyed two thirds ownership) did not install its own Chairman. Only 13¼ miles long with running rights over 54¾ miles of other companies' lines, it had a disproportionate importance as providing a connection between the Northern and Western main lines and the docks along the Thames and the goods depots of the City. The NLR eventually formed a link in a chain of lines circling London to the North and, as such, was potentially useful to Watkin's plan if a connection could be made off the MetR lines. Whilst Watkin was Chairman, the NLR enjoyed a profitable existence, declaring healthy dividends up to 7½ per cent from the conveyance of both goods and passenger traffic.

Great Eastern Railway
Watkin's role as a Director of the Great Eastern Railway (GER) brings together the influence of the Manchester Shareholders Association (MSA), an indication of how far Watkin's career as a Member of Parliament had progressed and his 'eye' for expansion of the MS&LR interests. As already noted, the GER had overstretched itself in pursuit of access to the coalfields of Yorkshire and in 1866 found itself in need of significant funds and parliament – in the midst of a short term monetary crisis – refusing permission to seek to raise the necessary funds. In summer 1867, Watkin was offered the post of chairman and though rejecting it, held out the prospect of nominating an excellent chairman, though subject to the Board of the GER being reconstituted. Members of the GER Board did not like such a proposal, but under pressure from the MSA, the Board resigned. Six new directors were elected, two of whom were Watkin and the 36-year-old Lord Cranborne (later Marquess of Salisbury and a great Prime Minister who had been caught up in the financial crisis and needed a job!) Cranborne had reservations about the relative strength of the GER accounts, their past management and faced a range of financial and administrative challenges. Cranborne's regime was extremely effective; in 1868 the Official Receiver was discharged, the following year the GER resumed paying a dividend and talk of re-expansion started anew. The talk of re-expansion started with a conference between Watkin, Rothschild, two other bankers and Salisbury. In 1869, he was thinking again about its aspirations to gain a connection with the Yorkshire coalfields. Because of the parliamentary jostling in 1864/65, the GER Board was suspicious about what they perceived as Watkin's divided loyalties (to the MS&LR and to the GER) and his association with the GNR. The coal mine owners of South Yorkshire complained in 1870 about the GNR and the MR joining together to give preference to coal from the North East and Derbyshire. In October 1870, Watkin proposed to the Board of the MS&LR a new coal railway which would be promoted by the South Yorkshire coal owners, but supported by the MS&LR and, he hoped, also the GER. This was an interesting early example of Watkin perceiving the role of the MS&LR as a carrier of traffic over a railway (promoted and with its capital provided by a third party) rather than over its own railway. The GER was prepared to back the proposal in principle, but preferred that the line would end East of the proposed Huntingdon. In March 1871 a Bill was prepared, argued in parliament, but rejected. The problem of the South Yorkshire coal owners had become acute; coal sent to London by rail had increased from 1.4m tons in 1862 to 3.7m tons in 1870, but the proportion from South Yorkshire had fallen from one sixth to one sixteenth and the three main carriers (GNR, MR and MS&LR) were in disputes over pricing. The rate cutting continued into 1871 and with the GNR and MR engaged in a commercial war, Watkin hardly helped by advising the GNR that unless they provided for some freedom for future coal traffic emanating from South Yorkshire that the MS&LR would have no alternative to establishing independent access to the market over another railway (the MR, which had its own route to St Pancras and, therefore, no longer relied upon the GNR for access to its tracks South of Hitchin). However, Watkin also said that in the short term the MS&LR would be satisfied with running powers over the GNR lines South of Doncaster and Lincoln. The wider railway 'picture' of that time featured potential amalgamations and the three chairmen (GNR, MR and MS&LR) were involved in discussions, driven perhaps also by the GNR and MR tiring of the antics of their smaller contemporary, but the mood of parliament (as evidenced in 1872 by the withdrawal of Bills for the proposed amalgamation of the LNWR and LYR, plus the MR and Glasgow & South Western Railway) was against such, at least at that time.

In February 1872, Salisbury resigned and Watkin followed in the August. Watkin waived his fees as a Director of the GER, either by returning them or giving them away to charity. The Board of the GER had a change of heart in 1876 and offered Watkin the Chairmanship, declined as it would then have been his fourth concurrent role as a railway company Chairman. He did, though, rejoin the Board as a Director for some 15 months from summer 1876. Though it increased the standing of Watkin in political circles and his involvement assisted the recovery of the GER, that railway was not really in his scheme of future things. In August 1878, he accepted the Chair of the East London Railway, having been asked to be the Official Receiver of that Company which formed a link between his SER and his MetR. Now that was certainly in his scheme of future things.

Measures of the relative success of a Chairman of a railway include safety of its day to day operations and its financial performance. Shortly following his election as Deputy Chairman of the SER, there occurred at Staplehurst, Kent, a serious accident which was caused after the civil engineers removed sections of rail. Ten people were killed and about fifty injured when a train, on which Charles Dickens happened to be travelling, derailed at speed. Two other serious accidents occurred within the territory of the MS&LR; firstly at Bullhouse, near Penistone on 16 July 1884, when a broken axle caused a derailment on an embankment with 24 lives lost, and at Hexthorpe, Doncaster, on 16 September 1887, a rear end collision being found to be the fault of the enginemen of the MS&LR train and causing 25 deaths. To place those statistics into a wider context, the period 1870 to 1887 inclusive saw 28 accidents of a serious nature involving a total of 351 deaths. The response of the staff of the MS&LR to support and help the railway was noble; the men at Mexborough met and decided to offer a full week's pay towards the cost of claims resulting from the incident. Staff at other centres followed their example, but whilst appreciating the gesture, Watkin asked that the Board might be allowed respectfully to decline it. Strange, though, that the Board could not grasp the opportunity to turn back nascent trade unionism. As it was, the employees of the railway – the driver and fireman of the MS&LR locomotive – faced charges of manslaughter and were represented in court by lawyers engaged by the Associated Society of Locomotive Engineers and Firemen (ASLEF) and not by the MS&LR. With the evidence that 'block' working over the sections in question had been suspended and the train not been stopped in order that the driver could be informed, the pair were acquitted. Membership of ASLEF leapt almost overnight.

A more favourable light can be shone on the MS&LR in regard to taking a lead in 1887 in the provision of continuous, automatic vacuum braking of all passenger carriages and also in the general extension of the block signalling with interlocking of points and signals.

In 1837/39 there were eleven directors of railway companies who were also Members of Parliament; by 1847 it was 80, 96 by 1859 and peaked in 1873 at 132 (at which time the House of Lords had forty-four railway director peers). Whilst not working in unison, their collective voice had to be taken into consideration by parliament and this so called 'railway interest' began to insert itself into the parliamentary process. In 1855, a committee including all railway directors sitting in either House was established to keep an eye on all business affecting them; in 1870 it became a Railway Companies Association and lasted until 1947.

Watkin's strongly held beliefs led him in early 1857 to be nominated to stand as a Liberal candidate for Great Yarmouth. He was one of two candidates elected and took his seat in parliament. However, his agent had been alleged to have been involved in election process irregularities and when this was proven, the election was nullified in the summer of 1857. Watkin failed to be nominated to stand for Great Yarmouth in 1859 and declined an invitation to stand for Salford. Any political aspirations were then paused due to his role with MS&LR, in Canada and having a young family, but were awakened a decade later when he stood unsuccessfully for Cheshire and also unsuccessfully for Exeter in 1873. However, for the General Election of June 1874 (when as Chairman of the SER he had improved the fortunes of that railway) he stood for – and was elected unopposed – to represent the united Borough of Hythe and Folkestone, a process repeated in similar circumstances in 1880 (at which time he was heavily committed to a tunnel to France). In 1885 and again in 1886 he was elected to the Hythe Division of Kent, but from 1888 (the year of the death of his first wife) his 'drive' for his political work declined, though he was re-elected for what became the 1891-95 term.

In the House of Commons, he spoke regularly upon the interests of the ordinary working man, but did not offer his support to the then nascent trade union movement. Watkin was a strong supporter of the Co-operative Society and held a belief that where there were conflicts between capital and labour, the mutual interests could prevail provided they had mutual trust. During his time as an MP he would have seen legislation passed in 1889 for all railways carrying passenger traffic to be worked on the 'block' system of signalling and all such trains to be fitted with instantaneously working continuous brakes, for limits to be placed on total hours to be worked over a given period of time and – for an industry characterised by a high incidence of accidents –the Safety of Servants (Railway Companies Prevention of Accidents) Act.

In 1857, he had seen an article in the *Illustrated London News* about de Gamond's plans for a tunnel to link his country with England and in 1860 Watkin had visited Paris. Various Anglo-French companies were formed, but the Gallic need for speed of action as strongly expressed in 1874 unsettled the British Foreign Office and the Treasury with the inevitable delay and political uncertainty. Watkin, though, was convinced and in 1875 on behalf of the SER/LCDR he submitted to parliament the Channel Tunnel Company Bill proposing a twin tunnel bore arrangement. The Bill received Royal Assent allowing land to be purchased. Unfortunately the site at Dover proved unsatisfactory and the Frenchman who had produced the original plans died during the same year.

Watkin was undaunted by these setbacks and in 1881 formed the Submarine Continental Railway Company, commenced the boring and invited Ferdinand de Lesseps (builder of the Suez Canal) and all and sundry of the political and social chattering classes to visit: and no doubt to be asked to support. Attempts to persuade the Board of Trade to support the venture with public finances failed and the questions of whether to proceed or not to proceed were debated. Boring continued; 1,840 metres from the French side by March 1883 (when work stopped) and despite an injunction on further workings in July 1882, a similar distance from the English side. For good measure, Watkin's equivalent chairman at the LDCR had become involved in a rival company known as the Channel Tunnel Company, but following that became moribund for several years. Watkin took it over in 1887 and his Submarine Continental Railway Company Ltd then became the Channel Tunnel Company Ltd. (which remained extant in the UK Stock Exchange until being re-named Channel Tunnel Investments in June 1971). Finance for this venture had started in March 1875. The Board of the SER agreed, with government authority, to make a grant of £20,000, with the proviso that the LCDR did the same and that the SER would not be bound to any further expenditure. Having failed in his bid for public funding (via the President of the Board of Trade) Watkin sought to attract a £250,000 public subscription for his venture which took over the SER then existing shafts and headings from the end of 1881. By summer 1883, some £100,000 had been expended. The public debate – though not physical works – about the pros and cons of having or not having a tunnel continued until 1895, when Watkin ceased to be an MP and he no longer had a platform from which to introduce eleven Parliamentary Bills and Motions, all of which were either defeated or withdrawn. One of them, the Channel Tunnel (Experimental Works) Bill of 1894, was sent by the Treasury to the War Office. The Permanent Secretary was 'strongly opposed ... on military grounds'. A by-product of the tunnelling was the discovery of a coalfield of some 200 square miles, 56 being under the sea. Though not in the lifetime of Watkin, forty Kent coal companies were registered and in 1984 production was over one million tons/year. The first trains through a rail only tunnel ran on 19 May 1994; Watkin's great-granddaughter being in attendance.

Watkin's wife died in March 1888. He married again in 1892, Ann, the widow of his friend Herbert Ingram (founder of the *Illustrated London News*) but sadly, she died four years later.

Throughout the period of Watkin's chairmanship, the town and port of Grimsby had grown. The expansion of the SAMR in 1847 had included the Sheffield and Lincolnshire Junction Railway and also the Grimsby Docks Company. The arrival of the railway and its ability to move perishable foodstuffs at speed to new markets rejuvenated the old fishing port of Grimsby. Shortly after taking over the Grimsby Docks Company, the MS&LR had built and opened a new fish dock in 1856, enabling the tonnage of fish landed there to increase from around 200 to 5,300 in 1861 and 64,000 in 1891. Not that fish was the only product; cargoes of coal, cotton, salt, iron and machinery were handled and there was a weekly passenger service to Hamburg, Rotterdam and later Königsberg. In 1856, £1m worth of goods was exported, by 1875, £10m and the tonnage using the port had increased over that period six-fold. This provided an example of Watkin at his best. He further developed the commercial approach by persuading the MR and the GNR to join with the MS&LR (and the SYR) to form a joint stock company known as the Grimsby Deep Sea Fishing Company. This became established and at that point the railway companies sold it to local merchants as being the sound basis for Grimsby's future prosperity. Some good business thinking in generating profitable railway traffic by making available venture capital until such time as the project was proven and then recouping the capital.

The MS&LR sought and received from parliament its Steamboats Act of 1864, enabling it to offer passenger and cargo services to the foreign ports already mentioned, plus eight more, including St Petersburg. In fact, since 1855, the MS&LR had promoted with French interests the Anglo-French Steamship Company and in 1865, the MS&LR bought out the Anglo-French and purchased four new vessels, two of which were built at Hull. Two iron paddle steamers were added to the fleet which by 1868 boasted ten ocean going vessels all sailing out of Grimsby. Quite the opposite of the fish trade, the ocean-going services were unremunerative, subject to international conflicts disrupting trade, competition from other railway companies, particularly the GER using the rapidly developing port of Harwich and collisions arising out of misadventure. However, the venture proceeded and in the 1880s, eight new ships replaced earlier 'sisters' and sufficient justification existed in 1890 to allow a further four new steamships into service.

Traction and rolling stock

The MS&LR had its own workshops at Gorton (Manchester), opened in 1848 as the 11th railway company locomotive building workshop and produced its first locomotive in 1858. Gorton produced locomotives, carriages and wagons on a site that was constrained and eventually a separate carriage and wagon build and repair workshop was opened in 1910 at Dukinfield, Manchester. From time to time, the requirements of the traffic department of the MS&LR caused the Board to authorise build programmes of locomotives, carriages and wagons by private contractors. The majority of the traction and rolling stock was acquired by outright purchase, though there were exceptions, such as wagons by hire purchase in the 1860s and a considerable volume and value for those destined for use on the London Extension from 1899, which were purchased, owned and leased to the GCR by the Railway Rolling Stock Trust Ltd. At the end of 1863, the MS&LR had 113 locomotives, 401 carriages and 4,333 wagons.

Charles Reboul Sacré had been appointed as the Locomotive Superintendent of the MS&LR in 1860, aged 29, with responsibilities also embracing civil engineering, canals and docks. He was conservative in his approach, favouring double framed locomotives, staying with single driving wheeled types longer than many peers, preferred fixed wheelset carriages (rather than have four or six wheel bogies). However, he quickly saw the advantages of steel over iron for rails, switches and crossings. His locomotives were long lasting; typical lives being 35 years. Between 1864 and 1870 (excluding 28 acquired with the lease of the SYR) 115 locomotives were added to stock, of which 67 were built by private contractors. However, from 1871 to 1889 production was almost exclusively by Gorton of an average of 20 locomotives a year.

Production of carriages during the same period was low until the changing requirements of the commercial and traffic departments resulted in the Board authorising expenditure. For services to King's Cross from 1873, Sacré built some fixed wheelbase 28ft 9in long vehicles, but bogied stock was still five years away when four composites appeared, followed by four more in the next two years. In 1884 and in agreement with the GNR, a first-class dining car with six wheel bogies was produced. In that same year, Gorton turned out eight first class lavatory carriages, a feature applied also to the earliest third-class saloons (for party travel), two of which were completed in 1886. For the CLC services, the arrangement was for the MS&L to provide the motive power whilst the GNR and MR provided the rolling stock. In 1888, twenty-four carriages were turned out for the Chester and Connahs Quay/Hawarden loop lines plus two more dining cars for joint use with the GNR for King's Cross Services.

Hire purchase of wagons (begun in 1860) was extended in 1864 by ten-year arrangements with the Gloucester Wagon Company and the Manchester Railway Steel & Plant Company for 200 coal wagons and 100 wagons for timber respectively. The rate of expansion of goods traffic is evidenced by 1.639 million tons in 1867 and 2.333 million tons in 1871. During that time, Gorton produced some 1,200 wagons and private contractors another 500 (Bury Railway Carriage & Wagon

Co. and Lancashire and Yorkshire Wagon Co.). Almost forgotten was the need to have an adequate supply of goods braked vans (eventually fitted with stoves).

By the time Sacré resigned in 1886, the stock position had increased to 540 locomotives, 835 carriages and 12,573 wagons. 70 per cent of the locomotives were double framed. 596 carriages were purely for passengers and 2,589 of the wagons were for coal and coke.

The elevation in 1886 of Thomas Parker (who had joined in 1858 as carriage and wagon foreman) to the role of Locomotive, Carriage and Wagon Superintendent also saw a separation of the engineering responsibility for civil engineering with which Sacré had previously been charged.

The arrival of Thomas Parker bought a recommendation to use single frames for new build locomotives and re-constructed, older types. He also inherited a design for a passenger 4-4-0 locomotive, the first of which was built by Kitson & Co. in 1887, exhibited at the Jubilee Exhibition in Manchester then stripped down at Gorton so that a complete set of production drawings could be made. Twenty-four more of the type were built in three batches, two of six by Gorton and one of twelve by Kitson & Co. during Parker's tenure. After a lull in new locomotive orders between 1886-88 (only twenty built, all by Gorton) the years 1889-93 witnessed an influx to meet the needs (184, of which 19 were by Gorton) and included 0-6-0s for main line work and tank engines

Above and opposite: During the early years of Edward Watkin's employment with the railways the finest locomotives of the London and North Western Railway along the Trent Valley were of the type depicted at photograph 8. As was typical of the era *Cornwall* – built 1847 – had one pair of large diameter driving wheels (8 feet 6 inches) with adhesion assisted by the weight of the boiler. The locomotive is now in the National Collection and is seen here during a rare venture outside the museum at Shildon. The large diameter single driving wheel designs of passenger locomotive continued to be favoured (a dozen were built for the MS&LR in 1882/3) and the Great Northern Railway No. 1 – also part of the National Collection – appeared from Doncaster Works in 1870 and is seen there in 2005.

for suburban and short distance passenger and goods work. Amongst these there was the first locomotive on any British railway to be equipped with a Belpaire firebox. Parker's last design was an elegant 4-4-0 with seven feet diameter driving wheels and Belpaire fireboxes (Class 11).

Carriage production and modifications continued apace. Forty-eight third class carriages were outshipped together with eight passenger brakevans in 1889-90 and eighteen third class saloons (for party travel) in 1890-91. Slip carriages were produced in 1892/94 to speed up six King's Cross services (four slipped at Worksop, one at Godley and one at Huddersfield) and in 1892 the Westinghouse and 'through' brakepipe was fitted to thirty-six carriages for inter-workings with the North Eastern and Great Eastern railways.

Wagon production at Gorton during the period included 50 butter wagons, 50 more for meat, 86 for Chester and Connahs Quay (1888), 520 various (1889) for margarine and for glass traffic (1893) plus orders in 1891/93 for a total of 1,632 wagons by Ashbury's Carriage & Iron Co. Ltd. (1,000 of which were for coal).

Henry Pollitt was appointed at a time when the needs for the London Extension services were being progressed. He continued to add to the classes introduced by Parker and not until 1897 did locomotives of his own design emerge from Gorton; a dozen 0-6-0ST and two 4-4-0s. Eleven more Class 11A 4-4-0s followed in 1898. Between 1894 and 1899, Gordon turned out 83 new locomotives and Beyer, Peacock supplied 153. The BP examples included 109 for the London Extension traffic which were purchased by the Railway Rolling Stock Trust Ltd. and hired to the Great Central Railway. The same trust also purchased, owned and hired to the GCR 228 passenger carrying vehicles and 5,658 non passenger carrying vehicles and wagons. The carriage construction was spread across Gorton and five private contractors (Craven Ltd., Ashburys Carriage & Iron Co., Brown Marshalls Ltd., Lancaster Carriage & Wagon Co. and Gloucester Carriage & Wagon Co.) providing a total of 502; the first two named private contractors also supplied a total of 5,521 wagons. By means of the Trust, capital expenditure of around £1 million was avoided at cost to a later annual charge against income. To assist with the logistics of the coal traffic, from 1895 Gorton turned out 1,000 coal wagons with side, end and bottom doors. Also of note is the fitment to 100 cattle wagons of vacuum brakes.

Many railway companies also favoured designs with double frames and many were produced for the MS&LR between the 1860s and 1888. Midland Railway 2-4-0 locomotive 158A was built in 1866 and is shown working with a vintage train of restored vehicles at the Midland Railway Centre. Although the locomotive appears to be in steam it was just rags burning in the smokebox plus a helpful breeze to add to the effect.

The railway companies promoted their individual identities through distinctive liveries. As shown at photographs 8-10, the passenger locomotives were smartly turned out, as were the humble goods types as shown here. 484 of this type were built from 1889.

Right and below: The construction of passenger carriages with bogies started in the 1870s and the first four of the MS&LR appeared from Gorton Works in 1878; two years later the first MS&LR bogied vehicles with lavatories were built and the first type with three axle bogies followed in 1883. Photograph 12 depicts a teak bodied electrically lit, steam heated, bogie carriage built at the end of the nineteenth century for the comfort of passengers on the Metropolitan Railway (which, together with several others, enjoyed something of a charmed life until sale in 1969 to the Bluebell Railway). The Directors of most railways had built for their exclusive use a saloon vehicle; in the case of the MS&LR in 1890. Photograph 13 shows the saloon built in 1897 for the Directors of the Great Northern Railway. The vehicles at 12 and 13 are at the Bluebell Railway.

South from Beighton to Annesley

After considering alternatives with others, the MS&LR decided to build its own line initially from Beighton to Chesterfield via Staveley. However, that proposal was rejected by committee in the House of Commons in 1888. Undaunted, the MS&LR returned in the following year with a Bill for a railway from Beighton to Annesley, with a branch to Chesterfield. The MR had been awkward the previous year and this second attempt by the MS&LR empowered it in March 1889 to negotiate certain reciprocal running rights with the GNR and LNWR, including the MS&LR running its trains into Nottingham (from Annesley on existing tracks). The LNWR accepted, but the GNR initially wanted more running powers (west from Retford) and also that under the term of the GNR/MS&LR agreement of 1860, the MS&LR should not promote (or assist any other company to promote) any extension South of Nottingham. That was unacceptable to the MS&LR and a second rejection looked probable. However, whilst the Bill was before the House of Lords committee the GNR accepted the terms of Pollitt's offer and withdrew its opposition. The construction of the Beighton-Annesley line was authorised by the MS&LR Act of 1889, giving access also to Chesterfield and several collieries.

Contracts (two) were let for construction from each end of the line, with a target completion within 18 months of Feb 1890. As it turned out, the first section of main line (Beighton to Staveley Works) was brought into use on 1 December 1891. At Staveley, a new locomotive depot, with two turntables, a shed capable of holding 60 locomotives, workshops for running repairs and 99 staff cottages were built. The next section, Staveley to Annesley junction, was opened on 24 October 1892, when MS&LR goods and coal trains began running to Nottingham and beyond by a few miles to Colwick yard. Colwick, instead of Doncaster, now became the exchange point with the LNWR for coal traffic from South Yorkshire. The branch from Staveley to Chesterfield had been extended by 4¾ miles to form a loop and re-joined the main line at Heath junction.

The remainder of the Derbyshire lines were short branches to give access to 15 collieries, providing a source of profitable compensation for the loss of some 140,000 tons annually from collieries closed down elsewhere.

Watkin must have been pleased with these developments, but he had wanted more co-operation from the GNR in the form of a new route to London, arguing that the existing routes (MR, LNWR and the GNR itself) would have to continue with expensive widening schemes and enhancing traffic facilities to meet likely traffic levels. Correspondence between Watkin and his opposite number for the GNR – Colville – had been exchanged in 1889 and early 1890, with the latter indicating on behalf of the GNR that the integrity of the 1860 agreement was paramount and all of the various optional ways forward proposed by Watkin were non-starters. Watkin had indeed proposed various combinations of traffic unions and junctions involving the MR, SER, MetR in addition to the GNR and MS&LR. The GNR was upset, feeling that arrangements for interchange of through traffic could be made between the GNR, MS&LR, SER and MetR without constructing a new line in 'direct hostility' to the GNR and in direct violation of the 1860 agreement. For Watkin, any hopes of a traffic union concept with the GNR were at an end; if the MS&LR wanted its own line to London, it would be on its own and along the parliamentary process he could expect fierce opposition.

The big steps along the way for Watkin were first to seek the support of his Board, followed by advising the shareholders to the intention, then to seek and gain parliamentary approval and then raise the capital required.

First then, the Board of Directors. As at March 1890 the Board comprised: Chairman, Edward Watkin; Deputy Chairman; Lord Wharncliffe (3rd Baron), a Director since August 1864; Directors, Sir John W. Maclure, a Director since October 1864, also a Director of the Cambrian Railways and Neath and Brecon Railway, Conservative MP 1886 Stretford Division of South East Lancashire, chairman of Ashburys Carriage & Iron Company, a likely beneficiary company for rolling stock build contracts; Lt. Col. George Morland Hutton, a Director since 1868; Sir Gilbert Greenall, a Director since July 1877, an old friend of Watkin's father Absolom and representative of 'the Liverpool' investors in railways; Edward Chapman, a Director since April 1878, son of a former chairman and holder of a large holding of Ordinary (share) stock; Tom Harrop Sidebottom, a Director since December 1878, cotton manufacturer and nephew of three uncles who had been directors of the SA&MR, also a Director of the St Helens & Wigan Junction Railway; Charles Henry Firth, a director since January 1881 and son of former director Mark Firth, Master Cutler and former Mayor of Sheffield; Rt. Hon. Sir Richard Assheton

Cross, a Director since 1884, a Lancastrian born lawyer and banker and MP who served as Home Secretary for Disraeli and Salisbury; Henry Davis Pochin, a Director since 1889, also a director of the MetR from 1872 and introduced Watkin to that Board. Representative of the Manchester investors in railways, previously Mayor of Salford and MP for Stafford; and Col. Charles Freville Surtees, a director from March 1890.

Watkin as a chairman with grand plans could proceed only with the necessary support of his Board; Wharncliffe, Maclure and Hutton had a long association with Watkin, knew his ways, had seen his development, knew his strengths and record. Greenall and Pochin would have known well how certain investors in Watkin's railways had benefitted from the results of his Chairmanship (SER 1870-74 gross return on capital 9.29 per cent, dividend of 7.5 per cent; MetR 1872-77 dividend increased from 1 to 5 per cent; NCR 1880 – dividend consistently 7.5 per cent; ECR/GER improved fortunes; MS&LR holders of debentures /preference shares). Chapman would have been fully aware of the reasons why holders of Ordinary stock had not fared as well as others with stock in certain other railways. Harrop and Sidebottom were 'safe' in that they were unlikely to form an alliance against the Chairman. Cross would have noted everything, knew the process had some way to go and would await with interest the final, crucial stage. Surtees (and Pochin) would be expected to gain the support of the SER/MetR boards to subscribe a significant sum at the appropriate time. Watkin had gathered around him some widely experienced and sound minds.

Assuming that it was an objectively managed meeting, the Board may have considered a wide range of factors, each of which could affect individual or the corporate view on whether to proceed as proposed by the chairman.

- general position
  Statistics as below did not support the view that there was a trade depression:

  As much as 50 per cent of the world's visible international trade was done by four industrialised countries: Britain, France, Germany and America.

  Britain was not at war.

  The population was increasing, demanding products and warmth in winter.

  In the larger cities, particularly London, there was an increasing trend to live away from the centres of work and travel to/from work from the suburbs.

  Inflation was low and in the mid-1880s had been negative.

  The cost of borrowing money was low and therefore the attraction to investors of a return higher than the Bank of England rate or from purchasing government 'consols' was high.

- MS&LR position:
  A line of its own directly and maybe through London to the South Coast (via the MetR/SER) would allow it to respond to potential mineral and perishable goods traffic, benefit from the increasing suburban traffic and compete for long distance passenger traffic.

  The railway was already well placed for coal, coke, iron ore and fish traffic; an extension would open up colliery traffic from Nottinghamshire and allow further expansion for other traffic for export and conveyance of imported goods.

  The competitors – particularly the GNR, MR and LNWR – would mount opposition to any Bill and seek to protect their commercial/financial positions.

- railway traffic and finance from 1870

	Length of line open to traffic	Total passengers carried (excl. season tickets)	Weight of goods and minerals conveyed	Gross receipts	Working expenses	Net receipts
	Miles	Millions	Tons/million	£m	£m	£m
1870	15,537	336.5	235.3	45.1	21.7	23.4
1880	17,933	603.9	303.1	65.5	33.6	31.9
1889/90*	20,073	817.1	424.9	71.9	43.2	36.8

NOTE:
* I have assumed Cross would have been able to seek guidance on trends from the Board of Trade.

- Railways' position generally
  Safer due to technical improvements to braking and signalling.

  Very few new railways had been built since 1875 - MR Settle and Carlisle 1876; Hull and Barnsley, Barry in the 1880s.

  The MR had faced cost overruns with its London extension.

  An increasing trend (though not supported by parliament) of railway companies to wish to amalgamate rather than work inefficiently with under-utilised facilities.

  Working costs increasing rapidly (rates, taxes, coal, labour).

  Restrictions on hours of working.

  Receipts per train mile declined in the 1880s by 8 per cent, MS&LR by more.

  In terms of the net return on capital in the late 1880s there was a fall to 4 per cent with the MS&LR at the average.

  Passengers were expecting higher standards in carriages, e.g. lighting and catering. However, the bulk of the increased numbers travelling were in third class carriages and benefitting from cheap fares and competition through excursion traffic for recreation/holidays.

- Structure of the MS&LR balance sheet:
  The percentage of total capital bearing fixed interest via debentures and preference shares may become a concern.

  Between 1880-89 total expenses had increased by 22.2 per cent, passenger revenue by 15.8 per cent, goods revenue by 20.1 per cent and net revenue by 13.4 per cent.

Whatever the discussion covered or did not cover is irrelevant. Watkin got his way, his dream was still alive and in the July of 1890 he formed with Wharncliffe, Hutton, Chapman and Pochin a committee to whip up support from industrialists, traders and civil representatives of cities/towns along the projected route.

Big step two – the seeking of parliamentary approval to a Bill – could now proceed. Pollitt was instructed to deposit a Bill for discussion in the 1891 parliamentary session. Fierce opposition was expected and to assist his committeemen, Watkin put in place a group of outsiders with experience of such processes. The 'consultants' included the Members of Parliament for Newark, Sheffield Brightside, Leicester and Nottingham East, plus a Queen's Counsel to guide upon the legalities. All that guidance and advice would have needed to be heeded as, following the case 'for' the Bill being put to the Parliamentary Committees between 17 April and 13 May 1891, the case 'against' was heard from 1 June; a very high total of 49 petitions sharing objections to the proposals in the Bill had been received and were to be considered. Proceedings ended on 16 June with the Committee finding 'against' the Bill. The Board of the MS&LR responded quickly and on 19 June the Directors resolved – subject to the agreement of the Shareholders – to renew its efforts. First, the opposition of the GNR needed to be negated and that was achieved by agreement on new running rights, in particular allowing the GNR to work over the MS&LR lines north of Nottingham and west of Sheffield, and for the MS&LR to be able to access north of Doncaster and into the West Riding by the GNR lines. They also agreed joint ownership of the projected new stations at Nottingham and Leicester. The MR was not so flexible and offered to withdraw its opposition if the MS&LR opted to use its existing Leicester-Rugby line. Far more positively, both the SER and MetR had agreed to subscribe to the capital, as had Staveley Coal & Iron Co. and Sheepbridge (Chesterfield) Coal & Iron Co.

By the end of March 1892, it was known that most of the 31 petitions 'against' were at the London terminal end, some were variously placated by proposals for tunnelling and re-housing. The case was considered in the first two weeks of April and by the 19th passed it completely. Passage through the Lords, though, was obstructed and then a General Election was called, halting all unfinished legislation, and it was not until 28 March 1893 that Royal Assent was granted, with eleven railways authorised to bring the MS&LR to London.

Whilst the London Extension Bill was being progressed, the MetR reached Aylesbury, there effecting a junction with the Aylesbury & Buckingham Railway (A&BR) which ran Northwards to join the LNWR at Verney Junction. The A&B was the line that the London extension was to meet at Quainton Road and was to be doubled in anticipation.

Attention then turned to big step three; raising the capital. The estimate in 1892 for the construction had been £6m. 1893 was a difficult time at which to raise money and in May, Pollitt had to tell the Board that potential financiers had advised against any attempt to create new capital. A dispute in the coal mining industry resulted in a strike by the miners with serious repercussions for the MS&LR, and holders of seven Preference Share stocks who, along with holders of Ordinary stock, were denied a half yearly dividend.

1894 brought better news; the £600,000 cash from the deal with the Sheffield & South Yorkshire Navigation and the mining dispute had been shelved for the time being at least.

Watkin, then 74, had given everything in support of his dream and at that stage started to relax the reins and let Pollitt (and Bell at the MetR) take more decisions. On 19 May 1894, Watkin resigned from his chairman roles at the MS&LR and MetR and, whilst this chapter is about him, it will continue and record how the London extension was taken to London.

At the same MS&LR Board meeting that accepted Watkin's resignation and extended a hope that he would remain as a director (which he did), Lord Wharncliffe was elected chairman and Pollitt was able to convey news that the raising of the capital would soon become a reality, thanks to a financier, Alexander Henderson.

Alexander Henderson was a Scot who joined Deloittes at the age of 21, been elected a member of the London Stock Exchange at age 24 and had built a reputation as a stockbroker. He lived at Buscot Park, Berkshire, which, prior to his arrival, featured a six mile 2ft 8in estate railway worked by three steam locomotives. Whilst the railway remained, motive power was – during his tenure – by horses.

Henderson's interest in railways extended beyond the UK. As stockbroker and accountant he had a long association with the Buenos Aires Great Southern Railway, its auditors and consulting engineers. Though never a director of an Argentine railway company, he was a director of Railway & General Stores Contractors which facilitated the supply of locomotives, rolling stock and infrastructure materials.

On 15 June 1894, Henderson outlined to the Board his plans to set up a syndicate. By the end of the month, some £4m had been underwritten and it was decided to create capital totalling £6.2m entitled 'London Extension Stock', of which all but £2m was to be issued at once. Interest on the newly issued capital for the Extension would be paid out of capital. Pollitt's suggestion to divide the eleven railways as authorised into individual construction contracts was adopted and by early October contracts worth £3.18m in total had been awarded to six different contractors for the 93 miles from Annesley to Quainton Road. The majority of the ensuing challenges were concentrated at the 'neck end of the bottle', i.e. the London end where it would be necessary to work with the MetR, including its ex-MS&LR Chairman (from 1894) James Bell who earlier in his career had had some personal rivalry with Pollitt at the MS&LR.

The process of drafting the eleven railway contracts individually resulted in that intended to be number ten not reaching completion whilst an overlapping addition eventually appeared numbered twelve. Railways six and seven became an eight mile connection between the MS&LR and GWR (Culworth Junction to Banbury Junction opened 1900), railway twelve never progressed to physical work, leaving eight, nine and eleven to occupy minds in 1895 and 1896. The Bell/Pollitt animosity did not help, landlords were as ever aware of the value of their property, competing railways protected their commercial positions and cost overruns emerged also with one contract let in 1894 for work at the London end. Railway eleven was simply a line less than half a mile long to a prosperous coal yard and was run from railway eight which (eventually) left the MetR at Canfield Gardens. It is worth explaining in some detail as it goes some way to explaining why the original cost estimates became so badly overrun.

First, the railway went into a covered way for 700 yards, then crossed the LNWR at what became South Hampstead station, then another 500 yards of covered way and into a tunnel 723 yards long through London clay, followed by another 67 yards of covered way. At that point, it was near Lord's cricket ground and the authorities there had originally been vociferous objectors to the MS&LR extension. Watkin had placated them with a route which ran for 200 yards under Lord's but did not interfere with the main playing area; a strip necessarily cleared for a covered way to be completed was relaid with turf taken from the land of Morley's Cricket Ground which had been purchased by the MS&LR for use as the Neasden locomotive depot and yards. Work at Lord's was out of season, between September 1896 and May 1897. South of the cricket ground the railway's works were somewhat less constrained and without a need for tunnelling, it was possible to lay out multiple tracks for the crossing over the Regents Canal. Provision for entry into the terminus allowed for up to fifteen tracks; but it was decided that five would suffice.

Railway number nine and its routing/junctions were particularly important to Watkin as it would enable a connection to the North London Railway and the London docks. The agreement of the LNWR was necessary and they were strongly opposed. Eventually, the MS&LR and MetR found something that was just mutually acceptable. It involved the MS&LR having its own two tracks between Preston Road Junction and Canfield Place Junction (railway number eight) but no station of its own South of Harrow, thus denying it lucrative suburban traffic. The access to the North London Railway was not made.

For the record, railway number twelve was a proposed cross London link for City and goods traffic off the MS&LR using a new link tunnelled (what became the Great Central Hotel) to join the MetR and give access to the London, Chatham & Dover Railway/other South of England routes. The MetR advised such a link could be available between 10pm and 5am, a maximum of twenty trains each way hauled by MetR locomotives and at exorbitant rates. It was out of the question for the MS&LR and encouraged support for railways six and seven, a developing relationship with the GWR (which finished up paying for the construction) and an exchange of goods traffic at Banbury Yard or at Reading for railways in the South of England. Watkin's dream had died; there would be no 'through' route from the north to the Channel.

Particularly in the London area – and also in Nottingham for the construction of the new station – the landlords and arbitrators had field days. Pollitt – to his credit, but several years late – identified the problem of a serious flaw in the original cost estimates. His revised estimate (at December 1895) was that the ultimate outlay would reach £11.477m and with total capital and borrowing powers presently authorised to only £8.2m.

All of the experience of Henderson was then called upon and he came up with some novel ideas and doubtless used all his contacts in the City. For the rolling stock requirements (109 locomotives, 228 passenger carriages and 5,658 wagons) a Rolling Stock Trust was formed. The purpose of that 'vehicle' was to avoid initial capital expenditure at the long term expense of hire purchase arrangement costs deducted as a charge against receipts. The financial arrangement between the Company and Trust was that interest of around £40,000 per year would be payable until 31 December 1902 and then a half yearly sum of £100k was payable until outright purchase was completed. It was the sort of investment that would present low risk as the assets were largely transferable and easily understood by new backers. The Rothschild family were long term friends of the Watkin family and it is recorded that Ferdinand de Rothschild offered his support at least for the idea of the Extension. His nephew Nathaniel – quoted as saying 'Never allow yourself to get caught without a loose million handy' – was MP for Aylesbury, Lord Lieutenant of Buckinghamshire and, like Ferdinand, lived close to the route, could also have been attracted. The rolling stock contracts placed were predominantly with private contractors and included £345,000-worth with Ashbury's Carriage & Iron Co. (Maclure being Chairman) and a remarkably low figure of £62,000 for 128 carriages from the MS&LR's own works at Gorton. Beyer, Peacock was the contractor of choice for locomotives, varying in cost between £2,200 and £3,500 each. Arbitration awards from disputes with landlords contributed, councils were doubtless prevailed upon to offer favourable local taxes for at least an initial period and the matter of the costs of re-housing some 3,000 occupants of those affected by necessary demolitions at the London end was managed by the Wharncliffe Dwellings Company, in Wharncliffe Gardens (Wharncliffe being Chairman of the MS&LR).

At the end of January 1896, it was decided to create the remainder of the capital authorised in 1893, some £2m. It was decided that rather than place the total amount into one offer, it would be equally divided. The reaction of the marketplace to the first tranche would largely determine the timing of any second tranche and, given the financial performance of the company in regard to dividends on Ordinary shares, there was a risk of failure. Perception of a marketplace is, though, unpredictable. One million pounds of stock was offered to the public in February and was subscribed three times over. The balance of another million was offered in the May and even more heavily over-subscribed. The strength of desire to obtain Ordinary stock was, presumably, driven by the same motivation as applied for railway shares in the 1840s; pursuit of a 'sure thing' and following others in the rush. Such pursuit flew in the face of considered advice as available from guides for shareholders prepared following analyses of annual Board of Trade Returns and half yearly meetings of the company involved. 'Home Railways as Investments 1897' stated:

> 'Under the circumstances it would be imprudent to purchase the Ordinary or Deferred stocks even at the recent low prices. This applies to the Preferred Ordinary

as well, for though an attempt is being made to improve the position of this stock by conversion, it must for some considerable time be a very risky holding.'

Market demand is frequently irrational. Thus the MS&LR London Extension moved forward and in 1897 became the Great Central Railway. Its momentum heavily mortgaged its future ability to meet from receipts a high level of debt to holders of fixed interest stock, an ability to secure running agreements on joint lines and to secure profitable traffic against competitor railways and parliamentary attention which seemed to favour traders. Interest in Spring 1898 on the debt was £1,000 per day; Pollitt needed trains asap.

Matters with the MetR worsened, particularly with regard to coal traffic and proposed new depots at West Hampstead and Willesden Green and, more significantly, for the movement by the GCR of coal to be exchanged with the GWR at Aylesbury, or to be worked to MetR country stations or to destinations south of the Thames. The GCR 'won' the first, but lost the second; the new line with the GWR from Culworth Junction would enable the exchange with the GWR, but was 2½ years away. Another victory for the GCR over the MetR was the sanctioning of a Neasden-Northolt line (1898) and in October 1898 a traffic exchange agreement with the MR and L&SWR for a new connecting curve to the MR Cricklewood-Acton Wells line at Neasden.

The first trains to use the extension were coal and ran in July 1898 and the new Marylebone station was opened on 9 March 1899. With Watkin in attendance, Marylebone goods station opened in April 1899. The coffers were drained and the GCR was quite unable to seek to match the symbolic gestures of wealth at the LNWR Euston and the MR's Grand Hotel fronting St. Pancras. However, the modest frontage of Marylebone was later masked by the building of the Hotel Great Central, though delegated to an independent company.

Above and overleaf pages: These three photographs show the present-day entrances to the termini of the Great Northern Railway, the Midland Railway and Great Central Railway at King's Cross, St Pancras and Marylebone, London, respectively. Originally from 1852/67 and 1899 they show well the scale of the 'statements' made by the GNR and MR (only half of the frontage is shown) and the relatively modest effort of the GCR. Each station also offered a hotel, that for St Pancras being as shown and that for both King's Cross and Marylebone being to the left of the area photographed.

Henderson had become Chairman in 1900 and with Pollitt as his able General Manager, set about taking the railway forward. He will have recognised the need to replace (and reward with a seat on the Board) Pollitt, he would need also a new solicitor, Chief Mechanical Engineer and Signal and Telecommunications Engineer. All would be done within months. He also needed to consider the structure of his Board. Over a period of time in came: Clement Molyneux Royds, MP for Rochdale 1895-1906; A. Percy Allsopp, MP for Taunton 1887-95; Edwin Arthur Beazley, Australian, ship owner; William Purdon Viccars, ex-military (became Deputy Chairman 1906); Sir Edwin Henry Fraser, Mayor of Nottingham 1896-99 and 1910 (helped with setting up Sectional Boards); Robert Nassau Sutton Nelthorpe, a Director of Humber Railway and Dock Company (son of Lord Auckland who had died in 1890); Sir Henry Wilson Worsley-Taylor, MP for Blackpool 1900-06 (son in law of Sir Edward Watkin); Walter Burgh Gair, a Managing Director of Barings bank (Deputy Chairman from 1918); the Earl of Kerry; Sir Berkeley George Digby Sheffield, MP (son of steel-maker at Scunthorpe); and Sir William Pollitt (ex-General Manager).

Anyone who thought that with the death of Watkin in 1901 the policy of expansion would lose strength was well wide of the mark.

It was a good time to be a senior railway official and through the reign of Edward VII and into that of George V, it was a period when the railways had achieved a high level of mechanical efficiency and with encouragement from parliament were improving their record keeping and learning from others. Safety of passengers had not been a recent concern (not a single passenger killed in 1901 due to railway negligence) and the serious accidents that did cause multiple fatalities (Salisbury, Grantham and Shrewsbury) each had excessive speed as an influencing cause.

The political world was changing as working men realised their collective strength in unity to demand improvements and women too began the fight for a say at the ballot box. As detailed in chapter 2 the GCR management made huge developments in their business up to 1914 when the First World War shattered the railways just as it shattered much else. Physical damage from bombing was minimal, but the strain put onto the railways to support the war effort was immense. The period of war included the sweeping away of the Liberal ideology that had sustained Watkin, was funded on a combination of loans, new taxes and inflation and in regard specifically to railways, convinced the government that a large-scale amalgamation of remaining companies and/or nationalisation should be considered. Judgements about the performance of the GCR cannot usefully extend beyond 1913.

Watkin died, peacefully, on 13 April 1901. The death certificate recorded the cause of death as 'cardiac failure, sickness, exhaustion'. He had 91 eventful years and was certainly one who followed his own convictions, including his liberal ideology, his Methodism, his Victorian spirit in pursuit of free trade, his acceptance of positions of authority only when backed by others, his strong moral compass, his support for the co-operative movement and in his role as a quiet benefactor, a husband and father. The key word was 'exhaustion'.

I have just returned from Paris using the Eurostar to St Pancras and passing under the English Channel. Whilst in Paris, I went to see the Eiffel Tower and watched the crowds who simply came to wonder at its creation now 130 years distant. Watkin was not deluded; he was a visionary.

Above and opposite: The availability of electricity enabled the development of tramway systems which in the main supplemented railway services in cities and major towns. Two early examples are depicted; Sheffield 74 and Glasgow 812, both dating from 1900, though neither being in the covered upper deck condition as now in the collection at the Tramway Village, Crich.

CHAPTER 2

SIR SAMUEL (SAM) FAY

It was with great pride and celebration that the Great Central Railway opened its New & Direct Route between Manchester and London (Marylebone). 1900 was the first full calendar year of passenger services.

This is the armorial device of the Great Central Railway. The word Forward was later adopted by the LNER and the BTC. The helmet in the centre is that of Mercury and above it are parts of the arms of Manchester, Sheffield, Lincoln and Leicester. Below the helmet are daggers and the hollow cross of London.

Samuel Fay was General Manager of the GCR from 1 January 1902, taking over from William Pollitt who had held that post for 16 years of a career with the MS&LR of 45 years. Apart from a spell at the War Office during the First World War, he remained in the position until the end of 1922. Together with his Chairman (Alexander Henderson, later, from 1916, Lord Faringdon) and the Company Solicitor (Dixon Henry Davies), Fay fronted a formidable commercial team for the GCR and was intent upon expansion. In support of that team were two fine, forward thinking engineers; John G. Robinson, recruited from Ireland (having served an engineering apprenticeship with the GWR) in 1900 and who became Chief Mechanical Engineer from 1902, and Arthur F. Bound who, progressively from 1903, developed into the role of Signalling Superintendent, having originally been recruited from the British Pneumatic Company. No disrespect to the civils here; simply that major works are recorded as being committed with contractors.

The post-Watkin era was well under way and from 1903 the administrative headquarters were based at Marylebone.

Samuel Fay was born in 1856 at Hamble-le-Rice in the New Forest, the second son of farmer Joshua Fay. He attended Blenheim House school, Fareham, and at the age of 15 joined the L&SWR as junior clerk at Itchen Abbas. A move took him to Stockbridge as a relief clerk and from there in 1881 to Kingston upon Thames. Whilst there, he collaborated with two clerks in the General Manager's Office at Waterloo to write and launch the *South Western Gazette* newssheets for staff, followed two years later by a personal initiative to write a book. His flair with word and pen as an editor brought him to the attention of the management of the L&SWR and in 1886 he was moved to a post in the Traffic Superintendent's Office, there quickly being promoted to be Chief Clerk. He had married in 1883 and his wife Frances produced for him a family of six children, most of whom were conceived during a particularly happy period of his life whilst living in Cirencester. Early in 1892, he was promoted to be Secretary and General Manager of the financially over-stretched Midland & South Western Junction Railway; at that time controlled by a Receiver. Relishing the challenge of improving the fortunes of 'his' railway, Fay managed the task so well as to be able to relieve the Receiver of his obligations and proceeded to run the show for six happy years. He was recalled to Waterloo HQ in 1898 as Superintendent of the L&SWR Line.

As an applicant for the role as General Manager of the GCR Fay enjoyed the support of his L&SWR GM, who at an earlier stage in his career had been a respected Goods Manager for the MS&LR and his recommendation would carry weight in the competitive process. It did indeed carry weight and Fay was successful.

The four sub-chapters of chapter 3 describe in detail aspects of the work of the GCR of particular interest. Here, the intention is to outline the range and scale of the principle activities taken up by the Board of Directors (with the support of the proprietors/shareholders in the Company) and then implemented by Sam Fay and his team. As such it is a study of the business of the railway which seeks to test the damning statements made by many a railway historian who have asserted that because the GCR did not declare a dividend for holders of Ordinary Shares, it was, therefore, a failure.

Although the GCR remained in existence until the end of 1922, the First World War resulted in the railway being managed for the duration by the Railway Executive Committee. Following the end of the war, the government introduced into parliament 'The Ministry of Transport Bill' which became law in 1919. That Act paved the way for the Grouping of the many railway companies from 1 January 1923 and with it the end of the GCR as a separate, corporate entity. Therefore, the years during which the Fay era Board and management of the GCR had control over its activities were 1900-13 and that is where my interest is focussed.

Between 1900 and 1913, the principal activities and policies which Fay implemented on behalf of his Board were both wide-ranging and challenging. The entire network was his to oversee, the workforce to motivate and encourage, new opportunities to be explored and cases for capital investment made, threats of a loss of business to competitors to be countered. Fay relished the individual and collective challenge.

The network included the new main line to London, the coalfields of the North Midlands and South Yorkshire, the industrial heartlands of Lancashire, the fishing industry of the East Coast. The approach to life in Edwardian times was more relaxed than in the nineteenth century of Victoria and desired more time for travel and enjoyment.

Following the resignation of Watkin in May 1894 as Chairman of the MetR, John Bell (who had been transferred from the MS&LR at the request of Watkin and had been Company Secretary) took over the joint roles of Chairman and Managing Director. He did not see eye to eye with William Pollitt, GM of the GCR, and consistently favoured the development of the City end of the MetR rather than that into still-rural Buckinghamshire. The years 1894-1901 were, therefore, difficult. The two railways were not neatly compatible in terms of their future plans; the MetR with its many stations, stopping passenger service timetable with peak hours traffic flows, gradients dictating point to point timings, and the GCR with its longer distance express passenger trains (in competition with the GNR and MR for timings) and freight trains into both Neasden and Marylebone. Recognising this, in 1897 the MS&LR had successfully approached the GWR with a view to constructing a largely new railway. That new railway as proposed would run a very few miles to the south

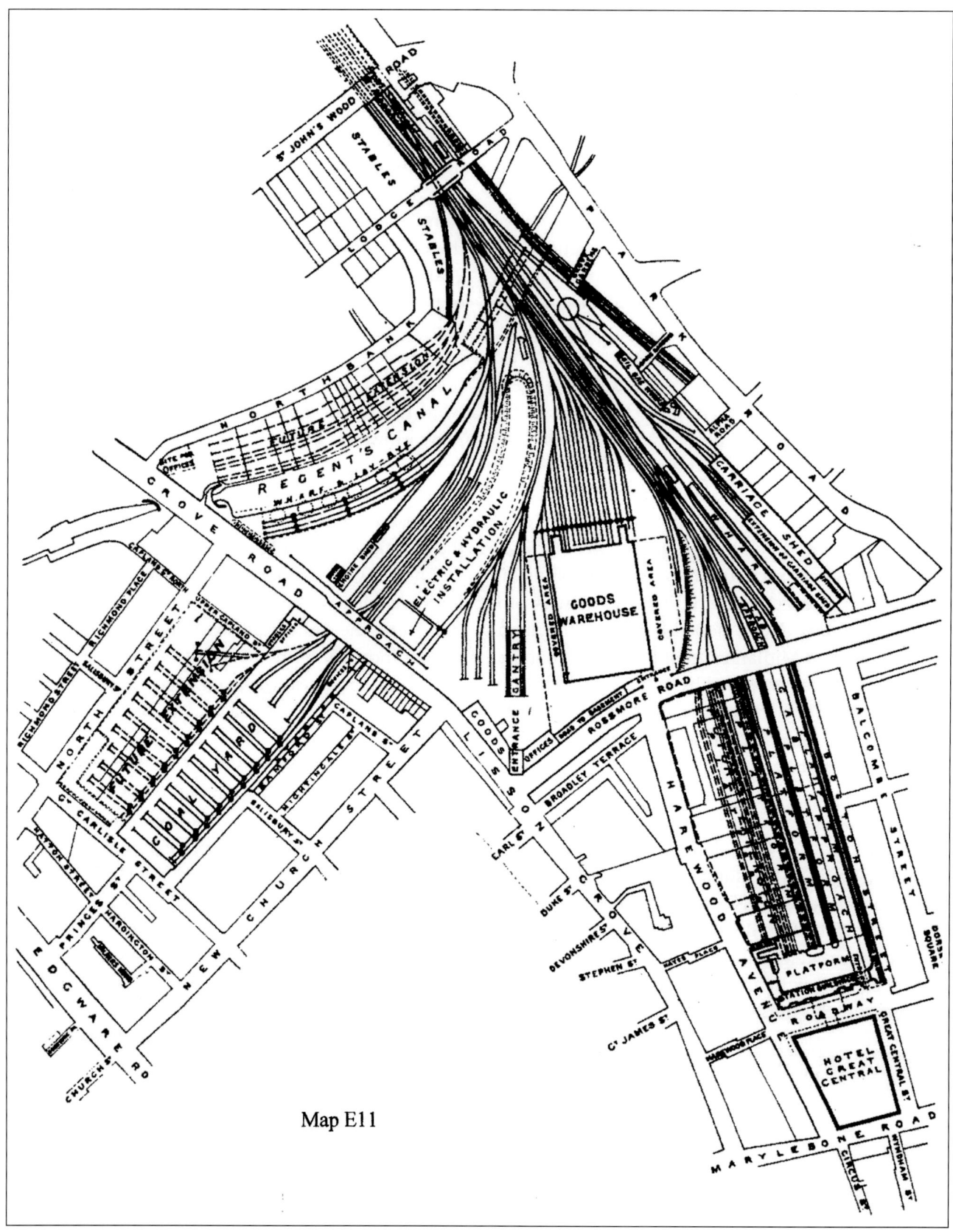

Map E11

The layout at Marylebone showing the coal yard, proximity of the Regents Canal, the limited number of passenger train platforms and the location of the Great Central Hotel, later HQ of the British Railways Board.

west of the Aylesbury to Marylebone route which would provide the GCR with a second, slightly longer, but operationally better route to Northolt Junction, 11½ miles from Marylebone. From that Junction, the GWR would make its way to Paddington and the GCR would run alongside the MetR for the final few miles to Marylebone. The medium-term attraction of the idea to the GWR lay in the potential for a faster 'short line' route from Birmingham (Snow Hill) to Paddington (via Aynho to Ashendon Junction, thence 34 miles via Princes Risborough and High Wycombe to Northolt Junction). For the time being, the plan was for the new line to diverge from the GCR line at Grendon Underwood Junction (some 47 miles from Marylebone via the 'old' MetR route, 50 miles via the 'new' GW/GC route).

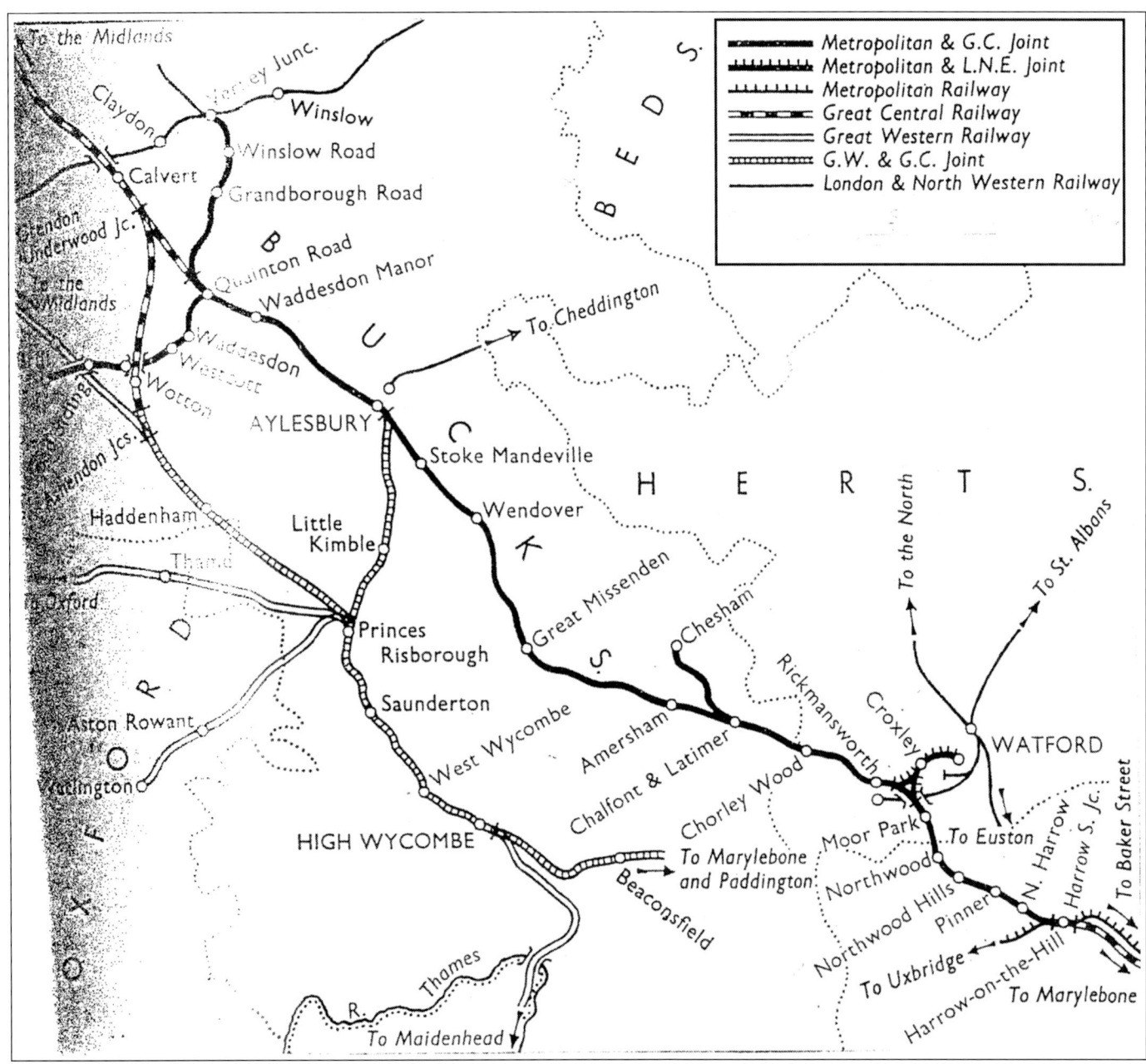

The two routes available for the final approach to London; the Metropolitan & Great Central Joint via Quainton Road and Aylesbury and the slightly longer, but more easily graded Great Western & Great Central Joint via Princes Risborough and High Wycombe. Map E10 and Chapter 8 are also relevant.

Through these arrangements, the GCR had a shared interest in the traffic planning for the MetR and GW/GC routes and opened up a new suburban area to the GCR. Work on the GW/GC route commenced in 1901 and continued in stages (including the doubling of the High Wycombe-Princes Risborough section) to enable completion and opening to goods traffic in November 1905 and was available for passenger trains from April 1906. In March of that year, the GCR had begun a service of suburban trains between Marylebone and Aylesbury/Chesham and from June the GCR ceased to work freight trains to the GWR via Quainton Road/Aylesbury.

The 8¼ mile link between Culworth Junction and Banbury Junction resulted from an agreement between the GWR and the GCR in 1899 which enabled in June 1900 the exchange of wagons between the two companies (60,796 in the first six months and some 90,000 by 1904) and the inauguration of a non-stop two train passenger service between Oxford and Leicester from August of that year using GWR locomotives, rolling stock and guards. Later in the year the GCR added three passenger trains offering connections with others at Woodford and Banbury.

The growing demand for the transport of coal for consumption in the UK and for export represented an opportunity for any railway company owning (or having running rights over) lines to/from collieries, to ports and/or to the main railway routes to London. Colliery owners were supportive of railway promotions to access new mines and to increase the flow of their product particularly in the months of winter.

Whilst competition existed between the various railway companies, it applied also between all of those companies and operators of coastal shipping down the East Coast to London; the rail share of total tonnage declining from 62 per cent in 1888 to 49 per cent in 1901, and 45 per cent in 1905 (of an annual total tonnage of roundly seven million).

The management of the GCR developed their interest in meeting demand at home and on the near continent via jointly owned line initiatives (partly to assist in repelling advances by new competitors) and by taking over lines with a strategic value. First, the lines jointly owned and operated in agreement with other railway companies. With the MR, the Great Central & Midland Joint Committee for a line from Shireoaks to Laughton in 1902. This gave access to new collieries at Dinnington and Thurcroft. It also repelled the North Eastern Railway (NER) and L&YR, at least for a time. With the MR, GNR, NER and L&YR to promote a new railway – the South Yorkshire Joint Railway (SYJR) – in which each would participate equally (1903). Opened in 1909, it ran from Dinnington through Maltby to Kirk Sandall, thence via the GC to Grimsby. With the GC, MR and Hull & Barnsley Railway (H&BR) Joint Committee (1907) for a line from Anston Junction to Braithwell Junction and Thrybergh Junction opened in 1909. With the H&BR (1909) for a line between Braithwell Junction and Aire Junction to give access to collieries at Bullcroft, Bentley, Yorkshire Main (and Thurcroft on the GCR/Dinnington on the SYJR). The GCR took a half share in this line (1910) mainly to keep the NER out and it became the Hull & Barnsley & Great Central Joint Committee. Reference to maps, as included, will assist an understanding of how the various independent and joint railways enabled coal to be moved away.

Secondly, the new (to the GCR) lines. The only section of the Lancashire, Derbyshire & East Coast Railway (LD&ECR) to be constructed was eventually between Chesterfield (Market Place) and Langwith Junction, thence East to join the GNR and GER joint line near Lincoln, and North towards Beighton (and via the Sheffield District to the attractive destination of Sheffield). The main line West to East was opened in 1899, giving access to multiple collieries. The GCR and LD&ECR came to an agreement to allow the latter's coal traffic to run to Grimsby (effected 1901). The value of this 38 mile 'main line' of the total route may be judged by the tonnages carried in 1897 (when the GNR received running powers and the LD&ECR was allowed to access the GNR Leen Valley extension when completed (effected from 1902) and 1905: 477,374 tons and 2,317,714 tons respectively.

The GER was not so fortunately placed. For its own needs and those of its customers, the GER needed to draw annually some 3.7m tons of coal and its system was not served by a single colliery. To assist in meeting its obligations the GER subscribed £250k to the LD&ECR. The LD&ECR certainly needed help; at end 1899 it had just 23 locomotives (37 in 1906), all Kitson. By 1905, it was clear to the Board of the LD&ECR (including two of the GER) that the Company would never fulfil its original intentions and they resolved to offer the railway to the GNR (7 November 1905). The GNR found the terms unacceptable and at a further

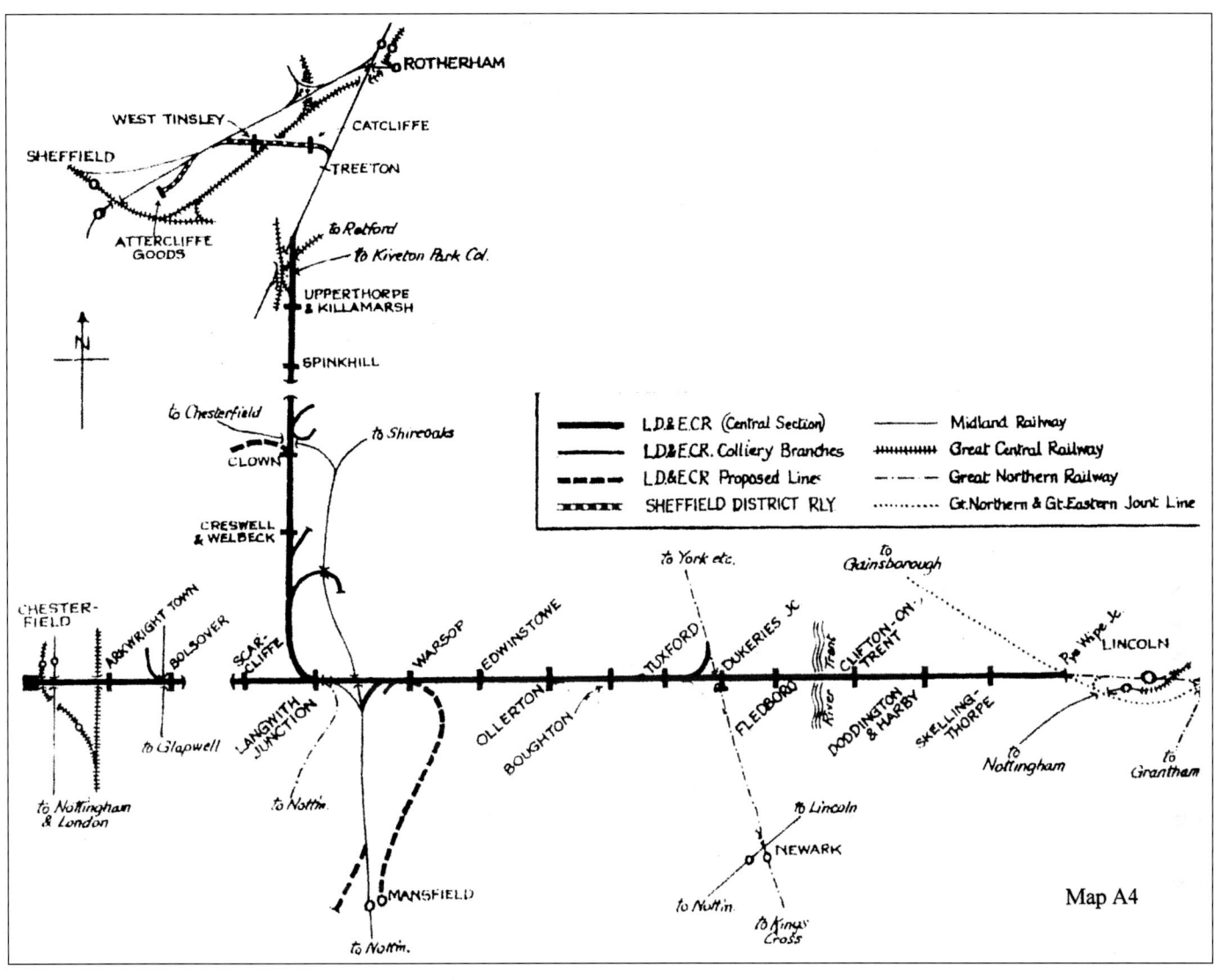

The Lancashire Derbyshire & East Coast Railway was of strategic importance to the fortunes of the Great Central Railway, taking coal South and East via Lincoln, providing a connection into Nottinghamshire and the London extension, and North to Sheffield/Rotherham.

meeting the LD&ECR Board considered an offer from the GCR. The GCR took over the LD&ECR as a going concern as from 1 January 1907.

The developments with the LD&ECR resulted in 1906 with influential business interests in north Nottinghamshire approaching the GCR with a proposal that a new line – to be worked by the GCR – should be built from Clipstone to the 'main line' at Annesley. For the GCR, the suggestion had commercial and operational merit. Commercially, the GCR would not be exposed. It would be allowed to tap into the production of additional collieries and would also allow the owners of the railway to restrict running rights (particularly the MR and GNR who were dominant in north Nottinghamshire) and, operationally, to allow coal to be moved to Immingham/Grimsby for shipment, for other coal to be moved as may be necessary south via Annesley and, thirdly, because it reduced the route mileage between Grimsby and London by five miles. The commercial details including sole running rights (except by agreement of the GCR) were agreed in 1910 after the passage of the Mansfield Railway Act earlier in that year and secured for the GCR not less than half a million tons annually from the pits of the Bolsover Colliery Company (Mansfield, Rufford and New Crown). The first trains ran in 1913, the GCR working the railway for 60 per cent of all gross receipts except rents from surplus lands.

In 1905, the GCR Board committed to a new works programme developed by Fay. This involved a new gravitation yard to be built at Wath-upon-Dearne

In the early years of the twentieth century it became fashionable for certain railways – including the GCR – to operate rail cars; both steam and petrol driven. Three steam rail cars were built at Gorton, two in 1904 and one the following year. The photograph depicts an example of a type of steam railmotor – essentially a self-propelled carriage – built in 1908 for the Great Western Railway.

The early years of the new century also saw various locomotive designers for railways at home and overseas developing classes of locomotives with 4-4-0, 4-4-2 and 4-6-0 wheel arrangements. Lightweight passenger trains competing on speed of journey became heavier, with greater comfort and better facilities becoming priorities. The first locomotive to attain 100 mph in the UK was reportedly *City of Truro* (built 1903) in 1904. Although the Great Western rebuilt a class of locomotives in 1938 with retained double frames, that era of design was over. The photograph was taken at Bewdley, Severn Valley Railway.

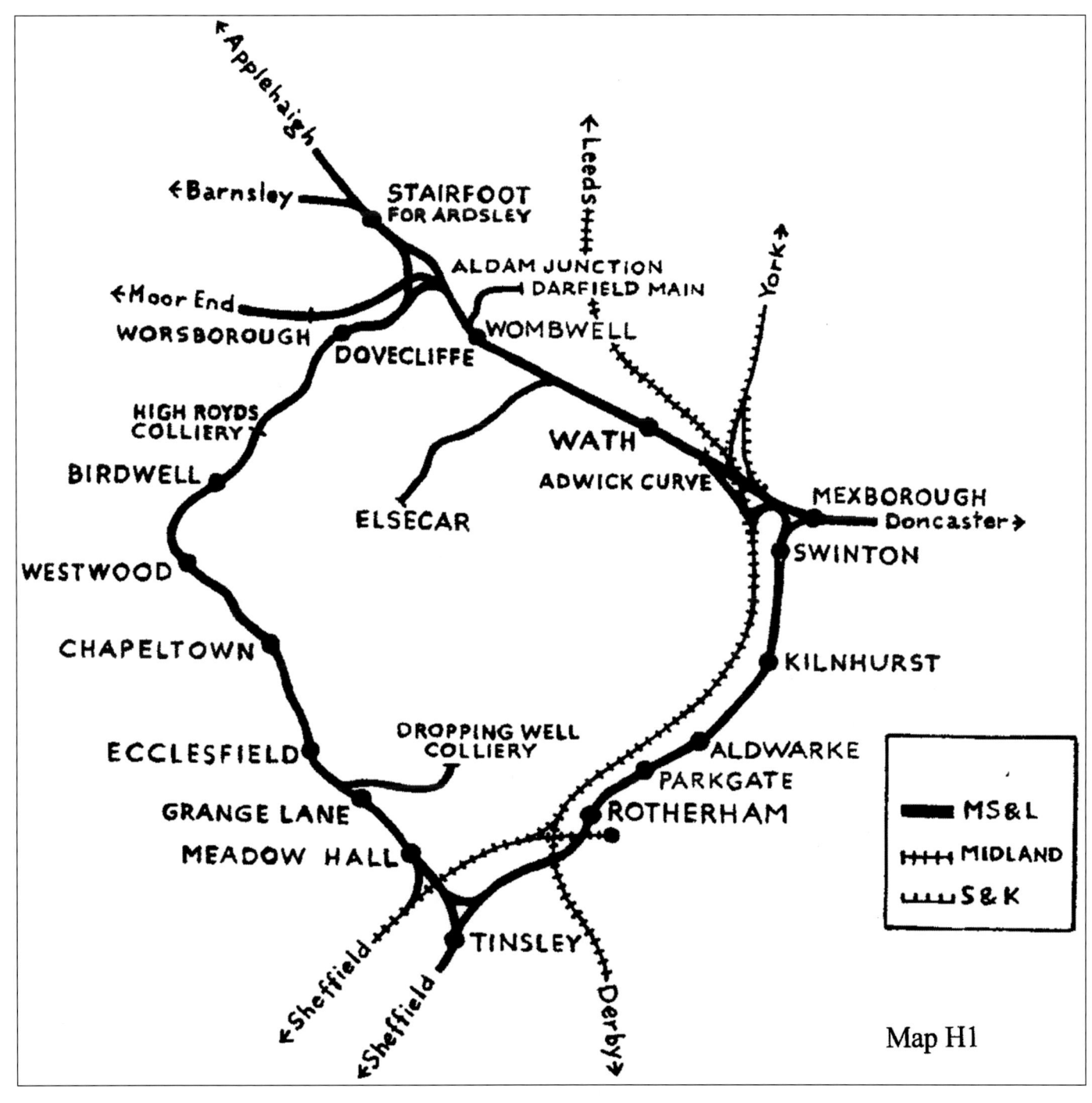

Map H1

(between Barnsley and Doncaster) in the midst of the South Yorkshire coalfields and with 45 collieries generating coal for movement. The benefits of having a concentration yard were perceived as savings in sorting privately owned wagons at collieries and an increase in the efficiency and utilisation of assets whilst moving loaded or empty trains within the constraints of motive power and line capacity. Wath was the ideal place, with the aim of a daily throughput of 5,000 wagons over three shifts each involving 35 men. The yard was brought into full operation in November 1907. A smaller yard was brought into use at Worksop. By 1903, it was clear that Doncaster represented an operating obstruction which would be best avoided by construction of a double track

54 • THE GREAT CENTRAL RAILWAY: WHAT REALLY HAPPENED

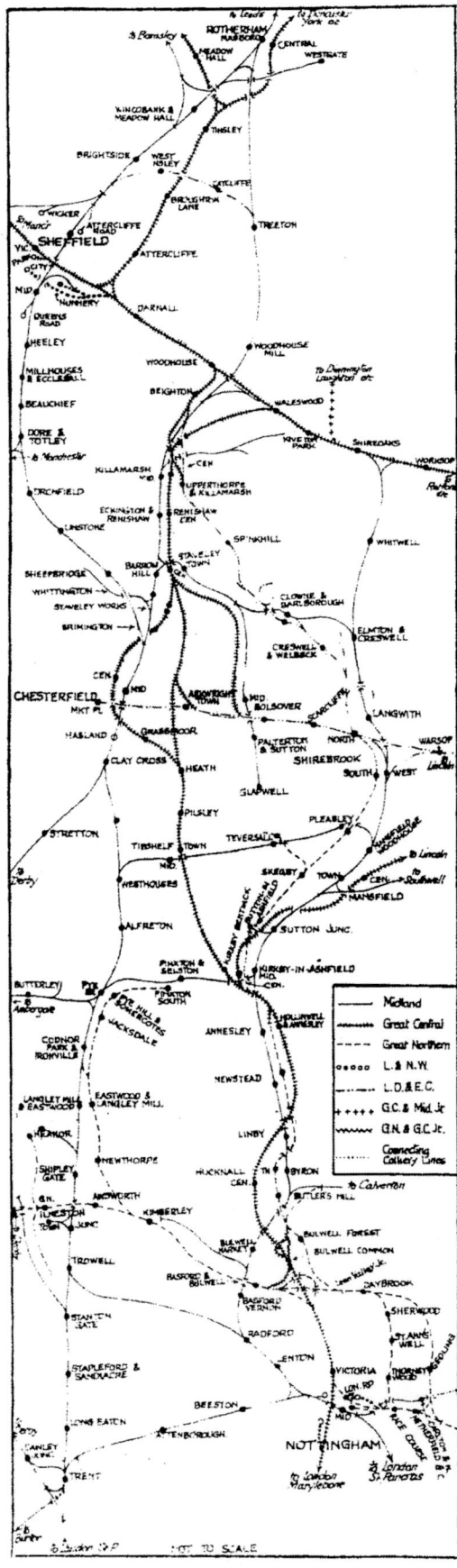

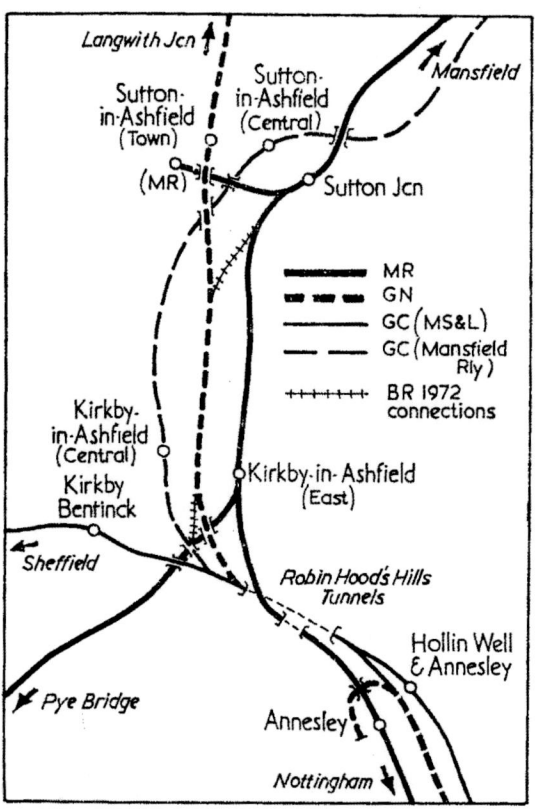

The coalfields of Nottinghamshire and Derbyshire attracted in turn the Midland Railway, the Great Northern Railway and the Great Central Railway. The close proximity of the tracks of the competing companies can be seen on this map together with the section as enlarged. The enlargement also serves to show how in the days of British Railways connections were usefully added.

Map B3

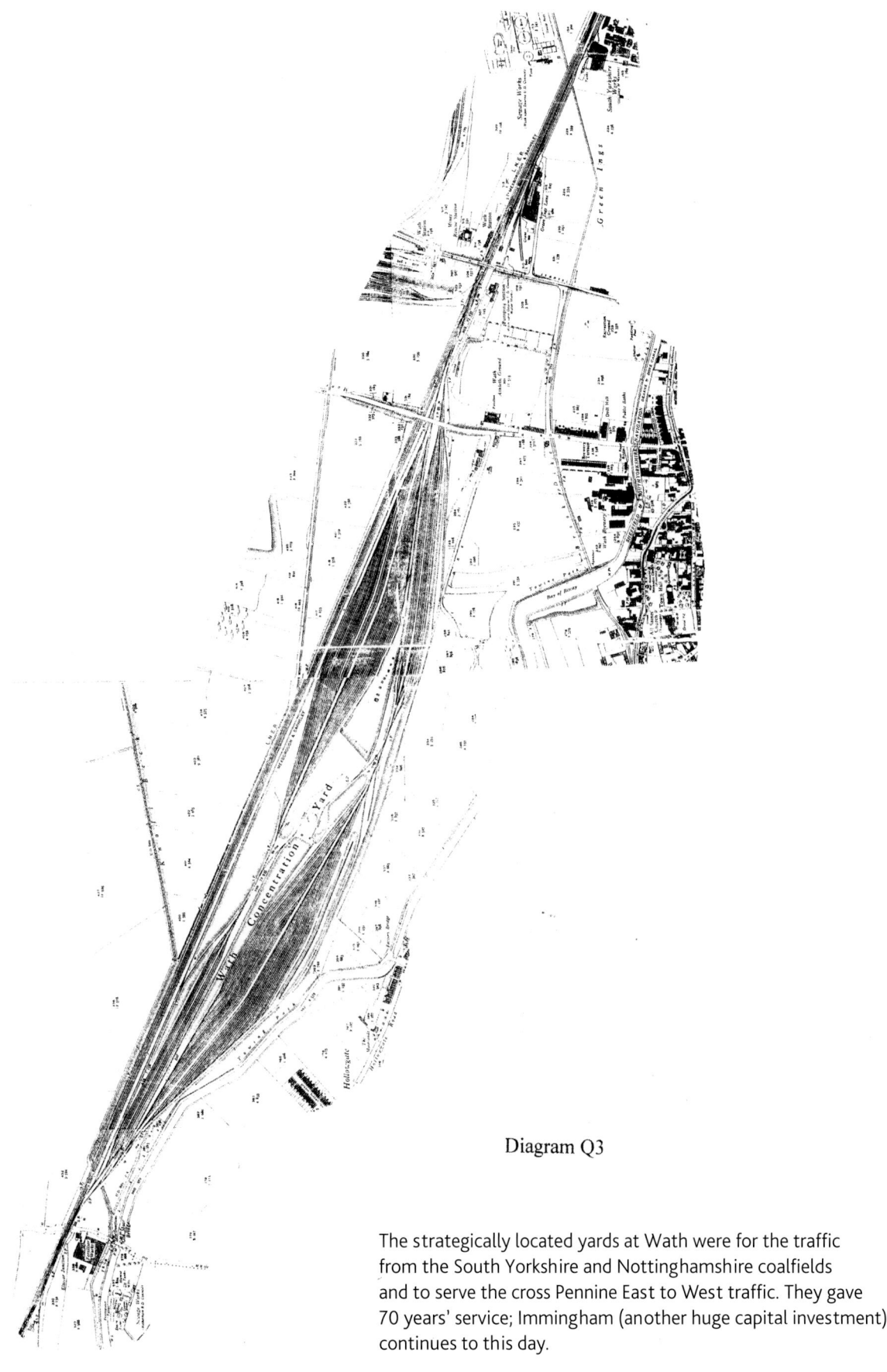

Diagram Q3

The strategically located yards at Wath were for the traffic from the South Yorkshire and Nottinghamshire coalfields and to serve the cross Pennine East to West traffic. They gave 70 years' service; Immingham (another huge capital investment) continues to this day.

avoiding line. The construction was authorised in 1903, but it was not until 1910 that it was opened. In that year, some 700 trains a day passed through Doncaster station area. The Mansfield Railway linked Clipstone (on the LD&ECR) to the main line South at Annesley, tapping more collieries including Mansfield, and the New Crown. GCR operated the line for 60 per cent of gross receipts. Each of the railways covered in this sub-section conveyed a limited service of passenger trains at one time or another, but as a proportion of the total traffic it was not significant within the total activity.

A further challenge was the management of two separate agreements over lines in Lancashire and Cheshire. The Cheshire Lines Committee (CLC) was an amalgam of interests of the GCR, MR and GNR, with services principally between Manchester and Liverpool/Chester, whilst the shorter Manchester South Junction & Altrincham (MSJ&A) was jointly between the GCR and LNWR. The arrangements for the CLC included the provision by the GCR of the 200 or so locomotives required to work the services and also the provision of some of the rolling stock. In 1900, the Liverpool-Manchester services benefitted from some new 12-wheel carriages, followed for more general service in 1904 by some composite, third class and third brake carriages, all being built by contractors.

Above and opposite: Developments in carriage design evolved to meet the needs of different bases of customers and generally became longer (as determined by track geometry), heavier and with better facilities. The GCR range of bogie carriages – all electrically lit after 1900 – included saloons for business travellers, open seating for excursions and compartment. Whilst the GCR continued to use hardwood species for carriage bodies, other companies were moving towards steel. The examples depicted are a 1912 Club saloon of the Lancashire and Yorkshire Railway (at the Keighley and Worth Valley Railway) and a 1915 steel panelled body compartment carriage of the Great Western Railway (Severn Valley Railway).

The availability to the GCR from 1910 of a carriage and wagon new build and repair workshop enabled production there of nine, five carriage trains for the Liverpool-Manchester expresses from May 1914.

The MSJ&A (jointly with LNWR) benefitted from five new 7-carriage trains of bogie carriages from 1911; capable of running as short sets in the off peak they allowed the release to the Isle of Wight of some ancient 4-wheel carriages. The final three sets were produced at Dukinfield; Wolverton having provided the initial pair.

The Wrexham, Mold & Connahs Quay Junction Railway (WM&CQJR) had formed part of Watkin's vision of a route into and through Wales. All in, its total route mileage was twenty-eight. From 1890, it had been under the control (by shareholding) of the MS&LR (now GCR) and as the 1890s progressed matters deteriorated. In 1897, the GCR had appointed a receiver who identified considerable debts. The only acceptable way out was to transfer the undertaking to the GCR, effective 1 January 1905.

The growth of Grimsby brought with it a need for relief by the availability of new dock facilities. Henderson was keen for the GCR to be the facilitator, but required the tangible support of the business interests of Grimsby and its people. The site chosen was Immingham, six miles upriver from Grimsby. Following a difficult parliamentary process, physical work commenced in summer 1906 and the first consignment of coal dealt with four years later. Three new railways were built locally; one of 5¾ miles initially to convey workers to and from the docks and, as such, the GCRs first 'light' railway, the second new railway of 8¼ route miles enabled coal to be brought to the Western jetty, the third, also 8¼ miles, to give Hull a link via New Holland. An electric tramway was laid to run parallel with the first of these lines and opened in November 1913, drawing its current from the railway's power station installed at Immingham.

The scale of the development at Immingham was immense. The dock estate covered 1,000 acres, with a

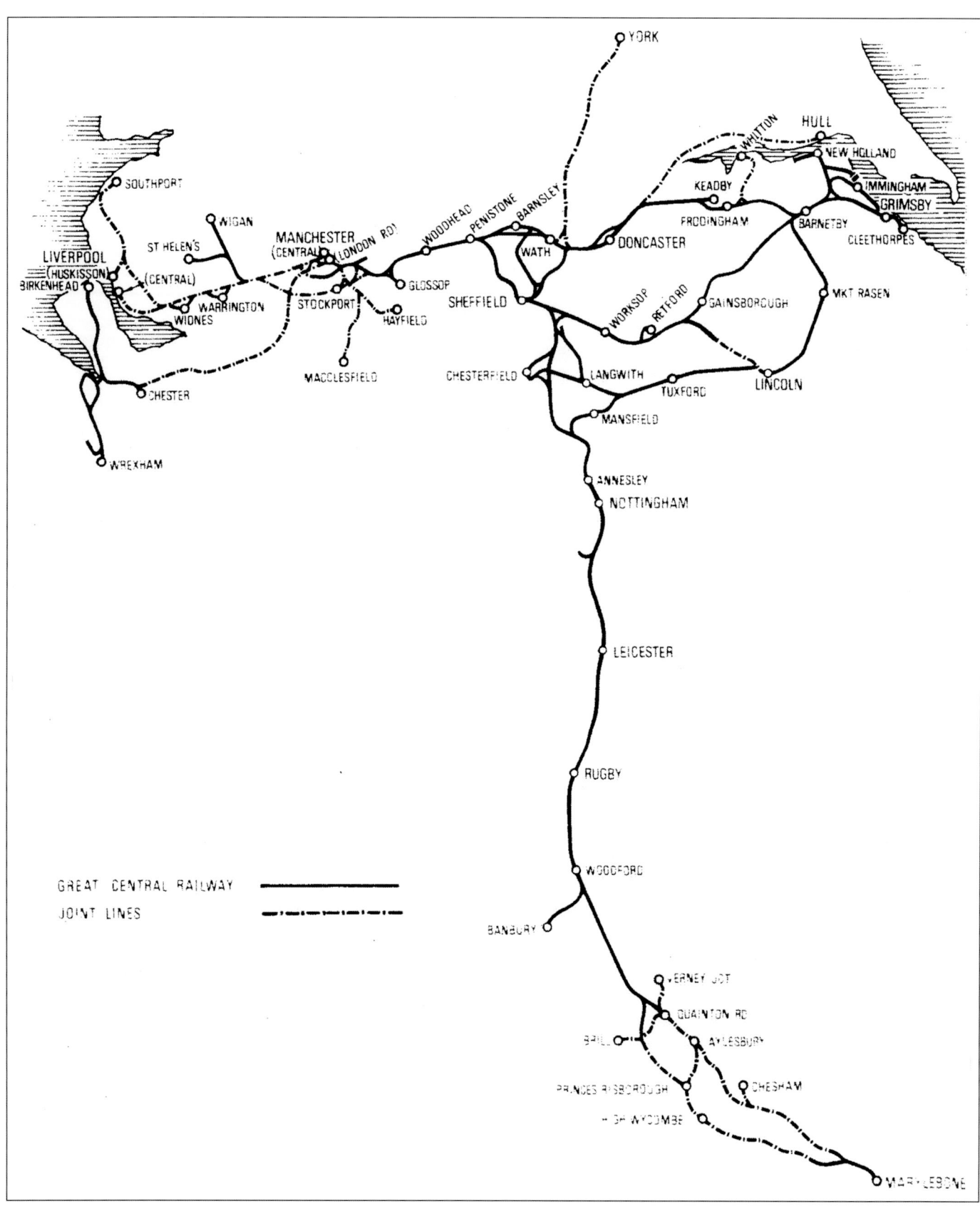

With the acquisition of the Lancashire, Derbyshire & East Coast Railway the shape of the Great Central Railway was all but complete. The empire of Henderson and Fay extended from the West coast to the East coast and South to London. The huge investment projects at Wath (top, centre) and Immingham (top, right) would follow.

For the Grimsby & Immingham Tramway the GCR had batches of vehicles built. Tramcar 14 was in the second batch (1913-15) and was built at Gorton with electrical equipment from Brush Loughborough and Dick, Kerr motors, with rheostatic and magnetic braking; when new the cars were painted in the GCR reddish-brown railway carriage livery. The vehicle is part of the National (railway) Collection and as depicted is in the later livery of British Railways, similar to that used for electric multiple unit vehicles.

length of 2½ miles, a breadth of one mile and two jetties fanned out into the river either side of the dock entrance. The East jetty was used by passenger trains/ships and the West jetty had a coaling hoist for bunkering coal at a discharge rate of 700 tons per hour. Along the length of the Southern quay were seven other coal hoists each of 700 tons/hour capacity, each hoist being fed by eight gravity sidings accommodating 320 ten ton wagons. Reception and storage sidings could hold a further 9,120 wagons. Sidings and other lines were illuminated and 'totalling 170 miles' could hold 16,850 wagons.

Grimsby was not totally neglected, additional timber yards, a coaling appliance, a new lock pit plus a deepening of another and a new quay wall being examples.

Between 1903 and 1914, the continental (Antwerp Rotterdam/Hamburg) fleet was enhanced by the construction of eight passenger and two mainly cargo ships together with three for short distance river crossing services Hull-New Holland. Passage times, accommodation and cargo handling facilities were all improved over the period. Upon the outbreak of war, three steamships were seized by the German authorities and their crews interned for the duration.

Fay's principal passenger train service obligations may be summarised as suburban, local, inter-urban (CLC), main line to London and inter (geographical) region. Suburban included into and out of Marylebone, into and out of Manchester; local (CLC, MSJ&A, limited services over predominantly goods lines); inter regional

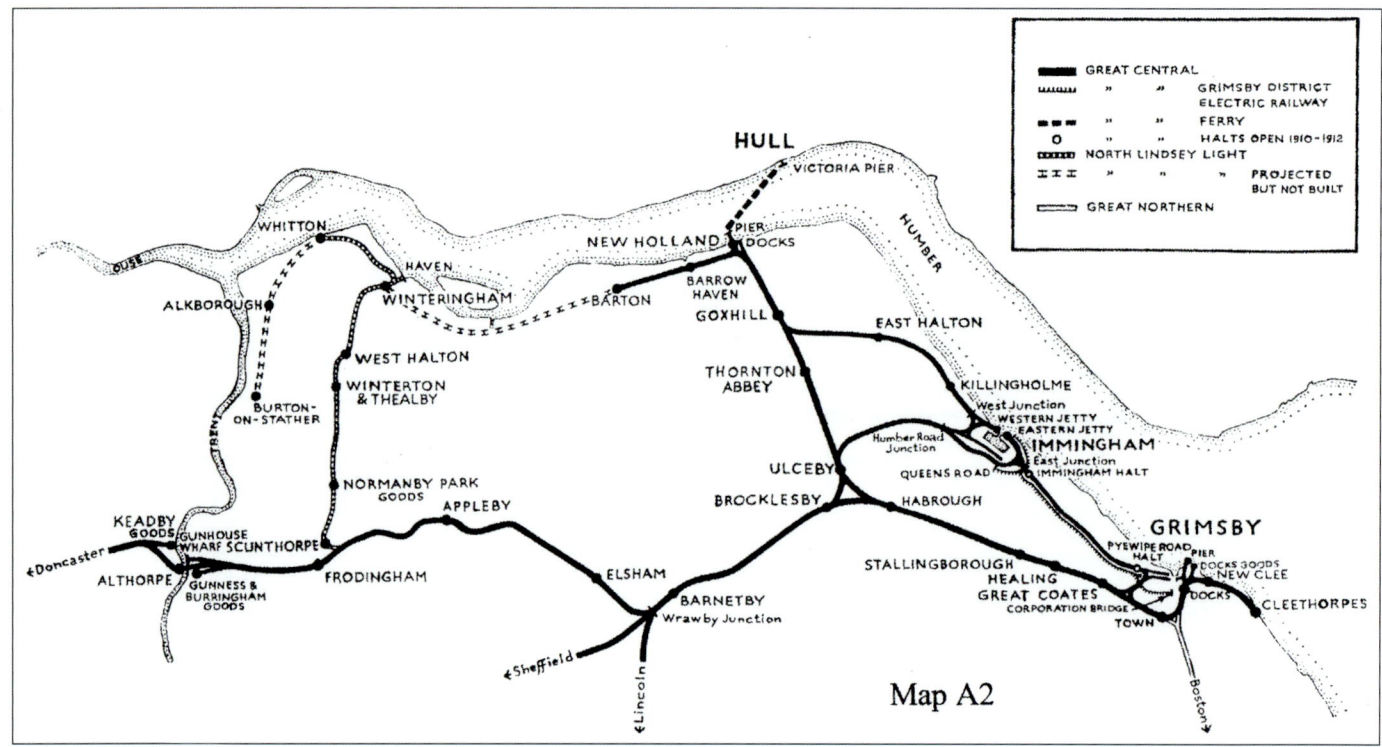

The area between Keadby and Grimsby was beneficially developed by the Great Central Railway and included the fishing port of Grimsby, the pleasure gardens and beaches of Cleethorpes, the docks of the new facility at Immingham and the development of the iron and steelworks around Frodingham/Normanby Park.

Steam powered road wagons were produced in quantity in two distinctive types; the undertype (as shown here) with the 'engine' below the chassis and either a vertically or horizontally mounted boiler/firebox to raise the steam and the overtype (see photos 43-45). The GCR employed some steam road wagons for cartage/collection/delivery. The example depicted was built in 1916 and the threat its type represented to traditional railway business is obvious.

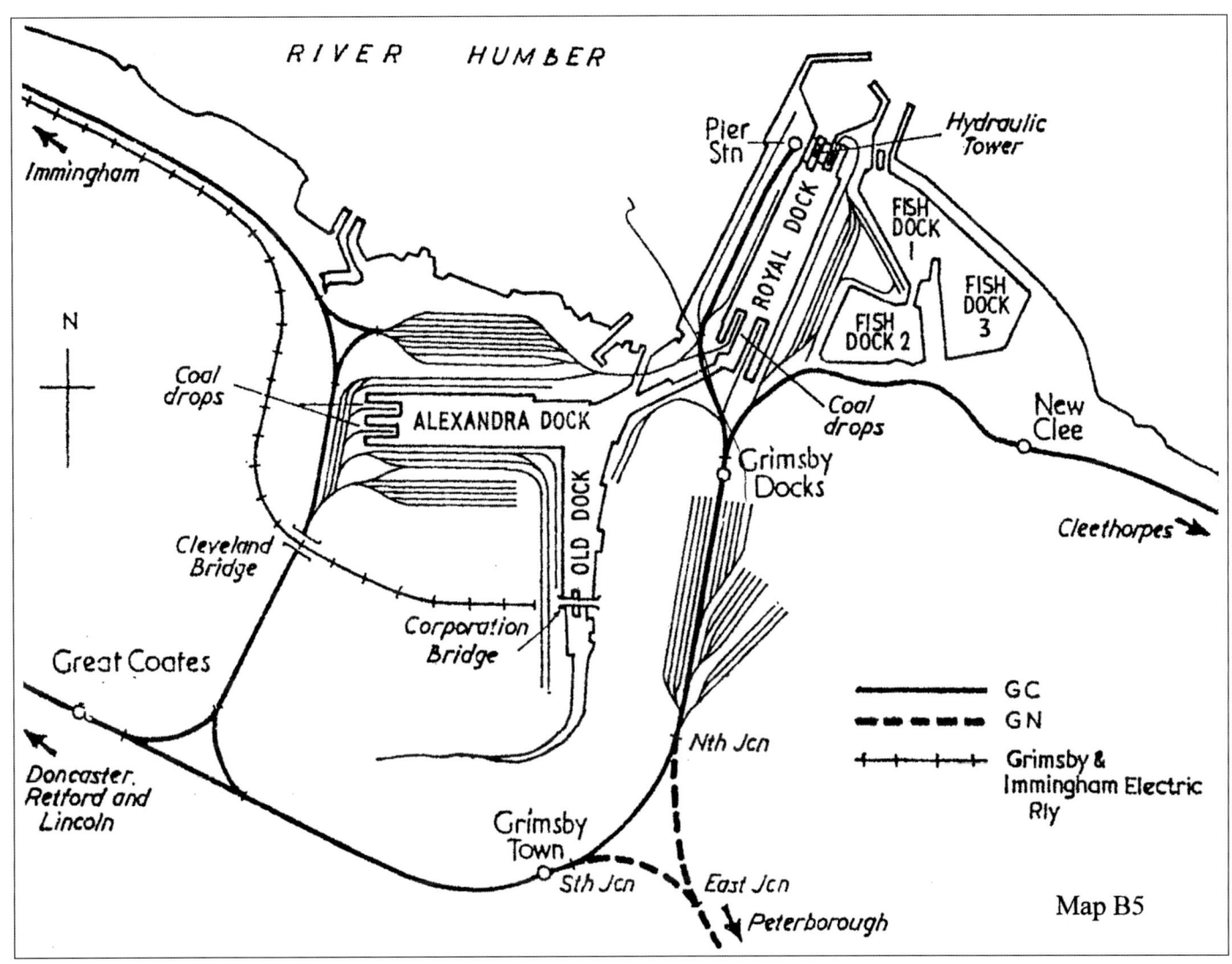

The expansion of Grimsby as a fishing and coal export docks brought operational problems for the Great Central Railway, leading to a high number of level crossings and manned signal boxes. The lesson was learned by the Company and South of Nottingham there were no level crossings for road traffic on the London extension.

extending well beyond the GCR routes. In meeting these obligations and competitive demands to provide a high standard of comfort for longer distance travel, Fay and Robinson had to contend with limited carriage and wagon building and repair facilities at the company's main workshop at Gorton, Manchester. Relief came in 1910 with the opening of a bespoke facility at Dukinfield. Prior to that year (and for some builds beyond it) contractors were used, particularly Birmingham Carriage & Wagon, Metropolitan Carriage & Wagon, Cravens and Brush Electrical Engineering Company. Between 1902 and 1905, orders were committed for a total of 222 carriages of types ranging from third class non-corridor to restaurant and slip coaches. Of that total, 26 were specifically for the London suburban route (1904). Also built were three steam rail cars (seeing service on New Holland-Barton, Wrexham-Seacombe/Brymbo and, briefly, Marylebone-South Harrow) and motor push/pull trains (steam at one end) which were employed between Marylebone and South Harrow. For completeness of record, 1912 saw the introduction of a single petrol-electric rail car which remained as a unique example in service in the Manchester and London areas.

To provide an indication of how Fay developed the passenger business the following summary has been included; year on year responses to the demands of Edwardian society in what many have referred to as the Golden Age of Railway Travel.

Left and below: Cessation of hostilities allowed a resumption of more pleasurable activities with some of the railways engaging in the charabanc outings and entering agreements with bus operators for inclusive rail/bus tours (Crich Tramway Village recreation).

Year	Developments

1900	(Pollitt) Basic London Extension services unchanged at 5/day giving daily coaching stock mileage of 400, comparable to LNWR/MR.
	
	Summer:
	    Leicester/Nottingham - Blackpool/Fleetwood
	    Sheffield - Blackpool
	    Leicester - Banbury - Oxford - Southampton

1901	Summer: Through carriage Marylebone - York – Scarborough

1902	(Fay) Breakfast and lunch Newcastle - Bournemouth
	
	Summer:
	    Nottingham/Leicester - Bournemouth (extended to/from York/Scarborough)
	    Marylebone - Stratford upon Avon

1903	Water troughs at Charwelton available. Non-stop running Marylebone - Sheffield and v.v. possible. 164¾ miles in 3 hrs 10 mins (up), 3 hrs 12 mins (down). Sheffield - Wakefield - Leeds services re-introduced. 'Slip' carriages ordered to supplement total available. New Breakfast car Wakefield (through carriage from Leeds) - Sheffield (connections from Barnsley/Hull/Lincolnshire lines) - London with carriage slipped at Nottingham (thence to Leicester). Return service slipped carriage at Leicester (thence Nottingham/Gainsborough/Grimsby). Liverpool - Cromer (via Sheffield/Lincoln/Yarmouth/Lowestoft) Manchester - Hull Manchester - Bournemouth From October London services ex-Sheffield speeded up by ten minutes. Manchester - Deal (via Sheffield/Woodford/Banbury/Reading/Folkestone/Dover)
1904	New stock for London suburban services ordered (steam heat/electrically lit) Two steam railcars delivered ex-Gorton (Wrexham - Brymbo, New Holland - Barton, Wrexham - Seacombe) +1 in 1905 Summer: Halifax/Huddersfield/Leeds/Wakefield - Bristol (via Sheffield/Banbury/Didcot/Bath).
1905	Through carriage Leicester - Aberystwyth (via Sheffield and Cambrian Railways) Summer: Cleethorpes/Grimsby Docks - Manchester (via Doncaster/Sheffield) Main line passenger services from Marylebone up to twelve, spread between 2.45am and 10pm.
1906	Sheffield - Llandudno GW/GC route towards London opened. Three GC services routed that way in each direction. Sheffield - Mansfield service discontinued. Summer: York - Cardiff (through carriage ex-Newcastle) (via Sheffield/Banbury/Cheltenham/Gloucester/Newport) (extended to Barry and with carriage ex-Hull from 1909) Motor push-pull services Marylebone - South Harrow.

Year	Developments
1907	Carriage for Stratford upon Avon slipped at Woodford at 6.20pm ex-Marylebone.
	Winter: Slip carriage in suburban working (for Amersham/Great Missenden).
1908	Leicester/Nottingham - Cleethorpes (via Duckmanton curve and LD&ECR).
	Carriage slipped at Penistone at 3.15pm ex-Marylebone.
1910	Summer: Rail and sea trip services to Isle of Man.
	Electric tramcars for Grimsby District (+4 more 1913)
1911	Summer: New 7am Breakfast service Sheffield - Marylebone (via GW/GC) Leeds - Bristol extended to Taunton/Ilfracombe Manchester - Grimsby - Cleethorpes accelerated.
1913	7.50pm Bristol - Leicester extended to York.
1914	GCR operating 20 restaurant car services, two with a shared responsibility (GWR).
	Southampton services improved with connection at Lymington for Isle of Wight.

The transhipment of fish from Grimsby represented a commercial opportunity that outweighed the operational constraints and costly manning of signal boxes at multiple road intersections in and around the town. The gross tonnage of fish landed at Grimsby continued to grow year on year:

1890	71,382 tons
1897 (10 months)	74,342 tons
1900	133,791 tons
1910	179,792 tons

Gross receipts for rail borne traffic in 1911 was £293k of which the GCR amount was £202,000. To cater for this traffic the GCR had built in 1902 17 bogie vans (Birmingham Carriage & Wagon) and in each of 1904 and 1905 one hundred (all by Cravens) conventional four wheel vans.

The GCR was well positioned to benefit from centres of production of iron ore, steel, gypsum, wool, cotton, chemicals, leather, hosiery, leather, for raw materials being imported (grain, timber) and exported (pig iron), semi-finished products and finished products. To meet this demand a fleet of specialist wagons was provided, included refrigerated trucks.

With the benefit of rising real incomes, the desire of the public to travel, explore and enjoy holidays and recreation was a great bonus for the railways. It was, therefore, natural that railway companies able to give access to places of natural charm or at the seaside should encourage that trade. The GCR bought out a travel agency by the name Dean & Dawson in 1904. In 1900, that firm had arranged for Lever Brothers of Port Sunlight an excursion to Paris for 1,500 passengers. Efforts were made to develop the business via 24 offices in England and Wales plus one each in Hamburg and Paris.

Fay was not too keen on third parties promoting trains and Dean & Dawson were reimbursed for them only by bookings; wet bank holidays were totally at the risk of the promoters.

Whilst Fay with his Board and management team were busily developing their business interests, most of their contemporary companies were doing similarly. Those wide developments had included many mergers and acquisitions. By 1906, there were fewer than 20 major companies controlling some 80 per cent of the total railway mileage. The days of fierce rivalry had been replaced by a more mature approach as to how matters may be improved to mutual benefit.

There were always claims and counter claims to be settled at chairman level and at one such meeting between Fay and his opposite number at the GNR (Oliver Bury) in 1906/7, a further item for discussion was the end of the fifty-year commercial agreement entered into in 1858. The two came around to the idea

During the Edwardian era the age of the motor bus for conveyance of passengers also arrived in earnest. Mike Sutcliffe MBE lovingly restored a collection of pre-1925 examples and in 2006 brought them to the Crich Tramway Museum where they were photographed. The GCR embraced in a small way the new traction; in 1906 it owned three motor buses.

Thorneycroft (1896) and Albion (1899) were, by the early 1900s, producing ranges of commercial vehicles for owners keen to enter the world of transportation. The examples shown here were photographed at Beamish Museum.

Illustration J3

The Great Central Railway was always keen to utilise its rolling stock to the greatest commercial advantage. Horse racing in midweek as well as at weekends attracted a healthy following.

of an amalgamation; 40 per cent of the total route mileage of the two systems carried joint running rights, joint lines totalled 177 miles and both companies enjoyed identical running powers over 41 miles of other companies' systems. Prior to the end of 1907, Heads of Agreement had been drawn up, the basis year would be 1906 and future division of profits would be based upon the proportional split of up to the total net receipts from 1906 (£3.8m; 57 per cent having been earned by the GNR and 43 per cent by the GCR) after deducting 3½ per cent interest upon their respective capital expenditure amounts for 1907. From any balance above the £3.8m the GCR would receive in each year £100,000 in respect of capital expenditure which had not produced any substantial revenue in 1906, such as the GW/GC joint line South from Grendon Underwood. Henderson presented the proposal to a meeting of shareholders in December 1907 and following approval, it was put forward to the Railway & Canal Commissioners in March 1908. There were 27 objections, ranging from other railway companies concerned with a threat to their business levels, traction and rolling stock builders, municipal authorities and, for good measure, the Board of Trade. The proposal was turned down and that decision upheld by the Court of Appeal. As well as the MR, the GER had been an objector; both were later invited to join and though the latter did agree, the MR did not. So the three (GCR, GNR, GER) re-submitted the proposal in the form of a Bill. For the second reading there were 52 objections and during the debate such was the level of hostility that the President of the Board of Trade, Winston Churchill, could see no prospect of the Bill being passed. The three companies thereupon withdrew their Bill. All a question of time and circumstances, it would be very different after the First World War.

During his time as General Manager, Fay had considerable involvement with matters affecting staff. The first branches of the Associated Society of Locomotive Engineers and Firemen (ASLEF) had been formed in 1880 (the first considered to have been at Sheffield, MS&LR) and with attitudes such as those which followed the accident at Hexthorpe in 1887 and the solidarity which was established during a strike on the MR in the same year encouraged membership. By 1903, membership exceeded 30,000 and the union became affiliated to the forerunner organisation of the Labour Party. The National Union of Railwaymen (NUR) began life in 1872 as the Amalgamated Society of Railway Servants. Its main concern was a limitation on hours of work as a means of reducing the high level of accidents; in 1875, 767 railwaymen were killed. By 1890, the union had 26,000 members.

Above, left and opposite: War brought an abrupt end to the development of the manufacture of road vehicles for private individuals and non-military connected concerns. Many buses – as depicted here with London General LH-8186 – were requisitioned for military use. Road lorries requisitioned took on the overall drab khaki.

In 1906, 30 Labour Party MPs were elected to a parliament which passed the Trade Disputes Act, restoring the rights of trade unionists broken in 1901 by a court ruling in favour of the Taff Vale Railway Company. In 1913, the NUR was formed through a merger of the Amalgamated Society of Railway Servants with the General Workers Union (workshops and poorly paid) and the United Pointsmen and Signalmen's Society, giving by the end of that year an organisation with 267,611 voices.

In January 1907, all railway company General Managers received a copy of a new All Grades Programme including an eight hour maximum working day for traffic grades. Apart from the North Eastern Railway, the railway companies' managements were opposed and in a good example of bargaining power working with a pragmatic politician (Lloyd George as President of the Board of Trade), a compromise was reached in the form of Sectional (i.e. grade of worker) and Central Conciliation Boards with arbitration available.

Fay established six Sectional Boards (A to F) covering locomotive drivers, signalmen, guards, carriage and wagon examiners, porters and permanent way gangers. Representation on each Board was equal as between the staff and management. Above, there was a Central Board made up of two Directors, the General Manager, a chief officer, a district officer and a staff clerk for the management and one representative of each Board on the employee's side.

The subsequent award of the arbitrators reflected the companies' loss of revenue in a slump in trade and the average weekly wage of the railway workers in 1910 (£1 5s 9d) was one penny less than in 1905. Also, there were 1,000 fewer men employed on the railways in 1910 than in 1907. At that time many railway companies – though not the GCR – were declaring dividends and building reserves of cash.

On the GCR, the conditions of the wages grade staff compared well with others and it was not surprising that further concessions could not be made in 1910. The mood nationally was hardening and fused with a refusal of the companies to meet representatives of the employees, all labour was to be withdrawn within 24 hours of 16 August 1911. The GCR fared very badly as they moved a lot of perishable traffic, but it was all over within two days. The government having turned away from repression, opened the door to industrial bargaining and also sealed the fate of the Liberal party for it could no longer count upon the support of the working class votes.

Fay was in his pomp; he had a supportive chairman above and to his staff he was a highly visible practical railwayman who was fair in his dealings and sensitive to the changing times. In a period when chief railway officers lived like demi-gods, he was perceived by the press and public as enterprising and adventurous. His flair for communications (started when at the L&SWR) was shown via the staff 'newsletter', *The Great Central Railway Times* in 1905, the same year that a Pension Fund for staff was established. Younger staff were encouraged to study the theory and practice of railway administration and the GCR met half way the costs of organised lectures in London and Manchester. In 1908, those staff who excelled in passing examinations and those who could produce matriculation certificates from schooling were placed upon a four year management training course involving time in nearly every department of the railway.

To assist the operating of the GCR, Fay was instrumental in the programme to install powered signalling, initially by a low pressure pneumatic system he had seen during a visit to the USA and also installed at certain locations on the L&SWR. With the technical advice and support of Arthur Bound (Signal Superintendent 1906-22) Fay convinced Henderson of the benefits – a saving of six mechanical signal boxes – and, eventually the system was applied along the intensively used section between Ardwick and Hyde (over 500 trains each 24 hours at Guide Bridge), at Wath Yard, Woodhead 'up' tunnel and at Manchester London Road station.

Locomotives and rolling stock were, from 1902, the responsibility of John G. Robinson who had served an apprenticeship with the GWR and been recruited by the GCR from a role in Ireland. He inherited a less than ideal set of circumstances. Although the previous occupant of the role had recognised the difficulties and taken steps to improve workshop facilities and practices at the GCR workshops at Gorton, Manchester, the position with locomotives was that of the total of some 900 (10 per cent being now for the London Extension), 246 were passenger engines, 474 were goods and 65 for shunting. The balance was the total owned by the Rolling Stock Trust Ltd.; 39 passenger engines and 69 goods engines.

To meet traffic requirements of 751 trains/day, he had to press into service locomotives that needed attention to safeguard the long term life of their boilers and fireboxes. The Board was responsive and agreed the money for 100 boilers and fireboxes plus a new order for 25 passenger locomotives. The MS&LR typically enjoyed over 30 years of service from their locomotives and with a progressive cycle of new, overhaul, perhaps modify or re-build, deploy on less demanding duties (perhaps on the CLC rather than over the Pennine routes) through a cascade arrangement when the next new class appeared. As at 31 Dec 1922 the GCR had a total stock of 1,358 locomotives.

The new build programme is interesting in that it clearly represented a sensitivity to meeting the needs of the GCR as being dependent upon freight for its continued livelihood and, being fully aware of the characteristics of the routes and traffic conveyed, Robinson responded with some very successful designs. He was prepared to experiment with compounding, pioneered in the UK the use of Belpaire fireboxes, debated long and hard the respective merits of 4-4-2 and 4-6-0 types, worked with private contractors (particularly Beyer, Peacock, which had its own workshops very close nearby to the Gorton works) who at that time were developing locomotives for specific route/traffic requirements in the British Empire countries particularly.

The approach is best summarised by reference to the two types of principal traffic (goods and passenger) plus the mixed traffic type. In addition were pure shunting locomotives, a collection of types which arrived with the WM&CQR and the LD&ECR (the latter all Kitson designed tank engines) and the very few railcars (steam and petrol/electric) with which the GCR experimented.

Goods Locomotives

Building Period	GCR Class	LNER Class	Wheel Arrangement	Number Built	Initial Builder
1901-1910	9J	J11	0-6-0	174	NR
1902-1911	8A	Q4	0-8-0	89	NR
1902-1904	8	B5	4-6-0	14	NR
1906	8F	B4	4-6-0	10	BP
1911-1919	8K	O4	2-8-0	126	GC
1914-1917	1B	L1	2-6-4T	20	GC

Passenger Locomotives

Building Period	GCR Class	LNER Class	Wheel Arrangement	Number Built	Initial Builder
1901-1910	11B, 11C, 11D	D9	4-4-0	40	SS
1903-1907	9K, 9L	C13, C14	4-4-2T	52	GC/BP
1903-1906	8B	C4	4-4-2	27	BP
1903-1904	8C	B1	4-6-0	2	BP
1905-1906	8D, 8E	C5	4-4-2	4	GC
1911-1926	9N	A5	4-6-2T	45	GC
1912-1913	1	B2	4-6-0	6	GC
1913	11E	D10	4-4-0	10	GC
1917-1920	9P	B3	4-6-0	6	GC
1919-1922	11F	D11	4-4-0	11	GC
1924	11F	D11/2	4-4-0	24	GC/LNE

Mixed Traffic Locomotives

Building Period	GCR Class	LNER Class	Wheel Arrangement	Number Built	Initial Builder
1906	8G	B9	4-6-0	10	BP
1913-1915	1A	B8	4-6-0	11	GC
1918-1921	8N	B6	4-6-0	3	GC
1921-1923	9Q	B7	4-6-0	38	VF

NOTES:

Locomotive builder code letters: BP Beyer, Peacock; GC Great Central Railway; LNE London North Eastern Railway; NR Neilson Reid; SS Sharp, Stewart; VF Vulcan Foundry

For passenger coaching stock the position at end 1899 was a total of 1,192, of which the majority were third class only (709) and a total in the types owned by the Rolling Stock Trust Ltd. of 228. Catering vehicles (for passenger use (14) and kitchen cars (4)) make up a total of 1,210. By the end of 1922 the total was 2,727 (including 43 restaurant cars). Again, it was a combination of Gorton plus private contractors that produced the new builds and these are identified later (in chapter 4). The significant features of the span were the vastly improved interiors of both classes and comfort facilities, debates about fixed wheelsets or bogies (and if the latter, four or six wheeled), braking and special adaptations for 'slip' coach working. Such were the demands placed upon the increasingly cramped conditions at Gorton that the Board authorised the building at Dukinfield (Manchester) of a bespoke carriage and wagon new build and repair workshop. Sadly, funds never extended to the provision of undercover carriage sheds.

Wagon stock quantities totalled 19,937 at end 1899 and 35,330 at end 1922. The developments included bogie coal wagons for locomotive coal, refrigerated vans, fish vans and eventually a stock of goods brakevans at a ratio of 1:50 wagons in total. Some details of the build programme are provided later (in chapter 4).

Fay retired in 1922, had ten years as Chairman of Beyer, Peacock Co. Ltd. and a Director of two railways in the Argentine. He died on 30 May 1953 aged 97 at his home at Awbridge in his native Hampshire.

Left and above: The tenure of Mr John G. Robinson as Chief Mechanical Engineer of the GCR was predominantly successful and two examples of his work were selected by the British Transport Commission for retention in the National Collection. His Class 8K 2-8-0 goods engines started appearing from 1911 and his Class 11F 4-4-0 passenger engines from 1919. Both classes achieved longevity through successive ownership periods into the 1960s and both examples saved have since been restored at and for use at the Great Central Railway. Photo 39 showing BR 04 63601 also serves as the cover for this book.

CHAPTER 3

THE GREAT CENTRAL RAILWAY'S FINANCIAL STRUCTURE AND PERFORMANCE

Many, probably most, readers of this book will be those who are particularly interested in railways in general and the GCR in particular. An interest in railways is often associated with a good memory for numbers; for example, famous locomotives, depot codes, speed records and distances. This chapter is dominated by a necessary consideration of numbers and, though related always to railways, they relate to financial performance of the MS&LR/GCR.

I cannot promise that for all it will be an 'easy' read, but I would encourage you to carefully follow the content, because it provides the answers to some of the questions asked about the financial performance of the Company and how it treated its shareholders.

Both of the long term Chairmen of the MS&LR/GCR (Watkin and Henderson) believed in expansion of the business and constantly sought – and received – the backing of their Boards of Directors and the investors who provided the capital. Over a period of years, the capital was invested in the business and was required to make a 'return' for the investors. The return was money from profits made; that is income from sale of tickets and transport of goods, plus catering and hotels less the costs of labour, materials and other areas of spend such as maintenance. In a successful year, it may be possible to pay the holders of all 'stock' bearing a fixed rate of interest and declare a dividend for holders of shares. Ideally, all investments in the company would have produced quick and healthy returns, but railways are long term businesses (which in the period under review were highly competitive between themselves) that require large scale investments with time needed to generate income from increased traffic.

Beyond the cold figures and statistics the warmer story of the progressive and very deliberate expansion of the GCR by Henderson – ably assisted by Fay, Robinson and Bound – will unfold. Whilst Fay – possibly like many readers now – found statistics difficult, Henderson had the ability to listen and respond to the needs of his General Manager, his senior engineers and traffic managers, as well as the needs of his investors, and skilfully guide the GCR through difficult times with considerable success.

Railway companies were statutory bodies, their powers being conferred directly by parliament. To provide authority to seek to raise capital with which to build a line, each aspirant company had first to seek and obtain an Act of Parliament. The legal obligations within these Acts came progressively from the Standing Orders of both Houses of Parliament and various general railway Acts. The Standing Orders set out the particulars and plans which would be required. Prior to bringing to parliament a private bill, a notice stating that intention needed to be published in either October or November in (the case of the MS&LR/GCR) the *London Gazette*, plus in newspapers with a circulation in the districts affected by the bill. By 30 November, a copy of the plans, books, maps and notice in the *Gazette* had to be lodged with the County Officer, with a copy also to the Board of Trade. By 15 December, details of any intended compulsory purchase of land and/or houses had to be lodged together with the responses of those potentially affected. Finally, by 17 December, the bill needed to be deposited in parliament by the company's agent, with a copy to the Treasury and other public bodies. The next stage was the deposit by the promoters of the bill of 5 per cent of the amount of the estimated expense. In the case of existing railway companies, the shareholders were protected by the need for a special meeting called for the purpose of seeking their approval; such meetings being known as Wharncliffe meetings, after Lord Wharncliffe, who established the rule.

By the end of January, a decision would be taken as to which House should first consider the bills deposited. Those not considered contentious would be directed to the House of Lords. The bills were thus divided between the two Houses. If in the Commons, the first purely formal reading would be followed by a second, during which principles involved would be discussed, prior to submission to a Committee (usually the General Committee on Railway and Canal Bills). During February, parties wishing to be heard against the private bill were required to deposit their petitions, stating exactly their objections. Unopposed bills were then dealt with separately. The Committee dealing with opposed bills would then hear from witnesses and counsel for and against the measures and then declare whether the preambles in the bill were found to be proven or not. If not proven, the bill would be dead, at least for that session of parliament. If proven, the bill came up for a third reading and, if it progressed, would be referred to the House of Lords where the process would be repeated. Finally, if successful in completing the process, the bill would be submitted for Royal Assent, when it became a statute of the country.

If in the House of Lords, the bill would first be considered by a committee of five peers not locally or otherwise interested (in the Commons, four members, plus a 'referee' if local or otherwise interests were present) and follow the same process as that applying to bills dealt with in the Commons.

The total process occupied six to twelve months, partly because of a stipulation that required defined periods between the readings of bills and consideration of reports.

In private (railway) Acts prior to 1844, there was no uniformity of approach to provisions relating to accounts or to the determination of profits. As an example, for the Stockton & Darlington Railway (1821) an obligation was to keep 'proper Books of Account' and, separately empowered the company to pay dividends. With one eye on the monopolistic practices of some owners of canals, the Act for the Liverpool & Manchester (1826) was more specific on profits and dividends. If a dividend exceeded ten per cent, the rates to be charged by the company were to be reduced by five per cent for every one per cent of dividend above ten. For the Great Western Railway (1835), accounts were required to be made up half yearly and dividends could be declared from the 'clear' profits. Since each Act also laid down maximum charges that could be levied, payment of interest on loans to the company was to be a prior charge (on receipts). Sometimes a proportion of the gross profit had to be reserved for contingency funds.

The government sought to protect the public interest via the Railway Department of the Board of Trade. The Railway Department was under the direct control of the President (by the early nineteenth century a member of the Cabinet) and consisted of an assistant, a junior assistant and a nine strong inspectorate. The duties of the inspectorate were to:

- advise Parliamentary Committees as required.
- ensure the provision of accommodation under the terms of the Cheap Trains Act for the movement of the working classes.
- inspect all new railways and either grant or refuse permissions to operate.
- investigate the causes of accidents and, when an enquiry followed, to make recommendations suggested thereby.
- specify the content and collate statistical returns.
- supervise the companies' relations with their workforce, including claims relating to the hours required to be worked in a week.
- act as an intermediary between the companies and traders with regard to rates charged.
- sanction bye-laws for stations.
- consider provisional orders made by the Light Railway Commissions.'

It did not take parliament long to spot an opportunity to raise funds for the Treasury via a passenger duty (Railway Passenger Duty Act 1842) and thereby required railway companies to maintain books giving details of receipts for carriage of passengers. The 1844 Act (popularly known as the Gladstone Act) was, however, subject to criticism because it failed to incorporate provisions to establish a systematic control over a method by which profits were to be calculated.

What was deemed good legislative practise for railway companies was also extended to include wider commercial applications. The Companies Clauses Consolidation Act 1845 required that a book keeper be appointed, that the balance sheet be examined by at least three Directors and signed by the Chairman or

Deputy Chairman. Auditors holding at least one Share in the company though not holding any office were to be appointed and to offer guidance upon depreciation of assets.

Parliament progressively attempted to limit the powers and activities of railway companies, not only in terms of restraining commercial freedoms and financial regulation, but also safety. Increasingly, therefore, the railway companies came to be treated as public utilities. Gladstone made the threat that if the railway companies put profit before safety and efficiency, nationalisation would follow. Thereafter, accidents would be matters for public enquiry.

The MS&LR acknowledged the role of auditors and in 1861, Watkin gained experience by being the auditor to the Oldham, Ashton-under-Lyne and Guide Bridge Junction Railway. His knowledge, together with the lack of clarity in the relevant Acts, provided for him opportunities to be legally creative with the compilation of trading accounts and balance sheets.

The Regulation of Railways Act 1868 provided to the 'by then' many railway companies some of the guidance that had been lacking in regard to the form and content of published accounts which were required to be compiled on a half yearly basis. In particular, the companies were required to adopt a 'double account' (double entry, credit/debit) system. That legislation further raised the status of auditors, particularly in regard to checking on the charging of all expenses to revenue account. The Act did not settle all of the problems and difficulties of railway accounting, the form of accounts which it prescribed remained unchanged until the Railway Companies (Accounts and Returns) Act of 1911, though refinements were made in the Railway Regulation Act 1871. The Schedules to the 1911 Act provided templates for the Forms of Financial Statements and Statistical Returns. Although returns to the Board of Trade had been made by the railway companies annually throughout the periods of the MS&LR/GCR, the Board wished to extend the fields of data to capture the work of ancillary business activities. The 1868 and 1871 Acts had required data for activities including steamboats, harbours, canals, hotels and catering, but in the interim some railway companies had added omnibus operations and at least one was contemplating the acquisition of a golf course. A copy of each annual report of the Board of Trade containing the data/information is held at the National Railway Museum and a study of those reports provides the factual basis for this chapter.

The Act of 1911 took a considerable time to reach the Statute Book. One reason was a sticking point around the inclusion or omission of a statistic which was extensively used by mainland European railway administrations and in North America: ton-miles. Ton-miles was simply a calculation of tons of goods conveyed multiplied by the distance in miles, and passenger miles. The fundamental units were respectively one ton carried one mile and one passenger carried one mile. Application of such a statistic would enable the calculation of:

- 'the average train load of goods and of passengers obtained by dividing the ton mileage and passenger mileage by the train mileage.
- the average wagon load and average carriage load obtained by dividing the ton mileage and the passenger mileage by the carriage mileage.
- the average length of haul obtained by dividing the ton mileage and passenger mileage by the total tonnage and total number of passengers carried.
- the average receipts per ton mile and per passenger mile obtained by dividing the goods receipts by the ton mileage and passenger receipts by the passenger mileage.
- the average density of traffic per mile of railway obtained by dividing the ton mileage and passenger mileage by the length of railway.'

Apart from the North Eastern Railway, the companies were not willing to compute the data and came up with 23 reasons why, including practical (rather than statistical) usage, cost and they favoured train miles. The matter rumbled on and Sam Fay tabled at the International Railway Congress in Berne in July 1910 examples – which may well have been based upon the GCR – of the complexity of some railway operations. In his examples, a train commenced its journey at a depot owned by company A, then passed on to a docks company (toll payable), then to company B's line (fixed toll payable per ton), then over a distance of company A's line, then over company C's line (one third ownership held by company A), then over a further section of company C's line (half owned by company A), then on to further railways for varying distances, some with reciprocal running rights. In summary, he provided a journey of 120 miles and one chain over eight different ownerships and eight varying methods of division of receipts and expenses. Far-fetched? Not really. Think in terms of a GCR owned depot, a train running then over the lines of the Manchester Ship Canal, the Cheshire Lines Committee, the Manchester South Junction and Altrincham, the Great Northern Railway, etc, before concluding its single journey. Those who were still awake could do no more than agree that it would be pragmatic to await a simplification of the organisation of Britain's railways.

The statisticians and economists were frustrated in being unable still to ascertain a measure of relative efficiency, of the product of all the expenditure of capital and revenue of each company, of establishing a measure of reasonable rates of labour and reasonable hours of work, of the cause of the constant rise in expenditure in proportion to gross receipts and it would remain impossible to isolate the reasons for unprofitable working.

The railway companies would, therefore, find it difficult to convince the Board of Trade of the basis for claiming a need for increases in rates to be charged and the traders would, at every turn, seek the protection of the public interest.

Ton mile statistics became *the* measure for UK railways, though not until after the Grouping following the Railways Act of 1921.

The motivations for the building of the early railways included a desire to speed up the transport of goods and materials for industrial production, a frustration with the canals and the commercial practices of some of their proprietors and for some a more altruistic approach to improving the prospects of localised industry. Quickly, a profit motive emerged, partly as a necessity to attract cash from investors. Railways were expensive to build; the Manchester & Leeds of 1835-6 attracted some £1.3m of subscriptions, about half of which was from subscribers inputting £2,000 and more.

High estimated costs initially (1831) put off the frustrated users of the canals system between Manchester and Sheffield but by 1836, influential men of Sheffield, Manchester, Ashton-under-Lyne and Stalybridge felt able to issue a prospectus showing the proposed capital as £800,000. Thus was born what became the MS&LR and later the GCR. Those promoters would doubtless have taken strength from the commercial success of the Liverpool & Manchester Railway (1830) and that having been widely noted in Lancashire spawned what would be a long lasting hotbed of financial support for railways and managers who could make them profitable. Half of the finance for the L&M had come from Liverpool and Manchester, with most of the balance coming from the Marquess of Stafford. The Liverpool Stockbrokers Association was formed in 1836 and one for Manchester followed later in that year. The extension south of the L&M towards Birmingham/London provides an example of how, for a short time at least, the profitable business of railways was largely confined to investors in the North West of the country. In 1836, the Liverpool share dealing price list named 71 companies, of which 38 were railways and, interestingly the 'old' canal companies were not included.

Until the coming of the railways, the London Stock Exchange was almost entirely a market for government stock and for historic, chartered companies. The era of raising capital for canal companies had not excited much interest and in 1825, initial dealings in the Birmingham & Liverpool, London & Bristol, London Northern and Kentish railway shares again did not cause wide interest. In 1830, of 205 active securities listed by the Exchange, only four were for railways; one being the Liverpool & Manchester for which speculative interest in its potential resulted in a price being recorded on 28 days.

By 1839, some railway companies were issuing preference shares which, by their title, ranked above ordinary shares by being better placed for dividend payments. Initially, they were used to attract capital for use in funding the construction phases of the new railways and offered a rate of interest just slightly above that generally available to the public. They became more popular later in the century particularly after the bases of railway accounting were strengthened by Act of Parliament (1871 Railway Regulations Act) which required the provision to the Board of Trade of statistical information.

In large provincial towns, it was the railway mania of the 1840s which stimulated the growth of stock exchanges and a huge bubble of speculation in railway shares expected to rise to a premium price. Edinburgh and Glasgow (1844), Leeds (also had a public stock exchange and an auction business in railway shares), Bristol, Birmingham and Leicester each followed in 1845. The mania or panic to buy railway shares is thought to

84 • THE GREAT CENTRAL RAILWAY: WHAT REALLY HAPPENED

	1864 £	1894 £
Total capital authorised	12,162,000	44,991,000
Total authorised for loans and debentures	2,939,000	12,158,000
Total capital paid up	10,011,000	32,830,000
Total paid up by loans and debentures[x]	2,562,000	8,766,000
Rates of interest payable on debentures issued at:		
3¾%	1,000	-
4 % (total)	368,641	79,577
4¼%	1,015,445	-
4³/8 %	60,000	-
4½%	1,075,449	8,342,392
4¾ %	58,631	-
5 %	62,154	300,000
Rates of interest payable on loans:		
4%	Nil	44,500
Rates of dividend (maximum) payable on preference shares issued at:		
(3¾ %)	366,698	366,698
(4 %)	-	5,278,980
(4½ %) all fully paid	-	1,797,428
(4½ %)	225,000	1,060,083
(5 %)	698,364	8,081,300
(6 %)	1,998,662	872,000
Dividend paid on ordinary shares?		
preferred	Yes*	Yes°
deferred	Yes*	No°

NOTES:
- x 25.6 per cent in 1864 and 26.7 per cent in 1894
- * a dividend of 2⅝ per cent was declared in 1864 for holders of ordinary shares to a nominal value of £4,090,732
- ø a dividend of 1½ per cent was declared in 1894 for holders of preferred ordinary shares to a nominal value of £2,213,620 and a dividend of ¾ per cent was declared in 1894 for holders of deferred ordinary shares to a nominal value of £2,213,620.

Additionally, in 1894, capital funds for the construction of stages of the London extension were attracted at varying rates of interest payable during those stages. The disparity in totals reflects monies 'called for', but not yet fully paid (e.g. loans and debentures in 1894).

Following the retirement of Watkin, the role of chairman was taken on in the short term by his previous deputy, Lord Wharncliffe. It was at a difficult time for the Board, with a need to press ahead with the London extension and its need for capital. General Manager Pollitt attracted the financier Alexander Henderson who accepted the challenge of securing the necessary funding and was later elected Chairman.

Henderson was successful in his efforts and by the end of 1899 when the London extension was opened, the capital structure had been changed from that applicable in 1894, the year Watkin retired. The relevant Act of Parliament had authorised additional capital and, strikingly, the total amount fully paid against that and previously unsubscribed authorisations had raised, between 1894 and 1899, some £8.75m. There were several categories of stock involved. Henderson had managed to restrict the proportion of the total amount represented by debentures and loans to 27.2 per cent (26.7 per cent in 1894) and, therefore, the source of much of the additional funding was from other categories of stock. Some £4m a large geographical region) had the lowest fares and highest dividends.

Parliament never totally trusted the railways and whilst accepting that further amalgamations were inevitable, it sought to lay down limits for those which were approved. In 1873, parliament turned down a proposed merger between the LNWR and L&YR which together worked one eighth of the railway mileage and owned one seventh of the total railway capital.

However, the natural course of economic activity and the relative strengths/weaknesses being exposed resulted, in 1906, with 223 of the 351 railway companies which existed in 1881 having disappeared from the scene and by 1913, 15 major companies controlled 84 per cent of the total railway mileage. The working arrangement conferences approach referred to earlier was extended in 1906 to the Humber ports, then about to embark on a massive expansion by the GCR at Immingham.

Nothing in the nature of a real monopoly existed so there was little possibility of outright exploitation and no British railway company ever made very large profits. Even in cases which appeared near monopoly, there is little to suggest it led to abuse.

As referred to in Chapters 1 and 2, the MS&LR/GCR pursued policies of expansion and, where necessary, expansion through operation of routes with others, amalgamation, absorption, acting as an operator of a line and through capital investment particularly in long term projects. Examples of the first are the CLC and MS&LA, of the second are the LD&ECR and WM&CQR, of the third around Immingham and for the Mansfield Railway and, finally, for the fourth Wath yard, marine activities, hotels and the London extension.

A long-term policy to expand the business of the company required capital funding. The potential sources of that funding were either from retention of net profits (and limiting dividends to certain categories of shares), or from an ability to attract new funds into issues of debentures/stock, or from a combination of both. For the MS&LR, the attraction of new funds was pursued and it is a tribute to Watkin that he carried with him his Board of Directors and his loyal group of investors in the long term success of the company. Indeed, the support of the backers extended to other railway companies which Watkin chaired. From the Board of Trade returns, it is possible to identify the starting and end positions (1864-94) for the period of Watkin's stewardship of the MS&LR.

Eastern Railway (without any other competition within exploitation of a new stronger position and the North The amalgamations thus far had not generated the 12,414 out of the 15,537 miles of track open for traffic. ments. By 1871, 28 of the 100 major companies worked another 383 were passed to establish working agreements. Between 1860-70, 187 Acts were passed containing provisions for amalgamations and a monopoly position. Between 1860-70, 187 Acts were facilities and increase efficiency than create and exploit was driven more by a desire to reduce duplication of trend towards consolidation of resources proceeded and on the part of railway companies. However, the natural interests of users against the monopolistic tendencies Parliament's concern was in the main to protect the general statutes had been passed relating to them. of economic activity in Britain; by that time over 200 By 1914, the railways were the most regulated form

most trains and fell further to one halfpenny. the standard third class fare was reduced to 1d/mile on for workmen, members of the armed forces and police, ger duty was reduced in return for concessionary travel for excursions and recreation. After 1883, when passenger new class of traffic, encouraged by special, cheap fares The 1860s onwards brought into existence an entirely price of a penny halfpenny per mile. a steady growth of third class patronage at an average railways but through the nineteenth century there was Initially, the wealthier members of society used the and also the passenger duty. inconvenienced. The 1844 Act has already been covered dealing with the passenger service pricing were far less By contrast with the goods side of the business, those traffic produced a return of 4s per mile. 7s per mile, whilst the 240 million miles of passenger million miles of goods traffic produced a net return of traffic and 47 per cent from passenger traffic. The 155 companies was around £100m; 53 per cent from goods At 1900, the total annual revenue for all the railway (see chapter 2) being the South Yorkshire Joint Railway. and receipts became more of a norm, a good example ing arrangements between railways, pooling of traffic market smaller than that of the supply side. Joint workgreatly reduced and been replaced by a demand side By the turn of the century, true competition had been the rates quoted were on such a basis. quote exceptional, special rates. By 1914, 80 per cent of competition from coastal shipping – to continually

House (RCH) to facilitate 'through' traffic bookings and administration. The RCH grew and in 1850 received statutory blessing and by 1887, it listed 2,753 articles under seven classifications. Coal and minerals were in the first classification, to which the lowest rates were applicable. A Royal Commission in the 1860s heard from railway company witnesses suggestions of a maximum charge of ninepence per ton for minerals, but this was deflected by the owners of the collieries, leaving only the unsatisfactory direction of the President of the Board of Trade (1866) that a 'reasonable charge shall be levied'.

By 1870, the longer established railway companies had several Acts empowering them over time to build or acquire new lines and/or enter joint line arrangements. The Midland Railway had Acts authorising rates for coal at one penny per ton/mile and, in another case, a penny halfpenny. In all, there had, by that date, been 900 Acts, each of which complied with the prior legislation. At that time, there was still no general economic criteria upon which railway rates were based other than the RCH classifications; a recipe for the forces of market competition to be fully applied at risk of retaining the traffic at an uneconomic rate. Local agents wanted the business and could not be expected to understand cross subsidisation of traffic flows.

Prior to 1881, the legal position may be summarised as maximum charges (for the combined track, locomotive and conveyance) were stated, undue preference between individual traders was prohibited and terminal charges were required to be reasonable. A parliamentary select committee of 1881 heard evidence of pricing policies. The conclusion reached was that, while pricing policies reflected what the market would bear above the level at which the railway business would be unprofitable, most railway companies were also mindful of the wider needs of their customers and the general development of the area the railway served. Examples had been given in evidence of raw materials being conveyed into an area at a low rate in order to help the production of finished products – also conveyed by rail – to be at a price competitive in the wider market. In order to avoid cutthroat competition formal meetings had been arranged to settle rates between and within competitive parts of the country. The Liverpool, London and Manchester conferences held in 1860, at Normanton in 1865, English and Scottish (1869) and West Riding (1875) had been useful in reducing the number of rates whilst

leaving goods agents scope to offer concessions on special facilities. Adjustments were also recognised where a particular company had a shorter route to the end customer and/or where alternative water transport was possible. It seemed that changes in the market price of the 'goods' conveyed did not affect the rate for conveyance; for example, the higher market prices for coal in the early 1870s.

The question of pricing for empty wagons being returned to their owners, cross subsidisation of certain traffics, marginal pricing for adding an additional vehicle(s) to a timetabled service train (e.g. for mail) were not explicitly raised.

The outcome of the parliamentary select committees in 1881 and 1882 suggested a uniform classification and a maximum level of charge for terminals. The Railway and Canal Traffic Act 1888 accepted the suggestion and required the railway companies to submit a revised classification to the Board of Trade. The laborious task was completed in 1892 but having resulted in more than four thousand objections from traders, the ensuing Railway (Rates and Charges) Order Confirmation Acts of 1891 and 1892 did not come into effect until 1 January 1893. Conveyance and terminal charges (except collection and delivery) were kept separate with both subject to a maximum, undue preference obligations were made more explicit, but competition was recognised as a justification for differential pricing as long as the public interest was safeguarded thereby. There was also something new; the taper rate. Instead of the charges increasing with each mile of distance beyond six as applied previously, the principle was adopted that the rate per mile should reduce with increased distance. The tapering scale imposed a certain rate per mile for the first 20 miles, after which it diminished as the distance increased, thus acknowledging for the first time the relationship to railway operating costs.

A further outcry from traders ensued, driven of course only by those rates that had been increased, and resulted in the Railway and Canal Traffic Act 1894 which prevented the railway companies from raising charges above the 1892 rates unless they could provide justification to the Commission. This reduction of flexibility was onerous for the railway companies and no relief was afforded until 1913, when they were allowed to raise their rates by 4 per cent to cover recent wage claims. The commercial reaction to this 1894-1913 period was for the railways – in the face also of increased

THE GREAT CENTRAL RAILWAY'S FINANCIAL STRUCTURE AND PERFORMANCE • 81

Year	Inflation %	Bank rate range %	Notes
1907	1.2	4 - 5½ - 7 - 5	
1908	0.5	2½ - 4	
1909	0.5	2½ - 5 - 4½	
1910	0.9	3 - 5	
1911	0.1	4 - 3½	
1912	3	3 - 4 - 5	

As can be seen in the table, 1894 and 1895 were good years in which to seek new capital, whereas 1890 was less so. During the period 1880-1893, the MS&LR were authorised to create £7.6m of new capital and did so without resorting to debentures and loans.

At a national level, railways were first taxed in 1832 at a rate of one halfpenny on every four passengers carried. This 'passenger duty' did not discriminate between classes and was felt to be unfair to the poor. The 1844 Regulation of Railways Act recognised this and made provision of an exemption for all fares at a penny a mile or less when travelling on specially cheap 'parliamentary trains'. The tax remained payable for those paying higher fares and on other train services. In 1869, the Chancellor of the Exchequer offered to abolish the tax, in return for agreement on other matters, but nothing changed until 1883 when passenger duty on all fares up to one penny a mile was repealed altogether, in return for which many railway companies introduced 'workmen's trains' embodied in the Cheap Trains Act 1883. For higher fares, the duty remained until 1929, thus ending the direct taxation of railways, the revenue instead being capitalised by the government to form a fund for the improvement of railway transport.

At a local level, rates were a bone of contention, particularly as the railways contributed so much to the localities they served and in so doing raised rateable values of properties. The Local Government Act 1858 limited railway assessments to a quarter of net annual value, but valuations tended to be disproportionate with the contribution made by the railways. As an example, in 1909, the GCR closed its locomotive depot at Queen's Walk Nottingham and transferred locomotives and men to Annesley following a dispute over rates payable. Throughout the period of the MS&LR and the GCR up to 1913, taxation and duty payments were, within

the scale of gross expenditure, insignificant and, whilst unwelcome, would not have concerned Henderson.

In the same way that the Railway Clauses Consolidation Act of 1845 had clarified to some extent matters for accounting, so too did it for pricing policy. The pricing policy for railways was not adopted by conscious decision, but grew with the development of the railway system out of the canals, turnpikes and stage coaches. Following the precedent of the canals, the early railway Acts had contained a simple classification of goods expected to be carried by rail and for each classification a maximum charge was prescribed. Maximum charges varied from Act to Act, and therefore between companies, complicated further whenever 'through' goods were necessarily transferred to another company for forwarding. Also complicating matters up to 1845 was the ability of the railway companies to make three separate charges; for use of the track, use of the locomotive and for the conveyance.

The maximum rate clause of the 1845 Act combined the three charges and introduced the principle of equal mileage rates to check discrimination. The Railway and Canal Traffic Act 1854 defined the duties of the railways to the public, laid down terms and conditions upon which traffic was to be accepted and conveyed, forbade undue preference and directed the railways to offer reasonable facilities. That left 'terminals' charges (e.g. collection, warehousing, loading, covering, cartage, delivery, transfer and demurrage) unclear and not limited by a maximum rate. Because there was no necessity for railways to publish tariffs, there was no readily available basis upon which traders could compare. These areas were addressed in Acts of 1868 and 1873, the latter setting up a Railway Commission which, amongst other things, was to settle inter-railway disputes by, if necessary, arbitration.

To assist matters between themselves, in 1842 a few railway companies established a Railway Clearing

80 • THE GREAT CENTRAL RAILWAY: WHAT REALLY HAPPENED

Year	Inflation %	Bank rate range %	Notes
1880	3	3 - 2½ - 3	
1881	-1.1	2½ - 5	
1882	1	6 - 3 - 5	
1883	-0.5	4 - 2½ - 3	
1884	-2.7	3½ - 2 - 5	
1885	-3	4 - 2 - 4	
1886	-1.6	3 - 2½ - 5	
1887	-0.5	4 - 2½ - 4	
1888	0.7	3½ - 2½ - 5	
1889	1.4	4 - 2½ - 6	
1890	0.2	5 - 3½ - 6 - 5	
1891	0.7	4 - 5 - 3 - 2½	
1892	0.4	3 - 2 - 3	
1893	-0.7	2½ - 5 - 3	
1894	-2	2½ - 2	MS&LR sought funding for London Extn
1895	-1	2½ - 2	
1896	-0.3	2½ - 4	
1897	1.5	3½ - 2 - 3	Queen Victoria Jubilee
1898	0.3	4 - 3½ - 4	
1899	0.7	3½ - 6	Anglo-Boer War
1900	5.1	4 - 3½ - 5	
1901	0.5	4 - 3 - 5	
1902	0	3 - 4	
1903	0.4	3 - 4	
1904	-0.2	3 - 4	
1905	0.4	2½ - 4	
1906	0	4 - 3½ - 6	

thought fit, set aside contingency for enlarging, repairing or improving the works connected with the undertaking. Whilst that provided a starting point, the novelty of railways in their earlier days was such that no one could form a view on, for example, the longevity of iron rails or for the 'life' of a locomotive, rolling stock and replacement of such. Initially, the LNWR and GWR favoured a fixed per cent charge set against the profits, the MR introduced a fund for permanent way only in 1848, but having found its provision to be inadequate, withdrew it in 1857. Progressively, the general policy became one of charging repairs and replacements to revenue.

With expansion of their service provisions and infrastructure the railways also had problems with what costs should be allocated to revenue account; to charge the latter account (and thereby reduce net profit) with additions to rolling stock, stations and buildings would – some thought – be unfair to those who were interested in short term dividends rather than the longer term capital growth of their company. For these reasons, it is suggested that to draw comparisons between the accounts of different companies over any period up to 1882 at the very earliest is to produce meaningless data.

The timing of promotion of new ventures is always important in relation to the cost of borrowing money by the promoter and in subscribing money as an investor. In the period 1880-1912, of particular interest to this book, neither the prevailing rate of cost inflation nor the Bank of England minimum rates gave cause for particular concern in regard to, for example, delaying a proposal until the next year's parliamentary session.

THE GREAT CENTRAL RAILWAY'S FINANCIAL STRUCTURE AND PERFORMANCE • 79

The rate of return on capital invested varied between railways, but the general expectation at the end of the 1880s was probably no more than 4 per cent (and slightly lower in the 1890s). That, of course, has to be viewed against the Bank of England minimum rate (down to 2 per cent in each of the years 1884 to 88) and consols which held 3 per cent

In the early years, promotion of railways had been inclined to be conducted with few rules and there was a widespread practice to pay dividends out of capital, even though all calls to pay for subscribed shares had not been answered. Even by the 1867 Railway Companies Act, 'working expenses' were not defined and railway accounting remained more of a variable practice than should have been the case. As late as 1882, a parliamentary select committee reported that paying interest out of capital was based upon sound financial practice. Chairmen who were fortunate enough to pay dividends for all priorities of investments preferred and were allowed to declare a fixed dividend rather than one which fluctuated and although all investors would welcome any dividend, there were groups who expressed an opinion that all costs of rolling stock, stations and sidings should be charged to capital. Company practices varied on that and also on 'betterment' when, for example an aged locomotive was re-built to give further service.

The guidance on provisions for depreciation (1844) was that before apportioning the profits to be divided amongst the shareholders, the Directors may, if they

The conclusion from this comparison is that two of them had an ongoing obligation to pay, at fixed interest, 79 per cent and 80 per cent of the total capital issued. Those two companies were the GCR and the SER, both previously chaired by Watkin and heavily influenced by his approach to financial management. Of the other companies, the LNWR, MR and (sometimes) GNR were competitors to the GCR and with fixed interest obligations much lower at 54/58/67 per cent, it meant that profits could be distributed throughout their financial support base and holders of ordinary shares could enjoy dividends.

Watkin's own definition of a sound railway company was one which earned as a net profit the whole of the original capital cost in a period not exceeding 25 years; that is 4 per cent per year.

From figures published by the Board of Trade in 1902, it is possible to identify the average holding of railway stocks in different categories for particular railway companies. The average is smaller than may have been supposed. For the Great Central Railway it was:

Total holders		Debentures		Pref. and guar.		Ordinary	
No.	Av £	No.	Av £	No.	Av £	No.	Av £
30,035	1,451	7,968	1,677	15,779	1,303	6,288	1,537

For comparison purposes here are statistics for other, relevant railway companies:

Company	Total holders		Debentures			Pref. and Guar.		
	No.	Av £	No.	Av £	%	No.	Av £	%
Great Northern	33,049	1,738	5,827	2,478	18	16,011	1,406	49
Great Eastern	35,020	1,452	9,444	1,844	27	16,672	1,180	48
Midland	75,793	2,379	13,221	2,848	17	30,792	2,180	41
LNWR	78,165	1,541	14,809	2,581	19	27,007	1,458	35
Metropolitan*	11,003	1,192	1,805	1,889	16	4,308	922	39
South Eastern*	17,371	1,720	3,642	2,157	21	10,293	1,163	59

NOTE:
* Watkin was chairman prior to that year.

(1881-88), dropped below that figure and remained there until 1907.

voting rights at meetings of the company. On occasion, the Directors may have been prepared to take loans at agreed levels of interest.

From this process, a new venture would typically have a proportion of its capital in debentures and a proportion in ordinary shares. There would be far fewer debenture holders than those with ordinary shares, but it was the former who tended to be interested in the long term with a guaranteed rate of interest. In those days of steady interest rates, the probability of frequent fluctuations in bank rates was low, but the risk existed that 4 per cent at time of purchase may later prove to be out of step with interest rates consistently at, say, 6 per cent. For the 'average man' the alternative was to purchase government issue 'consols'; a form of tradeable investment at a given rate of interest which was sold as a method of financing military operations.

Watkin courted the wealthier backers and, having demonstrated over time his abilities as a railway manager, auditor and in the use of available money, established a loyal following of backers, particularly based in the North West of England.

Whilst the type of investor traditionally ranged through the classes of Victorian society and attracted the bankers/financiers, a slump in new construction in the 1850s brought forth a new type; the railway contractor looking for work at home rather than overseas. The contractors understood the risks inherent in civil engineering and the difficulty of cash flow and returns to investors becoming due before the new line was completed and generating income. They also wanted their labour and plant to be operational. Such arrangements did, though, bring a difficulty in terms of competitive discussions regarding which contractor would provide the best combination of shares, Lloyd's bonds and cash as opposed to supposed 'closed' tendering with, in many cases collusion as to rates for the job. The issue of loan notes (and IOUs) – a potential method of seeing companies through a difficult time – had been made illegal by the 1844 Act, but in effect were replaced by Lloyd's bonds (Lloyd being a barrister not connected with the insurer). Such bonds enabled the contractor to trade the value of the bond with a bank or capitalist to fund his work safe in the knowledge that the bonds were tradeable and have a rate of interest higher than debentures, an alternative form of investment.

Debentures were perceived as being very safe, at least until 11 May 1866, when the collapse of the Quaker-run City bank Overend, Gurney & Co. – a leading banker to the railway industry – shook confidence and resulted in a legal ruling that made holders of debentures realise that such were not as safe as previously thought and did not, in fact, have 'first claim' status on property after all. Lord Justice Cairns gave the judgment of the Court of Appeal in which he said:

'... the railway ... must not, under a contract pledging it as security, be destroyed, broken up, or annihilated. The earnings of the railway must be made available to satisfy the mortgage [i.e. debenture holders] but, in my opinion, the mortgagees cannot ... reduce the railway into its original elements when it has been completed. Under the [temporary] Railway Companies Act 1867 [made perpetual in 1875] the engines, carriages, etc constituting the rolling stock and plant of a railway company are not ... to be taken in execution.'

In the aftermath a leading civil engineering contractor – Sir Samuel Morton Peto – faced ruin and he felt obliged to resign as an MP, the London Chatham and Dover Railway remained insolvent for five years and the Great Eastern – formed only four years previously – also suffered. 27 per cent of railway capital was then held in debentures.

Typically, debenture and preference shares were issued in blocks of hundreds with voting rights for the latter increasing by volume held e.g. for 4 per cent preference stock one vote for every £100 stock up to £1,000, then one for every £500 up to £10,000, above that one vote per £1,000.

In the first half of the 1870s, over 30 per cent of all railway share issues were for the preference share. Following the mania, debentures had become more relatively attractive and enjoyed popularity up until the banking crisis of 1866. Legal matters and rulings having been clarified, debentures regained popularity; in 1870 they accounted for less than 10 per cent of total paid up capital, five years later around 20 per cent and by 1890 the proportion was around 25 per cent and roughly on a par with preference shares. What had declined were loans and to a lesser extent ordinary shares.

THE GREAT CENTRAL RAILWAY'S FINANCIAL STRUCTURE AND PERFORMANCE • 77

have been started by a remark by Gladstone in 1844 that in his view, readily available capital would be employed in building railways. When a senior politician made a comment such as that it inevitably found its way into the press and made the job of underwriters of stock that much easier. Once any particular new issue found initial interest from investors, the demand quickly grew, irrespective of the true worth of the company. That led to the issue of a huge number of prospectuses – many of a hugely dubious nature – capital being subscribed without any clarity on how it was to be used, where the risks lay and whether the monies subscribed in good faith were in good, safe (from misappropriation) hands. In 1844, 49 railway Acts were passed authorising the expenditure of over £20m, in 1845, 94 Acts/£59m (equivalent almost to the national income). In 1844, 755 companies were listed at the London Stock Exchange and although joint stock banks (417) was the largest group, their paid up capital was only £26m compared with £47m of the 66 listed railway companies. At such times, confidence is all and share dealerships gave an opportunity to make money out of subscriptions ('scrip'), exchanged later for ordinary equity upon incorporation of the new railway. Fine for a while, though not so when the bubble burst, as it did in the autumn of 1845. The bursting of the bubble ruined many and very probably hardened Watkin's view on speculators. It is possible to identify two distinct types of shareholder; the permanent investor with the long term in mind and the temporary investor (including speculators) seeking quick returns or timely dividend declarations. In his time of authority, Watkin was fortunate to have a solid support base of the first type of investor whom he sought to reward and my conclusion from the research is that, despite the large number of them, he really did not give a high priority to holders of Ordinary stock.

For some investors, railway shares or 'homerails' remained a potentially attractive proposition and the loyalty of the Lancastrians can be shown by their influence in Watkin becoming first a Director of the South Eastern Railway and quickly thereafter its financially successful Chairman.

The expansion of the railway system after the 1840s required huge capital investment necessarily drawn from a range of types of investor, from the working class to the banks, landowners, gentry and investment houses. Total gross capital formation of railways reached one peak in 1847 (almost £44m, of which £7m was for land purchase), with other peaks in 1865 (£28m) and 1874–5 (£24m). In the 1840s and 1860s, railway investments accounted for between 20 and 30 per cent of gross domestic investment and, at the end of the century, around 10 per cent. Of the £1,300m that approximates to the total gross capital formation of the UK railways between 1831 and 1914, the purchase of land took altogether less than £200m. Between 1870 and 1913 the total, paid up capital rose by £815m, of which £516m was for new investment for railway purposes, £150–200m represented nominal additions to capital and some of the rest was spent on ancillary activities such as shipping services, docks, hotels and road vehicles.

Railways in the mainland UK were built purely as industrial undertakings with a view to providing and selling to the public a commodity for which there was an anticipated demand, at a profit yielding a sufficient return to justify the risk of an investment. The railways of the UK were built with public subscriptions in response to notices of the promoters. By the early 1900s, more of the public were financially interested in railways than with any other industry in the country.

Raising capital for new railway ventures was a competitive business and promoters set out to attract capital in different forms aimed at particular types of investor. Wealthy investors would be attracted by debentures offering a fixed rate of interest payable half yearly or annually and available in large value blocks of hundreds of pounds. Debentures did not carry voting rights, but groups of holders could call meetings and, in the worst cases, could petition against the company. As already mentioned, preference shares were used to help fund the construction phase of the new railway; they carried an interest rate and voting rights and became popular with contractors. For the 'average man' who wished to invest in a railway company, ordinary shares would be available via stock exchange brokers. The face value of the share may be, say one pound, but the stock exchanges would take a view on the relative attraction of the venture and if demand for the shares was high the trading price would become higher than the face value and, of course, lower if the attraction faded. The ordinary shares could be in two categories; preferred (when dividends were to be made) or deferred (the lowest category which received a dividend payment only when all other categories had been paid). Ordinary shares carried came from preference shares and £1m from the issue of guaranteed shares which ranked above preference and ordinary shares if and when dividends were payable. It seems that Henderson had to placate some holders of preference shares (£367,000 at 3¼ per cent and £872,000 at a whopping 6 per cent) by converting them to guaranteed status.

Persuasion in business can be costly, particularly if investors are willing only in return for more security and by adding a new category of stock Henderson had further increased the annual burden of payments that needed to be paid, increased the risk of reduced dividends to holders of preference shares and of there being little left for the holders of ordinary shares, both preferred and deferred. Despite the record of poor and nil returns to holders of ordinary shares, the total nominal value of ordinary shares subscribed had increased from £4.42m in 1894 (and continued to grow up to a total of £10.64m in 1922). The assumption is that the bid prices of the stock market for ordinary stock reflected the progress made by the Company and the probability of healthy dividends being declared as the investments produced net revenue.

The table which follows shows that, although the amount of capital authorised by Acts of Parliament increased between 1898 and 1912, Henderson managed to attract far more from investors who were willing to subscribe for the new and old issues of stock. Between 1900 and 1912, Henderson lifted the percentage of capital fully paid up from 77 to 88 of the total authorised. Furthermore, he restrained the level of fixed interest stocks (of debentures and loans) to within the limits set by the various Acts. However, by issuing guaranteed stock he had lifted the proportion to as high as 51.5 per cent making the Company very highly geared.

The financing arrangements were high risk and for the self-imposed burden to be satisfied year upon year would require net revenue to be maximised.

Year	Capital authorised		Capital paid up		Loans & debentures & guarantee %	Inflation %	Bank rate %
	Total £m	Loans & debentures %	Total £m	Loans & debentures %			
1898	48.46	26.89	40.15	27.4	40.6	0.3	4/3½/4
1899	48.84	26.53	41.56	27.2	40	0.7	3½/6
1900	54.84	34.6	42.06	28.1	40.6	5.1	5/3½/4
1901	54.84	34.6	42.43	28.7	41.2	0.5	4/3/5
1902	55.24	34.5	43.77	31	43.1	0	3/4
1903	55.24	34.5	44.09	31.4	43.4	0.4	4/3
1904	55.24	34.5	45.64	33.8	45.4	-0.2	3/4
1905	56.55	36	46.68	35.2	46.7	0.4	2½/4
1906	57.18	36.8	48.04	36.9	47.8	0	4/3½/6
1907	59.8	39.5	51.47	39.4	49.8	1.2	4/7/5
1908	59.83	39.5	52.24	40.2	50.5	0.5	2½/4
1909	60.58	40.3	52.49	40.5	50.5	0.5	2½/5/4½
1910	60.58	40.3	52.6	40.7	50.8	0.9	3/5
1911	60.58	40.3	52.6	42	51	0.1	4/3½
1912	60.58	41.5	53.5	41.7	51.5	3	3/4/5

The thinking of the board behind the scenes regarding the recruitment of a new general manager to replace the hard working, long serving Pollitt must have been interesting. The identification and attraction from the LSWR of Samuel Fay was, either by accident or design, a stroke of collective wisdom. He proved to be the perfect 'action man' to implement the Board's policy of expansion.

Not at all interested in statistics, Fay became totally immersed in making the railway work. Henderson, though, was very much in tune with the statistical aspects of the business. The choice of investments to be made and the sourcing of capital to support them were all about the closeness of Henderson to his operational colleagues and then his ability to attract either new capital or fund work from capital 'called up and fully paid' from earlier issues of stock. As shown in the table above, the total new capital authorised increased between 1900 and 1912 by £5.2m, but via his efforts with promoters and existing holders of stock, he managed to increase the total capital available to be committed in the same period by £11.4m. Henderson and his team were in their pomp. A measure of his success is that the proportion of capital authorised that was actually paid up increased between 1900 and 1912 from 77 per cent to 88 per cent. In other words, investors wanted more and could see that the railway was heading strongly in the right direction. But throughout that period, Henderson was also increasing the proportion of the total capital paid up that was represented by stock bearing fixed interest payment obligations; with the preference shares that had guaranteed status, that proportion had reached a very daunting level of 51.5 per cent. The GCR was expanding fast, investments wisely made could be expected to make net income (for examples: more powerful locomotives hauling heavier trains, shipping, services to new destinations). The plan clearly was to 'outrun' the burden of fixed interest debt. If that plan could come to fruition, his hope would be that all holders of stocks and shares would benefit. As can be seen in the following table, the railway consistently made a profit but it was insufficient to meet in full the rates of interest for holders of some preference shares and not at all for the declaration of dividends for holders of ordinary shares. However, Henderson had managed to close the gap for preference shares from £500,000 in 1900 to £160,000 in 1912 and with every prospect of closing it further.

Year	Total obligation if all holders of interest bearing stock and shares were paid £m	Net income GCR £m*	Amount not paid to holders of some preference shares £m
1898	1.299	1.315	-
1899	1.468	1.228	0.329
1900	1.527	1.140	0.552
1901	1.499	1.188	0.530
1902	1.546	1.328	0.548
1903	1.558	1.375	0.352
1904	1.594	1.421	0.325
1905	1.665	1.564	0.256
1906	1.694	1.638	0.233
1907	1.786	1.736	0.259
1908	1.813	1.726	0.304
1909	1.822	1.831	0.274
1910	1.836	1.831	0.199
1911	1.836	1.953	0.139
1912	1.777	1.982	0.160

NOTE:
* including contributions from shared ventures.

It is of relevance to cast an eye on the capital structures of the railway companies who were competitors (LNWR and MR) and the sometimes competitor, the GNR, together with the UK in total. Each of the LNWR, MR and GNR had a proportion of paid up capital held in the form of debentures and loans. The proportions were:

Year	LNWR	MR	GNR
1900	32.1%	20.3%	25.1%
1905	31.8%	21.3%	25.4%
1910	31.3%	21.3%	25.6%

For the UK in total, it was 26.4 per cent in 1900, 26.5 per cent in 1905 and 26.9 per cent in 1910. (For the GCR it was 28.1 per cent, 35.2 per cent and 42 per cent.) By adding in guaranteed shares, some of which the LNWR and MR owned, the relative positions became:

Year	LNWR	MR	GCR
1900	44.6%	29.8%	40.6%
1905	44.2%	30.4%	46.7%
1910	43.2%	30.7%	50.8%

Of further relevance is that although the GCR was able to meet its obligations in full to some 75 per cent of all its investors, that pales against the record of the LNWR, MR and GNR to pay dividends all the way down the list of categories to holders of deferred ordinary shares.

Company	1900		1905		1910	
	Pref %	Def %	Pref %	Def %	Pref %	Def %
LNWR	6¼		6⅛		6⅝	
MR	2½	2¾	2½	2⅝	2½	3½
GNR	4-6	Nil	4	1½	4	2¼

These relatively high interest rates paid in dividends to holders of ordinary shares alerted the representatives of the wealth creating workforce regarding the strongly held views that certain companies could and should find a more equitable distribution of profits than that which was being applied. By contrast, when matters reached a crisis at national level, the representatives of the main grades at the GCR acknowledged that they were and had been fairly treated. As an example the starting weekly wage of a Locomotive Driver with the GCR in 1904 was £1 10s, rising to £2 8s; the latter being higher than the rate paid by the GER, L&Y and MR, and on a par with the GNR and LNWR. GCR Firemen on express passenger workings fared well, at £1 10s a week. In the same year, the common working day was 10 hours, but 11 on the GCR, and with no paid holidays and no provision of overalls.

The chairmen of the GCR were faced with a need to raise capital at particular times; they did not have the benefit of forward knowledge of how the guideline Bank of England interest rate for lending may fluctuate and thereby influence others in the competitive world of borrowing and investing. One of the reasons that the LNWR, MR and GNR had been able to afford to pay dividends to holders of ordinary shares was that the fixed rates applicable to debentures, loans and for guaranteed shares were generally favourable over time whilst the same could not be stated for the GCR with its 'top end' obligation.

Company	Debentures %	Loans %	Guaranteed %
LNWR	3	5	4
MR	2½	2½	2½
GNR	3	5	n/a
GCR	3½-5	4-5	4-6

At a national UK level, the fixed percentage rates payable on debentures in 1900 ranged from zero to not exceeding six (with 62 per cent of those then paid up being between two and three) and loans ranging from one to not exceeding eight (64 per cent between four and five).

The detail of the uses for which the available new capital was attracted is given below. The following is a summary of expenditure of capital upon the railway and its ancillary activities up to the end of 1913.

Expended upon	£
Lines belonging to the GCR	34,282,431
Lines leased	88,553
Lines jointly owned/leased	1,621,552
Rolling stock	7,931,598
Manufacturing/repair facilities	953,802
Steamboats	687,832
Canals	910,174
Docks, harbours and wharves	2,262,622
Hotels	132,149
Electric power stations	125,013
Land, property (non railway)	2,953,180
Subscriptions to other companies	709,188

The Great War was funded, like all wars, by taxes, price increases and inflation. For example, the standard rate of income tax, which was 6 per cent in 1914, stood at 30 per cent in 1918 and the tax affected an additional 1.87 million individuals. Inflation in 1914 was -0.3 per cent but in the next years was 12.5 per cent, 18.1 per cent, 25.2 per cent, 22.0 per cent, 10.1 per cent and 15.4 per cent respectively. Steel rails increased in cost by 57 per cent. Salaries and wages also increased whilst the loss of manpower was equally significant; in the first six months of the war, 3,778 enlisted (11 per cent of the then workforce) and by autumn 1916 the number had passed 7,000. The Railway Executive Council assumed control of the railways for the government, effective from the outbreak. In 1917, Fay was asked to take over the post of Director of Movements at the War Office and in March 1918 he became Director General of Movements & Railways, with a seat on the Army Council. Amongst the contributions made by the GCR to the war effort were the building by various contractors and the GCR of a total of 521 of Robinson's Class 8K 2-8-0 locomotives (chosen by the Ministry of Munitions as a standard type for war service), Immingham became the headquarters for the Admiral of Patrols and was also used as a base for submarine, torpedo craft and mine laying destroyer ships and Grimsby was similarly used for coal storage and as a base for minesweeping trawlers.

Investment in the GCR continued through the years of the war and included extensive work to cross the River Trent at Keadby (1916); the quadrupling of tracks between Wrawby junction and Brocklesby, also between Doncaster and Thorne (1916), the strengthening of viaducts at Etherow and Dinting (1918/19) and the necessary remedial work at Wembley Hill following a landslip.

Better news during the war was the elevation to a peerage for Sir Alexander Henderson, aged 66. He chose the title Lord Faringdon. Changes to the Board were necessary following the death of Viscount Cross in 1914, Colonel Sir Clement Royds in 1916 and the Deputy Chairman Purdon Viccarr in 1918. Gerard Powys Dewhurst joined the Board in 1914 and the Hon Eric B. Butler Henderson of Stafford became a Director in 1918 and in the same year Director Walter Burgh Gair became Deputy Chairman.

Following the Armistice, Fay was released from War Office duties and returned to the GCR in May 1919. He had an Assistant General Manager, Mr E.A. Clear, previously Assistant Superintendent of the Line (Doncaster), Assistant Goods Manager (1902) and Assistant to the General Manager (1912).

Whilst the politicians debated the future organisation for the railways, the GCR Board responded to the urgent need for restorations, particularly the operational fleet of locomotives and rolling stock, plus the fleet of steamboats, and improvements, particularly at Grimsby. Capital investment was limited to dock works at New Holland and Grimsby, to civils and signalling work in connection with the British Empire Exhibitions at Wembley.

With effect from 31 December 1922 the GCR ceased to exist and became a constituent of the new LNER organisation. The final capital structure was:

Nominal rate of interest or dividend	Description	Amount of capital issued	Amount upon which interest or dividend was payable*
4	Debenture	79,577	79,577
4½	Debenture	11,367,341	11,367,341
5	Debenture	300,000	300,000
3½	2nd Debenture	11,383,060	11,383,060
3½	2nd Debenture Redeemable	742,730	742,730
4½	1st Prefce G'teed	1,035,000	1,066,083
3¼	Prefce G'teed	366,698	366,698
6	Prefce G'teed	872,000	872,000
5	G'teed	577,506	628,300
4	G'teed S. Yorks Rent Charge	448,980	448,980
5	Perpetual Prefce	1,008,000	1,008,000
5	Irredeemable S. Yorks Rent Charge	490,000	490,000

Nominal rate of interest or dividend	Description	Amount of capital issued	Amount upon which interest or dividend was payable*
4¼	S. Yorks Perpetual Rent Charge	1,501,020	1,797,428
4	Prefce	1,000,000	1,100,000
5	Convtble Prefce, 1872	1,000,000	1,000,000
5	Convtble Prefce, 1874	1,080,000	1,080,000
5	Convtble Prefce, 1876	1,500,000	1,500,000
5	Convtble Prefce, 1879	1,000,000	1,000,000
5	Convtble Prefce, 1881	1,380,000	1,380,000
4	Prefce, 1889	1,500,000	1,500,000
4	Prefce, 1891	2,230,000	2,230,000
5	Prefce, 1894	3,100,000	3,100,000
6	Prefd Ordy	5,318,490	5,318,490
-	Defd Ordy	5,339,530	5,339,530
		54,619,932	55,098,237

NOTES:
Nominal additions/deductions not shown.
* as listed in Board of Trade return

Each area of the business received, over time, a share of the available new capital. The fine detail of expenditure in each year is at Appendix 1.

Year	Locos £	C & W £	Infrastructure £	Shipping £	Marine installations £
1900	159,170	25,000	-	-	-
1901	186,280	-	342,000	-	-
1902	256,815	191,930	49,550	77,450	20,000
1903	159,950	176,540	81,905	-	16,720
1904	249,795	248,656	149,030	-	70,000
1905	113,970	78,320	552,434	20,000	41,000
1906	162,000	4,800	111,333	147,200	21,000
1907	212,900	-	-	-	-
1908	42,750	-	164,500	-	-
1909	68,250	-	11,700	80,250	-
1910	100,950	93,375	5,000	83,108	-
1911	75,000	117,950	11,329	38,000	-
1912	427,076	7,730	-	19,915	97,091

For that outlay of some £5.5m, the railway received around 600 new locomotives, 4,500 wagons, 300 carriages, nine ships, a new carriage and wagon workshop, new shunting yards, an avoiding line for always congested Doncaster and multiple civil engineering/signalling improvement works.

By adding the capital cost of the acquisition of the LDECR, the investment in the development of the Humber Commercial Railway and Dock Co., the capital expenditure necessary to make the WM and CQR workable, plus some capitalised rent charges for access to sites in South Yorkshire, the total of £11.4 million is reached.

Quite how Henderson decided upon the course to be taken for the development of the business is one of many unknowns. In retrospect, the 1900-1910 decade was looked upon as the Golden Age of railways in the UK, but at the time he could only seek to gauge the activities of the railways in total, the post-Boer war, the economy, anticipate the changing nature of Edwardian society and their expectations of higher standards for business and recreational travel. He would have had reasonably-based expectations of an increasing urban population (and would hope that Sheffield, Nottingham and Leicester would prosper), a continuation of the national advantages accruing from the free trade arrangements (which he would gauge from his involvement as a significant investor in the successful Manchester Ship Canal), demand for export of coal and other minerals (to boost activities at Immingham) and the general optimism of the times.

Having confidence and optimism for the short/medium term future were legacies of the Victorian era which were sustained, at least until 1910. The changing political moods in continental Europe then started to raise concerns and social changes (hours of work, national insurance legislation and labour/material cost increases) at home added costs which were not readily recoverable by the necessary but slow process of Board of Trade agreement to national increases. Henderson, with his senior management team, would have to 'out run' the onset of increasing real costs by expanding the business and taking every possible saving from increased efficiencies.

Robinson, the Chief Mechanical Engineer, inherited a fleet of locomotives in urgent need of replacements. He correctly identified the need for locomotives suitable for goods traffic as being the priority over passenger and mixed traffic. In the three categories, the totals built by and for the GCR in Robinson's tenure were 433, 227 and 62. The expectation would very probably have been for a life of some 25 years and both Robinson and Henderson would have been very satisfied with the fact that many of the 9J (LNER J11) and 8K (LNER 04) locomotives (a total of 300) carried on moving the goods well into the 1950s and in some cases the 1960s. The goods engines also included a small batch designed specifically for fish traffic. In the passenger category, the 9K and 9L (LNER C13, C14), 9N (LNER A5) and 11E/11F (LNER D10, D11) also saw very long lives of good service into the 1950s. The National Collection of locomotives under the management of the Science Museum, National Railway Museum, includes an example of an 8K and an 11F, both of which have been restored to steam in the preservation era. At the time of writing, the 8K is at the Great Central Railway, Loughborough, and the 11F is at Barrow Hill, near Chesterfield. Together with the 109 new locomotives made available for the London extension under a ten year hire purchase arrangement, the investment programme in locomotives was a success (though with a few costly experiments on the passenger fleet), aided by close association with private builders (such as Beyer, Peacock and those forming North British) who were exporters of similar designs for the overseas market. The success overseas (and with the GWR 28XX) of the eight coupled driving wheels of small diameter, together with Belpaire fireboxes, superheating (with consequential reductions in coal consumption) and piston valve locomotives encouraged Robinson to follow a similar successful course with his Class 8K 2-8-0s, North British building 48 of the initial production batch.

The capital expenditure on wagons was product and market driven, examples being fish, covered vans and an early venture into refrigeration. Whilst the vast majority of coal wagons were owned by the proprietors of the collieries, the GCR invested in some four wheeled varieties for general use and (because very few collieries could manage them) larger capacity bogie types mainly for conveyance of coal to locomotive depots. The GCR was at the forefront, with the move from grease to oil lubrication of axle boxes and in the design of wagons having side, bottom and end doors to ease discharge, particularly at docks.

The decision to promote long distance passenger trains necessitated an acknowledgement of the need to compete by the provision of high levels of comfort and refreshment facilities. The question of demand for out of season travel to holiday destinations and consequential underutilisation of stock must have troubled Henderson and Fay. Excursion traffic similarly was a risk whilst stock principally for European émigrés to North America (travelling between Grimsby and Liverpool) was opportunistic. The profitability of the CLC owed something to the cascaded use of older vehicles displaced elsewhere whilst the MSJ&A ran and ran until replacement was absolutely necessary.

The civils and S&T works included the major developments at Wath and Immingham, the widening of routes at particularly busy points on the network and the avoiding line at Doncaster together with improvements and not savings from advances in signalling technology promoted by engineer Bound.

Infrastructure and plant included the new carriage and wagon new build and maintenance works at Dukinfield which released capacity at Gorton for locomotive work and reduced the dependence upon private contractors. Also, the power generating plant at Immingham and shipping for passenger services together with hotels provide an example of how the GCR (and the GER, GWR and SECR in particular) sought to extend these activities via ancillary operations. Having the facilities at Grimsby for fish, coal and timber traffic would have allowed a better case to be made for the investment in steamboats and crewing of timetabled services to near Continental Europe, but a riskier venture than for the core railway business. Expectations of 20-25 years' service lifetime during which a high capital cost would need to be recovered were exceeded, at least in peacetime conditions. Of the early acquisitions, *Huddersfield* gave 31 years' service before becoming wrecked, *Ashton* 32 years prior to being sold and *Lutterworth* 41 years before being sold. Of the later acquisitions four lasted until the late 1950s (*Macclesfield*, *Bury*, *Accrington* and *Dewsbury*), whilst two were sunk by enemy action during the second World War (*City of Bradford* and, particularly cruelly, *Stockport*, which had been converted to be a convoy rescue ship, was torpedoed off Iceland with the loss of all on board including survivors from earlier sinkings by U boats).

The capital cost of the acquisition of the LDECR would have been justified based upon its financial performance, its operating ratio and its 'fit' with the wider traffic flows of the GCR. The decision to purchase that railway as a going concern with effect from 1 January 1907 was sound. The annual returns of the Board of Trade contained the data as to how the short, operational sections (Chesterfield to Lincoln Pyewipe Junction, plus a branch from Langwith Junction to Brightside Junction, Sheffield area and access to multiple collieries) was worked efficiently with a fleet of tank locomotives. Its main West-East line was double tracked and gave an outlet for loaded traffic to the lines of the GER, which enjoyed running rights. Relationships with the GCR had improved from 1900 when Dixon Davies relinquished his role as Legal Adviser to the LDECR and joined the GCR as Solicitor; a running rights agreement quickly followed. The line was opened in 1896 and its progress would have been noted with interest by both the GNR and the GCR.

Year	Minerals, tons carried	Net receipts £	Operating ratio %
1902	1,495,163	48,121	59
1903	1,785,791	56,083	56
1904	1,920,482	56,610	57
1905	2,242,124	63,522	57

However, all was not well within the LDECR as it had become clear that its extremely optimistic plan (to link Warrington with Sutton-on-Sea) was never going to be realised. A majority of the directors (though not those representing the interests of the GER) agreed in 1905 to a sale to the GNR on the basis of terms to be stipulated being agreed. The GNR found the terms unattractive and the GCR very promptly made an offer which was accepted (again, by majority) by the LDECR.

In contrast, the basis for the absorption of the WM&CQR would have been very different; it was heading towards being a bad debt written off. A cost of some £110,000 was needed to make it workable and safe to the extent of making a small contribution on revenue account.

From the foregoing, it is clear that Henderson – with the support of investors – was setting out his stall for the long term. The period before those investments would produce a return would vary, but the obligation remained to pay the fixed rates of interest within the total capital as paid up in the form of debentures, loans and guaranteed stock.

With such an overcapitalised company – in modern words, highly geared – Henderson would not have wished to add to the annual payments to holders of fixed interest stock. For pure railway activities, like the LDECR, he could not avoid it and would expect an early return from the investment. For the development of Immingham as a dock and railway facility he had needed to find another method that gave control to the GCR without adding to its financial burden.

The GCR would facilitate the enterprise, but the company – initially Commercial Dock Co. Ltd. – later Humber Commercial Railway and Dock Co. – would need to be promoted by the interests of Grimsby. The GCR was represented on the Board by W.P. Viccars, Director (to 1906), Deputy Chairman (from 1906), and R. Sutton Nelthorpe, Director and a man of Lincolnshire, son-in-law of a previous Deputy Chairman, Lord Auckland. Capital authorised was £1.77m and gradually paid up in line with physical work (£300,000 in 1905/06, £799,000 by end 1907, £1.17m 1908 and £1.58m by end 1909). Shareholders in the GCR were given the opportunity to invest and – as a measure of soundly based confidence – the return for guaranteed shares was a minimum of 4 per cent, the minimum being adjusted upwards depending upon tonnage throughput (which was achieved). The dock facility was opened in July 1912, Fay was knighted on that occasion and the facility in part remains in use over a century later.

Whilst investment of capital was a strong feature of the GCR policy of expansion, another route to improve the 'bottom line' of the Balance Sheet was through increased efficiency; for example, through better use of all resources, train weights to match the power of the freshly available locomotives, rostering of men and machines, improved line capacity through better signalling, combining fish traffic vans with passenger trains to same destination. The fact that the GCR and GNR had joint running rights over nearly 40 per cent of the total operating mileage of the two systems, plus joint lines, in 1907 prompted thoughts of an amalgamation. Although the idea received the backing of both Boards – and one of the original objectors, the GER, agreed to participate – such was the strength of opposition that the bill submitted to parliament was withdrawn by the three companies in early 1908.

Turning now to revenue expenditure – expenditure incurred on a day to day basis in the operation of the business – the Board of Trade returns identify costs under several headings. The principal cost areas were for labour in five departments and materials in four categories.

The uncontrollable variables within revenue costs represented a serious threat to Henderson's ability to meet the GCR's minimum level of fixed interest payments to stock holders. A detailed analysis of costs to identify volume and real cost increase variances is not possible, given that the scope and scale of the GCR changed so much. For example, the number of miles of line open increased from 383 in 1897 to 757 in 1912, locomotives 775 to 1,233 over the same period, passenger carriages 960 to 1,486 and wagons 17,748 to 32,693. Legislation affecting maxima for working hours, for conciliation boards and for National Insurance contributions by the employer added to the burden for direct labour. For strategic materials (permanent way, maintenance and repair) the trend up to 1907 was consistently upwards, though thereafter some reductions were achieved. For coal and coke for locomotives, fluctuations in the price at the pit head occurred, but the uncertainty was an unwelcome factor for budgetary purposes.

Working expenses for the period 1897 to 1913 were as follows:

Year	Total £m	Year	Total £m
1897	1.48	1906	2.9
1898	1.62	1907	3.2
1899	2.02	1908	3.2
1900	2.33	1909	3.1
1901	2.34	1910	3.2
1902	2.41	1911	3.4
1903	2.46	1912	3.5
1904	2.50	1913	3.9
1905	2.7		

As can be seen in the table, revenue costs increased year on year from £1.48m to £3.9m. Some of that increase was to be expected from the expansion of the Company's activities and some from increases in the costs of materials. The worrying aspects for Henderson would have been inflationary increases without him being able – in a regulated and competitive industry – to cover the additional costs through increases in traffic conveyed, efficiency savings, passenger fares and goods rate increases. His working margins were already slim, and I would suggest that it was a combination of these factors that may have shaken his confidence and prompted the discussions with the GNR (and later the GER) about seeking parliamentary approval to an amalgamation.

Henderson would also have kept an eagle eye on the income that the company was generating from its various activities. Total income minus total costs would provide him with a figure of profit (or loss).

Prior to a consideration of income streams, it is necessary to explain and identify the different sources.

Over the period of interest, the GCR worked, absorbed, acquired, jointly leased and granted/enjoyed reciprocal running rights over various railways. The income from some, though not all, of these ventures were included/incorporated in the annual returns. For example:

- included throughout the Wigan Junction worked by the GCR.
- included throughout a proportion of the West Riding and Grimsby Railway.
- included from acquisition/absorption of the Wrexham Mold & Connahs Quay, the Liverpool, St Helens & South Lancashire, the Lancashire, Derbyshire & East Coast and the Sheffield District railways.
- included from opening the half shares from the Great Western/GC, the GC and Midland, the Metropolitan Railway/GC and GC and West Riding and Grimsby joint lines.
- included from opening the Barton and Immingham Light, the North Lindsey Light and the Humber Commercial Railway and Dock Company.

The annual returns also listed railways in which the GCR had a shared interest, participated in and which generated (in most years) an income for all participants. The railways concerned were:

- Cheshire Lines Committee with the GNR and MR
- Manchester South Junction & Altrincham, with the LNWR
- Oldham, Ashton-under-Lyne and Guide Bridge, with the LNWR
- Macclesfield Committee, with the North Staffordshire Railway
- South Yorkshire Joint Line Committee, with the GNR, L&YR, MR, NER
- GC, Hull & Barnsley and Midland Committee
- GC and Midland Joint Committee
- Not yet open, The Mansfield Railway would be worked by the GC for 60 per cent of gross receipts.

Towards the end of the period under close review, the development of the iron and steel making industry around Frodingham intensified and was boosted as the thoughts of the government turned towards a need for naval and military hardware. Winston Churchill's declared objective was to have built two new warships to every one built by Germany. The GCR was well placed to contribute to and benefit from this concentration of effort.

The listings of profit from the two accounting sources are shown below. For the income from shared operations (e.g. CLC and MSJ&A) a proportion is included and for the CLC an estimate has been included for the provision by the GCR of locomotives. In the circumstances in which Henderson found himself, a contribution of around £150,000 per year was welcome and enabled more holders of stock to be paid. The right-hand column of the listings shows the annual total amounts that the GCR was obliged to pay to holders of fixed interest stock. For example, in 1905 profits totalled £1.564m (£1.4m + £164,000) and the obligation to pay totalled £957,000. That left (£1.564m - £957,000) £607,000 to pay the holders of preference shares and, if any money was left, to declare a dividend payable to holders of ordinary shares. The usual situation was that the holders of preference shares received either the full percentage, a proportion (say 3½ per cent instead of 5 per cent) or none. The holders of ordinary shares had to rely upon trading at stock market prices for any income.

Net income (that is gross receipts less 'expenses') for the two Groupings of contributors were:

Year	Included in the GCR return £m[+]	Included separately to the GCR return £m[*ø]	Obligation to pay holders of debentures, loans and guarantees £m[//]
1898	1.16	0.155	0.746
1899	1.07	0.158	0.76
1900	0.983	0.157	0.819
1901	1.03	0.158	0.791
1902	1.17	0.158	0.838
1903	1.22	0.155	0.849

Year	Included in the GCR return £m ÷	Included separately to the GCR return £m *ø	Obligation to pay holders of debentures, loans and guarantees £m //
1904	1.26	0.161	0.885
1905	1.4	0.164	0.957
1906	1.5	0.138	0.986
1907	1.6	0.136	1.078
1908	1.6	0.126	1.105
1909	1.7	0.131	1.114
1910	1.7	0.131	1.128
1911	1.8	0.153	1.128
1912	1.8	0.182	1.069

NOTES:

÷ first charges obligation to GW/GC and Metropolitan/GC
* amount shown is one third, one half or one fifth as appropriate
ø amount for CLC includes estimated amount for provision by GCR of locomotives
// increased margin allowed payments to more holders of preference

When viewed against the obligation to meet the fixed rates of interest payable on debentures, loans and guaranteed shares, the margins within which Henderson had to work were minimal. Any surplus was directed towards paying to the maximum extent possible the holders of preference shares as identified earlier in this chapter.

'First charges' were applicable to the arrangements entered with the Great Western and Metropolitan railways. The GW paid for the costs of the construction of the Banbury branch (opened to goods traffic June 1900), the GW/GC joint line with its connections at Northolt junction and Ashendon junction (opened to goods November 1905 and to passenger traffic in April 1906) plus the section between the latter junction and Grendon Underwood junction which was transferred to the GC in 1907. By the end of 1906, advances of the GW to its partner were £1,136,107 bearing interest at 4 per cent. The GC paid interest on half the capital spent upon the joint line by the GW, this being a first charge on the traffic receipts of the GC for the enterprise until the loan was repaid.

The disturbance occasioned to the Metropolitan Railway by the developments from the GW/GC Act of 1899 resulted in a claim by the former upon the GC for £1,037,000. The matter was resolved by the transfer to the GC of the Metropolitan widened line from Canfield Place to Harrow South junction on a lease of 999 years for an annual rental of £120,000 and the transfer of Met lines from Harrow South junction to Verney junction to a Met/GC Joint Committee. An annual rental of £44,000 would be payable, plus responsibility for the Brill branch line.

1913 was the first year for which the provisions of the Railway Companies (Accounts and Returns) Act of 1911 produced far more information than that hitherto. Leading up to that point, the position of the GCR in pure revenue terms was:

Year	Goods £m	Passengers £m
1898	1.85	0.66
1899	2.00	0.78
1900	2.12	0.88
1901	2.07	0.93
1902	2.20	0.98
1903	2.05	1.03
1904	2.30	1.06
1905	2.51	1.09
1906	2.75	1.22
1907	3.05	1.27
1908	2.95	1.33
1909	2.99	1.32
1910	3.16	1.37
1911	3.35	1.42
1912	3.42	1.42

From that can be deduced that in revenue terms, the GCR was predominantly a goods railway; some 73 per cent to 27 per cent. That, of course, does not mean that the same percentages applied to profit, the capital employed to produce the revenue, or the physical effort involved in producing the revenue/profit/return.

The 1913 returns include references to the average receipts per ton from merchandise as nine shillings and one halfpenny; from coal, coke and patent fuel as two shillings and a fraction of a penny; for other minerals two shillings and six pence and a fraction of a penny. For passenger traffic, the average receipts per ticket issued were for first class two shillings and ten pence plus a fraction; second class one shilling and eight pence plus a fraction; third class nine pence and a fraction. By taking the figures for goods traffic, the GCR was at the low side of the average. There are reasons why that should be.

Pricing for all categories of goods was, to a large extent, controlled by Acts of Parliament, but as has been noted earlier there was a reliance upon 'reasonable' rates being levied for many factors, including the use of wagons, collection, stowage, warehousing, cartage, sorting/shunting and charges levied by other railway companies necessarily used to reach the destination.

These pricing complications were a legacy of the way the railway companies had developed and, to some extent, the unwillingness of the Board of Trade Committee to legislate for all and every eventuality, preferring to let the companies compete and establish what the competitive demand side would bear. Clearly, any railway company that had control of 'through' traffic routes was well placed in terms of journey times and priorities, and pricing which benefitted them alone, without the need to pay third parties. In MS&LR days, Watkin had voiced his frustration at the many hindrances to his movement of goods (particularly towards London) and that was probably a factor in his resolve to have his own line, and a self-contained one at that.

In the circumstances, there were winners and losers. For coal, coke and patent fuel the MR fared well, the GCR not so well. Similarly, the lines that acted as part of the total conduit were able to benefit from what amounted to a facility fee, examples being the GW/GC and MetR/GC joint lines and the North London which did not originate traffic, simply moved it along.

For goods traffic along the London extension, the tonnages and train gross weights were crucial. For coal headed towards London, the GCR was competing from Nottinghamshire and Derbyshire with the MR (running rights with the GNR and from 1907 the GER lessened the competition) and made the most they could from the new deeper collieries of the Leen Valley and those owners of collieries who were disaffected by the level of service provided by the MR with access to both railways. However, the colliery owners knew very well the position the GCR was seeking and that hard-headed approach would have applied to negotiations on price and contract durations. Similarly, the colliery owners and landowners of South Yorkshire were supportive of the London extension, but at a cost level acceptable to both parties, but mainly to them. The capital structure of the GCR includes three, hefty South Yorkshire rent charges totalling £2.44m at annual rates of interest of 4 per cent, 4¼ per cent and 5 per cent. I assume much of that is for access to the area around Wath, where the new marshalling yard was constructed. For goods traffic generally, the link from Culworth Junction to Banbury gave access to the GWR line and marshalling yard at Banbury, whilst a spur off the GCR at Woodford gave access to the East & West Junction Railway (in 1909, the Stratford-upon-Avon & Midland Junction Railway) upon which 'through' goods traffic to Bristol and South Wales was routed without a need for Banbury. The tonnages of goods traffic carried over the GW/GC Joint Committee and the MetR/GC Joint Committee routes in 1913 totalled 1,320,716 (34,149 originating) and 564,931 (79,375 originating) respectively, reinforcing why the GWR were so keen for the Banbury branch to be built. The statistics also put into context the tonnage of coal carried forward from Woodford via the MetR/GC line. The total of 274,000 tons was around 1,000 tons per weekday within a grand total of some eight million tons carried by rail into London during that year. No statistical information has come to light for the route from Woodford to Stratford-upon-Avon and beyond, or via Aylesbury to Princes Risborough single line until the opening of the Banbury branch.

Average receipts per ton	£	s	d
Midland Railway		2	3
GCR		1	6
North London			10
Great Northern		1	10

Further clues were to be found in the Returns in respect of the tonnage carried which originated on the railway company's own lines. Again, this was an area which Watkin found irksome and frustrating; an expectation to convey traffic for others at less than that he felt was equitable, but which was the maximum the market would bear. Examples are (for coal, coke and patent fuel):

GCR	14,920,952 tons originated on GCR lines of a total of 38,649,389 tons carried.
Midland	27,338,480 tons (originated on the MR) of a total of 31,302,458.
GW/GC	185 tons of a total of 837,575.
MetR/GC	6,993 tons of a total of 273,631.
North Ldn	Nil tons of a total of 1,399,714.

Watkin had realised how the North London was so successful; do the thing you are best at. Henderson also realised it and, for example, worked the Mansfield Railway (one million tons output annually) for 60 per cent of gross receipts.

On the passenger side, the challenges included trying to isolate the increase brought about solely due to the London extension. As can be seen in the table, there was an increase year upon year 1898 to 1899 (line opened March 1899) and 1899 to 1900, but to claim this for the extension would need far more than the statistics in the Board of Trade Returns and, indeed, the lukewarm remarks of the Chairman in the Great Central Staff Journal. George Dow quotes figures for exchanges of wagons with the Great Western in the first six months of operation as 60,796 (1900) and by 1904 the annual figure nearer to 90,000. By the outbreak of war, the annual figure had grown to some 252,000 (492,000 in 1916).

The Returns for 1913 also gave an indication as to revenue streams for ancillary businesses, including steamboats, hotels and refreshment facilities on and off trains. Steamboats produced net receipts of £13,350 against gross receipts of £295,437; hotels and refreshments £12,556 on a gross of £115,091. A cross reference to other railway companies offering similar facilities shows:

Steamboats

Company	Gross receipts £	Net receipts £	% return
GER	376,604	50,111	7.5
GWR	180,729	(27,630)	-
SE&CR	341,815	125,580	36.7

Hotels, refreshment rooms and restaurant carriage services

Company	Gross receipts £	Net receipts £	%
GNR	195,948	23,324	12
GWR	291,711	66,330	22.7
MR	691,659	122,495	17.7
LNWR	467,840	95,934	20.5

Labour costs having increased as a result of nationally applicable Acts of Parliament, the railway companies were able to make a strong case for an increase in charges that they could levy. Writing about this in the Great Central Staff Journal, a member of the office of the Superintendent of the Line stated:

'a) that railway companies are not in a position definitely to ascertain the cost of production of any specified service they render to traders
b) the rates charged by the railway companies are not, and cannot be, based on any properly ascertained details of actual costs
c) charges have developed upon the basis of what the market will bear (for customer and supplier).'

It is my belief that the above position as stated stayed – for reasons of organisational complexity, volume of different categories of traffic effectively cross subsidising the weak and lack of action by the successive government administrations – unchanged for half a century. Add to that the statutory controls over pricing and fluctuations in the economic position of the country and the challenge for future management teams was clear.

The basic business model of the GCR was simply to expand its profitable activities and, also by improved efficiency, increase its net earnings with which to pay its capital debt, make a return for all shareholders and establish reserves.

The increase in paid up capital has been identified together with its allocation across the different activities of the business. The increases in revenue and net receipts have been identified. At the particular time period under close review, the practice of the profitable railway companies was to distribute net profits with only a small amount retained as a reserve.

From the investment summaries, it is possible to identify how the management of the GCR acknowledged the relative importance of goods traffic over passenger. It is also possible to identify the importance placed upon having port facilities at Grimsby and Immingham.

The investments made were generally sound and long term (marshalling yards, Immingham, route capacity) though the amount directed towards passenger steamboats would have been very unsound unless the services had use of the company's docks and facilities.

Long term investments in railways in a competitive, regulated environment cannot be expected to repay the capital debt over a short period. The fact is that the LNER, the publicly owned British Railways and, in the case of elements of the total business (railways and at Immingham), also the privatised (post 1994) railways of Great Britain all benefitted.

With regard to performance indicators, the first is did it make any money? Yes it did.

Year	Net receipts		Paid up capital		% dividend		Operating ratio	
	UK £m	GCR* £m	UK £m	GCR £m	UK	GCR	UK	GCR
1900	40.06	1.14	1,176	42.06	3.41	2.71	62	70
1905	43.47	1.56	1,272	46.68	3.42	3.34	62	66
1906	44.45	1.64	1,286	48.04	3.45	3.41	62	66
1907	44.94	1.74	1,294	51.47	3.47	3.38	63	67
1908	48.49	1.73	1,311	52.24	3.32	3.31	64	67
1909	45.14	1.83	1,314	52.49	3.43	3.49	62	65
1910	47.36	1.83	1,319	52.60	3.59	3.48	62	65
1911	48.58	1.95	1,324	52.90	3.67	3.7	62	65
1912	47.33	1.98	1,335	53.50	3.55	3.7	63	66

NOTE:
* including contributions from shared companies

On that measure, Henderson with Fay, Davies, the principal engineers and staff had made huge strides to successfully develop the business.

It is useful to be able to turn to published sources of financial advice offered to potential investors in 1911 and 1913. In 1911, the Society of Railway Stockholders voiced in their *Universal Railway Manual* a view that 'the prospects for the Great Central … are very good … income is increasing faster than fixed charges … the 1891 preference is worth buying as a speculation … in the same way the 1894 preference … in 1915 … would give a handsome profit on the present price of 55.'

Two years later the *Financial Times* stated that '… one of the leading UK railway companies … the position of the company … promises well in the near future … traffic returns have shown continued healthy expansion' and further, highlighted 'the exceptional prospects of this undertaking.' With those expressions of sentiment, it is probable that the price of ordinary shares on the stock exchanges would have reacted favourably. Henderson and Fay must have been pleased that their considerable efforts over a decade and more looked likely to mature; the word then used was fructify.

CHAPTER 4

LNER TIMES

This chapter covers the period 1923-47 and therefore, periods of economic downturn, some recovery, years of war and needs for the railways to adapt to changing circumstances. For enterprises with a high proportion of fixed costs in physical and human assets, particularly the need to maintain their networks, the desire for investments would have to be reduced. Revenue as available would be allocated to meet day to day expenses and keep at least some stockholders content with a return on their investment.

The Liberal led coalition government of David Lloyd George (1916-22) was concerned to ensure that the lessons learned and benefits from unification of control of the railways during the First World War were not lost. During summer 1918 the government appointed a Select Committee on Transport. The Committee concluded that a return to a pre-1914 status would be wrong and submitted for consideration three alternative ways forward, leaving the government to choose. The alternatives were:

a) further amalgamation of companies as a step towards unification.
b) unification accompanied by private ownership and commercial management.
c) unification by means of nationalisation followed by:
   - establishment of a government department to manage the railways.
   - constitution of a Board of Management not directly represented in parliament.
   - leasing the system to one or more commercial companies.

The government decided as a first step to create a new Ministry (Ministry of Transport Act 1919) which, initially amalgamated the former Roads Board and the Railway Division of the Board of Trade. The first Minister was Sir Eric Campbell Geddes, formerly of the NER and latterly, during the war, in various roles culminating as First Lord of the Admiralty in 1917. At the Armistice, Geddes was placed in charge of the co-ordination of demobilisation; a role for which his ability to sort through multiple matters, identify those having an importance and then deciding the appropriate action to be taken was well suited. He set about reorganising the railways in accordance with government policy. That policy eventually favoured the first alternative put forward by the Select Committee and would include the companies of Scotland, rather than establish a separate company for north of the border with England.

In due course, the Railways Act 1921 was passed, setting up four amalgamated companies. The companies were identified as Western (became the Great Western Railway), Southern (Southern Railway), North Western, Midland and West Scottish (London Midland and Scottish Railway), North Eastern, Eastern and East Scottish (London and North Eastern Railway) and thereby amalgamated the assets, liabilities and networks of some 130 individual companies, including 27 subsidiaries.

Rather than adopt a French style territorial organisation, the railway map for the mainland UK had the LNER extending into the LMS network at Rugby, Stafford and Fort William, had a gap between the former Great North of Scotland Railway at Aberdeen and the North British at Dundee under control of the LMS, but its main lines included the (GNR) East Coast from King's Cross to York (and Leeds), Newcastle and Edinburgh (393 miles), on to Aberdeen (130 miles), the (GER) lines from Liverpool Street into East Anglia and the (GCR) line from Marylebone to Nottingham, Sheffield and Manchester (206 miles). In all, 6,307 route miles, some 500 less than the LMS.

The constituent companies of the LNER had, in aggregate, the most complex capital structures with various types of 'share' issued over some 65 years. (See chapter 3 for the capital structures of the MS&LR and GCR.) The following arrangement was used as the capital formation of the LNER:

Stock	Nominal value £
3% debenture ranking	66,352,793
4% debenture ranking	33,617,629
4% first guaranteed	29,838,251

Stock	Nominal value £
4% second guaranteed	27,329,739
4% first preference	48,145,988
4% second preference	65,683,531
5% preferred ordinary	41,873,116
Deferred ordinary	35,514,228
	348,355,275

The capital (amount upon which interest or dividends was payable) for the main constituent companies was:

	£
NER (incl H&B)	92,617,528
NB	66,459,893
GNR	61,533,235
GCR	55,098,217
GER	55,073,850
GNSR	8,117,060

For interest, the Humber Commercial Railway and Dock Co., Mansfield Railway and the Nottingham (Victoria) station joint committee were listed separately with subsidiaries, though with rights to 7 per cent loans payable to holders in the Humber company, 5 per cent to debenture holders in the Mansfield and 3 per cent to debenture holders in the station committee.

Net receipts followed a similar ranking, with the NER (including H&B) at £4,723,209 and the GCR at £2,363,304 (1913).

The Railways Act of 1921 created an Amalgamation Tribunal which included in its remit the establishment of an arrangement whereby shareholders in the 'old' companies were to exchange their shareholdings for new ones in the LNER. There was no cash alternative and shareholders in the largest (in terms of balance sheet strength, net receipts in the base year – 1913 – and capital fully paid up) company, the NER, fared best in the process. The GCR was ranked lowly (after the NER, GER, GNR and North British) and received an allocation of stock. For example, the shareholders in the NER received, for each £100 of NER stock, £100 of the 4 per cent second preference stock, plus £50 of the 5 per cent preferred ordinary and £40 of the deferred ordinary. As ever, the stock exchanges took a view on the prospects and 'wrote down' the stock to give purchase prices per nominal £100 of between £88 and £33.10s. Investment in railway companies was not attractive, given that gilt edged securities were offering a return of 5 per cent.

Formal approval of the Tribunal's arrangement was required at Wharncliffe and Extraordinary General Meetings which, for the GCR, were held on 17 November 1922. Just 69 proprietors attended the EGM; a paltry number given that the register of shareholders the previous year listed 45,273 (26,215 held ordinary shares), but the necessary approval was given. For the many holders of GCR debentures at 4 per cent to 5 per cent, guaranteed stock at 4 per cent to 6 per cent and (some) preference shares at 4 per cent to 5 per cent, the good times of steady railway returns were gone forever.

The LNER was immediately an over capitalised highly geared company that would struggle to generate funds to both satisfy the shareholders and also invest in its future. For the Chairman, Directors and management of the former GCR it must have seemed a very familiar set of circumstances.

The characteristics of the main constituent companies varied; the GNR had the main line to Sheffield (at Retford), Leeds, York, Newcastle and Berwick as far as Shaftholme junction (near Doncaster), where responsibility passed to the NER. The GCR had its main line to Leicester, Nottingham, Sheffield and Manchester as well as its cross country route West from Grimsby. The GER extended into Cambridgeshire, Suffolk and Norfolk with its strong seasonal agricultural base, whilst the GER had in London an increasingly intensive suburban network with which to contend on a daily peak basis whilst the demand from North London via the GNR increased with the urban spread of the 1920s/30s. Important though passenger traffic was, it never represented as much as one third of the LNER annual gross receipts, the lowest proportion of all four grouped companies. The LNER was heavily reliant upon the movement of goods in its various forms; coal, coke and patent fuel, other minerals and general merchandise. The years of economic depression in the 1920s/early 1930s hit the traditional industries and their workforces particularly harshly and the LNER felt the full force in terms of tonnages of goods requiring movement and passengers seeking travel for both work and pleasure. The NB had the East Coast main line North from Berwick to Dundee, the borders, across the lowlands of Scotland, the coalfields of Fife and North to Fort William, Mallaig and Fort Augustus. The smallest of the constituents, the GNSR, confined its activities to Aberdeenshire, Banffshire and Morayshire.

The first Chairman of the LNER was a Scottish landowner with industrial interests and someone who felt comfortable in the ways of operational railways, William Whitelaw. He had been Chairman of the Highland Railway and, latterly, the North British. His appointment owed something to the ages of his peer group; the GER's Lord Claud Hamilton was 79, the GNR's Sir Frederick Banbury 78 and Lord Knaresborough of the NER 76. Whitelaw, at 61, was in his pomp and had as his Deputy Lord Faringdon (then aged 72) with a particular remit regarding financial matters. The structure of the 26-strong Board reflected the relative strength of the constituent companies; the NER had nine Directors, followed by the GNR, GER, GCR and NB each having four and the GNSR just one. The Directors previously with the GCR were Walter Burgh Gair (69), a Managing Director also of Barings bank; Edward Beazley (66), a ship owner and shipping insurance broker; and the last Director of the GCR, elected in 1918, the Hon. Eric B. Butler Henderson (39), the seventh child of Alexander Henderson (Lord Faringdon).

The Board decided upon a form of decentralised management organisation, acknowledging the need to retain morale throughout the new railway and avoid any overly NER 'diktat'. There were to be three main areas; Southern (the GNR, GER and GCR), North Eastern (North of Shaftholme junction near Doncaster) and Southern Scottish (NB) also with a provisionally temporary Northern Scottish (GNSR). The two Scottish Areas were managed by a General Manager and the English areas by Divisional General Managers. The reporting line of the DGMs/GM was to a headquarters Chief General Manager, Sir Ralph Lewis Wedgwood, and that reporting line was also applied to the Chief Mechanical Engineer, Herbert Nigel Gresley, to the Chief Accountant, C.L. Edwards, to the Chief Legal Adviser and to the Secretary. John G. Robinson of the GCR had been a 'possible' for the role of Chief Mechanical Engineer but opted to retire and recommended Gresley for the position. The locations of the various offices were at Marylebone (Chairman, Secretary, Board Room), at King's Cross (CGM and 'all line' officers, including Gresley), Liverpool Street (Southern Area), York (North Eastern), Edinburgh/Aberdeen (Scottish). Although there were later refinements, the starting organisation remained throughout peacetime years. One of the refinements, in 1927, was to divide the Southern area into two separate operating sections; the Eastern (former GER) and Western (GNR and GCR) with statistical information from each being provided for the annual returns of the Board of Trade.

At an operational level the former GCR was represented in key positions in the Southern Area: William Clow, Superintendent of the Line (1923-27) formerly Superintendent of the Line GCR (1910-22); Arthur Bound, Signal Engineer, initially for the GCR section, but from 1924 the entire Southern Area until 1929 when he became Signal & Telegraph Engineer for the LMS; W.G.P. Maclure, Locomotive Running Superintendent, formerly in the same role for the GCR; M. Robinson, son of John G., became District Locomotive Superintendent at Neasden; C.G.C. Dandridge, Advertising Manager.

Maclure did make some changes to allocations of locomotives, for example moving some large boilered ex-GNR Atlantics to Neepsend (Sheffield) for working across the Pennines, a handful of B3 4-6-0s to Doncaster to work re-routed fish traffic and a few B4 Class to March to help out there, although height restrictions restricted them to the GN/GE joint line. All ten of the B4 Class found work from the West Riding of Yorkshire on London King's Cross trains as far as Doncaster.

In the senior posts, Sir Ronald Matthews became Chairman in 1933, Sir Charles Newton became Chief General Manager in 1939 and Lord Faringdon died in 1934 aged 83. Even if the Board had desired rapid cross (former) company changes, it would have proven difficult. For example, the GER, NER and NB had adopted the Westinghouse brake as standard on 4,552 locomotives whilst the GNR, GCR and GNSR used the vacuum braking system on 2,931. There were also differences regarding the loading gauge – the GCR had adopted a width of nine feet three inches and a height of 13 feet and five inches – which prevented certain ex-GCR locomotives being used throughout the LNER system. It may well have been Watkin who directed the decision to build the London extension for those dimensions and thus allow 'through' international running; what is clear is that the GCR was not built in accord with the Berne Convention gauge as that was not agreed until 1913/14. The nature of the constituent companies was very varied, and the three Greats had little in common once the reciprocal running rights agreements became a thing of the past.

During the early years of the LNER very little changed and an observer at the lineside along the GCR lines would not have noticed much apart from the lettering on the tenders/tanks. In the background, in April 1919 ASLEF had secured full standardisation of enginemen's wages and conditions of service, embracing payment of a guaranteed week, paid annual leave and rest intervals. The other railway workers then demanded the same treatment via the NUR, achieved only after a nine-day general strike supported by ASLEF.

Before reviewing the financial performance of the LNER, it is appropriate to summarise the difficult times faced by the politicians wrestling with a range of economic challenges at home and influenced by turmoil in Europe and beyond. The collapse of the Liberal Party was extraordinary. In 1906, they won one of the largest landslide victories in history; 397 seats with Labour having 29. By 1929, Labour had won a parliamentary majority with the Liberals being in a poor third place. The Liberal stance around the expansion of democracy, industrialisation, free trade, home rule for Ireland and the creation of a limited welfare state had been successful only to the extent of widening the gap in the electorate (male and from 1928 female) between the wealthy and the rapidly more organised working-class seeking improvements to appalling social conditions. The passing of the Fourth Reform Act in 1918 tripled the size of the electorate, with Labour being the principal beneficiary. By January 1924, Ramsay MacDonald was able to form a minority administration, though it lasted less than one year, before the Conservative government led by Stanley Baldwin administered as best it felt able (including an ill-advised decision to peg sterling to the strong American dollar, weakening the trading position of Britain until 1931), before MacDonald won a General Election in 1929. After a full term, Baldwin returned for a third term (1935-37) and had the benefit of an improvement in economic conditions established around a policy of cheap money and the adoption of the economic theories of John Maynard Keynes. The final three governments during LNER times were those led by Neville Chamberlain (1937-40), Winston Churchill (1940-45) and Clement Attlee (1945-51).

An indication of the years of depression and the effect in the 1930s of a more stable economic policy can be gained from the statistics for inflation/deflation and the Bank rate for borrowings.

Year	Inflation/deflation %	Bank rate %	
1920	15.4	6/7	
1921	-8.6	7/5	
1922	-14.0	5/3	
1923	-6.0	3/4	
1924	-0.7	4	
1925	0.3	4/5	Note 1
1926	-0.8	5	Note 2
1927	-2.4	5/4½	
1928	-0.3	4½	
1929	-0.9	4½/6½	
1930	-2.8	5/3	
1931	-4.3	3/2½/6	Note 3
1932	-2.6	6/2½/2	
1933	-2.1	2	Note 4
1934	0	2	
1935	0.7	2	
1936	0.7	2	Note 5
1937	3.4	2	
1938	1.6	2	

NOTES:
1. adoption of Gold Standard linkage to American dollar
2. General Strike to highlight the wage reductions faced by coal miners
3. abandonment of linkage of sterling to Gold standard rate
4. unemployment at three million
5. constitutional crisis, abdication of King Edward VIII

The approach of the legislators to the financial management of the railways after the Grouping was that each would receive a 'standard revenue'. The basis of the standard revenue was to be the aggregate revenues for the constituent companies in 1913, the first year of the comprehensive annual returns to the Board of Trade, plus an allowance for capital expenditure. Those levels of standard revenue were to be produced by each grouped company and, if necessary, by manipulating charges levied. Failure in the early years to achieve the standard revenue would allow – from 1928 – relevant companies to apply to the Railway Rates Tribunal for authority to increase charges to an extent necessary to bring net revenues up to the standard.

Because of changing economic conditions and the growth of competition from alternative modes of commercial transport and delivery this arrangement – which may well have worked in Victorian times – was unrealistic in the circumstances that endured in the 1920s/30s and affected the LNER (with its dependence upon traditional industries requiring minerals) particularly harshly.

The standard revenue set for 1928 for the LNER was £14.8m (plus £429k capital allowance) and, if achieved, would have allowed payment of all the shareholders, including those with deferred ordinary stock just over 4 per cent. The actual figure for 1928 was £11.28m. Throughout its life, the LNER never achieved its standard revenue and in 1932, its worst year, it achieved less than half the target figure. However, it always made an operating profit.

Year	Net revenue earned
	£m
1923	13.2
1924	10.9
1925	9.2
1926	3.8
1927	11.2
1928	11.3
1929	13.1
1930	11.2
1931	9.4
1932	7.2
1933	7.7
1934	8.3
1935	8.4
1936	9.1
1937	10.1
1938	6.7
1939	9.3
1940	10.4
1941	10.6
1942	10.7
1943	10.7
1944	10.8
1945	11.0
1946	11.0
1947	11.4

During the 1918-38 period, certain sectors of the economy were affected adversely by unfavourable trends in the international economy. Britain's place of importance as an economic power declined rapidly after the war, partly because of the growing economic strength of other countries (the USA and Japan had been unaffected by the war) and also because of the new economic system 'model' which replaced free trade of goods and capital with commercial protective barriers. The insecurity provoked unhelpful governmental policies which caused the system to collapse and resulted in the international crisis of 1929-33. More and more barriers were placed and had the effect of previously interwoven trading agreements being negated. For Britain – so dependent upon trading – such events were catastrophic. Whilst trading across international borders was proving to be progressively more challenging, there were also problems in the home economy.

By 1911-13, two thirds of Britain's exports were in a narrow range of industries; principally coal, iron and steel, machinery and vehicles, shipping and textiles. In the inter-war years many of Britain's traditional markets were in countries which were by then able to develop increasing levels of self-sufficiency. Of the products, coal was under threat from oil and cotton from man-made fabrics such as rayon. Exports fell and, as demand reduced, unemployment in the producing areas of the UK increased. The inevitable consequence on the traditional transport system – railways and shipping – can be seen from the statistics for railway traffic.

Year	Coal (tons m)	Other minerals (tons m)	Merchandise (tons m)
1913	225.6	71.1	67.8
1924	209.2	65.4	60.9
1933	165.5	43.1	42.5

For the LNER, the figures were brutal.

Year	Millions tons of freight carried
1923	153.5
1933	114.7
1934	124.9
1935	124.3

For the LNER, freight in its various forms accounted for up to two thirds of its total revenue. That percentage – in the range 60-67 – represented the highest of the four grouped companies. In particular, the railway carried huge tonnages of coal, coke, other minerals, fish, meat, seasonal produce and general merchandise. Retaining and, ideally, growing that business was crucial to the fortunes of the LNER and its shareholders.

For the Board of the LNER, the business objectives were to move goods and passengers at rates regulated by statute and make a return for their investors whilst also investing in the development of the railway. Some understanding and financial relief was forthcoming though not until after 1928. The railway could move goods and passengers only to the extent that it was forthcoming either with or without competition (from other railway companies, commercial road vehicle operators and shipping) and was obliged to reduce its asset base (locomotives and shipping facilities), reduce its workforce, cut wages and conditions of service, reduce dividends and for investment increasingly rely upon government support.

Total number of locomotives (net)	
1925	7,456
1930	7,316
1935	6,787
1938	6,518

Workforce	
1937	207,530
1923	275,850

Wages were cut in all grouped companies by 2½ per cent from July 1928 to May 1930 and again (plus reductions in conditions of service) from 1931 until 1934.

Working in favour of passenger traffic was the increase in the population and particularly in and around the main cities.

Population (UK)	
1918	38,287,000
1925	45,040,000
1930	45,870,000
1935	46,870,000
1940	48,220,000

London	
1901	6,339,500
1921	7,480,200
1931	8,100,000 (est)
1939	8,600,000 (est)

NOTE:
The 1931 census was destroyed by fire and comparisons for populations of major cities are available only for 1901, 1921 and 1951.

	1901	1921
Leicester	211,600	234,100
Nottingham	239,700	262,600
Sheffield	409,100	490,600
Hull	240,300	287,000
Manchester	543,900	730,000

Working against the railway companies was the growth of commercial vehicles, privately owned cars and bus services.

By 1922, there were some 183 companies specialising in production of cars or components for them; by 1929 the effects of the economic strife had reduced that total to 58 and 60 per cent of UK production of new cars was by Morris and by Austin. However, by 1932, the UK was the largest producer in Europe (a position it held until 1955) and in 1937 produced some 380,000 new vehicles (15 per cent exported).

The grouped railway companies were affected to varying degrees by changes in economic conditions; the Southern was largely dependent upon passenger traffic, the Great Western had a well-balanced mix of passenger and goods, whilst the London North Eastern and London Midland & Scottish were hostage to the fortunes of heavy industry.

The companies sought help via the governments of the day with reaction times far too slow as the parliamentary process ground its way through annual tribunal hearings. The tribunals allowed the companies to table their grievances and seek relief from long-standing debts limiting their commercial freedom. Traditionally, parliament had tended to protect the rights of the customers of the railway companies for goods traffic. Some relief was afforded in 1929 to help the revenue account and in 1929/33 and 1935 to help with capital for investment.

The financial results of the LNER were the worst of the four grouped companies; their dividends to shareholders record similar. All the railways suffered the effects of increasing competition, the economic downturns and aftermath of the general strike, but none experienced the catastrophic drop in revenues as did the LNER between 1929 and 1932. The reasons were particularly the reliance upon areas of heavy and traditional industries (coal, steel, textiles) for traffic and the capital structure obliging the Board to make interest payments to holders of debentures and guaranteed stock, leaving (in 1932) nothing for holders of Ordinary stock and less than a full amount for Preference stock holders.

The average rate of dividend paid on issued capital was:

1923	4.43%	1931	2.50%
1924	4.41%	1932	1.90%
1925	4.26%	1933	2.04%
1926	2.99%	1934	2.22%
1927	3.03%	1935	2.22%
1928	3.03%	1936	2.41%
1929	3.34%	1937	2.63%
1930	3.02%	1938	1.76%

There were occasions up to 1932 when reserves were drawn upon to maintain a dividend to holders of Preferred Ordinary stock, a situation which infuriated the trades unions suffering a cut in wages/conditions. Equally unhappy were many stockholders who felt cheated by the 'standard revenue' model and the fact that the level was never achieved.

Revenue from the movement of coal was of critical importance to the balance sheets of the LNER and the LMS. In the UK there were eight main areas of coalmining: Northumberland, Durham, Yorkshire, Lancashire, Cheshire & North Wales, Derbyshire, Nottinghamshire & Leicestershire, Stafford 'Salop' Worcester & Warwickshire, Monmouthshire & South Wales and Scotland. Those coalfields as well as other English districts (for example Kent) produced the following tonnages:

On one of the two track sections of the GN main line, South from Peterborough towards London, a P1 2-8-2 has a slow-moving coal train approaching Hadley Wood. The problem for the operating authorities was fitting into the daily workings such trains amongst a series of faster moving services (Rail on-line).

Year	Total	Export	Taken to London by:	
	m tons	m tons	rail m tons	shipping m tons
1923	276	79.4	9.9	7.2
1924	267	61.7	10.1	8.4
1925	244	50.8	9.4	8.2
1926	126	20.6	6.2	4.2
1927	251	51.1	9.2	9.2*
1928	237	50.0	7.9	10.1
1929	258	60.3	8.4	11.2
1930	244	54.9	8.1	11.0
1931	219	42.7	8.0	10.7
1932	209	38.9	3.0	15.5
1933	207	39.0	3.0	14.8
1934	221	39.7	6.3	12.9
1935	222	38.7	6.4	13.3
1936	228	34.6	6.8	14.7
1937	240	40.4	7.1	15.2
1938	227	35.9	7.0	14.6

NOTE:
* Central Electricity Board formed (new power stations)

Of the eight main areas of production, four were more dependant than the others on the export market:

Area	1913		1919		1929	
	m tons	%*	m tons	%	m tons	%
Monmouthshire & South Wales	56.8	19.8	54.3	19.7	48.1	18.7
Scotland	42.5	14.8	38.5	13.9	34.2	13.3
Durham	41.5	14.4	34.9	12.6	39.0	15.1
Northumberland	14.8	5.1	14.3	5.2	14.5	5.6

NOTE:
* of total annual production for the UK

In addition, a proportion of the coal from Yorkshire collieries was exported from Humber ports, but the coalfield was less dependent upon export markets than the four above.

The LNER served six of the eight areas, competing with the LMS in four and to a small extent with private enterprises in two others. For the export markets, the tonnage moved to GCR/NER/NB ports in 1913 was 34 million and to those same ports in 1928 25.5 million. The decline in the total export markets was erratic; a slump in 1920/21 was followed by an upturn in 1923/24 to pre-1914 levels, then fell to a low plateau in 1925-28, during which the home market was badly affected by strikes/lockouts, unemployment and a downturn in demand in the textile and steel industries. The 1930s brought a further downturn for exports (1932/33 to 57 million tons from 82 million tons in 1929) and the export market remained stagnant until further falls were recorded in 1936 and 1938. The loss to the LNER from the reduction in movements of coal to the ports and for use of the facilities at those ports was huge. The Board of Trade returns (1927-37) include average journey receipts per ton of coal moved as being around three shillings and for 1923-29 the average receipt per ton mile at just over one penny; on that basis the average haul of coal was some 36 miles which seems reasonable when the proximities of coal fields to the ports is considered against the longer home market hauls along the London extension and to London via Lincoln/ Peterborough/ March.

For the home market the principal categories of consumption of coal were:

	1913		1929		1933		1938	
	m tons	%	m tons	%	m tons	%	m tons	%
Gas works	16.7	9	16.75	10	16.2	11	18.2	10
Electricity generation	4.9	3	9.8	6	10.3	7	14.9	10
Railways (locos)	13.2	7	13.4	8	11.7	8	12.5	7
Blast furnaces	21.2	11	14.5	8	7.4	5	11.6	7
Other iron and steel	10.2	6	8.9	5	5.9	4	7.2	4
Collieries (fuel)	18.0	10	13.7	8	11.6	8	11.9	8
Domestic	40.0	22	40.0	23	84.1*	57	96.9*	54
General manufacturing	57.7	32	55.0	32				

NOTE:
* includes General manufacturing

Of interest is the relative increase over time of fuel to generate electricity, the dips in demand for steel making and the steady proportion accounted for by domestic and general manufacturing. Domestic and general manufacturing followed the economic cycle of the 1930s. The position of the LNER as prime mover of coal was – as for the export markets – seriously affected. The LNER served the inland fields of Fife (which had benefitted from reorganisation, mechanisation and exploiting richer seams), Northumberland and Durham (for which the inland market was shattered by the collapse of heavy industries), Lancashire and Cheshire (with the LMS, the old and geologically troubled fields suffered by being dependant to a large extent upon the textile industry and progressively under competitive threat of coal from South Yorkshire). Between 1913 and 1929, the output of the Lancashire and Cheshire fields fell from over 24 million tons to roundly 15.7 million tons and its labour force declined by some 30 per cent.

However, it was not all bad news. The better news emanated from South Yorkshire and the East Midlands. In those areas, the successful development of fertile seams (Barnsley/Silkstone) which straddled North Derbyshire, Nottinghamshire and South Yorkshire had started before 1914. With the benefit of private capital investment, though, easily worked seams could be reached 2-3,000 feet underground, the coal produced being ideal for households, locomotives and coking uses. The most significant developments were under Sherwood Forest in the Dukeries (LDECR/GCR/South Yorkshire Joint Rly) of Nottinghamshire. There, between 1919 and 1925 several major colliery and iron/steel companies from Derbyshire and Yorkshire began the sinking of seven huge pits: Barber Walker & Co. Ltd., Harworth; Butterley Co. Ltd., Ollerton; Bolsover Colliery Co. Ltd., Thoresby and Clipstone; Stanton Iron Works Co. Ltd., Bilsthorpe; Staveley Coal and Iron Co. Ltd., Blidworth; Staveley with Sheepbridge Coal and Iron Co. Ltd., Firbeck Main.

Each new colliery cost £1-1.5 million (raised by shares) and each was designed and laid out to produce around one million tons annually. Between 1913 and 1929, South Yorkshire and Nottinghamshire coalfields increased their share of total British coal production from 14 per cent to almost 19 per cent and of the labour force, from 12 per cent to over 18 per cent. Together with the production from the Leen Valley extension and from other collieries, the former GCR lines were very well placed to contribute (with those of the GNR and shared within the former South Yorkshire Joint) to the revenue of the LNER. Although the days of intensive price competition between the GCR, GNR and NER had been negated by the Grouping, colliery owners' rights to retain prices in contracts remained as did competition, though not between the LNER and the LMS. Competition for the tonnage out of the new pits did not extend to each railway company building its own line to Harworth (1924/29), Firbeck (1926), Ollerton (1931) and Clipstone (1928), but did do so for Bilsthorpe (LNER 1928, LMS 1940), Blidworth (LMS 1925, LNER 1934), whilst Thoresby remained served by the LNER only (1926). A proposal for a Mid-Notts Joint Railway (mid 1920s) did not develop.

The negotiating position of the owners of the collieries was favourable to them; alternative routes to their end customers were a complexity for the competing railway companies, the fleets of wagons were largely their own and, being unbraked, could be hauled by any locomotive of suitable power, and statutory regulations on railway rates limited the 'hands' of the railway companies.

At times of lower demand for coal and as the larger pits produced a higher proportion of the total conveyed by rail there was a benefit to the railways in terms of the necessary shunting (sorting of wagons to enable them to be correctly returned). Giving evidence to the Royal Commission on the coal industry in 1925, Sir Ralph Wedgwood of the LNER said that the total freight shunting hours in 1924 had been some 23 million. Of that total, ten million hours were chargeable to owners or private wagons, nine tenths of which were engaged in the coal trade. If all wagons were railway owned, there would be considerable savings in sorting and making up trains, exchange operations at junctions and sorting/classification at distributing yards. He estimated the saving at 1.2 million shunting engine hours, in addition to better use of rolling stock and a reduction in empty wagon haulage, to produce annual savings of £0.6-1 million. The colliery owners did not favour the transfer of ownership, claiming that 'common pool' ownership could starve certain pits at times, but also because their own wagons could be used for stockpiles along the railway-owned sidings. No transfer of ownership took place, but the Commission recommended a review of the equipment for 20 ton wagons at ports, railway terminals and collieries and the standardisation of the types of wagons to enable more pooling of them.

There were also other developments within the coal industry that hardened feelings and positions taken about future ownership. The Coal Mines Act 1930 sought to facilitate the maintenance of wage rates at a time when hours/shifts worked were cut back but could do so only by the introduction of schemes for the control of output and sales. Whilst successful, it created a clear route to the formation of cartels and price 'maintenance'. It was a political/ industry trade-off between levels of prices, profits and wages with levels of output and employment.

It is difficult to find any basis for stating that in commercial terms and financial performance the railway companies benefitted, except by the availability of train load traffic, at least ex-colliery. Ownership of mines became more concentrated. Using one of the same companies as previously mentioned, Staveley Coal & Iron Co. Ltd. operated five collieries and, via share holdings, exercised control over seven other colliery firms (some of which were grouped for selling purposes within the Doncaster Collieries Association) and its leading entrepreneur, Charles Markham, had involvements with collieries producing some ten million tons annually. In 1925, a survey of 572 firms producing 200 million tons of coal found that over half of the 2,365 directors involved were also on the boards of other colliery companies.

One measure of the relative success of some of the firms listed previously can be gained from their record of dividend payments through this period of wider general strife, unemployment and social deprivation.

Year	Bolsover Colliery Co. %	Butterley Co. %	Staveley Coal & Steam %	Sheepbridge Coal & Iron %
1920	20	10	11¼	10
1921	13	8½	10	n/a
1922	3½	11¼	7½	6
1923	16	15	7½*	7½
1924	14	12½	7½*	7½
1925	8	6⅔*	7½	5
1926	15	6⅔*	5	2½
1927	6½	5	7½	7½
1928	1½	2½	5	2½
1929	3¾	5	5	2½
1930	2½	5	6	5
1931	7	5½	6	n/a
1932	7½	5	5	5
1933	7	5	5	5

Year	Bolsover Colliery Co. %	Butterley Co. %	Staveley Coal & Steam %	Sheepbridge Coal & Iron %
1934	8	5	6½	5
1935	9	6½	8	6½
1936	10*	8	9	10
1937	10*	8	10*	10
1938	10*	6½	11	12½

NOTES:
* = including bonus payments.

In common with the wider economy, the coal industry experienced a marked recovery from 1934, largely based upon improvements in home markets where demand increased rapidly.

From the Board of Trade returns for 1929 and beyond, it is possible to identify the net ton miles of coal, coke and patent oils taken via the former GNR and GCR routes as against the GER routes (the reason being the formation of the two operating sections of the Southern Area of the LNER) and also conveyed in the (former NER) Northern Area.

Year	via GER routes net ton miles, millions	via GNR/GCR routes, net ton miles, millions	via NER routes net ton miles, millions
1929	409	1,676	911
1930	402	1,620	806
1931	402	1,555	684
1932	373	1,448	615
1933	353	1,388	626
1934	374	1,475	696
1935	369	1,466	683
1936	385	1,546	721
1937	399	1,607	797
1938	386	1,549	672

For this slow-moving traffic conveyed in unbraked train loads, the main GNR route to London (New England, Peterborough, to Ferme Park) was – due to lengthy two track sections and both passenger and braked goods trains competing for track access – unsuitable. To overcome that problem, and also the growth in bricks traffic from Fletton, near Peterborough, coal southbound on GNR routes could be routed via Colwick, Nottingham area up the former GN/LNW line to Market Harborough, Welham junction or, if from further north, via Doncaster/Lincoln and up the former GN/GE line towards March and Whitemoor yard. The conclusion from this is that the former GCR routes (including the LDECR) must have conveyed the highest tonnage of coal, coke and patent fuels and, therefore, made – from this classification of traffic – the highest contribution to gross receipts.

Taking the other classifications of traffic – merchandise (excluding classifications 1-6) and livestock, and other minerals (classification 1-6) – the following applied (columns (a) are for merchandise and (b) for other minerals):

Year	via GER routes net ton miles, millions		via GNR/GCR routes, net ton miles, millions		via NER routes net ton miles, millions	
	(a)	(b)	(a)	(b)	(a)	(b)
1929	297	161	654	557	600	392
1930	285	178	617	545	543	336
1931	269	163	566	468	496	268

Year	via GER routes net ton miles, millions		via GNR/GCR routes, net ton miles, millions		via NER routes net ton miles, millions	
1932	223	132	495	390	438	129
1933	220	160	507	469	449	217
1934	226	165	531	575	495	263
1935	216	171	528	569	518	256
1936	224	175	574	600	568	300
1937	225	154	587	645	606	331
1938	209	121	542	578	542	269

As for coal, coke and patent fuels, the other minerals classifications (iron ore, pig iron, iron and steel, limestone, etc), columns (b), indicate the effect on heavy industries which particularly affected the former NER and the dependence of the LNER upon the former GNR/GCR routes. Again, the route capacity restrictions affecting the GNR South of Peterborough apply.

In terms of revenue from these traffics, for the LNER the average receipts per net ton mile were (for the key year of 1928 in pence):

i) coal, coke and patent fuels in LNER wagons 1.53
ii) coal, coke and patent fuels in privately owned wagons 1.06
iii) iron ore, railway wagons, 6 tons + 1.20
iv) iron ore, private wagons, 6 tons + 0.78
v) limestone in bulk, railway 1.12
vi) limestone in bulk, private wagons 1.28
vii) vegetables, station to station rate, 4 tons + 1.88
viii) textiles and clothing, station to station rate 5.19

In comparison, the LMS achieved slightly higher rates for i), ii), v), viii) with the first two being particularly significant in the competitive environment of the North Midlands coalfield.

By 1928 – five years after the Grouping and in the midst of economic, industrial and social strife – most people connected with the railway industry were concerned as to the situation. The owners of the LNER (its shareholders) were unhappy with the level of dividends, the trades unions were unhappy with the dividends that had been awarded whilst their members suffered from cut backs in wages and conditions of service, the traders as ever argued against any increase in rates and the management were doubtless frustrated by traffic losses over which they had no control. In each year since the Grouping, the Railway Rates Tribunal had heard evidence and dealt with outstanding claims, but with national rates for charging generally took the line that the Railway Act 1921 had stated 1928 as the key year for decisions. An attempt in 1928 to introduce a new structure of freight rates and restrict the growth of exceptional rates proved to be ineffective and this, together with obligations to accept any and all traffic offered, provide a reasonable level of service, avoid undue preference in the treatment of customers, left the railways commercially vulnerable. That evident vulnerability was able to be exploited by encroachment into the merchandise and perishable goods traffic by road competition less constrained and more flexible in their business arrangements. Road competition had arrived and with it a new challenge for the government. The progressive erosion of the railways' performance can be measured in the increase in the operating ratio (63 in 1913, 81 in 1934-38), the reduction in the average rate of return on capital raised (fell to 3.16 per cent) and the returns made by shareholders.

Tellingly, in 1927, 45 per cent of goods train receipts came from merchandise traffic which accounted for only 29 per cent of total train miles operated (coal, coke and patent fuel 38 per cent/52 per cent) and in 1932 for merchandise traffic 42 per cent/28 per cent and for coal, coke and patent fuel 43 per cent/56 per cent. For the ongoing business, it was essential that the LNER retained and developed its merchandise business and used the staple, long term movement of coal to cover as much of the fixed cost base of the business as was commercially possible. Both traffics were under threat; the first from road hauliers, the second from entrenched, legacy positions.

The Grouping brought together considerable steamboat services, harbours, docks and wharves (the world's then largest railway dock owner in terms of length of quays at 38 miles) and hotels. From ports at Leith, Newcastle, Middlesbrough, Grimsby and Harwich it offered sailings for passengers to the near Continent and Scandinavia, with some vessels also offering cargo facilities. It also offered train ferry services from Harwich and coastal shipping along and north of the Clyde, and across the Firth of Forth/Humber. The company also owned the small port of Silloth in Cumbria and was well represented in the major ports of Liverpool, Birkenhead, Manchester and Glasgow. The fleet totalled up to 59 vessels of varying types and gross tonnages. Within the portfolio of 20 company hotels were the Great Eastern and Great Northern in London, the North British in Edinburgh, the Royal Station at York and Newcastle and Royal Victoria Station at Sheffield, twelve of these hotels still continuing in operation.

In terms of financial performance, the businesses fared well (in terms of return upon net receipts; capital employed being difficult to identify) in the 1920s, but all suffered in the early 1930s, just as did the main railway business.

Year	Steamboats		Docks harbours and wharves		Hotels	
	£k	%	£k	%	£k	%
1923	80	8.4÷	660	25.7	300	14.0
1924	104	10.7	584	17.0	313	14.4
1925	133	13.7	153	7.1	309	14.3
1926	54	5.9	186	10.0	292	14.1
1927	203	20.0	146	6.4	309	14.7
1928	164	16.2	(74)	ø	191	9.2
1929	131	13.1	198	6.1	210	10.0
1930	98	9.9	207	6.8	175	8.8
1931	18	20	90	3.3	101	0.5
1932	(76)		52	2.1	50	0.2
1933	(95)		95	3.9	86	0.3
1934	(98)		151	5.7	125	7.1
1935	(44)	*	115	4.4	125	6.8
1936	21	2.6	183	6.7	164	8.4
1937	49	5.6	247	8.8+	165	8.0
1938	(18)		83	3.4	133	6.5

NOTES:
÷ Includes The Wilson's & North Eastern Railway Shipping Co. Ltd., Hull and Hull & Netherlands Steamship Co. Ltd., Hull, managed by LNER 1923-35.
* Associated Humber Lines formed to manage the fleet based there.
+ Tyne Dock sold to Tyne Improvement Commission.
ø Costs that year assumed to reflect relocation of Zeeland Shipping Co. and Vliessingen services from Folkestone to Harwich Parkeston Quay.

When allowed by statute, the LNER invested in the bus industry (as opposed to bus services) and on net receipts of around £200,000 in each of 1936, 1937 and 1938 made returns of 15.9 per cent, 19.3 per cent and 19.1 per cent respectively.

The Board of Trade returns continued to record statistics for the traffic carried by the GW/GC joint lines (Banbury branch from Woodford Halse, and via High Wycombe) and by the MetR/GC route (via Aylesbury and Amersham). Because the tonnages followed patterns similar to those recorded in this section, I have included only six of the years.

Year	GW/GC			
	Revenue receipts	Tonnages of traffics		
	£'000k	(a)	(b)	(c)
		'000 tons		
1923	268	984	288	614
1926	241	706	223	590
1928	310	166	242	664
1930	593	980	256	685
1935	551	857	237	691
1938	589	900	260	775
	Met R/GC			
1923	113	297	299	141
1926	89	160	271	111
1928	97	339	194	114
1930	371	389	215	123
1935	341	324	228	117
1938	350	320	50	126

NOTES:
a) coal, coke and patent fuels
b) other minerals (classification revision 1928)
c) general merchandise (classification revision 1928)

It is also possible to identify the revenue expenditure for these joint lines; the costs being predominantly for upkeep of the track and for total traffic expenses which I assume includes staff, stations, signal boxes, locomotive and depot costs. Revenue expenditure was (1938):

	GW/GC	Met R/GC
	£	£
Track	51,234	66,835
Traffic	55,662	62,739

When viewed alongside the revenue receipts as shown on the previous sheet, the net benefit to the operating companies from this traffic was relatively high. However, the capital debt, (first charge) provisions from GCR days still applied and required the LNER to pay the GWR £185,700 and the London Transport Passenger Board (as successor body to the Met) £114,338.

In its efforts to reduce costs, the LNER sought to increase the total train miles operated whilst reducing operating expenditure; in both areas it was successful, the increase/decrease in numbers being plus 11 per cent and minus 16 per cent respectively (1923-37). However, whilst various indicators could be explained by the erratic economic slumps in demand for coal to be moved (down from 98.5 million tons in 1923 to 86.6 million tons in 1937) the drop in average consignment load of general merchandise was due to road hauliers 'picking off' the lorry load consignments and leaving uneconomic smalls to the railways. The railway companies felt and argued strongly about what they considered to be unfair competition from the fast-growing road transport industry.

The effect upon the railways of the growth of road transport is considered in three groupings: bus services; road haulage; and privately owned cars.

The LNER inherited road vehicles from its constituent company; acquiring 58 motor buses, 28 horse buses and 200 or so goods and parcels cartage vehicles. In South Lancashire, the GCR had engaged (and owned shares in) Thompson McKay & Co. to manage the collection and delivery of goods and parcels; the railway also leased from that company its horses and road vehicles. As successors to the GCR, in 1928 the LNER purchased holdings in several, small scale bus companies through Thomas McKay, all monies being passed over by that company and shares held by it. The LNER then purchased shares in United Automobile Services Ltd. which was the leading operator in the north east. Collaboration between the LNER and LMS for bus services made both common and economic sense. That approach was also applied for the building of certain new sections of railways from a main route towards new sources of coal, whilst leaving the final connections to each colliery as a matter for commercial agreement between the owners of each colliery and whichever railway company was favoured with the contract for movement. The bus service collaboration agreement with the LMS was progressively extended to include: W. Alexander & Sons Ltd.; Eastern Counties Omnibus Co. Ltd.; Eastern National Omnibus Co. Ltd.; East Midland Motor Services Ltd.; Hebble Motor Services Ltd.; Lincolnshire Road Car Co. Ltd.; North Western Road Car Co. Ltd.; Scottish Motor Traction Co. Ltd.; Trent Motor Traction Co. Ltd.; West Yorkshire Road Car Co. Ltd.; Yorkshire Traction Co. Ltd.; Yorkshire Woollen District Transport Co. Ltd.

In addition to United, as previously mentioned, the LNER had non-controlling interests in East Yorkshire Motor Services Ltd. and Northern General Transport Co. Ltd.

The initiation of long-distance coach services designed to compete with passenger train travel was a predictable extension of the business aspirations of bus companies. It caused all four of the grouped railway companies – and the Metropolitan Railway – to contemplate the acquisition of powers beyond those granted by the Railways Act 1921. In November 1927, each had deposited with parliament a Bill seeking powers. During difficult Committee stages, the railway companies gave assurances about not exploiting their positions of ability to take controlling financial interests and, therefore, monopoly powers. The Bills were enacted in August 1928. Thereafter, the railway companies were able to quote for the provision of services and the LNER was successful for nineteen services, ten of which replaced uneconomic train services. To avoid saturation of the building capacity, the railway companies entered agreements with the three principal financing combines/holding companies – British Electric Traction Co. Ltd., Thomas Tilling Ltd. and Scottish Motor Traction Co. Ltd. – as to which railway would invest in which bus company and the extent of the investment.

The Road Traffic Act 1930 put in place for passenger-carrying vehicles a system of licensing, speed limits, age of drivers limitations, testing, insurance and taxation on fuel used (although the Local Government Act of 1929 had given railways and farmers rating relief on that taxation).

Above and opposite: By the late 1920s, forward control, driver by engine layouts for buses were commonplace and offered seating for between 30 and 40 passengers. During the Second World War, many were converted for use as ambulances.

The challenge of the rapid development of the road haulage industry prompted the Railway Companies Association (representing the interests of shareholders) to convene a working group of the four Chairmen, to persuade the government of the need for more equitable regulation and taxation arrangements. At the same time, they would wish to benefit from the statutory restrictions on charging for freight unchanged, despite the railways losing their perceived monopolistic powers over traders.

The Road & Rail Traffic Act 1933 went some way to meeting the legitimate concerns of the railway companies and completely changed the outlook for the road transport of goods. It made the operation of goods vehicles, whether for hire or reward or for ancillary purposes, illegal except under one of three classes of licence: A, public carriers, valid two years; B, limited carriers, valid one year, own or others goods; C, not allowed to carry goods for hire or reward (i.e. own goods only), valid three years.

The Act also sought to limit total hours worked by drivers. Objections to applications could be lodged by persons already providing facilities, whether by road or any other kind of transport. The railways took full advantage of their powers of objection and for the first year or two almost every application for a new licence or for additional vehicles or relaxation of conditions attached to a 'B' licence was opposed, with a high degree of success. The Act also gave the railways a significant concession; it allowed them to quote rates in the form of 'agreed charges', by which the whole of a trader's traffic could be carried by a railway company at a negotiated rate and irrespective of distance. However, the railways struggled with those traders who opted to build up their own fleets to carry their own goods ('C' licence), the control and management becoming an extension of their main business of production/manufacture. The other new area of competition with which the railways struggled to compete was for (in railway terms) wagon load traffic for short and medium distance traffic. It was a case of finding the railway rate applicable and undercutting it. The road hauliers had few fixed costs beyond the licence itself and for the vehicles/drivers/ maintenance facility and were, therefore, very well placed to nibble away at the railways' highest earning traffic. The railways' attempts to compete included a move into containerisation (see later).

The number of licence holders were:

Year	A	B	C
1936	27,722	27,017	26,956
1937	34,100	34,061	34,120
1938	161,221	186,481	178,298

The number of vehicles authorised and in possession:

Year	A	B	C
1936	90,493	91,081	93,216
1937	52,809	53,775	54,906
1938	316,714	362,380	365,025

The demand for private ownership of cars grew relentlessly. In 1913, Henry Ford's new factory in Manchester was helping him become the leading UK-based producer, with 7,310 vehicles. Other manufacturers contributing to a total production of some 16,000 were Wolseley, Humber, Rover, Sunbeam and Riley. Production of private cars came to a virtual standstill throughout the First

Above and opposite: By 1930 only half a dozen manufacturers built steam wagons, including Fodens Ltd. (examples at 43) and Sentinel Waggon Works Ltd. (44/45). All types shown were built between 1931-35 but production rates declined with increasing competition from petrol and diesel lorries with more comfortable cabs, cleaner fuel technology and relative ease of start-ups.

44

45

Left, below and opposite: The development of road motor vehicles for commercial and private use was relentless; colliery to consumer (46), producer to consumer (47), wholesale to retail (48) and pure freedom (49), all to some extent taking traffic from the railways' own transport organisations.

GENERAL CARRIERS
J. Brevitt
WILLENHALL STAFFS
GOODS AND PARCEL SERVICES.
CARRIERS OF REPUTE SINCE 1836
Phone
631211

48

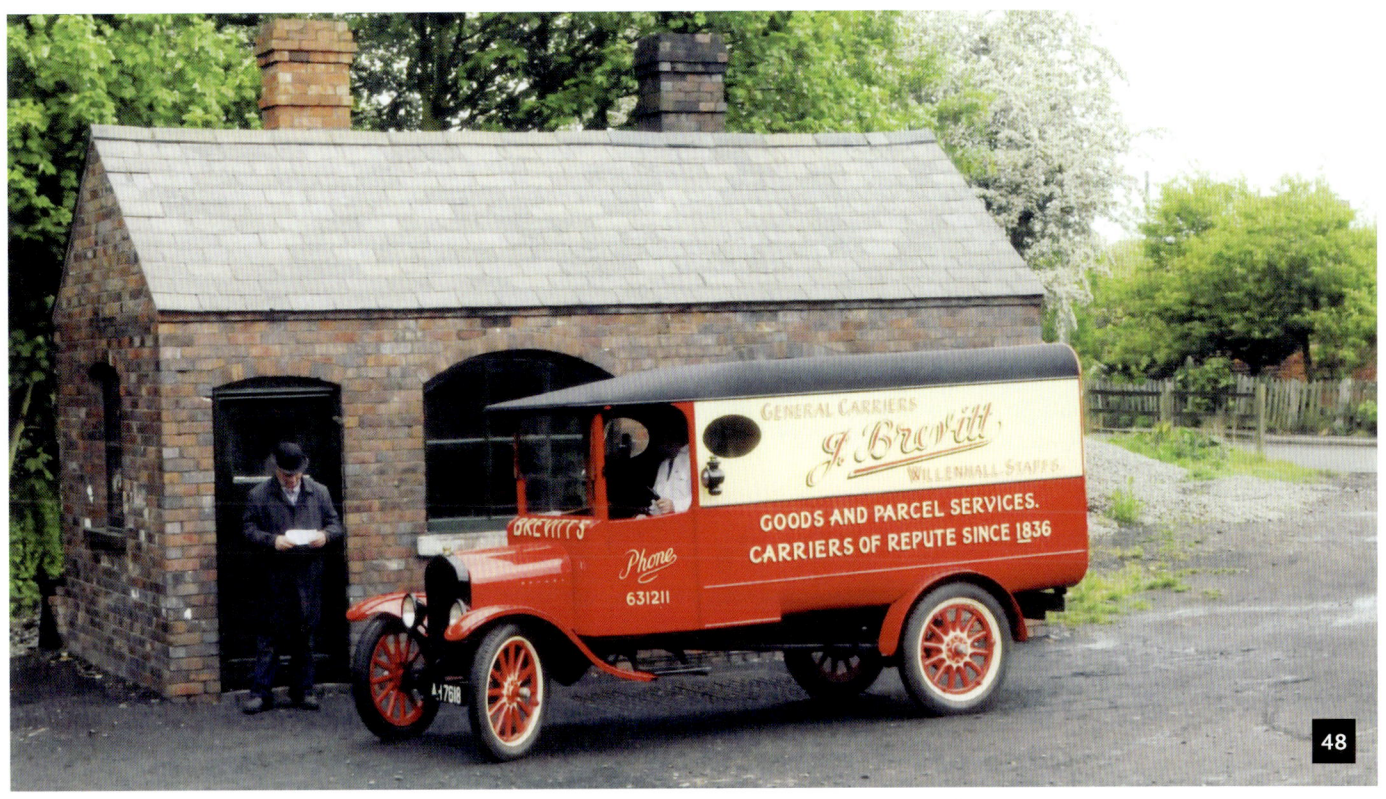

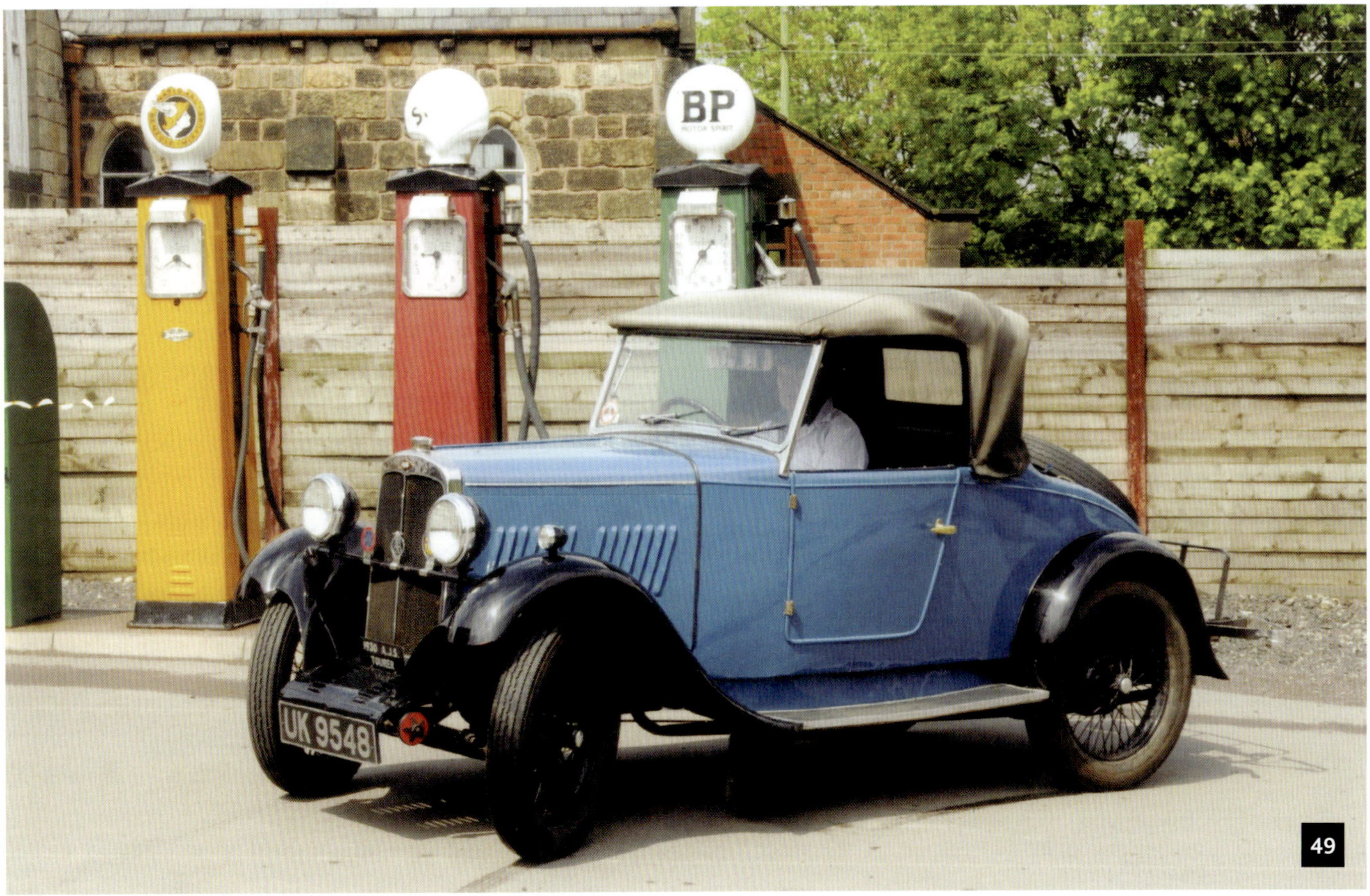
BP
UK 9548

49

World War, but then quickly resumed. A rapid growth in the number of motor companies by 1922 resulted in there being 183, though the economic slump of the 1920s reduced that number to 58 in 1929, by which time 60 per cent of total production was from Morris and Austin. By 1932, the UK was Europe's largest volume producer of cars (and remained so until 1955) and in 1937, 379,310 new passenger vehicles and 163,946 commercial vehicles were produced. Of the world's total exports of vehicles, the UK represented 15 per cent, a proportion that by 1950 had grown to 50 per cent.

The totals of various types of vehicles between 1928 and 1936 were:

Year	Cars '000	Motor cycles '000	Tramcars '000	Goods vehicles '000
1928	884	713	14	303
1929	980	731	14	326
1930	1,056	724	14	345
1931	1,083	627	13	357
1932	1,128	600	12	366
1933	1,203	563	12	383
1934	1,308	548	12	404
1935	1,477	517	11	422
1936	1,643	506	10	445

Wherever they looked, the LNER's management would have seen what we know now as market share being eroded, controls over much of their pricing and a fixed cost base that was much more restrictive than that of their main competitors. For a railway dependent upon freight revenue far more than passenger, it would have been of great concern.

This section has given precedence to considerations of freight traffic, bringing receipts as it did of nearly two thirds of the annual totals. That imbalance of consideration will be corrected later in this Chapter (traffic flows and planning, investment), but here is a simple list of passenger traffic receipts for selected years:

Year	£ million
1923	22
1926	19*
1928	20ø
1930	18
1934	16 ÷
1938	17

NOTES:
* general strike
ø abolition of passenger duty from first class fares
÷ excursion tickets valid on normal service trains

Finally, it is worth noting the contributions made by certain classes of 4-4-0 locomotives built in MS&LR/GCR days which gave good service well into, and in some cases, beyond the time of the LNER.

Shortly after the Grouping, the LNER took some fundamental decisions on traffic flow and planning:

a) it adopted as standard the vacuum brake rather than the Westinghouse air type
b) it adopted standard loading gauge measures. That necessitated changes to certain classes and sub-classes of locomotive in the form of reductions to the overall height to the top of the chimney, dome, safety valves, whistle and cab, a reduction in the width over the cab footsteps, relocation of front footsteps and cutting away quadrant sections of buffer beams. The modifications allowed, for example, the A1/A3s to work through beyond Newcastle onto the former NB to Edinburgh
c) it established at York an all line, central wagon control centre which sought the full employment of approximately 300,000 wagons (of which 100,000 were for coal, 30,000 covered goods wagons and 120,000 open goods wagons, 17,000 rail and timber wagons and 7,000 cattle wagons). The centre was managed by the Traffic Department which accepted equal responsibility for loaded and empty wagons. The line of communication was to/from the 24 district superintendents, each of whom sent a daily summary report for co-ordination at York and the sending of instructions for priority movements of stock. From the daily reports a 'picture' was readily apparent as to where the operating constrictions lay and why goods train traffic flows needed urgent attention. From the information it was possible to make the case for investment (1928) in a new yard at March and for a down yard specifically to sort

privately owned empty wagons into loads which could be better sent on their way to Lincoln, the coalfields and collieries of the Midlands/Yorkshire without incurring delays later in their journeys. Similarly, a case could be made later for a new yard at Mottram to assist the flow of traffic coming over the Pennines and destined for multiple destinations in small units throughout Lancashire and Cheshire

d) (together with the other grouped companies) it contributed to the construction and maintenance of a common pool of ordinary open goods, coal and mineral wagons, together with non-(brake)-fitted covered goods vans owned by the railways, in proportion to the freight it carried. The LNER was then at liberty to load and despatch any common uses vehicle regardless of its (previous) ownership and, of course, the LMS, GWR and SR did likewise. The theory was that the traffic flows would lead to a mix of wagons spread across the country in proportions of the four grouped railways' total stock

e) It implemented a method of classifying different types of freight trains into those which should usefully be formed of braked vehicles representing different proportions of the total number and those which, of necessity, would be unbraked. The brake force as available and the maximum number of wagons/weight would allow trains to be expected to meet calculated section (e.g. between loops, refuge sidings or yards) allowances and be written into the Working Timetable alongside all the other traffics of varying types, weights and expected section timings. By this method fast, fully fitted goods trains conveying fish, meat and perishable traffic could be accommodated whilst unbraked coal trains could occupy a length of line of some 74 miles for over seven hours. The classifications were:

    No. 1 goods, fitted, 50 mph (BR Class C)
    No. 2 goods, minimum of one third total vehicles fitted, 40 mph (BR D)
    No. 3 express goods, unbraked, 35 mph. Maximum load 45 wagons loaded, 50 empty. (BR E)
    Class A express goods not fitted with continuous brake
    Class B through goods
    Class C mineral or empty wagons
    Class D stopping (pick up) goods

To assist signalmen and other operating staff, the locomotives carried headlamps in different positions to denote the classification of train. Looking forward from the locomotive cab the position for a No. 1 was centre and right-hand side above bufferbeam, No. 2 was top of smokebox and right-hand side above bufferbeam, No. 3 was centre and left-hand side above bufferbeam. As confidence grew in having locomotives suitable for the projected timings available it was possible in 1932 for major timetable changes to be made:

f) it decided that each former constituent company would be responsible for the control, upkeep and overhaul of its own fleet of coaching stock. It also sought to agree with other railway companies the use of sets owned by each for lengthy cross-country journeys such as those operated along the former GCR route. For example, a GW set would work North on Tuesdays, Thursdays and Saturdays and a GCR set on Mondays, Wednesdays and Fridays

g) it replaced green aspects in GER distant signals with yellow.

Consideration is now given to how the former GCR lines contributed to the business of the LNER and how, in turn, the management of the LNER supported those former GCR lines. The outline of the network of the former GCR was basically like a capital T with the vertical running north to south from Sheffield to London and a thicker horizontal being the routes from Grimsby and Immingham across to the West coast at Liverpool/Chester/Wrexham, having crossed the Pennines en route between Sheffield and Manchester. Around Manchester and extending to Chester and Northwich, the LNER had a shared interest with the LMS in the CLC and over the short but busy MSJ&A to Altrincham also with the LMS.

The consideration is based upon the six principal traffic flows of the former GCR. Those traffic flows were firstly for passenger trains along the three main routes (Manchester/Bradford/Sheffield/London; west to east between Liverpool/Manchester/ Cleethorpes/Humber long distance cross country services), passenger trains along the jointly owned lines and the considerable seasonal and excursion trains from centres of population and, secondly, for goods. The goods traffic flows were principally along the same axes as the passenger services

Classification of goods trains: LNER

In LNER times the distinction between Numbers 1, 2 and 3 Express Goods trains was the number of wagons in the train and the number of wagons fully braked (Numbers 1 and 2) and braked (Number 3).

Wagons	No. 1	No. 2	No. 3
12	9	2	-
18	-	-	0
19	-	-	1
20	15	5	-
24	18	-	-
27	-	8	2
30	23	9	-
40	31	15	6
48	38	16	9
60	47	20	12
68	-	-	16
75	-	-	20

LNER GOODS TRAIN HEADLAMP CODES

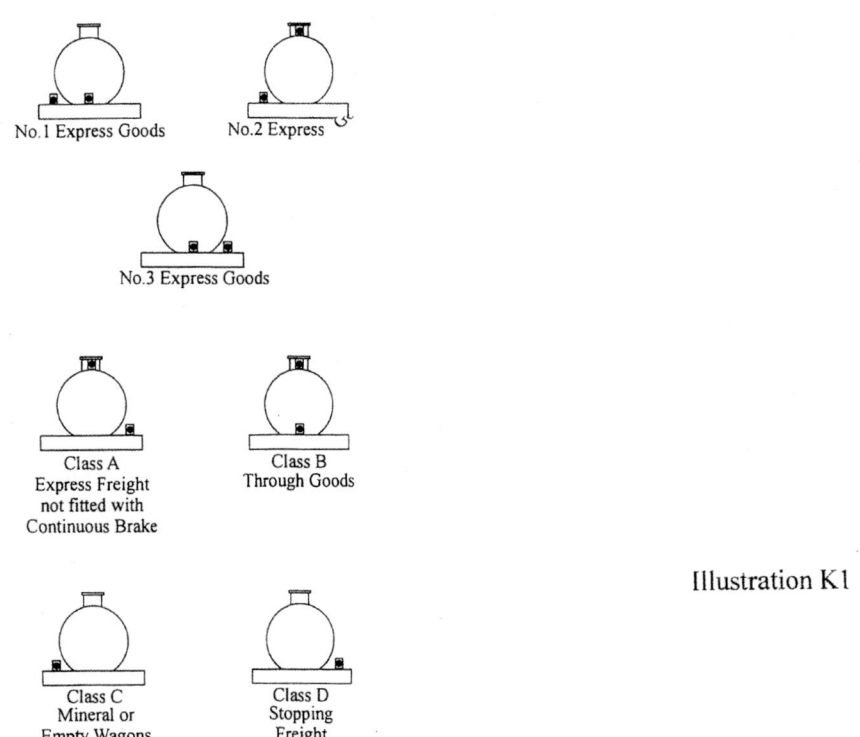

Illustration K1

The correct identification of goods trains by means of placement of headlamps on the front of the locomotive was influenced by the extent to which the train had braking power to assist the Driver and Guard. Guards anxious to reach their destination earlier were always keen to find a few extra braked vehicles allowing higher speeds.

with a proportion of consignments for other railway companies.

Each of these traffic flows is now considered and starts the three main line service routes. The reason for considering all these under one heading is that all passed through Sheffield (Victoria) and, as such, represents a traffic hub; trains were split there, carriages brought in from elsewhere were added, others despatched after the main train had departed, locomotives were sometimes changed (ones from the North Eastern Area relieved by others from the Southern Area and vice versa), refreshment cars replenished, mail and luggage transferred and a multitude of the travelling public moved along.

The days of the former GCR attempting to compete on speed with the LNWR, MR and, at times, the GNR for Manchester/Yorkshire passenger traffic to/from London were gone and whilst the basic pattern of train services remained largely unchanged, an early post-war re-introduction of slip carriage workings had doubtless pleased the well-heeled daily travellers heading home from London to Stratford upon Avon (1920, carriage slipped at Woodford), Brackley/Helmdon (1921) and at Finmere (1923), where the case was helped by one of the regular travellers being a Director of the LNER. The slipping arrangements lasted until 1936, when a rear end collision between the main train having been brought to a stand 'in section' (following a brake fault) was hit by the following slipped carriage. Whilst it lasted, the slipping of carriages supported the operating of two afternoon lightweight fast trains from Marylebone, which called briefly only at Leicester and Nottingham. Other Marylebone services were routed in accordance with pre-Grouping agreements via either the GW/GC joint or the MetR/GC joint and, in the same vein, it remained possible to travel to London King's Cross (GNR) and if heading west to Manchester/Liverpool, passengers could on certain trains reach Oldham and Stockport without a change of train. In general, it was for many years a time of very little change and with the retention along the line of something of the GCR days. The Marylebone services did, though, see changes in motive power. The workings were predominantly for Gorton-based locomotives driven and fired by men in the No. 1 link. Prior to the Grouping, D10 4-4-0 locomotives (built 1913) handled the traffic until the newer D11 class took over around 1919/20 and ruled the roost for up to 15 years. A Neasden-based D10 or D11 did, however, work the fast mid-afternoon service on three days a week, returning the following morning. The Manchester-Marylebone express services did not change locomotives at Leicester until much later. The D11 class were eased out following the arrival at Gorton of enough of the new B17 4-6-0 class to take on the new heavier workings. They in turn were relieved from 1938-9 by the arrival upon the scene of eight A3 class 4-6-2 locomotives; their availability due to the streamlined A4 pacifics supplementing the stud of the A3 class working the GN main East Coast Anglo-Scottish traffic. Because there is a high level of interest in the A3 class working along the former GCR route to London, here is the full list of those allocated.

BR number	Name	Depot	Period allocated
60039	Sandwich	Leicester	10/56 to 4/57
60044	Melton	Leicester	11/53 to 3/55
		Neasden	3/55 to 3/56
60047	Donovan	Neasden	6/39 to 2/41
		Gorton	2/41 to 12/42
		Gorton	7/44 to 10/44
60048	Doncaster	Leicester	2/49 to 11/55
60049	Galtee More	Leicester	2/49 to 6/55
			10/55 to 9/57
60050	Persimmon	Neasden	2/49 to 7/55
		Neasden	10/55 to 6/56
60051	Blink Bonny	Gorton	7/44 to 10/44
		Neasden	2/49 to 11/53
60052	Prince Palatine	Gorton	5/49 to 7/54
		Neasden	12/54 to 8/55

BR number	Name	Depot	Period allocated
60053	Sansovino	Neasden	6/39 to 11/42
		Leicester	12/49 to 5/45
60054	Prince of Wales	Leicester	2/49 to 6/56
60055	Woolwinder	Gorton	8/39 to 11/42
60059	Tracery	Gorton	9/38 to 12/42
		Leicester	3/51 to 4/57
60061	Pretty Polly	Leicester	2/49 to 6/50
		Neasden	7/51 to 2/53
60062	Minoru	Gorton	7/44 to 10/44
60063	Isinglass	Leicester	8/39 to 12/39
		Gorton	2/41 to 11/42
		Gorton	7/44 to 8/44
		Neasden	2/53 to 3/55
		Neasden	3/56 to 6/56
60090*	Grand Parade	Leicester	2/49 to 5/49
60102	Sir Frederick Banbury	Leicester	5/49 to 7/54
		Neasden	7/54 to 11/54
		Leicester	11/54 to 9/57
60103	Flying Scotsman	Gorton	7/44 to 10/44
		Leicester	6/50 to 11/53
60104	Solario	Gorton	5/39 to 2/43
		Leicester	6/50 to 7/54
		Neasden	7/54 to 12/54
		Leicester	12/54 to 9/57
60105	Victor Wild	Gorton	2/39 to 8/39
		Leicester	8/39 to 12/39
		Gorton	12/39 to 11/42
60106	Flying Fox	Gorton	7/44 to 10/44
		Leicester	8/55 to 9/57
60107	Royal Lancer	Gorton	7/44 to 10/44
		Leicester	6/50 to 7/52
		Leicester	8/52 to 9/57
60108	Gay Crusader	Gorton	12/41 to 1/43
		Neasden	9/52 to 3/53
		Neasden	11/53 to 7/55
		Neasden	10/55 to 1/57
60109	Hermit	Gorton	3/39 to 11/42
60111	Enterprise	Neasden	7/49 to 3/55
		Leicester	3/55 to 9/57

NOTES:
a) * left hand drive.
b) All named after racehorses which won principal races, apart from 60102 and 60103. 60103 is preserved and part of the National Collection under the public ownership of the National Railway Museum.
c) Allocations 7/44 to 10/44 for U.S. military movements following D Day landings.

The coaching stock utilised gradually became of the Gresley designed types and train weights in wartime were far higher than hitherto.

The Liverpool/Southport/Manchester to Cleethorpes/Hull trains were worked principally by Gorton No. 2 link, with Neepsend (Sheffield, Darnall from 1936) having a few turns and Immingham men working the weekly Orient Line Boat Train (eastbound train on Fridays, returning on the Saturday). There was no question of the stock of the Boat Train waiting quietly for its return; that afternoon it formed a Liverpool-Hull service (non-stop Manchester-Sheffield) and was returned early the following morning in time to work the eastbound Boat Train service. Neepsend turned out large boilered 4-4-2 (Atlantics) for their turns until the 1930s, when resident D11 and B17 classes appeared. In

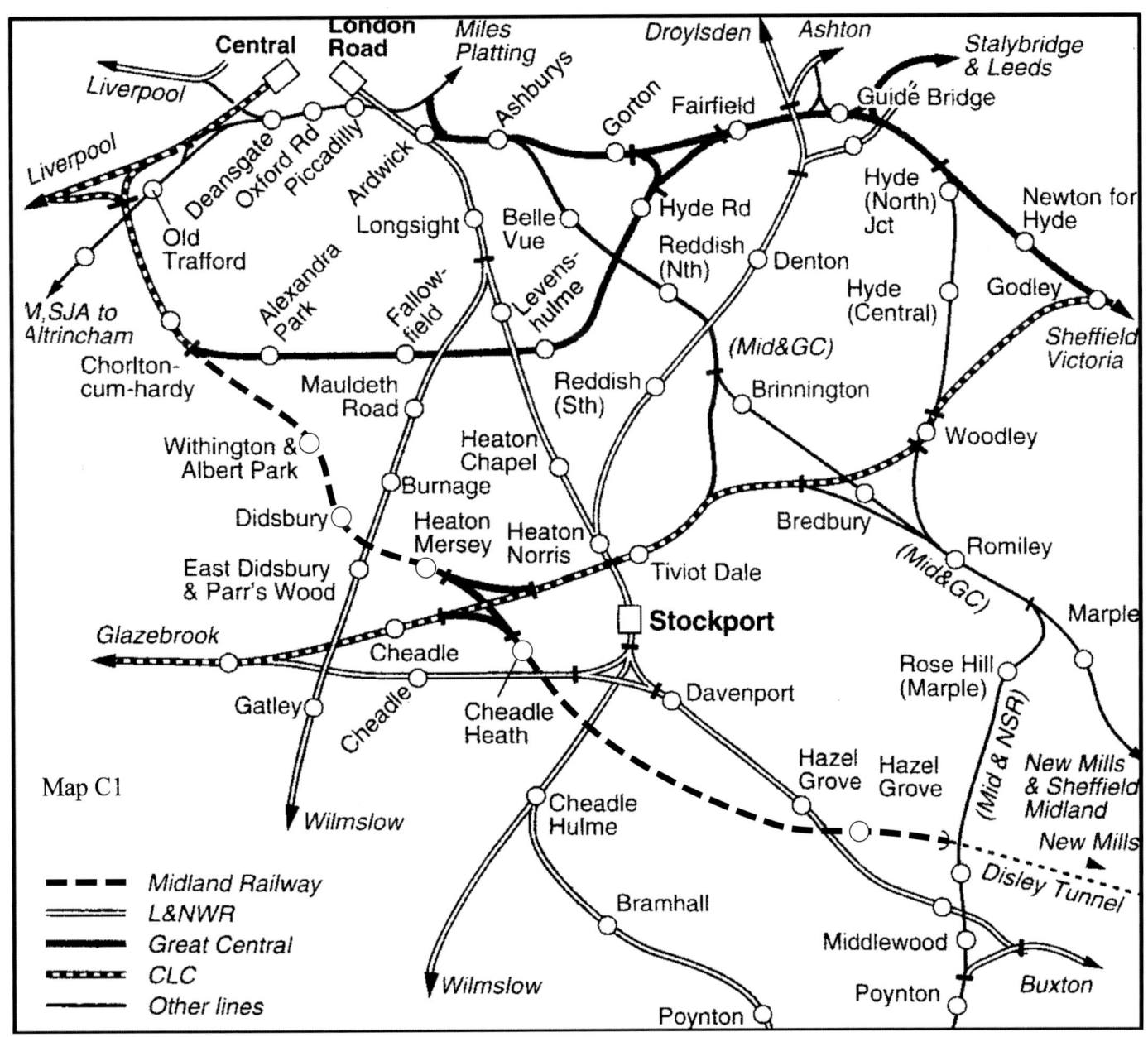

This map serves to illustrate how the Great Central Railway routed its passenger trains for Liverpool (via the Cheshire Lines Committee) between Fairfield (top, right) and Manchester (Central) where a reversal took place. GCR trains to Manchester (London Road) continued via Ashburys. The map also shows how the CLC route between Godley (top, right) and Glazebrook (centre, left) via Stockport (Tiviot Dale) could be used for trains for Liverpool and also the short Manchester South Junction & Altrincham line (top, left).

all, there were seven or eight return services daily, with the flow augmented on Summer Saturdays by four additionals. The routes taken varied, with Stockport having a service in each direction (and not calling at Manchester) and others went via Stalybridge to Huddersfield, then on to Sheffield.

For its main line passenger services terminating and passing through (with a reversal) Manchester, the LNER inherited and utilised the same, limited facilities as the GCR. London Road (in modern times Piccadilly) was a terminus dominated by the needs of the LMS and where just three platform faces were available to the LNER. Central was also a terminus (in modern times a convention centre) which the GCR had shared with the GNR and the MR as partners in the CLC and at which the Cleethorpes-Liverpool trains would receive a fresh locomotive upon arrival and from which fast CLC services to Warrington and Liverpool (45 minutes or 40 non-stop) departed. The MS&JA (with which the LNER shared an interest with the LMS) operated its busy short line services to/from Altrincham from a platform adjacent to the London Road terminus, whilst suburban services to Glossop, Macclesfield, Guide Bridge and Stockport kept platform 3 busy.

The longest distance worked by a locomotive and crew to/from Manchester was from/to Ipswich on the service to/from Harwich: 216 miles. Through engine workings began in 1927 and to work the train after April, Gorton was allocated B12 8557. Gorton and Ipswich shared this working, out one day, lodge, and return the next. A very reliable performer, 8557 was replaced in March 1928 by 8538, which stayed until it was replaced in February 1929 by a then new B17. Upon arrival at Sheffield (earlier at Lincoln), a portion for/from York was detached/attached, the train prior to 1927 having been a Harwich-York working. Whilst Gorton men also had the high mileage London turns, for Ipswich men the Manchester job handsomely exceeded on a mileage basis anything else the depot had to offer. Reflecting the importance, both locomotives used were kept in immaculate condition. However, how the mighty fall; after servicing at Trafford Park shed, the arriving locomotive was used on a peak hour stopping service from Central to Guide Bridge and back. That idea appealed to the management and from 1938, the locomotive additionally worked a later train through to Leicester (arrival at 10.47pm), returning to Manchester on the 12.25am from Leicester. Arrangements at Ipswich were for the incoming locomotive to be disposed and when examined in readiness for its next round trip north.

Throughout the period up to the outbreak of the Second World War, the LNER continued to operate the longer distance cross country train services. As at the winter timetable 1938/39, the Sheffield (Victoria) hub dealt with trains as follows, all of which conveyed a Restaurant Car:

Time	Service
11.22am – 11.37	Newcastle-Bournemouth
12.23pm – 12.27	Plymouth-Manchester (joined with service ex-London Marylebone at Woodford)
12.42pm – 12.46	(Harwich-Liverpool)
12.51pm – 1.00	Newcastle-Barry Docks/Bournemouth/Portsmouth
1.51pm – 2.00	Southampton/Cardiff-Newcastle and Berwick
3.03pm – 3.10	Barry Docks/Bournemouth-Glasgow
4.13pm – 4.26	Glasgow-Swansea/Bournemouth
4.16pm – 4.21	(Liverpool-Harwich)
4.57pm – 5.2	Manchester-Swansea/Bournemouth (joined with service to London Marylebone to Woodford)
5.40pm – 6.7	Bournemouth/Swansea-Newcastle
7.37pm – 7.44	Aberdeen-Penzance
10.05pm – 10.17	Penzance-Aberdeen

Together with the London Marylebone passenger services, these trains were afforded a high priority along the London extension as far as Woodford, with locomotive exchanges with the GWR taking place at Leicester Central rather than Woodford. For many years, Leicester had an allocation of aged Atlantics, but by 1937 that shed had been given an allocation of eleven B17 class 4-6-0 which could handle a dozen bogie carriages south of Nottingham and ten north along the more demanding route to Sheffield/Manchester. All of the locomotives as received were from the 1936/37 new build batch with greater water capacity tenders. Around that time, B17s were plentiful, with Doncaster allocated examples working fish trains to Banbury, three new to Darnall, one to Neasden and four to Gorton. Doncaster quickly lost

Four months before the Second World War one of the then new V2 2-6-2s has the 6.20pm Marylebone-Bradford express approaching Saunderton (Rail on-line).

their triplets, receiving new V2 2-6-2s as replacements: not all LNER/GWR through trains exchanged locomotives prior to crossing the boundary; a Darnall B17 and men worked the York-Swindon forward from Leicester to Swindon, the men lodged and worked through to Sheffield with a corresponding service the following day. That arrangement also applied to a GWR locomotive coming through to Leicester as part of a wider, periodic arrangement to protect lucrative mileage bonus payments for enginemen. Whilst Leicester's main passenger work was the former GCR routes to/from Marylebone/Sheffield/less frequently Manchester, its men had – in 1937 – a night turn with a B17 through to Newcastle, lodge and return the following night for a handsome 390 miles. That turn was part of an initiative by the LNER to offer cheap overnight travel, re-introduced in later years as the Starlight Specials. As at the end of 1938 the allocations of B17s to the former GCR route were:

Leicester (BR numbers)	61648	*Arsenal*
	61649	*Sheffield United*
	61651	*Derby County*
	61652	*Darlington*
	61653	*Huddersfield Town*
	61654	*Sunderland*
	61656	*Leeds United*
	61661	*Sheffield Wednesday*
	61665	*Leicester City*
	61667	*Bradford*
	61668	*Bradford City*
Woodford Halse	61647	*Helmingham Hall*
	61650	*Grimsby Town*
	61655	*Middlesbrough*

Neasden	61657	*Doncaster Rovers*
	61666	*Nottingham Forest*
Gorton	61634	*Hinchingbrooke*
	61660	*Hull City*
	61662	*Manchester United*
	61664	*Liverpool*
	61669	*Barnsley*
	61671	*Manchester City*
	61672	*West Ham United*

Of these, 61634 had been built in 1931, 61647 in 1935, 61648-61 in 1936 and the rest in 1937. Unfortunately, even from new they all had a reputation for rough riding. With the arrival of the A3 pacifics, Leicester was relieved of all of its B17s in 1940, but when the A3s themselves were re-allocated in 1942, eight B17s were returned, though all to Gorton, for GC line work. A further shuffle took place in 1944 with an influx of V2 2-6-2s, leaving only a few B17s along the GC line and the final three went from Gorton towards the end of 1946.

Before moving to consideration of goods traffic flows it may be useful to refer to the total allocations of locomotives at former GCR motive power depots. The large concentrations are an indicator of the areas where the traffic was originated and was destined.

Depots having less than 20 locomotives:
Bidston, Chester, Leicester, Wigan

Depots having between 21 and 50 locomotives:
Liverpool (Brunswick), Northwich, Staveley, Stockport (Heaton Mersey), Wrexham

Depots having between 51 and 100 locomotives:
Annesley, Frodingham, Immingham, Langwith Junction, Neasden, Woodford Halse

Depots having over 100 locomotives:
Gorton, Mexborough

For interest and of relevance to wider traffic flows (as at end 1947):
Colwick (Nottingham) 198
Doncaster 174
March 209
New England (Peterborough) 201

At the Grouping, the LNER and LMS inherited the CLC and the MSJ&A lines. The LNER picked up the prime responsibility carried by the GCR and provided the bulk of the motive power for the CLC, whilst costs of replacement/upkeep of coaching and wagon stock would be shared. For many years following the Grouping, the CLC continued just as before; a mixture of aged rolling stock plus the nine 5-car sets built at Dukinfield in 1914, hauled mainly by 4-4-0s. Class D6 (Pollitt design of 1895), of which all 33 were on the line until the first withdrawal in 1930 – fourteen more expired between 1931 and 1933, nine survived until the outbreak of war – and D7 (Parker 1887-94) of which Northwich had half a dozen in the 1920s. The passage of time saw a progression to D9, D10 and D11 classes. Manchester Central to Liverpool Central services were very smartly timed at 40 minutes non-stop and five minutes longer with a stop at Warrington. The coaching stock position was improved in 1937 by the authorisation of the building by Craven of Sheffield of twelve articulated twin carriages to form three, eight car sets, each of which did three return journeys each day. Turning facilities at both Liverpool and Manchester were improved in the late 1930s assisting the use of the B17 class.

The MSJ&A soldiered on regardless; its nine miles dealing with some 160 trains each day (6am to 11pm) and its passengers suffering in the generally aged rolling stock. Relief at last arrived in 1911, with two 7-car 488-seater trains (capable of being split in quieter times of the day). Electrification of the line in 1931 came as something of a relief to everyone.

The nation's appetite for fish remained strong and healthy, prompting the LNER to approve the building of an additional fish dock at Grimsby in 1934. Reaping (or perhaps trawling) the benefit of the GCR investment in bogie fish vans and the four-wheel variety fitted with vacuum braking, the LNER promptly decided that the Grimsby-London fish trains would be re-routed from 1924 to take the GN line, depriving Immingham men of work. At the Grouping, up to eight fish trains were despatched daily from Grimsby bound for London, Manchester, Liverpool, the Midlands and the West Country. In addition, four wheeled vacuum braked vans were added to many passenger trains. The locomotives used on the fish only trains were, in GCR days 4-6-0s of classes 8 and 8F (GCR classes) which became B5 and

B4 respectively in LNER days. The primary function of the B5 Class was to haul fish trains, but when built, the 1902 batch were the largest engines on the GCR and consequently were deployed between Marylebone and Leicester on passenger work. However, as newer classes emerged, the B5s gravitated north and by 1922, the total of fourteen was divided between Gorton, Immingham and Mexborough. However, the arrival upon the scene of the LNER K3 2-6-0 class from 1924 displaced the B5s from their traditional role. It was a similar case with the ten B4 class; at Grouping all were at Neepsend, Sheffield. To one of the B4s fell the distinction of being the final GCR 4-6-0 to work an express passenger train over the London extension; July 1949, forward from Leicester with the twelve carriage Newcastle-Bournemouth. The final withdrawals of these two classes were in 1950, the war years having provided a final opportunity for the B5s to demonstrate their capabilities on heavy passenger trains between Sheffield and Hull with service lives of up to 47 years.

Excursion traffic varied from a short-lived experiment in the summer months of 1925 to extend a London King's Cross-Sheffield Victoria Pullman train to Manchester to race day specials to Haydock Park, Doncaster and Aintree, to day trips to Southport, the East coast resorts and to Belle Vue pavilions and gardens. Grand National day generally produced sixteen longer distance trains from far and wide. Occasionally, there would be something extraordinary. On 22 June 1935, some 90,000 members of the Independent Order of Rechabites (i.e. teetotallers) held their first centenary celebrations and selected Belle Vue for the occasion. Watkin would have been pleased.

The planners at the LNER had grand ideas for the development of the former GNR main line from King's Cross. With one eye on what the opposition half a mile along the Euston Road in London were thought likely to do to attract a larger share of the Anglo-Scottish passenger traffic, as well as their own company's aspirations, meant that slow moving traffic would not be a welcome entry in working timetables from 1932. The movement of unbraked coal/mineral trains has been referred to earlier in this chapter and although the growth in the traffic flow of bricks from Fletton to London was assisted by use of vacuum piped wagons, the gross weight of each loaded wagon at 67 tons made acceleration of a train load a timing curve challenge.

Other traffic could and was moved. For example, the iron ore trains from High Dyke (south of Grantham) were diverted off the main line at Barkston and followed new, equally challenging, routes involving at least one reversal before finally reaching the steel making complexes around Scunthorpe/Normanby Park served from 1932 by the new depot at Frodingham (Keadby then closed).

The planning for the movement of goods traffic along the GN line from 1932 also incorporated thoughts to recast the Annesley to Woodford Halse coal workings. In 1931, Annesley received three K3 2-6-0s and initially they were diagrammed to work two return trips daily. Having proven the arrangements, the workings were increased to four, with 50 loaded wagons Southbound and 55 empties for the returns. The B7 4-6-0s helped out and by 1935, with a handful of B8s, had totally replaced the K3s. By 1943, all eleven B8s were at Annesley (see later under wartime for further locomotive allocations along the route.) The 4-6-0s of classes B3, B7, B8 and B9 all followed a similar pattern of movement to reach final deployment on CLC mixed traffic duties, with condemnation postponed due to the demands of wartime for all available traction and rolling stock.

Whenever there were paths available during the day time and as soon as the frequency of passenger services started to decline, there were timetabled goods trains either ready to go, newspapers being printed, mail being sorted for transit overnight and, every evening, the three to five tanks of milk for Marylebone wending their way from Dorrington (Church Stretton). The railway companies thrived on regular traffic flows such as the fish from Grimsby, meat from Scotland, meat imported into Liverpool from Ireland, seasonal traffics such as potatoes, fruit and other vegetables from Norfolk, Suffolk, Lincolnshire, the West Country and had a network of timetabled No. 1 and No. 2 goods trains from all of the major centres. Gorton shed had a group of enginemen with wide route knowledge known as the piped train link who worked overnight No. 1 and No. 2 goods to Marylebone, Lincoln, Grimsby, Ardsley and York, whilst from Liverpool, trains at 5.25pm and 6.10pm left Huskisson goods with up to 40 refrigerated vans bound for York. From Woodford, men had lodging turns at both Doncaster and Grimsby (for fish). From Lincoln to Manchester and vice versa came fitted goods via the GE/GN and, to avoid the congested area around Staveley, traversed the Midland route in part to reach Chinley/Stockport. Additionally, from Deansgate, Manchester, two fitteds went over the Woodhead route to Sheffield and thence York, presumably via the S&K, and from Ardwick two more went to Lincoln/Marylebone respectively. From Marylebone the 10.50pm SX (11.0pm SO) Marylebone to Manchester and Liverpool (split at Godley) mail and the 2.32am to Sheffield (newspapers) were particularly of importance. Trains out of Wath yard or bypassing it daily in 1932 were 61 Westbound and 64 Eastbound (1943 57/72 see later).

The complex nature of timetabling, rostering of men and locomotives made for an organisation that did not welcome change. Trains which were not required were shown in the working timetable as 'suspended', the paths seemingly protected for future reinstatement. Other trains were provided for as Q; ran when required.

Major changes to traffic flows and timetables – both public and working – needed careful planning. One such change was in connection with the introduction of high speed, streamlined locomotive hauled expresses along the former GNR/NER main line from King's Cross to Newcastle in the late 1930s. This initiative will be described more fully under investment but culminated in the world speed record of 126 mph being attained on 3 July 1938 by *Mallard*. Operating trains at over 90 mph required additional headways to be established in the working timetable and signalling to be suitable for the braking distances. The solution was a successful 'double blocking' i.e. the section to be signalled for the high-speed trains would be two block lengths rather than one. All very good for the small percentage of total travellers/freight along the route, but a headache for the operators and timetable planners. The ex GNR main line became an even less welcome route for slow moving traffic such as minerals which would be obliged to continue to use the alternative routes, irrespective of improvements along the GN.

The effect on the Annesley-Woodford route as a direct consequence of the high-speed policy is difficult to identify, but as a line with its own operating challenges including some long block sections, adverse gradients and few refuge sidings/loops it was certainly busy.

For Tuesdays to Fridays in 1939 (summer) the traffic flow dealt with was:

Class of train	Direction		Of which, Banbury line	
	From North	To North	To Banbury	From Banbury
No. 1 Goods	7*	4ø	3	3
No. 2 Goods	3	4	3	-
Class A	9	10	2	4
Class B	1	-	-	-
Class C	14	16	13	13
Class D	1	1	-	-

NOTE:
* 8.17pm   Doncaster-Banbury (fish) GWR line. 40 vans (B17)
* 7.50pm   Ardwick East-Marylebone Goods
* 9.23pm   Godley-Marylebone Goods
* 11.40pm York-Marylebone Goods
* 12.35am York-Marylebone Goods
* 3.32pm   Doncaster-Banbury (fish) GWR line. 45 vans (K3)
* 6.27pm   Grimsby-Banbury (fish) GWR line. 37 vans (GC B18)
ø 9.50pm   Marylebone Goods-Ardwick
ø 4.05am   Banbury-York
ø 6.05pm   Banbury-York
ø 9.07pm   Banbury Junction-Stainforth

12 of the 35 trains from the North and eight of the 35 going North were 'through' workings which passed through Woodford; all of these were either No. 1 goods, No. 2 goods or Class A. The balance of the totals was dealt with in the yards at Woodford.

From Grimsby, train loads of fish were also despatched to the North East and Scotland, to Manchester and Liverpool, to Western counties and Birmingham, and to the West Riding of Yorkshire. In addition to the train-load traffic, vans would be added to certain passenger train services. The railway thrived on regularity and efficient train management.

Throughout its existence, the LNER consistently made an operating profit. However, that profit (expressed as net revenue) was soon at a low level where dividends could not be paid to holders of ordinary shares, followed by a withdrawal of dividends to holders of second preference stock. In circumstances that would have been familiar to the Deputy Chairman Lord Faringdon, holders of debentures were always paid, good housekeeping and efficiency initiatives were pursued with vigour, but finding finance for capital investment was an increasingly difficult challenge. As a hostage to the fortunes of the national and, for coal exports, international economy and particularly exposed to erratic downturns in the traditional industries requiring transport, the LNER suffered. Through the first seven or eight years of their existence, the grouped railway companies felt increasingly constrained by the provisions of the Railways Act 1921, the slow mechanism of the annual Railway Rates Tribunals and the impracticability of the 'watershed' year of 1928 whilst their emerging competitors nibbled away at the more lucrative goods traffic without similar statutory restrictions.

The governments of the 1923-47 period – there were eight, five Conservative, two Labour and one wartime coalition – had to contend with far more than the position of the railways, but enacted legislation which went some way to addressing the concerns of the railway companies in relation to competition and also made available access to finance on favourable terms as part of a wider initiative to reduce national unemployment and enlarge the gross domestic product.

In terms of capital investment, the period 1923-38 can be divided into the years before government help was enabled and, secondly, the years in which government funds were successfully sought. In each of those two periods some £8 million was invested.

With its five constituent companies each in need of some investment, an eye on what the opposition for Anglo-Scottish traffic were perhaps planning at Euston, shareholders expecting returns on their investment, the trades unions seeking to at least retain hard won gains on conditions of service, traders always unhappy and the travelling public expecting decent levels of comfort, the Board of the LNER had at 1923 a huge challenge.

The former GCR – with its London extension at 1923 less than one quarter of a century old and with the benefit of the good work of John Robinson and Arthur Bound – certainly had its needs, but against those of the GNR voices (competition from the LMS must be countered), GER (East London suburban traffic expansion), NER (Tyneside electrification schemes extensions) and NBR (passenger and goods locomotives) its representatives on the Board would struggle to make competing claims for scarce finance.

This book is primarily about the former GCR and in reviewing the capital investment made by the LNER the benefit or disbenefit to the GCR lines will be identified.

The Board of the LNER was nothing if not well organised and in approaching the consideration of capital investment it adopted a well-structured approach. The consideration of expenditure committed is in eight areas: locomotives; carriages; wagons and containers; marine shipping; marine installations; major new works; minor works; ancillary businesses.

Locomotives

In approaching the consideration of future locomotive policy, the LNER Board turned to Sir Vincent Raven, the retiring Chief Mechanical Engineer of the NER, to produce a report on the organisation of the mechanical engineering department. His report made recommendations; firstly, that there should be a separation of responsibility between the Chief Mechanical Engineer (Gresley) and the locomotive running department and, secondly, there should be a Locomotive Committee. There would be a joint committee consisting of representatives of the locomotive department and the traffic department. That Committee would draw up annually a list of aspirations for new motive power to be built to meet the expected needs of the railway and replace obsolete stock. Only when the Committee's proposals had been authorised would the Chief Mechanical Engineer and his team respond with design proposals to the outline specifications of need and identify a cost (perhaps by inviting quotations from private contractors) to be submitted for approval by the Board. For example, traffic wanted goods locomotives that could take loads of 50 wagons rather than 40, they wanted locomotives and wagons with vacuum brakes to work 'fitted' (braked) trains that could be accommodated in a congested working timetable, the locomotive department wanted designs that would ease the burden of mechanical component failures, the Board wanted locomotives that would compete with the LMS, ASLEF wanted some form of automatic warning system. Of course, we now have the benefit of hindsight and what a wonderful position that is. In the 1920s/early 1930s the LNER Board had to take decisions based upon available finance and their collective judgement. Not for Gresley the big production builds; small class sizes, rebuilds, modifications, second-hand reconditioning. He would have his moment in history, but it would have to wait until well into the 1930s. What he actually came up with is as follows:

Year	Goods			Mixed traffic			Passenger		
	Class	Qty	Note	Class	Qty	Note	Class	Qty	Note
1924	O2/2	14	A	K3/2	172		D11/2	24	F
	O4	125	B	B16	32	D	N/7	93	
	O4/6	13	C	B7	10	E			
1925	P1	2	G				A5	13	
	O4/2	11	A/H				N2	107	
	U1	1	I						
1926	O4	48	B						
	J38	35	J						
	J38	289	K						
1927	O4	100	B				A3	78	A
							D49/1	34	
1928							B17/1	16	
							D49/2	41	
1929				K3/3	30				
1930							V1	72	
1931				K2/1	9		A8	45	C
1932	O2/3	39	A						
	O4/5	6							
	S1	6							
1933							D16/3	5	D
1934	J19	35	C				P2	6	L
1935							A4	34	M
1936				V2	184		D16/3	5	C
							B17/4	24	
							D20/2	4	C
1937				K4	7	C	B17/6	6	
				B16/2	7	C	W1	1	C/M
1938							D16/3	34	C
1939	O4/7	40	C				D16/3	1	C
							V3	20	A
1940									
1941							V4	2	

NOTES:

Table does not include small shunting locomotives (72)

A Development of earlier design
B Purchased following war service and reconditioned
C Rebuilt
D NER Class
E GCR classification
F Development of GCR Robinson design. Built to Scottish loading gauge
G Booster fitted for New England – Ferme Park mineral trains
H Modified for standardised LNER loading gauge
I Garratt for Worsborough incline work
J For Fife coalfield work
K Build batches spread over 15 years
L For Edinburgh – Aberdeen trains
M Streamlined
N For use in Scotland

Classification wheel arrangements:

A 4-6-2
B 4-6-0 (also GCR B16)
D 4-4-0
J 0-6-0
K 2-6-0
N 0-6-2T
O 2-8-0
P 2-8-2
S 0-8-4T
U 2-8-0 0-8-2
V 2-6-2
W 4-6-4

Right, below and overleaf: For its front-line fleet of passenger locomotives the LNER chose a livery of apple green lined out in red, black and white. Shown to good effect are a B12 (50), an A3 (51), both way from home at the Severn Valley Railway, plus a V2 (52) at the North Yorkshire Moors Railway. For humble goods locomotives, plain black was lifted somewhat by the attractive shading of the numbers and letters (53); shown here on a J17.

132 • THE GREAT CENTRAL RAILWAY: WHAT REALLY HAPPENED

Of particular interest is the purchase in three batches of 2-8-0 locomotives which had seen service during the First World War. The purchase of the initial batch of 125 was purchased and reconditioned, the Locomotive Committee stipulating a maximum cost of £3,500 per locomotive and to include the fitment of copper inner fireboxes in place of steel. The second batch (48) was purchased from Cohen Armstrong Disposal Corporation for £1,500; with reconditioning costs, a total per locomotive of £2,741. In 1927, the final batch (100) was purchased from the Government Disposals Board for £340 each and with reconditioning costs probably no more than £2,000 per locomotive. Spare components were also purchased; some 370 tons of non-ferrous and ferrous items for £3,600. When first built, the 04 class (GCR 8K) cost around £4,500 and in the mid-1920s to secure 273 locomotives for £750,000 represented sound business. The 04s gave good service into the 1960s. The purchase of these 273 locomotives swelled the Class to a total of 421 and enabled some weeding out of older classes and redistribution of locomotives to where they were best able to contribute.

The former GCR lines benefitted only marginally from the build and re-build programmes; the B17s of 1928 being used as noted in Traffic Flows and Planning and later reference under Wartime will identify the role of the K3s.

Sadly, Gresley died whilst still CME, at the age of 64; he was succeeded by Edward Thompson. For his 4-6-2 developments and new build he retained three cylinders but replaced his predecessor's valve gear arrangement with his own. None of the A2 class rebuilds was a success. His one largescale new build was the 410 strong B1 class produced by LNER workshops at Darlington (60) and Gorton (10), plus contractors North British Locomotive Co. Ltd. (290) and Vulcan Foundry (50). He also designed a class of tank locomotives (L1), but beyond that was limited to rebuilds.

Year	Goods			Mixed traffic			Passenger		
	Class	Qty	Note	Class	Qty	Note	Class	Qty	Note
1942	J11	31	C	B1	410				
1943	J20/1	20	C				A2/2	6	C/O
	O2/4	4	C				B12/1	9	C
							B17/6	12	C
1944	J27	17	P	B16/3	17	C	A2/1	4	Q
	O4/8	18	C						
	O1	58	C						
1945				K1/1	1	C	L1	100	
							A1/1	1	C/S
							B2	10	C
1946							A2/3	15	R

NOTES (LETTERS AS FOR NOTES TO 1924-41):
O Rebuild of Gresley P2 class
P Modification work
Q Development of A2/2 with V2 boiler
R Development of A2/2 as new build
S Rebuild of Gresley A1/A10 of 1922

Classification of wheel arrangement: L 2-6-4T

Thompson's short tenure ended in 1946 and the incoming CME was Arthur H. Peppercorn. In the short period before impending nationalisation put a halt to new proposals, he designed the A2 4-6-2 of which fifteen were built (five later modified), the A1 4-6-2, of which 49 were built, developed the K1 design for 70 locomotives and had 22 of the B17/1 class reboilered using the successful B1 design.

During and after the Second World War, the LNER was able to utilise locomotives made available on loan either by the USA Transportation Corps (1943-44) or the Ministry of Supply. In addition, it was able to purchase

Wartime on Britain's railways included the use of types produced in the USA and shipped for use in Europe. 25 of the S160 type were allocated to Woodford Halse and used on specific trains to particular destinations. (62) The influence of the designers of the locomotives from the USA can be seen in a type designed by R.A. Riddles during the war and of which over 700 were produced. 200 of the type were purchased from the War Department in 1946 by the LNER (63 – Colour-rail). Unfortunately for those who admire the aesthetics of locomotive design, H.G. Ivatt, A.H. Peppercorn and F.W. Hawksworth then took hold of the final designs up to 1951.

some of the latter, known as Austerities. In early to mid-1944, Mexborough and Neasden had a total of 19 and by the end of 1946 that number had grown to 46 (Mexborough 10, Gorton 10 and Woodford Halse 26). By the end of 1947, the total was 75 of which 48 were loaned, all 48 allocated to Mexborough.

Apart from when the needs of the nation were at the forefront and the former GCR London extension plus the link to Banbury/GWR was at full stretch, it is difficult to look beyond the allocation of B17s and A3s as being the highlights of the locomotive policy of the LNER in as much as it benefitted the former GCR. That in itself is a compliment to Parker, Pollitt and Robinson, who together provided a fleet of motive power which continued to work well beyond their life expectations and at the end owed no one anything at all.

Designer	Class MS&LR/GCR	LNER	Built	Qty	Final withdrawal
Sacré	GB	D12	1887-90	12	1929(1)
Parker	GDB	D8	1888	3	1825
Parker	2/2A	D7	1887-94	31	1938 (2)
Pollitt	11	D5	1895	6	1932 (1)
Pollitt	11A	D6	1897-99	33	1946 (2)
Robinson	11B/C/D	D9	1901-04	40	1949 (7)
Robinson	11E	D10	1913	10	1954 (3)
Robinson	11F	D11/1	1919-22	11	1961 (1)

Carriages, wagons and containers

Four of the constituent companies of the LNER had experience of working together on the provision of shared coaching stock; the GNR, NER and NB for the Anglo-Scottish traffic in East Coast Joint Stock, and the GCR with the GNR (and MR) for CLC traffic. The transition into the grouped LNER was, therefore, eased somewhat and the Traffic Superintendents and Passenger Managers of all the constituent companies met in committee to make recommendations around passenger services and passenger rolling stock. The Committee met monthly from November 1922 until late 1947 and as soon as the first days of 1923 resolved that there should be no central control for rolling stock. The reason was that each operating area controlled its own vehicles and had a voice in the determination of the annual Carriage Building Programme (CBP). The individual Area maintained its own allocation and it was unusual for vehicles to be 'borrowed' by others except in unusual circumstances. Control over vehicles was of particular relevance to maintaining trains in particular formations. For example, the 4pm London King's Cross to Newcastle (and other destinations by through carriages).

Vehicles	To	Arrival	Weight	Seats		Note
			Tons	1st	3rd	
Engine						
Brake, composite, twin	Leeds	8.5pm	48	10	48	
Third	Leeds	8.5pm	31	-	48	
Brake, composite	Leeds	8.5pm	30	12	18	
Brake, composite	Bradford	8.25pm	29	8	24	
Restaurant car, third	Newcastle	11.29pm	31	-	36	A
Restaurant car, first	Newcastle	11.29pm	33	21	-	A
Brake, third	York	8.15pm	25	-	28	B
Composite	York	8.15pm	29	12	27	B

Vehicles	To	Arrival	Weight	Seats		Note
			Tons	1st	3rd	
Brake, composite	Scarborough	9.18pm	30	12	18	C
Brake, composite	Cleethorpes	8.17pm	33	12	18	
Composite	Cleethorpes	8.17pm	33	21	32	
Third, semi open	Cleethorpes	8.17pm	30	-	48	
Brake van	Cleethorpes	8.17pm	26	-	-	
Brake, composite	Horncastle	7.32pm	33	12	18	
			441	120	363	

NOTES:

Leeds and Bradford, Cleethorpes and Horncastle detached at Doncaster. York and Scarborough at York. Newcastle cars added to another working at York.

A Return on 10.20am Newcastle – King's Cross weekdays, 10.10am Sundays

B Return on 11.10pm York as far as Grantham weekdays, then attached to 8.30am Grantham – King's Cross weekdays. Return on 10.00pm York Sundays

C Return on 10.37am Scarborough and attached to 12.20pm ex York.

Understandably, the central distribution of coaching stock was not, apparently, discussed again until 1939, when all-line control was established. The area organisation was abolished in 1942 and a central rolling stock control office established at York.

21,000 passenger vehicles came under the responsibility of the CME in 1923, of which less than 20 per cent were electrically lit and many were of the four and six wheeled variety. Shortly after Grouping, a series of standard carriage designs was developed and these (for both corridor and non-corridor) lasted with some modifications until 1941. Initially, the LNER favoured all-wooden bodies, using teak which provided a quiet ride and on their welded steel frames with centre couplings were safe in the event of derailment. Gresley was also attracted to articulation, perhaps more by the needs of general management for the savings in cost from using one less bogie for a twin set, two less for a triplet catering car set and so on, rather than the engineering consequences of such a policy.

The annual CBP was for the year commencing 1 April and was passed to the CME only when approved by the Board. However, Gresley initiated the process by the production for the Superintendents' and Passenger Managers' Committee (SPM) of a programme of withdrawal of stock; passenger vehicles 40 years old, other coaching stock 33 years. That programme identified the number of seats to be 'lost' and also the CME's own thoughts on new stock and its design. The SPM considered its needs and having done so presented them at a meeting attended also by the CME or his representative. The final recommendation went to the Chief General Manager who, in turn, reported it to the Locomotive and Traffic Committee, chaired for much of its long existence by the chairman of the board of directors. Approval or otherwise was then given, sometimes following a referral on the question of finance allocation. Finally, the CME was given the CBP to progress. For 1923, the costed programme was for £545,983 and included the provision of ten sleeping cars. From 1934, the CBP was made effective for the calendar year.

A review of the CBPs identifies the extent to which the needs of the former GCR were recognised:

1924/25 Proposed a set for the new Newcastle – South Wales service.

1930/31 Transfer from the ECJS of some 1924/25 built, third class standard LNER designs.

1931/32 Proposed the construction of 400 vehicles for services including Liverpool-Hull, Newcastle-Bournemouth, Cleethorpes and Leicester-Manchester, Newcastle-South Wales. This CBP was amended as a result of commercial pressure to counter new builds by the LMS; new stock for the ECJS resulted in displaced, older stock being 'cascaded' to other Areas.

1935 Noted that 276 six wheeled carriages were still in booked workings and a further 312

	were also available as required. Board intention to replace all by end 1936.
1937	Ten, five carriage sets for the Marylebone suburban services.
1938	Teak bodied excursion stock.
1939	Four, five carriage suburban sets for the Manchester district. Ten, five carriage train sets, including articulated twins for Hull-Leicester/Sheffield workings. Conversions for push pull workings.
1940	Six, five carriage train sets with articulated twins for semi-fast services.

A summary of the coaching stock produced by the LNER between 1923 and 1944 is:

Year	Built by LNER		Built by contractors	
	A	B	A	B
1923	203	110	-	-
1924	247	171	-	-
1925	248	387	353	-
1926	174	41	139	-
1927	201	108	206	8
1928	201	270	23	26
1929	217	344	118	-
1930	202	298	56	-
1931	110	107	33	-
1932	53	12	-	-
1933	81	94	40	-
1934	246	109	24	-
1935	339	17	308	-
1936	354	341	304	-
1937	309	218	235	-
1938	327	263	384	446
1939	286	856	96	554
1940	179	34	-	-
1941	74	32	-	-
1942	56	5	-	-
1943	25	32	-	-
1944	-	6	-	-

NOTES:
A Passenger carrying vehicles including kitchen cars and electric multiple units
B Other coaching stock

Whilst the former GCR was not exactly starved of investment, it is clear from the CBPs that the former GNR/ECJS line always enjoyed the highest priority. The use of scarce capital to fund high speed services using streamlined locomotives will be reviewed later in this

Above and next page: For vehicles used in passenger trains the LNER continued with the use of hardwood, principally teak. When lined out and varnished they would have presented a fine appearance, although the age of steam hardly supported the roofs being white. Examples are shown here at the North Norfolk Railway (56), Severn Valley Railway (57) and Great Central Railway (58). The LNER also applied articulation to some main line and suburban carriage sets: twins, triplets and quadruplets (59). Articulated sets were used on the CLC and Marylebone suburban sets from 1935. The last two pre-nationalisation carriages to remain in service with British Railways were of the type shown at photograph 60; built in the Thompson design era they were used in the *Flying Scotsman* train formations. Photographed in the carmine and cream livery of British Railways at the Llangollan Railway.

sub section. As was the case with its fleet of locomotives, the GCR lines continued to provide a return on earlier investment with minimal new expenditure.

Wagons and containers

At the Grouping the former GCR had 31,026 wagons of three main types absorbed by the LNER: open goods wagons (19,455), covered goods vans (3,146) and mineral (8,425). The largest contributor to the LNER total stock of these types being the NER; 108,031 out of 254,536. Unlike the GCR, the NER owned most of the mineral wagons used on its system and made 56,692 available, including 18,306 of 20 tons and over load capacity. However, nearly 70 per cent of mineral wagons on the LNER that were owned by that railway were of a load capacity of 12 tons or less. The rail industry and the coal industry were not ready, unable to or did not wish to invest in facilities to receive and load larger wagons and, in recognition of this the Railway Clearing House issued in 1923 a new specification for a 'standard' 12 ton load capacity wagon. That initiative supported a move by the grouped companies to eliminate excessive empty mileage in returning wagons to their home territory by forming a common user pool of all railway-owned ordinary open goods, coal and mineral wagons, together with non-brake fitted goods vans. After 1923, each company contributed to the construction and maintenance of the common pool in proportion to the freight it carried. The LNER was the second largest of the four, at 38 per cent of the total.

Whilst that helped somewhat with railway owned wagons, the fleets of privately-owned wagons remained a major operational headache; at 1928 a national census revealed a total of 578,626 coal and coke wagons which, by 1937 had grown to 592,498 (with an average capacity of 10.91 tons).

The number of LNER wagons fitted with vacuum/Westinghouse brakes as at 1923 was less than 4 per cent of their total fleet and whilst it became the practice for any new builds to be through piped (i.e. able to pass air, but not apply brakes on the vehicle) to enable braked wagons to function, the rate of investment in the vacuum braking system was woeful. As at 1953, the number of fitted goods trains on the former GCR London extension had not moved on from 1939 with nine weekday (Tuesdays-Fridays) services, four of which were for fish (and a new one for Guinness).

One new area in which the LNER participated and invested was in the containered traffic. The build-up seems to have been concentrated on express goods services from King's Cross Goods. The Railway Clearing

House quickly saw the potential and produced a design for a container which could be carried on a flat, two wheeled wagon or in an open goods wagon. As the idea became more widely accepted and applied further types of container of varying capacities appeared; in the case of the LNER eleven variants for a vast range of goods such as furniture, bicycles, pianos, perishable meat and vegetables. The growth in the difficult economic times of the early 1930s demonstrated the potential for such containerisation:

Year	Total of containers
1931	6,290
1932	7,027
1933	8,553
1934	10,514
1935	11,269
1936	13,034
1937	13,845

For all of the former GCR lines, it is difficult to identify any clear benefit from the LNER wagon and container policies. Although common pooling may have made a marginal difference for the better the predominance of privately-owned coal and coke wagons continued throughout and required different areas of investment funding.

Marine shipping
The LNER sought to develop certain of its routes, particularly from Harwich/Parkeston Quay. In 1927, the Dutch Zeeland Shipping company relocated to Parkeston Quay from Folkestone, thus permitting a twice daily sailing service to the Vlissingen. To support this service, the LNER invested in new ships, *Vienna* in 1929, *Prague* and *Amsterdam* in 1930.

In addition, the LNER acquired the motor ferry *Brightlingsea* in 1925, the cargo carrier *Sheringham* the following year and three train ferries built in 1924; these last three having been previously owned/operated by Great Eastern Train Ferries Ltd. which ceased trading in 1932. To support the development of traffic from Harwich, the shipping company DFDS operated services to Esbjerg and in 1931 the three companies (LNER, Zeeland and DFDS) were together offering services to Vlissingen, Esbjerg, Hoek of Holland, Antwerp and Zeebrugge. Transferred from Grimsby (ex GCR) in the 1920s came *Accrington* and *Dewsbury* for Antwerp and excursion traffic, but the latter sailings ceased in 1931. Following the Second World War, *Arnhem* replaced *Vienna* (a war casualty in 1941). A further train ferry was added in 1947, *Suffolk Ferry*; two of the original fleet of three having been acquired for war service, converted as landing craft carriers and lost in one action or another. Scottish services were refreshed by the arrivals of *Jeanie Deans* (1931), *Talisman* (1935), *Thane of Fife* (1937) and the one which survives to this day as an ocean-going paddle steamer, *Waverley* (1947).

For the former GCR marine activities centred upon Grimsby, the approach was less supportive. From the Grouping, the LNER had taken under its managerial wing the fleets of The Wilson's and North Eastern Railway Shipping Co. Ltd. (eight ships) and the Hull & Netherlands Steamship Co. Ltd. (three ships). The ships and their service lives with the owners mentioned were:

Wilson's (all passenger and cargo carrying):

Hero	1906-24
Juno	1906-26
Otto	1906-35
Hull	1907-37
York	1907-37
Darlington	1910-35
Selby	1922-58
Harrogate	1925-58

Hull & Netherlands:

Whitby Abbey	1908-36
Jervaulx Abbey	1908-36
Melrose Abbey	1929-59

For its Hull-New Holland Ferry services the following were acquired:

Tattersall Castle	1934
Wingfield Castle	1934
Frodingham	1936
Lincoln Castle	1940

In 1935, a shipping managing company – Associated Humber Lines – was formed to manage the LNER's own eight-strong fleet, plus those of the Goole Steamship

Co. (which previously managed the seventeen-strong LMS Goole based fleet), Hull & Netherlands Steamship Co. and Thomas Wilson, Sons & Co. (the four remaining Wilson's fleet). Under the terms of the agreement the vessels remained in the ownership of the various companies until 1957 when – for those then surviving – Associated Humber Lines became the owner in its own name.

Marine installations

In pursuit of economies and cash, in 1937 the LNER sold Tyne Dock to the Tyne Improvement Commission for £650,000 and thus avoided an impending heavy maintenance outlay.

The revenue expenditure account for docks, harbours and wharves in 1928 recorded the only loss in the period 1923-38. This corresponds to the timing of the proposed transfer to Harwich of the Zeeland Shipping Co's sailings and support activities and also of the sailings proposed by DFDS. I assume, therefore, that the costs were charged to revenue account and no investment was involved.

One business case for investment that could hardly fail even in the difficult times of the early 1930s was that for a new fish dock (number three) at Grimsby. It was a scheme dating back to GCR days but was postponed and postponed until absolutely essential. Here, at least was a benefit to former GCR line services, but elsewhere under shipping generally it was – as for locomotives, carriages and wagons – a case of minimal rations.

Major new works

It quickly became apparent at the Central Wagon Control office at York that there were major problems with goods trains heading for London via the routes through March and that empty, privately owned mineral wagons arriving back into the yards serving the Nottinghamshire, Derbyshire and Yorkshire coalfields had taken far too long to be sorted at March and sent on their way back for loading. The problem at March was that the LNER had inherited four small yards, each having limited capacity, and with a need for 'trip' workings between each to assemble trains for different areas. The problem with the return empties was multiple private owners with a relatively small number of wagons in any number of daily arrivals. The single solution to both problems was via investment in a new 'up' yard at March (opened 1928) and a 'down' yard, completed in 1931, with Norwood yard (1933) on the 'down' side used for sorting empties before they were forwarded to either the next yard or final destination yard. At the up yard, there was a capacity for 3,311 wagons plus ten reception lines holding 80 wagons each, replacing the need for yards at Peterborough East, at Whitemoor and elsewhere at March. The new yard enabled coal traffic from Colwick to East Anglia to no longer travel via Grantham and the GN line to Peterborough, but instead go via Sleaford and the former GN/GE joint line to Whitemoor, the reduction of trains daily on the former route reducing from thirty-four to seven, whilst on the latter increasing from twenty-three to fifty-seven. A new locomotive running shed was built at March to service the 186 locomotives allocated there (107 in 1922). The reduction in the number of coal trains using the GN Grantham-Peterborough section was particularly useful to the LNER aspirations for that route.

The problem of sorting wagons was also acute along the eastern approach to Manchester off the GC Woodhead route. It was the norm for trains to stand for far too long awaiting access to small yards such as Godley having inadequate facilities. The need to sort traffic heading beyond Manchester was met by investment in a new, better equipped yard at Mottram.

The NER had been at the forefront of electrification schemes; its 650v d.c. North Tyneside system having been installed in 1904 and was developed (1913-16) with a 1500v d.c. (overhead) system for coal traffic between Shildon (County Durham) and Newport (Teesside). The line became redundant with the decline in demand and at the end of 1934 all ten locomotives were stored, serviceable. The potential conversion of the locomotives to diesel power for use between New England and Ferme Park was considered with English Electric but based upon the projected traction equipment and its weight, the project did not proceed. One of the locomotives was used at Ilford depot for shunting (1949-60), but the others were withdrawn. More fortunate was the MSJ&A line (shared with the LMS) which was electrified with the 1500v d.c. system and opened in May 1931 with 24 vehicles.

The Central Electricity Board's national grid then under construction would reduce/eliminate the need for costly, bespoke generating stations specifically for railway systems and future prospects for electrification (the Weir Committee on main line railway electrification).

Mottram yard was the first West of Woodhead at which traffic for the Manchester area and beyond could be segregated. The picture shows the control tower and the staff amenities block for inspectors, shunters and wagon chasers. The electrification masts had been in place for several years awaiting investment finance and with that having been made available the days of 04s heading through Woodhead tunnel were numbered (Colour Rail 306359).

The advice from the committee was that a 7 per cent return on capital investment could be expected. Apart from the Southern Railway, the other grouped companies were not particularly attracted to the idea of electrification, partly because of the financial implications and also that steam traction could be developed for the higher speed passenger services.

Electrification of the passenger system on South Tyneside was, however, authorised in 1935 and in order to be compatible with North Tyneside (and use reconditioned stock whilst the north received new twin unit replacements) was at 650v d.c. Of the two systems either side of the Tyne, the north was the larger; having 64 coaches in twins, two spares and two parcels vans whilst the South had 17 coaches and one parcels van ('live' 1938).

Larger scale schemes were also proposed and to use the 1500v d.c. overhead method. Firstly, Manchester-Woodhead-Sheffield/Wath was proposed, agreed and work had just started before the outbreak of war caused a lengthy interruption – it was completed in 1954 – and secondly proposed for the GER Liverpool Street-Shenfield, also started, but was deferred by the outbreak of war. The question of improvements for the northern suburbs along the GN route from King's Cross was not easily resolvable until the intentions for, and of, the London Transport Passenger Board were clearer and financial arrangements agreed with the London Electric Transport Finance Corporation.

How times and policies change and can be changed when politicians so desire. Stanley Baldwin enjoyed or endured three tenures as Prime Minister (1923-24, late

1924-29 and 1935-37). Only in his final stewardship were economic conditions improving both at home and internationally. The policy of a period of low interest rates, projects to reduce unemployment and pump incomes into the economy, the growth of new lighter industries and a more confident population in the south east of the country responding to the availability of mortgages for affordable properties within thirty miles of London and excursions by rail all helped 'lift' the approach to life generally. National esteem was also important. Having the fastest trains, holding the Blue Riband for the fastest transatlantic crossing by passenger liner (lost to the '*Normandie*' of France in 1934) were important to some, though not to most in the north east, Lancashire and the Midlands.

When Gresley returned in 1934 from a short visit to Germany where he had seen the high-speed running of the two car, streamlined, diesel powered '*Fliegender Hamburger*' between Berlin and Hamburg, he considered the possibility of introducing a similar service between London King's Cross and Newcastle. The makers of the railcar could offer an average speed for the 268 miles of 63 mph which Gresley thought could be bettered by steam. With board support (and

Above and opposite: As economic conditions improved after the mid-1930s the LNER and LMS embarked on a programme to introduce streamlined locomotives and high-quality express trains between London and Scotland plus, in the case of the LNER, particular cities in Yorkshire. To haul the trains Sir Nigel Gresley designed the A4 pacific locomotives which appeared first in silver grey and, later, in blue, lined out in white and red to enhance the streamlined front. One of the class – *Mallard* – attained in 1938 a World record speed for steam locomotives of 126 mph and is seen to the right of classmate *Bittern* at Barrow Hill roundhouse (54). Six A4s were preserved and the four in the UK have all seen activity on the main network and at heritage railways. Some impression of the power and physical attraction of an A4 may be gained from photograph 55, taken at the Severn Valley Railway.

54

presumably government support for making available funds on attractive terms) it was decided to introduce a high speed streamlined train in the Autumn of 1935 to be named *Silver Jubilee*, marking 25 years of the reign of George V. For the train, a new class of locomotive was designed (the A4) and the first one, *Silver Link*, was completed in September 1935 and test runs with the new passenger stock held on the 27th; seventy miles of the test run being covered at an average of 91.8 mph. The construction cost of the locomotive was around £8,500 and a further 34 were built before the end of 1938, 17 with government financial assistance. To run with the locomotive, a seven-carriage set was built in 1935 at Doncaster; two twins and a triplet restaurant car. This new set was to be regarded as East Coast stock and the cost was not to increase the costed build programme for 1935/36; achieved by the other areas of the LNER giving up new build vehicles in the programme. The *Silver Jubilee* was certainly a technical success and whilst the figures presented varied (Gresley claiming gross receipts per train mile from running the train of 13s 11d whilst operating expenses were no more than 2s 6d, and Bell, the Assistant General Manager, claiming 16s 2d (including catering) against direct expenses of 4s 2d, compared to 5s/2s 6d for the LNER average). They were, of course, much simpler times, without cause to examine pay back periods and opportunity costs.

Emboldened by the commercial success of the *Silver Jubilee*, the LNER developed the streamlined train concept by introducing the *Coronation* (two sets plus another as a spare for this), the *Silver Jubilee* and the then proposed Leeds service, the *West Riding Limited*. The *Coronation* service to Edinburgh was introduced on 5 July 1937 and the *West Riding Limited* to Leeds/Bradford on 27 September 1937.

Doubtless as part of the agreement with Railway Finance Corporation, orders for new build carriage construction in 1936 and 1937 were placed with Birmingham Railway Carriage and Wagon Co., Metropolitan Cammell Carriage Wagon & Finance Co. Ltd. and Craven.

The operation of the high-speed services caused difficulties to the operating department, in particular signalling headways (double 'blocking' being decided) and adequate braking distances. This latter requirement was met by converting some of the mechanical distant signals to ground level colour light type. The LNER mainly used single lens searchlight signals, the need for double yellow warning signals being met by a second, separate lamp head. The GCR had made a modest start with three-aspect automatic colour sight signals on the final approach to Marylebone. Shortly after that, the NER pioneered all electric relay interlocking which revolutionised the signalling and points of selected routes as shown on an illuminated track diagram. The first installation in 1933 was at Thirsk as part of the re-signalling of the 30 mile York-Northallerton route and was followed by a second, at Northallerton.

Having trains covering 70 miles at an average speed of over 90 mph was a mechanical triumph; the need for track to be maintained to allow such speeds was a civil engineering challenge that had to be overcome. Whether or not the civil or signalling costs were taken into account when assessing the return on the initial investment is unclear, but there surely must have been significant costs to upgrade and maintain the 393 miles to Edinburgh and the short section between Doncaster and Leeds. The actual amounts expended by the LNER on maintenance of way and works were (actuals, not adjusted):

Year	£
1927	6,000,297
1928	5,988,345
1929	6,015,405
1930	5,565,784
1931	5,078,157
1932	4,659,079
1933	4,460,499
1934	4,655,443
1935	4,837,661
1936	5,097,420

Nearly £1m less in 1936 than 1929. One conclusion that could be drawn is that whilst the GN/NER main line benefitted, those in the other areas and elsewhere in the Southern Area (the GER and GCR lines) suffered. Regarding civil engineering, it is worthy of note that no significant expenditure seems to have been needed to be expended upon the London extension of the former GCR, 1897 to 1937. So much for those who said it was a poor investment; hard usage in peace time and the war years to come would inevitably take its toll, but it continued in an uncomplaining matter of fact way, just as did its locomotives, rolling stock and workforce.

The LNER enjoyed a good safety record between 1928 and 1935, but in its total time accounted for the lives of 182 passengers and staff in 13 serious incidents. Having a system of automatic warning for drivers would probably have prevented 42 of the deaths and a system of track circuits approaching home signals another 38.

As early as 1895, a substantial portion of the NER main line was equipped with a mechanical system devised and patented by Vincent Raven; commonly known as 'fogging apparatus' it worked by a trip lever between the rails coming into contact with a 'shoe' under the locomotive. If the 'shoe' came into contact a linking rod actuated an audible warning in the cab and also started to apply the brake. The apparatus could then be re-set by the driver. Following the Grouping, the LNER continued with the system and in 1929 made a strong point when issuing an edict that Southern Area-based A3 pacifics on through workings to Newcastle *not* fitted with Raven Fog Signalling Apparatus must on no account be allowed to work trains over the line between York and Alnmouth. Nevertheless, to the dismay of ASLEF and its members, particularly on the LNER, the equipment ceased to be used on and from 30 October 1933.

A disastrous collision at Castlecary (between Glasgow and Edinburgh) on 10 December 1937 in falling snow occurred when two trains passed a distant signal which they testified was clear but may well have been affected by a build-up of ice and snow. Both trains then collided with another train ahead. 35 people lost their lives and the Chief Inspecting Officer made a pointed recommendation that the LNER should take a further look at automatic train control, which it did, the Hudd system, which worked on electro-magnetic inductive principles without any direct contact between locomotive fittings and track equipment. In times of financial stringency, the LNER Board placed a heavy burden upon the shoulders and eyes of its footplatemen and could/should have done more by investing in automatic train control.

National pride was well in evidence with the news in July 1938 that one of Gresley's A4s, *Mallard*, had attained a world speed record of 126 mph with a test train between Grantham and Peterborough. Furthermore, another beneficiary of the government's economic recovery programme – the RMS *Queen Mary* – had regained for Britain the coveted Blue Riband.

Minor works supported by government funding
Of note were station improvement works (though none being GCR), expenditure on locomotive turning facilities (including Neasden, Leicester, Manchester Central and Liverpool) and new mechanical coaling plants (including Gorton), doubling of lines and installation of running loops.

Ancillary businesses
The investment in bus companies has already been covered. An additional initiative was by all four grouped companies to acquire Pickford removals firm and also Carter Paterson, a parcels carrying firm in 1930.

Sadly, Europe was then enveloped by the threat of another war which duly came to pass. The proud streamlined, train services were operated for the final time on 3 August 1939; one *Coronation* set and the spare set were despatched to Deeside for storage at Ballater, the second *Coronation* set was stored at Doncaster where three vehicles were damaged by fire and the *West Riding* set was stored at Copley Hill, Leeds. Following cessation of hostilities, the state of the track made very high-speed train working impracticable. Vehicles from the *Coronation* set re-appeared in ordinary trains including the GCR line *Master Cutler* and between Manchester and Cleethorpes. Other vehicles found longevity on King's Cross-Edinburgh workings until 1963/64, whilst two caught fire near Huntingdon. The two observation cars survived into preservation; one being at the Great Central Railway at Loughborough, Leicestershire. The A4 pacifics saw service until the mid-1960s, *Mallard* plus five more surviving and including number 9 which saw service on the GCR line for a month in 1941.

For holders of LNER preferred ordinary 5 per cent stock (of which there was some £42m) the period from 1929 to 1939 was dire; the average dividend declared for 1924-34 having been 0.54 per cent and for 1935-39 zero. By comparison, the holders of ordinary stock in the Great Western had received 4.17 per cent and 2.8 per cent respectively, though both the LMS and Southern were less at 1.13 per cent/0.85 per cent and 0.63 per cent/0.65 per cent respectively. For the wartime years only, the LNER failed to be able to declare a dividend for those holders, the GWR again leading with 4.42 per cent, followed in 1946-47 by 6.14 per cent (LMS, Southern and LNE 3.82 per cent, 3.54 per cent and 0.41 per cent respectively).

In 1941, the government gave the railway companies a guaranteed net, annual revenue of £43.5m, with the government taking any surplus above that figure. It was, for the government, a very good deal. In 1941-45, the railways earned £412.6m, but £195.3m (47 per cent) was retained by the Treasury. At the same time, cost inflation was rampant. Recovery via charging was possible to only a limited extent (from July 1946) and then by only 7-14 per cent. A further adjustment was allowed from October 1947, but a large gap between charges and costs remained.

With the outbreak of the Second World War, the administration of the railways of Britain was placed with the Railway Executive Committee. That body had been sanctioned by an Order dated 24 September 1938 and acted in an advisory capacity until the Emergency Powers Defence Act of August 1939 empowered the Ministry of Transport to take over the railways and that was put into effect by the Emergency (Railway Control) Order of 1 September 1939.

The Committee was chaired by Sir Ralph Wedgwood (LNER) with Sir James Milne (GWR) as vice-chairman. The plans as then implemented included the withdrawal of luxury and non-essential passenger train movements to allow for troop trains, air raid precautions, restricted lighting for the black-out, speedy repair to damaged infrastructure and evacuation of much of the civilian population from Greater London, Merseyside, Manchester, Glasgow and Clydebank plus other cities and centres with a high probability of being targets of air raids. The plans also included the requisition of all privately-owned wagons, the withdrawal of most restaurant and sleeping car facilities and, from later September 1939, all special excursion trains, with a National Emergency Timetable introduced from 25 September 1939. Station name boards were removed in 1940 and flows of troops, munitions and military hardware routed mainly to Southampton, Dover, Harwich, Avonmouth and South Wales ports, whilst reinforcements for the garrisons in the Mediterranean and Middle East were mainly dealt with through Merseyside and Clydeside. Once the threat of invasion had receded, a daily Ashford (Kent)-Newcastle (and return) via Banbury (to which point a Southern Railway locomotive worked) train avoiding London was introduced for service personnel.

Operationally, the war brought improvements to the Nottingham-Woodford section. New up and down line loops were installed at Ruddington, Loughborough and Ashby Magna with new up loops also at Quorn, Rugby and Charwelton. New sidings were installed at Barby to serve a War Department facility and at Woodford the capacity of the yards was significantly increased by the provision of a new, 11 road up yard and a new four roads plus 12 siding down yard. These new facilities were to the north of the existing yards and to assist in the servicing of longer locomotives the facility of a 54-foot diameter turntable was augmented by a turning triangle. The big step forward was the reduction in need to propel goods trains into refuge sidings to allow faster traffic to be given priority. Lengthy block sections with the adverse ruling gradient of 1 in 176 (up direction) were the factors limiting route capacity, relieved to some extent by the installation of semi-automatic and intermediate block signals in the particularly difficult sections between Whetstone and Ashby Magna/Staverton Road and Charwelton, where the line climbed through Catesby tunnel. In common with much of the rest of the networks the maximum permitted speed for passenger trains was 60 mph (emergency timetable introduced shortly after the outbreak of war) and 40 mph for goods traffic. The consequential reduction in track maintenance led to the inevitable progressive worsening of condition, exacerbated north of Nottingham by mining subsidence.

During the war, carriage of some eight million tons of coal annually by sea from north east England ports to London/southern England was suspended. The bulk of the additional rail traffic was sent via Colwick (GNR) to Ferme Park as 'through' trains (40/week) and from Peterborough also to Ferme Park (about 100 trains/week). Even at that rate, the total additional demand could have been met only by using all the available routes, including those of the MR and GCR.

The final tremendous task of railway planning before victory was for the invasion of France in 1944; Overlord or D-Day. The planning and implementation provide an example of how the former GCR lines became very valuable to the national interest. Planning for an invasion of Europe with the support of US troops and material had been continuous since early 1942; code name BOLERO for the planning, ROUNDUP and SLEDGEHAMMER for the operational phases. The first BOLERO key plan (31 May 1942) was based upon 1,049,000 American troops and an invasion date of Spring 1943; to achieve that 100,000 to 120,000 men per month would be sent to Britain together with material, using 80 ships of some 40,000 dead-weight tons. To create temporary accommodation for the arriving troops, British personnel would be transferred away from the south west of England. However, a strategic decision to invade North Africa (TORCH) in Autumn 1942 placed BOLERO on hold and the planned availability of the 1,049,000 troops moved to end of 1943. That proved impossible due to planned operations in the Mediterranean (summer 1943), heavy losses in Atlantic convoys due to enemy action, priority lend lease of equipment to the Soviet Union and imports of foodstuffs to Great Britain.

The fourth and last BOLERO plan appeared on 12 July 1943 and projected an invasion in spring 1944 involving 1,340,000 US troops (and British and Allied forces) and requiring up to 160 cargo ships to arrive in the UK in April 1944. The number became 1,446,000 and the date slipped to 1 May 1944, but the plan was for real and, from late spring 1943, the ports and railways became heavily involved in the logistics.

The troops arrived predominantly at Glasgow and on Merseyside with other ports also on the safer, west coast of Britain – Bristol Channel and Belfast – taking large numbers. The volume and tonnage of material was such that continuously from summer 1943, the Humber ports of Hull and Immingham were called upon and shipments taken South by rail:

Month	Tonnage '000
July 1943	41
August 1943	48
September 1943	73
October 1943	73
November 1943	85
December 1943	94
January 1944	72
February 1944	46
March 1944	86
April 1944	120
May 1944	220
June 1944	217

Around the clock, a constant flow of these additional heavy goods trains and returning empties was directed towards the holding yards of Southern and South Western England, utilising the new yard (1941) at Woodford Halse and then being directed via Banbury, Didcot and Reading or via a new (1940) connection at Calvert allowing access to the Cambridge-Oxford line (see later reference in chapter 9). The railway operating authorities sought to match train loads to best available motive power. Between mid-1943 and mid-1944 Woodford Halse had an allocation of 25 of the USA Transportation Corps S160 2-8-0s which were used on specific services to a limited number of destinations. The UK Ministry of Transport Riddles designed Austerity 2-8-0s were becoming available but as at February 1944, the GC lines had just ten and all were at Mexborough (46 at the end of 1946, with 26 then allocated to Woodford Halse). Wartime requirements had also influenced the allocation to Annesley of K3 2-6-0s; 16 being based there in November 1943, doubtless as part of the planning. Their B7 4-6-0s went to Gorton and the build-up of the K3s at Annesley (and other former GC sheds) depleted the stock at Gorton from 31 (July 1943) to nil (November 1943). Darnall had nine K3s (1940-45), receiving them from York and Scotland, and Immingham 11, whilst Woodford Halse had up to seven (March 1943: but reallocated when the S160 class arrived. After the S160 class members were moved on the stock of K3s increased to 16 and they remained until 1944-49).

All of the industrial centres of Scotland, the north and Midlands of England and particularly London suffered from bombing and rocket attacks. The day to day railway operations in the London area called upon the resolve of management and staff to start each day with whatever circumstances faced them and somehow keep services running.

Of related interest is the effect upon the shipping fleet with some tragic losses through enemy action, scuttling of vessels to try (unsuccessfully) to prevent use by the enemy and one case of a sale which resulted in that ship (the renamed *Darlington*) being bombed and sunk off Malta in 1941 by allied bombing. The list is:

Amsterdam	mined, 1944, during D-Day operations as a hospital ship
Archangel	sunk off East Scotland, 1941
City of Bradford	sunk off Malta, 1942
Darlington	as noted above 1941 having previously been used as a blockade runner in the Spanish Civil War
Malines	torpedoed, 1943
Munich	scuttled off Amsterdam, 1940
St Denis	scuttled off Amsterdam, 1940
Stockport	sunk by enemy action having picked up survivors from convoy shipping, 1943
Train ferries 2 and 3	converted to landing craft carriers, lost off French coast, 1940/45

The heavy utilisation of the railways with reduced maintenance of the assets was inevitable, but a lack of maintenance over a period of time simply aggregated the scale of the developing problem. That the railways performed as they did is a great credit to them and to the wartime Railway Executive Committee. The degree of reliance upon the former GCR London extension should not be understated.

The demands placed upon the railways during years of war took their toll on the fleets of traction and rolling stock. Reduced levels of maintenance of a fleet, which in peacetime would have been replaced in part by newly-built stock, became more apparent through reduced availability. The building during the war of 1,300 new locomotives helped the motive power position but 40 per cent of the total stock was over 55 years old. Of the 563,000 privately owned wagons which

Following the end of the war, the four grouped railways started on the road to recovery/nationalisation. Gone were the days of streamliners and, to assist maintenance, the fairings on the A4s were removed. In later days, *Sir Nigel Gresley* is seen priming to great visual effect on a day otherwise too warm to produce steam effects at the Great Central Railway.

were requisitioned and pooled for the years of war, over 50 per cent were over 35 years old. The railway companies' own fleets of locomotives were superior to the Ministry supply and their age profile reflected the investment of the inter-war years. The continuous high demand for coaching stock, the use of railway workshops for production of military equipment and general shortage of materials/labour had resulted in very little new build of passenger vehicles. 21.6 per cent of the fleet of coaching stock was over 35 years old.

Despite the increase in traffic, renewal of the permanent way in 1940-44 was reduced to under 70 per cent of pre-war levels equivalent at end 1945 to a backlog of two years' work. Similarly, viaducts, bridges, tunnels and buildings had suffered a reduction in maintenance.

The wartime Railway Control Agreement between the government and the companies included trust funds and were based upon arrears measured against pre-war expenditure. The trust funds amounted to £56.6m; by 1945 the account (adjusted for inflation) stood at £148.2m. Of course, the companies never saw actual cash; only £2.5m was taken out of the trust funds and the balance credited to the British Transport Commission following nationalisation. The companies also pursued claims for abnormal wear and tear plus war damage. The former was settled at £46m and the latter deferred until a proportion was paid under a grant under the War Damage Act of 1949.

The LNER was – by any measure – in a very difficult physical and commercial position. However,

The first Summer following the War and a pair of GCR Class 8F 4-6-0s – then 40 years old and with their lives extended by the demands of wartime – have a long excursion train. The big event of the day was a horse race meeting at Lincoln and the train may well have originated at Cleethorpes. The first two carriages are Gresley design, the fourth has the shape of a Barnum saloon and the third – a twelve-wheeler – may well have been an aged GN/MS&LR dining car (Rail on-line).

some things just had to be done. The condition of the Woodhead tunnels was causing serious concern and in November 1947, the Works Committee approved the construction of a new, double line tunnel at an estimated cost of £2.28m. Contracts could not be let before nationalisation; that project had to wait, as did electrification of the route, the electrification of Liverpool Street-Shenfield, widening works on the GN – and much more.

CHAPTER 5

PROGRAMME OF NATIONALISATION AND PLANNING TO 1955

The scope of this book is now widened to include references to the development of two organisations which influenced the relative fortunes of British Railways in the period 1948-65: the National Coal Board (NCB) and the British Electricity Authority/Central Electricity Generating Board (BEA/CEGB). There is a view held by many interested in railways that somehow the industry existed and sustained itself in its own right; nothing could be further from reality. As this and subsequent chapters will seek to identify, British Railways needed to work far more closely with organisations upon which it relied than seems to have been the case.

The Second World War ceased in Europe several months before doing so in the Far East. To general relief, VE (Victory in Europe) Day on 8 May 1945 signalled the end of the horrific years of war. Winston Churchill, as Conservative leader of the national government, offered to Labour MP Clement Attlee, his Deputy Prime Minister who had very effectively managed 'home' affairs, an extension of the then existing terms of government until the expected victory in the Far East was achieved. Attlee declined and a General Election was called for 5 July: summertime. Because of the much awaited and enjoyed return to peacetime with its traditional holiday weeks, particularly in the industrial heartlands, and also because many thousands of the electorate were still overseas, the counting of votes (73 per cent turnout) and declaration of the result was delayed until 26 July. The result of the first General Election since 1935 was a landslide victory for the Labour Party; an 11.6 per cent voter swing away from the Conservatives and a majority in the House of Commons of 145 seats. Given that Churchill had so skilfully guided Great Britain through the war that, in itself, should reasonably have counted for more, but the electorate was distrustful of the Conservatives in peacetime regarding any potential return to mass unemployment and losses of hard-won social reforms.

Additionally, Attlee, Herbert Morrison (Home Office) and Ernest Bevin (Ministry of Labour) had, during the years of war, demonstrated their abilities and were ready with a compelling 'Let us Face the Future' manifesto that promoted: full employment; a National Health Service (NHS); a system of social security; a programme of nationalisation; economic planning; and the prospect of the country's gross domestic product and exports being boosted by improved industrial efficiency.

That manifesto proved more persuasive than the Conservative's 'Churchill Factor' and, subsequently, the Labour Party formed its first majority government. The programme of nationalisation was planned to include the following, spread over a number of parliamentary annual sessions: the Bank of England; coal; electricity; inland transport (principally the railways), docks and wharves, road haulage industry; omnibuses and tramways, air-ways, London's buses and underground railways; iron and steel; and cables and telecommunications.

With a full five-year term in prospect and with the considerable benefit of post-war Marshall Aid in the form of gifts and loans from the USA and the Commonwealth (totalling some £2bn) and international trade resuming, progress with the programme was made.

By the end of 1949, the Labour Party felt confident that rather than wait until the spring, they would call a General Election for 23 February 1950. For that election, changes were introduced which affected 170 constituencies and made the outcome more difficult to predict. As it turned out (83 per cent) Labour attracted the highest

The post (Second World) War political drive for a programme of nationalisation.

number of votes (46.1 per cent) but finished with a vastly reduced working majority of just eight seats. The programme of nationalisation featured in the electioneering, with the Conservatives saying that whilst they would retain the NHS and social security arrangements, they would end the programme as proposed to be extended by Labour (to include cement, sugar, chemicals, water and insurance). For the by then nationalised railways, the Conservative approach would have been to reorganise into a number of regional systems each with its own pride of identity and each administered by its own board of directors where members would have practical experience of serving public needs. Both parties promised mechanisms to restrict the powers of monopoly organisations. A probable influence on voting patterns and turnout was the increase in levels of personal taxation (to 40 per cent).

Whichever party was in power, the programme of reforms had to be paid for. Taxation – both direct personal and indirect – had been increasing. The number of tax paying families had increased and would continue so to do:

Tax year	Number of families paying tax (millions)
1938/39	3.8
1948/49	14.5
1958/59	17.7
1968/69	20.7

Assisted by a continuation of the policy of low interest rates, private housing development continued and with electrical supplies as standard. Despite material shortages and allocations hindering industrial recovery and rationing in place for certain foods and essentials, the country was starting to recover.

After only 20 months, a further General Election was called for 25 October 1951. The timing owed something to the failing health of George VI and plans for him to undertake a lengthy tour overseas; with a government having such a slim working majority he ideally would not wish to be away from the country. For the Election, Labour ran under 'Proud of its record, sure of its policies – confidently asks the electors to renew its mandate' and promoted four key needs, to: work for peace (the Korean War then progressing); work to maintain full employment and to increase production; reduce the cost of living; and build a just society.

The Conservative Party ran under 'Britain Strong and Free' and stressed safeguarding 'our traditional way of life'. Their intention would be to repeal the nationalising Steel Act and stop all further nationalisation. With another high turnout (82.6 per cent), the Labour Party, again polled the higher number of votes, but lost on the 'first past the post' in terms of number of seats won. The Conservative Party was back in power (and would remain so for 13 years) with Winston Churchill as Prime Minister. As will be referred to later in this chapter, the political changes of 1950/51 affected the organisation and planning for the British Transport Commission (BTC) more so than for coal and electricity and left them playing 'catch-up'.

Economic indicators of the period were:

Year	Annual rate of inflation %	Bank of England minimum lending rate %
1945	2.8	2
1946	3.1	2
1947	7	2
1948	7.7	2
1949	2.8*	2
1950	3.1	2
1951	9.1	2/2½
1952	9.2	2½/4
1953	3.1	4/3½
1954	1.8	3½/3
1955	4.5	3½/4½

NOTES:
* devaluation of sterling/redirection of resources to support export markets.

The pathway to nationalisation in 1947 was eased by two major changes made in earlier years. First, the Coal Act 1938 had abolished the private ownership of coal deposits and of coal royalties. The ownership of coal royalties and hence the power to grant leases for the working of coal passed in 1942 to the Coal Commission. Secondly, labour relation arrangements within the industry as between the workforce and the owners and also as between different local district branches of the Miners' Federation of Great Britain (MFGB) had been eased somewhat by an agreement to replace the MFGB with a National Union of Mineworkers (NUM), with

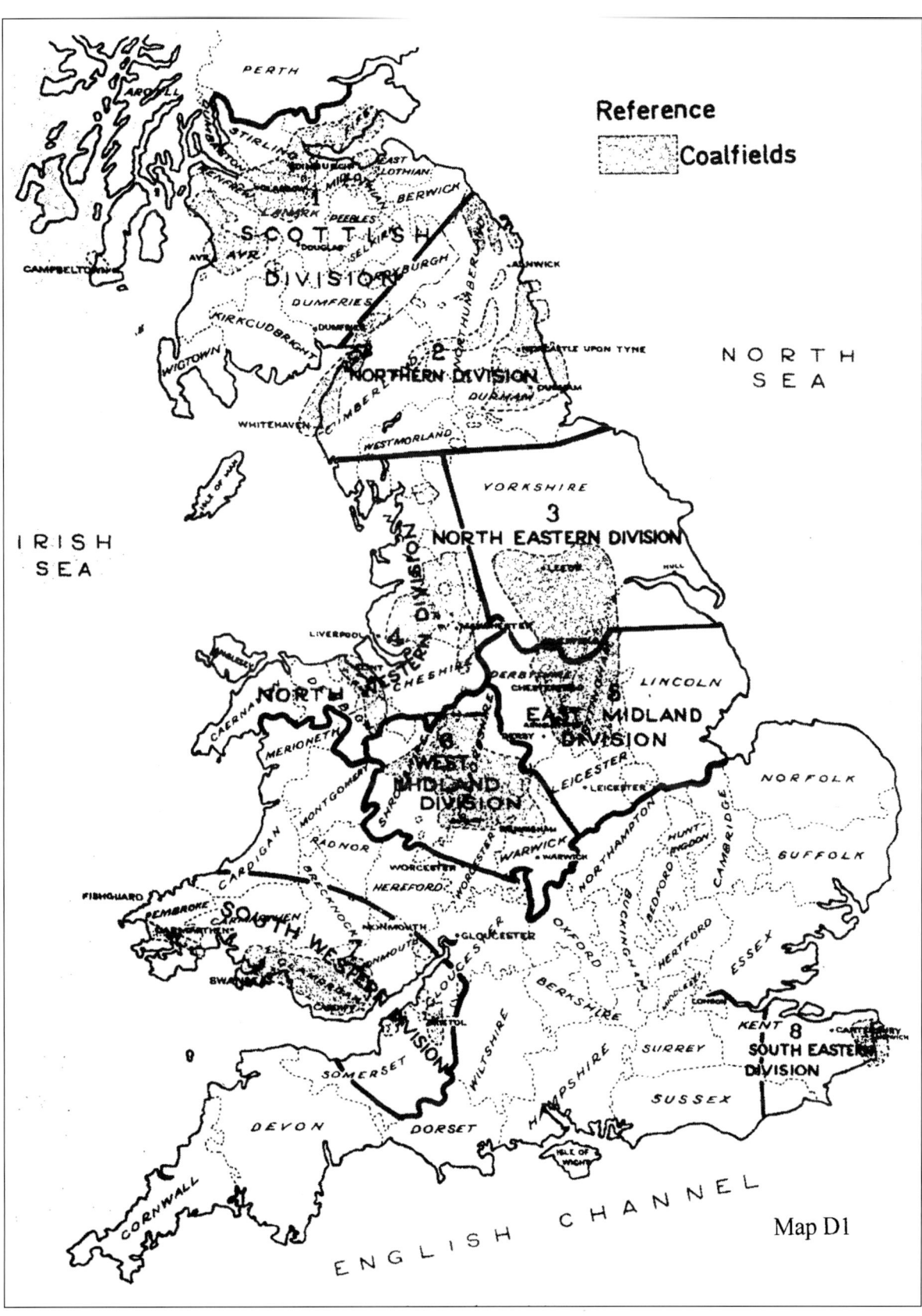

The Divisional structure of the newly publicly owned National Coal Board. Of particular relevance to this book are the East Midlands Division and the southern edge of the North Eastern Division.

responsibility for negotiating national agreements on wages, hours of working and related questions. The NUM had more than twenty areas, each of which had its own funds and could register separately as a trade union.

The scale of the industry was vast, with about 1,470 collieries of which about one third produced just one per cent of the total annual output. Quite in contrast were large scale interests of some dominant owners extending well beyond coal to include production of iron, steel and other basic commodities. Fourteen firms (less than 2 per cent of all firms involved) employed nearly 25 per cent of the total workforce, examples being Powell Duffryn (49 collieries, 27,000 men) and its subsidiary Cory Brothers (12 collieries) the largest, and – in our area of prime interest – Doncaster Amalgamated Collieries Ltd. (6 collieries and 16,000 men), Amalgamated Denaby Collieries (6 collieries and 9,000 men) and Bolsover Colliery Co. Ltd. with the same. The control over production was strongly evident in north Staffordshire (where 15 firms formed the North Staffordshire Land and Minerals Ltd. and accounted for 90 per cent of total production) and around Burnley (Hargreaves Collieries Ltd. owned 13 collieries). It all added up in 1943 to 90 per cent of the total output being produced by 46 per cent of the mines with 353 owning organisations.

Below ground level matters generally continued unchanged, mainly because many of the mines were too old or too small, or both, to justify investment with ownership scattered, making more efficient, larger replacement collieries for several smaller ones more difficult. Owners believed that modernisation would be resisted by the workforce, rendering investment unprofitable, besides lacking financial resources, and a lack of vision and drive by some mining engineers.

This combination of ills resulted during 1939-45 in a record of decline against almost every available measure; from saleable output for deep mined coal, to reducing levels of stocks against unforeseen demand, output per man-shift down (particularly when measured against similar conditions for mining in the Ruhr and the low countries), absenteeism had increased, total costs of production doubled and the size of the total workforce had fallen. Prime concerns were the need for mechanisation and for improvements to transfer the coal from face to the point where it could be taken to the surface. Research conducted during the war years under the chairmanship of Charles Reid (the Reid Report of 1945) concluded that most new output and most advances in efficiency could result only from large and, in many cases, reorganised mines and supporting organisations. As such, the Report was the strongest influence in persuading public and governmental opinion that the revived coal industry that was urgently needed could come about only following drastic changes to the existing organisation and financing of the industry.

The strong Labour Party of 1945 decided to nationalise the coal industry in its entirety and the Coal Industry Nationalisation Act was passed on 12 July 1946. With the NCB expressing in November a willingness to take over the industry from 1 January 1947, that became the primary vesting date. The intention was to ensure that all the physical assets directly involved in the business of coalmining passed to the NCB; assets used by composite firms for their iron and steel businesses were not transferred. Compensation of £394m was paid, mostly in the form of government stock, but some £66m in cash.

In 1947, the tonnage of coal produced was some 187.5 million tons. Of that total, the power stations took 27.5 million, gasworks and domestic took 43.2 million, coke ovens took 37.2 million and the railways consumed 12.2 million tons.

The reorganisation of the industry necessitated the selection of (and in some cases attraction of) candidates for senior roles of considerable responsibility and the balance of appointments was required to meet political aspirations by including representatives drawn from the wider workforce and not just previous owners. For some hard-line trade unionists, the idea of crossing the line to work in 'management' was too much, whilst others accepted on the basis that it represented an integral part of the achievement over half a century of hard-won progress within the aims of the Labour Party. The NCB was divided into eight production Divisions, each of which included a coalfield: Scottish; Northern; North Eastern; North Western; East Midlands; West Midlands; South Eastern; and South Western.

The Coal Board itself comprised a small group of men with a wide appreciation of the industry:

Chairman:
Lord John Hyndley: Managing Director of Powell Duffryn Ltd. since 1931 and who had undertaken government service work in relation to coal in both world wars.

Deputy chairman:
Sir Arthur Street: Career civil servant, latterly Permanent Secretary at the Control Office for Germany and Austria. Responsible for a stable and orderly institution and administration thereof.

Production:
Charles Reid: Formerly manager of Fife Coal Co., latterly Production Director of (wartime) Ministry of Fuel and Power. (Resigned 1949)

Sir T.E. (Eric) Young: Managing Director of Bolsover Colliery Co. Ltd., also latterly at Ministry of Fuel and Power. (Relieved of functional duties 1949)

Sir Humphrey Browne: From 1948, recruited from Manchester Collieries/NCB NW Division.

Manpower and Welfare:
Sir Walter Citrine: Trade unionist. Departed 1947 to be chairman BEA.

Replaced by –
Sir Joseph Hallsworth: Trade unionist. (Resigned 1949)

Industrial Relations:
Ebby Edwards: Trade unionist. Previously MP for Morpeth, Northumberland. Latterly General Secretary of NUM.

Finance:
Sir Lionel Lowe: Partner at Thomas, McLintock for colliery accounts work. Latterly at Ministry of Fuel and Power.

Marketing:
J.C. Grindley: ex-Powell Duffryn Ltd. Initially restricted by shortages and tonnage allocations.

Scientific:
Sir Charles Ellis: ex-Professor of Physics, King's College.

Legal:
Sir Geoffrey Vickers: ex-Slaughter and May, Solicitors. Also, part-time member of London Transport Passenger Board. Became responsible for Manpower and Welfare.

To this team was entrusted the bedding in of the new organisation, the control over policy formation and the planning for the future of their industry.

In 1949, the board was strengthened by five appointments, three of whom were prominent businessmen, J.H. Hambro of Hambro's Bank, Sir Geoffrey Heyworth of Unilever and Sir Godfrey Mitchell of George Wimpey & Co. The other two were senior trade unionists, Alderman Sydney Jones of the NUM and Gavin Martin of the Confederation of Shipbuilding and Engineering Unions.

In due course the East Midlands Division of the NCB was divided into six areas (Chesterfield, Edwinstowe, Alfreton, Ilkeston, Nottingham and South Derbyshire and Leicestershire) with a total of 89 collieries with a total manpower of 111,400. The North Eastern Division was divided into eight areas (Worksop, Doncaster, Rotherham, South Barnsley, North Barnsley, Wakefield, Castleford and Carlton), with a total of 112 collieries with a total manpower of 153,500.

Electricity industry

In the earlier stages of their political careers both Attlee and Morrison had served on municipal committees and were fully committed to extending public ownership within the industry. As architects of the progressing of the programme of nationalisation, their intention was confirmed in 1946, but had to await progress with the more pressing issues of coal.

Public sector involvement in the distribution of electricity had started before the founding of the Labour Party and quickly accounted for over 60 per cent of total sales. The remaining proportion – mainly in London and rural areas – was in the hands of franchised private companies. Private enterprise could see a future only in power generation (and bulk supply) where longer franchise periods applied and accounted for around one half of total production; municipalities individually generated the balance. In bulk supply, the Central Electricity Board (CEB), a public corporation established in 1927 by the Conservative government, had controlled the operation of power stations since the completion in 1933 of the National Grid transmission system. By 1945, two thirds of the capital in the industry was under public control.

As a 'new' industry largely already in the public sector and unencumbered by the industrial relations difficulties of coal, nationalisation (from 1948) was, therefore, less of a radical change than that for coal. However, it represented for the Labour Party a brightly shining example of how well-founded industrial policies could result in increased efficiency for the benefit of all. Based upon usage of coal, one ton produced in 1939 more than three times as much electricity as had been possible 30 years previously. For the same period, a typical, coal fired power station cost only half as much in real terms and in the inter war years wholesale prices had fallen by over 60 per cent (and retail by almost as much). However, wartime had halted further expansion, nearly one third of homes lacked a supply and, by 1945, there had built up a substantial backlog of investment.

The industry was hindered by the country having been divided into some 600 distribution areas and, largely because of that, a consensus within the industry that some form of reorganisation would be beneficial whilst building upon the existing culture of service, rather than profit. Questions about the form of organisation centred upon the extent of change that the politicians would seek to impose and the extent of control they would seek to exert in policy making. One concern evaporated with an announcement that the industry would be independent of gas and coal, and that electricity would not form part of a proposed National Fuel and Power Board.

During the 1946/47 session of parliament, the Electricity Bill was introduced and proposed the transfer of 200 companies and 369 local authority undertakings, plus the CEB and 300 power stations owned and operated by those organisations to form a new body, the British Electricity Authority (BEA). Within the BEA, a Central Authority would be responsible for running the power stations and the national grid, whilst the distribution and sales functions would be decentralised to fourteen Area Electricity Boards. Appointments to the Central Authority and Area Boards would be for the Minister to decide.

Following passage of the Bill, royal assent was received in September 1947, the vesting date was 1 April 1948 and the organisation remained in place until on 1 January 1958 it was replaced by the Electricity Council and Central Electricity Generating Board, CEGB.

As with the coal industry, appointments by the Minister to the 'centre' included men with long involvement in the industry, senior trade unionists, a skilled civil servant administrator and specialist support members. Again, as for coal several of the appointees had worked within the Ministry of Fuel and Power and had been involved together in an organising committee whilst the Bill progressed through parliament.

Chairman:
Lord Walter Citrine: Trade unionist. Previously Board member for Manpower and Welfare, NCB. Had demonstrated his skills with the nationalisation of the coal industry.

Deputy chairmen:
Sir Henry Self: Career civil servant responsible for policy development and administration.

Sir John Hacking: Formerly Chief Engineer, CEA. Responsible for operations, though not generation and transmission.

Labour relations and welfare:
Ernest Bussey: Formerly General Secretary, Electrical Trades Union.

These four full-time executives were joined on the board by eight, part-time members, four of whom were area board chairmen serving in rotation and who were either senior industry figures or trade unionists with varying attributes. The others were:

E.H.E. Woodward: Formerly General Manager of the North Eastern Electrical Supply Co.

Sir William Walker: Ex-Mayor of Manchester, engineer, former member of the CEA. Input on labour relations.

Dame Caroline Haslett: Engineer and founder Director of Electrical Association for Women.

Tom Johnston: Labour politician. Chairman of the North of Scotland Hydro-Electric Board.

Within the statutory powers regarding the Ministry's role on the authorisation of capital expenditure and the spheres of interest of the Central Authority and the Area Boards, the four full-time board members were charged with determining general business policy. In this they were afforded a high degree of freedom to provide an efficient, co-ordinated and economical supply of electricity and to extend that supply.

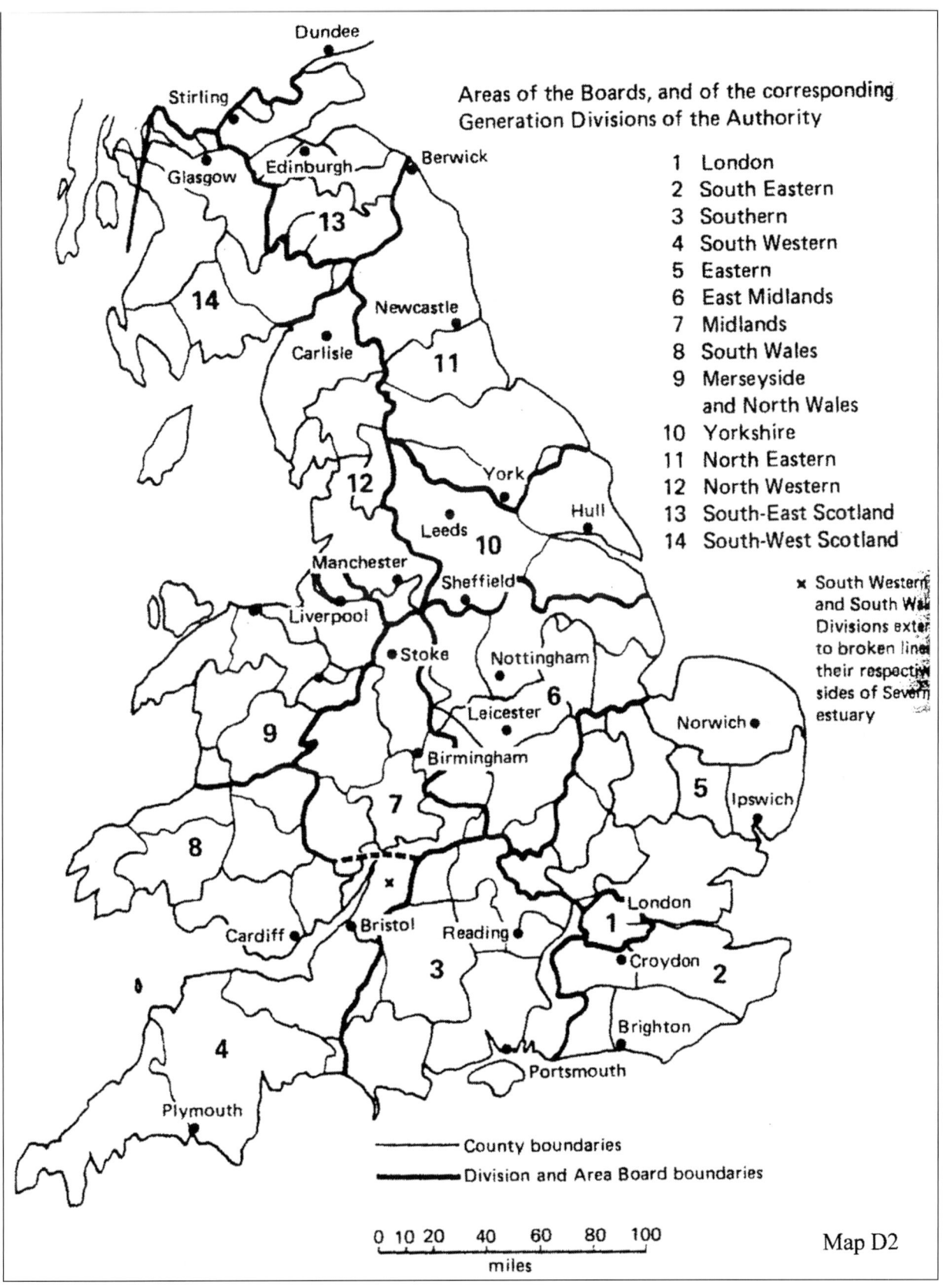

The Area Board structure adopted for the newly publicly owned electricity industry.

To address organisational issues V.A. Pask (ex CEB) was appointed Chief Engineer (reporting to Sir John Hacking) and the posts of Chief Accountant and Commercial Manager (reporting to Sir Henry Self) were filled by the ex-CEB men.

For generation, the Central Authority established fourteen divisions for the construction, management and operation of power stations; these were headed by former CEB managers (six), municipal engineers (six) and engineers previously with power generation companies (two). Of the area chairmen, five were from supply companies, five from public electricity authorities, two from the trade union movement and one from each of the engineering industry and civil service.

Between September 1947 and March 1948, the Minister made 140 appointments, 43 of which were full-time. The new organisation was ready to meet an early crisis of capacity, to lobby for allocations of scarce materials and to coordinate commercial matters affecting retail pricing. In the 1950s/60s, the electricity industry would expend the largest amount of capital of all UK industries; assets at vesting were £831m and planned investment put at £650m.

The decision to include in this chapter the coal and electricity industries was taken because their policies – and those of the governments of the day – influenced the role to be played by British Railways. As will become clear, certain railway routes benefitted from these policies whilst others did not.

In common with the coal and electricity industries, preparatory thinking for the re-organisation of inland transport had been developed throughout the years of the Second World War. However, the difference was that the owners of the largest share of inland transport – the four, grouped railway companies – were not in favour of any form of nationalisation. Following the 1945 General Election and an announcement on 19 November 1945 by Herbert Morrison as to the government's intention, the railway companies declined to become involved in the drafting of the legislation and reorganisation proposals therein.

Not a good start. The railways were still under government control, but the chairmen (representing the interests of their shareholders) felt it appropriate to resist – via the vehicle of the Railway Companies Association as a lobbying pressure group – the government's plans which started in 1943. Against the swell of support for change as evidenced in the 1945 General Election, it was always going to be a fruitless campaign, though certain changes to the scope of the draft legislation were made. Those changes actually did the railways no favours; Labour-controlled municipalities objected successfully to the handing over of their road transport undertakings and the Co-operative movement objected successfully to the inclusion of 'C' licence road transport hauliers. Despite these withdrawals, the legislation as drafted was still very extensive and incorporated the interests of the railways, docks and inland waterways, road transport, London's buses and underground trains, hotels and catering services, each of which would have an executive. The five functional executives would be placed under the overall control of the British Transport Commission (BTC).

The Transport Bill 1946 sought to establish the BTC with a general duty to provide an efficient, adequate, economic and properly integrated system of public inland transport and port facilities, and to cover costs taking one year with another. All assets were to be vested in the BTC which would determine overall policy, subject to Ministerial supervision. The Bill received royal assent on 6 August 1947 and the vesting date was 1 January 1948.

The railway companies viewed the two and a half years of peacetime operation prior to vesting day as purely transitional in nature; medium term and strategic planning was relegated below and beyond the day to day job of operations. Not for them any longer any concerns over pricing policy and finance generally; all were matters for the Labour government to sort out. Day to day communication from/to government throughout this time was via a continuation of the wartime Railway Executive Committee, chaired by the new Minister of Transport (Alfred Barnes). The companies had much to do simply in trying to reduce the backlog of maintenance to the infrastructure and fleets of traction and rolling stock. Sadly, there was also a spate of serious accidents claiming in 1947 a total of 121 lives, the second highest annual total in railway history. All the signs were – as with the coal industry in 1945 – that it was time to adapt to the inevitability of change, to reorganise and improve matters.

Barnes did not take long to announce his first appointment; on 8 August 1947 he appointed Sir (later Lord) Cyril Hurcomb – his Departmental Permanent Secretary – as chairman of the BTC. Hurcomb had been

Just prior to the Second World War, a small production batch of Bedford OB buses was produced. Following cessation of hostilities, production resumed and by the end of 1951 some 12,750 had been turned out. As such, the 27-seaters were one of the most popular types of bus ever produced.

heavily involved in the drafting of the Bill. He would be joined on the Board by four full-time members and one part-time member. They were:

Sir William Wood: President of the executive of the largest of the main line companies (LMS).

Lord Ashfield: Chairman of the London Passenger Transport Board (died in 1948).

John Benstead: Ex-General Secretary, National Union of Railwaymen (Deputy chairman from 1949).

Lord Rusholme (Robert Palmer): Ex-General Secretary, Co-operative Party.

Captain Sir Ian Bolton: Part-time. Accountant with McClelland Ker & Co.

The leader, in every sense, was Hurcomb and his first appointments were Miles Beevor, ex-LNER, as Chief Secretary and Legal Adviser and Sir Reginald H. Wilson, ex-Ministry of War Transport, as Financial Comptroller.

At their first meeting in August 1947, the intentions of the government were made clear. The BTC was a policy making and directing body acting collectively. To assist the Commission functional departments for the Chief Secretary, Finance and Public Relations were created, giving a total staff at end 1948 of 152.

Next to be appointed were the chairmen and members of the five Transport Executives. Like his opposite number at Fuel and Power, Barnes opted to do this from a list of recommendations and thereby meet the aspirations of the trade union movement for representation of the workforce. The careful profiling for and external recruitment of senior personnel for specific roles as for the coal and electricity industries did not appear to be replicated by Barnes for inland transport. The leading railway company manager (as chairman elect for the Railway Executive) was Sir James Milne of the Great Western Railway, but he was approaching retirement and declined the opportunity. The appointment made was Sir Eustace Missenden, chairman of the Southern Railway. The other appointees to the Railway Executive (RE) were six full-time and two part-time members:

Public Relations:
General Sir William Slim: Ex-Imperial Defence College (General Sir Daril Watson from 1949).

Operating (motive power shared):
Sir V. Michael Barrington-Ward: Ex-Divisional General Manager, LNER Southern Area.

Mechanical and electrical engineering:
(motive power shared) R.A. Riddles: Ex-Vice President LMS.

Civil Engineering:
J.C.L. Train: Ex-Chief Engineer LNER.

Commercial:
D. Blee: Ex-Chief Goods Manager GWR.

Staff:
W.P. Allen: Ex-General Secretary ASLEF.

Commercial (part-time):
C. Nevile: Chairman, Economics Committee, National Farmers' Union.

Sir Wilfrid Ayre: Chairman and Managing Director, Burntisland Shipbuilding Co.

Of these, the chairman and Michael Barrington-Ward had served together on the wartime Railway Executive Committee. The choice of David Blee perhaps reflected a desire to be seen to appoint someone from the most successful (in terms of dividends paid) of the grouped companies, even though two more senior colleagues had followed Sir James Milne in declining the opportunity (the Chief Civil Engineer and the Assistant General Manager). Except for Slim, the RE was essentially a body of lifetime experienced railwaymen of the old departmentally entrenched school, who knew very well their individual spheres of specialism. W.P. Allen deserves an additional note; as a boy engine cleaner at Hornsey (at tuppence halfpenny an hour) and the son of a driver, he campaigned successfully for a lodging allowance to be paid to Hornsey based cleaners (as applied at nearby King's Cross) and rose through the ranks to become a driver before being encouraged to take a full-time role in ASLEF. He was later elected General Secretary of that trade union and left that post to take up the role with the RE.

As for the BTC, a number of posts were allowed for departmental heads; each being a railwayman:

Chief Finance Officer	Ex-LMS
Legal Adviser and Solicitor	Ex-LNER
Secretary	Ex-LNER
Administration	Ex-LMS + SR
New Works	Ex-LNER
Public Relations	Ex-LNER

The total staff at June 1948 was 366.

The primary task at September 1947 of the RE was to be to unify the four railway companies in a real and operating sense whilst avoiding over centralisation. To satisfy these aims, a new, regional organisation would have to be devised. So, unlike coal and electricity, where clear lines of differentiation between the central policy making role and the functional, subordinate bodies existed, the new railway organisations would start with three levels of organisation (BTC, RE, regional).

To achieve the desired decentralisation, provide some devolution of authority and avoid departmental entrenchment, the RE felt that all of the departmental chief officers (e.g. mechanical and electrical engineering, civil engineering, operating, staff and commercial) would receive functional instructions from the 'heads' at the RE and at a 'regional' level, general managers would act as coordinators. In other words, the RE proposal was largely for a perpetuation of the then still existing railway companies; a status quo, though with five regions, the new one being Scotland, formed by merging LMS and LNER interests, might usefully be introduced on vesting day, then just three and a half months ahead.

In the early months following nationalisation of the railways, a K3 2-6-0 passes through Princes Risborough with the Niddrie-Marylebone fully fitted goods train. The first five wagons are flat with sheeted containers, probably with prime beef for Smithfield market. One of the commercial failures of the 1948-55 period was to be unable to build upon the success of the LNER in developing containerised traffic for distances of 300 miles plus (Rail on-line).

The BTC had other ideas and matters were settled during the Autumn. It was made clear to the RE that the BTC (and not the RE) would exercise functions similar to those of the four grouped companies, would be solely responsible for questions of policy including general financial control, the supervision of research and development, the preparation of a new charging scheme and arrangements for the coordination of transport. The RE would exercise the powers of General Managers and expenditure levels (for the RE) would be limited to £25k for renewals and new works, £5k for land transactions and £1.75k per yearly salary for staff appointments. Any adjustments to the railway regional structure, boundary changes, the closure of any railway line, dock, harbour hotel, steamer or ferry service was solely for the BTC to determine (with the Minister). Staff privileges and 'golden handshakes' were to be the subject of prior consultation with the BTC, as would any proposed leases exceeding 60 years. The only areas of policy that the RE could exert control over without BTC 'interference' were for operations, motive power and regional organisation.

Under the BTC plans, there were to be six Regions, each with a Chief Regional Officer reporting to and receiving functional direction from up to eight members of the RE. The Chief Regional Officers were all

Left and below: During 1948, a series of trials were held using locomotives along routes on Regions other than that on which the type was usually used. One of the classes involved was the West Country of the Southern, seen here passing Wortley (between Sheffield and Penistone) (Signalman Austin Brackenbury) and approaching Marylebone. (Rail on-line)

The Regional structure of the newly publicly owned railway industry. Note in particular the split between the Southern and Western Regions in South West England and the extension of the Eastern Region to Manchester. One of the political and organisational dilemmas was how to not simply replicate the four, grouped companies formed by The Railways Act (1921).

career served railwaymen who were capable of roles as General Managers rather than as co-ordinators across a number of departments. There were potential problems with boundaries being drawn geographically rather than along those of the systems of the former four companies. For the reorganisation of commercial departments that helped Blee, but for operations it recreated

for Barrington-Ward a range of problems. The RE eventually had to accept an uncomfortable and unsatisfactory compromise, in which operating and motive power were exempted from a strict geographical division. A number of penetrating lines was condoned for operating purposes only and pleased no-one. Amongst the penetrating lines were Manchester-Sheffield and Nottingham-Aylesbury; the former GCR route would traverse three regional boundaries and became managed by just one Region – the Eastern – and was controlled for operating purposes by that Region from Liverpool Street.

All in all, it was a new and unfamiliar organisation full of unseen conflicts, particularly as between the RE and BTC who did not play together very well.

Whilst the RE had been put in its place, it was a poor start to a new organisation and in contrast to both coal and electricity. That both the RE and the BTC had tried to reserve the policy making and planning rules reflected badly upon the early direction, or lack of it, given by the Minister.

Rushed policy-making rarely produces satisfactory results and, when it appeared, the regional structure could be officially justified only by emphasising its purely temporary nature, with modifications to be made later in the light of experience.

With regard to compensation to the shareholders in the former railway companies, the Ministry agreed to the use of market values, i.e. London Stock Market prices in particular weeks in 1945 and 1946 (the higher being applicable). However, by the time of the transfer date (1 January 1948) a rise in interest rates necessitated the issue of stock at 3 per cent, which was beneficial to the shareholders, but added to the BTC's interest burden.

By any measure, the nationalisation of inland transport came a poor third to those for coal and electricity; there had been no serious discussions about future deployment of transport resources, just political and administrative expediency.

The practical engineers on the RE at least made some progress with reducing the backlog of maintenance work. In November 1947, Riddles established a Wagon Repairs Committee which, within three months, had reduced the backlog by 20 per cent whilst Train tackled the more pressing infrastructure matters. In parallel, Blee successfully promoted a reduction in turnaround time for wagons and some weeding out of low capacity, grease lubricated ex-NCB wagons transferred (with the rest) to the BTC under the Transport Act 1947 (the NCB being compensated with 3 per cent Treasury stock). 1948 saw exchange trials of locomotives of similar power classifications which proved little and a range of new liveries was developed. In the short-term absence of a policy, the fleet of locomotives grew with the progressive introduction of some 1,500 new built to the designs of the previously grouped railway companies. In the policy vacuum, Riddles and his (largely ex-LMS) team were given a free hand to develop a range of designs for locomotives using standard components and, apart from one (of 999), all with two cylinders. Riddles was enthusiastic for steam and saw electric traction as the eventual successor, a view shared by the Treasury (1945) when Crompton Parkinson (electrical transmission package developer) raised the possibility of a supply arrangement with General Motors of the USA. The first standard class of locomotive – the Britannias – appeared in 1951 as did the first of many of the Mk1 passenger carriages, operationally very little changed apart from the return of mail trains and some restaurant/ sleeping car services.

Above, opposite and overleaf pages: These five photographs illustrate how the Railway Executive changed the liveries carried by the locomotives and how a unified appearance evolved. Early trials included different shades of green (65) and blue with red lining. For its fleet of mixed traffic locomotives, black lined out with white, grey and red was adopted and stood the test of time until the 1960s (66). Following the trials with blue/red a blue lined out with white and black was adopted for express locomotives (67) and all types of locomotive eventually received an emblem depicting a lion atop a wheel with the words British Railways. For the first of the BR Standard types a gloss black was adopted and with most externally placed copper pipework painted over (68). That in turn quickly gave way to a dark green lined out in orange and black (69).

The General Election of 1951 ushered in a new approach to the challenge of inland transport; the incoming Conservative government intended to create a new, competitive era. The legislative process resulted in the enforced sale of the BTC's road haulage interests (which became British Road Services) and placed into rail/road competition some £100m of general merchandise traffic, some of which traffic would inevitably be lost by the high fixed cost railway industry to the lower fixed cost base of the road haulier with more commercial flexibility. The railways would be exposed to competition and would need to adapt or wither.

The Transport Act 1953 received royal assent on 5 May 1953 and included compensation to the BTC only to the extent of the sale of assets, did not place any levy on the pricing of the successor road haulage body, removed the 25-mile restriction placed (1930s) on certain other holders of road licences, but did relax some of the restrictions on railway freight pricing.

In terms of organisation, the steps taken in the Act were draconian and sought to reduce the over centralisation which arose from the Transport Act 1947. Of the five Executives created by the 1947 Act, only London Transport survived; the others – including the Railway Executive – were abolished effective from 1 October 1953. The RE was abolished 18 months before a replacement organisation was put in place, during which time interim arrangements applied until 1 January 1955. The proposals of the Commission for the reorganisation were tabled in parliament in July 1954, debated in November and affirmed. The interim organisation included some former members of the RE (Train, Blee, Allen and Sir Daril Watson). Of the others, Missenden had retired and been replaced by John Elliot (ex-SR), Riddles and Barrington-Ward both retired.

Left and below: These photographs serve two purposes. Firstly, they show how the design of the Standard classes of locomotives had similarities to assist maintenance; a Class 4 in the dark green as also applied later to the pacifics (photo 68) and a Class 4 in the mixed traffic livery (70 and 71 respectively). Secondly, both locomotives carry the emblem introduced from 1956, Severn Valley Railway and Midland Railway Centre respectively.

PROGRAMME OF NATIONALISATION AND PLANNING TO 1955 • 169

No need to travel into town, we'll deliver it to you. The advent of the all-purpose delivery man with van which toured a local area, selling a range of everyday items and vegetables.

Above and overleaf: The combination of cheap fuel, an improving network of roads, a buoyant economy, changes to the licensing arrangements, avoidance of double or triple loading/unloading, a railway hamstrung by outdated commercial practices and higher overheads, all added up to the competition of the road haulage industry and their influential lobbyist the Road Haulage Federation.

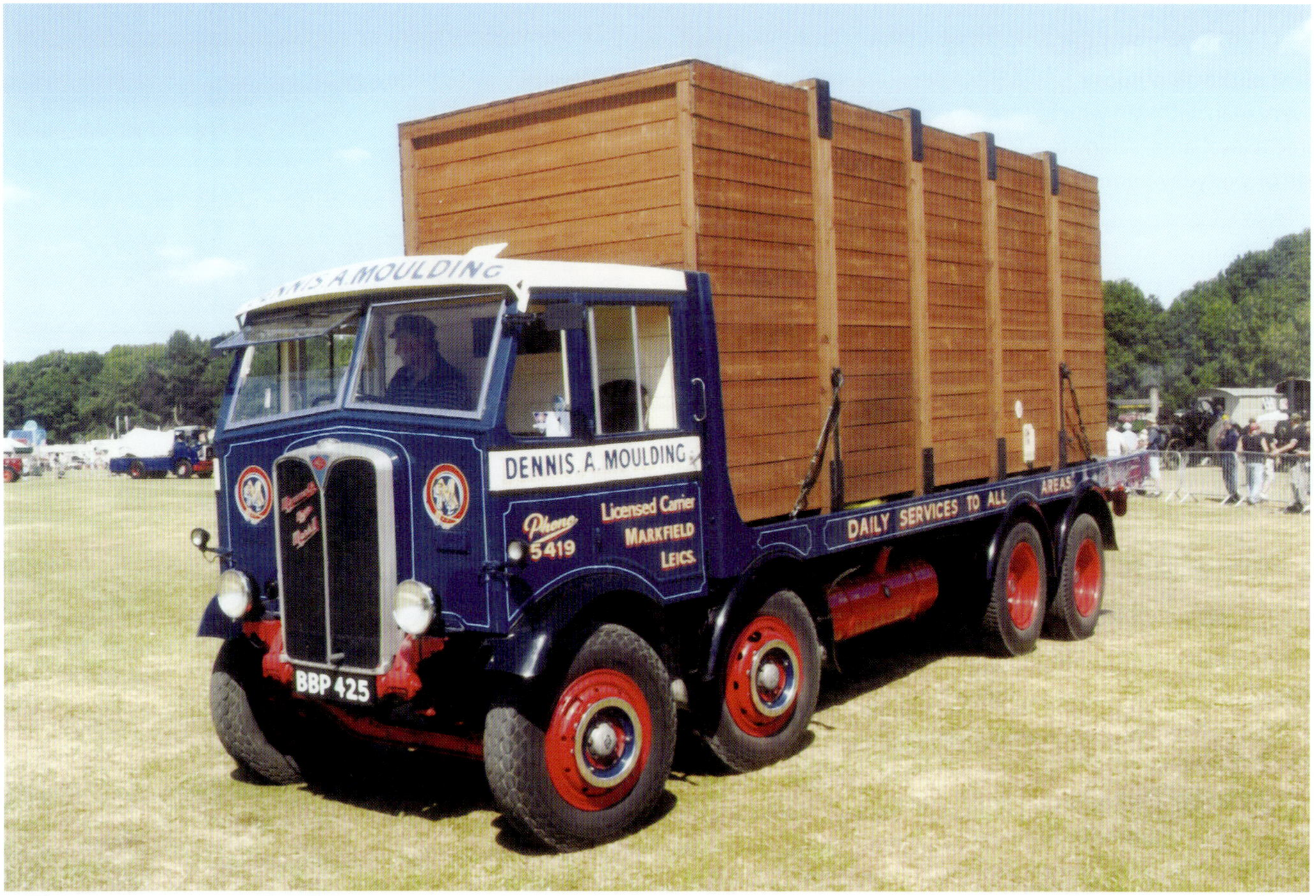
DENNIS. A. MOULDING
Phone
5419
Licensed Carrier
MARKFIELD
LEICS.
DAILY SERVICES TO ALL AREAS
BBP 425

TAUNTON CIDER
KYH 367
PLF 600

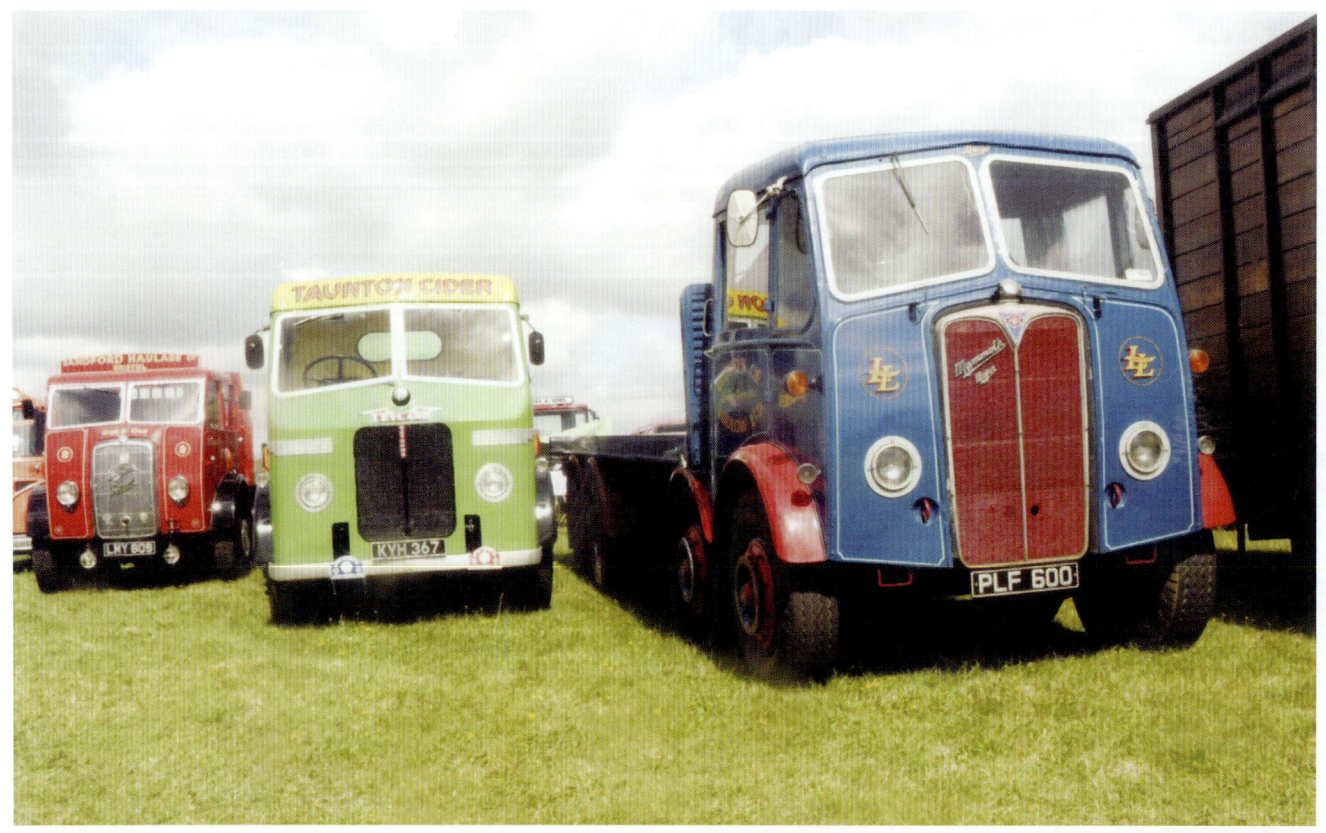

Sir Michael Barrington-Ward deserves a note as a career railwayman who was in a junior role with the GCR during the First World War and represented that railway with legal counsel in an action against Denaby Collieries, who were refusing to sell coal for locomotive use at cost price in accordance with government policy. Following the Grouping, he had been engaged in operational management within the Southern Area of the LNER (Western i.e. GNR/GCR lines from 1927) and as the Second World War approached, he was appointed Assistant General Manager (Operating) for the whole LNER system. During the war he served on the RE and oversaw the allocation/re-allocation of locomotives in line with strategic and crisis planning, including King Arthur (Southern Railway) locomotives to Tyneside and the changes affecting the former GCR lines (A3s/S160s). Post-war, he chaired the committee which determined the allocation of the new, Standard locomotives and was persuaded to allow 23 Britannias to be allocated to the GE line to Norwich to support a revised timetable. With his retirement went his knowledge of the role played by the former GCR London extension and of the route's strategic importance.

An organisation structure emerged, headed by General Sir Brian Robertson (from September 1953); an old soldier replacing an old civil servant. Sir Brian had a distinguished career in the Second World War, and it is likely that a further opportunity to command a labour force of some 850,000 (BTC total) would have attracted him. The organisation proposal was Robertson's rather than that of a Minister; the process of change not being assisted by there having been three Ministers of Transport (John Maclay, Alan Lennox-Boyd and John Boyd-Carpenter as well as, between October 1951 and September 1953, a Minister for Coordination of Transport, Fuel and Power). In those circumstances, Robertson relied upon what he said he had been instructed to do; provide leadership and inject some backbone into the Commission. This, though, seemed at odds with a view that the BTC would remain a policy unit with day to day management devolved to area authorities; the issue of centralisation versus decentralisation was far from settled. The Minister appointed 11 members to support Robertson; six full-time and five part-time, of which just three had prior experience of railway management. The members were:

Deputy chairman:
Sir John Benstead: Trade unionist on BTC since 1947.

F.A. Pope: Chairman, Ulster Transport Authority, on RE from 1951.

J.C.E. Train: Member of RE.

A.B. Valentine: Member of London Transport Executive.

Sir Reginald Wilson: Comptroller, BTC.

Part-time (all new appointments):
H.P. Barker: Engineering/household goods supply (prior role with BTC from 1951).

Sir Ian Bolton: Accountancy (prior role with BTC from 1947).

Lt Col. Donald Cameron of Lochiel: Army/Scotland.

Sir Harry Methven: Hotels/catering.

John Ryan: Metals industry (prior role with BTC from 1951).

If the right people were in place, they needed to guide the Commission throughout as long a period as possible. Robertson and Benstead remained until 1961, Lord Rusholme to 1959, Pope was part-time from 1955 to 1958 due to ill health, Sir Ian Bolton to 1959, John Ryan to 1956 and Sir Harry Methven to 1956. Cameron of Lochiel, Sir Reginald Wilson, A.B. Valentine and H.P. Barker remained until the abolition of the BTC in 1962.

Chief Officer roles included W.P. Allen (Chief of Establishment and Staff), D. Blee (Chief of Commercial Services) and Sir Daril Watson (Chief of General Services).

The creation of Area Boards opened the possibility of dynamic leadership talent from experienced industrialists, but it did not materialise to any great extent.

Chairmen appointed (part-time):

Sir Philip Warter	Chairman of Associated British Picture Corporation (Southern)
Sir Leonard Sinclair	Chairman, UK Esso Petroleum (Western)
Lord Rusholme	London Midland
Sir Reginald Wilson	Eastern
Sir Ian Bolton	Scottish
T.H. Summerson	North Eastern

The boards – which did not meet together – had 29 part-time members drawn variously from banking, finance, business, trade unions and academia. In practice, much of the day to day management and initiative was left to the Chief Regional Managers/General Managers.

The machinery of decision making was overbearing and limited by low levels of financial delegation to the area boards from the BTC. As an example, if a departmental officer on the western area wished to promote an initiative, it would need to pass through six layers of management before arriving at the BTC for approval or rejection. That was not decentralisation at all.

One policy area the BTC did tackle was that of the penetrating lines. It did that in 1955 by insisting upon geographical boundaries for the railway regions and included a statement to that effect in the Annual Report for 1955 (and again in 1958 and 1959). This proved to be very difficult to progress in two particular areas; Sheffield and Birmingham. For the former, the LNER line from Sheffield penetrated the LM Region territory to Manchester and, at the same time, the former Midland Railway/LMS and Great Central/LNER lines intertwined through a broad, common frontier between those two regions. The former GCR main line south from Nottingham was also an LNER line in the LMR geographical area. The matter was resolved between the two regions; Sheffield became Eastern Region for all purposes and the former GCR line (South of Heath, near Chesterfield) was transferred to the LMR.

With the concentration of minds over a lengthy period on the subject of organisation, there is no doubt that the railways suffered from being unable to concentrate on capital investment, costs, productivity and the control over pricing. Whilst both the coal and electricity industries came forward with credible plans to secure capital, the railways lost endless opportunities.

All three organisations – NCB, BEA and the BTC – faced common problems, which may be summarised as shortages of materials, particularly steel (where a quota system applied until 1953/4), governments wishing to support organizations which could export production and help prevent a balance of trade deficit (sterling was devalued in 1949) and government economic theory that placed at odds short term capital investment programmes to support employment rather than long term needs of the nationalized industries.

The coal industry

Against a background of estimated reserves for the whole of Britain of some 35,370 million tons of coal and a demand for coal for all its principal uses, the NCB produced in 1949 a Plan for Coal which was formally approved by the Minister of Fuel and Power in the following year. The Plan was based upon an expectation of demand for some 240 million tons being produced and sold annually in 1961-65, of which 210 million would be for home consumption and 30 million for export and bunkering. The planned output was 18 per cent higher than that in 1949 and to be achieved partly with new deep-mined coal becoming available. Manpower was expected to fall gradually from mid-1950 with productivity improvements more than offsetting that decrease. Plan for Coal was expected to cost, at 1949 price levels, £520m for collieries and £115m for other establishments. The rate of investment was intended to be at its highest between 1951-55, when £190m was suggested as the investment in collieries.

For the additional output, the Plan relied upon reconstruction of existing collieries and only to a small extent on new, providing a better rate of return. There were to be 67 major and 192 minor reconstructions, 22 new large collieries and 53 drift mines were indicated. Of the total output upon completion, 30 per cent would come from collieries with major reconstructions, 40 per cent minor reconstructions and 10 per cent from drift. The balancing 20 per cent would come from about 250 collieries continuing with little change. Between 350 and 400 collieries, mostly small, would be closed, though 90 would be merged with neighbouring pits.

Partly because of the overriding concern to maximise total output and to maintain the supply of coals of special quality, the strategy did not seek to achieve the greatest possible increase in efficiency. Coal is not a completely homogeneous commodity and for some purposes only certain types of coal will be suitable. Britain in the 1940s still had a demand for coal for all its principal uses (power stations, gasworks and coke ovens, domestic, steel making, railways), though reserves of particular types of coal varied in quantity across different coalfields and caused concerns over future supplies of prime coking coal for use in the iron and steel industry. Coal was ranked according to the content of volatile matter and their caking properties; low volatility would not produce coke of any commercial value but was given a high ranking whilst high volatility was given a lower ranking. The high-ranking coals tended to be found in locations with severe faulting and folding making extraction both difficult and costly. Complicating the science further was the fact that lower ranked coal may be cleaner when burned and come naturally in more suitable sizes. All in all, Britain produced 8 per cent very high rank, low volatile coals (anthracite and steam coal), 8 per cent of prime coking coal, 37 per cent of other coking coals, the balance being low rank coals. Most of the high-ranking coals were in the southern coalfields. Scotland, Northumberland and most of the Midlands had mainly low rank coals. Elsewhere, there was greater variety. The most abundant reserves, those of the Yorkshire and East Midlands coalfields, provided for nearly all uses; Nottinghamshire and North Derbyshire had mainly low rank coals suitable for general purposes whilst Yorkshire had plenty of nearly everything except high ranking, very specialised coals.

The planning, therefore, had to look beyond the simpler approach of investing where high productivity and lower costs of production could be achieved, i.e. in the East Midlands and Yorkshire. In fact, the degree of expansion originally proposed for the East Midlands and Yorkshire was reduced because of congestion on the trans-Pennine railway routes (later eased somewhat by electrification of the Woodhead route from 1954) and in the Humber ports.

Indicators of progress were:

Year	Total assets £m	Number of collieries	Total output m tons	Total manpower '000	Output per man year tonnes
1947	408	958	200	704	267
1950	n/a	901	206	691	298
1951	n/a	896	213	693	307
1952	n/a	880	214	710	302
1953	473	875	213	712	300
1954	519	867	215	702	306
1955	585	850	211	699	302

A new national price structure was introduced in two stages in 1951; for house coal in June and for industrial and carbonisation (used particularly by the Gas Boards) coals in December. The house coal scheme fixed delivered prices to the merchant's depot. The country was divided into 64 zones and a price for quality four (of eight) was fixed for each zone. The price differential between the eight grades was identical in all zones. The zonal price covered the cost of transport by rail. As the supplying collieries could vary from week to week, the previously applicable variations in price were avoided by using the delivered price basis. For the transport of house coal from collieries to merchants it mattered not to the NCB whether the BTC chose to take a longer route than that which appeared best.

The NCB contemplated the introduction of delivered prices for all coal but found this more difficult and less urgent for industrial users who were accustomed to buying large quantities from the same source over a period. In these cases, pit head prices applied and, in the case of the railways, the price was 'free on rail' with the BTC being responsible for the transport.

The electricity industry

As with coal, the BEA was obliged to seek from the Minister for Fuel and Power approval to their proposed, forward programme of capital investment and area budgets. Despite high demand for electricity and the areas wishing to sell more, the area budgets for 1950 and 1951 were severely cut back, though proposals for new power stations were generally accepted. Demand for electricity was outstripping supply and prior to the General Election of 1951, the area chairmen mounted a campaign against the Labour government. The arrival of the Conservative government brought little immediate change in the annual programmes of the level of investment sought and the industry generally managed to meet increased demand (1950/51 + 12.4 per cent, 1951/52 + 8.4 per cent, 1952/53 + 3.7 per cent) with fewer power cuts at times of high demand.

National economic matters improved from 1953 and allowed the Conservative administration to indicate that physical controls over forward investment plans could be replaced by responsible industry disciplines; in other words, the Ministry rather than the Treasury. This slight relaxation, though welcome, did though bring another problem; the government wanted the manufacturing base for generation equipment to have capacity for export, thus limiting the plans for UK development. Industries – both demand and supply – rather ignored the limits and in the 1950s there was real progress:

Year	Output capacity at year end megawatts	New fixed investment (current £s m)	Electricity share of UK energy markets %
1948	11,789	99	14.4
1950	13,518	138	15.7
1951	14,645	149	16.3
1952	16,079	159	16.5
1953	17,388	180	16.7
1954	18,806	215	17.5
1955	20,629	247	18.4

The British economy had long been built upon energy from coal and into the 1950s many commentators were convinced that this would continue for many years to come. The harsh winters of the early 1950s had seen the NCB provide the CEA with small tonnages of imported coal at subsidised prices. The electricity industry planners identified that by 1960, demand for coal would substantially exceed the estimates made earlier in the 1950s. That was due to demand exceeding efficiency gains and the 50 million tons expected to be required in 1960 (60 million tons 1965) was rather more than the NCB were planning to produce for them. Both the NCB and the Ministry were alerted and the latter, with the BEA examined a possible shift to alternative fuels.

In 1954, the government applied pressure to the Central Authority to adopt dual firing for either coal or oil in some power stations. That was opposed by the industry's engineers who preferred the use of imported coal, which at the time was a cheaper option than oil. Eventually, Lord Citrine and Sir Henry Self gained 'internal' support on 'national interests' grounds and a supply contract was committed with Esso Petroleum to supply oil from their new Fawley refinery to the nearby Marchwood (Hampshire) power station then under construction.

The politicians then became increasingly involved after the NCB advised a likely inability to meet demand in the 1960s. Dual firing would have the politically attractive route to taming industrial muscle of the unions and costs of oil were falling. Conversion costs were minimised by allowing for oil firing only in some stations and which were in southern England away from the coalfields which would have served them.

Oil was not, however, the only available answer to the anticipated coal shortage. The alternative – nuclear power – had initially seemed more attractive to most of the engineers, perhaps because it was new (in 1952 the first electricity was generated from a nuclear pile in the USA). The idea was attractive to the government as the military wanted a capability to produce weapons grade plutonium. The first site (Calder Hall, Cumbria) favoured the military need with electricity input into the National Grid from 1956 as a secondary consideration. Two further sites were announced in October 1955 (Berkeley in Gloucestershire and Bradwell in Essex, both being on river estuaries). The first contributions from these two sites were in 1962.

During the course of the 1950s, 39 conventional power stations of varying sizes were built and commissioned; three were capable of dual firing (coal/oil), one oil only and one for coal, oil or gas.

The CEA borrowed money to finance new investment (either short term from the banks or longer term through their public issues of fixed interest capital) and during the early years had benefitted from Labour's traditional view that interest rates should be kept down. On the six new long-term capital issues they made between 1948 and 1955 – each being for £100-£200m – they paid rates between three and four and a half per cent. However, Citrine and Self pushed their beliefs in low interest rates too far and with an optimistically low interest rate offered in August 1955 for an issue of £200m, most was unsubscribed and left in government hands. After February 1955, interest rates did not fall below the four per cent level.

As at end of 1955, coal was responsible for the production of some 85 per cent of the UK inland energy consumption with oil up to around 15 per cent and increasing.

The railway industry

Consumed by organisational and legislative matters, it took the BTC a very long time to come forward with a plan for capital investment; it was towards the end of the seventh year of its existence that proposals were submitted to the Minister. Starved of funds for capital projects since nationalisation, the Railway Executive had concentrated upon recovery from war damage to the infrastructure, building steam locomotives and operating the new railway organisation. Had the geographical area organisational arrangements worked more efficiently, the 'push' up to the RE of ideas and costed projects suitable for investment would surely have happened. As it was, it seemed that everyone at all three levels (BTC, RE and Chief Regional Officers) was waiting for someone else. Commission Comptroller Sir Reginald Wilson encouraged the BTC to summarise their expected capital requirements for submission to the Minister following the 1951 General Election. Subsequently he encouraged the RE to develop a plan; an accountant encouraging railwaymen to ask for money for their industry.

An RE committee produced 'A Development Programme for British Railways', though not until April 1953 and the timing of its submission to the BTC (May 1953) was unfortunate in that it coincided with the passage of the Transport Act 1953. The proposals were:

Spend area	Estimated cost £m
Electrification (all main routes out of London)	160ø
Improvements to track	60
Modernisation of signalling and telecoms	30
Re-siting and modernisation of marshalling yards	50
Rationalisation and modernisation of freight terminals	50
Continuous braking systems for freight rolling stock	40*
Introduction of diesel railcars	17
Reconstruction of passenger stations	40
Helicopter terminals and services	40
Marine services	13
	500

NOTES:
- ø Clearly the view remained that steam would be retained until electrification was widely extended.
- * development from recommendations of other groups.

By early 1954 (six years after nationalisation), pressure upon the BTC was starting to increase. Having seen the way in which the electricity industry had developed, the Treasury advised that it was ready to consider proposals for helping the railways but was opposed to any form of subsidy. The Ministry of Fuel and Power – with the full knowledge of the progress with low cost, efficient electricity and forward demand from the re-organised and more efficient coal industry – sought from the Ministry of Transport plans for the extension of electrification. From the geographical areas, the Western was organising a committee to explore the development of diesel services. Separately the BTC had in February approved the purchase of equipment for diesel shunting locomotives to be built by BR during 1955 and 1956.

Sir Daril Watson was instructed to set up a Planning Committee which he would chair. He did so and appointed thirteen (later fifteen) members, three of whom were from the Areas (one from the LM and two from the Western). Watson then set up nine sub-committees: forecasts and brief analysis of traffic; forms of motive power; modernisation of passenger and goods stations; modernisation of carriage and wagon fleets; modernisation and re-siting of marshalling yards; continuous braking of freight stock; permanent way and infrastructure works and signalling and telecommunications; technical staff requirements; ships and packet ports.

In the course of the late spring/early summer, the regional managements were invited to respond with their views on the emerging thoughts of the sub-committees. Responses received varied from well considered (for example the Western's own earlier work enabled them to respond fully on the development of diesel power) to hasty and limited (for example the vast London Midland came up with a one depot trial using 31 diesels to replace 41 steam). The Scottish (with hydro-electric supplies) wanted electrification with no zones being considered suitable for diesels.

The BTC considered the various outputs in November 1954 together with comments from the regional managers and members of the Commission. During the following week, the Plan was drafted and proposed an outlay of £1.17m between 1956 and 1970, of which a mere £300m was available from BTC depreciation and maintenance reserves. The balance of £870m would need to be borrowed. It had certainly been a long time coming and, in its favour, half the cost would be needed in any event for normal replacement of assets whilst the balance was for updating. The Ministry for Transport and the Treasury were in sympathetic mode, reasoning that as the railways were running at a loss and until modernised would be unlikely to improve efficiency. Also, a new charging scheme for freight would help (though it took BR until 1957 to produce it), as would deferring interest charges on borrowings. Treasury officials assumed the Modernisation Plan to be technically sound and that the prediction of an annual return of 17 per cent on investment would enable a modernised railway to pay its way.

The Modernisation Plan was published in January 1955 and in outline proposed:

	£m
Electrification:	
Main Lines. East Coast and West Coast to Leeds (possibly York), Birmingham, Manchester and Liverpool. Liverpool Street suburban extended to Ipswich plus branches	120
Suburban. Including Glasgow and some Eastern Region in a total of 390 route miles	65
Dieselisation:	
Main lines	125
Shunting and trip locomotives	25
Steam developments	10
Track and signalling:	
Improvements (of at least 100 mph on the main lines) and better use of track capacity	210
Passenger carriages and stations:	
Improvements including carriage cleaning and servicing depots	55
New passenger carriages, including multiple units and refreshment cars	230
Freight services:	
Construction/re-construction of 55 marshalling yards and closure of 150 yards	80
Reconstruction and mechanisation of freight terminals, improve transit times and exchange arrangements between rail/road	50
New and improved stock	150
Continuous braking systems on stock	75
Handling equipment/road vehicles	10
	1,240

The rushed manner in which the Modernisation Plan had been assembled had limited an opportunity to develop better based traffic forecasts and financial calculations. In fact, what was available was basic and hardly suitable for preparing the required 20-year traffic forecasts. The sub-committee to produce the forecasts was led by Mr Blee and included the Director of Costings and the Director of Statistics.

Unfortunately, the forecasts went badly astray for coal and for general merchandise. The sub-committee members deserve some consideration because, for coal, they used the NCB's production plans and estimated that coal carryings by rail would rise from 175m tons to 190-195m tons by 1964 (and possibly to 200-210m tons in 1974). In fact, carryings fell to 147m tons in 1964 and to 87m tons in 1974.

For merchandise traffic, the sub-committee felt that there was a case for retaining the existing market share, but in fact by 1962, the tonnage carried was down on the 1953 level by roundly 25 per cent. Based upon the output of the sub-committee the investment cases for more mineral wagons and for the fitment of vacuum brakes were bolstered.

There was certainly a case for wagons having a higher capacity. Although there had been a major culling of the 550,000 formerly privately-owned wagons requisitioned in 1939, there were still over 300,000 in use in 1953, about half of which were low capacity and grease lubricated. Since nationalisation, some 210,000 vehicles had been acquired and 338,000 scrapped, 9,000 second hand 16 ton mineral wagons were purchased from the French Railways.

If 'planning' is extended to include 'planning to recover cost increases' the record of the BTC up to the mid-1950s was poor, although in its defence the political mechanism was so slow and obstinate that approval of applications to raise freight rates and passenger fares always resulted in an increasing deficit of £70m between 1948 and 1955.

For reasons that in 2020 seem almost incomprehensible, the reasons given in 1950 for not raising the charges for profitable heavy freight traffic – coal, other minerals, iron and steel – were 'an anxiety about the effects on the industries concerned and fears about the likely reception of such rates by the government's

The Modernisation Plan of 1955 included proposals for both new and improved, existing marshalling yards. Some idea of the complexity of the legacy from pre-grouping and grouped railway company eras may be gained from this view of individual yards either side of the main lines in the general area of Temple Mills (Rail on-line).

Transport Tribunal'. The BTC was headed towards a financial disaster.

The former GCR routes were ideally placed to benefit from the investment made in the Yorkshire and East Midlands coalfields. Both the coal and rail industries should have done more to respond to the former industry's identification of capacity constraints for cross-Pennine and Humber ports traffic; the former only partially eased by the electrification of the Woodhead route.

For the traffic flow south, the demand for coal was predominantly for the domestic and industrial markets which initially remained steady and total demand for coal necessitated using all available ER and LMR routes. Specialist coking coals for the iron and steel industries of the East Midlands, Yorkshire and Humberside could be readily accommodated.

The expansion of the electricity generating industry and siting of new coal fired power stations was critically important, as was the type of coal that the BEA specified and the distance of the supply colliery. As examples in the Midlands, Castle Donington (1958), Drakelow A and B (1955/59), Hams Hall C (1958), Staythorpe (1950) and Willington A (1957) generally favoured the former Midland Railway/LMS served collieries rather than those of the GCR/GNR. The supply distances from collieries to these power stations was short, opening the possibility to improvements in wagon turnaround time.

Left and below: Electrification of the Woodhead route in 1954 provided an excellent example of progress; albeit long delayed by economic and wartime conditions. The earlier livery is shown at 73, an EM2 locomotive, whilst the dark green lined orange and black is shown at 74; an EM1 locomotive passing Torside … although in the second half of the 1950s, three of the first seven wagons are of the wooden body type (Photograph ColourRail DE435).

CHAPTER 6

DEVELOPMENTS FROM 1955 TO 1959 AND LONGER TERM CONSEQUENCES

In this period there were several developments which affected the future prospects of the former GCR lines, particularly South of Annesley. Those developments arose from a combination of political and industrial decisions plus some extraordinary weather conditions in London and the South East. It is appropriate to continue to record the progress made by the BEA/CEGB and the changing fortunes of the NCB (in that order because it was the former which dictated the direction taken) as both those organisations were important to the future role of the railways.

Throughout the period 1951-64 the Conservative party was in power. General Elections were held in 1955 (with Sir Anthony Eden as Prime Minister) and in 1959 (Harold Macmillan) with results which increased their overall majority of seats in the House of Commons to 49 and 88 respectively.

The first major political crisis of relevance to this book was an ill-advised military action with France in Egypt which resulted in the two former colonial powers being told by the United Nations to desist and the Suez Canal – crucial for the supply route for oil from the Middle-East to Europe – being closed due to blockages by multiple ships. The repercussions of that resulted in Eden being replaced by Macmillan.

Macmillan was rather fortunate in that his stewardship coincided with favourable economic conditions at home characterised by full employment, consumer confidence and, for most people, an increase in living standards. He remarked in January 1957 that 'most of our people have never had it so good'; a remark that shortly afterwards could equally apply to one of his senior colleagues, Ernest Marples, as described later. Never one to enjoy the moment, Macmillan worried about maintaining growth and full employment whilst restraining the threat from price inflation. Partly because of concerns about the activities of a trio of Ministers and also because of an unpopular wages freeze, the party felt a need for a change and prior to the 1964 General Election, Alec Douglas-Home was elected to replace Macmillan.

The General Election of 1964 was won by Labour by a tiny overall majority with Harold Wilson as Prime Minister. All three of our industries of interest were influenced and directed to varying extents by the politicians.

From nationalisation to 1964 there were seven different Ministers of (Fuel and) Power; three for Labour and four for the Conservative governments. Geoffrey Lloyd (1951-55) did not have a seat in the Cabinet, but via colleagues campaigned for the greater use of oil in power stations. Lloyd had charge of petroleum policy in the Second World War and was fully aware of its potential. The Chairman (Citrine) agreed – against the opposition of his engineers – to experimental conversions to oil of a few new power stations mainly upon the advice of the Ministry that oil prices would fall relative to coal.

Lloyd was still Minister when a White Paper announced in January 1955, the dawn of a civil, nuclear power age. The pursuit of this ideal up to a projected input annually of some 6,000 MW in the time of Sir Percy Mills as Minister of Power and with a seat in the Cabinet, only for the next incumbent, Richard Wood, to lead the retreat to a far lower figure. The Clean Air Act 1956 was useful in supporting the move by the BEA to site new power stations away from the major load centres.

The Electricity Act 1957 paved the way for the introduction of the Central Electricity Generating Board to take over some 262 conventional power stations and 6,000 route miles of Grid and Supergrid.

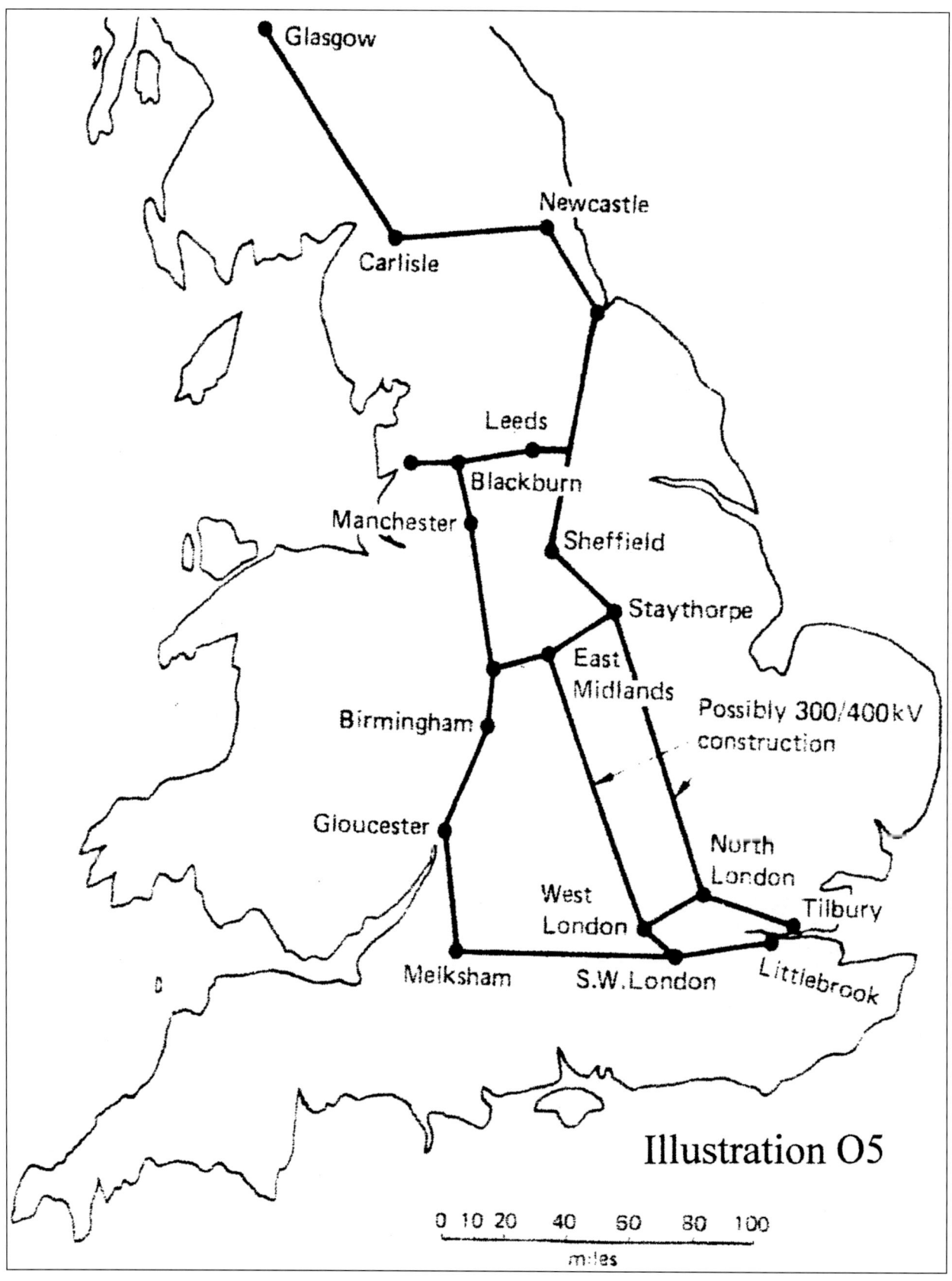

An outline of the proposed Supergrid for supplies of electricity. At that early stage power station output was only some 20 per cent of what became available with technological advances over the following decade.

Because of efficiency gains and forecasts of further growth in demand, the investment case for the industry was strong. The cost of new power station capacity was still the same in 1957 as it had been a decade earlier, despite material and labour cost increases.

The ideals of pricing policy from nationalisation as pursued by the Labour party and vigorously implemented by Citrine and Self (now at the end of their tenure; the former being replaced as chairman of the 'lead' organisations by Sir Christopher Hinton) were distant from those of the Conservative party of the late 1950s. In November 1957 and again in 1958, the three principal nationalised industries were required to accept Cabinet decisions on price freezes. The Chancellor of the Exchequer felt that both prices and profits should be increased to extract a high rate of return on the large loans being made to fund the growth of the industry; by 1960 these were at 6¼ per cent to 6¾ per cent per year. Something had to give. Policy instructions to increase expenditure on capital projects, freeze prices, increase the proportion of capital raised by self-financing and make the return required by the Treasury were incompatible. From spring 1958, pricing controls were relaxed, surpluses accrued, but were largely hidden by provisions for depreciation, and allowed self-financing to contribute 43 per cent of the total capital spend of £1,551m between 1958/59 and 1962/63; boom years for the industry.

The CEGB was in a good financial shape acceptable to the government of the day. This was a government more interested in public industries making returns on capital investment made available through Treasury-backed stock and with revenues going directly into the Treasury rather than simply breaking even taking one year with another.

Making the same formula work for the coal industry and the railway industry would be far more difficult.

As the coal industry was the responsibility of the same Ministers for Fuel and Power as for electricity, it could reasonably be assumed that it would be apparent that the policy decisions affecting the latter would inevitably impact upon the former. The move to experiment with oil was largely due to a forecast shortfall in future availability of the required tonnage of coal. The case for nuclear was founded upon growth in total demand and as a by-product of military programmes.

The politicians would doubtless have seen a larger total fuel requirement for the electricity industry and felt comfortable that coal would be a major supplier. However, the strategic decision on nuclear in particular inevitably disturbed the planning and investment case processes, leading to inevitable inefficiency in retention of older collieries, more men and working practices that would benefit from re-equipping with modern technology and better handling of coal to the surface.

The industry needed time for Plan for Coal to deliver benefits and the politicians seemed to recognise that, at least until 1957. In as far as it had been completed by 1957, the Plan was looking more like a safeguard against decline rather than a recipe for expansion. After 1957, market conditions for expansion of the industry were never present; of the six areas of sales only one – electricity – was a growth market. All the rest were certain to decline; steel, railways, private industry, gas and the domestic market.

In recognition of their changing market, the NCB produced in 1959 a Revised Plan for Coal which set lower annual production tonnages, sought new capital investment funding, proposed more closures of collieries and – in line with CEGB siting policies – proposed to source proportionately more of the revised production tonnage from the three low cost divisions.

Revised Plan for Coal coincided with a Treasury-led appraisal of the differing trading positions of the three principal nationalised industries. The Treasury felt that individual Ministers were not prepared to face up to the need for unpopular price increases to fund at least some of the total need for investment. The Treasury was seeking a net annual rate of return on investment of 8 per cent and hoped that it would act as an encouragement to managements – presumably aimed at the NCB and BTC rather than the CEGB – to deliver greater efficiency. The NCB response was apparent in that the investment schemes that produced quick returns (e.g. coalface machinery) were favoured over largescale major colliery projects. As for the electricity industry, the political strength of the Treasury brought some beneficial results, though for the coal industry in very different trading conditions.

Since nationalisation, the financial results of the coal industry up to 1957 were not far out of line with that statutorily required; at the end of that year the profit

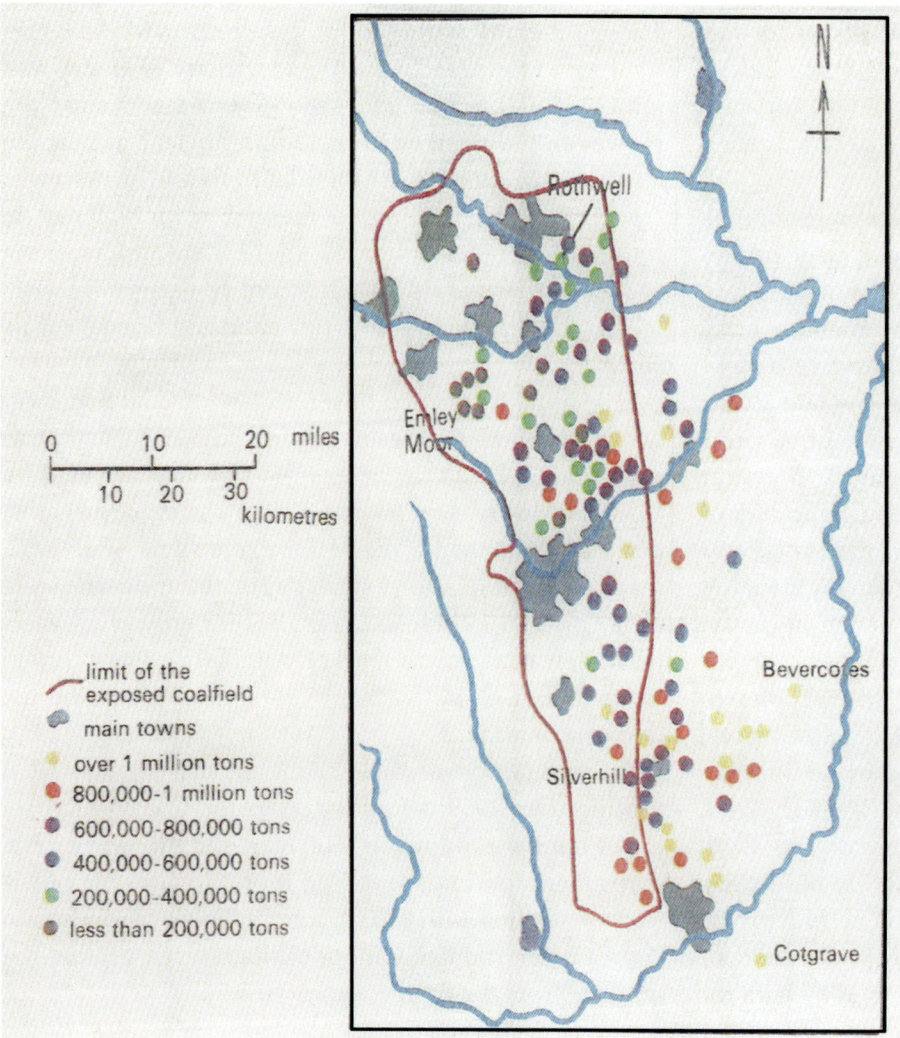

Left and Opposite: This is the same area as at Illustration O1 and shows the siting of the CEGB power stations. The coal for these power stations was mined in Nottinghamshire and Yorkshire and represented an increasingly higher percentage of total demand for coal. As the markets for domestic and industrial use coal fell, particularly in the South of England, the need for large tonnages by rail to London also fell. The peak demand for domestic coal was 1957 and, apart from stockpiling and the needs in the severe Winter of 1962/63, the decline was secular. The need for the London extension of the GCR was thus weakened.

and loss account had an accumulated deficit of £29.2m due in the main to poor years in 1947 and 1955. To achieve that position, price increases had been agreed to offset increases in costs, particularly for labour. The big increases in efficiency (expressed as output per man shift) were delivered between 1960 and 1970 (58 per cent).

On 1 October 1960, Alfred Robens (later Lord Robens) joined the NCB as Deputy Chairman and Chairman Designate, replacing James Bowman after a period of four months working together.

In spring 1961 (around the time of the wages freeze), a White Paper on the Financial Obligations of the Nationalised Industries set out new ground rules for higher financial returns. In so doing the consequences in social terms were more far reaching than pure returns to the Treasury.

By a combination of the easing of the material supply position and better coordination of effort, delays in the completion of power stations were progressively reduced in the 1950s from eleven to eight months. However, new constructions were still taking on average more than five years to commissioning. This was due in part to overcoming problems with movement and installation of the power 'sets' to provide the desired output, up from 60 MW to 100 MW (Castle Donington 1956) and (with a span of nearly seven years from order) 120 MW (Blyth).

Despite these problems, the BEA was able, in the first ten years of nationalisation, to double the capacity of the National Grid power stations. The size and capacity of the National Grid was another challenge faced, with decisions having implications for meeting demand in decades ahead. The approach favoured by the BEA engineers was to break up the Grid into three quite separate systems

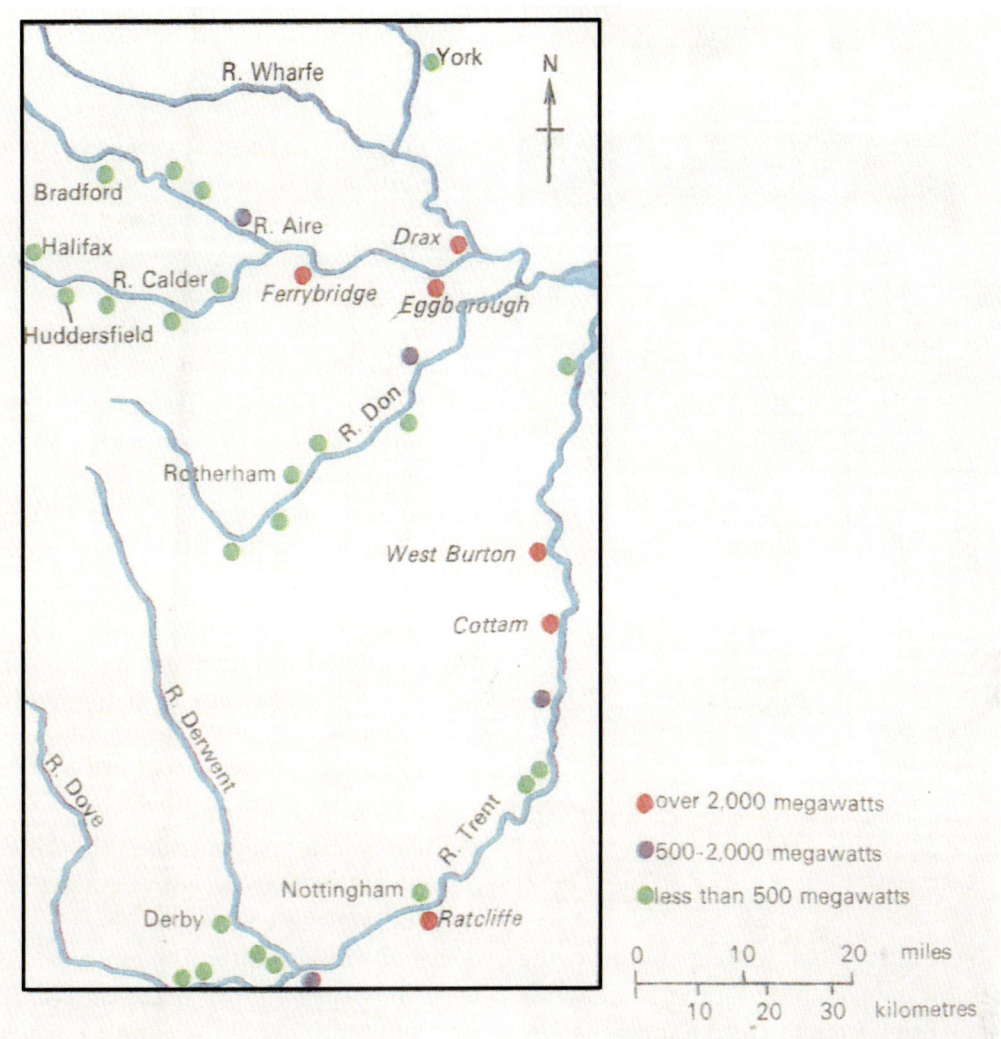

rather than raise the voltage and maintain the national system. An alternative approach was put forward by an independent consultant and suggested a higher voltage superimposed grid to extend the benefits of pooling demands nationally to gain economies of scale. He also suggested that there would be a good economic case with the higher voltage for transporting energy from coal mines to the load centres in the form of electricity cheaply via the grid rather than in expensive coal trains by rail.

The costing of the alternatives was difficult (both the NCB and RE refused to give guidance upon their future pricing), but by 1950, a BEA working party had concluded that on balance a higher voltage superimposed network – Citrine coined the name 'Supergrid' – would be worthwhile. In July 1952, the Central Authority agreed to invest £52m in 1,150 miles of Supergrid lines which would have six times the transmission capacity of the old lines.

The fact that demand for electricity built up faster than expected reinforced the economic case, as did the efficiency gains and by the end of the decade, the questions related to increasing further the voltage to be carried.

To feed the Supergrid, the BEA increasingly looked to sites more distant from the load centres, locating them either at the coast (where cooling water supplies were cheap and plentiful) or on the coalfields (where coal would be cheapest). Although the BEA failed to gain any understanding or commitments to future regional coal price differentials from the NCB, the discussions seemed to indicate (as in Plan for Coal in 1950) that there would be advantages in moving away from high cost coalfields of Kent, South Wales and Scotland towards the cheaper coal of the East Midlands and Yorkshire. As the 1950s progressed, investment in new power stations was increasingly concentrated in the Midlands and Yorkshire.

In the 1950-55 period new power stations had been opened as follows:

Location	Area	Capacity MW	Fuel	Year
Croydon B	Surrey	n/a	coal	1950
Staythorpe A	Notts	112	coal	1950
Westwood	Manchester	n/a	coal	1950
Dunston B	Tyne and Wear	300	coal	1951
Brunswick Wharf	London	340	coal/oil	1952
Keadby	Scunthorpe	360	coal	1952
Wilton	Redcar	197	coal/oil/gas	1952
Marchwood A	Hampshire	480	oil	1954
Barking C	London	220	coal	1954
Doncaster		122	coal	1954
Roosecote A	Cumbria	120	coal	1954
Stella North	Tyne and Wear	240	coal	1954
Battersea B	London	503	coal	1955
Drakelow A	Derbyshire	240	coal	1955
Portishead	Somerset	n/a	coal/oil	1955

Of interest are the three in London capable of being served by coastal shipping adapted for the Thames, the first major use of oil being from the Esso refinery nearby at Marchwood and the triple fuel options at Wilton for the ICI complex. With this programme, output capacity at year end 1955 was 20,629 MW compared to 13,518 MW in 1950.

As already referred to, the BEA increasingly looked to site power stations more distant from the load centres. Events between 4 and 9 December 1952 helped them make the case far more easily. Throughout those six days and nights, atmospheric conditions above London enabled the formation of dense, acrid and – for upwards of 10,000 people over a period of months after – deadly smog, a combination of fog and sulphurous coal smoke from industrial and domestic sources. At that time, most homes in London had more than one open hearth fire. The smog stopped road traffic and many railway movements, whilst theatres were closed as audiences could not see the stages. Astronomers at the Royal Observatory (founded in clear conditions of 1675) finally accepted the fact that since 1948 when a power station was opened nearby, their telescope had been obsolete due to being unable to provide any views of stars and abandoned the site.

In due course, a Parliamentary Select Committee was appointed to recommend ways of avoiding a repetition. The findings of the Committee prompted a Private Member's Bill which resulted in the Clean Air Act 1956. The Act – which had profound implications for the BEA, NCB and BTC – made provisions to limit the build-up of sulphur dioxide and, to do that, introduced controls, produced smoke free, prohibited dark smoke from chimneys, increased the height of industrial chimneys and for the siting of new power stations away from large conurbations. Local authorities were quick to use the provisions of the Act. In August 1956, the BTC was convicted and fined at Clerkenwell Court, London, for smoke nuisance at Camden and a similar case was brought in the following month for perceived transgressions at King's Cross.

The first half of the 1950s not only generated more electricity, but also considerable political interest and influence over the fuels to be used at power stations to generate the electricity. Those interests and influences are identified under political commentary and here the notes simply place on record what affected the demand for coal from the NCB and for movement of coal by rail.

The period 1958 to 1962 represented boom years for the electricity industry. Whilst the newly formed CEGB grappled with government policy decisions on nuclear power, demand for electricity continued to grow. The public at large was attracted by a culture of hire purchase agreements and between 1958 and 1960 the total hire purchase debt doubled (proving profitable for the area boards) as the proportion of consumers owning refrigerators rose from 11 per cent to 28 per cent, televisions from 47 per cent to 84 per cent and washing machines 22 per cent to 45 per cent. New housing was built with multiple access points for the ready supply of electricity; 'ready', that was, until Christmas 1961 and the severe winters of 1961/62 and 1962/63 when power cuts and voltage reductions had to be applied.

The response of the BEA/CEGB was to increase as quickly as possible its generating capability and total capacity from its power stations. The timescales from commitment of the build contract to commissioning of plant for conventional power stations was over three years and perhaps twice that for nuclear. Of the total of 57 conventional power stations built in the 1950s/60s by the BEA/CEGB, 48 were designed to burn coal. Reflecting the Clean Air Act and the policy to site new power stations away from the load centres and develop the Supergrid, only five of the coal only power stations were built south of an imaginary line drawn between Birmingham and Norwich. With the benefits of technological, material and manufacturing industry advances, the new capacity of some of the new stations built in the 1960s exceeded 1,000 MW and by the end of the decade would reach 2,000 MW.

A summary of the programme up to 1964 is:

Location	Area	Capacity MW	Year
Carrington	Manchester	240	1956
Stella South	Tyne and Wear	300	1956
Huncoat	Accrington	150	1956
Ince A	Ellesmere Port	240	1957
Hackney B	London	92	1957
Meaford B	Staffs	240	1957
Padiham	Lancashire	240	1957
Willington A	Derbyshire	400	1957
Wakefield B	Yorkshire	224	1957
Hams Hall	Birmingham	357	1958
Blyth A	Tyne and Wear	480	1958
Shoreham B	Sussex	342	1958
Drakelow B	Derbyshire	480	1959
Elland	Yorkshire	180	1959
Ferrybridge A	Yorkshire	300	1959
High Marnham	Notts	945	1959
Willington B	Derbyshire	400	1960
Bold	Lancashire	300	1960
Staythorpe	Notts	354	1962
Blyth B	Tyne and Wear	1,750	1962
Agecroft B	Lancashire	120	1962
Agecroft C	Lancashire	240	1962
West Thurrock	Essex	1,700	1962
Rugeley A	Staffs	600	1963
Rugeley B	Staffs	1,006	1963
Thorpe Marsh	Doncaster	1,100	1963
Drakelow C	Derbyshire	1,450	1964

Conventional power stations with a 2,000 MW capacity were very much in mind and each would require some five million tons of coal per year. A combination of decisions on the siting, planned output into the Grid and source of power for each new power station had implications for the BTC. Those decisions took into account ready availability of river water for cooling, types of coal needed, productivity of coalfields in the East Midlands/Yorkshire and enabled capital investment planning of the NCB to be progressed. Whilst having a Minister for Fuel and Power undoubtedly supported the coordination of policy between the CEGB and NCB, it left the BTC in a position of playing 'catch up' at best and, at worst, being left with a probably out of validity NCB annual output projection lacking detail. The forward production tonnages would not have declared the dilemma being faced within the NCB; that of their six markets for coal only one (that for power stations) was forecast to grow over the course of the next investment cycle. [new para] Had the portfolio of the Minister been extended to include keeping the BTC advised, that would surely have helped; it was not and it did not. For the BTC there were opportunities and threats. Opportunities to work with the CEGB/NCB on rail geometry at new power stations, better discharge facilities and improved wagon utilisation (as for the steel industry at Consett from Tyne Dock and for Stonebridge Park power station from Pilsley colliery). Threats included the gradual reduction of traffic for the other five markets, being left with a too large fleet of unbraked, mineral wagons and missed planning opportunities to better access available timetable paths for use by faster services.

In the decade to 1960, the annual burn of oil in power stations had increased from 0.2 million tons of coal equivalent to 9.2m and, at least whilst oil remained a low cost alternative, would provide a useful bargaining tool. In the mid-1960s, the fuel supply position would become more complex following the discovery of North Sea gas.

The 1960s saw a retreat from a politically led pursuit of nuclear energy. In addition to Berkeley, Bradwell and Hinckley Point, new stations at Transfynydd, North Wales, and Dungeness, Kent, were committed, but delayed and only three more were committed (Sizewell,

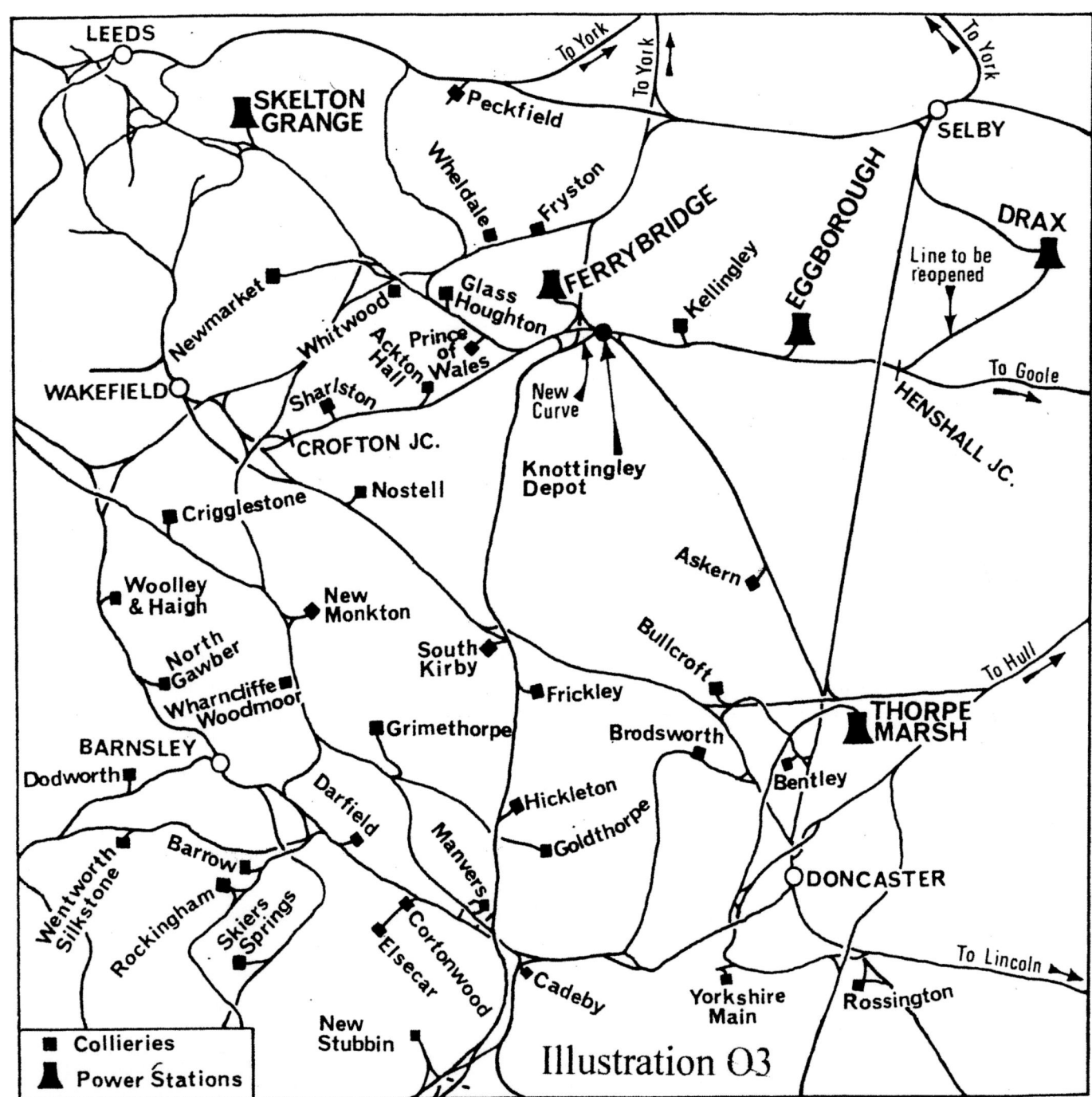

A further illustration of the policy of the CEGB to build high power output, conventional stations close to coalfields. The power stations shown in bold letters were in the last round of capital investment expenditure to feed the National Grid irrespective of where the consumer lived and worked.

Suffolk, Oldbury, Gloucestershire, and the final one, Wylfa, Anglesey, in 1964). A total of 4,455 MW was therefore expected to accrue by 1970.

From an output capacity of 20,629 MW at the end of 1955, the CEGB lifted that to 36,534 MW by the end of 1963 and to 56,057 MW by the end of 1970. Over that same period, the spare capacity margin to meet total demand was at lows in 1962 (minus 2.1 per cent) and 1961 (3.9 per cent), but by 1970 was a healthy 17.2 per cent.

The benefits to industries such as ICI and the Ford Motor Company which had invested in their own power producing plants extended via the availability of the Grid and Supergrid to railway power plants. From pre-Grouping days, the LNWR/LMS/BR and LSWR/SR/BR had power producing plants at Stonebridge Park, North London, (for the Watford line d.c. electric route to London Euston) and at Dunsford Road, Wimbledon, (for the Waterloo route), both of which became candidates for closure. Similarly, the London Underground system plants.

Coal industry

In financial terms, the NCB progressed Plan for Coal between 1950 and 1955 to be within £20m of that forecast to be spent. Capital investment committed was, at 1949 price levels, £248m and would in all probability have been more if the number of planning engineers and co-ordinators had been greater. As it was, around half of the 281 principal projects were works in progress rather than works completed.

Meeting the projected total demand for 240m tons of deep mined coal in 1965 was thought to be achievable only by a contribution from opencast mining of ten million tons, the retention of some 54,000 more men than had been envisaged, the completion of all the principal schemes then in progress and the start of 100 more schemes to enable a target of 250m tons by 1970 to be met. At that time (1955) the industry was planning for expansion. The manpower statistics were of concern and were formed by allowances for absenteeism, disputes and a lack of efficiency within the older collieries yet to benefit from investment. The proportion of the total tonnage raised from the faces that was saleable actually reduced. The additional capital cost to realise the revised Plan was put at £1,000m at then current prices.

To make up the shortfall in tonnages of large domestic and industrial use coal available, it was necessary between 1955 and 1957 to import. The ports were ill equipped to handle the tonnages involved (11m in 1955) and beyond 1956 no further contracts were placed. Between 1959 and 1970/71, the entire coal supply for the UK was home produced.

From 1951 to 1957 inclusive, coal input remained on a plateau; always above 225m tons, but never more than 228.4m. In 1957, home consumption was 5.3m tons less than in 1956 (partly because of a warm summer) and began a long downward trend, not a brief fluctuation. The industry was essentially demand market driven and after 1957, the market conditions for expansion were never present.

In 1959, the Revised Plan for Coal was produced and adopted by the NCB. The new target for production was to produce 200-215m tons annually by 1966 (previously 240m) with a projected investment (1960-65) of £535m at 1959 price levels. That £535m was in addition to the £886m already invested. The Plan also proposed the closure of 450-500 collieries (previously 350-400) and to source more of the revised total tonnage from the three lowest cost divisions (Yorkshire, East Midlands and West Midlands) plus special coal products from South Wales. However, the idea of providing entirely new capacity was not totally discarded, Kellingley being the last new colliery to come into production (1965). By 1965, 258 major colliery projects had been completed (out of 328 approved) and the industry had enough primary production capacity to meet all foreseeable needs but needed yet more investment to increase efficiency and add competitive strength against rival fuel sources.

A summary of production for 1956 to 1962 is:

Year	Deep mined coal m tons	Total coal m tons	Import m tons	Exports m tons
1956	210.7	225.6	5.3	9.9
1957	210.8	227.2	2.9	8.0
1958	202.2	219.3	0.8	5.0
1959	195.7	209.4	0.1	4.4
1960	186.8	196.7	-	5.6
1961	182.7	193.6	-	5.8
1962	190.7	200.6	-	4.9

As at 1957 the regional/divisional output percentages were:

Scotland	10.1
Northumberland and Durham	18.0
Yorkshire	20.9
North West	7.7
East Midlands	18.8
West and South Midlands	12.2
South West	11.4
Kent	0.9

NOTE:

In line with the Plan the three lowest cost divisions produced 64 per cent by 1972/73.

The implementation of the Plan came with the costs (financial and social) of closures:

Year	Closed on economic grounds	Closed for other reasons, e.g. geological
1959	36	17
1960	6	29
1961	4	25
1962	15	37
1963/64*	15	25
1964/65*	13	27

NOTE:
* accounting period

There were six principal home markets for coal in the 1950s: generation of electricity; production of steel; railway locomotives and power plants; private industry power plants; production of gas; domestic use.

Of these, only the generation of electricity represented a growth market (and would grow continuously into the 1970s). The others were under threat from various developments; steel from electric arc furnaces and imports, railways due to dieselisation and electrification, private industry from oil and electricity, gas due to the Clean Air Act (and later North Sea gas), domestic from smokeless zones and electricity/gas.

The timescales for change in each of the markets varied; railways a gradual reduction (which accelerated as the Beeching Plan/Transport Act 1962 became effective), private industry gradual and allowing scope for negotiation, gas also gradually (but accelerated after 1965) and domestic also gradual and allowing time to develop smokeless fuels.

Various smokeless fuels (Phurnacite, Roomheat, Homefire, Sunbrite and Multiheat) were developed by the NCB whilst private contractors (Rexco and Coalite) developed similar products from coal drawn from Mansfield, Ollerton and Thoresby collieries.

By around 1961 it was clear that the railways were about to face major changes and that opportunities would arise to introduce revised logistical arrangements to the benefit of the CEGB, the NCB, BRB and taxpayers alike.

Railway industry
For BR/BTC, the period between 1956 and 1960 was particularly challenging. On the one hand, a rapidly worsening financial position emerged from years of weak pricing policies, a lack of understanding of costs and profitability, intervention by government added to a downturn in the economy and of a principal customer (NCB). On the other hand, the acceptance by the government of the proposals for modernisation and the making available of capital had given the management an opportunity not to be squandered.

A fundamental problem throughout the 1950s was that neither the BTC nor BR really established and understood the various traffic flows of the railways, how each contributed to total surpluses/deficits, how best to allocate costs between the traffics and how best to set pricing policies which Transport Tribunals would find acceptable. To be fair to the BTC/BR, the Transport Act 1953 did them few favours; as a 'common carrier', the railways were obliged to accept all reasonable traffic offered (whilst road hauliers had the choice and priced accordingly) and were encumbered by unrepealed provisions dating back into the mid-nineteenth century requiring them to be non-discriminatory and to publish tariffs. The Act of 1953 went further; it required that the BTC 'must provide railway services for Great Britain' and in performing its duties the BTC must '… have regard to the needs of the public, agriculture, commerce and industry'.

Therein lay many of the problems. There was a big gap between recognising the problems of the railways as they started to manifest themselves and being able to take positive steps – for example axing clearly unprofitable services and/or by discriminatory pricing. Prior to the Act, the freight business had benefitted from four separate price increases (1950-52, plus 48 per cent in total) and, as traffic levels were sustained, the BTC were somewhat appeased. However, no one really understood the contributory or otherwise nature of the various traffics, passenger (fast/semi-fast, stopping, suburban), freight (coal/coke, minerals, merchandise).

The BTC had a Head of Costing and a Head of Statistics who had from 1949 started a process of gathering data, particularly for the railways. A Passenger Census was undertaken in 1952 and at least two of the Regions undertook further census work (the Eastern in 1955/57/60 and the Southern in 1958 and 1960). Work by the BTC between 1954 and 1956 suggested that in the latter year, BR's passenger services lost £76m, the parcels business was profitable (though reliant to an extent upon using facilities on passenger trains to convey much of its traffic) and, by calculation, freight had lost £4m.

In 1954, there had been an intention to have a Freight Traffic Survey. However this was delayed by higher priority being afforded to passenger traffic and by very protracted work to produce a revised charging scheme for merchandise freight (which appeared in print in 1957, see Appendix 2 for an example of its approach) and never reached the appropriate committee of the BTC. Spare a thought too for the difficulty arising from the areas/regions each having arrangements for accountancy and statistics based upon the former companies (LNER, LMS, GWR, SR) and the Board of Trade. From this, the costing/statistics teams at the BTC had to produce their results and encourage greater uniformity in regard to costs, allocation of costs and generation of new data.

How times changed is perhaps better explained first by reference to increasing the charges for transport of coal and minerals in 1949; a 50 per cent increase in rates would have been extremely supportive of the BTC position, but were not proceeded with on the basis of a possible loss of business, an anxiety about the effects on the industries concerned and fears about the likely reception of such rates by the Transport Tribunal. Secondly, by 1960 and armed with the results of their traffic census of 1960, the area board of the Southern Region resolved to reduce the number of marshalling yards, close one half (350) of its freight depots and public sidings by 1964 and cut the number of stations handling small sundries traffic from 130 to 25.

Gradually, a unified approach to some costs emerged and assisted the understanding of where the problems truly lay. The costs of the BTC also had to be reflected as central charges; BR as the largest body carried some 70 per cent of the total.

For its collection and delivery services, BR had a fleet of three-wheel mechanical horses which towed/detached, dropped off trailers. Bluebell Railway.

Traffic volumes and total market share statistics were:

Period	Passenger traffic mileage	Market share %	Freight traffic ton-mileage	Market share %
	('000m)		('000m)	
1954-56*	24.2	18.9	21.7	40.5
1957-59*	25.3	17.9	19.0	35.1
1960-62	23.5	14.3	17.5	29.2

NOTE:
* Suez crisis effect following rationing of petrol during part of 1956 and 1957.

The financial operating performance statistics were:

Year	Gross revenue £m	Net revenue £m	Central Charges £m	Overall balance £m
1955	453.9	1.8	42.2	(40.4)
1956	481.0	(16.5)	45.5	(62.0)
1957	501.4	(27.1)	45.5	(72.6)
1958	471.6	(48.1)	46.4	(94.5)
1959	457.4	(42.0)	46.7	(88.7)
1960	478.6	(67.7)	50.1	(117.8)
1961	474.7	(86.9)	53.7	(140.6)

NOTES:
( ) = deficit

For 1959 the fuller picture was:

Traffic	Gross revenue £m	Direct costs £m	Margin £m	Joint costs £m	Profit/loss £m
Passenger:					
Fast/semi-fast	89.3	58.0	31.3		
Stopping	23.3	62.3	(39.0)		
Suburban	31.3	30.1	1.2		
Total	143.9	150.4	(6.5)	74.7	(81.2)
Parcels	54.1	36.6	17.5	8.4	9.1
Freight:					
Merchandise	101.1	125.7	(23.6)	25.8	(49.4)
Minerals	45.8	33.4	12.4	9.8	2.6
Coal/coke	111.5	68.9	42.6	18.9	23.7

NOTES:
a) Direct costs were train working, marshalling, infrastructure, terminal and documentation costs, loss and damage, commercial costs and road conveyance. Interest at 3 per cent was added on the value of assets employed.
b) Joint (or indirect) costs were track and signalling, general administration and the balance of central charges not absorbed by interest charged directly. These were apportioned on the basis of share of gross ton-miles for track, track miles for signalling. General admin costs were spread proportionately to the allocation of direct costs. Some allowance was made for the additional costs incurred by passenger traffic on account of speed, safety and superior facilities.
c) Parcels statistics exclude the costs of parcels carried in passenger train guard's vans.

Clearly, the problems lay in particular with the stopping passenger services and with merchandise freight. Central charges too seemed to be in need of restraint.

The cost of labour represented some 60 per cent of total operating expenses and between January 1954 and January 1956 – a period of disturbed labour relations culminating in a strike by ASLEF in mid-1955 – five pay increases were agreed. The average weekly earnings increased at a rate far higher than the increase in retail prices, but in a 1960 comparison with ten other industries, railway workers fared worst (Guillebaud report). For other areas of costs (using an index of 100 at 1956) coal per ton increased to 118, steel rails per ton to 110 and electricity per unit to 105 by 1960. Diesel fuel oil per gallon fell to 78 (1956-1960).

Not unreasonably, the BTC sought to recover increases in costs by increases in fares and charging rates, though for the latter, commercial pressures at local level to retain business or attract new could lead to less than the total increase allowed actually being levied. There was a time lag between increase in and recovery of costs. The statistics also needed to reflect the government's intervention in 1956 to restrain increased charges (an application in February for a 10 per cent increase in freight charges was met by an award of 5 per cent) which resulted in no application for an increase in passenger fares during that year. In return, the government made financial concessions that were incorporated in the Transport (Railway Finances) Act of 1957. Whilst the provisions of that Act supported the modernisation programme, it did nothing to prevent further operating deficits. An era of deficit financing had arrived and the BTC was being led down the pathway to ever-mounting deficits by a government concerned about the 'over heating' of the economy, Macmillan at that time being Chancellor of the Exchequer and Harold Watkinson the incoming Minister of Transport. In real terms (i.e. not allowing for inflation) railway freight rates in the late 1950s were little above those applicable 20 years before and there having been a re-negotiation of the rate for coal following the NCB national zonal distribution pricing based upon delivered prices to merchants' depots.

BR had recognised that clearly unprofitable services and facilities needed to be withdrawn and proceeded accordingly:

Year	Route-miles authorised for closure			Stations and depots closed (numbers)		
	Passenger only	Freight only	Passenger and freight	Passenger only	Freight only	Passenger and freight
1953	162	68	12	21	9	15
1954	308	44	57	27	17	10
1955	100	56	118	37	38	13
1956	97	12	43	58	33	3
1957	67	2	40	28	23	8
1958	169	155	199	76	31	18
1959*	206	141	111	47	96	18

NOTE:
* including the closures of the Midland and Great Northern Joint line (East Anglia) and Hull and Barnsley.

It was a timid approach based in the main on the perceived contribution of branch line traffic to overall main line operational revenue and, particularly in Scotland, to a social obligation. The provisions of the Transport Act 1953 were being overtaken by changing social and economic circumstances of the nation. The difficulties facing the BTC and the government were to understand those changes, the pace of them and to place capital investment into areas likely to generate the greatest return for users and taxpayers.

Above: The railways into the 1960s continued to carry specialised traffic, including milk. The GC at Marylebone included facilities for a daily milk train which originated at, and was returned to ('without fail'), Dorrington in rural Shropshire. South Devon Railway.

Opposite: Competition for the railways' local passenger traffic intensified as the networks of bus operators were expanded and seating capacities increased (86 and 87). The 1950s saw the peak of the growth of the trolley bus system (88). Excursion and advertised longer distance road transport also grew (89 and 90).

The railway remained a substantial presence in the transport market, though a declining one. Traffic carried by BR:

Year	Passenger	Freight net ton – miles		
	miles	Coal/coke	Merchandise/livestock	Minerals
	millions	millions	millions	millions
1955	20,308	10,191	6,087	5,075
1956	21,133	10,248	6,008	5,217
1957	22,591	9,869	5,944	5,068
1958	21,725	8,927	5,231	4,268
1959	21,845	8,004	5,376	4,331
1960	21,143	8,105	5,706	4,840
1961	20,675	7,749	5,553	4,289

The big hope lay in the delivery of the second of the two big challenges faced by the BTC between 1956 and 1960: the Modernisation Plan which the government had somewhat unwillingly 'bought' in a reasonable expectation of wise management. Capital sourced, a business to be at least stabilised, a debt to be serviced, a return to be made on the investment – roll back the clock to 1900 and it is Henderson and the GCR all over again!

DEVELOPMENTS FROM 1955 TO 1959 AND LONGER TERM CONSEQUENCES • 193

Both the Treasury and the Ministry of Transport had concerns about the defects within the Plan and particularly the basis upon which a saving of £85m would accrue. Nevertheless, the Plan was accepted and, later, defended in the House of Commons. It would have been difficult to justify the government's investment of £400m in a new roads programme whilst turning its back on an industry which had suffered from financial parsimony in the past.

The BTC certainly knew how to spend money. Gross investment in railways 1955 to 1959:

Year	Current prices	
	Rolling stock £m	Total investment £m
1955	55.7	71.3
1956	66.1	89.0
1957	89.9	125.9
1958	87.4	141.0
1959	97.8	167.8

As with the BEA and NCB, government interventions into the plans of BTC were via the annual rounds of investment controls and targets, and an interest in the ordering of new equipment. For the BTC, there was a third process and that intervention was to review the Plan as the financial position of the commission – and particularly the railways – deteriorated.

Taking these in turn, there were cuts to the amount available in annual spending allocations (in February 1952 by 12 per cent, in September 1957 a cut of 5 per cent for the forward programmes for 1958 and 1959) and some relaxation to an earlier cut (May 1958, some relaxation for 1959). The scale of investment in the railways for 1954-62 represented between 3 per cent and 4 per cent of UK gross domestic fixed capital formation and, for the public sector in isolation, some 20 per cent for the same period. Of the £1,240m total, some £400m had been 'raised' internally by depreciation provision, leaving the balance to be raised by borrowings. The borrowings would bear interest charges and, therefore, the projected savings from the investment were crucial to its initial acceptance by government, a figure of £85m or 7 per cent on the total/10.5 per cent on the new borrowings. From 1956, all new capital for the public sector industries was raised directly by the Treasury (as part of the public sector borrowing requirement) and then lent to each industry. The interest rate on the first tranche was 5¼ per cent (the highest the BEA had ever incurred) and with the requirements of the NCB and BTC, a concern for government. The records of the BEA and, to a lesser extent, the NCB may just have led the Treasury towards a softer approach with the BTC than was justified.

The ordering of new equipment provided for plenty of interest. The needs for passenger traffic included diesel multiple units and diesel main line locomotives. Of these two, the understanding of BR was more advanced for the diesel multiple units. In 1951, the RE had set up a Lightweight Trains Committee which resulted in 219 vehicles being built, using light alloy, at Derby (BR) Carriage & Wagon Works. By 1954 suppliers (BUT and Rolls-Royce) had developed higher power output engines which enabled construction of the vehicles to be with steel, then becoming more readily available. BTC approval in principle to the ordering of vehicles had pre-dated the announcement of the Modernisation Plan and with that came confirmation that 844 vehicles would be built as a first tranche. In the four consecutive years 1955-8, the totals of new vehicles grew progressively from 111 to 1,070 and totalled 2,360. 1959 and 1960 saw further large-scale build programmes (832/575 vehicles) and in all 4,077 vehicles were built (51 per cent in BR workshops). The new trains proved popular with the travelling public and generated additional revenue; a 413 per cent increase for Leeds-Barnsley and over 200 per cent for Birmingham-Lichfield and Leeds-Harrogate. These results provided encouragement, but left questions unanswered, questions around revenue covering all direct costs.

With regard to its strategic policy for a fleet of main line diesel locomotives, the BTC proposed initial builds which would be subjected to trial running. Having evaluated the results of the trials, those types of locomotives with their power units and transmissions systems that emerged as being successful and affordable would be ordered in production quantities. Following representations from the Locomotive Manufacturing Association, orders were placed in 1955 with six different main contractors for a total of 174 locomotives in three different power ranges, eight different engine manufacturers and eight different suppliers of transmissions. The maximum number of locomotives of one type was twenty. With that combination of firms feeling their way in diesel manufacture and equipment not tested as a 'power system' (i.e. engine plus transmission), a period of years to build up mileage in traffic, assess reliability and total costs in comparison with other (competing) types was necessary. Such an approach was swept aside as the BTC tried to respond to its worsening financial position. The government's first request for a review of the Plan was in October 1956 (Proposals for the Railways) and outlined a 'thorough and selective trial' for the new diesels. Of the fourteen classes in the pilot scheme, ten had follow on orders without an adequate proving period.

Type	Series	Initial order quantity delivered year(s)	Follow on order(s) quantity delivered year(s)
1	D8200	10	1957-58	34	1959-61
1	D8000	20	1957-58	208	1959-68
2	D6100	10	1958-59	48	1959-60
2	D6300	6	1959	52	1959-62
2	D5000	20	1958-59	457	1959-67
2	D5300	20	1958	76	1959-62
2	D5500	20	1957-58	243	1959-62
4	D200	10	1958	190	1959-62
4	D800	3	1958	68	1959-62
4	D1	10	1959-60	183	1960-63

Above and overleaf: Transition from steam power. Photo 75 shows one of the early Derby lightweight diesel multiple unit vehicles which would, in the 1950s, have formed one half of matching twins, but seen here with a later build. Photo 76 shows one of many more types of diesel multiple units that were produced from 1957 as part of the Modernisation Plan and found favour with the travelling public. The hope for rural branch lines (under the provisions of the 1953 Transport Act at least) lay with the use of railbuses (77). Photos taken at the Ecclesbourne Valley Railway, Severn Valley Railway and Keighley and Worth Valley Railway respectively.

76

77

Above and overleaf: Dieselisation formed a significant part of the capital expenditure in the Modernisation Plan. The English Electric Company was quick off the mark to demonstrate with its prototype *Deltic* the advantages over steam (79). The London Midland Region proposals for its main line diesels envisaged two power range types; the type 4 (80) and type 2 (81); 2,300/2,500hp and 1,250hp respectively. Photograph 82 depicts the first type of main line diesel used on main line passenger trains on the GC; the English Electric type 3 as used on the Newcastle/York-Bournemouth service. Shildon, Midland Railway Centre and Severn Valley Railway, North Norfolk Railway respectively.

Beyond the classes in the pilot scheme, further types and classes were added and in quantity terms to the main contractors whose earlier builds had proven themselves; English Electric (EE) and Brush Traction (Brush) who together produced 1,544 of the total of 2,768.

North British Ltd. (D6100 class) went into liquidation and Birmingham Railway Carriage and Wagon Ltd. (D5300 class) was advised that no further orders for locomotives would be placed with them after completion of the D6500 series order.

Type	Series	Quantity	Year(s) delivered
2	D6500	98	1960-62
2	D7000	101	1961-64
3	D6700	309 (EE)	1960-65
4	D1000	74	1961-64
4	D1500	51 (Brush)	1962-68
5	D9000	22 (EE)	1961-62

The BTC paid the price for their headlong rush. The payment took various forms from withdrawal and replacement of steam to re-allocation due to being too heavy for the intended routes to a learning curve around maintenance, reliability, availability and lack of commercial warranty protections. With the benefit of experience and a greater reliance upon the advice of the manufacturers, some success stories did eventually emerge; the 22 Type 5 Deltics for the Eastern Region and in the longevity of the 512 type 4 D1500 series.

Between 1954 and 1962, 6,802 new passenger vehicles (loco hauled) and 3,816 new electric multiple unit vehicles were produced, largely without serious problems (71 per cent and 68 per cent respectively built in BR workshops). The BTC took a decision to standardise in future on 25 kv a.c. (except on the Southern Region) and accepted the consequence that the Eastern Region's schemes for Shenfield to Chelmsford and Southend would be electrified in the 1,500v d.c. system

Above and overleaf: In the space of a decade, the LNER had been replaced by BR (83 and 84 being the same locomotive) and steam gradually being replaced by cleaner technology and newer rolling stock (83 and 85 being the same location), North Norfolk Railway.

84

85

The romance of railways; forget it. Daily life around the clock at a locomotive running depot was a generally dirty and unpleasant environment. Engines having fires lit and steam raised for the day ahead represented tasks for those either starting a career, or just looking for any job and some who, for whatever reason, were not able to continue with footplate duties. When diesels and electrics threatened the traditional lines of promotion, BR found it increasingly difficult to attract and retain artisan staff who could find similarly or better paid work in clean, new industries. Barrow Hill roundhouse.

prior to later conversion. For reasons explained earlier, the government was keen that electrification schemes should proceed; Enfield-Bishop's Stortford, Colchester-Clacton, Glasgow suburban area, Kent Coast lines and Manchester/Liverpool-Crewe all proceeded, some 550 route miles (1959-62). The Southern Region had two main lines (Bournemouth/Weymouth and Salisbury/Exeter) for which steam was retained; pacific classes of 86 locomotives being rebuilt for the purpose.

Steam developments included the modification of some classes of express passenger locomotives (Western and Eastern Regions) and experiments with fourteen of the 9Fs, two of which were unsuccessful (Crosti pre-heat boilers and Berkeley mechanical stokers) and one which in time may have offered savings (the oblong ejector) from savings in fuel. Of the 999 standard locomotives built between 1951 and 1960, all but two (saved for preservation within the national collection) had been withdrawn by 1968.

Between 1955 and 1959, 239,222 new wagons and service vehicles were built and by 1962 a total of some 320,000 vehicles were equipped for continuous braking with a total fleet of 849,000 (down from 1,107,000 in 1948). However, the percentage of low capacity wagons (under 14 tons) was 46 per cent of the total fleet as the average capacity increased to 16.6 tons. There were various attempts to fit brakes to the fleet of mineral wagons – both BR and privately owned – none of which (screw couplings, instanter link couplings, clasp brakes) were successful and incurred heavy costs.

Track renewals continued at the rate of 1,500 miles per year, semaphore signals were replaced by colour light signals at a faster rate (1,300 track miles in 1959-62 compared to 600 miles in 1955-58) and, importantly, the new system of automatic warning system was installed on 1,200 route miles from 1957.

Station improvement works and new marshalling yards proceeded slowly but of the three yards completed by end 1959, one was Temple Mills (East London).

In the period 1956-58, £221m was advanced under the Finance Act 1956 and a further £191m under the Transport (Railway Finances) Act 1957. Meanwhile, the BTC had revalued the cost of the Plan at £1,500m plus an additional £160m for new projects. The operational deficits of 1956 and 1957 totalled £125.6m and in 1958, when the recession had a serious effect on the freight business, the deficit was £90.1m. The already serious financial position worsened and was hardly helped by agreement to extend the limit on deficit advances and increasing general borrowing powers. Two reviews of the Plan were undertaken, the second of which in the first half of 1959 was published as a White Paper, 'Re-appraisal of the Plan for the Modernisation and Re-equipment of British Railways'. In parallel with this the NCB was developing its revised Plan for Coal which, when it appeared, recognised and reacted to changes in demand.

The BTC re-appraisal reflected a fall in expected receipts from some coal traffic but felt they would be matched by increases in revenues in minerals and general merchandise. Similarly, the BTC forecast an increase in passenger revenues. In fact, all sources of revenue declined.

The timing of the separate appraisals by the NCB and BTC was unfortunate because the chairman of the NCB was unable to supply the BTC with a revised forecast of coal production for the years to 1963. As it turned out, the commission's estimate of 200-210m was close; 202m being the actual production in 1963.

This chapter has brought us to a point where the short/medium term plans of the CEGB and NCB were clear and the BTC was struggling to adapt to changing requirements for its passenger and freight services. The policy decisions of the CEGB and NCB having been made clear, there is no further need to refer to these organisations in detail. It is the consequences of those decisions that now take precedence as the remaining chapters concentrate on how the BTC (later BRB – chapters 9 and 11) and particularly the former GCR lines were affected.

CHAPTER 7

THE FORMER GCR LINES IN THE 1950s

This chapter identifies the role played by the former GCR lines within the nationalised railway network of the BTC. The content draws upon references to Working Timetables for 1951, 1953, 1957/58 (as part of the Eastern operating area) and for 1959/60 when control had passed to the London Midland Region as part of revisions to boundaries.

The chapter includes a model seeking to identify the net financial contribution of the main traffic flow (coal) along the London extension and to explain how a measure of profitability could have been identified.

Whilst the organisation and re-organisations of the BTC and RE stuttered in proceeding, the Eastern got on as best it could with the day and night job of running their areas of the new British Railways. The Eastern was essentially the routes of the GER, GNR and GCR that had formed the LNER.

24 May 1952. This photograph has been included to show how well the permanent way was maintained; a perfect shoulder of ballast as A3 *Flying Scotsman* approaches Staverton Road signal box (North of Woodford Halse) with the now (compared to mono photograph 1) much heavier 6.20pm Marylebone-Bradford. The now named express of eleven carriages included a restaurant car and the set was generally of Thompson design steel sided vehicles (R.J. Blenkinsop).

A lovely Spring morning; 27 March 1954 and the photographer was south of Rugby (Central) where there was a lengthy maximum speed restriction of 50 mph due to drainage problems. The Civil Engineer's lengthman has his piles of fine aggregate with which to 'pack up' under the sleepers. *Persimmon* has *The Master Cutler* as it passes a Northbound train of empties headed by a K3. Note the finely graded shallow embankments and the ever-present pole route for signal and telecommunications (R.J. Blenkinsop).

A feature of the geometry of the GC line South from Beighton (Sheffield) was the graceful, wide-sweeping curvature, as shown to good effect near Staveley. A V2 in black lined out in grey, white and red mixed traffic livery heads South (Rail on-line).

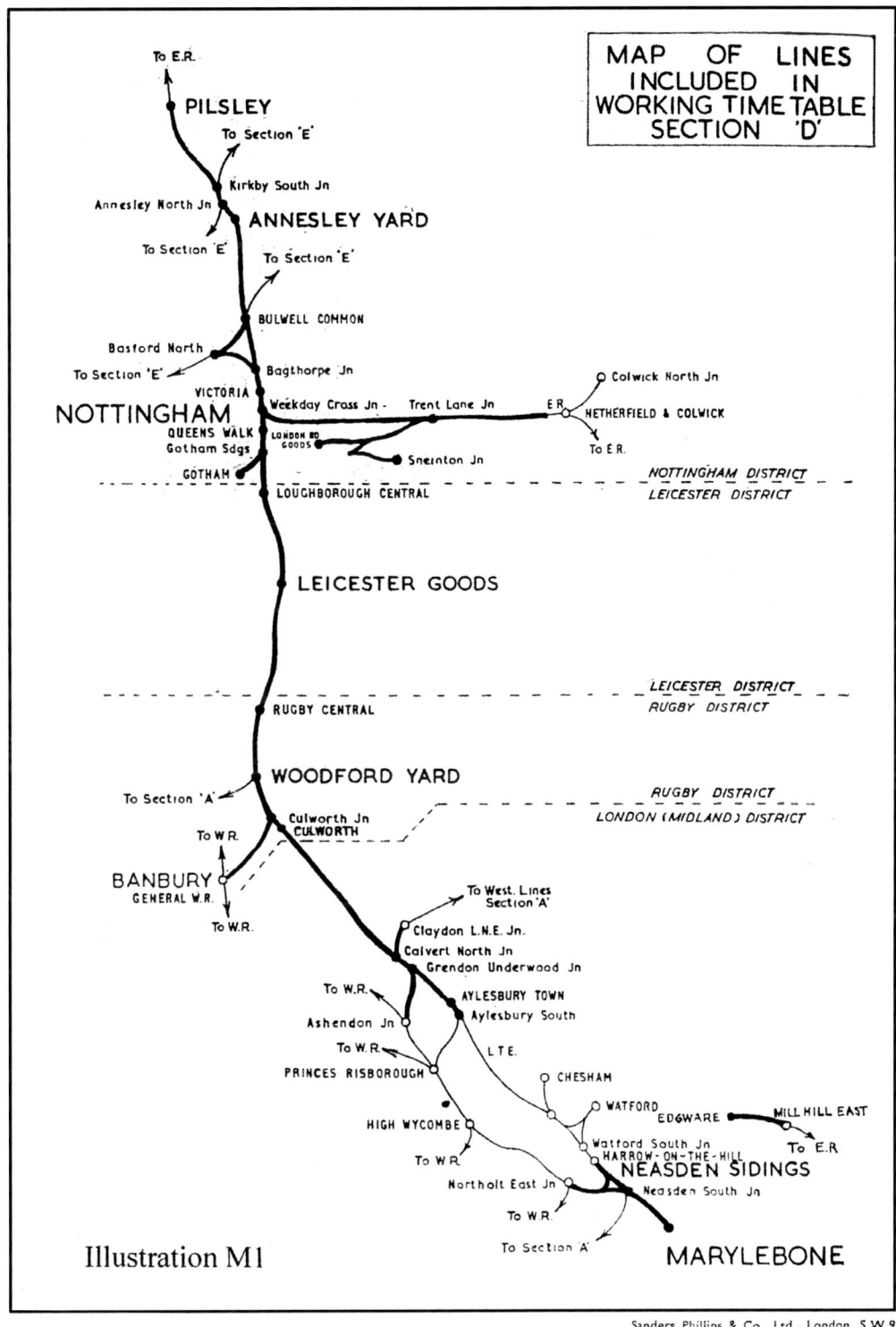

Illustration M1

Regional Working Timetables were in Sections. The London Midland Region WTT incorporated the operational arrangements of the Pilsley-Marylebone route into Section D. Colleagues managing neighbouring Sections A and E of the London Midland Region would be in communication as required as would colleagues in neighbouring Regions. The planning and timing of trains running through several operational Sections, together with locomotive and train crew arrangements, resulted in a way of management that was best suited to continuity without change. The relatively self-contained GC route South from Annesley was an example of an operationally straight forward route with 'out and home' locomotive/train crew workings. Whilst demand for the products being conveyed remained steady the route just got on with it, day in day out, night in night out.

With the experience of wartime operations along the London extension, the benefit of the improvements to Woodford Halse yard and the additional loops, it was possible for the timing graphs forming the Working Timetable to allow extra 'paths' for goods trains. During a 24-hour period (weekdays) in 1951 there were just eight 'down' line 'through' passenger trains from Marylebone:

1.30am	Nottingham
7.45am	Leicester
10.00am	Manchester
12.15pm	Manchester
3.20pm	Manchester
4.50pm	Bradford
6.15pm	Sheffield
10.00pm	Manchester
10.30am	Bournemouth-York and
9.40pm	Swindon-York.

Additionally, there were stopping services North from Woodford Halse:

5.45am	Nottingham
6.35am	Nottingham
10.00am	Nottingham
5.30pm	Nottingham
7.5pm	Leicester … plus one parcels train at
7.11am	Sheffield

Apart from these services, the line North from Woodford Halse was available for the 'lifeblood' of that part of BR; principally slow moving (average speed 25 mph), unbraked trains, plus empty fish trains and several at least partly loaded freight trains able to be timed at higher average speeds due to vacuum braking and locomotive power. All of these trains were 'balanced' by loaded Southbound services into, or through Woodford Halse.

In summary, the Working Timetable for these goods trains was established around the use of three classes of locomotive: V2 2-6-2, K3 2-6-0 and 01 2-8-0. For example, a V2 with a fully fitted class C train of 40 vehicles with oil axleboxes was timed at an average of 50 mph, class D (approx. 30 per cent vehicles brake fitted) 45 vehicles with oil axleboxes at 40 mph, a K3 would be timed at an average of 30 mph (class F) with 55 unbraked vehicles, an 01 25mph with 70 empty wagons (or 60 goods vehicles, various types) and class F, with 80 empties or 78 goods as class J.

On a typical day (Tuesday-Friday) the number of trains of the various classes heading North from Woodford Halse was:

Class	1951
C	2
E	2
F	35 (the majority of which were empty wagons)
K	1 ('pick up' goods calling along the route)

As a legacy or consequence of Watkin's desire for a self-contained railway, there were few operating constrictions from additional traffic joining, leaving or crossing the route; once on the move, the only obligation was to ensure that paths for passenger trains were kept clear. It was a simple length of operational railway.

The daily pick up goods would take its time and be available for collection/dropping off wagon load traffic from:

Location	Distance from Woodford Halse miles	Traffic
Charwelton	2½	Parkgate Iron & Steel Co.
Rugby North	14	Cattle
Lutterworth	21	Followes-Wycliffe Foundries
Leicester Abbey Lane	33÷	Distribution sidings
Swithland	39¾	Granite
Loughborough Central	44	Moss & Sons Tuckers Brick & Tile
Hotchley Hill	49½ *	British Plaster Board Marblageis Ltd.
Gotham	51	Gotham Co. Ltd. & 3 private sidings
Wilford	56	Brickworks

NOTES:
* trip workings plus 'pick up' goods
÷ block working, petroleum

Classification of goods trains: BR (ER/LMR)

In early BR times there were 9 different classifications.

3   Express goods or ballast train authorised to run at a maximum speed of 35 mph

4   Parcels, newspaper, fish, meat, fruit, milk, horsebox, cattle or perishable traffic composed of vacuum braked stock with brake pipe connected to the locomotive. Also, Express Goods train; livestock, perishable or ballast train with not less than one third of the vacuum braked vehicles connected to the locomotive

5   Freight, mineral or ballast train. Train of empty wagons carrying a through load to destination

6   Express goods, fish, meat, fruit, cattle train or ballast train not running under Class 3 or 4 headlamps

7   Through fast trains not running under Class 3, 4 or 5 headlamps

8   Goods, mineral or ballast train stopping at intermediate stations

9   Ballast, goods or inspection train requiring to stop in between signal boxes.

These numeric classifications were later superseded by letters C – F, H, J and K. Later still, BR reverted to train descriptions based upon four characters (numeric 0-9 for class of train, letter for the destination and double numeric for the train number (e.g. 4V72 was a fitted goods bound for the Western Region).

BR GOODS TRAIN HEADLAMP CODES

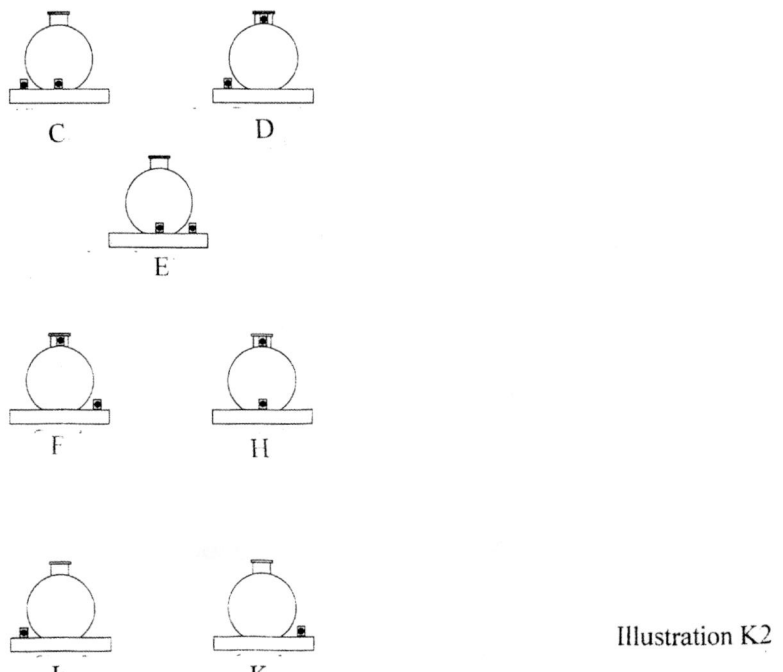

Illustration K2

This illustrates the developments in operating arrangements and train classifications over time.

Wagon storage – particularly in the summer months – was available at Staverton and Shawell.

Apart from Hotchley Hill, there is very little evidence that – in peace time – the smaller intermediate places along the London extension ever generated significant goods traffic flows beyond coal and minerals. The merchandise trains may well have had wagons added or detached but originating trainload traffic was always sparse. The criticism of the London Midland Region commercial managements for the line in this regard is baseless; the traffic was never there in GCR/LNER/BR ER days.

The destinations for the empty coal wagon trains were many and a surprisingly high number of them were destined directly for collieries, there no longer being a need (after nationalisation) to sort former privately-owned wagons. The collieries of Nottinghamshire featured strongly (Newstead, Bestwood, Kirkby Bentinck, Butler's Hill, Annesley) whilst other destinations were further afield (Ardsley, Selby, Newport, York, Stairfoot) and other trains went either to Annesley Yard (6-8) and other holding/distribution points at Staveley Town, Markham Jn and Bentley Jn.

Typical journey times for loaded class F trains between Annesley and Woodford (66 miles) were 3 hours and 15 minutes. Following a break for the footplatemen/guard and turning/servicing the locomotive, the return journey was similarly timed and would not allow a complete round trip within a normal shift. For that reason, many train crew turns either started or finished at Bulwell (with the staff train being used as a shuttle).

South and South West from Woodford Halse the operating arrangements were influenced by the needs of the former Metropolitan Railway services, the constriction represented by Banbury (Western) and the gradient profiles of the two routes to London; the original MetR/GC and GW/GC 'new' line.

Langwith Junction shed was always worth a visit. Here, five classes are represented; from left to right an 04/3, a K1, a K3, an Austerity and a J11 (Colour Rail 16444).

Of the eight main line through express passenger trains Northbound (1951), all but two (the 12.15pm and 6.15pm) were by the Metropolitan route which in addition also offered eleven trains during the day which terminated variously at Great Missenden, Aylesbury, Brackley or Woodford Halse.

From the Banbury direction came the expresses from Bournemouth and Swindon, both terminating at York. Three stopping services from Banbury to Woodford Halse were offered, plus the parcels train.

The principal flows to Woodford Halse were goods:

Via route	Class of train and quantity			
Metropolitan via Aylesbury	E 1	F 2		
GW/GC via High Wycombe	E 1	F 6	J 2	K 1
GW/GC from Banbury	C 1	F 2	H 1	J 16

Although the GW/GC route via High Wycombe was slightly longer than via the Metropolitan route, its attraction lay in its easier gradients (the Met being restricted to 40 wagon loads) and less competing traffic. The Woodford Halse stud of some 20 or so WD 2-8-0 locomotives were able to handle up to 70 wagons via High Wycombe. Some tonnage was tripped from Woodford Halse to Quainton Road and handed over there to the Metropolitan.

Half of the daily total of trains along the three routes was via Banbury. The sorting yards at Banbury represented an operating constriction, competing daily with the Western's own requirements and priorities. The total number of wagons exchanged between the Eastern and Western operating areas at Banbury in 1951 was 586,995 (378,788 in 1957), of which marginally more than half came from the Western. Wartime had involved a peak of 689,605. In the yards at Banbury, some regular traffic had to be reversed (for example if headed for South Wales or Bristol via Leamington) and for some (for example coal for gas works at Southall, Slough and Kensal Green) it would have been commercially preferable for it to have been routed from Woodford Halse via the GW/GC line via High Wycombe. New traffic flows to South Wales from mid-1951 prompted necessary changes.

The building by the Steel Company of Wales (briefly nationalised by the Labour government but in such a way that the Conservative government of 1951 was able to easily return it to the originating companies) of a new steel strip mill facility at Margam/Port Talbot created traffic flows of steel slabs and ingots from East Yorkshire (Frodingham, Scunthorpe) and – until higher quality ore could be shipped in sizeable, sea-going bulk carriers – iron ore from the Banbury area. To avoid a reversal at Banbury and a route to South Wales thence via Leamington Spa/Hatton, it was agreed with the London Midland that five trains daily would be routed from Woodford Halse via the former Stratford upon Avon and Midland Joint route to Stratford upon Avon, thence Broom (which was as far as Woodford Halse footplatemen worked), to Ashchurch where the former Midland line to Gloucester was accessed. Demand was quickly such that a sixth daily train (which could not be accommodated via the SMJ) was routed from Nottingham via the former GNR route to Derby (Friargate), Egginton Junction, Stafford and Shrewsbury to Pontypool Road.

Adding to the pressure on the timetable planners were requests for paths for seasonal traffic trains of, for example, vegetables from Cornwall, tomatoes from the Channel Islands, bananas imported through Avonmouth and/or Southampton and sugar beet being directed to a processing plant at Colwick near Nottingham. Whilst some of these trains ran during months when coal traffic was somewhat less, others simply added to the weight of timetabled trains and caused delays from attaching/detaching. It was, though, traffic that British Railways needed to retain.

In 1952 and 1955 there was a total of three accidents affecting passenger trains using the London extension.

On the evening of 30 June, the down *South Yorkshireman* from Marylebone to Sheffield/Bradford loaded to 11 carriages. Locomotives were changed at Leicester (Central) with class 5 B1 4-6-0 61126 assisted forward by a pilot locomotive in the form of A3 60054 *Prince of Wales*. Despite a permanent way temporary speed restriction between Leicester and Belgrave & Birstall, the train approached Nottingham (Victoria) – a distance of 23½ miles – in just under 27 minutes. The point to point (signal box) timings confirmed an average speed of over 70 mph between Rothley and Loughborough, but as that part of Leicestershire had some of the best available stone for track ballast there was no suggestion made in the report as to excessive speed. As the express approached its booked stop at Nottingham, the signalman of the North end was incorrectly proceeding with a train movement whereby a B1

210 • THE GREAT CENTRAL RAILWAY: WHAT REALLY HAPPENED

12

13

Right, below and opposite: During the BR era there were two accidents in the vicinity of Nottingham Victoria. At the North end, 60054 *Prince of Wales* (piloting a B1) on *The South Yorkshireman* ran beyond the platform signal to the right of the second carriage in photograph 12 and with 60054 continuing to a point adjacent to the smokebox of the D11 in photo 13. At that latter point the collision occurred with the incorrectly authorised propelling movement of an empty train into the centre track.

At the South end of the station the signal box was within a very confined area sheltered from all but Northerly winds. In those circumstances fog, snow, smoke and steam could prevent a clear view of passing trains. Such was the case when a goods train, which had become parted, passed and the signalman had no idea whether the final vehicle was a brakevan. In fact, the rearmost part of the train was a little beyond and that is where a collision occurred. Photo 14 was taken on a very dull day, but has been included to illustrate the point about how confined and sheltered was the signal box and its occupants. The lower image above, was taken in far better conditions, but shows the confined area of tracks. The signalman is keeping a watchful eye on the cameraman and his safety as A3 Tracery passes (Rail on-line).

was to propel carriages into the station. With the unfortunate timing that seems to characterise many railway accidents, the driver of 60054 either misjudged his stopping distance, misjudged the brake force of his train or expected assistance from the steam brake on the B1, with the result that the train passed beyond the signal protecting the incorrectly authorised propelling movement, with a consequential side on collision.

Later that year – on Sunday 7 August – single line working due to engineering work was in operation South from Rugby (Central). That meant that all trains used the 'down' line and 'up' trains heading for Woodford Halse and beyond would return to their correct line by means of crossover points. A 50mph speed restriction applied, a pilot rode with the footplate crew and instructions were given verbally at Rugby. The Weekly Notice of all planned work had been provided to footplate staff at Neasden depot where the crew of recently ex-Doncaster Works overhauled V2 60828 booked on duty to work to Leicester that morning and return with the same locomotive with the 10.35 ex-Manchester London Road passenger train. The Weekly Notice showed the single line working section as being between Rugby and Braunston & Willoughby; it having been thought at the time of printing that the crossover at Barby Sidings (between those two stations) had been removed earlier that summer. In fact, the crossover was still operational and at a late stage it was decided that the Barby Sidings crossover would be used and a 'Late Notice' of changes was displayed at the locomen's signing-on lobby at Neasden and elsewhere. The speed limit of the Barby Sidings crossover was 10 mph. For whatever reason – and as he died in the ensuing derailment no one ever knew for certain – the driver approached the crossover at line speed and perhaps a little more, with the inevitable derailment. In evidence it emerged that the verbal reminder instruction at Rugby was given at a time when the safety valves of the locomotive were lifting and may well not have been fully heard by the driver of the left-hand drive locomotive. The accident did not reflect well on the pilotman.

In dense fog on the early morning of 20 January 1955, an unbraked train of 61 mineral wagons became divided at Weekday Cross Junction, half a mile south of Nottingham (Victoria) station. The locomotive continued with a portion of the train for some 20 minutes and passed three signal boxes without any of the signalmen noticing and sending the appropriate bell code forward for the train to be stopped due to no 'tail lamp' and advising the previous box. The 7.28am Leicester (Central) to Manchester London Road passenger train ran into the wagons at Weekday Cross Junction. In evidence, the three signalmen all gave plausible reasons for being unable to be certain the freight train had a brakevan attached. The footplate crew were exonerated.

By 1953, matters nationally had improved for the population; rationing was less acute, material shortages were less, the war in Korea had ended and with the coronation of Queen Elizabeth II, the general mood was good. Thoughts naturally turned to holidays and British Railways responded with the re-introduction of holiday trains, particularly on Summer Saturdays and, to give an extended weekend, also on Friday nights. The Great Central line was heavily involved with these trains as follows:

Fridays only
9.40pm   Marylebone – Liverpool (via Met)

Fridays and Saturdays only
9.45pm (2)   Marylebone – Edinburgh (via GW/GC)
10.5pm   Marylebone – Edinburgh (via GW/GC)

Saturdays only
7.20am   Leicester-Cleethorpes
7.45am   Leicester-Scarborough
8.25am   Leicester-Scarborough
11.50am   Rugby-Manchester Central
8.5am   Bournemouth-Newcastle
10.28am   Poole-Bradford
11.5am   Swindon-Sheffield
11.55am   Marylebone-Nottingham
11.16am   Bournemouth-York
12.10pm   Ramsgate-Nottingham
12.20pm   Margate-Leicester
7.00am   Basford-Mablethorpe
7.10am   Tibshelf-Skegness
7.55am   Heath-Blackpool
9.44am   Basford-Scarborough

A new class C (fully brake fitted) service was introduced on Tuesdays and Fridays only; the 4.46pm Park Royal to Newcastle trainload of Guinness conveyed in tanks which were demountable for onward delivery to their final destination. Stops were made to change locomotives at

Woodford Halse, for water at Loughborough and Darnall and to change crews at Annesley. With a V2 it was often the case that, if the driver had enjoyed a good run, he would 'catch' the tail lamp of the preceding passenger train (Woodford Halse-Leicester) and be running under caution signals between Ashby Magna and Leicester Goods. Such were the difficulties in all Working Timetables.

The pattern of goods services between Woodford Halse and Annesley in 1953 remained closely aligned to that applicable in 1951, though with adjustment to some final NCB destinations which probably reflected Plan for Coal developments and an easing of rationing supply to the domestic market.

At the North East locations of the former GCR network traffic flows in 1953 were equally healthy. Taking Immingham as the example for mineral trains, Grimsby and New Clee for fish and Cleethorpes for Summer Saturday passenger traffic the flows were:

Immingham, Tuesdays-Fridays:
(Reception sidings)
29 arrivals from 14 originating points; mainly GCR but including Lincoln LMR, Whitemoor and Colwick. Five of these mineral trains were Q (ran as required) and as all were for coal it is probable that restrictions on exports resulted in their suspension.

There were six daily iron ore workings (three Q) from Immingham Mineral Quay to Frodingham (five: two Q) and Normanby Park.

Grimsby/New Clee fish train departures:

1.5pm	New Clee-Banbury
4.48pm	Grimsby-Nottingham
5.13pm	Grimsby-Ashton Moss (Manchester)
5.30pm	New Clee-London East Goods (King's Cross)
5.58pm	New Clee-London East Goods
6.18pm	Grimsby-Cambridge
6.25pm	Grimsby-Banbury
7.6pm	Grimsby-King's Cross Goods

Summer Saturdays only passenger trains from Cleethorpes were:

7.28am	Blackpool
9.5am	Leeds
9.14am	Manchester
10.00am	Rotherham
1.30pm	Leicester
1.40pm	Bradford
1.50pm	Bradford
2.00pm	Sheffield
2.54pm	Barnsley
5.38pm	Doncaster
6.32pm	Doncaster

These were balanced by inbound trains, with two Q from London King's Cross (depart 3.59pm and 4.25pm).

Of interest, the weekdays 8.57am Cleethorpes-King's Cross passenger train was timetabled to run at over 60mph.

Direct benefits from the re-starting of capital investment projects dating from pre-war were apparent in the completion and opening in 1954 of the electrification between Manchester and Sheffield/Wath yard plus to a minor extent at Woodford Halse with the arrival in autumn 1953 of five diesel shunting locomotives. The RE/BTC had embraced diesel shunting locomotive technology, but Annesley waited and waited until 1959. New fish vans were ordered in 1954 and testing – particularly on the Midland lines of the London Midland Region – of improved braking and coupling systems progressed with mineral wagons, but without ultimate success.

Industrial relations on BR deteriorated in 1954/55 as the railways slipped down the pay 'league' in comparison with other industries. This simmered and in spring 1955 finally boiled into a 17-day strike by members of ASLEF who represented 80 per cent of footplate crews. Depending upon the number of NUR footplatemen (who did not support the strike) at different depots, services were either reduced or completely lost to users of the railway. Amongst the users were those wishing to move perishable traffic: fish, fruit, vegetables and meat. The opportunity was taken by the road haulage industry – benefiting from the licencing provisions of the Transport Act 1953 – to secure contract work to initially help (for example at Grimsby and New Clee) through the crisis, but with reasonable requests for a proportion of the tonnage beyond the crisis. The Midlands cities and towns were within the reach of the East Coast of England fishing ports and were easy targets: Nottingham, Leicester, Birmingham, Derby, etc.

The progressive introduction from 1951 of the new BR Standard classes of steam locomotives eventually included allocations to some of the former GC routes, particularly the London extension and, initially and only briefly to a minor extent, for iron ore traffic for the steelworks around Scunthorpe.

New from the Doncaster Works built batch of seventeen, a total of five Standard Class 5 locomotives was allocated to Neasden; 73155-58 arriving in December 1956 and 73159 in the following month. With their arrival, the last of the Neasden A3 pacifics (60108) left in February 1957 and although one V2 was allocated in May of that year, it departed two months later, leaving the London end of the route with a total of eleven class 5s (the other half dozen being B1s) as the 'front line' power. The Standard 5s settled in and typically worked double 'out and home' trips to Leicester, accumulating some 400 miles daily. At the start of 1957, Woodford Halse had six V2s (reduced to four during the year) and five K3s (increased to seven) to work the fitted freights in particular.

The first few of the class 9 2-10-0 locomotives (which eventually totalled 251) designed for heavy freight work had appeared in early 1954 and, following proving trials around Crewe, had been allocated to South Wales for steelworks traffic. Further allocations in 1954 benefitted Eastern Region depots at March (eight) and Peterborough New England (eleven), supplemented in 1955 by two more to each depot, plus Doncaster (three) and (North Eastern) Tyne Dock (seven). The London Midland Region received its first allocation in 1954 with seven to Wellingborough followed in 1955 by fifteen more (including the ten fitted with Franco-Crosti pre-heat boilers) and ten to Toton, between Nottingham and Derby. The total of twenty-six locomotives built in 1956 went to Tyne Dock (three), Wellingborough (nine), Toton (12) plus first allocations to London Cricklewood (two) and Westhouses near Chesterfield (six). All were put to work on heavy minerals traffic between docks and steelworks and between coalfield yards and intermediate or destination yards, quickly winning plaudits (to a lesser extent in the case of the Franco-Crosti batch). From Summer 1957 some of the LM based locomotives were deployed on Saturdays Only passenger traffic when their lack of steam heat apparatus was unimportant; the Eastern Region quickly followed the lead.

The traffic management team of the Eastern Region recognised the potential beneficial use of Class 9s on the Annesley-Woodford Halse coal traffic and planning started for their intended use from mid-1957. Amongst the potential benefits was an improvement in the round-trip timings, allowing a single crew to achieve it within a single shift without the previously necessary change of crew at Bulwell. With 45 loaded mineral wagons (or 60 goods/70 empties) trains timed as Class E (average speed 30 mph) would – subject to the WTT requirements to accommodate express and stopping passenger services, fitted goods trains and the 'pick up' goods trains – achieve a 'standard' timing of 2 hrs 39 minutes in running the 66 miles. A necessary re-drafting of the timing graphs (refer to Appendix 3 for an example) allowed for 31 trains. (Note: the WTT for 16 September 1957 to 8 June 1958 shows the trains as Class H). With their high capacity water tanks, stops for water at Loughborough would be less frequent, though still desirable as the water quality at both Annesley and Woodford Halse was very poor and caused firebox and boiler problems.

To work the service from spring 1957, Annesley depot received an allocation of 9Fs. In February 1957, the first ten arrived (four from March and six from Doncaster), followed in April by twelve more (all from Doncaster), in May by five (one from March and four from New England) and five more in July (two from March and three from New England), a total of thirty-two all from the Eastern Region. In addition, two newly built examples arrived; 92095 and 92096 in March and April respectively, giving by summer a total allocation of thirty-four. The donor depots did not miss out; both Doncaster (for the March/Whitemoor workings) and New England received newly built 9Fs in late 1957 and early 1958.

Up to the time of its closure, Annesley had a total of 37 different 9Fs for varying durations. The depot workforce included a Fitter's role solely for changing worn brakeblocks, the average block life being every two and a half round trips to Woodford Halse.

The allocation of the 9Fs allowed the re-allocation of 32 2-8-0s (all Class 01) mainly to March, leaving 20 at Annesley (all but one of which was from the batch rebuilt in 1944 and well described as 2-8-0 B1s) for North/East bound mineral traffic.

For interest the other GC route depots that also received 9Fs during their brief service lives of less than 12 years were:

Frodingham	5	3 briefly in 1959 and 3 from Winter 1963
Immingham	20	mainly in two batches, from 1959 and 1963

Staveley Barrow Hill	2	1965
Woodford Halse	1	short period in 1959
Mexborough	2	short period in 1958
Langwith Jn	23	short periods in 1965

In addition to the Class H freights along the London extension and the WTT for 16 September 1957 to 8 June 1958, the pattern of goods services was similar to that for 1953. The steel traffic to South Wales remained augmented by the sixth service routed via Derby Friargate. There was an additional fish train (1276 6.25pm ex-New Clee) to Leicester and a new class C (777 5.30am ex-York Dringhouses) to Cardiff which after a 53-minute sojourn at Woodford Halse for examination was on its way.

The passenger services also generally remained as four years previously, but the choice of service available for passengers between London, Leicester, Nottingham, Sheffield and Manchester was widened. The reason for that lay in a proposal to electrify the section between Manchester London Road and Crewe (via Wilmslow), to be followed by Liverpool Lime Street to Crewe that had been accepted as part of the Modernisation Plan and prompted the London Midland Region to protect its traffic. The planning of the LMR involved a speeding up of services from London St Pancras and the transfer of Class 7 Royal Scot locomotives to work to Manchester. Departures from St Pancras to Leicester, Sheffield/Leeds/Bradford and Manchester were:

7.25am	Manchester
7.55am	Manchester fast, *The Palatine* (arr. 11.45am)
9.15am	Edinburgh via Nottingham, *The Waverley*
10.15am	Glasgow via Leicester, *The Thames-Clyde Express*
10.25am	Manchester
12.15pm	Sheffield/Leeds/Bradford
12.25pm	Manchester
2.15pm	Sheffield
2.25pm	Manchester
3.15pm	Sheffield/Leeds/Bradford
4.15pm	Sheffield
4.25pm	Manchester
5.05pm	Sheffield/Leeds/Bradford
6.33pm	Derby
6.42pm	Sheffield, 124 mins to Nottingham
6.50pm	Manchester

The respective departures from London for either Sheffield (Victoria) via the GC routes or Sheffield (Midland) via either Leicester or Nottingham via the Midland Railway routes were:

Marylebone	St Pancras
10.00am	10.15am *Thames – Clyde*
12.15pm	12.15pm
3.20pm	3.15pm
4.50pm *The South Yorkshireman*	5.05pm
6.18pm *The Master Cutler*	6.42pm

If the analysis is extended to include the GN route from London (King's Cross) via Retford, the 8am departure would have a traveller in Sheffield at 11.07am.

The BTC discussions and decisions around the commercial aspects of the 'penetrating lines' (as in Chapter 6) tended to be concentrated on the West Midlands areas around Birmingham and Wolverhampton. Thereabouts, the potential for new traffic and the risk to loss of existing traffic to road was huge and the case for the former weakened by commerce and industry not knowing with whom to deal and in many cases receiving approaches from both the LM and Western Regions. Unfortunately, the two regions could not and did not agree a way forward.

To a large extent a similar commercial situation existed within a radius of 15-20 miles of Sheffield. In addition to two Regions (Eastern and London Midland), the former Midland routes to London (St Pancras) and cross country between Bradford/Leeds to Bristol/Cardiff, the former Great Central route from Manchester (London Road) to London (Marylebone)/Cleethorpes were multiple shunting yards dating from pre-Grouping days, Wath yard, between 50 and 60 collieries, steel works and, as in the West Midlands, commerce and industry needing better commercial arrangements.

The Eastern Region recognised the need and the potential and, as part of the wider BTC moves to address their concerns over penetrating lines – created a new District centred upon Sheffield. The District encompassed Barnsley, part of the Doncaster District and the former Midland Railway LMR routes south as far as Chesterfield. The new arrangements became effective from February 1958 and at that time the LMR took over from the Eastern responsibility for the Great Central line South of Heath near Chesterfield and for the electrified

Rothley, Leicestershire, was a typical single island platform GC station with modest facilities for goods traffic. One traditional railway feature nowhere to be seen South of Nottingham was a level crossing for road traffic. A K3 calls with a Leicester – Nottingham stopper. The station is available to be enjoyed these days as part of the preserved Great Central Railway (Colour Rail 98074).

route through Woodhead/Penistone between the tunnel (inclusive) and Manchester.

The new Sheffield District offered massive scope for capital investment schemes in the form of diesel locomotives, diesel multiple unit services, an initial reduction in duplication of shunting yards followed by a new marshalling yard at Tinsley. In the nationalised era, the scope for the BTC/ER/Sheffield District provided a particularly rare example of successes out of the 1955 Modernisation Plan.

With the worsening financial results of the BTC in mind, regional management became far more aware of the need for originating traffic receipts and by working more closely with commerce and industry. The Scunthorpe-South Wales flow of steel trains provided an example. Rather than send the trains in stages between yards at Annesley, Woodford Halse, Gloucester/Stoke Gifford and (if via Shrewsbury at Pontypool Road/Severn Tunnel Junction) it would have been far better for everyone to route the trains via Birmingham and with a change of locomotives/men there. That attractive option was apparent, but pathing of additional trains via Derby and Birmingham was not possible, at least for a few years.

Equally, the routing of coal traffic needed to be reconsidered in the light of nationalisation of both the NCB and BR. With regional zone pricing including transport, routing was of concern to the NCB only if complaints were received about late arrivals at the consignee's yard. If BR wished to send trains via Lincoln, Sleaford, March, Peterborough rather than a shorter mileage route with fewer shunting yards that was entirely up to them.

When the BTC addressed the 'penetrating lines' crossing regional boundaries and the London Midland Region assumed control over the GC route as far as Heath (near Chesterfield) and between Woodhead tunnel and Manchester, the two named expresses were downgraded and business travellers offered the alternative route. Both names survived and run as current day services between Sheffield and London St Pancras International.

1957 placed unusual demands upon the railways. Petrol rationing because of the Suez crisis remained in force until mid-year and resulted in millions of additional passenger journeys and the strengthening (i.e. additional carriages) of services. It was also the first year in which demand for coal fell, a traffic position for the railways that was of concern and one which was worsened as an economic recession took hold in 1958.

The changes to regional boundaries did not, initially, affect locomotive allocations or the workshop responsible for overhauls and supply of consumables/spares to depots. The replacement for any locomotives withdrawn before the end of 1959 would be the responsibility of the previous owner. Motive power depot codes were changed; Annesley became 16D, Woodford Halse 2F, Neasden 14D and Leicester (Central) 15E.

Physical change occurred at different rates but over a period of a few years the general appearance was transferred from ex-LNER to ex-LMS, plus plenty of BR types.

Depot	Year	Allocation (steam)		
		Total	ex-LNER	ex-LMS
Annesley	1959	79	32	7
	1963	67	nil	28
Leicester	1959	22	19	3
	1963	14	nil	12
Neasden*	1955/56	69	48	11
	1959	61	6	35
Woodford Halse	1959	51	20	5
	1963	49	2	15

NOTE:
* including Aylesbury and Chesham.

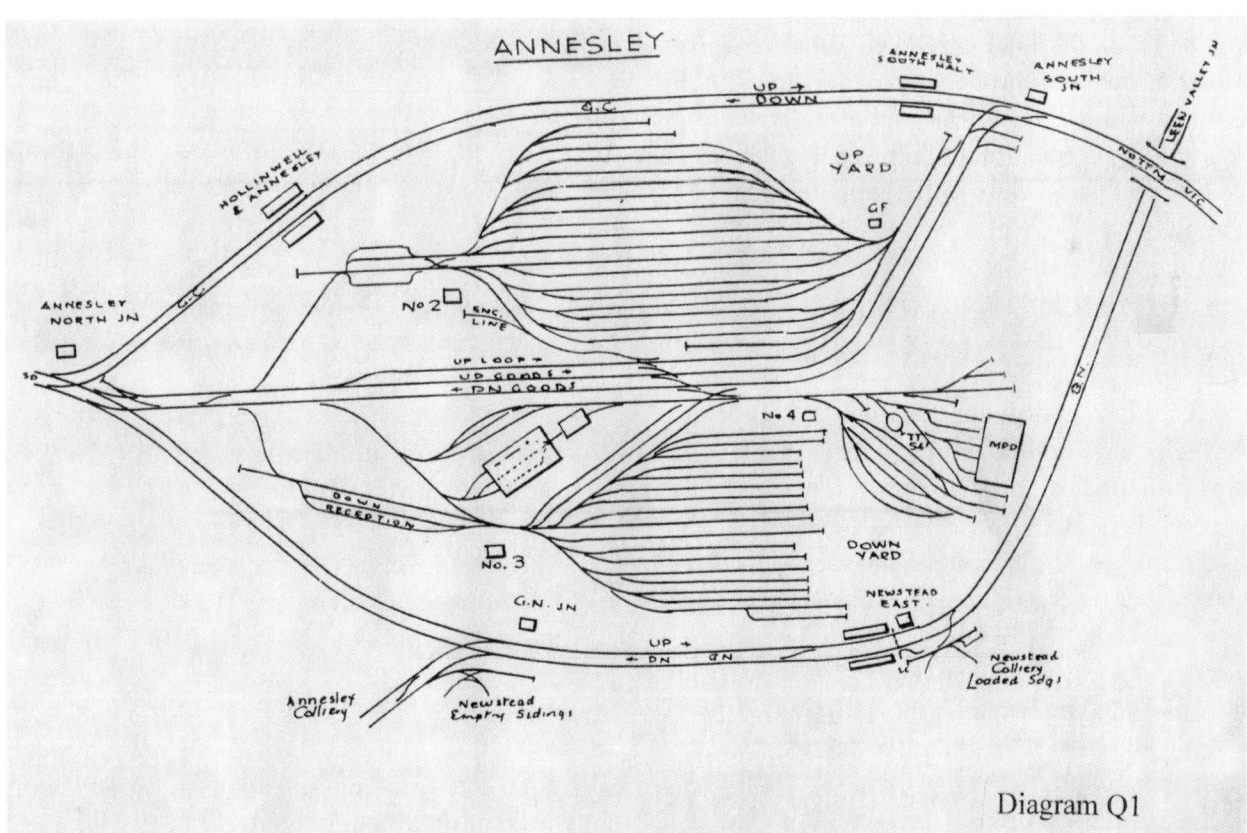

Diagram Q1

An outline of the yard, depot and wagon repairs arrangements at Annesley. Ideally, through goods traffic would be routed between Annesley North Junction and Annesley South Junction via Hollinwell & Annesley. However, in many instances Drivers would whistle up and request the up goods to get coal and/or water at the motive power depot. Trains of loaded wagons would be formed in the up yard and leave at Annesley South Junction. The wagon repair shed is centre, lower. The former GN line (Leen Valley) can be seen passing under the GC line, serving Newstead and Annesley collieries and then – under a running rights agreement – joining the GC line at Annesley North Junction.

With the exception of two of the years of the Second World War, it is probable that 1957 represented the year when the London extension was utilised to best effect.

Day in night in, day out night out, just doing the job. As explained in chapter 6, the BTC was struggling to provide meaningful statistical information about its various traffic flows and to translate whatever information it had into measures of profitability. Whilst it is correct to say that measures of profitability were difficult, it is also correct to say that the Annual Report and Accounts of the BTC contained a wealth of financial and statistical detail. From those details, it is possible to develop a model to seek to identify the profitability of the Annesley Yard-Woodford Halse Yard section for the coal traffic.

The bases upon which it is possible to build a model are:

- there was one principal customer: the NCB
- in the main the coal conveyed originated from collieries geographically close to Annesley and shunted/tripped by Annesley locomotives
- the 'through' coal trains between Annesley and Woodford Halse were uniformly formed of 45 wagons
- intermediate coal traffic (e.g. for Nottingham, Leicester) was worked separately
- locomotives allocated to the main line and trip workings were within two classes; the 9Fs and the O1s (Late 1957 allocations were used)
- the Annual Accounts and Report of the BTC for 1957 provided information for average:
  - receipts per ton
  - receipts per loaded wagon forwarded
  - load per wagon (Figures for the Eastern Region were used)
- the Annual Accounts and Report of the BTC for 1957 provided information on working expenses:
  - train and vehicle operating expenses
  - maintenance of rolling stock
  - other traffic expenses
  - signalling expenses
  - maintenance of way and structures
  - general

The model seeks to identify the income from the coal traffic flow and then the working expenses that need to be deducted to provide a measure of either profit or loss; that measure is simply an operating profit or operating loss. Beyond the operational level the BTC had other costs, including central charges and the cost of borrowing money to fund modernisation work.

The same approach would be less applicable for other freight traffic flows (e.g. fish, minerals, steel and merchandise) because they were not self-contained, had multiple customers, originating points, destinations, variable tonnages and quantities of wagons. The model would not be applicable for passenger traffic flows.

Any model which relies upon averages is open to question and provides more than ample interest for accountants and economists. For that reason, all the assumptions I have made are included. The model is built around income and costs.

INCOME

Income (all at 1957 prices) for coal/coke/patent fuel:

	£	s	d	tons
Average receipt per ton	1	0	4	
Average receipt per wagon forwarded	10	13	3	
Average load per wagon				11.93

Assumption:
- discrepancy between receipt per ton x 11.93 and receipt per wagon forwarded due to commercial rebate payable to NCB

Quantity of trains run on weekdays: 27
   Loaded wagons per train: 45
   Total number of loaded wagons per day:
     (27 x 45) 1,215
   Total tonnage of coal moved (1,215 x 11.93) 14,495
   Total income per day (1,215 x £10-13-3) £12,955

Assumption:
- even flow of traffic throughout year. Proportion of total coal for industrial use as opposed to domestic market unknown.

At this stage, it has been identified that the income generated each weekday was £12,955 and the coal has arrived (70 miles) at Woodford Halse. The average receipt per wagon forwarded by the NCB is based upon their charges 'delivered by rail to user or merchants' depot'. The wagons of coal would then be shunted/re-marshalled into trains for onward movement:

- to Quainton Road/London via Metropolitan Rly route via Aylesbury (roundly 70 miles)
- to London via High Wycombe (GW/GC route) (roundly 70 miles)
- to Banbury and beyond (WR route or via SMJ to Stratford/Ashchurch/Gloucester) (average to destination 35 miles)

Therefore, the income figure of £12,955 has to be reduced to take account of the forward movement to final destination.

Assumption:
- based upon the WTT for the London routes and the GW/GC route the proportion of the tonnage destined for London was 40 per cent and with 60 per cent via the GW/GC.

Assumption:
- the traffic originated on the Eastern Region and the revenue was retained by that Region. The commercial arrangements with the Western Region for taking forward the wagons i.e. in trainloads is unknown.

COSTS

The model now considers costs, again at 1957 levels. For BR in total the proportions of total working expenses were:

Cost element	% of total
Trains and vehicle operating expenses	36
Maintenance of rolling stock	21
Other traffic expenses	16
Signalling expenses	7
Maintenance of permanent way and structures	16
General	4

The Annual Accounts and Report of the BTC for 1957 provided statistical details:

Number of steam locomotives	17,250
Number of wagons	1,100,000
Cost of repairs plus depreciation for steam locomotive fleet	£39,769,508
Cost of repairs plus depreciation for wagon fleet	£43,132,139
Cost of other traffic expenses	£82,185,065
Total track mileage	51,079
Total route mileage	18,965
Signalling expenses	£35,925,649
Permanent way expenses	£84,775,787
General (admin, police, rents, rates insurance, etc)	£18,181,763

Average weekly earnings for particular grades of staff:

	Weekly	Daily*
	£ s	£ s
Locomotive Drivers	13 17	2
Locomotive Firemen	11 7	1 12
Guards	11 19	1 14
Depot staff (averaged)	11 18	1 14
Carriage & wagon	11 15	1 14
Control staff	14 5	2 1
Yardmasters/Foremen/Inspectors	14 15	2 2
HQ operating staff	15 9	3 1
Clerical staff	11 18	1 4
Average fuel consumed per mile (ER)	60.44 lbs	
(Not in Report) Cost per ton of coal	£4	

NOTES:
* rounded

For train and vehicle operating expenses, the model is concerned only with identifying an amount for steam traction enginemen, guards, fuel for steam traction, servicing 'cleaning' lubricating and other depot expenses for steam locomotives, shunting expenses for freight and admin. The following estimates have been made for Annesley to Woodford Halse:

- number of main line trip workings and shunt locomotives — 45
- staff train Bulwell Common locomotive — 1
- number of Drivers/Firemen in Woodford Halse plus local trip workings 'links', plus shunting yard — 60
- number of Guards for Woodford Halse plus local trip workings 'links' — 45
- number of wagons in 'circuit' (colliery to destination yard and return) — 15,000
- fuel consumed by locomotives Annesley – Woodford Halse and return plus 'lighting up' — 4 tons

- fuel consumed local trip workings/shift
  plus shunting plus 'lighting up' 3 tons
- number of motive power staff directly
  involved 45
- number of C&W servicemen involved 21

Assumptions:
- locomotives 28 9Fs, 15 01s, 2 J39s daily
- Drivers/Firemen 60, to include allowances for rest days/sickness/holidays
- Guards 45, to include allowances as for enginemen
- wagons 15,000 to allow for 10-day round trip, unloading, collection, sorting, re-marshalling, return empty
- fuel 4 tons main line round trip plus lighting up, 3 tons local trip working plus lighting up/day
- mpd staff 45 (3 shifts) to include boilerwashers, coalmen, fitters, firedroppers, steamraisers and shedmen
- wagon shops servicemen 21 (one shift)
- shunting yard 27 (3 shifts)

Further assumptions affecting calculations of costs:

- costs for passenger, parcels, merchandise minerals, fish and steel trains (full and empty) excluded
- costs for stations and station staff excluded
- proportion of total cost for signalling, permanent way, administration, general expenses charged as for line usage

Calculation of costs per day:

Train and vehicle operating expenses: £
Enginemen   60 Drivers at £2   120
             60 Firemen at £1-12s   96
Guards   45 at £1-14s   76
Fuel   28 at (4 x £4) £16   448
             17 at (4 x £3) £12   204
Servicing locomotives (£21,761,391 ÷ 17,250)
  per year £1,261. Per day (£1,261 ÷365)
  £3-9s. Total for 45 locomotives (45 x £3-9s)   169
Servicing wagons (£13,575,087 ÷1,100,000)
  per year £12. Per day (£12 ÷ 365) 8d
  Total for 15,000 wagons (15,000 x 8d)   500
Shunting expenses   (est)   330
Maintenance of rolling stock expenses:

Locomotive (steam) repairs and depreciation
  cost per year (£39,769,508 ÷ 17,250) £2,305
  Average cost per day (£2,305 ÷ 365) £6-6s
  Total for 46 locomotives (46 x £6-6s)   290
Freight wagon repair and depreciation cost
  per year (£43,132,139 ÷ 1,100,000) £39-4s
  Average cost per day for 15,000 wagons
  2s (15,000 x 2s)   1,500

Other traffic expenses: (est)   50

Signalling expenses:
  Average cost per year per route mile
  (£35,925,649 ÷ 18,965) £1,814-6s
  Average cost per day (£1,894-6s ÷ 365)
  £5-4s
  Total for 70 route miles Annesley
  area collieries to Woodford Halse
  (70 x £5-4s) £364. Proportion charged
  to coal traffic only 50 per cent   182

Permanent Way:
  Average cost per year per track mile for
  permanent way and structures
  (£84,775,787 ÷ 51,079) £1,659-14s
  Average cost per day (£1,659-14s ÷ 365)
  £4-11s. Total cost for 140 track miles
  Annesley area collieries to Woodford
  Halse (140 x £4-11s) £637. Proportion
  charged to coal traffic only 50 per cent   319

General expenses (e.g. police, rent, rates,
insurance, admin) (est)   200
                                    Total: 4,484

The model has identified income of £12,995 and total working expenses costs of £4,484 per day. However, the costs identified are for the journey as far as Woodford Halse. Costs for onward transit to final destination need to be identified.

Assumptions:
- based upon the WTT the London routes took 40% of the total traffic (486 wagons) and the GW/GC route to Banbury and beyond 60% (729)
- the trains forward would be worked to London by Woodford Halse locomotives and to Banbury also by Woodford Halse locomotives

- the proportion of track utilisation via the Metropolitan route via Aylesbury for coal traffic was low, via the GW/GC higher. The average mileage is as for Annesley area – Woodford Halse.

Calculation of costs per day:

		£
Enginemen	45 Drivers at £2	90
	45 Firemen at £1-12s	72
Guards	36 at £1-14s	60
Fuel	30 at £16	480
	4 at £8 (diesel)	32
Locomotive servicing	30 at £3-9s	
Wagon servicing	nil (Annesley)	
Locomotive maintenance	30 at £6-6s	
Wagon repair	nil (Annesley)	
Signalling Met route	20% of (70 x £5-4s)	73
Signalling GW/GC routes	50% of (70 x £5-4s)	182
Signalling Banbury route/SMJ	50% of (35 x £5-4s)	91
Permanent way Met route	20% of (70 x £4-11s)	64
Permanent way GW/GC route	50% of (70 x £4-11s)	159
Permanent way Banbury/SMJ	50% of (35 x £4-11s)	80
General expenses	(est)	200
	Total	1,583

Total working expenses (£4,484 + £1,583) £6,067

Total income less total working expenses (£12,955 - £6,067) = £6,888 per day (£2.4 million for the year). Even if costs were double that shown, the traffic was still 'in the black'. The fact that the GC routes produced a positive operating margin from coal is not surprising as coal traffic generally produced operating surpluses and made a major contribution to an otherwise depressing picture. Minerals traffic, fast/semi-fast passenger and suburban passenger services and coal and coke were the flows in the black, whilst stopping passenger services and merchandise traffic were very solidly in the red.

Chapter 6 provides more detail on the deterioration in the late 1950s of the BTC finances and the central charges, central administration charge and interest payable on capital borrowed to finance the Modernisation Plan that applied.

To complete the record, mention must be made of two accidents. In 1957 and 1961 an accident occurred at each of Leicester (Central) and between Rugby (Central) and Lutterworth.

Overnight 18/19 February 1957 heavy snowstorms brought down the telegraph wires linking the signal boxes at Leicester North and Belgrave & Birstall. A system of trains being allowed to move between the two points was implemented on a timed interval basis. Visibility at Leicester was particularly difficult and a B1 (61269) ran into the rear of a stationary goods train. On that particular morning, the woes at Leicester were compounded by a derailment of a locomotive at the south end of the station.

The second accident occurred between Rugby and Lutterworth during the night of 10/11 February 1961. The 36-wagon 1.50am Woodford Halse-Mottram partially vacuum fitted freight train became divided between the unbraked 25th and 26th vehicles, but because the vacuum braked portion of the train (vehicles one to twelve behind the locomotive) remained intact, the driver was unaware of the separation. Within a matter of minutes, the lack of a brakevan tail lamp would alert the signalman at Lutterworth, but cruelly not before the 10.25pm York-Swindon passenger train had entered the signalling section and was heading towards the derailed portion of the freight train. Unfortunately, the derailment had left the 26th vehicle standing foul of the 'up' line and in the ensuing collision and derailment the driver of the passenger train lost his life. For the record, the locomotive of the passenger train was a Western Region Hall Class, 6902.

For the Woodford Halse to Annesley section, the WTT for November 1959 to June 1960 (LMR) showed a number of changes to the previous pattern of freight traffic. For example, in 1953 between midnight and 6am, there were eight Class H trains of empty wagons (trains 3504/12/6/86/20/4 for coal) and three vacuum fitted trains (two Class C, one E). In 1959, there were no coal empties departing until 6.5am. Thereafter, during the rest of the day there were thirty-two services (five fitted, twenty balanced coal empties, six steel empties and the pick up goods).

In the 'up' direction, there was a reduction in trains on Saturdays; eight coal and four fitted being 'suspended'. The trains of merchandise showed some changes (including the reduction in fish trains, down to two) in terms of quantity as well as originating points and destinations. The trains from Manchester (Ardwick) and Niddrie (West) were gone, but new were four heading variously from the York area to Banbury/Bristol/Cardiff and a Sheffield to Colwick Class D. The fact that the LMR did not use numbers to identify trains in the WTT does not assist in tracking the 'what happened?' questions.

Some explanation for the changes can be found in the state of the economy, which in 1958 was affected by recession in heavy industries and which then took some time to recover, and in works underwritten by the Modernisation Plan. The statistics underline the national position for coal and coke:

Year	Millions of tons carried
1957	167
1958	153
1959	144

Year	Loaded wagons forwarded (millions)
1957	14.2
1958	12.8
1959	11.7

Year	Reduction in loaded wagons forwarded (thousands)
1958-59	118 (3.8% down on 1957-58)
1959-60	(5.7% down on 1958-59)

Year	Improvement in average wagon load (tons)
1958	12.88
1959	13.17
1960	13.38

As the coal carried along the route was principally for the domestic and industrial markets, the effect of the recession would have been less than elsewhere, but the effects of the implementation of the Clean Air Act were becoming apparent in London and the South East as smokeless fuel/oil/electricity made gains in the heating markets and for power generation.

For merchandise traffic, the volume reduction was not so severe, but there is little to support a theory that the 'new' fitted trains resulted from an increase in demand. It is far more probable that the re-organisation of yards in the Sheffield area and the Midland division of the LMR struggling with line capacity between Stenson Jn and Washwood Heath (i.e. Derby to Birmingham) as new power stations came on stream that a diversionary route was sought. These trains were worked by Eastern Region locomotives (frequently V2s) as far as Woodford Halse with a change of crew at Annesley.

Passenger traffic in summer 1959 is considered in three areas: timetabled weekday services, seasonal extras and excursions, mainly sporting.

Excluding the intermediate stations stopping service the pattern at Rugby (Central) was:

Time	From	To
12.16am	Marylebone	Manchester/Liverpool
12.40am MX	Swindon	York
2.43am	York	Swindon
2.48am (pass)	Liverpool (Central)	Marylebone
3.49am	Marylebone	Leicester (Central)
9.44am	Sheffield (Victoria)	Marylebone
11.40am	Manchester (London Rd)	Marylebone
11.56am	Marylebone	Manchester (London Rd)
1.43pm	Bradford (Exchange)	Marylebone
2.07pm	Newcastle	Bournemouth (West)
2.12pm	Marylebone	Manchester (London Rd)
3.49pm	Bournemouth (West)	Newcastle
5.11pm	Manchester (London Rd)	Marylebone
5.21pm	Marylebone	Manchester (London Rd)
6.42pm	Marylebone	Bradford (Exchange)
7.20pm	Manchester (London Rd)	Marylebone
8.08pm	Marylebone	Manchester (London Rd)
10.09pm	Swindon	Sheffield (Victoria)
11.14pm	York	Swindon

In summary, not a lot of change from the 1920s.

Dated Summer Saturday, balanced additionals from Leicester (Central) were:

Time	From	To
12.05am	Nottingham (Victoria)	Portsmouth Harbour
1.00am	Leicester	Ramsgate
1.30am	Derby (Friargate)	Ramsgate
1.50am	Sheffield (Victoria)	Hastings
3.24am	Nottingham (Victoria)	Bournemouth (Central)
5.20am	Leicester	Llandudno
7.45am	Leicester	Scarborough (Londesborough Rd)
1.26pm	Bradford (Exchange)	Poole
1.59pm	Sheffield (Victoria)	Bournemouth (Central)
3.28pm	Newcastle	Swansea (High St)
10.38pm	Scarborough (L Rd)^ø	Swindon
11.55pm (FO)	Sheffield (Victoria)	Portsmouth Harbour

NOTE:
ø carriage(s) added to York-Swindon train.

Excursion traffic for enthusiasts increased in the 1950s. Very well turned out D11s 62662/4 worked one leg of an out and back tour from London with an A4 to Sheffield, an EM2 to the outskirts of Manchester, the D11s back to Sheffield (via Todmorden and Barnsley) and the A4 back to London. The two D11s were turned at Rotherwood and that is where *Princess Mary* is seen (David Marriott).

Trains to Skegness and Mablethorpe were operated out of Leicester (Belgrave Road) with Leicester (Central) crews along the former GNR route to join the GN/LNWR line at John O'Gaunt before heading to Melton Mowbray (North).

For that year I do not have details for Summer Saturday services from Nottinghamshire and Derbyshire but by that date the two principal operators of bus services – Trent Motor Traction and Midland General – had been co-operating to mutual benefit by offering express services on Summer Saturdays and 'through' services on other days. In 1955, the year of the ASLEF strike, services on Saturdays had been introduced to supplement that to Rhyl (introduced in 1949):

- X13 Alfreton-Great Yarmouth
- X17 Loughborough-Great Yarmouth
- X18 Loughborough-Blackpool
- X19 Derby, Nottingham-Clacton-on-Sea
- X20 Nottingham-Cromer (ran to Hunstanton on Thursdays and Sundays).

For the 1956 peak season, Midland General proposed – though eventually did not proceed with – express services from Mansfield to Torquay and to Bournemouth. The services as proposed would have supplemented existing year-round daily services operated under a pooling of vehicles/mileage accumulated arrangement between Associated Motorways and certain Yorkshire operators who were naturally wary of those seeking to cream off the summer traffic.

1956 did see the introduction of a Nottingham-Blackpool service operated by Trent, North Western, Ribble and Lancashire United via Manchester, Chorley and Preston with connecting services to Liverpool, Kendal, Keswick, Morecambe and Scotland.

The operators of long-distance summer services were fortunate in that the restrictions on fuel due to the Suez crisis affected them only between December 1956 and April 1957. They were less fortunate when the major bus operators were afflicted by an all-out strike between 20 and 28 July 1957.

Like the railways, the operators of long-distance bus services were starting to face the rapidly increasing threat to their businesses from the number of families able to own a car and enjoy the freedom of choice as to when they travelled. However, sporting fixtures continued to attract train loads of fans.

With Wembley Stadium in North London being conveniently placed to the GC line, many sporting excursion trains used the route. Of particular interest were Football Association Cup Finals, Rugby League Challenge Finals and England versus Scotland association football matches. When Nottingham Forest reached Wembley in 1959, a total of 23 specials ran; 13 being routed via the GC line mainly with Immingham and Colwick B1s. A few weeks prior to that – on the night of 10/11 April – a succession of trains was worked from Scotland for the international versus England. Of those that came from the East Coast of Scotland, four used the GC route from Mexborough and exchanged locomotives there. Any local spotter at Mexborough shed later that morning would scarcely have believed his eyes as he looked upon four Haymarket pacifics; two A4s and two A3s. The Rugby League challenge final could produce a mid-morning rush; 1959 (Hull v Wigan) bringing a repeat of the Immingham stud from the FA Cup Final the previous week. Out of context here, but relevant nevertheless were the arrangements for Leicester City's appearances at Wembley in 1961 and 1963. Both the Midland and GC routes were used; motive power being three Royal Scots and one Patriot plus a V2 on the latter route in 1961 and two Jubilees in 1963.

At the end of the 1950s, the London extension was particularly busy with coal, mineral and merchandise freight trains, retained 'through' passenger services, parcels and mail trains. The predominant traffic flow was coal for the domestic and industrial markets to the south and south west of the Nottinghamshire coalfield. The warning signs for the future were appreciated by the NCB but their response – with the BTC/BRB – in the form of a new approach to marketing smokeless fuel and regional coal distribution depots to replace direct deliveries to thousands of small stations/merchants' yards would necessarily occupy the planners.

In 1959, the BTC re-appraised the BR Modernisation Plan of 1955. The chairman announced at a press conference in July that the 1955 Plan was soundly based and there was no need for any fundamental changes; it was (in the view of the BTC) a sound investment from the country's viewpoint. Subsequent events since 1955 made some modifications desirable, but they were few and aimed chiefly at accelerating the implementation. It was a sign of myopia.

Sir Brian Robertson went on to say that no closures of main lines were envisaged between 1959 and 1963 (the period covered by the re-appraisal). That included the GC main line, over which Sir Brian said a great deal of freight would be diverted, while the Crewe-London Euston main line was being electrified. He actually said that the GC line would be 'loaded' with goods traffic after withdrawal of its through passenger services at the end of the summer timetable (September) and their replacement by three daily workings in each direction between Marylebone and Nottingham. Because of a dispute in the printing industry, new timetables could not be made available and the winter timetables did not take full effect until 2 November.

The proposals for the withdrawal of through passenger working had first been announced in the summer and eventually involved over two stages, there being no service from London (Marylebone) venturing further than Nottingham (Victoria), no local services between Nottingham (Victoria) and Sheffield (Victoria), the reduction and downgrading of services between Marylebone and Nottingham and very little for Yorkshire folk who had used *The South Yorkshireman* service. The only marginal beneficiaries along the GC route were those at intermediate stations: Harrow-on-the-Hill, Aylesbury, Brackley, Woodford Halse and Lutterworth.

For the short time that it would run, the train in the evening for Sheffield/Manchester was retimed from 6.18pm (as for *The Master Cutler*) to 7.15pm and re-routed via Aylesbury where a stop was inserted into the timetable. Arrival at Sheffield (Victoria) was at 11.13pm.

Between Nottingham, Chesterfield and Sheffield the proposals were to run diesel multiple units between the Midland stations; two in the 'down' direction and four in the 'up', with a call at Chesterfield. Passengers for Halifax and Huddersfield would – subject to the proposals for the GC line being accepted – be accommodated in through carriages attached to trains from/to London (St Pancras). A service across the Pennines between Sheffield (Victoria) and Manchester (London Road) would continue.

Predictably, the proposals brought forth objections and the matter was referred to the Area Transport Users Consultative Committee (see later chapter 10). Perhaps because of that, in September BR carried out a passenger census. That census had shown that the average number of passengers in the five trains then running between Marylebone and Sheffield (Victoria) was below 80 in every case. In the 'up' direction, the average was 66 between Manchester, Sheffield and Nottingham, 66 between Nottingham and Leicester and 78 between Leicester and London; similar in the down direction. Between all these cities, BR offered a good alternative service and there was no justification for a duplication of services between Nottingham, Chesterfield and Sheffield.

The London Midland Region had also announced a Freight Traffic Plan, under which parcels traffic would be concentrated on six centres: London, Birmingham, Leicester, Liverpool, Manchester and Nottingham – at which more than 90 per cent of the Region's parcels then originated. That, at least, was potentially good news for the GC line with its connections to four of the six centres.

There were other signs as to the future in the authorisation of capital expenditure for particular marshalling yards. The BTC's Modernisation Plan included support for a London outer ring freight route. Improvements along this route – from Cambridge to Ashford via Bletchley, Oxford, Reading and Tonbridge – had been advocated in 1949. The existing line passed under the GC line near Calvert (between Woodford Halse and Aylesbury) and the two routes had been connected during the Second World War. The intention of the 1950s scheme was to relieve congestion at London junctions by keeping north-south freight traffic (wagon load) out of central London. In furthering the scheme, a 'flyover' bridge was built at Bletchley (£1.6m) and land acquired at Swanbourne (Buckinghamshire) for use as a marshalling yard. If the scheme – which the BTC recognised was 'never expected to show a direct financial return' – had survived later scrutiny (see later in chapter 9), the future for the London extension would have been better safeguarded. That it did not survive the scrutiny was nothing to do with the London Midland Region.

What was very much to do with the London Midland Region was their successfully made investment case for dieselisation of Midland Division services out of St Pancras to the Midlands, Sheffield, Leeds and to Manchester. Major investment in a new diesel depot at Toton (between Nottingham and Derby) was sanctioned, as was a new suburban diesel multiple unit service between St Pancras and Bedford (Midland) and out of Marylebone to Aylesbury with a new maintenance facility at Cricklewood, North London.

Change – massive change – was just around the corner and it was triggered by the result of the General Election held in October 1959.

CHAPTER 8

MOVEMENT OF COAL SOUTH BY RAIL

As outlined in chapter 7, the flow of coal was the principal southbound traffic along the London extension of the former GC line as far as Woodford Halse. This chapter seeks to identify the relative importance to BR in the 1950s of that GC line for the proportion of the total tonnage carried to London yards (the coal flow for destinations West of Woodford Halse via Banbury will be covered in chapters 9 and 11). The identification of the relative importance of one particular route and tonnage destined for domestic/household use and for industrial users involves a necessary consideration of the other flows by rail required to meet the total demand.

Until the mid-1950s, the industrial strength and wealth of the UK together with the warming of its population was heavily dependent upon coal. Although the industrial revolution was established and developed in areas having ease of access to coal, large areas lacked a nearby coalfield. Centres of administration, finance and trading arrangements – particularly London – relied upon transportation of coal by sea/river/canal and rail. Places such as Lincoln – with no easy access to a coalfield – quickly responded to becoming a centre at which various railway companies exchanged their traffic.

London, as the fast-growing seat of government promoting free trade within and beyond the British Empire, was servicing the needs of its commodity markets and its concentrated local population. The coalfield that supplied the needs of the domestic population of London and of the industrial users/private generators of power was that of Nottinghamshire. Later, as demand grew and that coalfield was tapped by more railway companies, new railway routes were opened. Although the Midland Railway, established in the 1840s, had a strong presence along the Erewash Valley of Nottinghamshire, it did not have a direct route to London until 1867. Until that time, it relied upon commercial arrangements to use the tracks of other railway companies.

Chronologically, the GNR, with its main line from London King's Cross to Doncaster, was first, in 1852, to establish a link for coal to be taken south via Peterborough and Hitchin. Meanwhile, the MR developed its network and connections in the North Midlands and initially agreed with the LNWR to use a route south via Hampton-in-Arden and Rugby, a route already becoming congested and suffering – as far as the MR was concerned – from unfair priorities being assigned. The MR route via Bedford to Hitchin (1857) suffered from there to London the same pressures and from 1868 the MR had its own route into London (St Pancras/Somers Town) from Bedford.

Such was the growth in demand and, therefore, the commercial attraction of the movement of coal, that over a period of decades the GNR, Great Eastern (GE), LNWR, MS&LR/GCR and Lancashire Derbyshire & East Coast Railway (LDECR) each sought to challenge – (via parliament if necessary) – the MR, which considered Nottinghamshire and its coalfield to be its lucrative territory. The costs to the 'invaders' varied from civil engineering costs (particularly viaducts and tunnels) to commercial concessions in negotiations with colliery owners as providers of the product and railway wagons. Chapters 1 and 2 explained the attraction to the MS&LR/GCR and the risks accepted by its chairmen and shareholders. Appendix 4 shows how the hold of the MR was weakened over time and how, after 1922, the LMS/LNER co-operated to jointly access output from new and deeper coalfaces.

Operational change by the railways was generally slow and well into the BR era very long-standing arrangements for motive power, manpower, routing through junctions, exchange arrangements en route to destinations and timetabling enjoyed priority over efficiency. There were exceptions; the 1947 and 1957 improvements for Annesley-Woodford Halse workings were good examples, a reorganisation of yards at

Above and overleaf pages: Coal for London. The lure of lucrative traffic out of the coalfields of Nottinghamshire encouraged competitors to the Midland Railway to invest heavily; as an example the Great Northern thought little of the cost of a viaduct such as that shown at photo 17 to access Pinxton (Colour Rail 98166).

For every loaded coal wagon Southbound there was, several days later, that same wagon being returned empty. Here a 9F has a train of empties at Charwelton. The sidings to the right were used for locally originating iron ore traffic (Photo 19 Colour Rail 381926). Photo 20 shows a loaded coal train on the Midland between Trent and Syston. Photo 21 is of interest as it shows the block train of 16 40-ton wagons which ran between Toton and Stonebridge Park power station between the late 1930s and early 1960s, routed via Market Harborough and Roade to gain the former LNWR main line. As with photograph 4 here was a solution to the problem of slow moving, unbraked coal trains between specific collieries and specific destination customers … a pioneer merry go round type operation. Photo 22 shows one of the many trials undertaken by BR in an attempt to improve matters with screw couplings and vacuum brakes; eventually abandoned for most mineral traffic and with the NCB and CEGB banning wagons so fitted.

Peterborough (1953) and at Temple Mills, GER (1954/9). As a self-contained operation, the GC London extension as far as Woodford Halse offered relative attractions but, as will be explained, it also suffered from operational weaknesses generally common to all routes; multiple customer (coal merchants) destinations for small numbers of wagon load consignments of domestic coal from multiple collieries requiring shunting/sorting at least once during the journey. From 1948, the problems of privately-owned wagons and ownership of collieries had disappeared, potentially providing BR opportunities with the larger tonnage consignments to industrial users and for its own internal use (e.g. steam motive power depots and power generation plant at Stonebridge Park and Wimbledon).

There were several routings by which coal reached the railway yards north of the Thames in the London area:

Eastern Region:
   a) the former GN/GE Joint line from Doncaster via Gainsborough initially to March/Whitemoor (in Cambridgeshire) where incoming traffic, either loaded or empty, was re-sorted prior to onward movement. This flow was enhanced along the way at Sykes Jn (where traffic from west of Retford joined) and at Lincoln (from various collieries in Derbyshire and Nottinghamshire via Killamarsh and Mansfield areas). From Lincoln the trains could be routed via Sleaford (incoming traffic from South Nottinghamshire/Leen Valley collieries via Colwick) and Spalding or via Boston and Spalding (in this latter case, a few trains going on to Peterborough (New England) rather than Whitemoor). Traffic from Leicester (LMR) via Peterborough was also routed to Whitemoor.
   b) the former GN main line from Peterborough (New England) to London (Ferme Park).
   c) the former GCR line from Annesley initially to Woodford Halse where incoming traffic either loaded or empty was re-sorted prior to onward movement (London Midland Region responsibility from 1958).

Eastern Region/London Midland Region:
   a) the former GN/LNWR Joint line from near Nottingham to Welham near Northampton, via Market Harborough.

London Midland Region:
   a) the former MR lines South from Toton (between Nottingham and Derby) via any of three routes; viz Nottingham and Edwalton to Rushton near Kettering, via Trent and Syston to Manton there to join the route via Edwalton and via Trent, Syston, Leicester, Wigston (traffic joining from Leicestershire coalfield and diverging to Rugby), Market Harborough (traffic diverging to Northampton and Rugby) and Rushton where all three routes converged initially to Wellingborough (Northamptonshire). At Wellingborough most southbound coal trains at least exchanged locomotives and train crews.

The geological formation of England meant that the routes further towards the east provided fewer obstacles in the

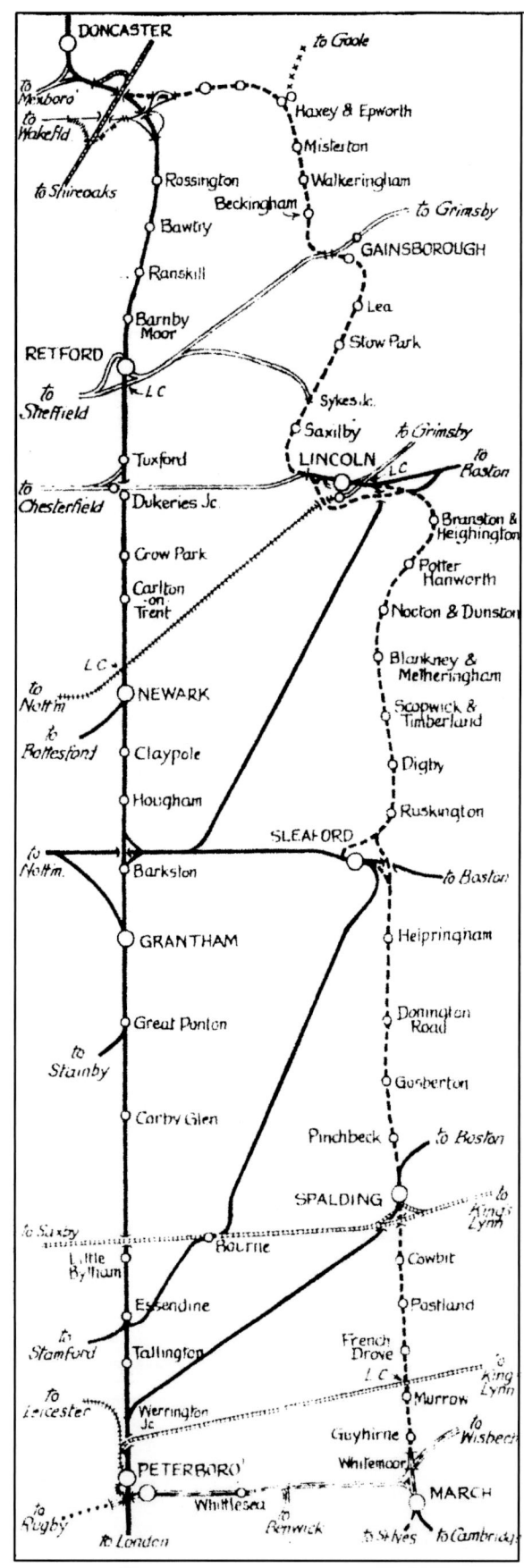

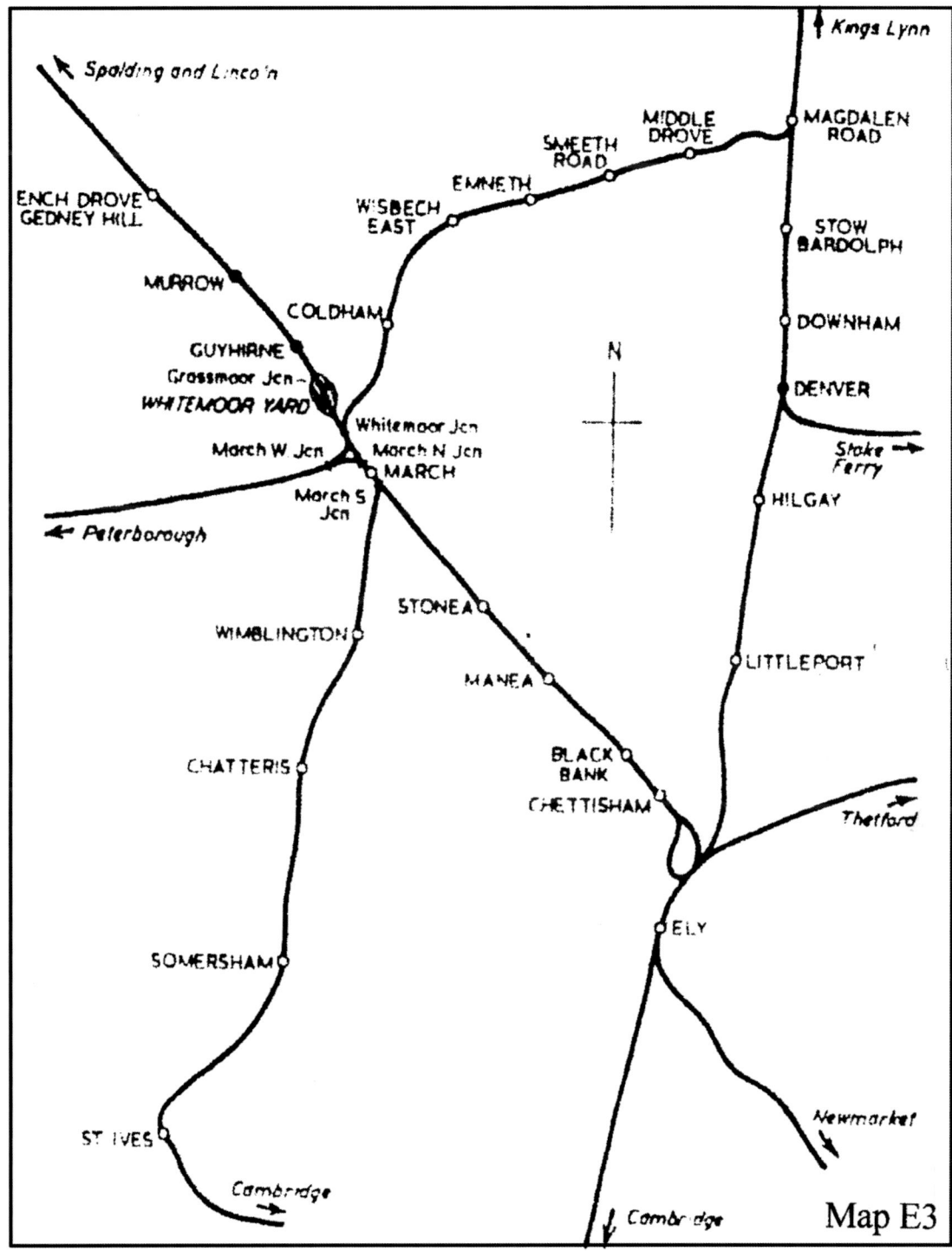

Having arrived (map E1) from multiple originating points and having been sorted at Whitemoor yards for onward movement, coal traffic for London Temple Mills yards could be forwarded via alternative routes.

Opposite: This map shows the main Great Northern Railway route between Doncaster and Peterborough. Slow moving trains of coal were not welcome on such a section used by passenger trains and, instead, were routed via Lincoln, Sleaford and Spalding to the yards at March/Whitemoor. The map also illustrates how coal traffic from elsewhere could join the flow at Lincoln, Sleaford, Spalding and via Peterborough.

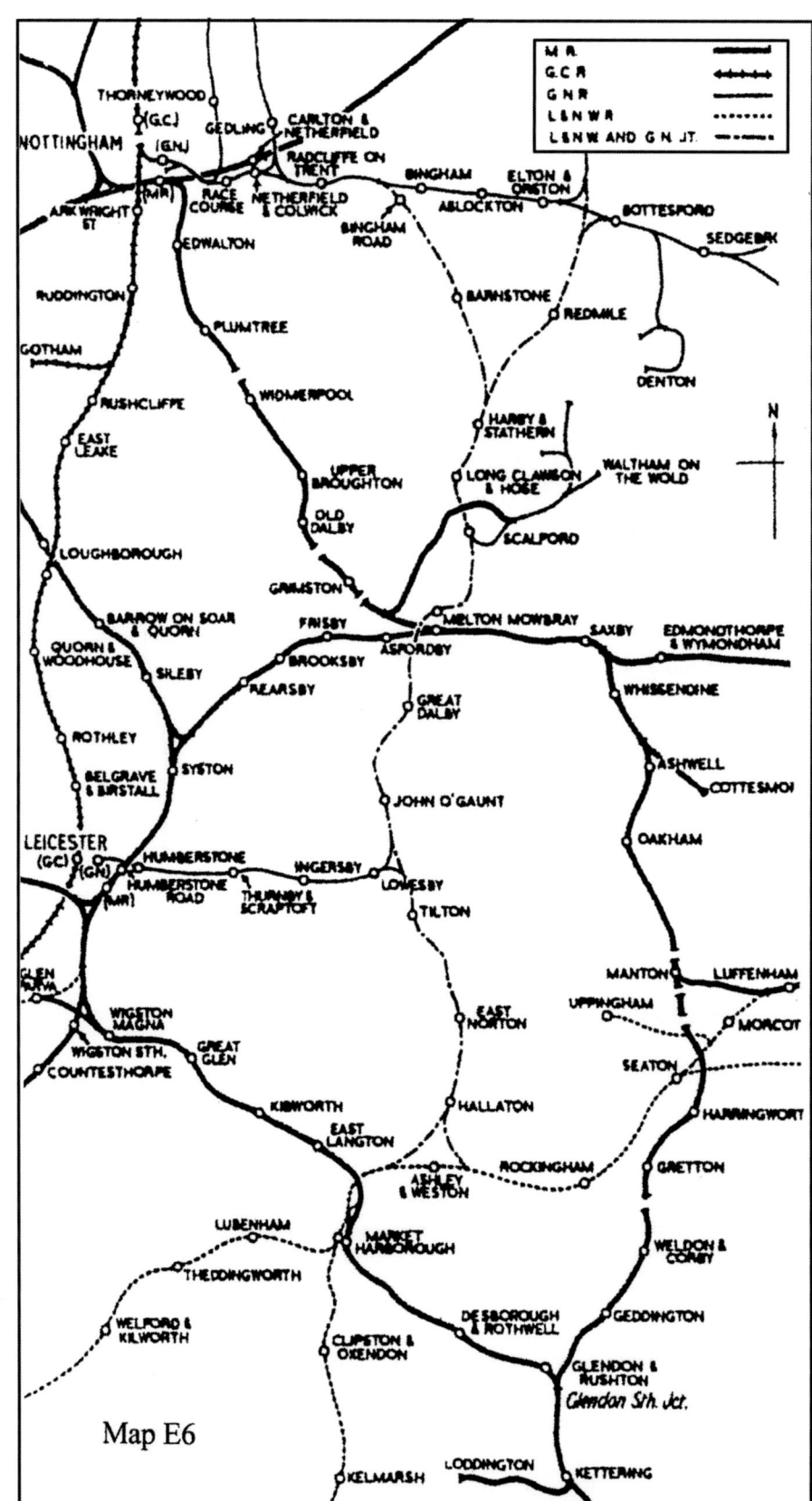

This map provides greater detail for the working of the coal trains through parts of the East Midlands. No single route could have met the total demand up to the end of the 1950s.

MOVEMENT OF COAL SOUTH BY RAIL • 233

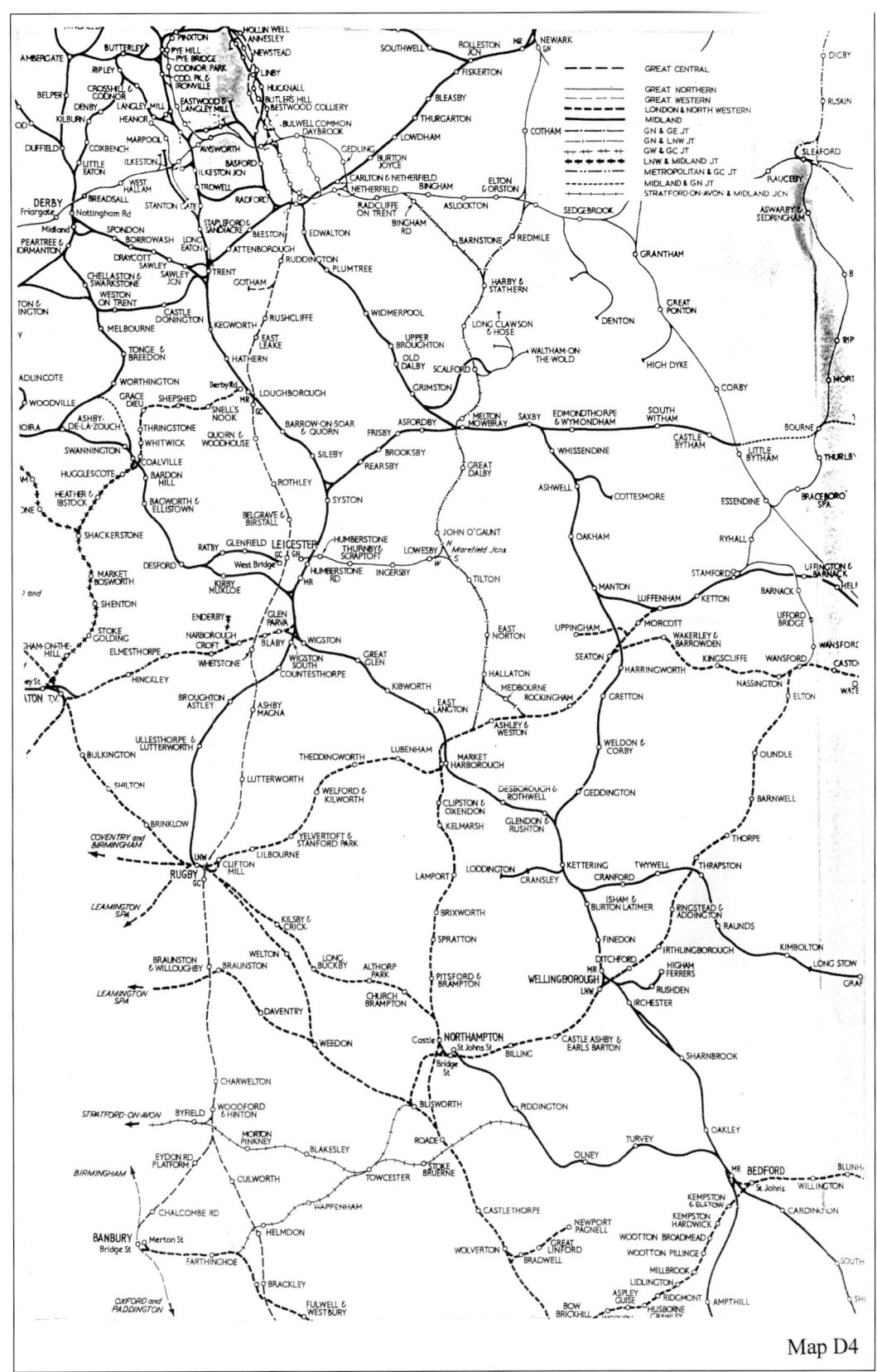

Map D4

The East Midlands showing the railway routes as built by the original private companies. The map shows routes taken by coal trains heading South; via the Great Central, the Midland and Great Northern/London & North Western in particular. The Great Northern/Great Eastern Joint route is shown at map E1.

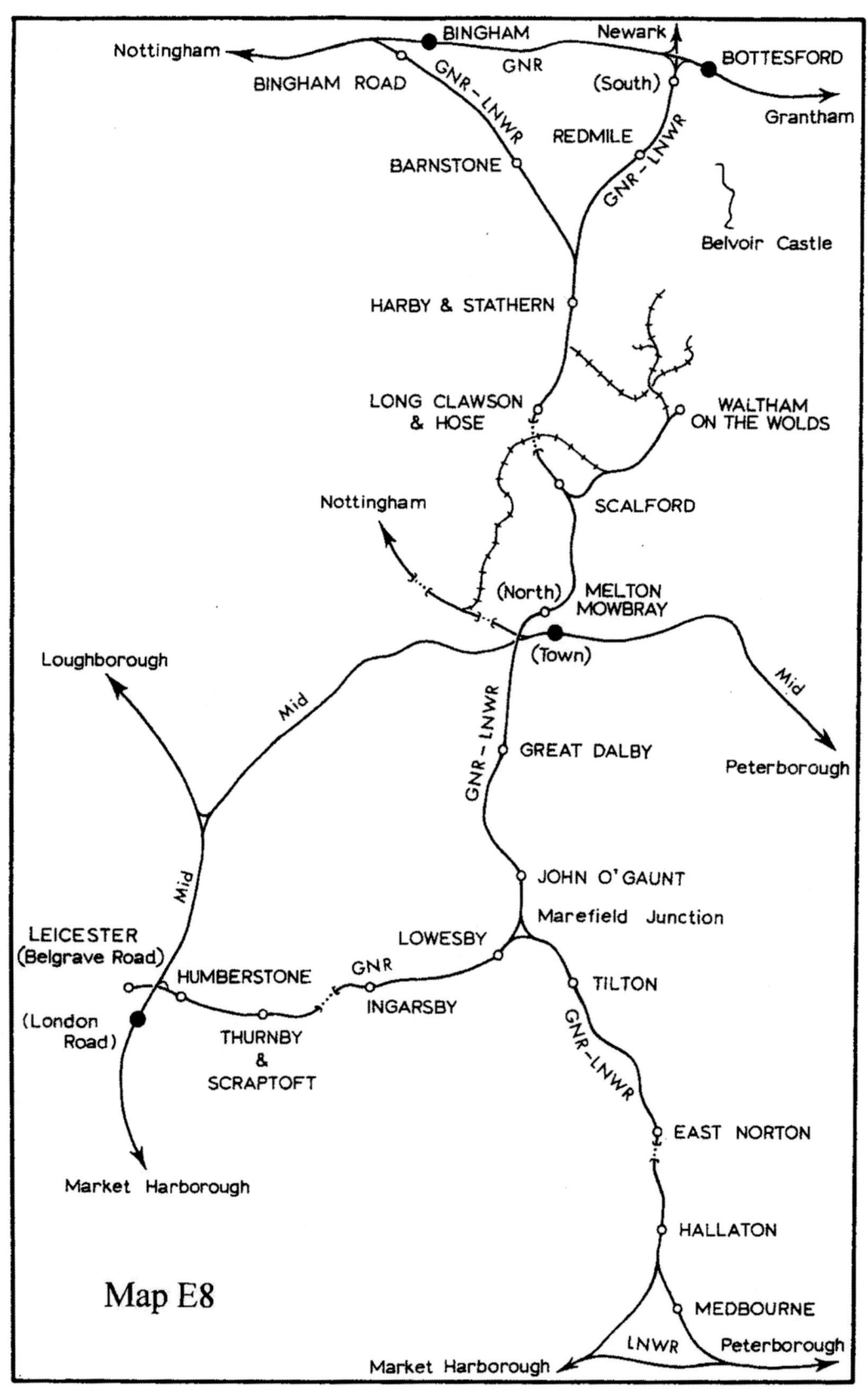

The reason for inclusion of this map is to show the triangular junctions allowing access to the GN/L&NW Joint line for coal traffic leaving Colwick yard.

form of adverse gradients for heavy southbound traffic. In that regard, the MR routes fared worse; from the undulations of its main line south from Leicester with its climbing to Desborough north from Market Harborough (4½ miles for which 19 minutes were allowed), the climb from Irchester to Sharnbrook (which resulted in a diversion via Wymington and a tunnel) and its long slog up from Elstow near Bedford towards Leagrave, to its Nottingham-Rushton line with nine tunnels and the 45 arch viaduct at Welland. The GC line a little to the east was very well engineered to a ruling gradient of 1 in 176, but still had a long climb up through Staverton towards Charwelton and undulations along the MetR route beyond Woodford Halse. The GN line authorities made operational use difficult for themselves with long stretches of two track route suitable for high speed running, seven refuge loop sidings available for slower moving traffic, the two-track viaduct at Welwyn and tunnels at Potters Bar.

Irrespective of the routing, the coal for London arrived in yards within a handful of miles and was distributed from there. Cross London traffic is dealt with later in this chapter.

Each route is analysed in turn. For the analysis, the years 1953/54 have been used; a year for which many WTTs (though not all) are available, at which time the NCB Area organisation had settled, when the CEA policy and growth profiles were still somewhat constrained by lack of capacity and the RE/BR Regions were hamstrung by BTC matters and coming to terms with The Transport Act 1953. Developments later in the 1950s in as much as they affected the coal traffic and the individual routes are also dealt with later in this chapter.

Eastern Region route a (from Doncaster, Sykes Jn, Killamarsh, Mansfield, Colwick, Peterborough):

The small town of March in the Fens of Cambridgeshire was an unlikely place at which to find a huge, mechanised marshalling yard, a locomotive depot with an allocation exceeding 100, a passenger station boasting four through platforms plus three bay platforms, trains converging from five directions and employing between 15 per cent and 20 per cent of the total population of around 13,000. Trains approached from the North (from Lincoln/Spalding), the East (King's Lynn), the South East (Ely), the South (Cambridge) and the West (Peterborough). The majority of the trains were freight classes D to J, but the station also handled balanced express services. The Colchester-Newcastle, Harwich Parkeston Quay-Liverpool (Central) and Lowestoft/Yarmouth (Vauxhall)-York were all long-standing services which ran throughout the year; Summer traffic to the East Coast resorts swelled the flow. It is, though, the freight traffic that is the main interest of this book, particularly the flow of coal arriving from the North and West to be sorted and despatched into East Anglia or forwarded to Temple Mills, London. To maintain consistency, the trains for Tuesdays-Fridays have been identified.

From the Doncaster area came 18 coal trains via Gainsborough, Lincoln and Spalding taking some four and three-quarter hours. At Sykes Jn, six miles North of Lincoln (Pyewipe Jn), the flow was enhanced by four workings from either Staveley and/or Worksop via the GC Retford line. From Lincoln six of the 22 trains took the route via Boston and Spalding and three of that six were destined for Peterborough (New England), taking six hours. The larger balance of 16 trains took the route via Sleaford and Spalding.

From Langwith Jn and, separately, from Mansfield Concentration Sidings, came a total of 12 trains. Coal from Warsop, Langwith, Cresswell and Shirebrook collieries was tripped to Langwith Junction and coal from Ollerton, Thoresby, Welbeck, Bilsthorpe, Blidworth, Clipstone and Rufford was tripped to Mansfield Concentration Sidings. The history of the development of these GN flows is included later in this Chapter (under the Eastern Region/London Midland Region Joint route). All were routed to Lincoln and from there ten were sent to Whitemoor via Sleaford and Spalding (four and a quarter hours) and two went to Peterborough (New England) via Boston and Spalding (four and a half hours). These trains used the former LDECR/GC line through Tuxford.

From Colwick (Nottingham) came a further 12 services routed via Sleaford (three hours and forty minutes).

A further flow of trains came from holding sidings in the Lincoln area; a total of seven.

To complete the summary, a total of 18 trains arrived from Peterborough (Stanground), having originated on the London Midland Region. The points of origin suggest that four may have been for minerals traffic rather than coal. For the 13½ miles from Peterborough, one hour was allowed, 22 minutes of which were to allow time for the hard-pressed signalman at Twenty Foot signal box to arrange access into the up yard via his counterpart at March West.

In aggregate, 59-63 arriving trains loaded with coal. A small proportion of the total tonnage would be for BR internal use, but the larger proportion was for domestic and industrial users.

Upon arrival at March/Whitemoor, the loaded trains would be routed into one of ten reception sidings for examination. The train locomotive would then be released to go to March depot for servicing and turning as necessary. The loaded train would then be split (in accordance with the wagon labels from originating point) into 'cuts' for sending over a hump to run into any one of the 40 sorting sidings; retarders slowing the progress of the wagons as they gained speed down the initial gradient after the hump. This manually intensive work involved shunters lifting the coupling between each 'cut'; a train of 60 wagons requiring between 40 and 50 'cuts' could be handled in seven minutes. Each of the sorting sidings was for a particular destination route, e.g.

Siding 11:
Althorne, Angel Road, Battlesbridge, Billericay, Burnham-on-Crouch, Cricksea Siding, Down Hall Siding, East London line, Fambridge, Hockley, Hogwell Siding, Mountness Siding, New Cross Depot, Park Yard, Ramsden B Siding, Rayleigh, Rochford, Southminster, Tottenham, Tufnell Park, Wickford, Woodham Ferrers.

Siding 12:
Blackwall, Canning Town, Chingford, Clapton, Hoe Street, Noel Park, Palace Gates, Seven Sisters, Thames Wharf, Victoria Docks, West Green, Wood Green, Walthamstow.

When a siding had accumulated a train-load, it became a WTT booked service and, as departure time approached, would be coupled up, drawn forward into one of ten departure sidings and a brakevan then allowed by the guard to run down an incline and onto the rear of the train. The impact that vacuum brake fitted mineral wagons would have made in terms of time for connecting/disconnecting hoses and brake testing was never felt and, as it was, many vacuum braked merchandise services left the yard at least one classification lower (e.g. C as a D, D as an E) than it could have been.

The volume of wagons dealt with daily at Whitemoor up Yard was regularly in excess of 3,000 and a similar number in the two down Yards (down plus Norwood). The mechanised down Yard (with two retarders compared to four in the up Yard) dealt with vacuum brake fitted traffic whilst Norwood Yard marshalled empty coal wagons for despatch in trainloads directly wherever possible to collieries. To handle the 70 daily departures March motive power depot was able to find locomotives with wide route availability; only its six V2s being restricted by axle weight to route availability nine (the most restricted). As the 1950s progressed Doncaster, March and New England received allocations of the Class 9F 2-10-0s which were well capable of handling the loads.

The coal destined for Temple Mills (most 'through', whilst a few were held at Cambridge/Broxbourne whilst passenger train occupation was at a high level) was marshalled into 21 daily departures. The Loads Book information is not available.

Prior to the second half of the 1950s – when a rationalisation and a Modernisation Plan funded project had improved matters – Temple Mills did not fit the popular description or shape of a marshalling yard. In fact, it was an historical ribbon development of ten yards, extending from Lea Bridge to Stratford either side of the main line. For up side traffic there were seven yards: coal yard, Blackwall yard, Old Laughton, New Laughton, Old Suburban, New Suburban and Colchester. Old and New Suburban were actually for down traffic (secondary sorting and holding sidings for wagons awaiting Control instructions) and Colchester yard was located on the down side together with Cambridge yard, New Connection yard and River (Lea) yard.

To compound the difficulties, the low-lying areas were subject to flooding. This unsatisfactory arrangement whereby wagon(s) load traffic would typically need shunting more than once before heading for the final destination was first addressed in 1930 (LNER). At that time Cambridge yard was upgraded to operation by hump/incline mode. The 1954 (BTC/ER) scheme resulted in a continuous, two miles long yard with 52 miles of sidings (12 reception and 52 sorting), realignment of the main line to one side of the yard rather than through its midst and incorporation of the marshalling work undertaken previously at Mile End, Thames Wharf, Goodmayes up, Park (Tottenham) and Broxbourne. Progress was slow, but eventually completed in 1959 by additional capital expenditure (Modernisation Plan ER scheme) on two, new power signal boxes. This investment scheme was one of many which were subjected to scrutiny by various bodies in 1959/60 (referred to in chapters 6 and 9) and demonstrated the uncertainty of the cases. Most of the internal data produced to justify major schemes in the 1950s were limited to estimates of the likely improvement in net revenue. Some projects promised to return a reasonable proportion of the capital outlay. In the original submission for Temple Mills, an investment of £2.5m (of which £2.1m represented betterment) was expected to yield a return of 6.6 per cent on the net outlay, or 13.5 per cent on the betterment portion.

After the scrutiny, a final estimate raised both costs and savings, altering the expected return to 7.9 per cent and 12.8 per cent respectively. Nearby Ripple Lane, Barking, which arguably had a brighter future from the oil facilities at Thames Haven and cost a similar amount to Temple Mills offered 5.3 per cent and 6.3 per cent on the net outlay and betterment portions respectively. Regional managements started to look for ways to maximise profitable traffic flows and if the Eastern Region still had responsibility for the London extension of the former GC line it is quite possible that a greater tonnage would have flowed via Whitemoor and into Temple Mills.

Eastern Region route b (from Peterborough to Ferme Park, North London):
The difficulties of finding paths for unbraked and slow in accelerating freight trains over this route were outlined in chapter 4. By the early 1950s, nothing had been changed to disturb the status quo; not only were express and stopping passenger trains competing for paths, but so were vacuum brake fitted fast freight trains with time sensitive perishable traffic and a constant flow of trainloads of bricks. Southbound as far as Langley Junction the adverse gradients were no more severe than 1 in 200 though with lengthy climbs from Connington to Abbots Ripton and from Arlesey to Stevenage, the latter with refuge for water at Hitchin. At Langley Junction, the slow-moving traffic could be routed via the Hertford loop and thus avoid the operating difficulties of the two track sections over Welwyn Viaduct and through Potters Bar/Greenwood. The Hertford loop offered no panacea as it had other traffic to accommodate. Apart from one short distance at 1 in 100 the adverse gradients were no more severe than 1 in 198 and – at 22 miles to Wood Green – just half a mile longer than the main line. The loop was first used from 1918 (freight) and 1920 (passenger); the latter in difficult operating circumstances following a collision in Welwyn North tunnel. At that time, the 15-mile section between Langley Junction and Cuffley was single track only; a matter quickly addressed by doubling and construction of a fly-under to the down side at the junction. A mile or so onwards from Wood Green brought the coal trains to Ferme Park yard (fitted traffic being handled at East Goods, King's Cross goods yard).

Wartime contingency planning resulted in a useful link between Bounds Green (half a mile North of Wood Green) and Temple Mills via Palace Gates and allowing an alternative route into/out of/between strategic yards and routes.

As at 1953, just eight coal trains were tolerated in the WTT; four before noon and four thereafter (Tuesdays-Fridays). Some four and a half hours were allowed for the journey with stops at Hitchin and any combination of delays occasioned by the four, two track sections and how faster moving traffic was performing on any particular day.

The arrival upon the scene of the new Class 9F locomotives offered some potential improvements to point to point running times. Trials held in late 1954 with 45 loaded mineral wagons (60 empties Northbound) suggested that 26 minutes could be timetabled for the 15½ miles Northbound between Huntingdon and Fletton Junction. At that time the BTC was keen to develop improved methods of managing minerals traffic (see also later reference to trials on the London Midland Region), but it became an expensive failure. Later in the decade it probably helped the Eastern Region case for investment at Temple Mills to be accepted based upon maximum tonnage being directed via Whitemoor.

The needs for coal and coke for the domestic market in North London prompted the principal distributing merchant in the area – Charrington – to fund and open in 1958 a concentration depot on the site of the (GE) Palace Gates yard. This depot took an average of 1,000 tons each week in block trainloads, with bagging and onward delivery by Charrington and replaced the need for coal facilities (wagon load) at New Southgate, Oakleigh Park, Noel Park, Wood Green, Stoke Newington, South Tottenham, Hornsey, Granley Gardens, Muswell Hill and Highgate. As such the initiative by Charrington provided the NCB with a blueprint for the future (see later, chapter 11).

Eastern Region route c (from Annesley area collieries initially to Woodford Halse for sorting into London area traffic and that for destinations via Banbury):

The traffic flows on this route are detailed in chapter 7. Here, it is important to highlight the extent of coal traffic sent forward to London by the two routes. The two routes to London (Neasden) were via either the route through Quainton Road and Aylesbury shared to a large extent with the Metropolitan Railway or the route through High Wycombe shared with the Western Region. Use of the former route was restricted by the need for passenger services and the limitation to 40 loaded wagons because of adverse gradients. The GW route allowed trains of up to 63 loaded wagons but was slightly longer.

From the very earliest of days of the arrangement between the GCR and the Metropolitan Railway (chapter 1) the latter company wished to have a commercial role with coal. As part of this, coal trains were still sent from Woodford Halse to exchange sidings at Quainton Road from where the Met provided wagons to Aylesbury and the 14 stations to Neasden. The 'through' trains to Neasden were just four and ran before and after the passenger services took precedence. The GW/GC route via High Wycombe had six 'through' trains (1013/49/93/1101/11/3540), one of which was coal for locomotives and ran as either Class H (63 loaded wagons) or Class F (higher speed, but limited to 45 wagons).

The yard space at Neasden (shared with the Metropolitan Railway) and the coal depot at Marylebone were adequate for the volume of tonnage, but both were modest in size; the coal depot and sidings had a capacity of 220 wagons, but did offer at Marylebone a useful exchange facility to the Regents Canal. Although there were trains daily between Neasden and Brent/Cricklewood there was no significant involvement with Cross London flows. At quiet times a Metropolitan Railway electric locomotive would convey coal to Chiltern Court and the overall impression is of localised distribution plus the industrial users and constantly replenishing the stocks on hand at Neasden motive power depot. As the final entrant into London and having to overcome considerable resistance to the siting of its terminus, the scale of GCR operations, though considerable, paled against those of its near neighbours.

The GN/LNW Joint

There was a further route in which the Eastern Region had an operational interest; jointly with the London Midland Region, it extended from Newark to Market Harborough, Northampton, Roade where access to the former LNWR main line was gained and allowed traffic to reach Sudbury Junction/Willesden yard in North London. Part of the route – from Marefield to Welham – formed part of the GN/LNW Joint line and, as will be explained, allowed coal traffic to flow not only through Newark (ex-Doncaster/Retford) but also out of Colwick, Nottingham, and iron ore traffic to flow in the opposite direction.

For convenience of readers, a summary of the development of the GN inroads into Nottinghamshire is included and explains how GN traffic from North Nottinghamshire (ex-Mansfield Concentration Sidings and Langwith Junction) contributed to Eastern Region route a.

The Ambergate (Grantham), Nottingham, Boston & Eastern Junction Railway (ANB&ER) had opened a line from Grantham to Colwick in 1850 and the expectation was that in due course the ANB&ER would become leased by the MR; however, by share trading with the GNR it was able to usurp the Midland position and to the consternation of the latter Company was able to work trains into Nottingham. A very unhappy arrangement was resolved only by Act of Parliament (1853) for the construction of a new line between Colwick and Nottingham (London Road), opened in 1857.

Having established itself in the area during the 1860s, the ambitious plans of the GNR to further exploit the area were developed in the 1870s and 1880s. The developments eventually gave access to collieries in both South and North Nottinghamshire as well as Derbyshire and exits from Colwick in the south and from Mansfield Concentration Sidings and Langwith in the north; the latter forming part of the aggregate flow identified at Eastern Region route a. The developments are dealt with chronologically first for those affecting Colwick.

In 1871, a Bill was deposited in parliament by the GNR for consideration in the session of 1872. The Bill was in two parts. Part one proposed the construction of a line from Colwick to Awsworth from where a branch line to Pinxton would be constructed, whilst the main project was pushed West towards Derby and Egginton/ Burton-upon-Trent. The Midland Railway was not at all impressed. Part two of the Bill proposed a line from South of Newark to Leicester, via Bottesford.

In 1872, the GNR purchased 150 acres of land at Colwick where sorting yards, a replacement engine shed, workshops and employee accommodation were envisaged. In the same year, the GNR (Derbyshire & Staffordshire) Act was passed allowing the lines to be built Westwards via Awsworth, Ilkeston to Derby (Friargate) and Egginton (opened in 1878) and the branch from Awsworth to Pinxton (opened fully from 1876). Also in 1872, the GNR obtained powers for the line from south of Newark towards Leicester, through the Vale of Belvoir, via Bottesford, Melton Mowbray and Marefield, but when the Bill came before the House of Lords the section from Marefield to Leicester was deleted. In the following two years the GNR made further efforts to reach Leicester and, as part of these efforts, proposed jointly with the LNWR to connect also with the Market Harborough-Peterborough line at Welham (Junction). To counter this threat, the MR joined with the MS&LR to promote the alternative route from Doncaster to Rushton, near Kettering. A battle royal ensued involving all four protagonist companies in Parliamentary Sessions and whilst the MR/MS&LR emerged with a Bill, its depletion along the way rendered it so distant from the original intent that it was abandoned. Not to be outdone, the GNR and LNWR joined forces and in 1874 secured an Act for the Marefield-Welham line; the then existing line between Bottesford and Marefield becoming the joint property of these two Companies, as did the connection from Harby & Stathern to Saxondale Junction. In readiness for coal flowing out of Colwick to increase traffic heading for the Eastern counties a direct line from Allington Junction to Barkston East Junction was built in 1875. The Newark-Welham line was opened in stages between July 1878 and December 1879 with the GNR services finally reaching Leicester in 1883. As a result of these considerable efforts both companies accrued benefits; the GNR had an alternative if lengthy route to London with new markets along the way, it had a route for iron ore to new developments in Nottinghamshire and passenger traffic (particularly in the summer) from Leicester, the LNWR had access to a coalfield in Nottinghamshire that offered quality coal for domestic, industrial and its own internal needs. Wider arrangements between the GNR and LNWR gave the former running rights over the system of the latter as far West as Wellington (Shropshire).

The potential to further tap into the coalfields of Nottinghamshire and thereby enhance the flow from the Pinxton line, resulted in an Act of 1880. Under the provisions of the Act the GNR was authorised to build a six-mile line from near Basford (Colwick-Kimberley line) along the Leen Valley to Newstead, with short branch lines to connect with collieries at Bestwood, Hucknall (3), Linby (2), Newstead and Annesley. Coal traffic from various collieries began in October 1881. A further branch was added in 1886 to Shipley (Nutbrook colliery) and later extended to Heanor (goods from 1892).

These developments resulted in the yards at Colwick being extended in 1889-91. Not only was the tonnage of coal increasing; so too was that of iron ore, necessitating widening of the route to four tracks between Saxondale Junction and Radcliffe-on-Trent.

As the GNR made progress along the Leen Valley, Edward Watkin, chairman of the MS&LR (GCR from August 1897), was developing plans to progress south from Beighton, Sheffield (chapter 1). The MS&LR eventually passed beneath the sandstone ridge of the Robin Hood Hills to connect at Annesley with a short extension of the GNR from Newstead and opened up various mutually beneficial running powers. The GNR was granted running powers to Sheffield over the MS&LR, the LNWR similarly benefitted (from agreement with the GNR) and ran a goods service from Colwick to Sheffield and, from October 1892, the MS&LR began goods traffic to and from Colwick. Naturally, the MR was very upset by all this and their mood worsened when the Stanton Ironworks

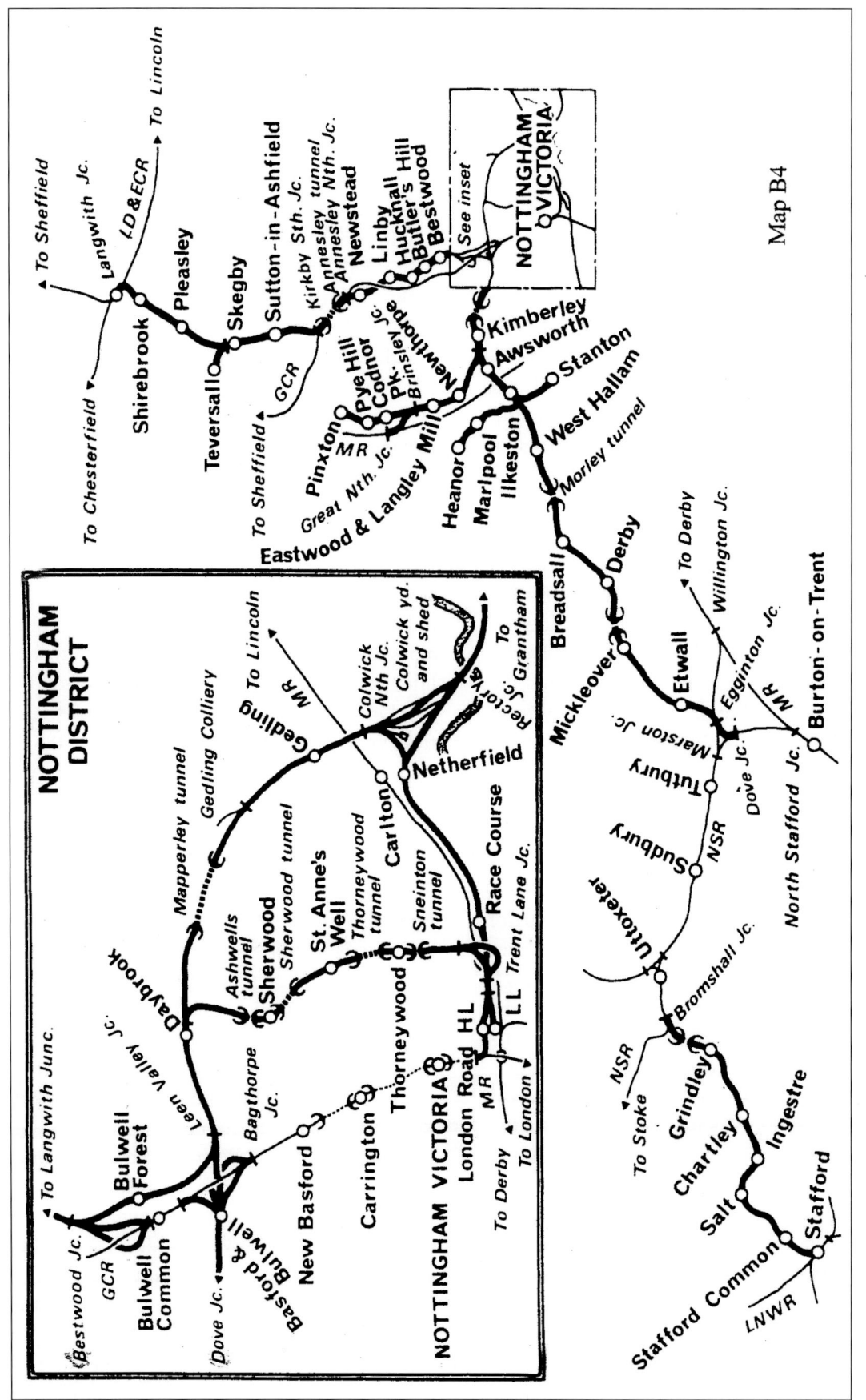

This map identifies the presence established by the Great Northern Railway around Nottingham and particularly the Leen Valley collieries, how it encroached onto an area previously dominated by the Midland Railway. The map also identifies the location of Colwick, the presence of the later arrival of the Great Central Railway and the GN route which extended via Derby (Friargate) to Stafford.

Map B4

Company pressed the GNR to extend the Leen Valley line to serve its collieries at Silverhill, Teversal and Pleasley. The GNR Act of 1892 gave powers for the 'Leen Valley Extension', ten miles from Newstead, via Pleasley, to the new LDECR line at Langwith. A further Act of 1896 gave access to collieries at Sutton and at Shirebrook whilst other developments allowed access to the considerable source of coal at Kirkby (from 1896) and Butcherwood collieries. Contractor and geological difficulties delayed matters and it was 1897 before commitment of a contract for the Pleasley-Langwith Junction section. The line was opened in sections; from Pleasley to Shirebrook colliery in 1900 and traffic to Langwith from May 1901. Further south and conveniently close to Colwick, a new colliery was opened at Gedling in 1903.

By 1900, Colwick yard was the largest on the GNR system, capable of housing 6,000 wagons. In the following year, Colwick motive power depot had an allocation of 200 locomotives, the largest shed by allocation on the GNR (231 in 1927, 199 in 1950 and 146 in 1959).

In LNER/early BR days, Colwick was a Locomotive District Centre (code 38A) with Annesley, Leicester, Staveley and Woodford Halse subordinated as 38B-E respectively.

At the time of our main operational consideration – 1953/4 – there were three routes out of Colwick for loaded coal trains and empty wagons being returned:

1) the GN route to Grantham, thence to Peterborough via the GN main line and then via Eastern Region routes a or b above
2) the GE route via Allington Junction and Barkston to Sleaford and then via Eastern Region route a above (12 trains daily)
3) the GN/LNW route via Saxondale Junction and Welham to Rugby/Northampton, Bletchley, Watford and Willesden/Sudbury Junction.

Whilst the main loaded coal train flows were west to east, trains from Newark to Welham were received at Stathern Junction and, if headed for Colwick, used the connection at Bottesford. Ore trains for the iron and steelworks of the North Midlands, Yorkshire and Humberside provided for considerable loaded tonnage to the west and north.

The exchange point for coal traffic between the GN and LNW was at Welham, near Market Harborough. From there the LNW would take forward trains sorted for the Rugby and Northampton directions which diverged at Number 1 Junction, just South West of Market Harborough. Off the GN to Welham came eight (coal) trains daily (Tuesday-Friday), two of which originated at Doncaster and the remainder from Colwick. Only two of the eight were 'through' trains and both were destined for Willesden/Sudbury Junction yard. Coal trains which originated at Welham and were taken forward by the LNW routes could have been formed of loads received from Toton (six) or Colwick (four), but for destinations at Foleshill Gas Works and Northampton Electricity Works Sidings as well as Bletchley (one), Watford (one) and Willesden (one).

The planned NCB extension Eastwards in the Nottinghamshire coalfield would involve the sinking of a new colliery at Cotgrave, a new rail connection at Radcliffe-on-Trent and an awful lot of politics before a new power station capable of burning 5m tons of coal annually would be built.

London Midland Region lines South from Toton:

To the Midland Railway, any other railway company seeking to gain access to their strongly held territory in the North and East Midlands from the 1840s was an invader. The MR first went to extraordinary lengths to repel the advances of the GNR at Nottingham, fought parliamentary 'battles' against the GNR with the LNWR in the early 1870s and tried hard to thwart the MS&LR as it advanced South from Sheffield in the early 1890s. The monopoly powers of the MR were weakened partly by a reaction of colliery owners and those of other industries who encouraged competition; the hand of the former group being strong as owners of the product, means of transportation (wagons) and also the end base of customers. In 1881 the MR tried, unsuccessfully, to purchase a large quantity of privately-owned wagons and did whatever it could to undercut charges of their emerging competitors. The GNR in response purchased coal at pithead prices and set up a wholesale/retail distribution network at certain destinations. For 120 years the MR and its successors in title enjoyed rich pickings from coal and seemed to be present wherever it was likely to be found. A railway tale suggested that when the first man stepped down on to the surface of the moon, he should not be surprised to find already there a Midland 3F, a brakevan and 15 empty wagons just in case coal deposits were found.

The Midland did not have its own terminus/goods depot in London (St Pancras/Somers Town) until 1868 and up to that time had relied upon other companies to allow its coal trains use of their routes.

A predecessor to the Midland Railway – the Midland Counties – opened between Nottingham and Derby in 1839. Extensions were made to Leicester and Rugby which made possible an exchange of traffic with the LNWR for onward movement to London. The commercial and operating arrangements left the MR frustrated and an extension south from Leicester to Hitchin in 1857 offered better prospects via running powers over the GNR. Although the prospects and actual performance were indeed better, they still left much to be desired, hence the direct line South from Bedford.

The volume of actual and projected traffic was such that the MR was soon contemplating additional routes and also to protect what it saw as its territory by thwarting the aspirations of others. That resulted in part in the parliamentary battles of 1872-74 (referred to earlier) and led to the MR dusting off a proposal first made in 1848 for a line from Manton (on the Leicester-Peterborough line) to Rushton near Kettering where it would join the main line from Leicester to London St Pancras. The necessary Act was passed in 1875, but it was not until November 1879 that 'through' goods services ran between Nottingham and Kettering.

The delay resulted from civil engineering works and two deviations from the original plans; the former involving nine tunnels, a very substantial viaduct at Welland and meeting a ruling gradient southbound of 1 in 200, the deviations were that the new line from Nottingham actually joined near Melton Mowbray rather than Saxby and joined the main line at Glendon South Junction near Kettering. Opening the route allowed slow moving coal trains to be kept away from the main line through Leicester and to assist in the regulation of traffic through Nottingham; an alternative route from the yards at Toton/Stanton Gate via Loughborough, Syston North to East Junctions to Melton Mowbray was also used.

Therefore, the MR had three routes to London from the sorting yards at Toton; via Nottingham and Manton to Kettering, via Loughborough, Syston and Manton to Kettering, via Loughborough, Leicester and Market Harborough to Kettering. South from Glendon South Junction all three flows shared common tracks and, from 1884, benefitted from the opening of the Wymington Deviation which was engineered to a ruling gradient of 1 in 200 at the expense of a tunnel.

Though not always parallel, the Midland and its successors had use of a four-track railway South from Trent Junction to the yards at Brent/Cricklewood, North London; a distance of 111 miles.

There were two further routings (south of Leicester at Wigston to Rugby and from Market Harborough onto the GN/LNW line) which will be explained later, but for now the concentration is on the three routes south through Kettering.

As with the Eastern Region routes south, the London Midland Region had an intermediate yard; for Whitemoor, New England and Woodford Halse insert Neilson's Sidings/Finedon Road, Wellingborough. Midway between Toton and Brent it was a natural railway point for examination of wagons and exchanges of locomotives, Enginemen and Guards.

Despite its reputation as a railway with a policy of double heading with small locomotives, the Toton-Wellingborough-Brent route of the LMS/first decade of BR years was the domain of Beyer Garratt 2-6-0 0-6-2 locomotives (of which starting with three in 1927 there were by 1931 a total of 33), Stanier 8Fs from the middle years of the LMS and, at the end of the steam era, the Riddles 9Fs plus the ten built to Franco-Crosti designs. The arrival of the 9Fs (as in chapter 7) allowed the withdrawal of the Garratts that then remained. By early 1956, one third of the Class had been withdrawn and, of the remaining 22, half were based at Toton. By the end of that year just three were at Toton whilst ten found employment working from Hasland, near Chesterfield, from where the last survivor – 47967 – was withdrawn in December 1957 and ran in steam via Derby to Crewe Works for cutting up. Throughout the LMS era and into that of BR, five and seven plank (high) sided wagons conveying eight/ten tons of coal (gross) were commonplace, those many with grease lubrication quickly being weeded out and the fleet strengthened by 16 ton mineral wagons, though still unbraked and with link couplings. A Garratt would cope easily with a train of 86 loaded wagons of the older type; the limiting factors being lengths of sidings, distances between access gates and strength of couplings. Northbound from Brent (on the four track railway) at least as far as Wellingborough a Garratt would take 100 empty wagons. The then modern equivalent – a 9F – would cope with 45-50 16 tonners with the plentiful 8Fs consistently reliable with similar loads. The principal depots supplying power from the North were Toton, Kirkby-in-Ashfield and Leicester. Wellingborough and Cricklewood dominated the Southern half of the route, locomotives being able on good days to achieve double out and home workings. The allocations of 8Fs and 9Fs (1959) to the main depots were:

Depot	8F	9F	Total depot Allocation
Wellingborough	14	35	63
Toton	55	12	98
Cricklewood	12	5	54
Leicester (Midland)	9	8	63
Kirkby-in-Ashfield	34	-	48
Kettering	19	5	39
Hasland	14	-	39

From the early days of its existence, the BTC, via the RE, was keen to improve operational arrangements with slow moving, unbraked mineral trains. For some years, trials on the Midland Division of the LMR were held to test the use of a new type of coupling and using the vacuum brake system as successfully and widely practised with many merchandise trains. The advantages were seen as allowing greater total brake force and shorter stopping distances from a higher line speed, particularly for trainload traffic such as iron ore for steelworks and coal for industrial users. The LMS had been ahead of the game; in the 1930s they had adapted a design from the railways of Germany and had built a unit train of 16 40 ton, bogie wagons equipped with vacuum brakes throughout. For workings from Pilsley Colliery to Willesden, North London, the coal was discharged for use at the LMS Stonebridge Park power station generating electricity for the Euston-Watford services. Pilsley Colliery was used because its loading screens had been designed to allow loading of high sided wagons with coal suitable for the purpose.

The trials were held in both static and running condition; the former mainly with locomotives fitted with air pumps (BR Standard Class 5 and BR L1 tanks) and the latter with Black 5s, Royal Scots and Britannia pacifics and 9Fs reliant upon creating vacuum and with a Standard Class 5 and Britannia pacifics equipped with air pumps. The testing typically used the Toton, Syston, Manton route to Glendon South Junction and thence via Wellingborough to Brent. Timings of these Sunday test trains was straight forward and was based upon those for weekday Class D traffic. For a pair of Britannias borrowed from the Western Region the start to stop time from Wellingborough (Finedon Road) to Brent (60 miles) with 61 loaded 16 ton wagons, plus dynamometer car and 20 ton brakevan, was 99 minutes, comfortably well inside the usual 2 hours. Further North the undulating 14-mile section between Wing and Glendon South Junction was timed at 20 minutes (compared to the usual 38) and must have been exhilarating throughout the seven mile climb from Harringworth to Corby and Weldon.

The trials came to nothing; heads rolled at HQ, the Westinghouse Brake Company had to be compensated, unbraked mineral trains continued to roll and, eventually, the BTC/BRB adopted the use of air braking systems to replace vacuum.

The only mechanised yard along the route was that at Toton, where a hump and retarder operation similar to that at Whitemoor was operated. In fact, most of the loaded coal trains were marshalled in Stanton Gate yard, one mile north of Toton.

Collieries contributing to the flow south from Stanton Gate included Annesley, Butler's Hill, Clipstone, Kirkby, Mansfield, Newstead, Linby, Sherwood, Rufford and Welbeck.

Density of southbound coal traffic via the three alternative routes (Tuesday-Friday, 1953/54) to Neilson's Sidings/Finedon Road yards at Wellingborough varied. Routed via Nottingham, Edwalton, Manton and Corby were nine trains, via Trent, Syston, Melton Mowbray, Manton and Corby were 16 trains and via Trent, Leicester and Market Harborough four (two of which probably conveyed internal user coal for depots along the route). Of this total of 27 (discounting the internal use), five were 'through' workings from Stanton Gate to Brent not requiring re-marshalling but requiring examination and changeover of locomotive and/or train crew. For completeness of record four of the trains originated from Chaddesden yard, Derby, with coal from Shirland, Ripley and Denby.

A reference was made earlier in this section to further flows of coal traffic from north to south. They were:

- from Toton and Nottingham (Beeston) via Trent to Leicester, thence to Wigston where they were routed to Rugby. Of the seven trains two were Toton to Willesden, North London, and five originated from Leicestershire (with coal which could have been mined either in Leicestershire or Nottinghamshire) for Rugby/Nuneaton.
- also from the Leicestershire and Nottinghamshire coalfields came trains routed via Wigston to Market Harborough and Desborough to Kettering/ Wellingborough. A total of eight trains plus one from Chaddesden, Derby via Trent and Leicester. Some of these workings were of the 'pick up' type, slow moving (19 minutes being allowed for the four mile climb from Market Harborough to Desborough and kept well clear of the faster, fitted freights which dominated the hours of night time)
- finally, a further 15 trains were routed via Wigston to Market Harborough from where they took the LNW routes to Rugby/Northampton and from the latter to Roade Junction with destinations of Northampton (three), Bletchley (one), Watford (two), Stonebridge Park power station (vacuum fitted, one, three times weekly) and Sudbury Junction/Willesden (eight).

It is now possible to identify the aggregate of loaded coal trains that were flowing South. Because the Midland routes were so relatively complex the 'staging post' of Wellingborough is used for incoming (from the north) and, following sorting, Southbound to London.

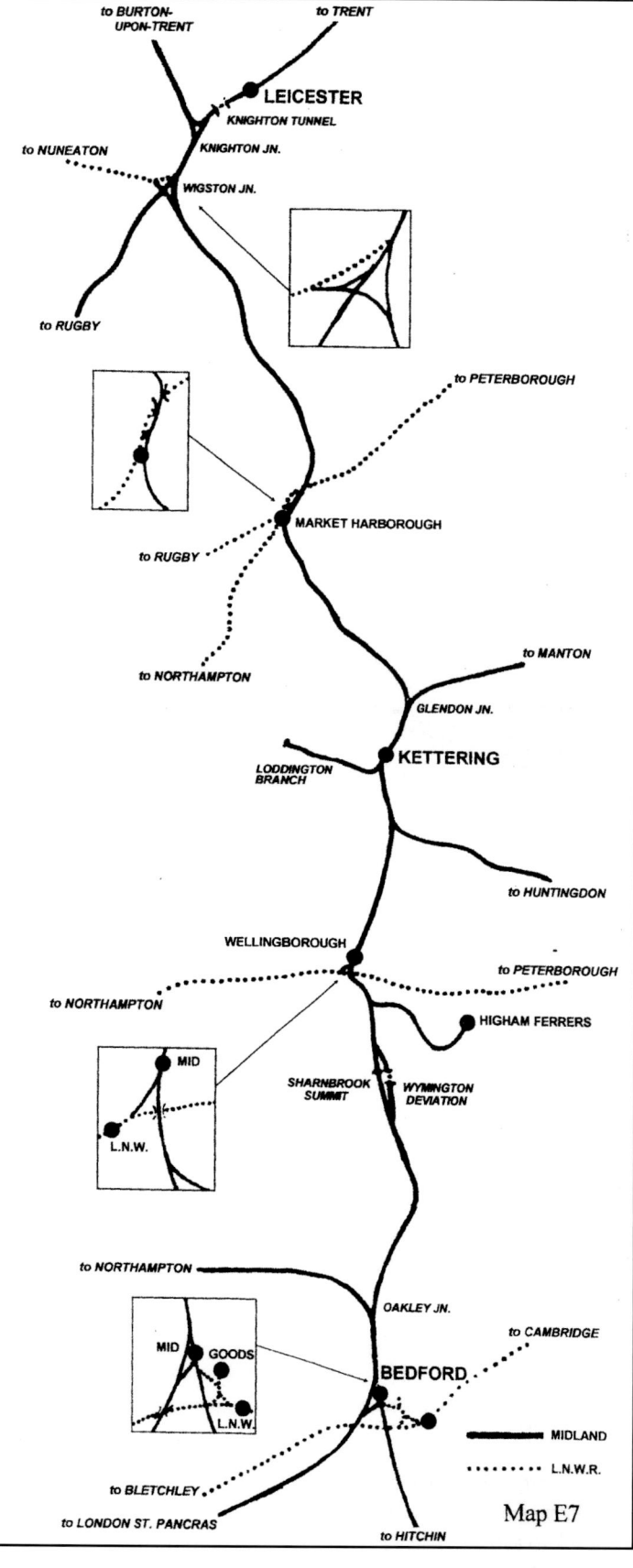

Map E7

MOVEMENT OF COAL SOUTH BY RAIL • 245

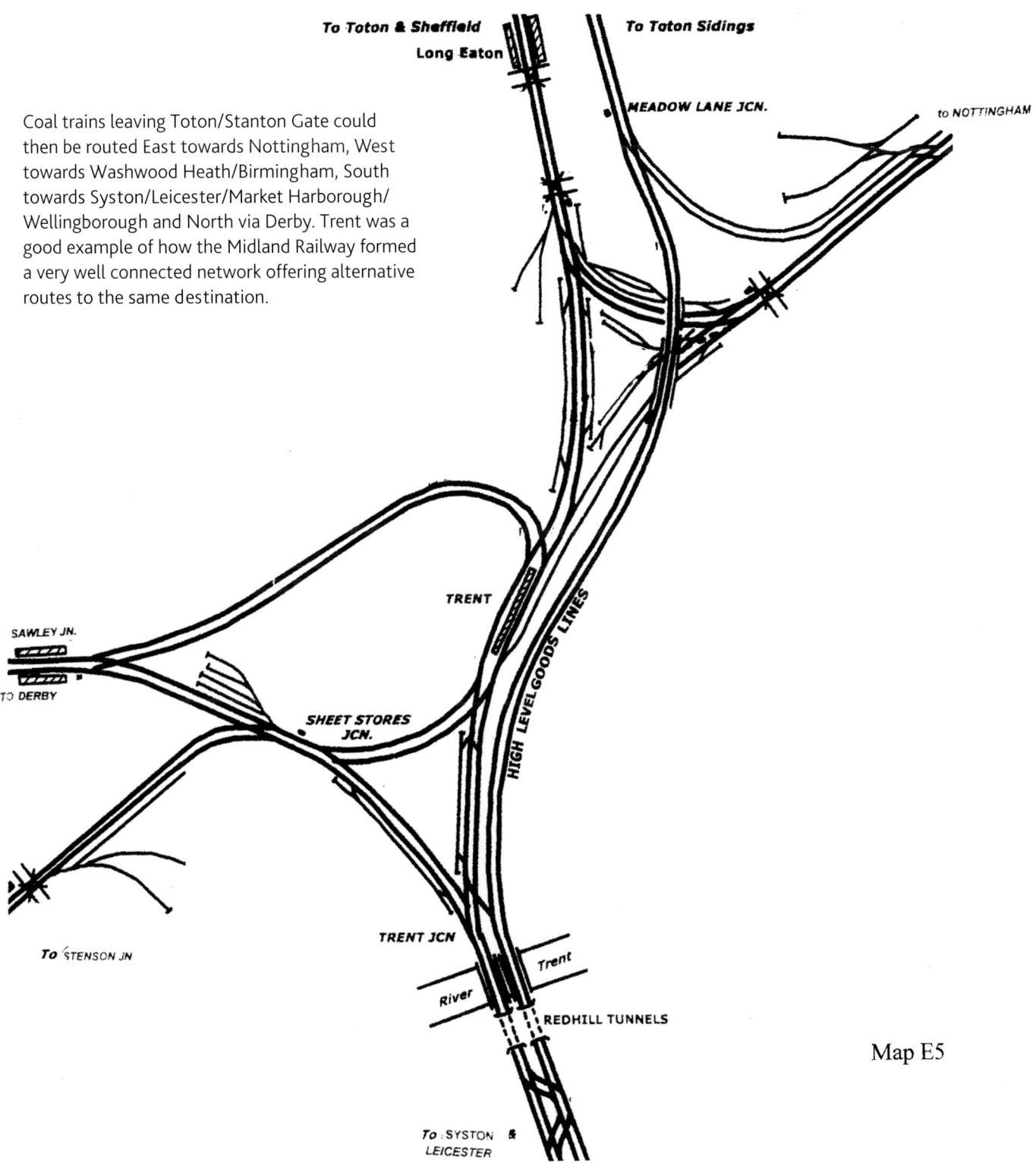

Coal trains leaving Toton/Stanton Gate could then be routed East towards Nottingham, West towards Washwood Heath/Birmingham, South towards Syston/Leicester/Market Harborough/Wellingborough and North via Derby. Trent was a good example of how the Midland Railway formed a very well connected network offering alternative routes to the same destination.

Map E5

Opposite: This map shows the Midland main line between Leicester and Bedford. Coal traffic from the Leicestershire coalfield could join at Wigston whilst that heading to Rugby could leave there. At Market Harborough traffic from the Great Northern/London & North Western Joint joined and then left towards Rugby/Northampton. At Glendon Junction traffic from Toton/Stanton Gate via Syston and Manton joined and went forward initially to Wellingborough. The map also shows the Wymington Deviation which coal trains generally took to avoid the climb to Sharnbrook Summit. Finally and of later interest is the Cambridge to Bletchley line at Bedford.

The aggregate of coal trains reaching Wellingborough was 38:

- from Toton/Stanton Gate via Edwalton   9
- from Toton/Stanton Gate via Syston   16
- from Toton/Derby via Leicester and
  Market Harborough   4
- from Leicester via Wigston and Market
  Harborough   9

Of the total, several would be for locomotive coal, several others would have dropped off wagons to merchants/industrial users and five were 'through' workings to Brent, London. Following examination of the 'through' workings plus re-engineering/change of train crew and the re-sorting of the other 33 trains, a total of 27 loaded coal trains left Wellingborough daily (Tues-Fri's) destined for Hendon or Brent yards, for which 140 minutes was a typical timing. Locomotives could, as required, work double out and home workings in 24 hours, with the majority of turns being for Wellingborough allocated locomotives.

The Regional flows in aggregate

Five London yard complexes received coal trains from the points of origination summarised in this Chapter: Temple Mills and Ferme Park (Eastern Region), Brent/ Hendon and Willesden/Sudbury Junction (London Midland Region) and Neasden/Marylebone (Eastern/London Midland Region 1958 changeover of responsibility). These yards were all within a very few miles of each other.

Originating from	Receiving yard	Trains
Whitemoor	Temple Mills	21
New England	Ferme Park	8
Woodford Halse (Met)	Neasden	4
Woodford Halse (GW)	Neasden	6
Wellingborough	Hendon/Brent	27
Welham/Leicester/Toton	Willesden area	15
		81

The various WTTs are helpful but are inconsistent in how the final destination of each train is shown and, therefore, it is difficult to isolate trains which ran to BR's own depots and power generating plant (except the Toton-Stonebridge Park workings). For the principal purpose of this chapter – to identify the relative importance to BR in the 1950s of the GC line – establishing a tonnage is secondary to establishing a proportion of the total trainloads received into London yards. The trainloads arriving were typically equivalent to 45-50 wagons of the 16 ton type and carrying an average of 10.95 tons (Eastern Region) and 10.94 tons (London Midland Region) in 1953. For the GC routes from Woodford Halse, the restrictions of the Aylesbury route were at least compensated by loadings via the High Wycombe route.

The proportion of train loads arriving via the GC routes expressed as a percentage of the total was 12.3 per cent.

For completeness of the record, there was a considerable flow of traffic between the yards of the four regions represented in the capital. In the quieter hours of night and in the middle of the day, a procession of trains would pass between Temple Mills, Ferme Park, Brent, Willesden, Acton (WR) and Battersea, Hither Green, Feltham and Norwood (SR), explaining why Southern Region locomotives were often seen at Cricklewood/Brent. Because the yard/depot/wharf at Neasden/ Marylebone were modest in size and the GCR was a late arrival into London when arrangements were well in place, Neasden featured to only a limited extent in cross London traffic with transfer trips to Brent/Temple Mills. Brent had 22 daily flows to the Southern Region with sidings in the yard strictly designated for sorted traffic.

Domestic household and industrial users represented around one-third of the total tonnage of coal moved by train. The decline in demand from all but the CEGB (power stations) market from 1958 was progressive, but for London and the South East was faster as implementation of the provisions of the Clean Air Act 1956 gathered support and momentum across various authorities.

The tonnages (millions of tons) moved by rail 1951-59 were:

1951	170
1952	171
1953	175
1954	173
1955	166
1956	168
1957	167
1958	153
1959	144

MOVEMENT OF COAL SOUTH BY RAIL • 247

Map E9

1   Temple Mills   4   Neasden
2   Ferme Park   5   Willesden
3   Brent

The five, big yards for receiving coal traffic into London are shown here: Temple Mills (principally from Whitemoor), Ferme Park (New England, Peterborough), Brent/Cricklewood (Midland routes via Wellingborough), Willesden/Brent/Sudbury junction (LNW routes from Roade) and Neasden (GC routes).

248 • THE GREAT CENTRAL RAILWAY: WHAT REALLY HAPPENED

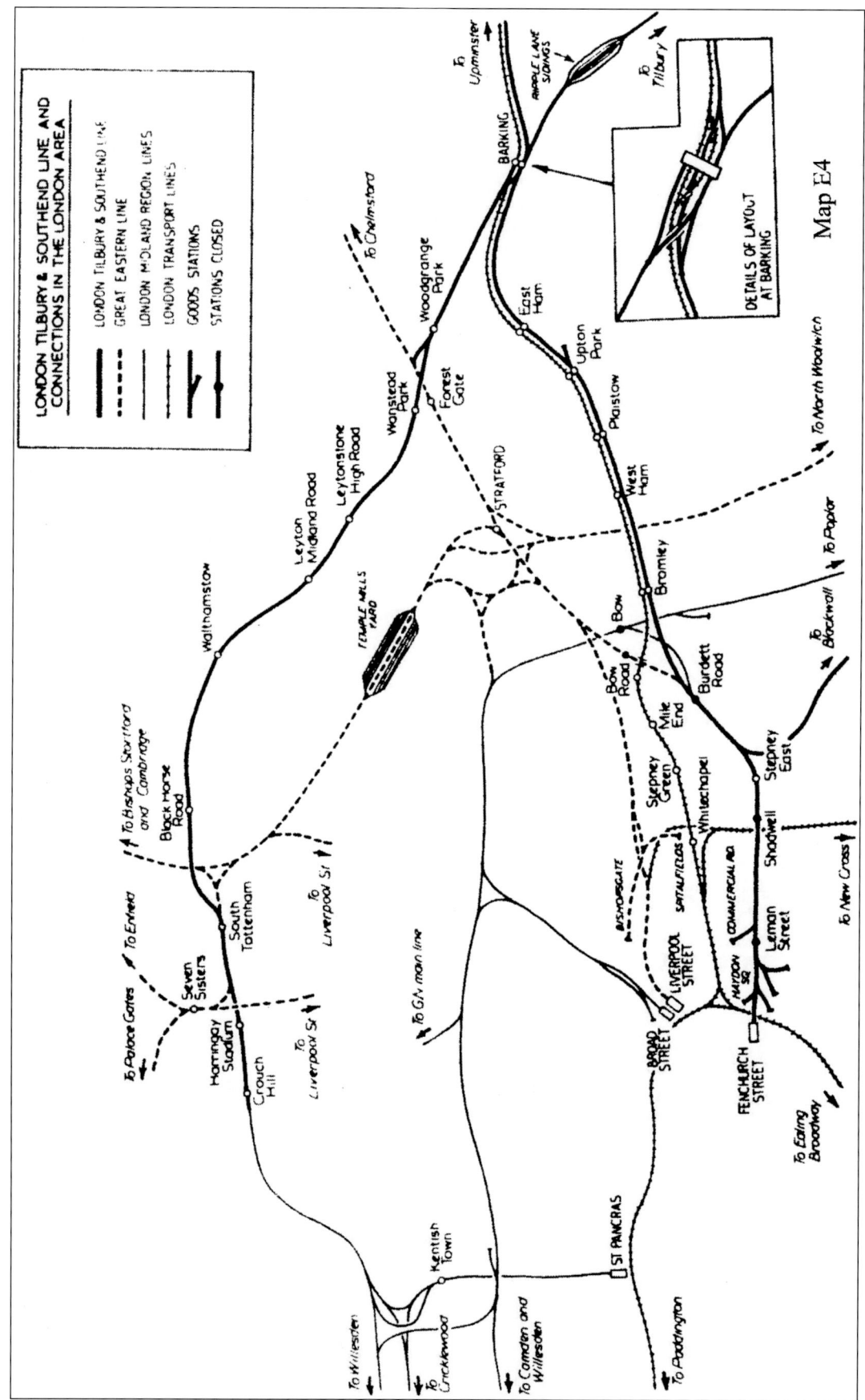

This map is included to illustrate the location of Temple Mills yards and how Cross London transfer goods traffic could be routed West.

MOVEMENT OF COAL SOUTH BY RAIL • 249

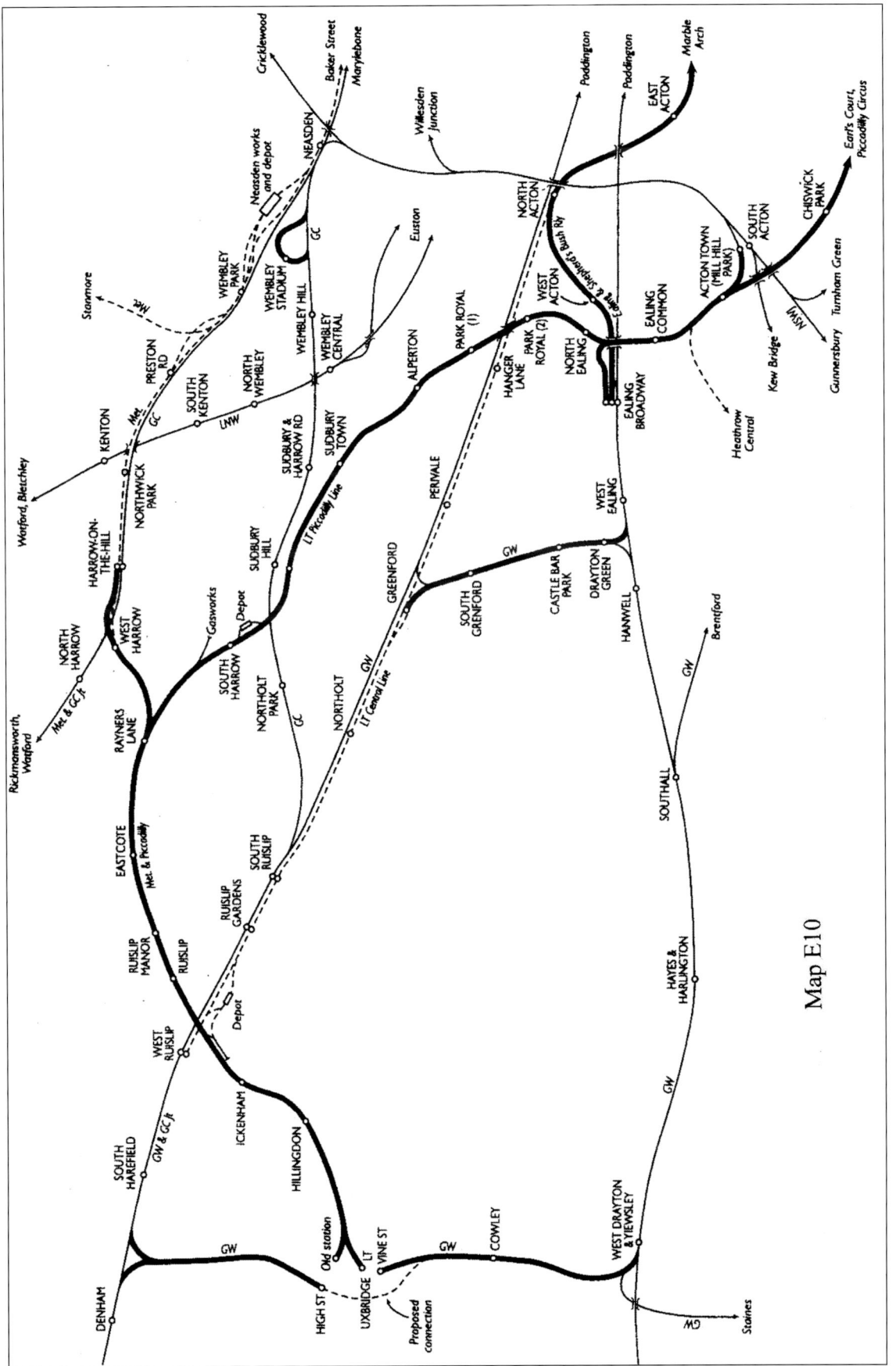

Map E10

This map shows the final approaches to Marylebone, the location of Neasden, its connections to yards at Acton and the loop line that served Wembley Stadium.

Industrial users were similarly faced with decisions on continued private generation of power or use of alternatives to coal.

BR relied upon the production forecasts of the NCB and designed its operational arrangements around those forecasts and areas from which the NCB wished to produce coal for its various markets. Up to 1959, the Plan for Coal provided the NCB with its production plan; the Revised Plan for Coal of 1959 recognised the changes affecting different markets.

Based upon the WTT information it is possible to identify the tonnage of coal moved by rail into London yards (Tuesday-Friday):

Total number of trains	81
Total number of loaded wagons est	3,645
Average tonnage per wagon	10.945 (ER/LMR average)
Total tonnage arriving est	39,894
Total tonnage arriving from Woodford Halse est	5,319
Proportion of total tonnage arriving at all yards that came from Woodford Halse:	13.5 per cent

Assumptions made:
  The WTT arrangements applied
  The average trainload was 45 wagons
  Average tonnage per wagon based upon BTC Annual Report

As the decade progressed, the average load per wagon increased to 12.62 tons in 1957 and by 1960 was 13.62 tons. Reflecting the slightly higher average loadings and also the downturn in demand for movement by rail, the reductions in loaded wagons forwarded within the LM Region were:

Year span	reduction in loaded wagons forwarded '000	% reduction on previous year span
1958 to 1959	302	8.9
1959 to 1960	118	3.8
1960 to 1961	169	5.7

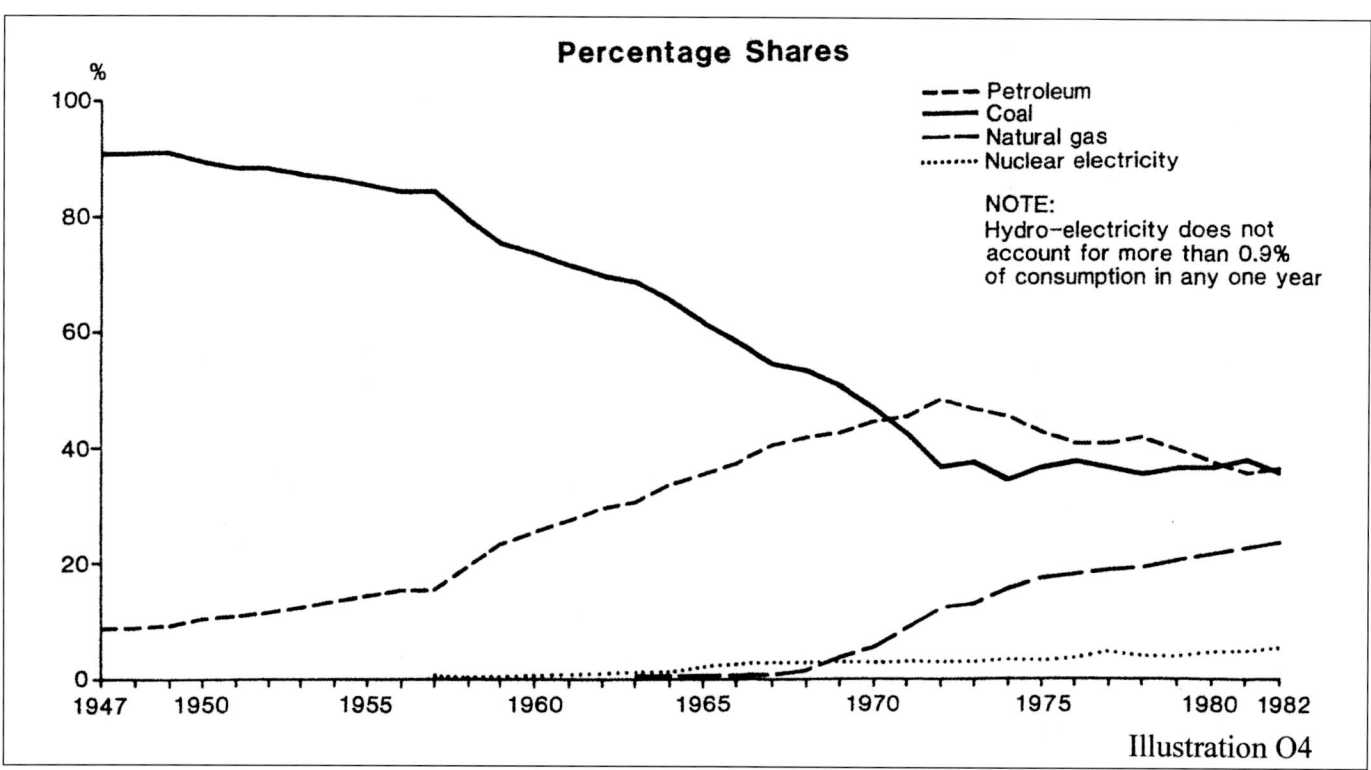

Illustration O4

Although the CEGB continued to take huge tonnages of coal the percentage share of sources of power changed over time as can be seen. With that change the challenge for the NCB was to compete; where they were able and allowed to do so and won contracts the railways were also able to contribute. Petroleum products became a new source of revenue for the railways, though not benefitting the former GCR routes until Killingholme (Immingham) came on stream.

The market was in secular decline.

The commercial policy of the NCB for zonal pricing including the cost of transport by rail rendered irrelevant the differing lengths of route taken by BR from particular areas of the Coal Board. As identified in chapter 7, the actual cost via different routes was largely unknown within BR and considered secondary to meeting the needs of the nation as in the Transport Act 1953.

Planning revolved around NCB forecasts for areas and particular collieries, the location of yards, motive power depots, motive power, train crew hours of working, route knowledge and other traffic requiring access to the routes. The output was the Working Timetable and Sectional Appendices thereto. Revisions to the WTT were made but the wholesale recasting by the LNER of the arrangements for the Annesley-Woodford Halse workings was a rare example within the overall scene of little change.

The WTTs as used for this and other chapters paint a very black and white picture of daily events. The day to day reality was frequently very different with bottlenecks (e.g. Staveley, Lincoln, Erewash Valley approaches to Stanton Gate/Toton) and NCB-based problems with geology within mines, subsidence, wagon storage and loading. The combination of these factors resulted in inefficiency, frustration and a statistic that a coal wagon made a productive roundtrip journey only in around 12 days. Up to 1957, all the BR routes had a contribution to make.

Whilst being primarily concerned with the London extension south from Annesley, it is relevant here to identify that the former GC lines north thereof were used for coal traffic routed to Lincoln and Retford, thence via the GN/GE route towards Whitemoor.

The route south from Annesley needs to be considered in two parts; firstly to and secondly onwards from Woodford Halse.

The largely intentionally self-contained GC line to Woodford Halse was one of the simplest on BR to operate and – as identified in chapter 7 efficient in utilisation of men, machines and its infrastructure. Upon arrival at Woodford Halse, the trains were sorted for movement forward to destination. A proportion of the total was for destinations via either the Aylesbury (Metropolitan) route or the High Wycombe (GW/GC Joint) route to the London area whilst a larger proportion was despatched via Banbury. Chapter 7 identified the geographical and operational constraints of the Aylesbury route and how the loadings were higher via High Wycombe. The markets for the coal despatched were domestic and industrial with the proportions between the two being difficult to identify. For those trains reaching Neasden yard/Marylebone Goods Depot/Regents Canal wharf, the total capacity – in the hundreds of wagons – paled in comparison to the other receiving yards for coal traffic. The restricted capacity was a limiting factor in determining the tonnage which could be sent, irrespective of the relative efficiency of the route north of Woodford Halse.

A reduction in total demand for coal of one million tons each year would be equivalent to six loaded trains of coal each weekday; as such not significant. A reduction of 19 million tons each year – 114 trainloads – was, however, significant.

With the timing of Revised Plan for Coal being 1959 and the official response of the NCB to a recognition of declining demand in all of its markets except power generation in the north of England, the BR planners deserve some sympathy for 1958/59. The dilemma of the planners was that of all forecasters; when does a blip become a trend and then become a terminal decline?

For the first time in over a century the planners were faced with a task of managing declining tonnages to a declining number of destinations

As described in chapter 6, finance was made available under the Modernisation Plan of 1955. Schemes put forward by the Eastern Region included improvement works at Temple Mills yards, a new yard at Ripple Lane, Barking, and electrification plus route improvements for the GN main line north from King's Cross. The latter scheme did not survive the review in 1959, but the work at the two yards was too far advanced to be altered. As the questions relating to returns on investments to be made became more challenging, it became more difficult for regional management to provide answers and seek justifications for cases already made. Having survived the scrutiny of the various bodies reviewing the Modernisation Plan, the yard at Temple Mills had a safeguarded future. Coal would continue to flow through there. Similarly, the West Coast line into London Euston required a maximum continuing contribution from coal traffic.

The London Midland Region had submitted proposals for a programme of dieselisation of the Midland Division using two types of main line locomotives; a

1-Co-Co-1 type 4 (D1>) and a Bo-Bo (D5000>) type 2, plus a major new maintenance facility. Early planning for this included 33 diesels for Annesley-Woodford Halse traffic and the building at Annesley of a diesel depot for £215k, but was not sanctioned. All of the routes except those south from Woodford Halse benefitted from the availability of recently introduced BR Standard freight locomotives.

The GN/GE route from Doncaster via Gainsborough, Lincoln and Sleaford to Peterborough would be required as the diversionary route for traffic between Doncaster and Peterborough via Retford, Newark and Grantham. Similarly, the Hertford Loop would enable essential works on the main line to be progressed.

The Midland main line from Manchester (Central) to London (St Pancras) would be upgraded and required at least whilst the electrification work between Manchester (London Road)/Liverpool (Lime Street) to Crewe-Stafford-Rugby, direct and via Birmingham (New Street) and London (Euston), was progressed. Similarly, the GW route (partly shared with the GC) from Birmingham (Snow Hill) via Banbury and High Wycombe would also be required.

The production plans of the NCB and the siting of new power stations to be commissioned by the CEGB favoured the Nottinghamshire and Yorkshire coalfields and the traditional railway routes to the east, west and north, but not south, or south west beyond the West Midlands.

Whilst the level of demand for domestic and industrial coal remained at the levels of 1953-57, the two GC routes from Woodford Halse to London had a role to play. The relatively efficient operation of the route from Nottinghamshire at least as far as Woodford Halse supported its continuation. As with all of the other routes to London, there were other traffic flows using the routes, the GN/LNW route being heavily dependent upon iron ore.

Any option to increase the tonnage of coal to London from Woodford Halse in years of increasing demand would need to recognise the limited capacity for coal wagons at Neasden/Marylebone depot plus Regents Canal wharf.

When demand for domestic coal and from industrial users started to decline, the rate of reduction in and around London was accelerated by the London County Council and other authorities, including BR, by use of diesel shunting and cross-London mixed traffic diesel types, implementing the provisions of the Clean Air Act 1956. Decline in demand was irreversible.

As an example beyond the closure of the London extension of the former GCR, the number of loaded coal trains heading south from Wellingborough daily (Tuesday to Friday) fell from twenty-seven in 1953 to eight in winter 1965 and with a Coal Concentration Depot at Walworth Road serving the residual markets of South London.

The lack of any alternative route for coal traffic from Nottinghamshire via Woodford Halse to Banbury and beyond, plus steel traffic from Humberside to Bristol and South Wales, safeguarded the GC London extension, at least in the medium term.

In the overall scheme of things in the 1950s, the relative importance to BR of the London extension for coal traffic to London was low, but at a time when no single route could cope with total demand it had a contributory role to play. As and when demand declined, so too would the level of comparative importance against those routes with better facilities and in receipt of capital investment. The GC routes were badly placed.

With the benefit of the Treasury's Review of Nationalised Industries in 1959, a stable government with a new term in prospect, a Minister for Transport keen to develop new policies and the BTC railway finances seemingly almost out of control, the politicians had an opportunity to address the future role of railways.

CHAPTER 9

DR BEECHING AND THE TRANSPORT ACT 1962

The political time span between the General Elections of 1959 and 1964 included considerable effort being directed towards matters related to the then current state and future role of the railways.

As part of the national review of the railways undertaken by Dr Richard Beeching, all routes and traffic flows were identified, including the former GC lines. From the review, some sections emerged with a strongly functional future, others with either an uncertain future or the prospect of no future.

This chapter has two aims. First, to identify the context within which policy decisions were formed (the political influences and drive). Secondly, to seek to identify why one scheme that could have supported any case for a continuing role for the London extension was actually not pursued. Matters that were pursued and which affected the future role of the London extension are identified and developed in chapter 11.

With the prospect of another five-year term in power from October 1959, the Conservative party – which had in its previous term approved the costly Modernisation Plan of the BTC – directed considerable effort and parliamentary time to the role of the railways.

The chronology of main events was:

Date	Event	Note
10/59	General Election	1
11/59	Appointment of Ernest Marples MP as Minister of Transport	2
11/59-5/60	Select Committee on Nationalised Industries	3
3/60	Prime Minister's statements(2) in House of Commons	4
4/60-10/60	Stedeford Advisory Group	5
8/60	Ministerial Group on (railway) Modernisation	6
12/60	Government White Paper. Reorganisation of Nationalised Industries	7

Date	Event	Note
3/61	Dr Richard Beeching appointed by Minister on 5-year secondment from ICI Ltd.	8
4/61	Government White Paper. The Financial and Economic Obligations of the Nationalised Industries	9
4/61	National (railway) traffic census undertaken by BTC	10
6/61	Dr Beeching succeeded Sir Brian Robertson as Chairman BTC/designate BRB	-
61	Drafting of Transport Bill	11
5/62-11/62	Interim BTC/BR Committee formed	12
9/62	Transport Act 1962	13
1/63	BTC abolished. BRB created.	14
3/63	The Reshaping of British Railways (Beeching) Report published	15
10/63	Prime Minister Macmillan resigns, succeeded by Alec Douglas-Home.	-
10/64	General Election	16

NOTES TO CHRONOLOGY:

1. Won by Conservative party with a healthy overall majority of 88 seats.
2. Harold Watkinson moved to Defence. Senior civil servants at Ministry in 1959 were James Dunnett (who upon his appointment in April to be Permanent Secretary made it clear that he was keen on the idea of moving towards a much smaller, but more cost effective railway system) and David Serpell who was transferred from the Treasury as one of the Deputy Secretaries. Both servants were heavily involved in the process of statutory change.
3. A Select Committee to examine BR/modernisation had been requested by the BTC in June 1958 but was not convened until after the BTC's own review of early 1959 referred to elsewhere in this Chapter. The Select Committee reported in July 1959.
4. The Prime Minister made two separate statements. The first related to a review of railway rates of pay and comparability with other industries which was expected to lead to a significant increase (actually 8 per cent). 'The Government accept the objective underlying the Guillebaud Committee – that fair and reasonable wages should be paid ... others,

also, must accept corresponding obligations, including a remodelling of the railway network, higher fares and rates, and a reorganisation of the structure of nationalised transport.' The second statement set out the intent to change. 'First, the industry must be of a size and pattern suited to modern conditions and prospects. In particular the railway system must be re-modelled to meet current needs, and the modernisation plan must be adapted to that shape.'

5   Referred to within this chapter.
6   Political manoeuvre to protect government position from internal criticism of management of Modernisation Plan.
7   Reflected some of the outputs of the Stedeford Advisory Group towards future organisation of transport and roles of the centre/regional managements.
8   Referred to within this chapter.
9   Applicable also to NCB and CEGB. Related in particular to breaking even over a five-year period and attaining defined rates of return on capital borrowed.
10 This was a BTC initiative aimed at understanding all categories of traffic flowing during the week commenced 23 April.
11 This paved the way for the new organisation of nationalised transport, the separation from the operating railway of the engineering workshops and the bases upon which objections to line/station/facilities withdrawals could be founded and reviewed by the Area Transport Users Consultative Committees.
12 Interim management arrangements until BTC formerly abolished and BRB created.
13 Having passed through the Houses of Commons and Lords, received Royal Assent on 1 August.
14 Referred to within this chapter.
15 Referred to within this chapter.
16 With a slogan 'Let's go with Labour for the New Britain' Labour won with an overall majority of four seats.

Many of the schemes put forward by the six railway regions for inclusion in the Modernisation Plan were submitted against a tight timescale and some were 'old' schemes not updated against whatever measures were available as regards a likely return on the estimated capital investment. Whilst much of the Plan was built upon foundations of sand, the lack of guidance from the commission reflected badly. The commission also felt that criticism of the deterioration on the revenue account was unfair as it had itself been failed by government. In that rather unsatisfactory state of affairs it is perhaps not surprising that firstly, in autumn 1958, the BTC requested that a Select Committee be appointed and secondly the government felt that the BTC should – like the NCB – conduct its own review and publish the outcome.

Trusting a schoolboy to set his own examination questions and then allowing him to mark his own answers would inevitably lead to a pass, with or without distinction. In July 1959, Sir Brian Robertson stated that the re-appraisal showed that the 1955 Plan was soundly based and that there was no need for any fundamental changes; it was, he said, a sound investment from the country's viewpoint. The main thrust was to speed up modernisation of the means to handle traffic for which the railways were best suited and also to eliminate more quickly railway facilities that were redundant in modern conditions. He went on to say that some 2,000 route miles of the network (10 per cent) would be closed between 1959 and 1964 (300 route miles between 1954 and 1958). The closures would not include any main lines. That included that GC line over which a great deal of freight would be diverted whilst the Crewe to London (Euston) electrification work was progressed to completion. The GC line would be 'loaded' with goods traffic after withdrawal of its through express passenger trains at the end of the summer timetable (i.e. September, though due to printing industry problems, postponed to November). Finally, he said that the GC and a few other duplicate main lines may be shut down after 1963; but in the meantime, consideration must be given to the industries they served and as diversionary routes.

There seems to have been no references to return on investment, the likelihood of wages rising by a significant amount, the ability or otherwise to negate the debt on capital account or the worsening financial position of the Commission.

How they must have groaned in Whitehall.

Ernest Marples – newly appointed – had an opportunity to influence the selection of the members of the Select Committee, but really wanted a hand-picked team of industrialists and some civil servant representation from his own Ministry and the Treasury (the latter having the benefit of working with both the NCB and CEGB).

By the autumn of 1959, political and civil service attitudes towards railway recovery were hardening. After the General Election of October, the Minister (Watkinson) was moved to Defence and his successor was Ernest Marples (first elected a Member of Parliament in 1945, Parliamentary Secretary to Harold Macmillan in

1951-54 and Postmaster-General 1957-59). He had also been successful in business and was founder of a road construction business, Marples, Ridgeway & Partners, which benefitted from contracts for flyover connections and the linkage of the southern end of the M1 motorway through Hendon. He found difficulty in letting go his lucrative business interests, seemingly ignored the obvious conflict of interest in his Ministry approving road contracts, was suspected of tax fraud and eventually fled the UK for the tax haven of Monaco where he died in July 1978.

Two enquiries into the commission's railway activities were established. The Select Committee on Nationalised Industries with thirteen members took evidence between January and May 1960. Whilst those proceedings continued, Marples received a memorandum from the Ministry of Transport and the Treasury which raised severe doubts about the over optimistic forecasts and under-estimated expectations of future wage costs. In March 1960, when an 8 per cent increase in railway wages was deemed by a separate enquiry to be merited, Marples moved to set up the Special Advisory Group to assist him in examining the 'structure, finance and working' of the BTC railway activities. The Group consisted of businessmen: Sir Ivan Stedeford, head of Tube Investments Ltd.; Dr Richard Beeching, ICI Ltd., Technical Director; Henry Benson, accountant, Cooper Brothers; and Frank Kearton, Courtaulds Ltd. as well as two civil servants, Matthew Stevenson of the Treasury and David Serpell, from Transport.

The timing of reporting by the public committee and the private group overlapped; a report from the former in July 1960 and an initial recommendation from the latter in June 1960 as their work progressed (until October 1960). The Plan was effectively stalled whilst a detailed enquiry was held into the viability of schemes in progress. The BTC submitted 120 projects (£227m) listed under four headings:

a) too far advanced to be sensibly stopped
b) self-evidently justified
c) unavoidable replacement
d) started, but not passed the point of no return.

The group recommended that most of the schemes in a) to c) should be allowed to proceed and all in d) should be halted. The committee accepted that it was difficult to measure the effects of the Plan as it proceeded and welcomed the fact that some schemes had produced good results in terms of revenue generated. However, it censured the BTC for inadequate financial testing of the predicted return (profitability) of individual projects. There was also criticism of how the commission had selected schemes to be given priority and lack of progress towards rationalisation of the network and improvements to freight operations.

The group heard from the Minister for Transport that his department was planning an extensive programme of road building which would limit the future prospects of the railways.

In a separate development, Marples set up a Ministerial Group on Modernisation to examine detailed aspects of the Plan, presumably to shield from the public the role of Whitehall departments in accepting the basis upon which the Plan had been allowed to start and proceed.

The BTC submitted a modified programme for the 1961-64 period. To what did all this add up?

- the BTC had wanted to modernise the railways after years of neglect. In so doing it was ill equipped for the changes from the obligations of the Transport Act 1953 to the demands for returns/profitability
- the public wanted the convenience of a railway of roughly the same size as in 1955
- the government wanted the BTC to fulfil its (1953 Act) obligation to 'break even'.

Reconciling these objectives was impossible. The railwaymen had lost their industry.

The membership of the Stedeford Advisory Group had originally included Sir Frank Smith who had recently retired from ICI Ltd. and it was Sir Frank who suggested Dr Richard Beeching. Dr Beeching had worked during the Second World War under the direction of Smith in a department responsible for the design of armaments. After the war, Smith returned to his former employment at ICI Ltd. and his place was taken by Sir Steuart Mitchell (later to be Deputy Chairman to Beeching at the BRB). In 1948, Beeching joined ICI as Personal Technical Assistant to Sir Frank; a position he held for 18 months until he was appointed to the Board of the ICI Fibres Division. In 1957, Beeching became Chairman of the

ICI Metals Division and Technical Director on the main board. In 1959, Sir Frank retired and in his apologies to the request from the Ministry of Transport, suggested Dr Beeching as an able replacement.

Having a group of four (the two civil servants had a watching brief) left open the possibility of two v two in terms of agreeing a way forward to a recommendation to the Minister. That proved to be the case for reviewing detailed aspects of the Modernisation Plan. Wishing to proceed, Marples asked the group to concentrate upon matters of the organisation and finance, though the group did take an interest in examining the 120 projects as already mentioned.

The same two v two divisions (Beeching/Benson v Stedeford/Kearton) emerged from discussions on future organisation; it was the seemingly recurring theme in British railway organisation history of the extent of the power to be withheld at the 'centre' and the consequential extent of decentralisation of functional authority. Beeching/Benson wanted a strong central Railway Board with functional responsibilities. Its membership, they contended, should be limited to professional railwaymen serving full-time, reinforced by a part-time element not including Regional Chairmen or Managing Directors of the non-railway constituents of the commission (London Transport, British Road Services, Road Passenger Transport, Docks, Inland Waterways, Thomas Cook). Stedeford/Kearton disagreed and at the end of the group's deliberations, seven recommendations were made unanimously and one (organisation) giving two options.

The BTC did not like either option. The upshots were; firstly, that when the White Paper 'Re-organisation of the Nationalised Transport Undertaking' appeared in December 1960, it took no more account of railway opinion than was apparent in 1952 when preparing the ground for the Transport Act 1953, and, secondly, that Marples had been impressed by the work and approach of Beeching. One thing that was abundantly clear from the two separate reviews of the Modernisation Plan was that the BTC's own review should be treated with scepticism.

With the railways, Marples was faced with multiple problems. He could not stop the outflow of capital into modernisation schemes and had to rely on the BTC to take a more proactive role in judging schemes. The revenue account for 1960 did nothing to inspire confidence, as the overall deficit reached £128.3m, freight having lost £47m despite coal/coke and minerals earning a surplus of £16m. Part of the increase in the deficit was due to a wage award of 8 per cent. He wanted to pursue organisational change, but Robertson would not be the man to lead it. He wanted to find the best 'shape' for the railways in the future.

Elsewhere in Marples' portfolio, his tenure coincided with the new age of road transport. It witnessed the start of the 'largest road building programme ever' which continued unabated for 15 years, an increase over that period in the number of road vehicles by 149 per cent and 57 per cent of households owning a car. Freight traffic by road was helped by the length of articulated vehicles being increased by 40 per cent (1955-68). In 1962, lorries over eight tons carried only 11 per cent of the total ton-mileage in 1962 and 62 per cent in 1976. Marples held a very good position in being able to foresee the threat to the market share enjoyed by the railways and also found difficulty in letting go his shareholding in a road construction company beyond transferring it to his wife.

To address the problem of the future role and shape of the railways, Marples turned to Dr Beeching, or rather he turned to ICI Ltd. with an offer of a five year secondment on a salary equivalent to that being paid by ICI; a figure that was nearly five times Marples' own salary as Minister, twice that paid to the chairmen of the NCB and CEGB and more than twice that paid to Sir Brian Robertson. Dr Beeching accepted the terms for a secondment to 31 May 1966 with termination at any time. An exceptional salary for an exceptional role, an expectation that Beeching would shake up the railways and was someone who would apply private sector strictures to public sector operations. He proved more than able to lead a managerial revolution at the headquarters; 222 Marylebone Road, the former Great Central Railway Hotel.

As a trained scientist, Beeching would naturally set out to raise empirical data, particularly so as, after briefing meetings with the Directors of Costings and Statistics, he would have been aware that the annual reports of the commission provided the best available information. Beeching was not fettered by the emotionalism that seemed to characterise so much railway work and managers; rather it was a case of rational thinking applied in a consistent manner. The national traffic census arranged for the April was authorised to proceed and, whilst the analysis would be a mammoth clerical task, it would provide information which extended beyond the regional boundaries that pervaded the accounting. In 1955, the Railway Clearing House had largely ceased its main role of allocating expenditure for transits over former boundaries.

Beeching was content to set the menu of questions and let others respond in time with answers. When his Report was published in March 1963 the majority of the traffic information was based upon 1961 and the layout of what was available followed the same approach to categories of traffic as had been introduced half a century earlier. For freight there was coal/coke and patent fuel, minerals, merchandise and livestock. Passenger traffic was categorised as fast and semi-fast, stopping and suburban. Similarly, track costs followed the approach as included with the accounts.

In summary the approach to that aspect of the wider brief was:

- to define the nature of the problem
- to analyse the problem
- to examine the present state of the railway in terms of organisational responsibility, types of traffic and how the physical network is used
- to analyse by types of traffic to identify their contribution to the revenue account
- having established a base of information, conduct deeper analyses to provide a basis for making rational decisions.

All of the foregoing would take time and, in the interim, Beeching turned his attention to people and to organisation. Strongly held views as argued within the Stedeford Advisory Group were maintained; Beeching wanted a strong board with functional duties and not decentralisation and regional autonomy. On the recommendation of Beeching, Marples appointed three new (non-railwaymen) members of the BTC: Leslie Williams, recently retired from Shell Chemicals (September 1961); Philip Shirley, seconded from Unilever to act as Member for Finance (October 1961); and Sir Steuart Mitchell, previously Beeching's Superintendent following the retirement of Sir Frank Smith post-war (February 1962). These men were to direct the reorganisation of the railway workshops under central (rather than regional) control.

Beeching also selected Sir Philip Warter – a part-time member of the commission – to be his deputy chairman from October 1961. Benstead, Sinclair and Grand retired from the BTC. Internal reviews were soon underway to reduce the multiplicity of committees, advisory panels, councils and conferences that seemingly supported each other.

The railways' publicity and press arrangements were revolutionised following the arrival of another Shell executive – S.K. Garratt – who, together with Eric Merrill, worked closely with Beeching to create a corporate approach to managing public aspects of the Report.

Between October 1961 and April 1963, nearly 40 officers were appointed from leading private sector organisations – Shell, ICI, General Electric, Lever Brothers, Jaguar Cars – three of whom became board members. Of course, they had difficulties of understanding how the railways needed to operate, but equally, some produced major benefits from initiatives to which BTC chief officers had a myopic outlook. Amongst these was the winning of ten major oil contracts, the innovations being that the oil companies owned or leased the wagons and the BTB did what it was best at, providing suitable motive power, train crew, a timetable for efficient movement of full and empty wagons from/back to oil company terminals.

Beeching needed someone who could advise him as necessary and to whatever detail he required about how the operational railway worked in practice. Robertson had Blee and Hollingsworth in that role and, when the latter retired in 1961, Robertson recommended Stanley Raymond. Raymond was appointed and, with his background of London Transport and road haulage as well as railway work, had the confidence of Beeching from July 1961 in giving impetus to the traffic studies then starting. His style impressed and, in January 1962, he was sent to Paddington as General Manager with an instruction to 'flush out the old guard'. The headquarters post of Traffic Adviser was then scrapped, leaving a post of Chief Operating Officer as the senior 'doer' in shaping the way forward. That post was filled from early 1962 by Gerard Twistleton-Wykeham-Fiennes – thankfully the T-W parts were not generally applied.

Fiennes had been educated at Winchester and Oxford University and was selected to enter service in 1930 as a Traffic Apprentice for the LNER. Following training in

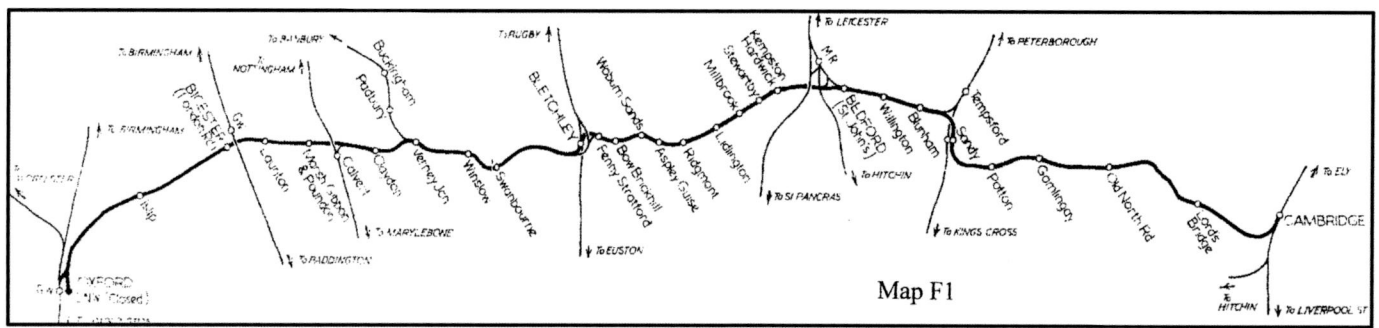

The Cambridge – Oxford line via Bedford and Bletchley which was so useful during the Second World War to route traffic for the South of England without crossing London. The 1940 connection with the Great Central line is shown at Calvert. Swanbourne is shown between Bletchley and Calvert.

operational functions of the railway and being passed out in rules and regulations, he spent the majority of his career within the three areas of the Eastern Region; the Great Eastern Lines out of Liverpool Street, the Great Northern Line out of King's Cross and for a relatively short time the Great Central line based at Nottingham. A career of progression had taken him, his wife and young family from home to home, irregular disturbance required of operational managers who were expected to live 'on the patch' and be 'on call'. A summary of his career:

1933	Assistant Yard Master, Whitemoor
1939-45	Variously: Edinburgh
	Cambridge – Relief District Superintendent
	York – Trains Assistant. BOLERO planning
	Shenfield – GE Wartime HQ
	Nottingham – District Superintendent
	Stratford – District Superintendent
1948	Assistant Superintendent, Liverpool St, GE lines
1957	Traffic Manager, King's Cross, GN lines
1961	Chief Operating Officer, BTC HQ

He had experienced a great deal of railway work, including the horrors of wartime, coping with the blitz, planning, fatal accidents and inquiries, planning the Liverpool Street-Norwich 'Britannia' timetables, the early GE suburban electrification investment schemes for the Modernisation Plan, the alternative 'Deltics' plan for the East Coast following the electrification scheme being rejected.

Of particular relevance to this book was his time at Nottingham, his knowledge of diversionary routes for avoiding London and his involvement with the new Sheffield District created in 1957/8.

Whilst at Nottingham, he recognised the potential for getting trains through the environs without the need for engines always seeming to need coal or water or both which saw them turned 'inside' at Annesley and delayed there. He wanted to do what was eventually done with the 'windcutters' and change crews at Bulwell. Further south, he recognised and tried (unsuccessfully) to find a way to improve matters at Banbury with through running of locomotives and trains to Swindon or Reading or Honeybourne.

The diversionary route of interest was a cross-country between Cambridge-Bletchley-Oxford.

The huge commercial potential of Shelfield/South Yorkshire was quickly apparent to Fiennes. In reviewing possible sites for a new marshalling yard (Tinsley), the closeness of the pre-Grouping railway company lines – MR, GN, GC – all of which were duplicating facilities, yards, motive power and commercial arrangements was clear.

By his own admission a 'doer' and not a 'planner', Fiennes arrived at HQ at a time when Raymond was Traffic Adviser to Beeching. However, from January 1962 until November 1963 (when he became Chairman and General Manager, Western Region and Stanley Raymond returned to HQ as a Board Member) Fiennes was instrumental in generating new ideas and putting a

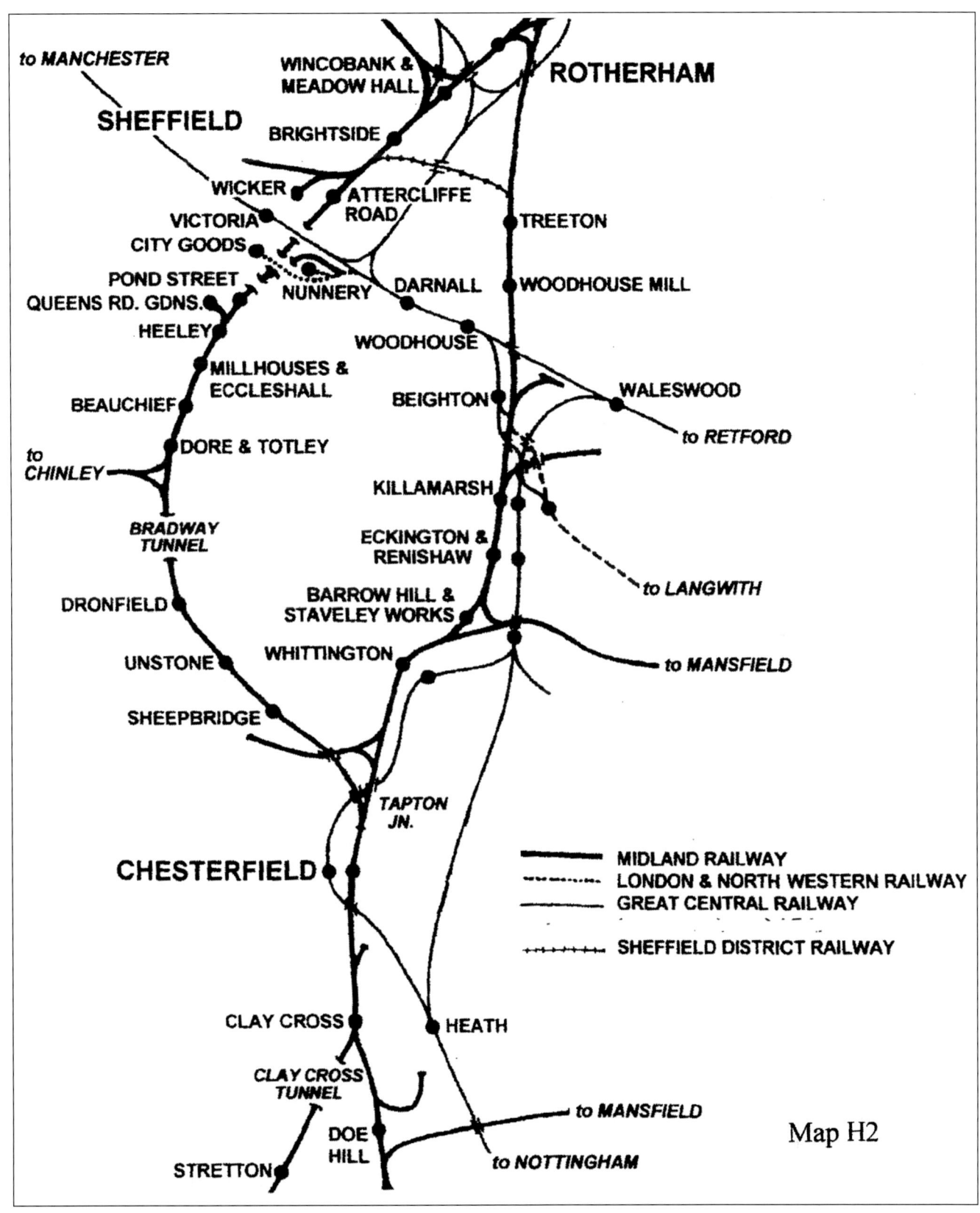

This map shows the duplication of routes between Chesterfield and the approach to Sheffield from the East at Waleswood/Beighton. With the traffic potential of the area and the need for economies and improved efficiency, the opportunity for investment and case for rationalisation could be made. Maps H3-H6 at Chapter 12 also refer.

stop to some bad ideas. Beeching, though, also wanted an experienced operator who could also take on an organisational and planning role. F. (Fred) Margetts, General Manager of the North Eastern Region, had impressed Beeching at an officers' conference in 1961 and was first appointed to the 'shadow' BR board during the interim period as the BTC was coming to an end. From that move – in July 1962 – it was clear that Margetts was destined for the operating functional role of the British Railways Board and Gerard Fiennes was not. However, for a period of approaching three years, Fiennes had and took an opportunity with others to develop some initiatives that would shape the way forward particularly for freight traffic. These initiatives included what he termed 'merry go round' high capacity coal wagons which would – with the necessary support of the NCB and CEGB – be run in circuits between collieries and power stations with automated loading from and discharge into bunkers. The second initiative was from a massive increase in containers of various lengths and capacities which would be transferable between road and flatbed railway wagons for transit over distances where the economics of rail transport bettered road; this became known as the Liner Train concept.

The limitations of the British railways' loading gauge and the desirability of conforming to the international standard size shipping containers then starting to gain rapid momentum caused this second initiative to falter and eventually be overtaken by a Freightliner concept linking ports with strategically placed rail/road interchange points.

Fiennes also had another role and that involved proposals made in the Modernisation Plan for new marshalling yards. His thinking – and this went back to his time at Whitemoor and his involvement with the constrictions of Annesley and particularly Banbury – was that, wherever possible, trains, once on the way from point of origin, should not need to be re-sorted in the traditional manner en route. The concept – strengthened by the outputs from traffic studies – was built around trainload rather than wagon load traffic running between a smaller network of yards. For example, a block of twenty wagons for Birmingham from Newcastle would be joined at Sheffield by an incoming block of twenty wagons from Wakefield; a network of brake fitted merchandise trains. There was a danger from the proposals in the Modernisation Plan that interchanges of traffic would be dealt with not where logic suggested they should be – at the centres of production and consumption (e.g. Sheffield, Newcastle, Middlesbrough, London) – but at inter-regional boundaries (e.g. Carlisle and Swanbourne). Swanbourne is the 'green field' site of interest here.

Swanbourne is three miles west of Bletchley in Buckinghamshire and was on the line offering a threatened passenger service between Cambridge and Oxford and some freight. Bletchley is also on the main line between London (Euston) and Rugby and to the west of Swanbourne the Cambridge-Oxford line passed under the GC line near Calvert, a few miles further west it passed under the GW line between Banbury and Princes Risborough, before later reaching the GW line between Banbury and Didcot at Oxford, 76½ miles from Cambridge. During the Second World War, a link between the east-west line and the GC line was installed at Calvert, with the strategic intent of allowing freight and defence movements between the north and south without passing through London. Improvements to this route to form a London outer ring freight route were advocated by the RE in 1949 and dusted off again in 1954. The BTC fully recognised that the cost of up to £15m was 'never expected to show a direct financial return'. It was too late to save the cost of a flyover bridge at Bletchley, but Fiennes put a stop to the scheme.

Had it progressed to fruition, a modern yard at Swanbourne would have opened the way for traffic along the GC route for Gloucester/Bristol/South Wales to be routed via Oxford, Didcot and the GW main line towards Swindon for the South Coast via Oxford, Reading, Tonbridge and Ashford, whilst London traffic would continue by the GC/Met route to Neasden/Marylebone. At the time there were daily nine trains of steel between Scunthorpe and Consett to South Wales routed from Woodford via the SMJ route to Stratford, thence a new connection towards Honeybourne, Cheltenham and Gloucester. Coal traffic for the west of Woodford Halse (the higher proportion of the total) would – because of the nature of its distribution for the domestic market – have needed the Banbury and SRJ lines, though trainload (industrial users) and domestic coal for London could have continued as before via the two alternative routes South from Woodford Halse. As the pattern of freight traffic flows became better understood and as the tonnages of different categories of freight changed over time, the decision to not proceed with greenfield new marshalling yards was correct.

Of related interest, but nothing to do with Fiennes, was the Freight Plan of the London Midland Region which envisaged a concentration of parcels handling depots at London, Nottingham, Manchester, Birmingham and Leicester. As four of those centres were on the GC route and the volume of parcels was considerable, that, potentially, offered additional traffic. As it transpired, there was one Oldham-London service and an enhanced former newspapers night service from London to Nottingham which loaded to twelve plus bogie vehicles and returned from Nottingham around mid-day loaded with parcels.

The short-term (which became medium-term) role of the GC route as envisaged by Sir Brian Robertson in 1959 ('loaded' with freight trains diverted due to electrification work) did not materialise. The main reasons for this were that the electrification work was progressed in stages, much of the route allowed short diversions (e.g. Manchester/Crewe to Stafford traffic could be routed via Stoke, Stafford to Rugby traffic flows could be routed around via Wolverhampton/Birmingham/Coventry and vice versa, Rugby to Roade via Northampton), a lack of paths available via the route over the Pennines to Sheffield thence the GC line, retaining the traffic on LM routes over which train crew turns could be protected and commercial control arrangements. Certain passenger services were diverted between Manchester and London, but only night sleeping car services used the GC route.

Fiennes, as a doer, became extremely frustrated by lack of progress with merry go round and Liner trains. Margetts – as the responsible board member – became more directly involved in the thinking behind a concentration for freight on a limited number of routes – a move to a 'doing' role was in order for Fiennes. In autumn 1963, Dr Beeching advised Fiennes that Stanley Raymond was returning from the Western Region to take a role as a board member and James Ness, General Manager (Scottish Region), was coming to HQ to develop freight liner routes strategy planning. Fiennes was invited to take the role as chairman and general manager of the Western Region, a promotion in seniority and an invitation he accepted. With the greater amount of management information that had become available from the traffic studies (which replaced a lot of uncoordinated regional data) the route's strategy and its detailed planning had emerged as the preferred way forward. Fiennes, Margetts and others needed to allow the planners time to do their job, including the establishment of a Central Wagon Authority under the very experienced and dependable Harold Hoyle. Ness relieved Margetts of his planning role, allowing the latter to concentrate upon aspects of the consequences of wholesale withdrawal of services as proposed in the Re-shaping of British Railways report announced in March 1963 (and given political force by the provisions of the Transport Act 1962).

It was the arrival of Ness that precluded further direct involvement for Fiennes and as the latter stated in his book *I Tried to Run a Railway*, he had taken from him a personal interest in closing the GC main line. The outcome of the work of Ness and its strong relevance to this book is told in chapter 11.

With all this activity at HQ, the regions – just as after nationalisation whilst the BTC and RE did not play together very well – did manage to make good use of some of the capital investment (continuous welded rails, colour light signalling, installation of an automatic warning system, lifting average speeds of passenger trains, station improvements) and ran a safe railway day in day out, night in night out, 365 days/year.

To round off the organisational debate, the new British Railways Board (fully assembled by November 1963) consisted of a chairman (Beeching), a deputy chairman (Steuart Mitchell), eight full-time members (including Margetts and Ness) with functional responsibilities and five part-time Members. Margetts and Ness were the two 'railwaymen', the others brought a wide range of other professional skills and contributions.

'The Re-shaping of British Railways' (Beeching) report has been the subject of many a comment and book; suffice here to say that the 'axe' was poised to fall on passenger services of relevance to this book; along the London (Marylebone)-Leicester-Nottingham (Victoria) and Woodford Halse-Banbury, Manchester

(Piccadilly)-Hayfield/Macclesfield, Barton-on-Humber-New Holland Town, Glazebrook-Stockport (Tiviot Dale), Wrexham (Central)-New Brighton and New Holland Pier-Cleethorpes (local). Something slightly less terminal was proposed for Lincoln (Central)-Market Rasen-Cleethorpes. Beyond the passenger services, the BRB would take decisions regarding its freight operations and routes in line with its financial obligations within the Transport Act 1962.

By mid-1963, Marples could consider that he and his senior civil servants had orchestrated a well thought through political process. The Transport Act 1962 had provided (at Section 56) the basis upon which objections to closure or amended railway passenger services could be considered by the relevant Area Transport Users Consultative Committee; that basis was one of hardship caused by the proposal. Beeching was made fully aware of this provision and the re-shaping report made reference to the very limited scale and degree of hardship which the proposals in the report were likely to incur. The arrangements for the GC main line proposal are referred to in chapter 10.

CHAPTER 10

THE POLITICAL PROCESS OF CHANGE FOR RAILWAYS IN THE 1950s AND 1960s

When the railways were taken into public ownership in 1948, the government established (under Section 6 of the Transport Act 1947) an organisation of Transport Users Consultative Committees. In order that the users of railways (and other public transport) should have some means of criticising the British Transport Commission and making suggestions for improvements, the Consultative Committees were established to represent transport users of all kinds. In the event that the BTC wished to withdraw a service, the procedure to be followed required the posting/publication of notices and an opportunity to make representations to the relevant Area Committee.

The Transport Act 1962 varied the grounds upon which objections to proposals could be founded and brought forth considerable criticism of the British Railways Board and Ministry of Transport.

This chapter examines the functions of the TUCC, particularly in regard to the closure of the GC main line, and also records how successive Ministers of Transport responded to the proposals arising from the Re-shaping of British Railways Report of March 1963.

The independent chairman and members of each committee were appointed by the Minister who sought to find a cross-section of representatives of transport users. No salary or fee (other than expenses incurred) was payable.

There were eleven areas including the East Midlands in which much GCR territory lay. The functions of the area committee were wide: '…may make recommendations in regard to any matter affecting the services and facilities provided … to which consideration ought to be given…'

The Transport Act 1953 extended the role of the Area Committees to include bus services.

The Central Transport Consultative Committee was set up in 1948 and had an independent Chairman and representatives as follows (all appointed by the Minister):

- agriculture (two)
- commerce and industry (five), including the NCB
- shipping (one)
- labour (two, nominated by the Trades Union Council)
- local authorities (five)
- British Transport Commission (two, including one who was a Member of that Commission)
- the Chairmen of the Committees for Scotland and for Wales.

The main role of the CTCC was to receive, consider and confirm or reject the recommendations of the English Area Committees.

The area committees had representatives as follows (all appointed by the Minister):

- British Transport Commission (two, including one who was from British Railways and – in the East Midlands Area the Divisional Manager of British Road Services)
- a cross section of transport users.

For the area committees, the BTC representatives may involve officials with particular knowledge useful in responding factually to questions or objections raised.

Following publication and posting of a proposal by the BTC regarding a service, the area committee would fix a date up to which representations could be raised and a place and time where such objections would be heard and considered. Cross examination of witnesses

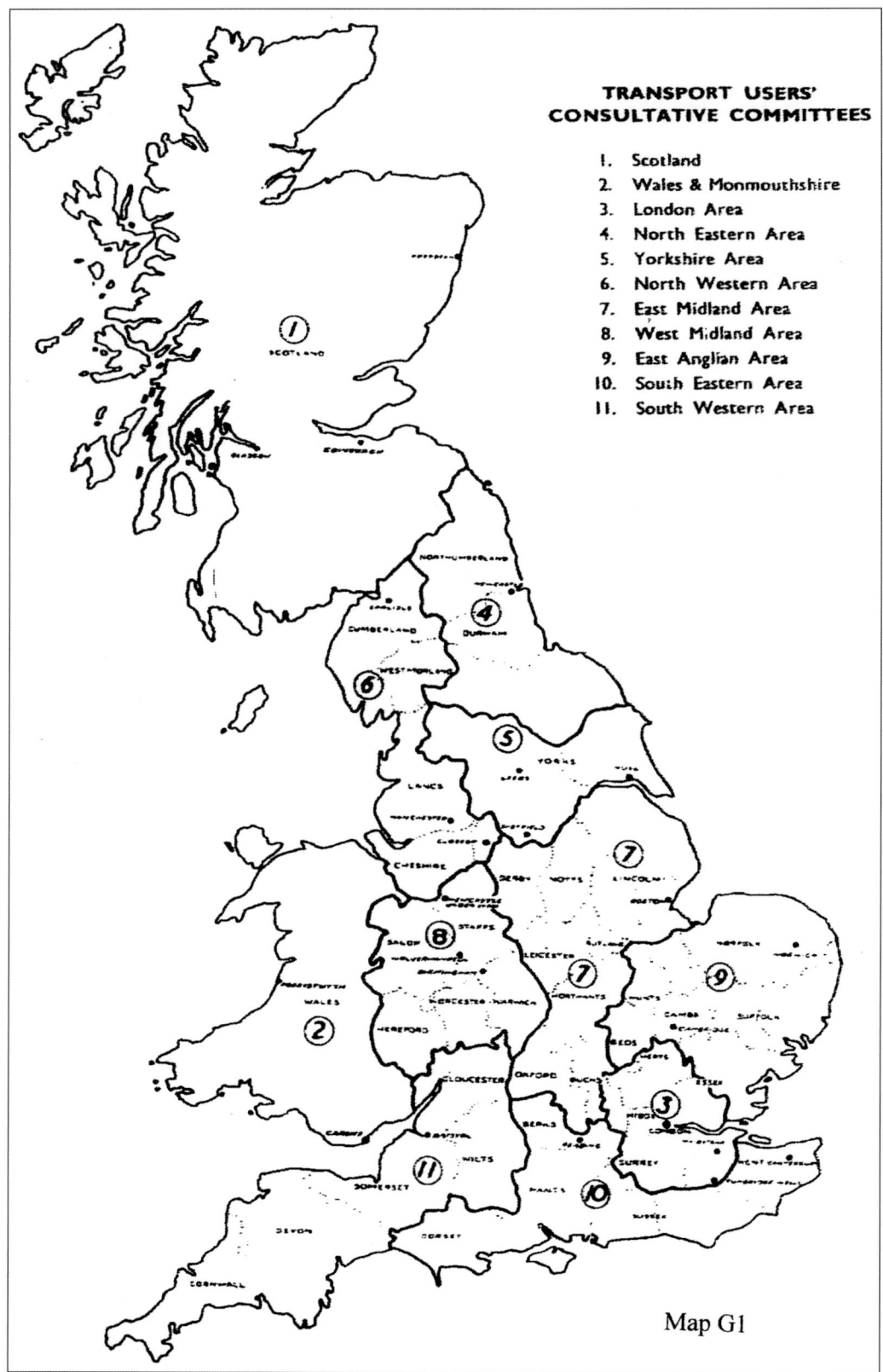

The organisation of the Areas of the Transport Users Consultative Committees. Area 7 covered the parts of the former Great Central Railway at most risk from proposed withdrawal of passenger services.

by solicitors or counsel was not allowed and such representatives were treated as spokesmen.

From their earliest days, the committees were criticised, mainly due to a lack of understanding of their role:

- the Committees were not subservient to management
- there were no compulsory powers to enforce their views; they were merely consultative
- the work of a Committee was not a form of arbitration tribunal.

In their first decade of service, the TUCCs investigated and agreed to the closure of just over 3,000 route miles of track and over 700 stations; the CTCC was generally supportive of the BTC and, as an example, encouraged the introduction and extension of use of diesel multiple units. Towards the end of the 1950s, there were signs of better co-ordination between rail and road services, particularly where rail services were pruned.

That generally mutually supportive arrangement would be sorely tested by the implementation of the vast range of closures listed in the re-shaping report of 1963. Minister Marples – in full knowledge of the weakness of the costing information available to the BRB – made a provision in the Transport Act 1962 which revised the basis upon which objections to the Board's proposals could be made; it limited that basis to 'hardship'. For good measure it was included in the re-shaping report. It was a perfect 'stitch up'.

> 'It would be folly to suggest that widespread closure of stopping train services will cause no hardship anywhere or to anybody, and the Transport Act, 1962 makes the consideration of hardship the special responsibility of Transport Users Consultative Committees, where objections to closures are lodged. For the purpose of judging the closure proposals as a whole, however, it is necessary to have some idea of the scale and degree of hardship which they are likely to cause'.

The paragraph then referred to bus services and concluded that:

> 'In most of the country, therefore, it appears that hardship will arise on only a very limited scale'.

Once the closure notices started appearing, the objections quickly followed. Most were based not upon hardship, but the perceived revenue/income/profitability/usefulness of such and such a service, many were directed not to the TUCC, but to the MPs, Minister or BRB. Dr Beeching was astute as regards public relations and his team was ready with 'standard' letters referring to the 'overall position' rather than questionable 'profitability' of a particular section. Good, accurate, corporate traffic and route costing data was something that neither he, the Minister nor anyone else had available; it was the Achilles heel and, thus, the avoidance of it. It did not reduce the welter of criticism and there was little incentive for the six regions to provide carefully formulated data. As far as they were concerned, the Act of 1962 had transferred the responsibility for public decisions on opposed closures from the TUCC to the CTCC to the Ministry and placed no obligation upon BR to publish any financial information in support of its proposals. The Minister was in a position of difficulty and after negotiations with the CTCC (itself finding difficulty in doing much other than referring matters to the Minister) agreed to supply rudimentary data, for line closures, on revenue and direct movement and terminal costs, together with track and signalling costs attributable to passenger train working. Estimated renewal and maintenance costs over a five-year period were also to be given. For station closures, originating receipts and direct costs were to be supplied. These figures were endorsed in October 1963 by Sir William Carrington, past President of the Institute of Chartered Accountants in England and Wales, in a report commissioned by Marples following criticism in both Houses of Parliament. The Minister had won the day, but only just. Thereafter it was no good Professor Hondelink, on behalf of the National Council on Inland Transport, or Lord Stonham and the Earl of Kinnoull getting excited; the legislation had been passed (not one Conservative MP voted against it) and any revision would come about only if the Labour party won a General Election with a manifesto pledging repeal. In the case of the GC main line, questions of hardship were largely resolved by the availability of alternative bus and rail services; Appendix 9 lists the bus services for the 1966 proposal.

Labour did win the General Election of October 1964, but with an overall majority of just four. Transport policy was a low priority and suggestions that they would halt major closures were never followed up with a working definition of what constituted a major closure.

448 closure proposals were made under the Transport Acts 1963 (and 1968) to the end of 1973. The number of proposals for closure made between 1 June 1961 (BRB) and the Transport Act 1962 taking effect – and therefore dealt under the 1947/1953 TUCC procedure – is not known, but there were 74 full or part closures. In the 18-month period from June 1963 to December 1965, some 330 closure proposals were processed. The most important period was 1964-66, when 258 closures were made, 'bridged' by two chairmen of BRB (Beeching returned to ICI Ltd. in 1965 at the end of his five-year period of secondment and Stanley Raymond succeeded him) and two Ministers of Transport (Thomas Fraser October 1964 to December 1965 and Barbara Castle). In his final months, Fraser gave his consent to the closure of such lines as the Somerset and Dorset (Bath to Bournemouth), Salisbury-Exeter (duplicate line from London to Exeter and Plymouth), Leeds/Lancaster-Morecambe and Heysham, plus the closure of termini including Glasgow's St Enoch and Buchanan Street.

When Barbara Castle became Minister, she was very nervous about proceeding with closures before her transport policy had been fully worked out, an attitude strengthened during the campaign leading to a decisive win by Labour in the General Election of March 1966 (96 seat overall majority). Nevertheless, she agreed to 71 proposed closures including Aberdeen-Keith-Elgin and Stanley Junction-Forfar-Kinnaber Junction, plus Manchester (Central) station. It fell to her to accept the proposals for the Great Central main line, 73½ miles in total. On average, Castle took seven months to process proposals and, at a time when there were suggestions of a shift in transport policy, she withheld her consent on 38 occasions, 18 involving complete refusals. MP for Blackburn, a third of these cases were in the north west of England: Manchester-Glossop, Liverpool-St Helens-Wigan, Liverpool-Fazakerley-Wigan and Liverpool-Chester (General).

For every refusal to give consent, the chairman of the BRB could actually afford a wry smile; unable to balance the books, Minister, due in part to your decisions. The age of the subsidised, grant-aided railway had dawned.

CHAPTER 11

THE FORMER GCR LINES IN THE 1960s

This chapter identifies the effects upon the former GCR lines of policy decisions of the BTC (up to mid-1961), the BRB, CEGB and NCB, plus the outputs from the work of Dr Beeching and the provisions of the Transport Act 1962.

Based upon the public statements of the Chairman of the BTC in Summer 1959 (following the Commission's own review of the Modernisation Plan) those close to the management of the GCR lines would, at the end of that Summer, have had several expectations:

- early withdrawal of through London (Marylebone)-Manchester/West Riding passenger trains North of Nottingham (Victoria)
- a reduction in the frequency and increase in journey times for a passenger service between Marylebone and Nottingham (Victoria)

The fireman of this 9F has filled the firebox and with the safety valves indicating a good steam pressure he probably thought his job was done before relief at Bulwell/Annesley. The train is approaching Barnstone tunnel, North of Loughborough. (Rail on-line)

An evening fish train approaching Belgrave & Birstall (Rail on-line).

- early withdrawal of the stopping passenger service between Nottingham (Victoria) and Sheffield (Victoria) with closure of stations
- a closure of the GC main line after the completion of the electrification work between Manchester (London Road/Piccadilly) and London (Euston) i.e. after 1963
- that the process of withdrawal of services would follow the provisions of the Transport Act 1953 and involve the relevant Transport Users Consultative Committee (TUCC). (As outlined in chapter 10)
- that the route would be 'loaded' with freight traffic diverted due to electrification work, would continue to act as a diversionary route and serve industries.

Beyond those expectations, planning (with London Transport) was advancing for the responsibility for track and services over the 38-mile section between Marylebone and Aylesbury and the early introduction by the LMR of a diesel multiple unit service.

The LMR plans for dieselisation of its Midland Division main line services based upon two types of locomotive were moving forward into the initial production phase and with a later intention to concentrate heavy maintenance at one new depot between Nottingham and Derby. The early planning involved diesel locomotives for the GC en route and for a new maintenance facility at Annesley.

The LMR was developing a network of parcels depots at major centres; four of which were served by the GC route (and the former Midland).

The Nottinghamshire coalfield was well placed to supply coal suitable to meet the increasing tonnage requirements of the CEGB for its network of power stations in the North Midlands.

The domestic and industrial power plant/gas works markets for coal were in secular decline, with the expectation of reducing demand for movement south and south west from Nottinghamshire. The use of unbraked wagons for much of that traffic did not fit well with the efforts of the BTC/BRB to timetable faster moving services through congested sections of routes.

Elsewhere – as outlined in chapter 9 – the recently re-elected Conservative government had the potential of a full five-year term in which to progress change in the way the nationalised industries met the needs of the nation. In the case of the railways, the extent of the change was to be profound.

Between 1960 and 1966, the former GC lines were enveloped in change; some sections thrived (at least in the medium term) whilst others were closed. The reasons for the changes were varied and frequently complex; some were within the direct control of the BTC/BRB (for example routes rationalisation) whilst many were not (for example, demand for particular products, policies of the NCB with the BRB on wagon load coal traffic, social change, road building programmes and political will). The 'key' aspects to be retained in mind as the developments are explained below:

- the BTC and its obligations under the Transport Act 1953 were displaced effectively from mid-1961 and replaced by the British Railways Board
- the developments between spring 1961 and end 1962 as Dr Beeching and his team worked to make proposals to re-shape British railways
- further developments of Dr Beeching with regard to the planning of main routes as the core of the future rail network
- the enabling legislation of the Transport Act 1962 which paved the way for the implementation of the Beeching Report of March 1963
- the former GCR lines were but one small part of much larger scale proposals, but received a disproportionate amount of attention
- there was no grand strategy for the closure of former GC lines around which other decisions were made; in fact, as developments outside the direct control of the BRB emerged it became more a logical consequence. It was the fact that it was the largest proposed closure that generated interest and prompted an enhanced level of attention at the Ministry and BRB
- the financial position of the railways continued to worsen in 1960 and 1961.

The focus of the chapter now concentrates on the day and night job of the GC lines. As before, the consideration is separated for passenger and for freight. The first stage will cover the period from 1960 to spring 1963 (when the Beeching Report was published). The second stage will outline how route rationalisation proposals and circumstances beyond the control of the BRB effectively sealed the fate of the London extension of the former GCR.

The review incorporates the end of the 'through' services to points north beyond Nottingham Victoria, cross country trains, seasonal and special traffic, and the Marylebone to Aylesbury suburban service. Along the way, references will be made to how alternative services were made available on other routes to meet the needs of through and intermediate passengers.

The final timetable (15 June-13 September 1959) for the through services between Marylebone and stations north of Nottingham (Victoria) was extended whilst the East Midlands Committee of the TUCC considered objections to the proposals made by the London Midland Region for the 'through' services and also the stopping passenger services between Nottingham (Victoria) and Sheffield (Victoria), the latter including Chesterfield (Central). The consideration merely postponed the implementation of the proposals. Keeping the public aware of the revised arrangements by the issue of the revised winter timetables was complicated due to a strike which severely affected parts of the printing industry. It was over the weekend of 2-4 January that the curtailment was actually effected and which resulted in the withdrawal of four through daytime services to Manchester (one starting from Leicester Central at 7.30am, Manchester 10.50am) at 10.00am, 12.15pm, 3.20pm and 18.18pm (arriving at 3.19pm, 5.40pm, 8.26pm and 11.24pm respectively). That pattern of services was very similar to that from the very earliest days of the London extension. In addition was the 4.50 ex-Marylebone which ran as *The South Yorkshireman* via Sheffield (Victoria) from where a portion was run onwards to Bradford (Exchange) arriving at 10.25pm. The replacement service (between Marylebone and Nottingham Victoria) was meagre; departures from the former at 8.40am, 12.40pm (12.25pm SO) and 4.30pm and taking around three hours, with three corresponding up workings at 8.45am, 12.30pm and 5.15pm. All services called at Aylesbury, Brackley, Woodford Halse, Rugby Central, Lutterworth, Leicester Central and Loughborough Central, whilst Harrow-on-the-Hill was served by the first down and final up service. These trains were planned to be worked with diesel multiple units but events elsewhere (see later) made that impossible. Whether, in the confusion and adjustments made to traction and rolling stock diagramming, word did not reach the train planners is not clear, but in the winter timetable of 1960/61, the three northbound services found themselves – over the 13 mile easily graded section between Lutterworth and Leicester (Central) – as the equal 40th fastest trains in Great Britain (60.5 mph average). Some of the drivers accepted the challenge. Train formations were reduced from six to four carriages with effect from the winter timetable 1963/64.

Any travellers from Bradford, Huddersfield and Halifax who retained any lingering loyalty to *The South Yorkshireman* were, initially, ill-served by an arrangement involving through carriages from the last two towns mentioned being added at Sheffield (Midland) to the 8.52am Bradford (Forster Square)-London (St Pancras) service. A balancing return service departed St Pancras at 5.5pm. For that traffic, the arrival of the Deltic locomotives on the GN line from King's Cross to Leeds allowed from September 1961 a far preferable service via Leeds whilst Sheffield also benefitted from a fast Pullman service via Retford (*The Master Cutler*) to/from King's Cross twice each weekday.

However, returning to the woes of early 1960, it was necessary temporarily, for four months, to start/terminate most passenger services to/from Sheffield (Victoria) at either Central or Victoria stations in Manchester whilst reconstruction work was progressed at London Road station. Steam traction was used to the first available exchange point with electric traction. One through train does seem to have survived the cull; the 9.55pm (10.40pm SO) from Marylebone which ran to Manchester (Central).

The consideration by the East Midlands Committee of the TUCC had been protracted and its recommendations were passed to the Central Transport Consultative Committee which co-ordinated the work of the areas. In due course, the CTCC endorsed the proposals made by the London Midland Region to withdraw the local passenger services between Nottingham (Victoria) and Sheffield (Victoria), subject to the provision of a bus service for Nottingham workers who travelled to/from work from Tibshelf, the withdrawal of stopping services between Aylesbury and Rugby (though with the provision of a bus service for Calvert) and the retention of a train service for people living between Nottingham and Rugby in addition to the three semi-fast services from/to Marylebone. The intermediate service of six-eight trains would serve East Leake, Loughborough (Central), Leicester (Central), Ashby Magna and Lutterworth. The CTCC recommendations linked to the endorsement of the LMR proposals were accepted by the Minister of Transport. The Sunday day-time services to/from Nottingham ceased from 10 March 1963 and the stopping services north of Nottingham were withdrawn from 4 March 1963. The summer timetable merged some of these services by inserting stops at Lutterworth, Ashby Magna and East Leake into the three Marylebone – Nottingham services with additional journey times. The three services ex-Nottingham were re-timed to 8.15am, 12.15pm and 5.15pm. Steam haulage remained with a wide variety of classes in evidence, if only temporarily. A Sunday service was retained for Marylebone-Aylesbury.

To round off this section, reference is made to sleeping car services from/to Manchester, Liverpool and Scotland which would normally have terminated at/started from London (Euston) which, because of re-construction work at that latter terminus, were temporarily diverted to Marylebone. At its peak (summer 1963), five services were accommodated though only one (11.55pm ex-Manchester Piccadilly) used the GC route throughout. Presumably, the others (ex-Glasgow and Liverpool) used the Bletchley-Calvert link. On occasions, the Midland main line was used by Euston line services south of Nuneaton, being routed to/from St Pancras via Wigston (Leicester).

For cross-country services there was the Swindon-York (MX) at 9.40pm from Swindon (4.59am arrival) – which was mainly for parcels and mail – plus the 7.30pm Swindon-Sheffield (due 12.38am). In addition, there was the Bournemouth (West)-Newcastle (11.16am/9.23pm) which, during the winter months, was truncated to run between York and Banbury only and was a North Eastern Region four car diesel multiple unit. (306 miles round trip.) The through service (from York) was reinstated from Summer 1961 to run throughout the year until September 1966, with diesel D6700 series as far as Banbury and return.

During the summer months, there was a further inter-regional service and one with its origins in the days of Fay; a York-Swansea which latterly was routed via Banbury, Oxford, Didcot and the Severn Tunnel rather than the previous route via Cheltenham Spa and Gloucester. Another long-standing service – the Continental, Liverpool/Manchester to Parkeston Quay saw a change of locomotives at Sheffield (Victoria) and, during the period under review the replacement of steam (then usually a Britannia of the Great Eastern lines) with one of the then new English Electric type 3 D6700 series which worked out and home (from Winter 1963) to/from Manchester (Piccadilly) where the train terminated at 1.40pm and returned at 2.42pm. Manchester (Central) had, therefore, lost a long-term service, as had Liverpool and BR had saved a change of locomotives at Guide Bridge and at Manchester (Central). Note: a connecting train from/to Liverpool to/from Manchester was introduced later.

Planning for future through passenger services between Humberside and Manchester strongly favoured a Hull-Manchester/Liverpool diesel multiple unit service via Leeds and Huddersfield rather than a Cleethorpes/Grimsby service via Sheffield.

Seasonal traffic was varied and, in the summer, abundant on all the former GC passenger lines. The established pattern of services to the east and south coast resorts continued though the Llandudno service seems to have become an early casualty. Longer distance Saturday trains were the Bradford (Exchange)-Poole and return, the Manchester (Piccadilly)-Hastings and return and the returning Ramsgate-Derby (Friargate) which went south overnight Friday into Saturday. By the start of 1961, the condition of the track between Leicester (Belgrave Road) GN station and the connection with the GN/LNW Junction at John O'Gaunt was raising concerns. A decision was taken that the summer seasonal trains to Mablethorpe and Skegness would start instead from Central, traverse the GC to Nottingham (Victoria) where engines would be changed and Colwick men would continue to enjoy an out and home trip. Passenger trains over the former LDECR section of the GC lines were irregular, but part of that route was used by Manchester (Piccadilly)-Skegness Saturday trains as far as Lincoln from where the GN route was taken via Louth.

The GC lines formed part of an Anglo-Scottish route taken by *Starlight Specials* and (a new initiative that proved popular), the car-sleeper services. The two were aimed at different segments of the market; the former enticing with cheap fares the opportunity of a weekend away in either Edinburgh, Glasgow or London and the latter aimed at car owning families who would use the train overnight between home and their touring start point. For the *Starlights*, Marylebone and St Pancras were the London termini and, rather like the waves of specials that would be run for football finals and international matches at Wembley Stadium, the start/end of the Glasgow Fairs holidays in July could produce up to 15 trains, all requiring a change of locomotive in either the Leeds or Sheffield areas. The network of car-sleeper trains included one train each weekday night, destined for either Glasgow or Perth from Marylebone, where a loading ramp was used to place cars into a string of covered vans with end doors, whilst the travellers were accommodated in the sleeping cars. These services were steam hauled with Class 7 power provided from Willesden working out and home plus, on occasions, a Holbeck Jubilee returning North. Elsewhere along the route a Newcastle-Dover/Newhaven car sleeper service was routed via Banbury, Oxford, Reading and Tonbridge.

Football (either Association or Rugby League) and hockey internationals/finals could produce extra traffic dependent upon which teams were successful. Leicester City reached the FA Cup Finals in 1961 and 1963 with trains using both the GC and Midland routes. England v Scotland in 1961 (9-3!) was the last of the 'waves' as domestic FA Cup Finals did not feature teams from along the route and the Rugby League Challenge Cup Finals featured Hull, Wakefield and Huddersfield which used the GN line rather than the GC. Not to be overlooked were the FA Cup semi-finals played at neutral grounds having high capacity stadia. Sheffield Wednesday's ground at Hillsborough was frequently used and Wadsley Bridge station dealt with special traffic. 31 March 1962 paired Manchester United (supporters using Manchester suburban sets of carriages via Woodhead) with Tottenham Hotspur. The original intention was to direct the seven trains for supporters of Tottenham Hotspur from St Pancras to Sheffield (Midland), but a docks strike and the directing of a particular ship to Tilbury during the night of 30/31 March meant that several (football) sets of carriages had to be used to convey ship passengers from Tilbury to Liverpool. As part of the re-arrangements, three trains ran from King's Cross to either Wadsley Bridge or Sheffield (Victoria) utilising two A4 and one A3 pacific locomotives.

From the early squabbles between the Metropolitan Railway and the Great Central Railway for the sharing of tracks over sections of the 44 miles into Marylebone (from Quainton Road) the GC/LNER/BR had always had to 'make do' with whatever the Met timetable allowed. Apart from some of the night-time, that left precious little and had resulted in the use of the GW/GC line via High Wycombe.

Finally, from 1951 – and 30 years too late – matters started to improve by agreement between the London Transport and Railway Executives within the BTC. At that time, LT (Metropolitan) assumed responsibility for Harrow-on-the-Hill-Watford and for the Chesham branch, to just short of Aylesbury (38 miles from Marylebone). However, the Metropolitan was, at that time, electrified only as far as Rickmansworth (17 miles), at which point steam replaced electric locomotives. The planning involved an extension of electrification beyond Rickmansworth along the branch to Chesham and along the main line to Amersham (effective from 12 September 1960). Until 1958, the Chesham branch had been operated with former GC C13 4-4-2 locomotives sub-shedded from Neasden. The 'bottleneck' was the seven mile section between Watford South Junction and Harrow-on-the-Hill where around 120 trains (predominantly Metropolitan, which always took precedence) of the two users passed in each direction daily. That, plus the fact that Marylebone had just four platform faces may help explain why, over the 60 years from 1899, the GC line carried so few through passenger trains. The problem of the 'bottleneck' was – belatedly – solved by the quadrupling of the tracks and allowing the LT and BR services to be more happily timetabled and controlled (1961). As part of this re-arrangement, BR planned and introduced a two-class diesel multiple unit service between Marylebone and Aylesbury; four cars being doubled in the peak travel hours. The start of the service of diesel multiple units was badly affected by problems elsewhere (particularly St Pancras-Bedford and short-term substitution of electric services from Liverpool Street by use of diesel units) and with a need for modifications at main works (Derby) of the bogies.

Finally, on passenger services there were two 'casualties'. Having been reprieved by the TUCC in 1959, the Grimsby and Immingham Light Railway ran for a further two years. 49 years of service with its fleet of 12 single deck cars augmented after 1948 by ex-Newcastle cars. Lest we forget that Nottingham (Victoria) station was jointly managed by the GN with the GC, the passenger service between that station and Pinxton was withdrawn on and from 7 January 1963.

The planned network of parcels trains (i.e. specific to parcels traffic not conveyed on passenger trains) did make progress, though the short distance traffic (e.g. Nottingham-Leicester) was immediately under threat from road competition. The down newspapers and parcels train from Marylebone to Nottingham returned during the middle of the day, an overnight Oldham-Marylebone through service started and a Crewe-Marylebone service used the Bletchley-Calvert route to gain access.

The categories of freight traffic carried remained as long defined by the Board of Trade, BTC and would be adopted by the BRB and Dr Beeching for his studies and analyses: coal, coke and patent fuel; minerals, including iron ore; merchandise, including fish and containerised produce.

Taking these in turn, we will start with coal. During the three years 1960-62, the total tonnage mined (including opencast and licenced operators) by the NCB was steady in the range 194-201 million tons. There were no imports and exports ranged between 4.9 and 5.6 million tons per year. After 1962, the NCB adopted a different accountancy period; figures for 1963 (and, therefore, including the effect of the severe winter of 1962/63) are not available for direct comparison.

Although in line with the NCB Revised Plan for Coal, the total production of coal was declining from its peak in 1957, the tonnage carried by rail in 1961 (133 million tons) was very similar to that in the previous year, due to demand from the CEGB growing at a faster rate than the reduction in demand from other sectors. The combined effects of the Clean Air Act 1956, the growth of oil as a source of power for private industry, electricity for heating domestic households and oil as a replacement for coal/coke town gas supplies inevitably reduced demand for coal. The tonnage of coal (including smokeless) for the domestic household market between 1956 and 1961 fell by 4 million tons/year (8 per cent), for town gas by 6.6 million tons (23 per cent), for iron and steel production and for coke ovens by 5.1 million tons (14 per cent) and for all other industrial users by 7.9m (23 per cent).

As identified in chapter 8, the London extension of the former GC conveyed coal principally for the domestic and industrial markets, with the higher proportion of the total tonnage forwarded from Woodford Halse being for the Western Region via Banbury. North of Annesley, the output from some collieries for the CEGB would have sustained traffic flows, with cross-Pennine traffic being at a rate that precluded serious consideration of diverting freight traffic normally using the Manchester-Crewe-London route. Both the NCB and CEGB had banned the use in their yards of BR mineral wagons having screw couplings, thus ensuring a continuation of slow-moving, unbraked trains reliant upon three link couplings manually lifted as necessary. The identification of reductions in tonnages on the various routes to London is difficult although the Leicester (Wigston)-Rugby line was at 31 December 1961 a casualty due to track condition and the GN/LNW Joint line saw a reduction in traffic. Banking of trains from Market Harborough towards Northampton – for which two 0-8-0s were retained – ceased and loads initially reduced, though later re-adjustments to traffic arrangements saw a short-term return to banking with what was locally available.

For coal traffic it can be concluded that, in the short-term, nothing was going to change very much; at least not until the doctor and his equivalent chairman at the NCB – Lord Robens – agreed a mutually beneficial way forward.

Dr Beeching's team quickly identified that for coal class traffic, 16 per cent of the total tonnage carried was being conveyed in small consignments to 72 per cent of the total station yards served (2,443). Such an arrangement – involving individual wagons from multiple originating collieries being sent to individual coal merchants via trip workings to/from yards and requiring re-sorting at one or more intermediate yards (Woodford Halse/Banbury) – was inefficient in the extreme and costly in terms of railway resources. The mutually beneficial scheme as agreed between Beeching/Robens was to introduce a number of coal concentration depots served by trainloads of coal and then despatched by road to destinations within a radius of up to 30 miles. As such it was an extension of the Charrington initiative at Palace Gates referred to in chapter 8. Developments beyond 1963 are dealt with later in this chapter.

Iron and steel products, plus scrap, together represented the highest annual tonnage of minerals (as defined by the railways) carried by BR; 19.1 million tons in 1961.

As identified in chapter 7 the GC lines had benefitted from consistent flows of semi-finished steel products (billets, blooms and slabs) between Scunthorpe/Normanby Park and South Wales, principally for Port Talbot where the hot strip mill was striving to meet increasing demand from the motor vehicle, domestic whitegoods and tin plate industries. Whilst adding to the cost of production, the carrying between production sites was unavoidable whilst old plant at Port Talbot was renewed and a cold strip mill added. Additional tonnage was added from Consett and at its peak (when stock piling of slabs was underway) nine trains daily were seeking paths via the GC at least as far as Bulwell (where the GN route via Derby Friargate could be taken). The traffic continued throughout the 1950s and, with the installation of a new link at Stratford-upon-Avon from 1960, could be routed variously from Woodford Halse to the Western Region destinations.

This traffic flow was dependent upon the continuous availability at Scunthorpe/Consett of suitable flat-bed wagons – particularly bogie bolster types – and journey times and constrictions to progress were a particular concern to the Regional Wagon Authority. An obvious and shorter (by 23 miles) alternative route – from Scunthorpe via Doncaster, Mexborough, Rotherham, Chesterfield, Derby, Birmingham and Gloucester – would enable radical improvements to be made, but until 1963 was difficult, due to pathing of trains, particularly between Derby and Birmingham. More detail will be provided later in this chapter, but for now, the change that was effected came about with co-operation of four regions (NER, ER, LMR, WR), the use of diesel locomotives with a change at Birmingham and a journey time (to Severn Tunnel Junction yard) of less than 12 hours. Empty wagons were returned by existing services to Birmingham, Barrow Hill and Staveley (both in the Chesterfield area) for movement forward to Scunthorpe.

Steelworks in the Sheffield/Rotherham area (Parkgate) were able to produce limited supplies of steel strip in coils and trains destined for the West Midlands were routed via Derby to either Washwood Heath or Bescot.

The individual mineral classification with the highest tonnage (almost half of the 1961 total of 34.4 million tons) was iron ore. The GC lines around and to the steelworks of the Scunthorpe area were increasingly drawn from the ore fields of Lincolnshire, initially via the GN (as described in chapter 4). A larger volume flow went from Northamptonshire to South Wales, but only a small tonnage was dealt with at Woodford Halse yard. Whilst European based steel producers struggled with post-Second World War conditions, the variable quality of the Midlands iron ore was accepted, but as demand for consistently better quality steel products and competition increased, the steel producers needed to respond. The two principal flows of interest here each declined as a result of decisions to build deep water bulk handling facilities at Port Talbot/Margam and (later) with the co-operation between the NCB, the British Transport Docks Board and the then nationalised British Steel Corporation, near Immingham.

The strikingly stark feature of the principal southbound fitted (Class C and D) freight trains using the GC line South of Sheffield in 1960 was that none originated along the route. All came from originating points in the North Eastern Region (or north thereof) with NER motive power (usually V2 2-6-2s) which worked through to Woodford Halse and had no need to bother Annesley Yard.

3.10am	York-Woodford Halse (London/WR)
3.55am	York-Banbury
5.20am	York-Cardiff
5.40am	York-Bristol
2.15pm	Newcastle-Park Royal Tu Tho (Guinness)
8.20pm	York-Banbury
9.40pm	York-Marylebone

In the down direction, there were seven principal fitted trains, one of which was the 9.00pm Marylebone-York and another the Guinness on MFO; the rest started from Woodford Halse with traffic predominantly from the Western Region.

Had paths been available in the WTTs for the various sections, all of these through trains could have been sent via other routes; the GC line was merely a conduit providing train crews.

Trains specifically for fish traffic originated from four principal docks: Grimsby and New Clee, Hull, Fleetwood and Aberdeen. From these four, the highest tonnage in 1962 was from landings on Humberside, 250,000 tons out of a total of 350,000 tons. Since 1954, the annual tonnage loaded to rail vans as consignments of wet fish destined for merchants/ distributors had been declining, offset to some extent by an increase in tonnage of processed at sea/frozen fish loaded into containers and then on to flat-bed wagons. The decline in tonnages was initially started by the 19-day ASLE&F strike of spring 1955, which alarmed the trade and prompted the start of alternative road distribution arrangements. The growth of processed tinned/frozen food had resulted in the use of some 250 containers per week and some were conveyed (usually marshalled next to the locomotive) on the 4.30pm and 6.25pm departures from Grimsby/New Clee. The fleet of conventional wagons used was specific to the traffic and was on average at less than half life; Aberdeen traffic had the benefit of roller bearing axle fitted wagons built in 1960 and (at least in the early months) distinctively white and denoted with a blue spot on the side.

The GC lines conveyed fish traffic West to Ashton Moss for Lancashire and North Wales, for Leeds and the West Riding of Yorkshire, and particularly South/South West as follows:

3.30pm	Hull-Plymouth via Doncaster, Tuxford, Mansfield, joining the GC at Kirkby South Junction. At Calvert this train left the GC by reversal onto the (Bletchley -) Oxford line, thence to the Western Region
4.30pm	Grimsby-Whitland via Lincoln, Mansfield and Kirkby South Junction to Woodford Halse, thence Banbury and the Western Region
6.5pm	Hull-Banbury*
6.25pm	New Clee-Banbury*

* These two trains were combined at Mansfield and ran forward as one train with vans detached at Nottingham (Victoria), Leicester Goods and Rugby for locally based merchants/road distribution.

The traffic was demanding upon the use of vans destined for particular stations and merchants, average loadings per van frequently being in the low tons. As the traditional charging basis was per consignment and not fully costed to reflect direct railway operating costs, the reduction in tonnage was serious for BR and fish merchants alike as the public expected a market price favourable to meat.

It would have been possible to identify the direct operating costs and revenue arising. Purely from a motive power and enginemen perspective, the traffic costs were:

Train	Motive power working (ER/LM only)	Enginemen arrangements (ER/LMR only)
3.30pm	Hull-Leicester	Hull-Doncaster
	Leicester- Oxford	Doncaster-Leicester
		Leicester-Oxford
4.30pm	Immingham-Banbury (General)	Immingham-Lincoln
		Lincoln-Leicester
	Class 7 from spring 1962	Leicester-Woodford Halse
		Woodford Halse-Banbury
6.5pm	Hull-Doncaster	Hull-Doncaster
	Doncaster-Mansfield (shunt/attach) – Leicester	Doncaster-Mansfield-Leicester
6.25pm	Immingham-Lincoln	Immingham-Lincoln
	Lincoln-Mansfield Stop	Lincoln-Mansfield

The arrangements for the returning empty vans was for the Western Region to work them to Woodford Halse, from where they were taken forward as part of ordinary freight trains (usefully forming a fitted head) or as the 1.22am (Grimsby), 3.35am (Hull), 5.10am (New Clee) or 11.59pm (Hull) fitted trains ex-Woodford Halse yard.

The 'Re-shaping of British Railways Report' made no mention of fish traffic and the tonnage carried by rail continued to fall.

A review based upon 1960-63 of freight traffic at or passing Annesley would have shown a generally static picture to/from the south and an increase (CEGB traffic) to/from the north.

To the south (Woodford Halse/Colwick/Derby direction traffic) there were 58 departures, 42 of which made their way to Woodford Halse whilst from the south 47 trains arrived, 43 of which came from Woodford Halse. Heading north were 64, 30 of which went towards Pilsley and the balance diverging for Shirebrook North (13), Mansfield (Central) (16) and to Colwick via the north junction.

At Woodford Halse, 44 northbound arrivals and 43 northbound departures were dealt with along with 42 southbound arrivals and 47 southbound departures.

The MetR/GC route (via Aylesbury) accounted for 15 trains in each direction, the larger proportion heading towards the Western Region either via the GW/GC route, Banbury or towards South Wales (via Stratford-upon-Avon), Honeybourne.

The freight trains between Annesley and Woodford Halse and vice versa were, therefore, the coal trains (25-27), steel trains (5), merchandise trains (8) and fish trains (4), the vast majority of which ran empty on the return.

If we undertook between 1961 and 1963 a hard-headed business review of this freight traffic our conclusions would probably have been:

Traffic	Analysis
Coal for domestic and industrial markets	NCB expectations of declining demands over a period of years. Wagon load traffic inefficient and costly in terms of use of infrastructure and other resources. Improved methods of meeting demand under discussion between BRB and NCB.
Steel semi-finished products to South Wales	Continuation of traffic in short/medium term. Capital investment at Port Talbot for new facilities, including a new strip mill, would allow production locally of semi-finished products.
Iron ore to Normanby Park/Scunthorpe and to South Wales	Continuation of traffic for certain grades in short/medium term. Capital investment in deep water bulk discharge facilities at Immingham/Port Talbot harbour to allow import of ore would negate need for UK ore.
Merchandise	Route used mainly as a conduit for through traffic which – subject to paths – could be directed elsewhere.
Fish	Tonnage declining. Van load traffic with small consignments to multiple destinations. Costly in terms of use of resources. Products had to have an affordable retail price.

From that analysis it may be concluded that unless new traffic flows could be found or directed to the route the future for the GC main line South of Annesley was largely out of the direct control of the BRB and more with the NCB, the Steel Company of Wales/British Transport Docks Board, the backers for the deep water facility at Immingham and the National Federation of Fishmongers and Poulterers. The railway was there to provide a service, but under the terms of the Transport Act 1962.

The development of the various classifications of merchandise traffic – particularly in bulk and over long distances – some 39 million tons in 1961, was an area under the control of the BRB and, in addition, there were new traffic flows. The approach for the merchandise traffic will follow, but the major new bulk traffic flow – oil – was of no benefit to the GC main line; a short-term supply to the Leicester area by rail was to be replaced by the siting of the UK's largest inland storage facility for petroleum products at Kingsbury which paved the way for road distribution. Beyond that, another short-term provision was for construction materials (sand and gravel) taken from Colwick to a temporary site at Ashby Magna for the M1 motorway. The self-contained nature of the GC main line (which was a policy of Watkin) had left it isolated and in something of a time warp; a steam worked stretch of railway used principally by slow moving, unbraked coal trains.

With the benefit of our analysis we could surely have had a job with Dr Beeching's team! It was at this time (August 1963) that Fiennes had taken from him 'an interest in closing the GC line' (chapter 9), Dr Beeching brought Raymond back to the BRB and drafted in James Ness, latterly General Manager, Scottish Region. The strongly functional board that Beeching had argued so forcibly for was showing its worth; Raymond took on the passenger and organisational aspects of the commercial function, allowing Leslie Williams (ex-Shell Mex & BP) to concentrate solely on freight. Ness took on the role of planning, allowing Margetts to concentrate on the implementation of the re-shaping of the network, i.e. reduction thereof. From October, the 15-strong board was in place.

The stage had been reached where the development of a small number of routes was *the* way forward for freight. In simple terms, a concentration of the maximum traffic along routes between major centres of population, commerce and industry, take the advantages accruing over road for bulk movements in fully brake fitted train loads over long distances and maximise the utilisation of the fixed costs. The re-shaping report had identified seven routes:

	Forward direction '000 tons	Return direction '000 tons	Total
London-Scotland	620	710	1,330
London-Midlands-S. Lancashire	4,880	7,160	12,040
London-Southampton/Portsmouth	230	360	590
London-Yorkshire-Tyneside	1,350	2,260	3,610
South Wales/Bristol-Midlands-Yorkshire-Tyneside	2,140	3,760	5,900
South Wales/Bristol-S. Lancashire -Scotland	1,480	1,780	3,260
London-South Wales/Bristol-Plymouth	1,460	1,350	2,810
Other			9,460
			39,000

Of these routes, the one of relevance to this book is South Wales/Bristol-Midlands-Yorkshire-Tyneside. The task facing Ness was the planning of the traffic flows in line with the objectives above. In some respects, he was fortunate in being able to benefit from other schemes that had been developed in isolation, but which would contribute handsomely in aggregate; the capital investment in the Sheffield/Rotherham area which had survived the various assessments of the Modernisation Plan and had been approved in 1961, the dieselisation of the cross-country passenger services along the route in question which had allowed the passenger timetable to be re-cast from September 1962, a reduction in slow-moving, unbraked coal trains between Derby and Birmingham, the reduced number of trains requiring banking up the Lickey incline between Bromsgrove and Blackwell, the adoption of oil by the West Midlands Gas Board in place of coal/coke and, importantly, that for a route encompassing four Regions (Western, London Midland, Eastern and North Eastern) multi-discipline teams had been working together for several years. Ness was indeed fortunate and within a very few months was able to advise Margetts as the board member responsible about what had become known as the NE/SW Route Rationalisation. A by-product of this was the way forward to propose the closure of sections of the GC main line.

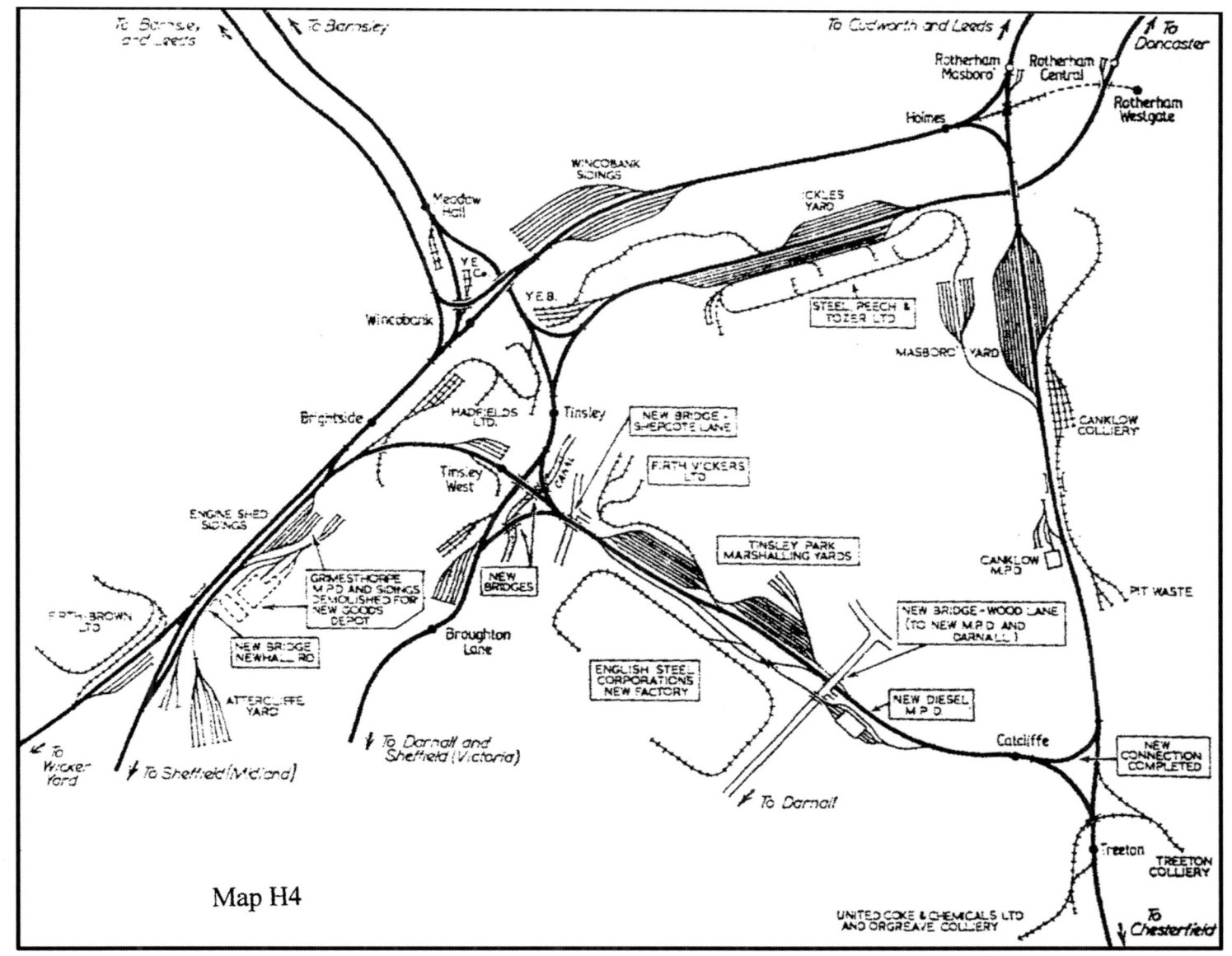

Map H4

The investment in the Sheffield and Rotherham areas was approved in 1961 and over a period of four years was expected to include the construction of a new yard and diesel depot at Tinsley and a new freight terminal at Grimesthorpe. Map H4 shows the location of the new yard, the feed lines to all four points of the compass and the sites of heavy industrial concerns that were good, long-term customers of BR. The new connections to the GC lines are to the left of the left-hand yard at Tinsley Park Marshalling Yards. The increasing number of Toton-Wath (thence cross-Pennine) coal trains would join at Catcliffe in the bottom right-hand corner and having passed through Tinsley would exit via (top left) the former GC route as shown 'to Barnsley'. Traffic from the North Eastern Region yards at Tyne (Newcastle), Tees (Middlesbrough area), York and Healey Mills (Wakefield area) would enter top left and right whilst through traffic for the Midlands/South West from the first three mentioned yards could be routed via the existing (Midland 'Old Road') from Rotherham (Masborough) via Treeton to Chesterfield (Tapton Junction). NE/SW passenger traffic would use the former Midland line as shown between Holmes and Brightside.

The spine of the cross-country route was part of the network of the Midland Railway: Bristol, Gloucester,

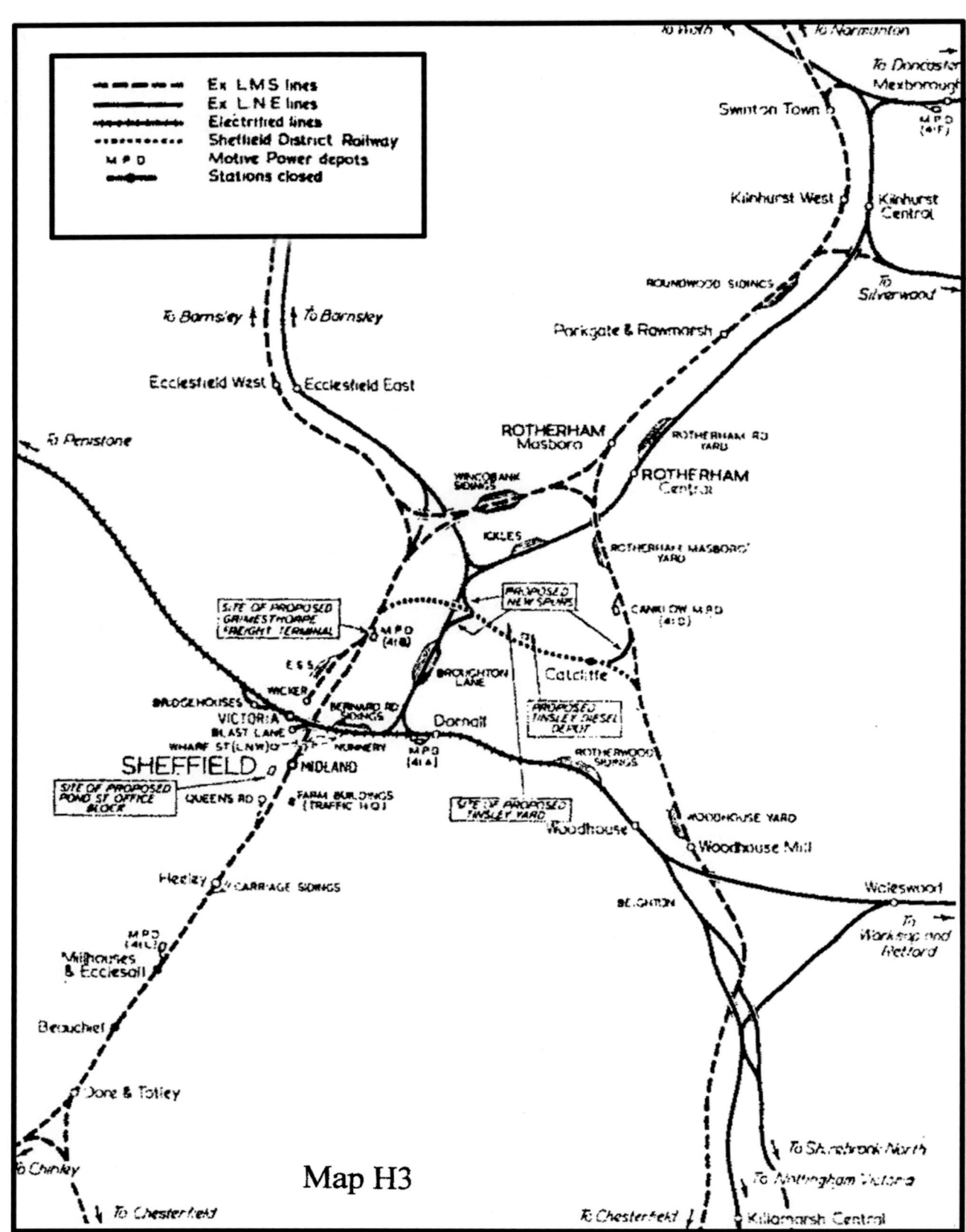

This map develops map H2 at Chapter 9.

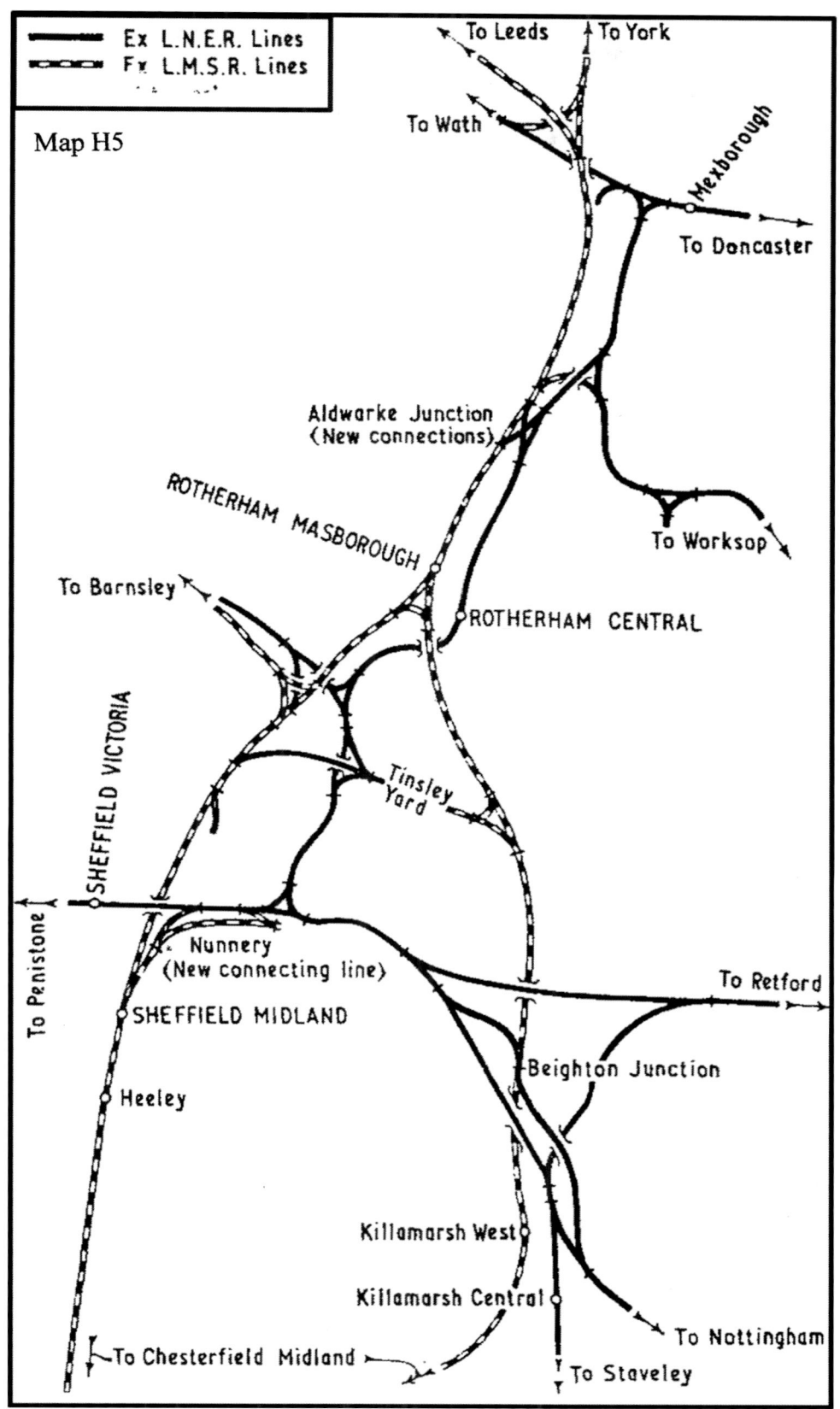

Further developments from maps H2 and H3.

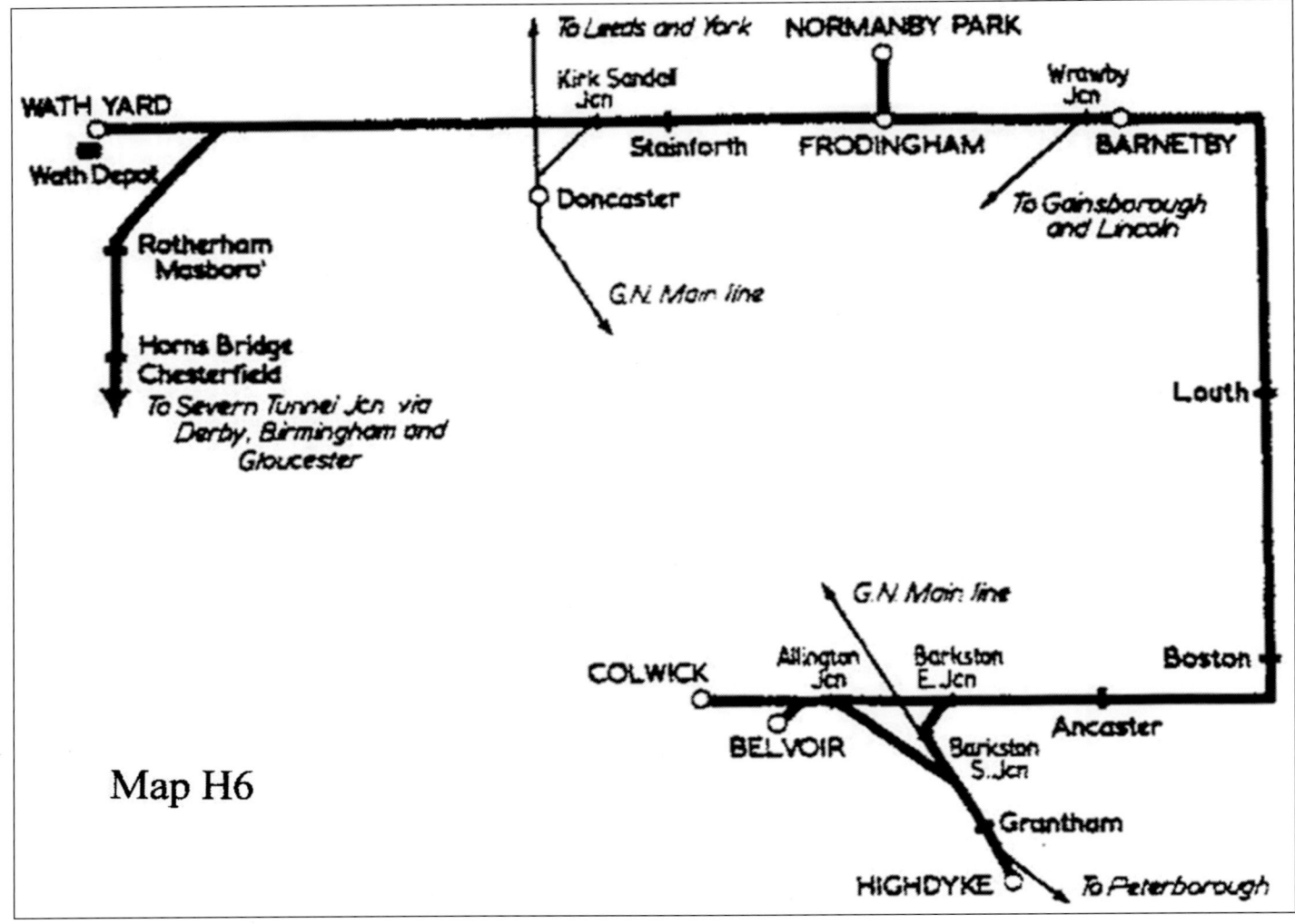

This map illustrates how iron ore, steel and merchandise traffic could be routed without any need to use the former Great Central route South of Heath.

Cheltenham Spa, Birmingham, Derby, Sheffield, Leeds/York. From a planning and operational policy perspective it had – until the 1958 change of regional boundaries – been the total preserve of Derby. By that time, the pattern of passenger services extended to Cardiff and to Newcastle, a distance of some 300 miles. Operating constrictions included the Lickey incline between Bromsgrove and Blackwell, where all trains were obliged to take the assistance of one or more banking locomotives and lengthy sections of two track railway with refuge loops allowing a maximum of 70 wagons. The passenger timetable had changed little since the Second World War and, for a route with few challenging gradients, apart from the Lickey, was well within the capabilities of Class 6 steam power. After 1958 planning for changes necessarily involved four regions (the London Midland as lead, the North Eastern, Eastern and Western) and needed to take account of the needs of the GPO/Royal Mail for which Tamworth and Birmingham were particularly important points of exchange of mail. The route between Derby and Birmingham was joined at Stenson Junction (4 miles from Derby) by tracks carrying slow-moving, unbraked coal trains for Willington and Drakelow power stations and considerable tonnages for Washwood Heath (Birmingham) yard for West Midlands Gas Board, industrial and domestic markets. Birmingham and Gloucester could both be 'avoided'.

The investment case for dieselisation of the Midland Division of the London Midland Region (that is St Pancras to Sheffield, Manchester, Leeds, Glasgow, Edinburgh and cross-country Newcastle/York/Leeds to Bristol/Cardiff as well as the GC main line to Pilsley) was made upon the provision and use of BR/Sulzer type 4 and type 2 locomotives. For the cross-country routes, the depots and men included Leeds (Holbeck), Newcastle (Gateshead), Derby and Bristol (Barrow Road), but required enginemen from many other depots (e.g. Kentish Town, Trafford Park, Nottingham, Saltley, Gloucester, York, Heaton, Carlisle (2), Polmadie and Haymarket) to receive three weeks of training. Detailed planning and training of the trainers started in 1960 with the aim of having the full allocation of locomotives available for a timetable based upon diesel timings from September 1962. Services from St Pancras were the first to receive the new locomotives and these worked alongside and frequently in place of the Metrovick type 2s which were proving to be unreliable. By mid-April 1961, a total of 23 turns were being worked by diesels and the plan was then for eight further locomotives to be working from Bristol and Newcastle. However, the needs of the WR and NER to have enginemen trained on other types of locomotive (EE types 4 and 5 on the NER and hydraulics on the WR) took precedence. The cross-country trains started to see the Sulzer type 4s in numbers from the start of the Winter timetable in September 1961. At that time, 59 turns had been allocated to diesels (27 on cross-country) with through working between Bristol and Newcastle and up to 20 hours in service out of twenty-four.

By February 1962, most of the available Class 4 and 5 fitted freight trains on cross-country had been handed to diesels, extended later to include Class 6 with a fitted head of a minimum of 20 per cent and loads equivalent to a Class 9 steam locomotive. From 12 March 1962, the banking of trains from Bromsgrove up to 12 carriages hauled by type 4 diesels ceased.

That left the Achilles' heel of the slow-moving, unbraked coal traffic between Toton and Washwood Heath. For those eight daily services, a plan was devised to use the initial build of ten locomotives (D1 – D10) when they were released from summer duties on the Liverpool-Euston expresses. That came to fruition, but quickly exposed the residual slow-moving power station and trip workings, requiring a further seven locomotives.

Full introduction of the diesel-based passenger timetable for cross-country came into effect as planned on 10 September 1962. Although based upon a low overall percentage availability per day, the rate of failures of the diesels was of concern and, throughout the harsh winter of 1962/63, steam came back to the fore. As an example of the difficulties faced, the old engine changing point for Newcastle/York-Bristol trains was Sheffield (Midland). The steam depot at Millhouses was closed in December 1961 and from then onwards until well into 1964, any steam locomotive arriving from the north would be required to work forward to either Derby or Birmingham. That brought forth all four types of LNER main line passenger pacifics and V2s. Another example was the re-allocation to Derby in early 1963 of eight Jubilee Class 6 locomotives.

The bounty from their endeavours was rich and was shared amongst the regions. The Western wanted paths for heavy trains of imported cocoa beans from Avonmouth Docks to Bournville (Cadburys), they were also content to go along with the re-routing of diesel multiple unit services between South Wales and Birmingham (later extended to Derby) to New Street rather than Snow Hill and accepted a new service from Leeds to Cardiff. The *Cornishman* (Penzance-Wolverhampton) was also re-routed to go to Sheffield. The Scottish Region used one of the four new Scotland-South West fitted freights (Edinburgh Lothian Road-Stoke Gifford) to return a diesel to Leeds and then proceed via the cross-country route. The North Eastern and Eastern Regions used paths for trains of steel to the West Midlands and South Wales. The London Midland Region had the problems with the new traction and also with the pattern of Nottingham-Leicester-Birmingham-Derby diesel multiple units. Finally, the Southern Region wanted to send Fawley (Esso) refinery-Bromford Bridge petroleum product trains via Bristol; acceptable as a stop gap before the route via Reading and Oxford with diesels became available. Progress was hard won, but progress it was.

Whilst since his arrival Ness would have been pre-occupied with the planning for the various routes, his 'pending tray' as left by Fiennes would have contained a Planning Report to the BR Board dated 18 July 1963. That Report included an 'examination of duplicate routes' (e.g. from London to Exeter via the Southern and Great Western routes) and stated that 'the case for closing a major portion of the ex-GC main line should be ready by October 1963'. The stage reached in autumn 1963 with the Sheffield scheme and the dieselisation of the Midland

Division responsibility lines enabled Ness to advise Margetts that the board could be updated with regard to the GC line. As at December 1963, Ness was confident he had the train paths he needed to transfer some freight traffic from the GC line to the NE/SW route whilst the residual flows naturally declined or were lost to road.

The Memorandum to the British Railways Board was dated 11 December 1963 and is included as Appendix 5. The Memorandum estimated net savings of £1.75m, an anticipated staff displacement (2,150) and the phasing of action. Movement towards closure would be gradual. Freight withdrawals and diversions would commence in June 1964, main line passenger train withdrawals and diversions would take place in 1964 and, with the withdrawal of the last of the local passenger services at an as then indefinite date, the ultimate aim was complete closure by June 1965. The Board was requested to note the intention ... 'to implement the first major scheme of main line route rationalisation as envisaged in the Re-shaping Report'. The Board noted accordingly.

The diversions referred to – and hence the need for additional paths in the WTT – were:

	Southward		Northward	
	Freight	Pass. & parcels	Freight	Pass. & parcels
Stenson Junction-Washwood Heath (Derby-Birmingham line)	11	2	8	1
Trent Junction-Syston Junc (Midland line from Toton)	5	3	2	3
Grantham-Ferme Park (GN route out of Colwick)	3	-	3	1
Rugby-Bletchley (LNW main line)	2	3	1	3

The estimated number of wagons in each direction daily was 1,200, which suggested mineral traffic (loaded 45, returning empty in longer trains of up to 70 also as limited by the length of refuge loops). The NE/SW fitted trains (including vacuum braked steel trainloads) were already accommodated within the NE/SW route WTT.

Therefore, at BRB headquarters the policy decisions had been taken; freight would either be diverted to other routes (fitted trains, including possibly fish) whilst unbraked mineral traffic (principally coal) was expected to have a reducing demand (see later ref NCB/BRB plans) and that remaining would be directed to the former Midland GN or LNW routes. Parcels and newspaper trains would be diverted with St Pancras assuming the role taken by Marylebone and similarly with the Midland line stations/depots at Leicester, Nottingham and Manchester. The passenger train involved was, presumably, the Manchester-Marylebone sleeping car service.

To round off the review, it may be useful to identify what had happened with passenger services on alternative routes and then review motive power arrangements along the GC main line.

From the perspective of a traveller between London, Leicester, Nottingham, Sheffield and Manchester via the Midland route, there were progressive improvements in terms of point to point timings and quantity of services. Nottingham-Loughborough-Leicester benefitted from the introduction of a diesel multiple unit, as had Nottingham-Chesterfield-Sheffield (all Midland). Rugby-London Euston services were subject to various levels of disturbance as electrification work progressed southwards.

The improvements had started in 1957 (as part of the LM Region response to electrification work), had developed as Class 7 steam power became available in quantity and, from Winter 1962/63 the full benefit of the policy of dieselisation. For that timetable the pattern of services to the main cities and average speeds was:

To London	Distance miles	Fastest service	Number of trains
Manchester	189	3 hr 10m (P)	1
		3 hr 35m (O)	10
Sheffield	158	3 hr	10
Nottingham	127	1 hr 55m (P)	1
	124	1 hr 59m (O)	9
Leicester	99	1 hr 23½ (P)	1
		1 hr 34m (O)	14

NOTES:
(P) Midland Pullman
(O) Ordinary services with catering

Finally, for 1960-63, a brief review of motive power arrangements for the depots serving the Marylebone-Nottingham services.

Neasden

In September 1960, the depot had an allocation of 69 steam locomotives including nine Standard Class 5s and six B1 4-6-0s. The only other LNER types were two L1 2-6-4 tank locomotives. Britannia Class pacifics were then allocated (ex-Newton Heath and Crewe North) to take on the Nottingham services and Summer seasonal night trains. The large stud of 2-6-4 tank locomotives was largely displaced by the progressive arrival of the diesel multiple units and, with that, it was possible to plan for the closure of the depot. That entailed Annesley becoming responsible for providing power for the London passenger services and, with a lack of coaling facilities at the Southern end, would require locomotives with large capacity tenders. The Britannias that had arrived in September 1960 had seven tons capacity, as did the Great Eastern (Norwich and Stratford) examples which were starting to need new homes. Neasden was closed in June 1962; the remaining Fairburn 2-6-4 tanks went mainly to Cricklewood and Woodford Halse, the BR Standard Class 5s to Woodford Halse and Leicester (Central) and the Britannias to Annesley. The depots 'on call' at the London end were, therefore, Kentish Town (also close to closure) and – with relevance to passenger traffic diverted from the Euston line – Willesden.

Woodford Halse

As at early 1963, there was within the allocation of 58 steam locomotives, 24 Austerity 2-8-0s, 14 Class 5 4-6-0s of various origins, seven Fairburn tanks (ex-Neasden) and three 8F 2-8-0s. The depot also serviced the 9Fs working in from Annesley, the NE Region locomotives arriving on the fitted freights and Western Region locomotives arriving from the Banbury and Gloucester routes.

Leicester (Central)

Leicester's traditional role as a place at which GC line locomotives were changed had ceased and its allocation at January 1963 totalled 11 Class 5 4-6-0s and three 2-6-4 tanks.

Annesley

With the closure of Neasden, Annesley locomotives worked the passenger services to/from Marylebone as out and home turns. The Royal Scot Class locomotives with nine-ton coal capacity tenders offered greater insurance cover than the Britannias fitted with a seven-ton capacity and, at January 1963, Annesley had nine Royal Scots including one (46126) which was a direct replacement for another (46143) which had become a total failure during the previous November. All of these locomotives were high mileage candidates for shopping into works for overhauls, but for which the Proposals had no chance of acceptance. As and when available, the London Midland Region Britannias with larger coal capacity tenders (nine- tons) were also used (70045-54). At the time there was some criticism of using Class 7 locomotives on 4/6 carriage trains; the criticism overlooked other services worked. For the Annesley-Woodford Halse freight services the depot at the former place still had 29 9Fs; completing the total allocation of the depot (67) were 19 8Fs (which had assumed the role of the LNER 01s), seven Black 5s and three 2-6-2 tank locomotives.

From 9 September 1963, Woodford Halse depot was re-designated 1G, Leicester (Central) 15D and Annesley 16B.

Coverage of this chapter can now be extended to include 1964-69. Activity may usefully be summarised:

What happened at BRB headquarters?

The follow-up to the Board Minute from 19 December 1963 was a meeting held on 27 January 1964 and attended by senior (Deputy General Manager) representatives of the four regions involved with the NE/SW route rationalisation. That meeting identified the procedures (including consultation with Trade Union headquarters and Regional Staff Councils, negotiating with freight customers, advice to local authorities, press notices and public notices). It was on 2 July 1964 that the Chief Operating Officer, BRB, advised all concerned of the decision that steps could be taken to proceed with the development of the closure proposals. Accordingly, a further meeting attended as for 27 January 1964 was held on 14 July 1964. A copy of the notes of that meeting are attached at Appendix 6. Consultation at various levels and advice to staff at local level happened 17 October 1964.

In parallel with that timescale, separate developments had occurred affecting domestic coal and fish trains.

The partial solution for domestic coal consigned in small tonnages to multiple stations and merchants was perceived by the BRB and NCB mutually to be inefficient and wasteful of resources. The response was to be in the construction on railway land of coal concentration depots with mechanised facilities to receive trainload consignments, transfer to bunkers holding different grades of coal, anthracite and smokeless fuel, which would be collected/bagged for merchants to collect and distribute. The plan envisaged 40 large depots also with stockpiling of up to 25 per cent of the expected annual tonnage throughout, plus up to 300 smaller depots; therefore some 340 sites replacing 4,000. The potential benefits to both the BRB and NCB were huge, though for the merchants less so and many baulked at the idea. The first mechanised depot (December 1963) was at West Drayton, West London, with an annual throughput tonnage of up to 200k, a peak weekly load of 6.5k (daily 1.2k) and displaced 21 former rail served depots. 23 qualities of fuel were offered, supplied from South Wales and the East Midlands in large capacity mineral hopper wagons. The initial arrangements for supply from the East Midlands involved three collieries (Gedling, Williamsthorpe and the huge, new Calverton); one train each from Gedling and Williamsthorpe weekly was merged into one and followed the GC route to Woodford Halse, thence via Banbury/Reading, and three trains weekly from Calverton via (the Midland route) Beeston, Stenson Junction, Washwood Heath and Banbury. The future intention for supply from the East Midlands was for one train daily marshalled at Toton with wagons from the same three collieries. The 'worst case' for the GC route was, therefore, the loss of one Annesley-Woodford Halse (conventional 45 wagon) coal train each day.

The second mechanised depot was sited at Leagrave near Luton on the Midland main line and opened in Summer 1964 with coal supplies from Maltby colliery (near Rotherham) plus anthracite from South Wales and smokeless fuels. The wagons from South Wales were routed via Oxford, Bletchley and Bedford. Another 150k tons/year, but this one and its distribution by road radius would barely have affected GC stations. Taunton depot followed later in that year with coal in trainloads from the East Midlands via Birmingham and Bristol where, at the latter, wagons from South Wales were added.

As an example of the smaller depots, the Birmingham Division of the London Midland Region (which also included some ex-Western Region territory) replaced 168 delivery points with 24 which extended as far as Leamington Spa and Stratford-upon-Avon. Quite how far West and South West of Woodford Halse went domestic coal from the East Midlands and quite how far East and South went domestic coal from South Wales is an unknown to me, but the withdrawal of goods facilities from stations along lines taken from Woodford Halse would suggest a significant effect in 1963/64:

Blisworth	Padbury	Charwelton
Olney	Brackley	Helmdon
Towcester	Farthinghoe	Finmere
Byfield	Aylesbury	Calvert
Fenny Compton West Kineton	Chipping Norton	Alcester
Ettington	Hook Norton	Hinton
Stratford-upon-Avon	Bloxham	Ashton-under-Hill
	Kings Sutton	Beckford Ashchurch

For winter 1965 the London Midland Region ran block trainloads of coal from Washwood Heath to Gloucester via either Honeybourne or direct. The loaded wagons became stockpiles for onward movement as demands from merchants arose more locally.

It was a good plan and good co-operation between two nationalised industries. However, by the end of 1965, only 14 fully mechanised depots were opened, 22 at end 1966, well short of the target. The market was declining. For the BRB it was too little, too late.

Amongst the revenue that the BRB could opt to lose as a result of closure of the GC main line was from fish traffic. The problem, as the BRB saw it, extended beyond Grimsby and New Clee to include the other ports from where fish was despatched daily: Fleetwood and Aberdeen. Proposals for a re-organisation of the traffic were presented on 4 May 1964 to the National Federation of Fishmongers and Poulterers by a representative of the BRB. Basically, the BRB wanted nine services instead of twenty-five and including a combined (at Doncaster) train from Grimsby and Hull going forward to South Wales/Midlands and South West/Midlands and South of England. The extremities would be Swansea, Plymouth and Southampton; thought to be justified by the fish traders due to Welsh and South West fleets preferring to serve the French and Irish markets rather than those more local. The Hull/Grimsby traders recognised the economics and established their own road distribution company Hull Fish Transport Ltd.

The supply of semi-finished steel products (blooms, billets and slabs) from Scunthorpe/Consett to Port Talbot was to cease following the nationalisation of steel by the Labour government and the availability at Port Talbot of the new harbour facility. Port Talbot became the most economical and the largest strip mill in the UK, making something of a mockery of the government's attempt to introduce competition in Scotland, North Wales, the Midlands and elsewhere in South Wales.

When and how did the London Midland Region headquarters become involved?

With regard to the second question, the London Midland Region was, of course, the messenger who stood every chance of being shot multiple times as the message was delivered. To the regional management fell the tasks of consultation (effectively communication and explanation) with the staff, input to the TUCC Area Committee, the issue of formal Notices regarding passenger services, working with other customers and managing the considerable human resource implications.

How did the incoming (Labour) Minister of Transport become involved?

The Labour Minister of Transport, the Right Honourable Thomas Fraser, had during the early months of his tenure from October 1964 been subjected to various pressures from objectors to the process being followed by the BRB; from MPs, Trade Unions and others. He wished to hear, and for his officials to hear, first-hand what were the proposals for the GC line and the stage reached.

Following the victory in the General Election, the Minister had required the BRB to submit proposals for withdrawals of passenger services and closures for Ministerial vetting before they were published. This became known as the 'early sift' and was introduced to prevent lengthy TUCC hearings of cases which were likely to be, in Fraser's words, 'non-starters' from the outset; in such cases the Minister would give his or her consent to the proposal made by the BRB. If the BRB hoped their proposals for the GC main line would be dealt with by the early sift their hope was soon dashed. The meeting held on 11 February 1965 was a clear sign that whatever had been provided by the BRB was insufficient or, perhaps, because it had excluded all but the proposals for passenger services, the hope and intent of the BRB being that by the time the passenger services were proposed for withdrawal everything else would have gone.

At a personal level, Fraser was in post until December 1965, at which time he was replaced by firebrand Barbara Castle, the first female Minister of Transport. Fraser – a Scotsman – resigned in 1966 and took on the role of Chairman of the Scottish Hydro Electricity Board.

A copy of the BRB notes of the meeting held on 11 February 1965 is in Appendix 7. Note: the reference to Lord Hinton (latterly Chairman of the CEGB) had nothing to do with Didcot power station (see later reference in chapter 12), but to do with the fact that he had been appointed by the Minister to advise him on the BRB Trunk Routes proposals which were available in draft form.

What was the reaction of Members of Parliament?

As part of the procedure agreed in January 1964, five Members of Parliament were briefed on 26 February 1965 by Margetts regarding the proposals to withdraw the passenger services and close sections of the GC main line. Four of the five MPs were primarily concerned in protecting the best interests of their railwaymen and railway women constituents. A copy of the notes of the meeting and the related press coverage in the *Nottingham Guardian Journal* is in Appendix 8.

The East Midlands Area of the TUCC conveyed the necessary hearings of objections to the proposal of the BRB (via the London Midland Region) to withdraw passenger services between Marylebone and Nottingham Victoria. As with many other such hearings (as referred to in chapter 10) there was considerable antipathy expressed towards the limitation of objections to 'hardship' and to the paucity of the rudimentary data about revenue, direct movement and terminal costs. The objections did though have some effect because the Minister pronounced there was a requirement to maintain a revised service of passenger trains between Nottingham and Rugby (Central) after the 'through' trains were withdrawn from 3/4 September 1966. Passengers for

Brackley booked to Banbury or Aylesbury, thence by bus. Brackley and Woodford Halse stations were closed and other stations along the route became unstaffed halts. The through service between Poole and York was diverted via Sheffield (Midland), Derby, Birmingham (New Street) and Oxford and parcels traffic was withdrawn from Brackley, Woodford Halse, Lutterworth, Ashby Magna, Leicester (Central), Loughborough (Central) and East Leake.

The alternative bus services offered are in Appendix 9.

What happened at an operational level?
The residual Rugby to Nottingham (Arkwright Street from 1967) service with conductor guards issuing tickets for journeys along the line only was operated by two or three car diesel multiple units and ran until 3 May 1969; the then Minister having given her approval to the proposal. The lingering potential death of the section allowed some enthusiasts with a vision of which Watkin would have approved to get together with an intention to save the Leicester to Nottingham section. It was the starting point for a long struggle towards eventual fine achievement; please refer to chapter 14 for more information. By that time the chapter of the subsidised, social railway had started to be written; the Marylebone-High Wycombe-Aylesbury service receiving in 1969 a grant of £552,000 (only Inverness-Wick/Thurso with £595,000 appears to have exceeded that amount).

On a brighter note, the former GC lines and depots north of Annesley had a good future. A new diesel locomotive facility was installed at Shirebrook to act as a satellite away from the major new depot at Tinsley. Production of coal from Nottinghamshire for CEGB use would be taken north to Wath/Tinsley, south via the LD&ECR route and to Immingham for export. For passenger services, Glossop (Central) survived a proposed closure, the CLC largely escaped the cull and the MSJ&A benefitted from capital investment in electrification to more modern standards

Operational review 'snapshots'
For the first time in this book the operational matters and what happened are secondary to the main theme of process. The following are 'snapshots' of developments of relevance to what was happening elsewhere to effect change:

- Leicester motive power depot was closed on 6 July 1964
- Cricklewood motive power depot which could 'cover' for failures at the London end closed in December 1964
- Willesden motive power depot was able to provide Class 7 'cover', usually, up to May 1965 in the form of Britannias until closure in September 1965
- Annesley received replacements for three Royal Scots withdrawn (46101/11/26 withdrawn, replaced by 45735, 46156/67), but following a further demise the cascade of power embraced Standard Class 5s with BRIC (nine ton coal capacity) tenders and finally Black 5s after the Standard 5s were re-allocated to Tyseley and Lancashire
- the appearance of V2s faded with the closure of Cricklewood
- Willesden and Cricklewood enginemen learned the GC main line in anticipation of diversions
- cross-country services utilised NER/ER/WR diesels on out and home workings using Leicester/Oxford as the points of exchange
- after the Summer Saturdays only passenger traffic had ceased from 6 September 1964, the timetable started to take on its final form for the following two years
- the GN Nottingham (Victoria) – Derby (Friargate) passenger service was withdrawn on 4 September 1964
- diversions of long-distance, overnight passenger trains to use the West Coast route (Euston) took place, including the car sleeper (Calvert/Bletchley), the Manchester sleeper, but in the Winter of 64/65 brought into Marylebone a sleeping car train from Glasgow
- Annesley motive power depot closed on 3 January 1966, Colwick remained open, explaining the appearance of ex-LNER B1s from time to time. Banbury also helped out with BR Standard types and effectively became the redoubt.

As at spring 1965 the allocations at ER depots of interest were:

Colwick: 15 B1, 9 04, 23 WD, 2 9F, 25 350 h.p.
Immingham: 13 B1, 14 WD, 9 9F, 5 Brush 2, 2 Brush 4, 32 350 h.p.

Langwith:	16 04, 10 WD, 19 9F, 10 350 h.p.
Canklow:	13 B1, 21 WD, 3 LM4MT
Darnall:	43 350 h.p.
Tinsley:	11 BP type 1, 23 EE type 1, 32 Brush 2, 46 EE type 3, 46 Brush 4, 38 350 h.p.
Frodingham:	5 K1, 10 04, 26 WD, 1 9F, 11 350 h.p.

- Colwick motive power depot closed in December 1966.

The WTTs for 1964/65 were, therefore, the last ones to indicate something of what the GC main line was well capable of handling:

Passenger trains	12
Parcels/newspapers/fish	5
Fitted freights	7 + 1Q (Barry Docks – Bradford)
Unbraked freights	27 (paths available, not all used)

The route also dealt with long-distance extras including racing pigeon specials and, increasingly, for railway enthusiasts. Of the latter, one in particular warrants a mention; the annual spring tour of the East Midlands branch of the Railway Correspondence and Travel Society. Over the years, the Society had organised tours to places of railway interest and with unusual motive power. They had taken a pair of 4-4-0s (a Southern Schools and a Midland 2P) to Darlington and for 1964 requested the use of a Princess Coronation pacific, ideally *City of Nottingham*. The London Midland Region obliged and sent the locomotive light engine to Bletchley, thence Calvert and on to the GC and North to Annesley. The following day (9 May) the locomotive ran the tour to Swindon and back. It was a significant day for Swindon as some of their remaining Castle Class locomotives worked a high-speed Paddington-Plymouth and return special.

Further rationalisation of arrangements was made in winter 1964/65 in the Sheffield/Rotherham area; at

The volume of commemorative railtours increased during the 1960s, with enthusiasts wishing to mark the passing of classes of locomotives and lines. Here, an 04 passes Whisker Hill Junction, Retford, with one such tour, 12 October 1963 (photo David Marriott).

Aldwarke Junction the former LNER/LMS routes were joined with new connections. An extension of electrified route over 16¾ miles from Woodburn Junction and Darnall Junction and North East over the former GC line via Broughton Lane enabled cross-Pennine traffic to be dealt with in the new yard at Tinsley (electrification extending to Catcliffe). Quite in contrast, the goods yard at Marylebone together with the Lisson Grove coal yard and nearby railway owned properties were sold to the local authority for housing developments. At that time the parcels concentration depot was still open and was retained temporarily pending completion of the Euston station reconstruction works. Further rationalisation was planned for Sheffield with a new connection at Nunnery proposed to allow passenger trains to be routed into Midland station. More positively, one of the former Woodhead tunnels (the up) which was closed and had its entrances sealed in 1954 was re-opened in 1966 to allow electricity cables between Thorpe Marsh power station (near Doncaster) with the switching station at Stalybridge, thus preserving the natural habitats of the Peak National Park. (Similar work was undertaken later with the electrified new tunnel.) Sheffield (Victoria) station closed on 5 January 1970 at the time the electrified service from Manchester was withdrawn. The station was re-opened very briefly in 1972 whilst re-signalling work took place at Midland station.

The diversion of freight traffic to the NE/SW route started in earnest in mid-1965. For the winter WTT 4 October 1965-17 April 1966 trains of interest from the North Eastern Region were:

Reporting number	
4V34	Tees – Cardiff
7M67	Tees – Washwood Heath
8M40	York – Annesley
4E52	York – Colwick (sugar beet)
8M59	Stockton – Stanton (iron works)
4M82	Stockton – Wellingborough (iron ore empty mins trainload)
7M88	Tees – Avenue (Chesterfield, iron ore empties)
8M64	Tees – Chaddesden (Derby)
4M89	Tees – Washwood Heath
4M77	Tyneside – Washwood Heath
6M82	Tees – Oxley (Wolverhampton, steel)
4M72	Tees – Wellingborough (as 4M82)

NOTE:
I do not have the WTT for traffic from the Scunthorpe direction of the Eastern Region.

The timetabling arrangements had, by that time, been further improved by the adoption of clockface departures from Birmingham to the north (00 and 35) and west (00 and 25) for main line services with similar arrangements for local diesel multiple unit services. Power signalling with three aspect colour light signals based upon three power signal boxes (Derby, Trent and Saltley, Birmingham) was introduced from 1966/67.

The closure of the GC Woodhead route came in July 1981, by which time it was freight only.

CHAPTER 12

ACCIDENTS OF TIMING

The core of this book is about 'what really happened', as a statement, not a question. This Chapter takes a brief look at things that could have and one that maybe still will affect parts of the route of the Great Central Railway.

Watkin's dream of an overland route to India
When Edward Watkin and his father attended the Great Exhibition of the Victorian era in 1851, they studied a display of Europe and beyond to India. An opportunity of free trade across such an expanse was immediately apparent. 'Impossible! A fantasy by a fantasist.'

On 18 January 2017, a freight train carrying containerised goods from China arrived in London. The train had travelled overland and undersea for 12,451 kms (7,780 miles) in 18 days.

Watkin's dream of a tunnel under the English Channel
In 1973, the third application by a UK government to join the then European Common Market of six economically strong Western European countries was accepted. With the appointment of President Pompidou (1969-74) matters between the UK and France had generally improved and led to discussions on linking the two countries by a tunnel under the English Channel/Pas de Calais. Although enabling works quickly started, they were equally quickly terminated due to difficult prevailing economic conditions. Later, tunnels from between Folkestone (close to Watkin's site of work) and Calais were bored and opened for rail traffic in 1994.

A railway route from the North of England/Midlands to the Channel Tunnel
Although the track gauge of the railway administrations of the UK and most of Western Europe is the same at 4 feet 8½ inches, the 'size' of the rolling stock that can be accommodated varies, for example, width, height and length. When it was planned, the Great Central Railway London extension was to be built with curves of one-mile radius and to a sizing (loading) gauge more generous than many of its then competitors. The gauge adopted was not, though, to the gauge adopted by several European railway administrations at a convention in Berne, Switzerland, in 1912. It was never the case that trains originating in Western Europe could run along the London extension without civil engineering projects for bridges in particular.

Although the London extension was intentionally an 'isolated' main line railway, a connection with the Cambridge-Bletchley-Oxford line was installed in 1940 at Calvert, near Aylesbury. That connection allowed traffic to flow east-west and enabled trains to be routed to Oxford-Reading-Tonbridge-Ashford-Channel ports without passing through London.

The Modernisation Plan of the BTC in 1955 envisaged a new marshalling yard at Swanbourne, between Bletchley and Calvert, but the scheme was cancelled.

The political process of closure of railways
The Transport Act 1962 paved the way for the re-shaping of the railways and limited objections to those based only upon 'hardship'. The entire process was determined by a lack of credible costing data which the BTB could consistently apply to all proposals. As the programme of closures was progressed the rail lobby became more aware and more authoritative as it became better informed, recruiting ex-railwaymen, professional economists, engineers, planners and environmentalists. The then new considerations of social or cost benefit studies started to emerge from local authorities and contributory income from branch lines to main lines started to influence thinking between the General Elections of 1964 and 1966.

Contrast the processes of 1964-68 with the concerted, successful opposition to the later proposal to close another duplicate main line, i.e. Settle to Carlisle. Consider, also, lines closed which have subsequently been re-opened.

Didcot power station
Although the planning for the programme of new power stations for the CEGB had essentially been completed by the early 1960s – and all were to be built on or close

to the coalfields that would serve them – two further applications for additional capacity were submitted in 1964. One was for Rugeley in Staffordshire and the other at Didcot in Oxfordshire.

Whilst Rugeley was close to the East Midlands, Didcot was a hundred miles and more from both South Wales and the East Midlands; as such it seemed a strange siting. The power station was designed for firing by either coal or oil, it being sited on the route of a wartime petroleum product pipeline from Aldermaston to bases of the U.S. Air Force elsewhere in the area. With a power generating capacity of up to 2 MW, Didcot would be a very large-scale consumer of coal; if using coal only, up to 5 million tons a year or roundly 14,000 tons a day. For comparison with the Annesley-Woodford Halse workings of 1957-60 (27 trains in each direction) the demand for Didcot alone represented the equivalent of 22 trains (of 45 wagons each carrying 14 tons of coal). That comparison is largely irrelevant because the larger capacity 'merry go round' wagons were being introduced and would be capable of faster round trip timings. What is relevant is that the Annesley-Woodford Halse-Banbury-Oxford-Didcot route could have been used as a long-term base traffic flow around which other traffic flows could also have contributed.

Coal was supplied from the East Midlands coalfield and was routed via Birmingham-Banbury and Oxford (1969).

HS2 rail route London-the Midlands-the North

At the time of writing, the authorisation of high-speed rail line 2 for north of Birmingham is the subject of considerable debate and criticism. If the northern cities of Sheffield and Leeds are to benefit (being 160/190 miles from London by conventional rail and road) a route will need to be found that also serves Nottingham. By combining the interests of Sheffield and Manchester with Leeds, maybe there is a future role for the Woodhead/Penistone routes; add a connection to the HS1 channel tunnel services and Watkin would be totally vindicated. Where are the men of vision?

CHAPTER 13

EXTANT/PRESERVED/RESTORED EXAMPLES OF ROUTE, ARCHITECTURE AND TRACTION AND ROLLING STOCK OF THE FORMER GCR

The railway network of the UK is now widely recognised as a national asset rather than as a liability. The current day custodians of the network face challenges in managing many routes which had their origins in the days of Watkin. It is still possible to travel over sections of the MS&LR, the GCR, the CLC and MSJ&A using public passenger services offered by holders of franchises. From time to time rail-tours are organised to travel over lines normally used by freight trains. Beyond that, there are some splendid examples of preservation and restoration to be enjoyed. This short chapter lists some of what can be seen and enjoyed.

For journeys on Network Rail

To research what is available reference can be made to two railway atlases, copies of which are generally available:

British Railways Pre-Grouping Atlas and Gazetteer by W. Philip Conolly
Rail Atlas Great Britain and Ireland by S.K. Baker (various issues)

A comparison between the two will enable journeys to be selected.

For journeys on freight only lines the website suggested for this is:

www.railtourinfo.co.uk/diesel_2020.html

Operators who favour freight only lines include:
Branch Line Society
Pathfinder Tours

Preserved sections of route

The Great Central Railway plc (www.gcrailway.co.uk) is the present-day operator of a mainly steam service between Loughborough (Central) and Belgrave & Birstall – known as Leicester (North) – an eight mile section of the former London extension. The section has a double track between Loughborough and Rothley with Quorn & Woodhouse as the intermediate station. The railway today is the culmination of the efforts started in 1969.

Each station depicts a different era of the history of the line; for example, Loughborough the 1950s and Quorn & Woodhouse the Second World War. A long-term aim of the Company has been to re-connect East of Loughborough with another extant section of route; that to Ruddington (Nottingham), a distance of nearly ten miles, part of which is still used by Network Rail freight trains (www.gcrn.co.uk). Trains are operated over both sections at weekends, mid-week holiday seasonal dates and Bank Holidays.

Restored stations/architecture:

There are two CLC stations to visit:

- Manchester (Central) now in use as a convention centre
- Irlam station (16 mins by train from Manchester Oxford Road station)

Main Line Preservation Group

President: The Rt. Hon. the Earl of Lanesborough, T.D., D.L., J.P.
Chairman: Richard J. Willis, M.A.

The Group has been formed in order to ensure that main line steam locomotives shall run again on a main line owned by enthusiasts. At present part of the former **Great Central** line from Leicester to Nottingham is the subject of negotiations with B.R. with a view to acquisition by the Group. This is the most modern main line which is likely to be available for our purpose.

The Last Main Line

Closure is imminent. By the time you read this the final date may have been announced.

Subscripton to the Group is only 10/-. This low amount has been fixed so as not to deter anyone from declaring his interest. Finance of any project of this nature must come from donations and loans. Send subscriptions, donations and offers of loans to the Treasurer or write to the Secretary for further information. S.a.e. appreciated.

Treasurer: R. W. Holmes, 　　　　　　　　Secretary: S. W. Smith,

Illustration P1

Men of vision. An early advertisement which is self-explanatory. Please refer to Chapter 13 for an impression of what was achieved.

Pages 291-303: The founders and long-term supporters of the Main Line Steam Trust would have been pleased with the progressive achievements in establishing and then extending the initial purchase of the Loughborough-Quorn & Woodhouse section to Rothley and then to Leicester North (Belgrave & Birstall). The basic infrastructure, the stations, the traction and rolling stock, the regulatory authorities, the willing base of volunteers, the colour of the final figure of the profit and loss account, the building of the balance sheet, the transition from a redoubt for steam enthusiasts to being a family day out attraction plus exceptional gala events ... quite a story and a very human story, characterised by successive management teams maintaining the spirit of what the GC was all about, a hard-working railway run by proud staff (and, also, the volunteers).

Over the years, locomotives from all the Regions of British Railways have been used on the GC. Here (99-102) are a Castle, a King, Hall and Manor of the Western (103-107), a Schools, King Arthur, two West Country light pacifics and a Merchant Navy of the Southern (108-111), a Black 5, Jubilee, Princess Coronation and an 8F of the LM (112-114), an A2, B1 and J52 of the Eastern (115-118), a Class 5, Class 4 and two of the same 9F representing the era of the BR Standard designs (115 Phil Jones).

The diesel era was represented by a multiple unit saved and maintained by a group of engineers from the LM Region as volunteers (119). Signalling includes example gantries and signal boxes saved/recovered and finely restored (120 and 121). The interior picture is of the newly built signal box at Swithland Sidings between Quorn and Rothley, largely the result of a benefactor and totally the result of a professional approach.

Each station represents a different era in the history of the line; Quorn (122) depicts the Second World War. Not only in those difficult times do so many now enjoy themselves because of the devoted service of a few.

EXTANT/PRESERVED/RESTORED EXAMPLES OF ROUTE • 293

99

100

101

102

EXTANT/PRESERVED/RESTORED EXAMPLES OF ROUTE • 295

EXTANT/PRESERVED/RESTORED EXAMPLES OF ROUTE • 297

107

108

EXTANT/PRESERVED/RESTORED EXAMPLES OF ROUTE • 299

113

114

EXTANT/PRESERVED/RESTORED EXAMPLES OF ROUTE • 301

115

116

EXTANT/PRESERVED/RESTORED EXAMPLES OF ROUTE • **303**

119

The clock tower of Nottingham (Victoria) station, Victoria Centre is preserved as a Grade II Building.

The station building at Brackley (Central) station is in use as a café.

The station frontage of Leicester (Central) station is the subject of a restoration development project (2019).

Great Central Hotel, Marylebone and station concourse, 222 Marylebone Road, London NW1 6JQ. The hotel and former railway headquarters offices is now a five-star landmark hotel.

A pair of gates from the entrance to Marylebone station are in use as the entrance gates at the Tramway Museum, Crich, Derbyshire.

Preserved rolling stock

Electric tramcars:

Three of the tramcars used on the Grimsby & Immingham Electric Tramway survived into preservation.

Car 14 was built at Dukinfield C&W Works, GCR in 1915 and is in the custody of the National Railway Museum.

Cars 5 and 10 were in the batch of 19 sold by Gateshead & District Tramways for use at Grimsby. 5 is in the custody of the Tramway Museum (https://www.tramway.co.uk) at Crich and number 10 is at Beamish Museum (https://www.beamish.org.uk)

Electric locomotives:

Three of the electric locomotives used along the Manchester-Sheffield-Wath line between 1954 and 1981 have been preserved:

26020 is at the National Railway Museum, York (https://www.railwaymuseum.org.uk)

27000 is at the Midland Railway Centre, Ripley (https://www.midlandrailway-butterley.co.uk)

27002 is at the Museum of Science & Industry, Manchester (https://www.scienceandindustrymuseum.org.uk)

Steam locomotives:

Two former GCR locomotives were preserved as part of the National collection. Both have steamed in preservation:

63601 GCR Class 8K, LNER/BR Class 04 2-8-0 is at the Great Central Railway, Loughborough

62660 GCR Class 11E LNER/BR Class D11 4-4-0 *Butler Henderson* is at Barrow Hill Roundhouse Museum, near Chesterfield (www.barrowhill.org)

Carriages:

Examples of carriages as used by the MS&LR/GCR/LNER/BR have been preserved:

6 wheel MS&LR carriage, numbered as 946, is normally at the Great Central Railway, Nottingham.

Four examples of GCR Barnum type carriages are at the GCR, Nottingham.

Two complete rakes of Gresley teak carriages can be seen and travelled in. One is at the Severn Valley Railway, Kidderminster (www.svr.co.uk), and the other at the North Yorkshire Moors Railway, Pickering (https://www.nymr.co.uk)

Shipping:

Two of the three paddle steamers used on the Hull – New Holland services survived into preservation:

PPS *Wingfield Castle* is at Hartlepool's Maritime Museum (www.hartlepoolsmaritimeexperience.com)

PPS *Tattershall Castle* is a pub/restaurant moored at the Victoria Embankment, London (https://www.thetattershallcastle.co.uk)

Other:

Aero research facility (private property) Catesby Tunnel, Charwelton, Northamptonshire, is in use for various testing purposes.

Woodhead Tunnel portals, Derbyshire, and Dunford Bridge, near Penistone. May be viewed from the Longdendale Trail footpath.

The Great Central Railway Society (www.gcrsociety.co.uk) was founded in 1974 and is open to all who are interested in any aspect of the Great Central Railway, its predecessors, successors and joint lines.

Above and opposite: Marine activities deserve a mention. LNER paddle steamer *Waverley* of 1946 has survived and offers a programme of excursions from various ports and harbours around the UK (97). The Humber ferry *Tattershall Castle* (registered Grimsby) – in an increasingly modified form – is moored alongside the Victoria Embankment, London (98).

124

CONCLUSIONS

Readers of this book will, doubtless, form their own views upon whether its content adequately describes what really happened. In so doing, readers who follow the chronology of events will be able to address the series of challenging questions I faced in researching the book and also follow the answers that I have offered. I am not the first to attempt such an exercise. Whilst the general questions of why a section of line was built and then closed have been covered, I am amongst a very few writers who have taken an analytical approach to the businesses of the railway and avoided the nostalgia for all things lost.

The tasks as presented include that the building of the Great Central Railway and its predecessor company was undertaken by use of private capital. Edward Watkin as General Manager and later chairman earned over a period of some four decades the respect and trust of investors who increasingly took little persuasion in committing funds. Watkin's moral code and compass provided a form of protection for those investors and with stock bearing fixed interest rates of return, they were rewarded over time. Watkin seems to have taken a rather different view of those who rushed headlong to the Stock Exchange in an irrational pursuit of Ordinary shares which they saw as a certainty from which to prosper. I have concluded that Watkin was a prime example of the embodiment of confident Victorian society; principled, a believer in expansion and international free trade bringing wide benefits. He was far more than the man who strove to link England with continental Europe and beyond; the book includes a listing of his considerable achievements.

Chairman Henderson with General Manager Fay – I have concluded that they could not have succeeded in isolation from each other – took on with relish the challenges of the then new Great Central Railway. It is clear that by 1912/13 they had established by wise operational decisions and long term capital investment projects a strong basis from which a successful corporate business would develop. Henderson was somewhat unfortunate in that at times when he needed to attract new capital, the cost of money as expressed by the Bank of England minimum lending rate was relatively high. That resulted in a heavy burden of debt repayable to investors whilst the benefits from costly investments had yet to reach maturity.

Revenue from transporting coal was crucial to the fortunes of the Great Central Railway. I have concluded that the owners of colliery companies generally outwitted their contemporaries in the railway companies as the latter competed for contracts. As a late entrant to an already competitive market in parts of Nottinghamshire, the Great Central was never able to secure a commercial position of strength. The company did prove more successful in its acquisition of the LD&ECR and in working the privately owned Mansfield Railway. The commercial pricing of coal traffic was never soundly based at any time up to the early 1960s.

The times of ownership by the LNER were characterized by the routes of the former Great Northern Railway being favoured for scarce investment monies, leaving the Great Central on meagre rations though never completely starved. During the years of war, the London extension and its route allowing access to the south coast without passing through London was of immense value to the national interest.

The period between nationalization of inland transport and the mid-1950s were characterized by poor leadership from headquarters whilst organizational turmoil took hold. The former GCR routes and particularly the London-Manchester/Sheffield/Bradford was avoided during that time, a focus that should have identified the extent of duplicated passenger services. However, any such focus would have identified the importance of the London extension and the link to Banbury for coal, steel and merchandise traffic. Whilst demand in London and the south of England for coal for domestic use, power generation and industry remained strong, no single railway route could supply the tonnage. In such circumstances, the GCR London extension and link to Banbury had a role to play. Demand for coal in these markets declined after 1957, though it took some time to recognize that the decline thereafter would be irretrievable in tonnage terms. That, together with the strategic decisions taken by the CEGB to build new conventional coal or dual fired conventional power stations close to economic coalfields north of the River Trent, effectively weakened the case for retaining the London extension. Apart from coal, the former GCR route south of Sheffield generated only a small tonnage of goods and the merchandise trains were using the route as a convenient, operational conduit.

The potential greater use of the Manchester/Sheffield and London Great Central route whilst the alternative routes via Crewe and Stoke on Trent were electrified, remained largely that; just potential that did not materialize to any great extent.

The fish traffic from Grimsby was a significant contributor to the fortunes of the GCR and LNER. The railway strike of 1955 irreparably damaged trust and that, together with the progression of the fishing industry and consumers to pre-packed at sea, frozen products and an unwillingness of all concerned to fund capital investment effectively handed the business to road hauliers.

The work of Dr Beeching's team of planners finally put into place some factual information about traffic flows and routes that had been so badly lacking and required a decade before. Once that information was placed alongside other work on investments in modern traction, signalling, other infrastructure improvements and projections of requirements from the CEGB and the NCB, it was clear that there was no future role for the London extension; other parts of the former GCR would, though, enjoy a continued role in meeting these requirements and still use Wath and Immingham.

The number of organizational, economic, political, industrial and social variables that were present in the late 1950s weaken the strength of opinions that held that the Great Central London extension was closed purely as a result of actions taken by the London Midland Region. The withdrawal of express passenger services from 1958 formed part of a wider programme of change to support the use of the St Pancras-Manchester/Sheffield route whilst the LNW routes were electrified. The Midland route beyond Derby suffered the same fate as the London extension of the Great Central; no economic case for retention, just nostalgia and emotion – at least in the eyes and minds of those trying to reshape British Railways at that time.

APPENDIX 1

CAPITAL EXPENDITURE 1900-1912

The following lists record the significant capital expenditure committed year by year, though because of time lag actual expenditure would have extended, in some cases, into different years. The lists cross refer to chapter 2.

CAPITAL EXPENDITURE COMMITTED IN 1900

			Total £	Note(s)
Traction and rolling stock				
Locomotives				
Class 9F	31:	15 GC @ £2750	41250	a
		16 BP @ £2995	47920	
Class 13	6:	6 GC @ £3000	18000	a, b
Class 15	20:	20 BW @ £2600	52000	
Coaching stock				
Dining cars ex-GN/MS&L 2 GC @ £2000			4000	a, c
Various for CLC				d
Wagons				
Fish vans (4 wheel) 50 B'ham C&W @ £210			10500	
Fish vans (4 wheel) 50 GC @ £210			10500	a
Civil and S&T works				
Culworth Junc – Banbury Junc				e
Gotham branch				f

CAPITAL EXPENDITURE COMMITTED IN 1901

		Total £	Note(s)
Traction and rolling stock			
Locomotives			
Class 9F	6 BP @ £3315	19890	
Class 9H	22 GC @ £3300	72600	a
Class 9J	22 NR @ £3445	75790	b
Class 11B	5 SS @ £3600	18000	b
Civil and S&T works			
Neasden – Northolt Junc		342000	

CAPITAL EXPENDITURE COMMITTED IN 1902

			Total £	Note(s)
Traction and rolling stock				
Locomotives				
Class 8		6 NR @ £3700	22200	
Class 8A		3 NR @ £3700	11100	
Class 9H		18 GC @ £3360	60480	
Class 9J	27:	18 NR @ £3445	62010	
		9 NR @ £3225	29025	
Class 11B		20 SS @ £3600	72000	
Coaching stock				
Total of 54 incl slip carriages. B'ham C&W, Metro C&W, Craven			108000	
Wagons				
Previously on hire		525	5250	a
Fish vans (bogie)		17 B'ham C&W @ £495	8415	
Mineral (10t)		500 Ashburys @ £70	35000	
Coal (10t)		400 Craven @ £69	27600	
Coal (bogie 30t)		30 B'ham C&W @ £255.10s	7665	
Marine shipping				
City of Leeds		Earles @ £38800	38800	
City of Bradford		Earles @ £38650	38650	
Marine installations				
Grimsby (herring trade improvements)			20000	
Civil and S&T works				
Shireoaks – Laughton GC share			49550	

CAPITAL EXPENDITURE COMMITTED IN 1903

			Total £	Note(s)
Traction and rolling stock				
Locomotives				
Class 8A		15 KN @ £3300	49500	
Class 9J	13:	2 GC @ £2850	5700	a
		11 BP @ £2850	31350	
Class 9K	20:	8 GC @ £2770	22160	b
		12 VF @ £2770	33240	
Class 11B		5 SS @ £3600	18000	
Coaching stock				
Total of 50, bogie, non-corridor				
B'ham C&W, Metro C&W			88000	
Restaurant cars 4 GC @ £2000			8000	a
Wagons				
Horse boxes		50 B'ham C&W @ £325	16250	
Parcels (bogie)		8 GC @ £800	6400	a
Brake vans		50 Craven @ £294.16s	14740	
Coal (steel, 20t, s.d.) 100 Leeds @ £190			19000	
Coal (steel, 20t, b.d.) 50 Leeds @ £200			10000	
Box vans (15t)		150 Metro C&W	11400	
		@ £205	30750	
High sided (10t)		100 RY Pckg @ £114		
Scrapped		1428	(28500)	a
Marine installations				
Cleethorpes (improvement works)			16720	
Infrastructure/plant				
Dukinfield C&W works, land			11000	
Civil and S&T works				
Charwelton (troughs)			6000	
Gorton (west of, track widening)			39405	
MSJ&A works GC share			25500	

CAPITAL EXPENDITURE COMMITTED IN 1904

			Total £	Note(s)
Traction and rolling stock				
Locomotives				
Class 8		8 BP @ £3325	26600	
Class 8A		18 KN @ £3300	59400	
Class 8B		5 BP @ £3750	18750	
Class 8C		1 BP @ £3370	3370	
Class 9J	44:	9 GC @ £2850	25650	
		15 VF @ £2895	43425	
		15 BP @ £2850	42750	
		5 YE @ £2850	14250	
Rebuild		20 GC	10000	a, g
Railcars				
Steam		2 GC @ £2800	5600	a
Coaching stock				
Corridor	76	B'ham C&W, Metro C&W	52000	
Non-corridor	72	B'ham C&W, Metro C&W, Cravens	132000	
CLC	178	GC (?MR/GNR), Glos C&W		d
Wagons				
Various		488 GC Gorton	40544	
Fish vans		100 Cravens @ £153.15s	15375	
Coal (bogie, 40t)		25 B'ham C&W @ £349.10s	8737	
Various (10t)	700	Various	55500	h
Various (10t)	450	Various	33300	h (300)
Van (refrigerated)		50 Metro C&W @ £205.2s.6d	10256	
Marine installations				
Grimsby (new lock pit)			70000	
Civil and S&T works				
Neasden Junc – Northolt Junc – 3 stations			17915	
Signalling:		Ardwick – Hyde, plus support for 15 years	46190	
		Woodhead tunnel 'up'	2100	
Gorton (east of, towards Guide Bridge, track widening)			54575	
Infrastructure/plant				
Gorton Works:		new wheel drop	10550	
		enhanced facilities	17700	

CAPITAL EXPENDITURE COMMITTED IN 1905

		Total £	Note(s)
Traction and rolling stock			
Locomotives			
Class 8A	5 KN @ £3400	17000	
Class 8B	12 NB @ £4050	48600	i
Class 8D	1 GC @ £3370	3370	j
Class 9J	5 YE @ £2900	14500	
Class 9K	10 GC @ £2770	27700	
Absorption	18 ex-WM&CQ		k
Railcars			
Steam	1 GC @ £2800	2800	
Coaching stock			
Dining cars	6 Brush		
Corridor composite 8 Brush			
Corr comps brake	2 Brush total	30410	l
Wagons			
Well, bogie	4 D'ton @ £675	2700	
Fish vans	50 various @ £146.16s	7340	
Fish vans	50 various @ £159.18s	7995	
Brake vans 100:	50 Cravens @ £290.10s	14525	
	50 Cravens @ £307	15350	
Marine shipping			
Wrexham	Raylton Dixon	20000	
Marine installations			
Grimsby (timber yard, coaling appliances)		41000	
Civil and S&T works			
Wath/Worksop yards		350000	
Grimsby Lt Rly construction		27834	
Infrastructure/plant			
Dukinfield C&W Works, construction		165000	
Gorton Works, new tooling		9600	

CAPITAL EXPENDITURE COMMITTED IN 1906

		Total £	Note(s)
Traction and rolling stock			
Locomotives			
Class 5A	6 GC @ £2650	15900	a, b
Class 8B	8 GC @ £3750	30000	a, i
Class 8D	1 GC @ £3500	3500	a, j
Class 8E	2 GC @ £3400	6800	a, i
Class 8F	10 BP @ £4200	42000	
Class 8G	10 BP @ £4110	41100	b
Class 9J	7 GC @ £2900	20300	a
Sacré 2-4-0	3 GC @ £800	2400	a, m
Coaching stock			
Motor sets	3 GC @ £1600	4800	a
Marine shipping			
Immingham	Swan Hunter	73600	
Marylebone	Cammell Laird	73600	
Marine installations			
Grimsby (new quay wall)		21000	
Civil and S&T works			
CLC:	Throstle Nest Junc – Trafford Park. GC share	15666	
	Manchester Central platform 9. GC share	3333	
GC and H&B Joint Anston – Roundwood. GC share		67697	
Gorton & Openshaw station		4637	
Infrastructure/plant			
Dukinfield C&W Works elec sub-station		20000	

CAPITAL EXPENDITURE COMMITTED IN 1907

		Total £	Note(s)
Traction and rolling stock			
Locomotives			
Class 8A	13 KN @ £4350	56550	
Class 8H	2 BP @ £4625	9250	b, n
Class 9J	35 GC @ £2900	101500	a
Class 9L	12 BP @ £3400	40800	b
Sacré 2-4-0	3 GC @ £1600	4800	a

CAPITAL EXPENDITURE COMMITTED IN 1908

		Total	Note(s)
		£	
Traction and rolling stock			
Locomotives			
Class 8H	2 BP @ £4625	9250	
Class 9J	11 GC @ £3000	33000	a
Civil and S&T works			
Doncaster avoiding line		164500	

CAPITAL EXPENDITURE COMMITTED IN 1909

		Total	Note(s)
		£	
Traction and rolling stock			
Locomotives			
Class 8A	15 GC @ £4350	65250	a
Class 9J	1 GC @ £3000	3000	
Marine shipping			
Accrington	Earles	41500	
Dewsbury	Earles	41500	
Northwich	(sold)	(2750)	
Infrastructure/plant			
Dukinfield C&W Works cost overrun		11700	

CAPITAL EXPENDITURE COMMITTED IN 1910

		Total	Note(s)
		£	
Traction and rolling stock			
Locomotives			
Class 8A	17 GC @ £4350	73950	a
Class 8J	9 GC @ £3000	27000	a
Coaching stock			
Braked	6 GC (Dukinfield) @ £2000	12000	a
Barnum excursion	23? GC @ £1500	34500	a
Wagons (all GC from Dukinfield)			
Fish vans (10t)	100 GC @ £80	8000	a
Cattle vans	25 GC @ £80	2000	a
Vans (15t)	50 GC @ £70	3500	a
Vans	100 GC @ £60	6000	a
High sided (10t)	50 GC @ £60	3000	a
Brake vans (12t)	5 GC @ £80	400	a
Various	500 Cravens @ £60.15s	30375	
Loco dept coal	60 GC @ £60	3600	a
Marine shipping			
Blackburn	Earles	-	
Bury	Earles	41500	
Stockport	Earles replacement for '*Blackburn*'	41608	q
Civil and S&T works			
Whitton branch (NLLR)		5000	

CAPITAL EXPENDITURE COMMITTED IN 1911

		Total	Note(s)
		£	
Traction and rolling stock			
Locomotives			
Class 8A	3GC @ £4000	12000	a
Class 8K	6GC @ £4500	27000	a
Class 9N	9GC @ £4000	36000	a, b
Coaching stock			
Various	72GC total	117950	o
Marine shipping			
Immingham/Marylebone mods total		38000	
Civil and S&T works			
Ashton Moss link to L&Y		11329	

CAPITAL EXPENDITURE COMMITTED IN 1912

		Total	Note(s)
		£	
Traction and rolling stock			
Locomotives			
Class 1	1 GC @ £5500	5500	a, b
Class 8K	89: 21 GC @ £4400	92400	a
	20 KN @ £4550	91000	
	48 NB @ £4512	216576	
Class 9N	6 GC @ £3600	21600	a
Railcars			
Petrol/electric	1 Westinghouse	2500	
Coaching stock			
MSJ&A	2 x 7 car sets GC share	7730	
Marine shipping			
Various, low tonnage 12 total		9915	
Humber river ferries 2 total		10000	a
Marine installations			
Grimsby (new fish dock)		-	p
Civil and S&T works			
Darnall (widening)		31400	
Wrawby/Barnetby/Brocklesby works		65671	

CAPITAL EXPENDITURE

Abbreviations and notes used:

Ashburys	Ashburys Railway Carriage & Iron Co.
B'ham C&W	Birmingham Carriage & Wagon Co.
BP	Beyer, Peacock & Co.
Brush	Brush Electrical Engineering Co.
BW	Burnham, Williams & Co. (Baldwin Works)
Cammell Laird	Cammell Laird & Co. Ltd.
CLC	Cheshire Lines Committee
composite	coaching stock offering more than one Class
Craven	Craven Bros Ltd.
C&W	Carriage and wagon
D'ton	Darlington Wagon & Engineering Co.
Earles	Earles Shipbuilding & Engineering Co., Hull
GC	Great Central
Glos C&W	Gloucester Carriage & Wagon Co.
GN	Great Northern
H&B	Hull & Barnsley
KN	Kitson & Co. Ltd.
Leeds	Leeds Forge Co.
L&Y	Lancashire & Yorkshire
Metro C&W	Metropolitan Carriage & Wagon Co.

CAPITAL EXPENDITURE

MR	Midland Railway
MS&JA	Manchester South Junc & Altrincham
MS&L	Manchester Sheffield & Lincolnshire
NLLR	North Lindsey Light Railway
NR	Neilson Reid & Co.
Raylton Dixon	Raylton Dixon, Middlesbrough
RY Pckg	RY Pickering & Co. Ltd. (Glasgow)
slip	carriage detached from main train
SS	Sharp, Stewart
S&T	Signal and telecommunications
Swan Hunter	Swan Hunter Shipbuilding Co.
'up'	line used by trains in direction of London
VF	Vulcan Foundry
Westinghouse	Westinghouse Brake and Signal Co.
WM&CQ	Wrexham Mold & Connah's Quay
YE	Yorkshire Engine Co.

NOTES:

a estimated
b first build of Class. Cost to include design, production drawings, jigs and templates
c conversion work to existing vehicles
d third of total cost (with GN)
e separate note applies to funding this line
f cost assumed to be included in London Extension
g rebuild programme spread 1902-06
h oil lubrication rather than grease
i 4-4-2
j 4-4-2 compound
k separate note applies to accounting
l production spread to 1909
m rebuild for motor train (push pull) operation
n first British 0-8-4T
o 12 vehicles for Newcastle and Manchester to Bournemouth service
    10 vehicles for London services (purchase rather than lease)
    8 vehicles for Newcastle to Barry service
    20 vehicles for Hull, Sheffield to Manchester and Liverpool services
    10 vehicles for London suburban services (purchased rather than lease)
    10 Barnum saloons for excursion and émigré services
    12 composite braked vehicles including 2 slip
p project and expenditure progressed in 1934
q 2 ships sold in 1910 (ages 27 and 33 years)

APPENDIX 2

EXTRACTS FROM BTC FREIGHT CHARGES BOOK 1957 BR 22415

In this modern age of charging by container size/cubic capacity and weight of goods to be carried, it is of little relevance to spend much time on how complicated British Railways made such matters in 1957.

With road hauliers all around looking for loads, one has to pity a BR Goods Agent faced with the complexities of different types of timber or for the huge range of items that could be put into containers, subject to levels of differential percentage increased charges which were agreed during the three years it took to produce the Book.

Appendix 2

BRITISH RAILWAYS

B.R. 22415

Instructions regarding the Charging of Timber

1. DEFINITION.

The term "Timber" means wood in an unmanufactured, roughly-hewn, roughly-sawn or planed state; it does not include any wood shaped, prepared or partially prepared, other than planing (except when specifically stated), nor any description of wood separately specified in the Index of Commodities.

2. TIMBER AT MACHINE WEIGHT.

The following are carried at actual machine weight only:—

African Whitewood (Obeche)
American Cherry, square-edged
American Chestnut, square-edged
Boxboards, tied in bundles
Boxwood
Canadian Yellow Pine, sawn 4 inches thick and under
Cedar, e.o.h.p.
Cocuswood
Cordwood
Cornel
Cratewood, round or split
Dogwood
Ebony
Fir Logs, peeled, not exceeding 14 feet in length, for the manufacture of Wood Wool
Firewood, unprepared

Flooring and Matchings, manufactured—
  Maple
  Oak
  Pitch Pine
  Pyinkado
  Tasmanian Oak
  Teak
Gaboon Wood
Gurjun
Hop Poles
Iroko
Kingwood
Lamao (White Lauan)
Lancewood
Lignum Vitae
Mahogany
Myall
Olive Wood

Partridge
Persimmon
Pit Props, not exceeding 14 feet in length
Poles for Rustic Work
Poles, rough, for Boat Hooks
Purpleheart
Red Lauan
Rosewood
Sandal Wood
Satinwood
Serayah
Silkwood
Sleepers, half round or waney edged
Snakewood
Stavewood, riven
Tulipwood

Mixed consignments of Sawn Planks, Boards or Scantlings of two or more species of Timber (mainly Hardwoods) and not fewer than three different thicknesses or widths.

Imported Timber, round, square or partly square, for propping or shoring in mines.

Timber in lengths of less than 3 feet; but this does not apply to cargo specifications of Fir or Pine Ends, which may contain a proportion of shorter lengths.

Also the following when conveyed between places in Scotland:—

  All Timber occupying one ordinary wagon.

  Round Timber not exceeding 7 inches in diameter to collieries and mines, loaded in—
    Swivel Bar or Twin Wagons, or
    One Rail Wagon, or
    Two Ordinary Wagons.

Timber not shown above or in Instruction 3.

3. TIMBER AT MEASUREMENT WEIGHT.

(i) **Round Timber,** as named hereafter in this Instruction, is charged on measurement weight only (except as provided for in Instruction 2) calculated as follows:—

Measurements to be taken by tape measure according to the following rules. Irregularities of shape and hollow places to be taken into account and addition or deduction made for them.

QUARTER GIRTH—

The girth to be measured over the bark when bark is present, and the quarter girth reckoned from this to the quarter inch.

Pieces of even shape: The mean girth of each piece to be taken.

Pieces of irregular shape: Each piece to be marked off into suitable sections lengthwise, the marks being put at even foot or half-foot points, and the mean girth of each section taken.

When a tree with bark on has had the bark removed at the proper girthing place for the purpose of ascertaining the measurement under bark, it is to be girthed on both sides of the stripped place and the mean of the two measurements taken.

LENGTH OF HALF-FOOT—

Pieces of even shape: Each piece to be measured from end to end.

Pieces of irregular shape: The length of each section as marked off for girthing to be taken.

Chopped (tapering) butts and slanting saw cuts to be measured from and/or to the middle of such cuts.

Fractions of length under half a foot to be dropped.

CUBICAL QUANTITY—

The cubical quantity must be reckoned from the measurements according to the Timber Measurement Tables provided for the purpose, and known as the 144 divisor tables.

These tables are calculated as follows:—

$$\frac{\text{Length to the half foot} \times \text{quarter girth} \times \text{quarter girth}}{144} = \text{Cubic feet}$$

The cubic contents of each piece must be recorded in feet and inches. These must be added together to ascertain the cubical quantity of a consignment consisting of several pieces.

A table for converting cubic contents into tonnage is shown at pages 5 to 12 of these Instructions.

MEASUREMENT—

The Railways' Timber Measurers will generally measure round timber consigned at measurement weight, and give to the Goods Agent particulars of the measurements, showing:—

(a) The description of Timber.

(b) The cubic contents.

(c) The pieces, if any, on which allowances have been made, the amounts of the allowances and the reasons for them.

In cases where the Railways are unable to provide Timber Measurers the Senders must give the above information when handing the traffic to the Railways.

When the quantity ascertained by the Railways' Measurer is greater than that declared by the Sender, the figures given by the Railways' Measurer must be used.

When a Trader asks to be supplied with the details of the measurements of the Timber, other than the total number of cubic feet in a consignment, these may be supplied on payment of a charge of 1s. 0d. per ton, minimum 9s. 1d. per consignment.

(ii) **Rectangular Timber (other than Logs)**, i.e. Deals, Battens and Boards, Planks and Scantlings, as named hereafter in this Instruction (except as provided for in Instruction 2) is charged on measurement weight only, based on the actual cubical contents, full measurements each way being taken by calliper or rule.

(iii) **Rectangular Logs and Defective Angle Logs, Sawn or Hewn on All Four Sides,** as named hereafter in this Instruction (except as provided for in Instruction 2) are charged on measurement weight only, calculated as follows:—

LENGTH to be measured to the half foot; fractions of half a foot to be dropped.

WIDTH AND THICKNESS to be measured by calliper in the middle of the log, to the quarter inch.

THE CUBIC CONTENTS of each piece to be ascertained according to the following rules:—

	To
Not exceeding 5 cubic feet	Feet and tenths.
Not exceeding 10 feet in length	Half foot.
Under 8 inches either side	Half foot.
All other logs	The foot.

The following allowances to be made from the cubical quantity of defective Angle Logs:—

(a) If the total width of the wanes is more than one-fifth of the girth an allowance of 10 per cent. is made.

(b) If the total width of the wanes is less than one-fifth of the girth no allowance is made.

(iv) **Weight.**—Weight under (i), (ii) or (iii) to be reckoned from the cubical quantity according to the table of feet to the ton shown at the end of these Instructions. A fraction less than half a cubic foot to be dropped and half a cubic foot or more reckoned as a cubic foot.

When Timber, carried at Measurement weight, is sawn and bound together again, it is charged as follows:—

When bound together and measured in the round form (boule)—

If measurement weight is obtained from details of each board comprising the boule prior to banding. As Sawn Timber.

If measurement weight is obtained from the boule in the round form. As Round Timber.

SECTION B.
Alphabetical list of Container traffics, conditions of acceptance as to risk, and differential percentages which must be added to the existing chargeable rates unless otherwise shown.

TRAFFIC	Differential Percentage
Accumulator Boxes	
Accumulator Lead Plates	
Accumulator Lead Plates (worn out)	—
Accumulators	
(*see* Electric Batteries and Cells, Accumulator).	
Acetylene, in cylinders	5
Acid, Boracic	
Acid, Citric	—
Acid, Tartaric	
In small cardboard cartons in paper parcels	10*
Advertisements, dummy, for shop display	10
Advertising Signs, metal and/or wood—	
With glass	20
Without glass	10
Adze Handles and Shafts	5
Aerated and Mineral Waters, in cases, casks, crates, hampers or jars	5
Aeroplane Flares, uncharged	10
Aeroplane Parts as listed in the Index of Commodities (except Cowls or Covers of Engines)	10
Aeroplane Parts—Cowls or Covers of Engines	25
Aeroplane Parts in mixed consignments	10
Agglomerate Blocks for Electric Batteries—(*see* Electric Batteries and Cells, Primary).	
Agricultural Draining Pipes	5
Air Chamber Receivers or Outlets for Humidifiers and Air and Dust Extraction Plant	5
Air Pipes for Ventilators	5
Albums	10
Alga Marina or Seaweed (dry)	5
Aluminium	
Aluminium Alloys	—
Bar, ingot, plate, rod or strip—	
In cases or crates	5
Not in cases or crates	10
Castings—(*see* Castings).	
Forgings, not machined, packed	5
Scrap	5
Tubes	15
Wire	5
Aluminium Bedsteads	10
(The headpiece to be detached and laid on top of the mattress; the legs also to be detached and packed inside the spring, the whole being wrapped in corrugated paper with an outer wrapping of kraft.)	
Aluminium Foil	10
Aluminium Tanks	5
Aluminium Ware—(*see* Hardware).	
Ambulance Stretchers—	
Rolled up	5
With wheels (not carriages)	25
American Cloth	5
Ammonia Solution, containing not more than 5 per cent. of Ammonia, in bottles in cartons	5*

TRAFFIC	Differential Percentage
Ammunition Boxes, iron or steel	5
Ammunition Carriers for Trench Mortars	10
Animal Gut Skins, dry, packed	5
Animal Offals, frozen, in cases or sacks, in heavily insulated containers (e.g., A.F. type)	25
Anti-freezing Fluids (Glycerine Solution), non-inflammable	10
Anti-Gas Celastoid Eye-Shields	25
Antimony Regulus, in casks or cases	5
Antique Furniture—(*see* Furniture).	
Antiseptic and Protective Soap Composition, in casks or drums	5
Archery Apparatus	10
Artificial Flowers, Fruit and Leaves	20
Artificial or Synthetic Rubber, raw, in slabs	5
Asbestic Bricks for Retorts	5
Asbestic Sheets, corrugated or flat	5
Asbestic Slates	5
Asbestos and Wool Mixture for use in Gas Masks	5
Asbestos Board	5
Asbestos Felt or Asbestic Cellular Sheets or Slabs, plain or faced with asbestic slate	5
Asbestos Steam-pipe Covering	5
Ash Trays, glass	5
Asphalt, fibrous, in rolls	5
Asphalt, solid, consisting of earthy matter impregnated with not more than 55 per cent. of Asphaltum (Bitumen) or Pitch	5
Automatic Delivery (Slot) Machines, metal	10
Axe Handles and Shafts	5
Axle Boxes, iron or steel	10
Axles, Perambulator	10
Backs and Sides, fireclay, for Grates, Ranges or Stoves	5
Bacon	5
Bacon and Hams, cured, in insulated containers other than heavily insulated (e.g., F.M. type)	10
Badminton Apparatus	10
Bags—	
American cloth, canvas, carpet or fibreboard	7½
Leather	5
Made from Gelatine or Cellulose Solution, for wrapping purposes	5
Paper, without flaps, packed	5
Shopping, plastic	7½
Soldiers' Kit	5
Workmen's Tool	5
Bakelite (Synthetic Resin)	15
Bakers' Oven Trays, woven iron wire	5
Balances, Chemical, packed	5
Balloons	20
Balls, iron or steel, rough, for crushing materials	5
Balusters—	
Concrete (cement) or ferro-concrete	5

APPENDIX 3

NOTES OF EXPLANATION ABOUT WORKING TIMETABLES

Several chapters of this book have included references to working timetables (WTT). As many readers will be unfamiliar with how railway timetables are traditionally drafted, two examples are included.

The first of the examples is for a basic, single track railway with two terminal stations and six intermediate stations. Three of the six intermediate stations have double tracks to enable two trains to 'cross'. It is factually based upon the Isle of Man.

The vertical axis is for distance and the horizontal axis is for time. As shown, a train (10) leaves Douglas at 10.00 hrs as another (11) leaves Port Erin at 10.00 hrs. The trains occupy their respective sections until 'crossing' at Castletown. It is a very basic operation repeated three more times during the day. An additional train (60) is able to be timetabled to leave Douglas and enter the section to Port Soderick only when train 12 has reached that station. Train 60 then has to wait at Port Soderick until train 13 has arrived from Port Erin and the section forward to Santon is clear. As a safeguard, drivers have to be in possession of a 'staff' for the section into which they are to enter and pass through.

The second example is for a multi-track section of railway and shows traffic in one direction only using one track. The vertical access is distance and the horizontal access is time. The example illustrates the difficulty of fitting into the timetable a slow-moving coal train which leaves Peterborough at 9.20 hrs and reaches its destination (73½ miles) at 3.50pm. The problem for the timetable planners is that during that time-span, 17 passenger trains need to be accommodated and the locomotive of the coal train will need water supplies at Offord and Hitchin. The route requires the coal train to stand awaiting the passage of faster trains at bottlenecks such as Arlesey (Note: this illustration was originally used in Vintage LNER journal Spring edition 2001.)

A similar situation along the London extension of the GC line was eased by there being less passenger trains to be timetabled.

320 • THE GREAT CENTRAL RAILWAY: WHAT REALLY HAPPENED

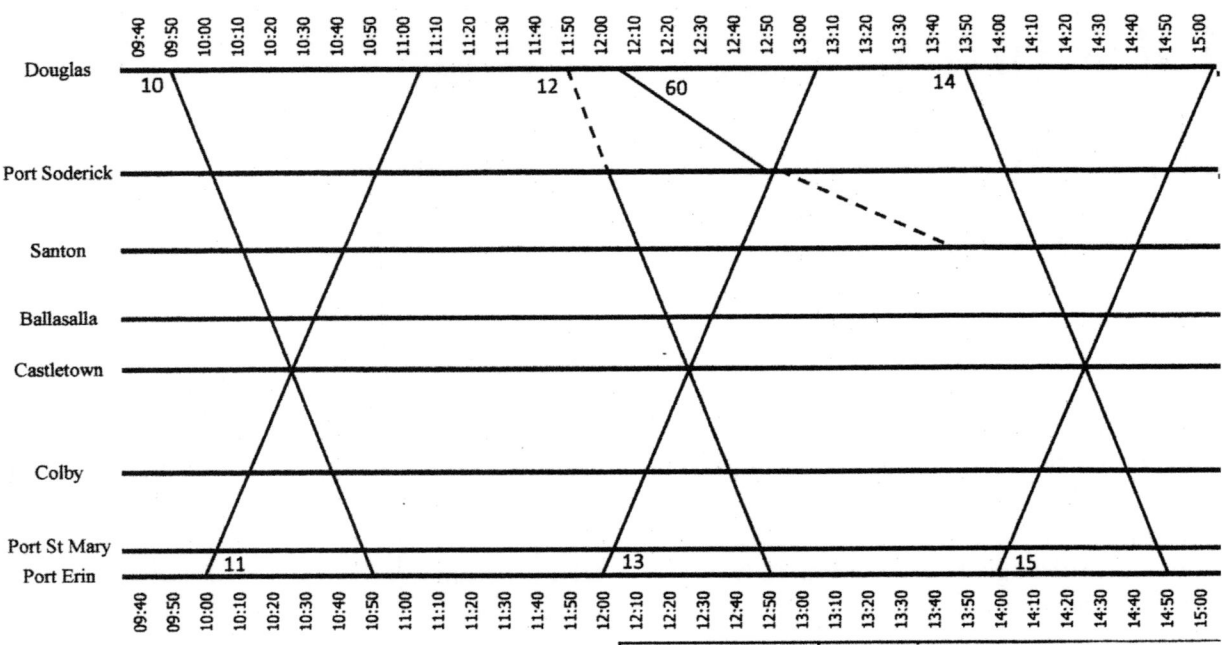

Appendix 3 – example one

Appendix 3 – example two

APPENDIX 4

DEVELOPMENT OF COMPETING RAILWAYS IN EAST MIDLANDS COALFIELDS

Starting in 1840, the Midland Railway enjoyed, at many collieries, a position of some commercial strength as being the only railway company able to move the coal. This led to complaints of poor service, slow return of wagons and many colliery owners seeking to encourage alternative providers of railway services to install connections and compete for the production.

The arrival onto the scene of the GNR (1872) resulted in new railways to tap coal from new sources rather than duplicate existing facilities at collieries served by the MR; West Hallam (MR 1870, GNR 1878), Nutbrook (1870/1886) being exceptions. The newly linked collieries were:

Mapperley	1872
High Park	1875
Lodge	1875
Plumtree	1875
Watnall	1875
Cinder Hill	1877
Linby	1881
Bestwood	1882
Manners	1886 (MR)/1897 (GN)
Hucknall	1898

NOTE:
The GNR built in 1883 a new link to the Stanton New Iron Works which replaced Stanton Old Iron Works, linked to the MR from 1872.

The extensions of the MS&LR/GCR South from Beighton resulted in large-scale duplication of facilities which, commercially, were more beneficial to the colliery owners than the two railway companies. The chronological progression can be understood from the following listing, the routes of the two railway companies being very close:

Colliery	Served by the MR from:	Served by both MR and MS&LR/GCR from:
Holbrook	1840	1892
Speedwell	1866	1892
Sutton	1866	1897
Langwith	1875	1896
Markham	1875	1892
Pleasley	1877	1897
Warsop	1879	1896
Langton	1885	1893
Hartington	1888	1892
Bentinck	1894/98	1898
Cresswell & Welbeck	1894	1898
Summit	1897	1897
Shirebrook	1898	1900

NOTE:
Once established, the GCR benefitted from arrangements whereby they worked the Mansfield Railway with a very significant annual tonnage from Mansfield, Clipstone and Rufford Collieries.

The Midland Railway made attempts in 1881 to purchase as many as possible of the then privately-owned coal wagons, but it proved a failure. Apart from wartime (when pooling of wagons was requisitioned) the sorting of individual wagons from/to owners/customers was a constant drain upon the resources and costs of the railways up to 1939 and briefly after the Second World War.

Following the Grouping of the railways (1923) and the changed economic circumstances of the 1920s/30s the LMS and LNE co-operated to the extent of building jointly owned lines whilst commercial arrangements were for each company to negotiate with the owner.

In the 1950s/60s, closures of collieries in Nottinghamshire were justified by the NCB as a result of a range of circumstances, from a dangerous deterioration of underground conditions, previously potentially economical seams becoming inaccessible and uneconomical due to geological fault lines, mergers with adjacent colliery workings, investment in new technology considered to be more worthwhile if directed elsewhere and concentration of resources at the then new deep pits to meet changing consumer demand patterns. The following is a list of colliery closures in Nottinghamshire which ended long standing transport arrangements and created a small number of new arrangements.

Colliery	Year sunk
Brinsley	1872
Clifton	1868
Cossall	1870-72
Firbeck	1923-25
Highpark	1860-66
Kirkby Summit*	1888
Langton	1844-46
Lodge (merged with Moorgreen)	1878-80
Oakwood Grange	1930-32
Radford	1897-1900
Selston	1872-74
Watnall	1874
Wollaton	1874

NOTE:
* 2,000 jobs lost

In Derbyshire it was a similar picture:

Colliery	Year sunk
Alfreton	1895
Blackwell (2)	1861/1880
Bretby	1875
Brookhill (merged with Bentinck)	1908
Church Gresley (merged with Cadley Hill)	1855
Coppice (2)	1900/1930
Cotes Park	1854
Denby	1854
Granville Swadlincote (2)	1854
Grassmoor (merged with Williamthorpe)	1854
Homewood	1874
Langton (merged with Kirkby)	1842
Mapperley	1870
Morton	1866
New Langley (merged with Ormonde)	1859
Park House	1880
Pilsley	1867
Pinxton	1938
Plymouth, Pinxton	1940
Ramcroft	1915
Shirland	1864
South Normanton	1895
Stanhope Bretby	1960
Stanley	1895
Swadlincote	1854
Swanwick	1854
Wingfield Manor (merged with Swanwick)	1908
Woodside (3) (merged with Coppice)	1930

Appendix 5 Memorandum dated 11th December, 1963 to British Railways Board

11th December, 1963

MEMORANDUM TO THE BRITISH RAILWAYS BOARD

EXAMINATION OF DUPLICATE ROUTES

In the Planning report to the Board dated 18th July it was stated that the case for closing a major portion of the ex-G.C. main line should be ready by October 1963. A little more time than was then envisaged has been needed.

The accompanying comprehensive memorandum sets out the case, an estimate of the net savings ($£1\frac{1}{4}$ m.), the anticipated staff displacement (2,150), and the phasing of action.

Movement towards closure will be gradual. Freight withdrawals and diversions will commence in June 1964, main line passenger train withdrawals and diversions will take place in 1964 and, with the withdrawal of the last of the local passenger services at an as yet indefinite date, the ultimate aim is complete closure by June 1965.

The Board is requested to note the intention to embark immediately upon the steps necessary, in the fields of consultation and public notification of intentions, to implement the first major scheme of main line route rationalisation as envisaged in the Reshaping Report.

F. C. MARGETTS

11th December, 1963.

MEMORANDUM TO THE BRITISH RAILWAYS BOARD

EXAMINATION OF DUPLICATE ROUTES
NORTH EAST/SOUTH WEST AXIS
PROPOSAL TO CLOSE THE GREAT CENTRAL MAIN LINE

1. Objective

It was decided at the end of 1962 that the North East/South West axis routes should be examined with the aim of closing as much as possible of the G.C.Main Line between Sheffield and Aylesbury.

2. Conclusion

This examination has shown that 111½ route miles can be closed between Renishaw and Calvert. Short sections connecting other lines converging on the G.C.Main Line will be retained at Staveley, Annesley and Nottingham. A broad estimate of the savings that will result from this closure is £3.3m. per year. Of this £3.3m. per year, £2.07m. would have been saved by conversion of the G.C.Line from steam to diesel operation, and £1.24m. is the net saving directly attributable to the closure of the line. About 2,150 staff will be displaced on the G.C.lines while about 345 extra staff will be required on the Midland lines.

    Appendix 'A' details the passenger and freight stations to be closed.
    Appendix 'B' details the passenger trains to be withdrawn or diverted.
    Appendix 'C' details the track mileage to be closed.
    Appendix 'D' details the annual savings by departments and estimated loss of revenue.
    Appendix 'E' details the staff to be displaced on G.C.lines and additional staff required on Midland lines.

3. Timing of Closures

    Local Traffic

Before the local passenger services on the G.C.Main Line can be withdrawn, it will be necessary to obtain the Minister of Transport's approval to the re-submission of the case for withdrawal of the Rugby-Leicester-Nottingham local services. In a letter dated 14th January, 1963, the Minister informed the Board that he

(i) accepted the recommendation in favour of the withdrawal of the local passenger services between Sheffield and Nottingham, on condition that a direct bus service will be provided between Tibshelf and Nottingham to meet the needs of persons using the present railway services to travel to and from work;

(ii) accepted the recommendation that a service of passenger trains should be retained between Nottingham and Rugby to meet the needs of users travelling to and from work;

(iii) accepted the recommendation in favour of the withdrawal of the local passenger services between Rugby and Aylesbury on condition that a bus service will be provided to meet the needs of users living at Calvert.

—continued—

3. **Timing of Closures**

   Local Traffic (Cont'd)

   Following the publication of the Reshaping Report, there correspondence between the Minister and the Board on the question of the inclusion in the Plan of the withdrawal of passenger services which, as at (ii) above, had previously been rejected by the Minister.

   It was subsequently agreed that the Board would not resubmit proposals of this kind unless there had been, in the Board's view, a material change of circumstances and that, prior to issuing press notices on the proposed withdrawal, the approval of the Minister to proceed with the submission would be sought. In order that the through passenger trains which are to be diverted or withdrawn may be left out of the re-submission of the proposals to withdraw the local services, it is proposed to divert or withdraw these through trains in September 1964 and to re-submit the case for withdrawing the local services after that date, with a view to implementation in June 1965.

   Before the local freight and parcels services are withdrawn and arrangements made for retention of some traffics at alternative stations, it is necessary to consult the traders who use the services. No particular difficulty is anticipated in handling that traffic which can be retained at alternative stations on other routes. There are a number of private sidings, however, whose location and/or traffic will not allow of transfer to another route, and this traffic will be lost. A broad estimate of the annual receipts from this traffic is £178,500. No traders have yet been approached and the final estimate of lost receipts may be different.

   Trunk Traffic

   A large part of the total traffic on the G.C.Main Line is through traffic and will be diverted to other routes, primarily the Midland routes to London and Birmingham, which are already heavily occupied. The number of passenger trains to be diverted is small, and it is proposed to divert these in September 1964. The through freight traffic, however, is heavy and the key to this closure is the implementation of the scheme to replace all steam locomotives on the Midland lines by diesel locomotives. This was approved by the British Transport Commission in February 1962, and the placing of orders for the 294 diesel locomotives (129 Type 4 and 165 Type 2) needed to complete the scheme has subsequently been approved by the Commission and the Board. Provided that the allocation of diesel locomotives continues as planned when these orders were placed, completion of delivery is scheduled for June 1965 for the Type 4's and the Type 2's. On 27th November, 1963, 53 Type 4 and 5 Type 2 of this order had been delivered. Associated with the delivery of these locomotives is the construction of diesel maintenance facilities. The completion of Toton diesel depot is an essential forerunner to the final closure of the G.C.Main Line.

   This depot is due to be completed in April 1965, by which time all the diesels allotted to the Midland diesel scheme and which are required for implementation of G.C.closure should have been delivered, if the anticipated delivery rate is maintained.

   It is recommended that final closure of the G.C.Main Line should take place in June 1965, and that this final closure should be preceded by a staged programme of diversion of traffic away from the G.C.line commencing in June 1964.

4. **Phasing of Action leading to Closure**

   It is recommended that the following lines of action, which will prepare the way for total closure, be followed:-

   (a) Staff consultation be initiated at B.R.B./N.U.R.level, followed by Regional/Sectional Council consultation.

   (b) Discussion with local authorities, and negotiations with traders about local traffic, be initiated to coincide as nearly as possible with Staff Consultation.

-continued-

- 3 -

4. **Phasing of Action leading to Closure (Cont'd)**

    (c) Through passenger train diversions and withdrawals be implemented in September 1964, followed by submission to T.U.C.C. of case for withdrawal of local passenger trains, with the aim of withdrawal by June 1965, if approval is obtained from the Minister of Transport.

    (d) Freight diversions, and withdrawal, be implemented in stages from June 1964 to June 1965.

5. **Capital Expenditure**

Other than the implementation of the Midland lines diesel scheme, and the physical work entailed in dismantling the G.C.line, no capital expenditure is directly associated with the closure of the G.C. line. The Midland lines diesel scheme includes provision for substitution of steam by diesel on the G.C.lines. 33 diesel locomotives had been allocated to the G.C. line at a capital cost of £3.04m. A diesel maintenance depot was planned for Annesley at a cost of £210,000. The diesel maintenance depots on the Midland lines will be able to absorb the additional locomotives required to work the diverted traffic over Midland lines. The number of additional locomotives required on the Midland lines has not yet been determined, but will probably be slightly less than would have been required on the G.C.lines.

The closure of the G.C. Main Line will not prejudice the closure of Snow Hill Station, Birmingham.

Because the Midland lines carry heavy and important traffic, the London Midland Region are making provision for Multiple Aspect Signalling on them, and plans are being prepared accordingly. Their introduction will underwrite the long term success of closing the G.C.Main Line.

6. **Further Action**

The closure of the G.C.Main Line will have far reaching effects on other lines and yards, notably, the G.N.line from Annesley to Eggington, the Woodford-Stratford-Gloucester line, Banbury yard, and lines and yards in the Nottingham area. It is proposed that the team who have examined the G.C.Main Line should now examine these lines.

F.C.MARGETTS

Appendix 6 Memorandum following meeting held at BRB Headquarters on 14th July, 1964 (including, at end, an extract from supporting papers)

CONFIDENTIAL

MEMORANDUM OF MEETING HELD AT 222, MARYLEBONE ROAD
14TH JULY, 1964

PRESENT:

L. W. Ibbotson, B.R.B. (Chairman)

C.S.McLeod	)	T.R.V.Bolland	Eastern Region
E.Merrill	)	R.L.E.Lawrence	London Midland Region
A.W.Woodbridge	)	D.M.Howes	London Midland Region
G.Crabtree	) British Railways	J.E.H.Skerrett	North Eastern Region
C.Haygreen	) Board	H.C.Sanderson	Western Region
L.J.Hamblin	)		
B.Seymour	)		
D.H.Coombs	)		
R.H.Johnson	)		
D.J.Finch	)		

ROUTE RATIONALISATION
EXAMINATION OF NE/SW AXIS ROUTES

1. **Purpose of Meeting**

    At the meeting held on 27th January, 1964, the procedures necessary to set in train the implementation of the proposals for the closure of the G.C. main line were worked out. No further action has been taken, pending a decision to set these procedures in motion.

    On 2nd July the Chief Operating Officer advised all concerned of the decision that steps could now be taken to proceed with the development of the closure proposals, but that the withdrawal of the local Rugby-Nottingham passenger services must be dealt with last.

    The purpose of the meeting was to review the procedures worked out on 27th January in the light of this decision, amend them as necessary and revise the time scale.

    During the course of the meeting it was confirmed that the decision was to be interpreted as meaning that the proposals should be developed and progressed on the basis that the local passenger service between Rugby and Nottingham remained in operation.

2. **Phasing of Withdrawals and Diversions**

    This was agreed as under :-

    Phase 1. Diversion of through merchandise services.

    Phase 2. Diversion of parcels services.

    Phase 3. Diversion of through mineral services.

    Phase 4. Withdrawal of local freight services.

    Phase 5. Withdrawal and diversion of express passenger services.

- 2 -

2. Contd. The aim should be to implement the first phase by the beginning of 1965 and to complete the whole sequence by the end of the year. The point was made that the diversion of the mineral services must be effective before September so as to avoid making the change when coal traffic is heavy and operating conditions difficult.

Phase 5 would be regarded as independent of the other four phases because of the different considerations involved – see Section 3.

One of the problems associated with the diversions would be the deployment of Type 4 diesel-electric locomotives to cover the services, but the representatives of the four Regions concerned were satisfied that suitable arrangements could be made.

In answer to a query by Mr. Skerrett, Mr. Lawrence said that the Midland route was considered to be capable of dealing with the additional volume of traffic which it would be called upon to handle. It should, however, be recognised that until proposals for the modernisation of signalling could be developed, authorised and implemented, the standard of operating efficiency might not be all that could be desired during periods of adverse weather.

3. Passenger Train Services

It was noted that certain of the express passenger services which are to be withdrawn or diverted contribute to the local Rugby-Nottingham service, and it would be necessary to augment the latter so as to maintain a service of the standard laid down.

Mr. Lawrence indicated that it would be desirable to terminate the local service at Arkwright Street so as to free Nottingham, Victoria (the new connection at Netherfield will be in use by the beginning of 1965 and would allow of the diversion of the Grantham service to Nottingham, Midland). He also sought some latitude in the way of service adjustments to achieve efficient utilisation of stock and men. Mr. Haygreen will seek confirmation from the Ministry that these steps will be in order.

The withdrawals and diversions will mean the complete withdrawal of services as between Banbury/Aylesbury and Rugby Central and between Nottingham (Victoria) and Sheffield (Victoria). This will necessitate the implementation of the laid down procedure; the aim will be to post public notices by 31st October, 1964.

4. Sequence of Procedure

It was agreed that the sequence of procedures should now be as follows :-

1. Consultation with Trade Union Headquarters on amended proposals.
2. Staff consultation (Sectional Council) on detailed proposals in each Region.
3. Opening of negotiations with interested traders.
4. Advice to Local Authorities and interested M.Ps.
5. Press announcement of initiation of enquiries.
6. Posting of public notices indicating express passenger train withdrawals.

- 3 -

4. contd. It was agreed that the "amended" proposals should be phrased in the following terms :-

> "The British Railways Board are studying the possibility of diverting through passenger and all freight traffic to other routes."

5. Timing

It was agreed that item (1) above should take place on Day "A", items (2), (3) and (4) on Day "B", and item (5) on Day "C". Item (6) can take place at any convenient date after Day "C".

Mr. Lawrence will indicate as soon as possible the suggested date for Day "A".

Mr. McLeod will advise Mr. Lawrence as to the information which is considered to be necessary to implement the consultation procedure at National level.

Mr. Merrill will similarly liaise with the Regions concerned in regard to the question of publicity.

6. General

Mr. Ibbotson undertook to seek clearance for the procedure which had been agreed and to advise all concerned when this was received.

Reference was made to the need to ensure that removal of redundant assets did not lag behind the withdrawal of services.

XO/31/5

719/7/4.

Freight traffic originating or terminating at depots on the G.C. line will be dealt with at alternative terminals on other routes. This is in line with the normal processes of rationalisation and concentration; handled traffic is already concentrated on Nottingham (Carrington Street), Leicester (Queen's Walk) and Rugby (Midland). It is probable that Nottingham (Queen's Walk) will be retained as a coal concentration depot and that a freight service will be provided to deal with gypsum traffic from Gotham.

Between Sheffield and Nottingham the line passes through the East Midlands coal field. With the exception of Arkwright Colliery all seventeen collieries affected by the proposals are dually served and the whole of their output can be dealt with by the alternative route. This will be an advantage rather than a drawback, particularly when it is borne in mind that the coal despatches to the south will dwindle and those to the new power stations will increase, and there is no question of adverse effect on the servicing of the coalfield. Provision is made to continue to serve Arkwright Colliery and also to maintain the convenient access to Bentinck Colliery.

The approximate extent of the diversion to other routes is 1,200 wagons per day in each direction. In the Up direction this is almost wholly loaded traffic; in the reverse direction it includes a high proportion of empty wagons. Some two-thirds of this traffic flows along the N.E./S.W. axis, and this will be diverted via the Midland route through Birmingham, thence via Gloucester or Banbury. The N/S traffic which makes up the other third will be equally spread over the former Great Northern and Midland routes to London.

The routes to be used are generally more favourable operationally than is that to be closed. Taken in conjunction with the higher haulage capacity of the diesel locomotives which are coming into use this enables the benefits of concentration to be exploited to the full extent, not only reducing the extent of intermediate marshalling but enabling the combined traffics to be moved with a comparatively small increase in the number of trains.

The diagramatic map which is being produced will show the scale of the additional services, but over the key sections of the main diversionary routes they will be :-

	Southward		Northward	
	Ft.	P & P	Ft.	P & P
Stenson Jct. - Washwood Heath	11	2	8	1
Rugby - Bletchley	2	3	1	3
Trent Junction - Syston Junction	5	3	2	3
Grantham - Ferme Park	3	-	3	1

Motive power to work the G.C. line freight services is mainly based on Annesley and Woodford depots. Steam traction is being run down and the substantial cost of conversion of facilities for dealing with diesel locomotives is avoided; the number of locomotives to be built is also less than would be the case if the G.C. route were retained.

APPENDIX 7

Appendix 7 Notes following discussion held at BRB Headquarters on 11th February, 1965 between representatives of the Ministry of Transport and representatives of the BRB

COPY NO. 5

NOTES OF DISCUSSION BETWEEN THE MINISTER
OF TRANSPORT AND REPRESENTATIVES OF THE BRITISH RAILWAYS BOARD
HELD AT B.R.B. HEADQUARTERS:
THURSDAY, 11th FEBRUARY, 1965.

Representing the Ministry of Transport :-

The Rt. Hon. T. Fraser (Minister)
Mr. I.T. Lawman
Mr. S.T. Swingler
Mr. R. Freeson
Mr. F.D. Bickerton
Mr. C.P. Scott-Malden

Representing the British Railways Board :-

Mr. F.C. Margetts
Mr. S.K. Garratt
Mr. G. Crabtree
Mr. D. Fenton
Mr. J.E. Dewdney
Mr. J.R. Legg

[handwritten note: Not a particularly true record of proceedings but may be helpful for our press release]

Mr. Fraser, Minister of Transport, after being welcomed by Mr. Margetts, said it would be helpful if he could hear from the British Railways Board, first hand, what their proposals were for the Great Central Line and the stage reached. The projected closure of the route had invoked much public discussion and he was subjected to pressures from objectors, M.Ps., Unions and others. Although statutorily freight closures were not his concern, he could not afford to give the impression of disinterest in view of wider national interests and particularly the task recently assigned to Lord Hinton. He thought that if the proposals were right then there was a good deal to be said for projecting a better public image of them so that there would be a clearer understanding of what the Railways were trying to do. This would help him as Minister as well as benefiting the Railways.

Mr. Margetts said that he appreciated Mr. Fraser's position and would be glad to explain what the British Railways Board was trying to do. He said that the Great Central line had been in mind for closure for some time and that the present proposals took account of the retention of the Rugby - Nottingham passenger service in accordance with the directions of Mr. Fraser's predecessor.

The Great Central had been built as a competitive route and the work on it could readily be encompassed in other ways. Detailed points made by Mr. Margetts, and supported subsequently by Mr. Fenton, were as follows :-

- Passenger train loadings were light, there was a duplication of passenger station facilities along the competing routes and there were excellent alternatives available.

- Most of the freight traffic was through-through and by concentration, use of modern diesels, etc. it could be handled readily on other routes with a relatively small increase in the number of trains. In actual fact, there were only 1,200 wagons per day to be diverted, of which 800 were to go to the Midland route via Birmingham.

2/Cont'd...

		£
Estimated loss of Receipts:		225,800
Estimated Savings:		
Train working	892,000	
Shunting (Motive Power)	110,000	
Provision & Maintenance of Wagons	42,500	
Station & Depot staff	567,500	
Maintenance & Renewal of track	384,400	
Maintenance, renewal, stores, etc. of stations & buildings	36,400	
Maintenance & renewal of signalling	30,800	
		2,071,600
		£1,845,800

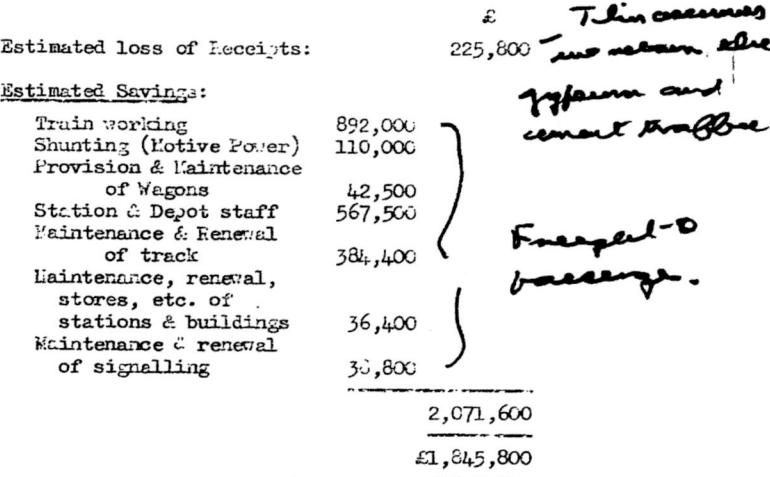

These figures were taken out in October 1964 and did not reflect the recent wage increase.

Mr. Fraser asked for details of the number of staff displaced, redundancy, etc. and was informed that the net reductions in numbers of posts estimated in October 1964 totalled 1,786. He was given details of the breakdown and phasing.

Mr. Fraser enquired regarding the progress of staff consultation and Mr. Fenton explained that this was almost complete. Mr. Scott-Malden said the impression given by the Unions was that they had been presented with a fait accompli, and he wondered whether any modifications were made as a result of implementing consultation. Mr. Margetts dealt suitably with this aspect of the matter.

Mr. Scott-Malden asked if the proposals took account of the position as foreseen over the next 20 years and Mr. Margetts confirmed that this was so.

Mr. Fraser thanked Mr. Margetts for the information which had been supplied and said that he would hope that a decision would be given during the following week on whether the proposals for passenger service withdrawals could be published. He thought that, following this, the British Railways Board would be well advised to get across to the public, in a more favourable light than hitherto, what they were trying to do and what they hoped to achieve.

Mr. Margetts accepted this suggestion and undertook to have a paper prepared, which could form the basis for publicity, explaining the object of the proposals, their scales and the benefits they would bring, as well as their effect on staff. The Ministry would be consulted regarding this and it would be necessary that any public announcement should be carefully timed, assuming that the Minister's decision in regard to publication of the passenger service proposals was favourable.

It was agreed that the exchange of views on the Great Central line had been most helpful and the meeting concluded with a brief explanation from Mr. Margetts on what the British Railways Board had in mind regarding the Broad Street - Richmond services.

- 2 -

- The freight facilities were also duplicated but special arrangements were being made to handle the traffic for the two big customers, viz., - British Gypsum Co., Gotham, and A.P.C.M., Whetstone, the latter moving to Syston.

- The proposals involved no capital expenditure and, indeed, avoided expenditure on new works and locomotives; there were net savings of the order of £1.6m. plus a substantial sum for site values.

- The Board was very conscious of the staff problem and special measures were being taken to deal with redundancy and resettlement.

Mr. Fenton indicated that allegations of congestion on the alternative routes were not justified by the facts. He explained the improvements which concentration of traffic and dieselisation on routes with more favourable gradients would bring, and demonstrated that the key points on these routes had handled substantially greater volumes of traffic under less favourable conditions.

Mr. Margetts summed up by saying that the British Railways Board were satisfied that the proposals were sound, reasonable and essential to progress. It was known that the staff were already leaving in anticipation of closure, no money was being spent to modernise the traction on the Great Central line because steam was on the way out and it was, therefore, undesirable that there should be delay in the implementation of the proposals.

Mr. Swingler, from his local knowledge of the area, amplified what the Minister had said regarding local objections. It was said that the rail forwardings from the East Midlands colliery area had fallen by 20% in the last three years because of the railways' inability to move the coal efficiently. It would be helpful if details could be given to counter this. It did seem to him that the line passed through an expanding coalfield and it would strengthen the railways' case if they could confirm that coal traffic would be satisfactorily conveyed.

It was explained to Mr. Swingler by Mr. Margetts, supported by Mr. Fenton and Mr. Crabtree, that the proposals did not sever access to any collieries; the majority of them were dually served, and concentration on one route should improve the service. A progressively increasing part of the output would go to power stations in the Midlands rather than to the south. The Minister could be assured, therefore, that the servicing of the coalfield would be adequately covered.

Mr. Fraser said that the map exhibited suggested that the Great Central route was more direct than the alternatives. Mr. Margetts explained that, in fact, the bulk of the traffic moved along the NE/SW axis, for which the Midland was the most favourable and direct route. The Minister's point on presentation was taken.

Mr. Lawman asked if details of the financial improvement could be given and Mr. Margetts put to him the following figures which took account of the probable retention of the cement and gypsum traffic.

3/Cont'd...

APPENDIX 8

Appendix 8 BRB Memorandum dated 26th February, 1965 following meeting held at BRB Headquarters on that day with Members of Parliament (including press coverage 27th February, 1965)

GREAT CENTRAL LINE

The following Members of Parliament visited the British Railways Board on February 26th, to make representations in regard to the projected closure of the Great Central Line:

    Mr. Michael English
    Mr. Tom Swain
    Mr. W.C. Whitlock
    Mr. Eric Varley
    Sir Barnet Jenner

They were received by Mr. Margetts, who was accompanied by Messrs. Johnson, Garratt and Ibbotson.

After welcoming the Members of Parliament, Mr. Margetts outlined the main reasons for the proposed closure of the Great Central Line and said that it was the intention of the Railways Board to remove the freight traffic from this line, the first stage of which would take place on Monday next.

The future of the passenger services was, of course, dependent upon the Ministry and T.U.C.C. hearings, if the Minister so decided.

Mr. Johnson outlined the situation, with particular reference to the accumulation of traffic on January 16th referred to by Mr. Whitlock in the enclosure to his letter of February 18th. He explained the abnormal circumstances which lead to this accumulation and the methods which were taken to handle it. He went on to say that the Railway were not unused to situations of this kind when they had to handle peaks of traffic and that the exceptional measures, which were necessary, were taken when required and quickly dispersed the accumulation as was done in this case.

Sir Barnet Jenner made specific reference to the diversion and cancellation of the passenger services around Leicester. Mr. Margetts reminded him that the future of the passenger services was a matter which the Minister of Transport and his Ministerial colleagues would ultimately have to decide.

The other four members were concerned primarily with the effect on their constituents who were Railwaymen, the redundancy arrangements and the collaboration with and information to the staff. Mr. Johnson outlined the steps he had taken to deal with this situation and Mr. Nicholson was called in to the meeting to explain the redundancy arrangements in greater detail. He undertook to let Mr. Whitlock have a note of what had been agreed with the Unions in this respect.

/ Continued

XO/31/5

- 2 -

During the course of discussion, Mr. Tom Swain, Member for Derbyshire N.E., referred to the Trunk Route Report and, in particular, drew our attention to Tables 5 and 6. While recognising that the figures given in the tables had necessarily to be assumptions, he would very much appreciate some further information as to the evidence which was used as a basis. Mr. Garratt undertook to supply this.

It was explained that in Stage I, which started on March 1st, 246 posts were to be saved. In accordance with usual experience in such cases, by the middle of February, 207 of these posts were unfilled and only 39 men remained to be placed. In the case of Stage II, planned for June 13th, 959 posts were to be displaced, of which one-third were already vacancies. The Third Stage, the date of which could not be calculated as it was subject to Ministerial decision, would displace 815 posts, of which at present only 68 were vacancies. The situation was changing all the time and Mr. Nicholson stated that there would be no difficulty in accommodating the remainder of the men displaced in Stage I, in posts in their immediate vicinity. He pointed out that in the Eastern Region in the Sheffield area, there were already 895 vacancies, whereas in the London Midland Region, Manchester and south thereof, there were 9,230 vacancies.

It was agreed that what had taken place at the meeting was not confidential. The Members of Parliament expressed their gratitude for this opportunity to learn more of the position and Mr. Margetts expressed his pleasure at being able to meet them.

E.W.K.

The Guardian Journal, Saturday, February 27, 1965

Plan to 'close' GC line starts now, MPs told

By Our London Correspondent

PLANS for the phasing out of the Great Central Railway as a main line between Nottingham and London were revealed to five East Midland MPs by officials of the British Railways Board in London yesterday. As a through main line it will cease to exist, but portions will be retained to carry freight.

The plan, which will lead to the displacement of 677 staff and the abolition of 1,205 posts, of which 528 have been left unfilled as they became vacant, begins next week.

The MPs, who spent two hours at the Marylebone headquarters of British Rail, were Mr. William Whitlock (Nottingham North), Mr. Michael English (Nottingham West), Mr. Tom Swain (Derbyshire NE), Mr. E. Varley (Chesterfield) and Sir Barnett Janner (Leicester NW).

Mr. Whitlock had arranged the meeting following discussions with railwaymen in Nottingham and a talk with Mr. Tom Fraser, Minister of Transport.

The meeting of the railwaymen took place at British Railways Staff Association Club at Bulwell on February 14 and was also attended by Mr. W. N. Warbey, MP for Ashfield.

'Line murdered'

At yesterday's meeting with the Railways Board Mr. Whitlock advanced the case put by the men that the Great Central line "had been murdered," but this was rejected by the representatives of the board.

Mr. F. Margetts, who is a member of the board and responsible for operating and rolling stock and other activities, was accompanied by Mr. H. C. Johnson, general manager of the London Midland Region and other advisers.

The MPs received maps which showed that the GC line would be discontinued over two or three stretches, for example north of Aylesbury to Rugby and at two points between Nottingham and Sheffield.

Other sections, as between Rugby and Nottingham, will carry passengers but not freight, and some stretches of the line will carry both freight and passengers.

In three stages

The expenditure involved would not justify maintaining "a meandering line" for odd occasions of congestion on other routes.

The board representatives outlined to the MPs a three-stage programme for bringing the GC line to an end as a main line.

The first stage will begin next week, when reductions in freight services will abolish 246 posts, of which 207 are already vacant and only 39 of the staff will have to be absorbed.

The second stage will be carried out in June and this will involve 959 jobs, of which 321 are already unfilled.

9,000 jobs open

The third stage, which would include, if the Minister of Transport consents under the powers he retains, passenger services, would be planned immediately his decision was known. This would include 815 posts and of these 68 are at present left unfilled. Thus the total of jobs finally dispensed with would amount to 2,020.

The MPs pressed the board representatives for information about the handling of redundancies which would follow this run-down. The officials said that there were 895 vacancies in the Sheffield area of Eastern Region and 9,000 jobs waiting to be filled on the London Midland Region south of Manchester.

Each man displaced would be offered all vacancies known and in prospect in his own grade and as far as possible in his own area.

Mr. English asked how Nottingham railwaymen would be affected and he was assured that sufficient railway jobs were available in the area to absorb the local men displaced.

The board representatives admitted that some railwaymen would have to be moved, but claimed that their plan for dealing with redundancies had been fully discussed with the trade unions.

The management replied that if reorganisation did not take place, and the drift from rail to road continued, a redundancy problem would still arise, with little hope of absorbing the men displaced.

Financial aid

For men who had to move they were offering lodging allowance of £4 4s. weekly for at least a year. If a man were a householder he would receive assistance in buying a new house and his legal costs for selling his old house would be paid.

Where a displaced railwayman elected to leave the service he would receive a generous lump sum as severance pay.

When Mr. Whitlock brought up the complaints of dictatorship and failure of adequate consultation which were raised at his meeting with the railwaymen's representatives at Bulwell on February 14, he was told that the trade unions were told of the proposals long ago.

It was admitted that initial difficulties might arise, but the reorganised system would carry all that the present system does and more.

APPENDIX 9

Appendix 9 BRB listing of alternative passenger transport facilities following proposed closure 3/4th September, 1966

ALTERNATIVE PASSENGER TRANSPORT FACILITIES

As has already been announced, the alternative transport facilities available have been considered. These include:-

(a) **By Rail**

At Sheffield, the services operating to and from Sheffield Midland.

At Nottingham, the services operating to and from Nottingham Midland.

At Leicester, the services operating from Leicester Midland.

At Rugby, the services operating from Rugby Midland.

(b) **By Road**

(i) Between Sheffield, Nottingham, Loughborough, Leicester and London

The service operated by Yorkshire Services.

(ii) Between Nottingham, Loughborough, Leicester and Brackley

The service operated by Associated Motorways via Northampton

(iii) Between Nottingham, Loughborough, Leicester and London

The services operated by Yorkshire Services and the service operated by the United Counties Motor Omnibus Co. Ltd.

(iv) Between Rugby and London

The service operated by the Birmingham and Midland Motor Omnibus Co. Ltd.

(v) Between Rugby and Woodford Halse

The service operated by K.W. Coaches Ltd.

(vi) Between Woodford Halse and Banbury

The service operated by Owens of Boddington

(vii) Between Brackley and Banbury

The service operated by the Birmingham and Midland Motor Omnibus Co. Ltd.

(viii) Between Brackley and Oxford

The service operated by the City of Oxford Motor Services Ltd.

(ix) Between Brackley and Aylesbury

The service operated by the Red Rover Omnibus Co. Ltd.

(x) Between Aylesbury and Banbury

The service operated by the Birmingham and Midland Motor Omnibus Co. Ltd.

(xi) Between Aylesbury and Oxford

The service operated jointly by Premier Travel Ltd. and Percival Motors (Cambridge) Ltd.

(xii) Between Aylesbury and London

The service operated by London Transport (Green Line).

Additional road services between Woodford Halse and Rugby and between Brackley and Aylesbury will also be provided.

BIBLIOGRAPHY

(Chapters 3-11 inclusive)

A Regional History of the Railways of Great Britain Volume 9 The East Midlands	R Leleux
Argentine Railways	S Damus

Board of Trade Annual (railway) Reports (various years)
Bradshaw's Railway Manual Shareholders' Guide and Directory (various years)
British Newspaper Library
British Passenger Locomotives — B Way, R Wardale
British Pullman Trains — C Fryer
British Railways Board Annual Reports (various years)
British Railways Board files (as archived)
British Railways Marshalling Yards — M Rhodes
British Railways: A Business History 1948-73 — T R Gourvish
British Railways Gradient Profiles — Ian Allan Ltd.
British Railways Pre-grouping Atlas and Gazetteer — W P Conolly
British Transport — H J Dyos, D H Aldcroft
British Transport Commission Annual Reports (various years)

Coal Mines and railways in the Leen Valley:
    Nottingham to Annesley — R Hibbert

Department of Transport archived material

Engineers, Managers and Politicians — L Hannah
Forgotten Railways Chilterns and Cotswolds — R Davies, M D Grant
Forgotten Railways The East Midlands — P H Anderson

Goods Traffic on the LNER — G Goslin
Great Central:
    Volumes 1 – 3 — G Dow
Great Central in LNER Days — D Jackson, R Russell
Gresley Locomotives — B Haresnape

Hansard (various dates, but particularly 20 December 1963)
History of the British Coal Industry:
    Volume 4: 1913-46 — B Supple
    Volume 5: 1946-82 — W Ashworth
History of the Great Northern Railway — C H Grisling
History of the LNER:
    Volumes 1-3 — M R Bonaviá
History of the Steel Industry in the Port Talbot area — S Parry
Home Railways as Investments 1897 — W J Stevens

House of Commons Parliamentary papers

I Tried to run a Railway	G T-W Fiennes
Lighted Flame (History of ASLE&F)	N McKillop
LMS & LNER in Manchester	R E Rose
LNER 150	D St. J Thomas, P Whitehouse
LNER Carriages	M Harris
LNER Handbook	D Wragg
Locomotives of the GCR	E M Johnson
Locomotives of the LNER	RCTS
London's Lost Railways	A A Jackson
Midland Main Lines to St Pancras and Cross Country Sheffield to Bristol	J Palmer
Midland Railway	C Hamilton Ellis
Modern Railway Operation 1926	D R Lamb
Modern Railway Working 1912	J Macaulay
National Archives, Kew (PRO)	
Nationalised Transport Industries	L C Hunter, D W Thompson
Organisation of British Railways	M R Bonaviá
Oxford Companion to British Railway History	
Passenger timetables of British Railways	GCR/LNER/BR

Periodicals:
- Backtrack
- Modern Railways
- Railway Magazine
- Trains Illustrated

Railways and the State	E Short
Railway Development in the Nottinghamshire Coalfield	Birks and Coxon
Railway Observer	RCTS
Railways since 1939	H C Casserley
Red for Danger	L T C Rolt
Re-shaping of British Railways (Beeching Report/Maps)	
Rise of Road Transport 1919-31	C Dunbar
Search Engine (NRM, York)	
Sectional Appendices to Working Timetables	BR, ER/LMR
Select Committees into Nationalised Industries	NCB/BR/CEGB
Signalling Record Society	
Staff magazines	

Ten Year Stint	A Robens
The Final Link	D Edwards, R Pigram
The New Competitor (RM October 1906)	W J Scott
The Railways of Great Britain. An Historical Atlas	Col M H Cobb
The Train that Ran Away	S Joy
Transport Acts 1921/53/62	
Transport Age	
The Yorkshire, Nottingham, Derbyshire Coalfield	G Macdonald
Trent (Motor Traction)	J Banks
Trent – Part Two, 1946-68	D Bean
US Army in World War II: The Transportation Corps Overseas	US Govt
Vintage LNER	Express Books
Working Timetables of railways	GCR/LMS/LNER/BR
Yeadons Register of LNER Locomotives	

INDEX

Accidents:
   Braunston & Willoughby 212
   Hexthorpe 29
   Leicester 221
   Nottingham (Victoria) 209
   Penistone 29
   Rugby/Lutterworth 221
   Weekday Cross 212
Acts of Parliament:
   coal industry 107, 152, 154, 183
   electricity industry 155, 179, 183
   inland transport 81-2, 112-3, 145, 148
   railways 15, 23, 30, 36, 38, 74-7, 81-2, 94, 98-9, 109, 113, 145, 158, 167 182, 188, 191, 202, 238, 253, 262
   road transport 112-3
Annesley:
   depot and yards 214, 217, 238, 251-2, 283, 286
   model of financial performance for coal 218-23
   Woodford Halse workings 127-8, 146, 206, 208, 213-4, 226, 230, 274-5, 290, 309
Associated Society of Locomotive Engineers and Firemen 29, 67, 101, 129, 191, 213-4
Aylesbury:
   Aylesbury diesel workings 268, 272

Banbury, see Woodford Halse
Barrington-Ward, M. Sir 160, 171
Beeching, R. Dr 253, 255-7, 265
Beighton – Annesley 36
Board of Trade 74, 79, 83, 105, 116, 189
Bradford 119, 215, 269-71
Braking systems and trials 29, 118, 127, 129, 138, 144, 201, 229
Brent (Cricklewood) yards 241-2, 246
British Railways Board:
   Members and officers 256-7, 276, 327-9
   organisation 256, 261
   finances 189, 269
   interface with Government 266, 331-3
   modernisation 260
   route planning 261-2, 277, 280-2
British Transport Commission:
   Members and officers 158-9, 171-2
   organisation 161, 163, 167, 171
   interface with Government 148, 172, 175-6, 188-9, 191, 194, 252, 254, 256
   interface with Railway Executive 161, 163
   route planning 216, 261
Bus companies and services 111, 224, 263, 265, 337

Calvert 147, 226, 258, 272, 289
Capital:
   investment 40, 103, 129-49, 152, 172-6, 181, 187, 194, 213, 251, 254-5, 310-4
   structures 84-9, 98-9
Catesby tunnel 146, 306
Channel tunnel 24, 30, 44, 289
Charwelton 146, 206, 306
Chesterfield 50, 172, 225, 269, 282
Classification of trains 119, 207
Clean Air Act 1956 179, 184, 246, 252, 272
Coal mining industry:
   Coal:
      concentration yards 235, 237, 273, 284
      export 50, 105
      market for inland 95, 105-6, 181, 188, 246, 251, 268
      movement South by rail 28, 36, 50, 95, 140, 216, 226-52
      production 102, 105-6, 148, 154, 173, 187, 222, 241, 246, 272
   Coalfields:
      development 23, 28, 30, 36, 50, 172, 321-2
      siting 104, 106, 153
   Collieries:
      ownership 106-7, 154
      own wagons 107
      profitability 107
   National Coal Board:
      formation 152-5
      interface with Government 172
      investment 172
      liaison with British Railways Board 188, 250, 269, 273, 284
      Members and officers 154-55, 183
      Plan for Coal 172, 181, 187
      Revised Plan for Coal 181, 187, 272
Colwick depot, traffic and yards 36, 238-41, 280, 286
Conciliation Boards 69

Conservative Party 129, 140, 150, 152, 179, 253, 265
Containerised traffic 135, 138, 274

Darnall 123-4, 287
D-Day planning 146
Didcot power station 289
Diesels for London Midland Region 226, 251-2, 280
Diversion of trains onto GC route 254, 261, 268, 270, 273, 282
Doncaster 53, 91, 100, 235
Dukinfield C& W Works 31, 61, 71
Duplicated main lines 254, 281, 323-30

Edwalton, see Manton
Electricity industry:
   British Electricity Authority:
      formation 154-5
      management 155-6
      National Grid 155, 179, 182
      planning 172-3
   Central Electricity Authority 156-7, 172, 183
   Central Electricity Generating Board:
      Members and officers 183
      organisation 183
      planning 179, 182
      production 182, 184-5
      siting of power stations 181-5, 252
      sources of power 177, 185, 250
      Supergrid 179-180
Electrification of railways 144, 149, 175
Excursion and seasonal trains 67, 127, 212, 123-4, 271, 286-7

Faringdon, A. Lord, see Henderson, A.
Fay, S. Sir 46-72, 84-97, 271
Ferme Park 148, 237-8
Fiennes, G. T-W. 257-8, 260
Financial performance 20-1, 28-9, 37-8, 40, 44, 47, 72-97, 99, 102-5, 107-8, 148, 163, 190, 221, 254
Finedon Road, (Wellingborough) yards 230, 243-4, 246, 252
Fish traffic 30, 128, 213, 274-5, 284

Gorton Works 31, 33, 70
Government Committees and Papers 98, 256
Great Central Railway Society 306
Gresley, H.N. Sir 129-33, 142
Grimsby and Cleethorpes 16, 30-1, 50, 57, 59-60, 64, 97, 110, 126, 129, 146, 213, 271, 284

Henderson, A. 39, 84-97, 128, 192
Hotchley Hill 206, 208
Hotels 40-1, 110, 256

Immingham 51, 57, 83, 87, 89, 92, 97, 99, 146, 177, 213, 215, 286, 309
International Railway Congress 75

Labour Party 69, 98, 101, 129, 150, 152, 179, 253, 265, 285
Langwith 215, 235, 241, 287
Leicester 124-7, 206, 217, 221, 223, 230, 269, 282-3, 286, 305
Lincoln 19, 28, 230, 235
London North Eastern Railway:
   carriage building programmes 135-7, 144
   finances 101-2, 109, 118, 145
   high speed locomotives and trains 128, 142
   maintenance 144, 148
   war-time 145-9

Main Line Steam Trust 291-2
Manchester 12, 13, 32, 59, 70, 123-4, 126, 225, 261, 282, 286
Mansfield Concentration Sidings 235
Manton 241-3
March/Whitemoor yards 108, 140, 214, 230-1, 235-7, 251, 266
Margetts, F C 259, 276, 323-6
Marine and shipping 30-1, 59, 89, 91, 96, 110, 139-40, 147, 306-7, 316
Market Harborough 242, 273
Marples, E. 254-6, 262, 265
Marylebone 41, 47, 59, 63, 127, 225, 268, 272, 288
Motor vehicles 103, 109, 113-4

National Union of Railwaymen 67, 69, 213
Neasden 38, 41, 126, 145, 217, 238, 246, 283
Neepsend 100
Ness, J. 261, 276, 280-2
New England, Peterborough 108, 226, 235, 237, 246
Nottingham 26, 40, 99, 172, 225, 261, 269, 282, 286

Parcels depots and trains 261, 268, 272
Parliament:
   process for legislation 28, 36, 38, 73-4, 281-2
   representation of railway companies 23-4, 29, 56, 70, 158
Penetrating lines 172, 215-6
Petrol railcar 61
Pilsley colliery 229, 243
Publicity 64, 97, 265, 336

Railway & Canal Commissioners 68
Railway Clearing House 81, 138-9, 256
Railway companies (principal ones only):
    Cheshire Lines Committee 23, 56, 119, 126, 286
    Grand Trunk (Canada) 19-20
    Great Central and Midland Committee 50
    Great Eastern 22, 28, 50, 67, 99
    Great Northern 16, 18, 21, 28, 36, 50, 67, 87, 99, 108
    Great Northern/London North Western joint 230, 238-41, 273
    Great Western/Great Central 47, 67, 94-6, 110-1
    Grimsby & Immingham 59, 64, 272, 305
    Lancashire, Derbyshire and East Coast 50-1, 70
    Liverpool & Manchester 12, 16
    London Midland and Scottish 109
    London North Eastern 98-149
    London North Western 15-6, 22-23, 80, 87
    Manchester & Sheffield 16, 28, 37
    Manchester Sheffield & Lincolnshire 12, 16, 17, 22, 23
    Manchester South Junction & Altrincham 53, 119, 126, 140
    Mansfield 51, 56, 83, 96, 99
    Metropolitan 25, 38, 47, 94-6
    Midland 15, 21, 28, 80, 87, 95, 321
    North Eastern 83, 99, 140
    North London 25, 95-6
    Oldham Ashton under Lyne and Guide Bridge 18, 75
    South Eastern 16, 24, 30
    Trent Valley 13
    Wrexham, Mold & Connahs Quay 23-4, 56, 70
Railway Executive:
    Members and officers 159-60
    interface with British Transport Commission 161, 163, 167
Railway Rolling Stock Trust Ltd 31-3, 40, 70
Railway Tribunals 99, 101, 108-9, 177, 188
Road building programme 194, 256
Robens, A. Lord 182, 274, 278
Robertson, B. Sir 171, 224, 254, 257
Robinson, J. G. 46, 70, 90, 135
Rugby 146, 206, 222, 242

Scunthorpe/Normanby Park 93, 273-4
Sheffield area (excluding Tinsley) 50, 121, 124, 215-6, 225, 269-71, 282, 288
Slip carriages 33, 121
Stanton Gate 242

Steam locomotives (particular classes only):
    A3 4-6-2 121-2, 214
    BR Standard 164, 201, 213, 237
    K3 2-6-0 127, 147
    S160 2-8-0 131, 147
    V2 2-6-2 125
    private builders 16, 50-1, 53, 133, 310-4
Steam railcars 63
Stedeford Advisory Group 253, 255
Steel traffic 209, 215-6, 252, 273, 281
Stock exchanges 76
Stonebridge Park 187, 227, 243
Strategic routes 269, 276, 280-2
Sudbury Junction/Willesden 246
Swanbourne 226, 258, 260, 289
Syston 230, 242-3

Temple Mills 177, 227, 236, 244, 251
Tinsley 258, 273, 277-81, 287
Toton 230, 241
Transport Users Consultative Committee 225, 243, 268, 270
Trent 230, 245
Trent Motor Traction Ltd 224

United States of America Transportation Corps 133, 146

Wagons:
    control authorities 118, 140, 163-4, 261, 273, 282
    private ownership 107, 119, 138, 147, 176, 227, 241
    public ownership 138, 176, 207, 227
    route specific 229, 243
Wath 33, 55, 128, 215, 280
Watkin, E. Sir 12-44, 75, 78-9, 90, 206
Welham 230, 241
Woodford Halse:
    depot and yards 127, 206, 215-7, 251-2, 275, 283, 287
    traffic:
        Annesley, see Annesley – Woodford workings
        Banbury and west 39, 41, 47, 50, 208-9, 222, 261, 275
        London via High Wycombe GW/GC 47, 50, 111, 208-9, 212, 238, 246, 250-2, 275
        London via Aylesbury Met/GC 38-41, 47, 49, 111, 208-9, 212, 235, 238, 246, 250-2, 274-5
Woodhead:
    route 16, 18-22, 128, 140-1, 177, 261, 288, 290
    tunnels 149, 288, 306